wisdom

《w 006 20 190

W0006515

the

wisdom

of solomon

authorized king james version

grove press
new york

with an introduction by | piers paul read

Introduction copyright © 1999 by Piers Paul Read
The Pocket Canon second series copyright © 2000 by Grove/Atlantic, Inc.

All rights reserved. No part of this book may be reproduced in any form
or by any electronic or mechanical means, including information storage
and retrieval systems, without permission in writing from the publisher,
except by a reviewer, who may quote brief passages in a review. Any
members of educational institutions wishing to photocopy part or all
of the work for classroom use, or publishers who would like to obtain
permission to include the work in an anthology, should send their
inquiries to Grove/Atlantic, Inc., 841 Broadway, New York, NY 10003.

a note about pocket canons

The Authorized King James Version of the Bible, translated between 1603 and 1611, coincided with an extraordinary flowering of English literature. This version, more than any other, and possibly more than any other work in history, has had an influence in shaping the language we speak and write today.

The books of the King James Bible encompass categories as diverse as history, philosophy, law, poetry and fiction. Each Pocket Canon volume has its own introduction, specially commissioned from an impressive range of writers, to provide a personal interpretation of the text and explore its contemporary relevance.

introduction by piers paul read

Piers Paul Read, the third son of the poet and critic, Sir Herbert Read, is the author of thirteen novels and four works of non-fiction, among them Alive: the Story of the Andes Survivors. *His novels have won a number of awards, among them the Hawthornden Prize, the Somerset Maugham Award and the James Tait Black Memorial Prize.* Alive *received the Thomas More Award for Catholic Literature in the US. He is a Fellow of the Royal Society of Literature and is vice-president of the Catholic Writers' Guild. His most recent book,* The Templars, *is a work of history. He is married with four children and lives in London.*

As a child I was greatly impressed by the story in the Bible of how King Solomon came to acquire great 'riches, and wealth, and honour' and innumerable concubines and wives. God appeared to him in a dream and promised to give him anything he asked for. Solomon chose wisdom which so pleased God that he gave him everything else besides. Here was the formula, surely, for the God-fearing hedonist to have his cake and eat it.

Despite Solomon's example, however, I suspect that few of us, if given the same opportunity, would make the same choice today. Wisdom has gone out of fashion. The very word is one of a number in the English language that we find frequently in works of literature but seldom in everyday life. In the half-century that has passed since I reached the age of reason, I can scarcely remember ever having heard a philosopher, statesman or indeed anyone else described as wise. Our most common terms of approbation tend to be 'intelligent', 'clever', 'astute', 'shrewd' or 'high-powered'. The skills of our rulers lie in reading the runes of focus groups and opinion polls, and the image they want to project is of someone vigorous, forceful, youthful, dynamic – not wise. In the academic world, professors are appointed for their specialist knowledge, not their overall sagacity, and university chancellors are chosen more for their abilities as administrators and fundraisers than as the elders of their people.

Even philosophers who, from the etymology of the word that denotes their calling (love of wisdom), might be expected to give it some meaning, are no longer wise. Continental philosophers spew out incoherent gibberish while British linguistic philosophers have narrowed their focus to the point of irrelevance. The Professor who taught me at Cambridge was actually called John Wisdom but he restricted speculation in our seminars to how we could know whether or not our desks existed. Bertrand Russell and A J Ayer were undoubtedly highly intelligent men but, to judge from their private lives, could not be called wise.

What do we learn about wisdom from *The Wisdom of*

Solomon? Had I read it as a child, I would have been disappointed to discover that it is not a handbook on how to have your cake and eat it. Nor was it in fact written by Solomon: his putative authorship was as a commonly used literary convention. Modern scholarship suggests that it was composed by a Jewish sage living in Alexandria [in Egypt] in the first century before Christ. Alexandria at the time had a largely Greek population and an essentially Greek culture: *The Wisdom of Solomon* was written in Greek and quotes from the Greek version of Scripture but it is addressed to Jews – reminding them of their special destiny and warning them against the spiritual and intellectual temptations that surround them – mysterious cults, pagan rituals, sophisticated philosophical systems. It has none of the anguish of the Book of *Job* or the pithiness of *Proverbs*, but it is fascinating first as a text that was familiar to the first Christians and then as a critique of the kind of sceptical, hedonistic society that we find in the developed world today.

The influence of *The Wisdom of Solomon* on St Paul and the Christian Evangelists, particularly St John, make it a link between the Old and New Testaments. The description of Wisdom could be that of the Holy Spirit: 'For she is the breath of the power of God, and a pure influence flowing from the glory of the Almighty: therefore can no defiled thing fall into her. For she is the brightness of everlasting light, the unspotted mirror of the power of god, and the image of his goodness … and remaining in herself, she maketh all things new: and in all ages, entering into holy souls, she maketh them friends of God, and prophets'. (7:25-27).

There is also the author's esteem for virginity: 'Better to have no children and to have virtue …' (4:1). 'Wherefore blessed is the barren that is undefiled, which hath not known the sinful bed: she shall have fruit in the visitation of souls. And blessed is the eunuch, which his hands hath wrought no iniquity, nor imagined wicked things against God' (3:13-14). This was a radical departure from the accepted notion in Judaism that fertility was a sign of God's blessing and sterility a sign of his disapprobation; and it echoes the passage in St Matthew's Gospel (19:12) where Christ blesses those who make themselves eunuchs for the sake of the Kingdom of God – the text that justifies celibacy as a Christian ideal.

The Wisdom of Solomon's critique of the permissive society of Alexandria in the first century BC goes some way to explain why, in an agnostic age, wisdom has gone out of fashion. To the author, God is the source of wisdom and it is vain to believe that we can reach a true understanding of our condition through the use of our own intellectual resources. 'For what man is he that can know the counsel of God? Or who can think what the will of the Lord is? For the thoughts of mortal men are miserable, and our devices are but uncertain. For the corruptible body presseth down the soul, and the earthy tabernacle weigheth down the mind that museth upon many things' (9:13-15).

Thus, to be wise, a man must be virtuous because sin blocks the conduit from God to man. A virtuous king will be a wise king and therefore a good king, benefitting the community he serves. 'But the multitude of the wise is the welfare of the world: and a wise king is the upholding of his people' (6:24). The benefits of wisdom accrue also to the individual and those around him while the sinners' families share their fate – their 'wives are reckless, their children depraved, their descendants accursed'.

However, the source of the happiness that comes with wisdom is not necessarily the riches, honour and triumph of a Solomon: wisdom will ensure that even if a man does not prosper in this life, he will find his reward in the next. Here we see how the Platonic distinction between body and soul solves the riddle posed by the earlier book of *Job*, and by our observation of the suffering of innocent people. In contrast to the prevailing Jewish view that prosperity and longevity are marks of divine approbation, the author warns the reader not to search for happiness in precisely those things that came to Solomon with his gift of wisdom – honour, riches, concubines and wives. The first twenty verses of the second chapter are in fact a satirical apologia of those who believe that we should eat, drink and be merry for tomorrow we die. 'Our life is short and tedious … the breath in our nostrils is as smoke … Come on, therefore, let us enjoy the good things that are present: and let us speedily use the creatures like as in youth. Let us fill ourselves with costly wine and ointments: and let no flower in the spring pass by us' (2:1-2, 6-7).

To the modern ear, there is something bleak and perhaps a little crabby about the teaching of this Jewish sage. Was he, one wonders, jilted in his youth or passed over for promotion? The nearest equivalent in the present day might be a disgruntled old Catholic priest in San Francisco or New York who feels that society has gone to the dogs – everywhere; 'manslaughter, theft, and dissimulation, corruption, unfaithfulness, tumults, perjury, disquieting of good men, forgetfulness of good turns, defiling souls, changing of kind, disorder in marriages, adultery, and shameless uncleanness' (14:25–6). He seems to relish the fate that awaits sinners: and is delighted that God vents his wrath on their children too, but he is not as vindictive as he at first seems. He wants to persuade his readers that they will benefit from Wisdom because it fosters temperance and prudence, justice and fortitude 'which are such things, as men can have nothing more profitable in their life' (8:7). In other words, wisdom, like virtue, is its own reward.

Although Wisdom is not given an existence distinct from that of God in *The Wisdom of Solomon*, it is personified in the female gender and there are passages, as in *Solomon's Song*, where the author uses the language of a male lover. 'I preferred her before sceptres and thrones, and esteemed riches nothing in comparison of her. Neither compared I unto her any precious stone, because all gold in respect of her is as a little sand, and silver shall be counted as clay before her. I loved her above health and beauty, and chose to have her instead of light; for the light that cometh from her never goeth out' (7:8–10).

In an age when enquiry is perceived as something aggressive that attacks the pit face of the unknown with the pick-axe of the intellect, or seeks to dissect the mysterious with the scalpel of an analytical intelligence, it is surprising to find knowledge presented as feminine – intuitive, passive, receptive. However, this conforms to the perception of one of the few thinkers in modern times who I *would* call wise – the psychoanalyst C G Jung.

Jung was a revered figure in my childhood: my father, Herbert Read, greatly admired him and published his collected works. But he balked at Jung's answer, when asked if he believed in God: *I do not believe, I know*. Like many in his generation, my father was a professed agnostic but, as G.K. Chesterton once wrote, when we cease to believe in God, we do not believe in nothing, we believe in anything – and the god worshipped by my father was art.

How is this relevant to *The Wisdom of Solomon*? In its final section, which describes the role of Wisdom in the deliverance of the Jews led by Moses from the Egyptians, there is a contemptuous digression on idolatry which, according to the author, brings all kinds of evils in its wake – fornication, adultery, orgies and infanticide. At first sight, it seems difficult to point to any modern equivalent to the worship of graven images: perhaps the closest, in a major world religion, is the Hindu's veneration of his different gods.

piers paul read

But if the author of *The Wisdom of Solomon* was to be miraculously transported into one of the great metropolises of the modern world, what would he think? In Wall Street or the City, would he not see a multitude worshipping a golden calf? And if he were to visit our great art galleries, with their august spaces and imposing portals, might he not mistake them for temples? Looking at the solemn, reverential expression of those studying the modern works of art, would he not suppose that here was the worship of idols – images a man 'hath carved … diligently, when he had nothing else to do, and formed … by the skill of his understanding, and fashioned … to the image of a man' (13:13-14). Would he not conclude, with some justice, that at the end of the twentieth century art has largely replaced religion as the object of popular devotion? Are not the great galleries our temples? And do not pilgrims stream to the shrines of culture – the Guggenheim Museum in Bilbao, the Museum of Modern Art in New York? Can we really say that idolatry is a thing of the past?

I ask this with some regret because my father devoted much of his life to the cause of contemporary art – and indeed came to be known in Britain as the apostle of modernism. But his was a god that failed. Towards the end of his life he wrote that he had always found less sustenance in the works of those who deny the reality of a living God – he cited Marx, Nietzsche, Freud, Shaw and Russell – than in those of writers such as George Herbert, Pascal, Spinoza, Kierkegaard, Gerard Manley Hopkins and Simone Weil who affirmed God's existence. He had come to realise, like the Jewish sage in Alexandria twenty-one centuries earlier, that wisdom is not a human accomplishment but a gift from God.

the wisdom of solomon

Love righteousness, ye that be judges of the earth: think of the Lord with a good heart, and in simplicity of heart seek him. ²For he will be found of them that tempt him not; and sheweth himself unto such as do not distrust him. ³For froward thoughts separate from God: and his power, when it is tried, reproveth the unwise. ⁴For into a malicious soul wisdom shall not enter; nor dwell in the body that is subject unto sin. ⁵For the holy spirit of discipline will flee deceit, and remove from thoughts that are without understanding, and will not abide when unrighteousness cometh in.

⁶For wisdom is a loving spirit; and will not acquit a blasphemer of his words: for God is witness of his reins, and a true beholder of his heart, and a hearer of his tongue. ⁷For the Spirit of the Lord filleth the world: and that which containeth all things hath knowledge of the voice. ⁸Therefore he that speaketh unrighteous things cannot be hid: neither shall vengeance, when it punisheth, pass by him. ⁹For inquisition shall be made into the counsels of the ungodly: and the sound of his words shall come unto the Lord for the manifestation of his wicked deeds. ¹⁰For the ear of jealousy heareth all things: and the noise of murmurings is not hid. ¹¹Therefore beware of murmuring, which is unprofitable;

and refrain your tongue from backbiting: for there is no word so secret, that shall go for nought: and the mouth that belieth slayeth the soul.

[12] Seek not death in the error of your life: and pull not upon yourselves destruction with the works of your hands. [13] For God made not death: neither hath he pleasure in the destruction of the living. [14] For he created all things, that they might have their being; and the generations of the world were healthful; and there is no poison of destruction in them, nor the kingdom of death upon the earth. [15] For righteousness is immortal. [16] But ungodly men with their works and words called it to them: for when they thought to have it their friend, they consumed to nought, and made a covenant with it, because they are worthy to take part with it.

2 For the ungodly said, reasoning with themselves, but not aright, 'Our life is short and tedious, and in the death of a man there is no remedy: neither was there any man known to have returned from the grave. ²For we are born at all adventure: and we shall be hereafter as though we had never been; for the breath in our nostrils is as smoke, and a little spark in the moving of our heart, ³which being extinguished, our body shall be turned into ashes, and our spirit shall vanish as the soft air, ⁴and our name shall be forgotten in time, and no man shall have our works in remembrance, and our life shall pass away as the trace of a cloud, and shall be dispersed as a mist, that is driven away with the beams of the sun, and overcome with the heat thereof. ⁵For our time is a very shadow that passeth away; and after our end there is no returning; for it is fast sealed, so that no man cometh again.

⁶'Come on therefore, let us enjoy the good things that are present: and let us speedily use the creatures like as in youth. ⁷Let us fill ourselves with costly wine and ointments: and let no flower of the spring pass by us. ⁸Let us crown ourselves with rosebuds, before they be withered. ⁹Let none of us go without his part of our voluptuousness: let us leave tokens of our joyfulness in every place: for this is our portion, and our lot is this. ¹⁰Let us oppress the poor righteous man, let us not spare the widow, nor reverence the ancient gray hairs of the aged. ¹¹Let our strength be the law of justice: for that which is feeble is found to be nothing worth.

¹²'Therefore let us lie in wait for the righteous; because he is not for our turn, and he is clean contrary to our doings:

he upbraideth us with our offending the law, and objecteth to our infamy the transgressings of our education. ¹³ He professeth to have the knowledge of God: and he calleth himself the child of the Lord. ¹⁴ He was made to reprove our thoughts. ¹⁵ He is grievous unto us even to behold; for his life is not like other men's, his ways are of another fashion. ¹⁶ We are esteemed of him as counterfeits: he abstaineth from our ways as from filthiness: he pronounceth the end of the just to be blessed, and maketh his boast that God is his father. ¹⁷ Let us see if his words be true: and let us prove what shall happen in the end of him. ¹⁸ For if the just man be the son of God, he will help him, and deliver him from the hand of his enemies. ¹⁹ Let us examine him with despitefulness and torture, that we may know his meekness, and prove his patience. ²⁰ Let us condemn him with a shameful death; for by his own saying he shall be respected.' ²¹ Such things they did imagine, and were deceived; for their own wickedness hath blinded them. ²² As for the mysteries of God, they knew them not: neither hoped they for the wages of righteousness, nor discerned a reward for blameless souls. ²³ For God created man to be immortal, and made him to be an image of his own eternity. ²⁴ Nevertheless through envy of the devil came death into the world: and they that do hold of his side do find it.

3 But the souls of the righteous are in the hand of God, and there shall no torment touch them. ²In the sight of the unwise they seemed to die: and their departure is taken for misery, ³and their going from us to be utter destruction: but they are in peace. ⁴For though they be punished in the sight of men, yet is their hope full of immortality. ⁵And having been a little chastised, they shall be greatly rewarded; for God proved them, and found them worthy for himself. ⁶As gold in the furnace hath he tried them, and received them as a burnt offering. ⁷And in the time of their visitation they shall shine, and run to and fro like sparks among the stubble. ⁸They shall judge the nations, and have dominion over the people, and their Lord shall reign for ever. ⁹They that put their trust in him shall understand the truth: and such as be faithful in love shall abide with him; for grace and mercy is to his saints, and he hath care for his elect. ¹⁰But the ungodly shall be punished according to their own imaginations, which have neglected the righteous, and forsaken the Lord. ¹¹For whoso despiseth wisdom and nurture, he is miserable, and their hope is vain, their labours unfruitful, and their works unprofitable. ¹²Their wives are foolish, and their children wicked: ¹³their offspring is cursed. Wherefore blessed is the barren that is undefiled, which hath not known the sinful bed: she shall have fruit in the visitation of souls. ¹⁴And blessed is the eunuch, which with his hands hath wrought no iniquity, nor imagined wicked things against God; for unto him shall be given the special gift of faith, and an inheritance in the temple of the Lord more acceptable to his mind.

[15] For glorious is the fruit of good labours: and the root of wisdom shall never fall away. [16] As for the children of adulterers, they shall not come to their perfection, and the seed of an unrighteous bed shall be rooted out. [17] For though they live long, yet shall they be nothing regarded: and their last age shall be without honour. [18] Or, if they die quickly, they have no hope, neither comfort in the day of trial. [19] For horrible is the end of the unrighteous generation.

4 Better it is to have no children, and to have virtue; for the memorial thereof is immortal, because it is known with God, and with men. ²When it is present, men take example at it; and when it is gone, they desire it: it weareth a crown, and triumpheth for ever, having gotten the victory, striving for undefiled rewards. ³But the multiplying brood of the ungodly shall not thrive, nor take deep rooting from bastard slips, nor lay any fast foundation. ⁴For though they flourish in branches for a time; yet standing not fast, they shall be shaken with the wind, and through the force of winds they shall be rooted out. ⁵The imperfect branches shall be broken off, their fruit unprofitable, not ripe to eat, yea, meet for nothing. ⁶For children begotten of unlawful beds are witnesses of wickedness against their parents in their trial. ⁷But though the righteous be prevented with death, yet shall he be in rest. ⁸For honourable age is not that which standeth in length of time, nor that is measured by number of years. ⁹But wisdom is the gray hair unto men, and an unspotted life is old age.

¹⁰He pleased God, and was beloved of him, so that living among sinners he was translated. ¹¹Yea, speedily was he taken away, lest that wickedness should alter his understanding, or deceit beguile his soul. ¹²For the bewitching of naughtiness doth obscure things that are honest; and the wandering of concupiscence doth undermine the simple mind. ¹³He, being made perfect in a short time, fulfilled a long time; ¹⁴for his soul pleased the Lord: therefore hasted he to take him away from among the wicked. ¹⁵This the

people saw, and understood it not, neither laid they up this in their minds, that his grace and mercy is with his saints, and that he hath respect unto his chosen.

[16] Thus the righteous that is dead shall condemn the ungodly which are living; and youth that is soon perfected the many years and old age of the unrighteous. [17] For they shall see the end of the wise, and shall not understand what God in his counsel hath decreed of him, and to what end the Lord hath set him in safety. [18] They shall see him, and despise him; but God shall laugh them to scorn: and they shall hereafter be a vile carcase, and a reproach among the dead for evermore. [19] For he shall rend them, and cast them down headlong, that they shall be speechless; and he shall shake them from the foundation; and they shall be utterly laid waste, and be in sorrow; and their memorial shall perish. [20] And when they cast up the accounts of their sins, they shall come with fear: and their own iniquities shall convince them to their face.

5 Then shall the righteous man stand in great boldness before the face of such as have afflicted him, and made no account of his labours. ² When they see it, they shall be troubled with terrible fear, and shall be amazed at the strangeness of his salvation, so far beyond all that they looked for. ³ And they repenting and groaning for anguish of spirit shall say within themselves, 'This was he, whom we had sometimes in derision, and a proverb of reproach. ⁴ We fools accounted his life madness, and his end to be without honour. ⁵ How is he numbered among the children of God, and his lot is among the saints! ⁶ Therefore have we erred from the way of truth, and the light of righteousness hath not shined unto us, and the sun of righteousness rose not upon us. ⁷ We wearied ourselves in the way of wickedness and destruction: yea, we have gone through deserts, where there lay no way; but as for the way of the Lord, we have not known it. ⁸ What hath pride profited us? Or what good hath riches with our vaunting brought us?

⁹ 'All those things are passed away like a shadow, and as a post that hasted by; ¹⁰ and as a ship that passeth over the waves of the water, which when it is gone by, the trace thereof cannot be found, neither the pathway of the keel in the waves; ¹¹ or as when a bird hath flown through the air, there is no token of her way to be found, but the light air being beaten with the stroke of her wings, and parted with the violent noise and motion of them, is passed through, and therein afterwards no sign where she went is to be found; ¹² or like as when an arrow is shot at a mark, it parteth

the air, which immediately cometh together again, so that a man cannot know where it went through: ¹³even so we in like manner, as soon as we were born, began to draw to our end, and had no sign of virtue to shew; but were consumed in our own wickedness.' ¹⁴For the hope of the ungodly is like dust that is blown away with the wind; like a thin froth that is driven away with the storm; like as the smoke which is dispersed here and there with a tempest, and passeth away as the remembrance of a guest that tarrieth but a day.

¹⁵But the righteous live for evermore; their reward also is with the Lord, and the care of them is with the most High. ¹⁶Therefore shall they receive a glorious kingdom, and a beautiful crown from the Lord's hand; for with his right hand shall he cover them, and with his arm shall he protect them. ¹⁷He shall take to him his jealousy for complete armour, and make the creature his weapon for the revenge of his enemies. ¹⁸He shall put on righteousness as a breastplate, and true judgment instead of an helmet. ¹⁹He shall take holiness for an invincible shield. ²⁰His severe wrath shall he sharpen for a sword, and the world shall fight with him against the unwise. ²¹Then shall the right aiming thunderbolts go abroad; and from the clouds, as from a well drawn bow, shall they fly to the mark. ²²And hailstones full of wrath shall be cast as out of a stone bow, and the water of the sea shall rage against them, and the floods shall cruelly drown them. ²³Yea, a mighty wind shall stand up against them, and like a storm shall blow them away: thus iniquity shall lay waste the whole earth, and ill dealing shall overthrow the thrones of the mighty.

6 Hear therefore, O ye kings, and understand; learn, ye that be judges of the ends of the earth. ² Give ear, ye that rule the people, and glory in the multitude of nations. ³ For power is given you of the Lord, and sovereignty from the Highest, who shall try your works, and search out your counsels. ⁴ Because, being ministers of his kingdom, ye have not judged aright, nor kept the law, nor walked after the counsel of God; ⁵ horribly and speedily shall he come upon you; for a sharp judgment shall be to them that be in high places. ⁶ For mercy will soon pardon the meanest; but mighty men shall be mightily tormented. ⁷ For he which is Lord over all shall fear no man's person, neither shall he stand in awe of any man's greatness; for he hath made the small and great, and careth for all alike. ⁸ But a sore trial shall come upon the mighty. ⁹ Unto you therefore, O kings, do I speak, that ye may learn wisdom, and not fall away. ¹⁰ For they that keep holiness holily shall be judged holy: and they that have learned such things shall find what to answer. ¹¹ Wherefore set your affection upon my words; desire them, and ye shall be instructed.

¹² Wisdom is glorious, and never fadeth away: yea, she is easily seen of them that love her, and found of such as seek her. ¹³ She preventeth them that desire her, in making herself first known unto them. ¹⁴ Whoso seeketh her early shall have no great travail; for he shall find her sitting at his doors. ¹⁵ To think therefore upon her is perfection of wisdom: and whoso watcheth for her shall quickly be without care. ¹⁶ For she goeth about seeking such as are worthy of her, sheweth

herself favourably unto them in the ways, and meeteth them in every thought.

[17] For the very true beginning of her is the desire of discipline; and the care of discipline is love; [18] and love is the keeping of her laws; and the giving heed unto her laws is the assurance of incorruption; [19] and incorruption maketh us near unto God: [20] therefore the desire of wisdom bringeth to a kingdom.

[21] If your delight be then in thrones and sceptres, O ye kings of the people, honour wisdom, that ye may reign for evermore. [22] As for wisdom, what she is, and how she came up, I will tell you, and will not hide mysteries from you; but will seek her out from the beginning of her nativity, and bring the knowledge of her into light, and will not pass over the truth. [23] Neither will I go with consuming envy; for such a man shall have no fellowship with wisdom. [24] But the multitude of the wise is the welfare of the world: and a wise king is the upholding of the people. [25] Receive therefore instruction through my words, and it shall do you good.

7 I myself also am a mortal man, like to all, and the offspring of him that was first made of the earth, ²and in my mother's womb was fashioned to be flesh in the time of ten months, being compacted in blood, of the seed of man, and the pleasure that came with sleep. ³And when I was born, I drew in the common air, and fell upon the earth, which is of like nature, and the first voice which I uttered was crying, as all others do. ⁴I was nursed in swaddling clothes, and that with cares. ⁵For there is no king that had any other beginning of birth. ⁶For all men have one entrance into life, and the like going out. ⁷Wherefore I prayed, and understanding was given me: I called upon God, and the spirit of wisdom came to me. ⁸I preferred her before sceptres and thrones, and esteemed riches nothing in comparison of her. ⁹Neither compared I unto her any precious stone, because all gold in respect of her is as a little sand, and silver shall be counted as clay before her. ¹⁰I loved her above health and beauty, and chose to have her instead of light: for the light that cometh from her never goeth out. ¹¹All good things together came to me with her, and innumerable riches in her hands. ¹²And I rejoiced in them all, because wisdom goeth before them: and I knew not that she was the mother of them. ¹³I learned diligently, and do communicate her liberally: I do not hide her riches. ¹⁴For she is a treasure unto men that never faileth, which they that use become the friends of God, being commended for the gifts that come from learning.

¹⁵God hath granted me to speak as I would, and to con-

ceive as is meet for the things that are given me, because it is he that leadeth unto wisdom, and directeth the wise. [16] For in his hand are both we and our words; all wisdom also, and knowledge of workmanship. [17] For he hath given me certain knowledge of the things that are, namely, to know how the world was made, and the operation of the elements; [18] the beginning, ending, and midst of the times: the alterations of the turning of the sun, and the change of seasons; [19] the circuits of years, and the positions of stars; [20] the natures of living creàtures, and the furies of wild beasts; the violence of winds, and the reasonings of men; the diversities of plants, and the virtues of roots; [21] and all such things as are either secret or manifest, them I know. [22] For wisdom, which is the worker of all things, taught me; for in her is an understanding spirit, holy, one only, manifold, subtil, lively, clear, undefiled, plain, not subject to hurt, loving the thing that is good, quick, which cannot be letted, ready to do good, [23] kind to man, stedfast, sure, free from care, having all power, overseeing all things, and going through all understanding, pure, and most subtil, spirits. [24] For wisdom is more moving than any motion: she passeth and goeth through all things by reason of her pureness. [25] For she is the breath of the power of God, and a pure influence flowing from the glory of the Almighty: therefore can no defiled thing fall into her. [26] For she is the brightness of the everlasting light, the unspotted mirror of the power of God, and the image of his goodness. [27] And being but one, she can do all things: and remaining in herself, she maketh all things new: and in all ages entering into holy souls, she maketh them friends of God, and prophets. [28] For God loveth none but him that dwelleth with wisdom. [29] For she is more beautiful than the sun, and above all the order of stars: being compared with the light, she is found before it. [30] For after this cometh night; but vice shall not prevail against wisdom.

8 Wisdom reacheth from one end to another mightily: and sweetly doth she order all things. ²I loved her, and sought her out from my youth, I desired to make her my spouse, and I was a lover of her beauty. ³In that she is conversant with God, she magnifieth her nobility: yea, the Lord of all things himself loved her. ⁴For she is privy to the mysteries of the knowledge of God, and a lover of his works. ⁵If riches be a possession to be desired in this life; what is richer than wisdom, that worketh all things? ⁶And if prudence work; who of all that are is a more cunning workman than she? ⁷And if a man love righteousness, her labours are virtues; for she teacheth temperance and prudence, justice and fortitude, which are such things, as men can have nothing more profitable in their life. ⁸If a man desire much experience, she knoweth things of old, and conjectureth aright what is to come: she knoweth the subtilties of speeches, and can expound dark sentences: she foreseeth signs and wonders, and the events of seasons and times. ⁹Therefore I purposed to take her to me to live with me, knowing that she would be a counsellor of good things, and a comfort in cares and grief. ¹⁰For her sake I shall have estimation among the multitude, and honour with the elders, though I be young. ¹¹I shall be found of a quick conceit in judgment, and shall be admired in the sight of great men. ¹²When I hold my tongue, they shall bide my leisure, and when I speak, they shall give good ear unto me: if I talk much, they shall lay their hands upon their mouth. ¹³Moreover by the means of her I shall obtain immortality, and leave behind me an everlasting

memorial to them that come after me. [14] I shall set the people in order, and the nations shall be subject unto me. [15] Horrible tyrants shall be afraid, when they do but hear of me; I shall be found good among the multitude, and valiant in war.

[16] After I am come into mine house, I will repose myself with her; for her conversation hath no bitterness; and to live with her hath no sorrow, but mirth and joy. [17] Now when I considered these things in myself, and pondered them in my heart, how that to be allied unto wisdom is immortality; [18] and great pleasure it is to have her friendship; and in the works of her hands are infinite riches; and in the exercise of conference with her, prudence; and in talking with her, a good report; I went about seeking how to take her to me. [19] For I was a witty child, and had a good spirit. [20] Yea rather, being good, I came into a body undefiled. [21] Nevertheless, when I perceived that I could not otherwise obtain her, except God gave her me; and that was a point of wisdom also to know whose gift she was; I prayed unto the Lord, and besought him, and with my whole heart I said,

9 ¹O God of my fathers, and Lord of mercy, who hast made all things with thy word, ²and ordained man through thy wisdom, that he should have dominion over the creatures which thou hast made, ³and order the world according to equity and righteousness, and execute judgment with an upright heart: ⁴give me wisdom, that sitteth by thy throne; and reject me not from among thy children. ⁵For I thy servant and son of thine handmaid am a feeble person, and of a short time, and too young for the understanding of judgment and laws. ⁶For though a man be never so perfect among the children of men, yet if thy wisdom be not with him, he shall be nothing regarded. ⁷Thou hast chosen me to be a king of thy people, and a judge of thy sons and daughters. ⁸Thou hast commanded me to build a temple upon thy holy mount, and an altar in the city wherein thou dwellest, a resemblance of the holy tabernacle, which thou hast prepared from the beginning. ⁹And wisdom was with thee, which knoweth thy works, and was present when thou madest the world, and knew what was acceptable in thy sight, and right in thy commandments. ¹⁰O send her out of thy holy heavens, and from the throne of thy glory, that being present she may labour with me, that I may know what is pleasing unto thee. ¹¹For she knoweth and understandeth all things, and she shall lead me soberly in my doings, and preserve me in her power. ¹²So shall my works be acceptable, and then shall I judge thy people righteously, and be worthy to sit in my father's seat. ¹³For what man is he that can know the counsel of God? Or who can think what the will of the

Lord is? [14] For the thoughts of mortal men are miserable, and our devices are but uncertain. [15] For the corruptible body presseth down the soul, and the earthy tabernacle weigheth down the mind that museth upon many things. [16] And hardly do we guess aright at things that are upon earth, and with labour do we find the things that are before us, but the things that are in heaven who hath searched out? [17] And thy counsel who hath known, except thou give wisdom, and send thy Holy Spirit from above? [18] For so the ways of them which lived on the earth were reformed, and men were taught the things that are pleasing unto thee, and were saved through wisdom.'

10 She preserved the first formed father of the world, that was created alone, and brought him out of his fall, ²and gave him power to rule all things. ³But when the unrighteous went away from her in his anger, he perished also in the fury wherewith he murdered his brother. ⁴For whose cause the earth being drowned with the flood, wisdom again preserved it, and directed the course of the righteous in a piece of wood of small value.

⁵Moreover, the nations in their wicked conspiracy being confounded, she found out the righteous, and preserved him blameless unto God, and kept him strong against his tender compassion toward his son.

⁶When the ungodly perished, she delivered the righteous man, who fled from the fire which fell down upon the five cities. ⁷Of whose wickedness even to this day the waste land that smoketh is a testimony, and plants bearing fruit that never come to ripeness: and a standing pillar of salt is a monument of an unbelieving soul. ⁸For regarding not wisdom, they gat not only this hurt, that they knew not the things which were good; but also left behind them to the world a memorial of their foolishness: so that in the things wherein they offended they could not so much as be hid.

⁹But wisdom delivered from pain those that attended upon her. ¹⁰When the righteous fled from his brother's wrath, she guided him in right paths, shewed him the kingdom of God, and gave him knowledge of holy things, made him rich in his travels, and multiplied the fruit of his labours. ¹¹In the covetousness of such as oppressed him she

stood by him, and made him rich. ¹²She defended him from his enemies, and kept him safe from those that lay in wait, and in a sore conflict she gave him the victory; that he might know that godliness is stronger than all.

¹³When the righteous was sold, she forsook him not, but delivered him from sin: she went down with him into the pit, ¹⁴and left him not in bonds, till she brought him the sceptre of the kingdom, and power against those that oppressed him: as for them that had accused him, she shewed them to be liars, and gave him perpetual glory.

¹⁵She delivered the righteous people and blameless seed from the nation that oppressed them. ¹⁶She entered into the soul of the servant of the Lord, and withstood dreadful kings in wonders and signs; ¹⁷rendered to the righteous a reward of their labours, guided them in a marvellous way, and was unto them for a cover by day, and a light of stars in the night season; ¹⁸brought them through the Red sea, and led them through much water. ¹⁹But she drowned their enemies, and cast them up out of the bottom of the deep. ²⁰Therefore the righteous spoiled the ungodly, and praised thy holy name, O Lord, and magnified with one accord thine hand, that fought for them. ²¹For wisdom opened the mouth of the dumb, and made the tongues of them that cannot speak eloquent.

11 She prospered their works in the hand of the holy prophet. ²They went through the wilderness that was not inhabited, and pitched tents in places where there lay no way. ³They stood against their enemies, and were avenged of their adversaries. ⁴When they were thirsty, they called upon thee, and water was given them out of the flinty rock, and their thirst was quenched out of the hard stone. ⁵For by what things their enemies were punished, by the same they in their need were benefited. ⁶For instead of a fountain of a perpetual running river troubled with foul blood, ⁷for a manifest reproof of that commandment, whereby the infants were slain, thou gavest unto them abundance of water by a means which they hoped not for: ⁸declaring by that thirst then how thou hadst punished their adversaries. ⁹For when they were tried, albeit but in mercy chastised, they knew how the ungodly were judged in wrath and tormented, thirsting in another manner than the just. ¹⁰For these thou didst admonish and try, as a father: but the other, as a severe king, thou didst condemn and punish. ¹¹Whether they were absent or present, they were vexed alike. ¹²For a double grief came upon them, and a groaning for the remembrance of things past. ¹³For when they heard by their own punishments the other to be benefited, they had some feeling of the Lord. ¹⁴For whom they rejected with scorn, when he was long before thrown out at the casting forth of the infants, him in the end, when they saw what came to pass, they admired.

¹⁵But for the foolish devices of their wickedness, wherewith being deceived they worshipped serpents void of

reason, and vile beasts, thou didst send a multitude of unreasonable beasts upon them for vengeance, [16] that they might know, that wherewithal a man sinneth, by the same also shall he be punished. [17] For thy Almighty hand, that made the world of matter without form, wanted not means to send among them a multitude of bears, or fierce lions, [18] or unknown wild beasts, full of rage, newly created, breathing out either a fiery vapour, or filthy scents of scattered smoke, or shooting horrible sparkles out of their eyes, [19] whereof not only the harm might dispatch them at once, but also the terrible sight utterly destroy them. [20] Yea, and without these might they have fallen down with one blast, being persecuted of vengeance, and scattered abroad through the breath of thy power; but thou hast ordered all things in measure and number and weight.

[21] For thou canst shew thy great strength at all times when thou wilt; and who may withstand the power of thine arm? [22] For the whole world before thee is as a little grain of the balance, yea, as a drop of the morning dew that falleth down upon the earth. [23] But thou hast mercy upon all; for thou canst do all things, and winkest at the sins of men, because they should amend. [24] For thou lovest all the things that are, and abhorrest nothing which thou hast made: for never wouldest thou have made any thing, if thou hadst hated it. [25] And how could any thing have endured, if it had not been thy will? Or been preserved, if not called by thee? [26] But thou sparest all, for they are thine, O Lord, thou lover of souls.

12 For thine incorruptible Spirit is in all things. [2] Therefore chastenest thou them by little and little that offend, and warnest them by putting them in remembrance wherein they have offended, that leaving their wickedness they may believe on thee, O Lord.

[3] For it was thy will to destroy by the hands of our fathers both those old inhabitants of thy holy land, [4] whom thou hatedst for doing most odious works of witchcrafts, and wicked sacrifices; [5] and also those merciless murderers of children, and devourers of man's flesh, and the feasts of blood, [6] with their priests out of the midst of their idolatrous crew, and the parents, that killed with their own hands souls destitute of help: [7] that the land, which thou esteemedst above all other, might receive a worthy colony of God's children. [8] Nevertheless even those thou sparedst as men, and didst send wasps, forerunners of thine host, to destroy them by little and little. [9] Not that thou wast unable to bring the ungodly under the hand of the righteous in battle, or to destroy them at once with cruel beasts, or with one rough word, [10] but executing thy judgments upon them by little and little, thou gavest them place of repentance, not being ignorant that they were a naughty generation, and that their malice was bred in them, and that their cogitation would never be changed. [11] For it was a cursed seed from the beginning; neither didst thou for fear of any man give them pardon for those things wherein they sinned.

[12] For who shall say, 'What hast thou done?' Or who shall withstand thy judgment? Or who shall accuse thee for the

nations that perish, whom thou hast made? Or who shall come to stand against thee, to be revenged for the unrighteous men? [13] For neither is there any God but thou that careth for all, to whom thou mightest shew that thy judgment is not unright. [14] Neither shall king or tyrant be able to set his face against thee for any whom thou hast punished. [15] Forsomuch then as thou art righteous thyself, thou orderest all things righteously: thinking it not agreeable with thy power to condemn him that hath not deserved to be punished. [16] For thy power is the beginning of righteousness, and because thou art the Lord of all, it maketh thee to be gracious unto all. [17] For when men will not believe that thou art of a full power, thou shewest thy strength, and among them that know it thou makest their boldness manifest. [18] But thou, mastering thy power, judgest with equity, and orderest us with great favour, for thou mayest use power when thou wilt.

[19] But by such works hast thou taught thy people that the just man should be merciful, and hast made thy children to be of a good hope that thou givest repentance for sins. [20] For if thou didst punish the enemies of thy children, and the condemned to death, with such deliberation, giving them time and place, whereby they might be delivered from their malice: [21] with how great circumspection didst thou judge thine own sons, unto whose fathers thou hast sworn, and made covenants of good promises? [22] Therefore, whereas thou dost chasten us, thou scourgest our enemies a thousand times more, to the intent that, when we judge, we should

carefully think of thy goodness, and when we ourselves are judged, we should look for mercy.

[23] Wherefore, whereas men have lived dissolutely and unrighteously, thou hast tormented them with their own abominations. [24] For they went astray very far in the ways of error, and held them for gods, which even among the beasts of their enemies were despised, being deceived, as children of no understanding. [25] Therefore unto them, as to children without the use of reason, thou didst send a judgment to mock them. [26] But they that would not be reformed by that correction, wherein he dallied with them, shall feel a judgment worthy of God. [27] For, look, for what things they grudged, when they were punished, that is, for them whom they thought to be gods; [now] being punished in them, when they saw it, they acknowledged him to be the true God, whom before they denied to know; and therefore came extreme damnation upon them.

13 Surely vain are all men by nature, who are ignorant of God, and could not out of the good things that are seen know him that is: neither by considering the works did they acknowledge the workmaster; ² but deemed either fire, or wind, or the swift air, or the circle of the stars, or the violent water, or the lights of heaven, to be the gods which govern the world. ³ With whose beauty if they being delighted took them to be gods; let them know how much better the Lord of them is; for the first author of beauty hath created them. ⁴ But if they were astonished at their power and virtue, let them understand by them, how much mightier he is that made them. ⁵ For by the greatness and beauty of the creatures proportionably the maker of them is seen. ⁶ But yet for this they are the less to be blamed; for they peradventure err, seeking God, and desirous to find him. ⁷ For being conversant in his works they search him diligently, and believe their sight, because the things are beautiful that are seen. ⁸ Howbeit neither are they to be pardoned. ⁹ For if they were able to know so much, that they could aim at the world; how did they not sooner find out the Lord thereof? ¹⁰ But miserable are they, and in dead things is their hope, who called them gods, which are the works of men's hands, gold and silver, to shew art in, and resemblances of beasts, or a stone good for nothing, the work of an ancient hand. ¹¹ Now a carpenter that felleth timber, after he hath sawn down a tree meet for the purpose, and taken off all the bark skilfully round about, and hath wrought it handsomely, and made a vessel thereof fit for the service of man's life; ¹² and after spending the refuse of his work to dress his meat, hath filled himself; [13] and taking the very refuse among those which served to no use, being a crooked piece of wood, and full of knots, hath carved it diligently, when he had nothing else to do, and formed it by the skill of his understanding, and fashioned it to the image of a man; [14] or made it like some vile beast, laying it over with vermilion, and with paint colouring it red, and covering every spot therein; [15] and when he had made a convenient room for it, set it in a wall, and made it fast with iron. [16] For he provided for it that it might not fall, knowing that it was unable to help itself; for it is an image, and hath need of help. [17] Then maketh he prayer for his goods, for his wife and children, and is not ashamed to speak to that which hath no life. [18] For health he calleth upon that which is weak; for life prayeth to that which is dead; for aid humbly beseecheth that which hath least means to help; and for a good journey he asketh of that which cannot set a foot forward; [19] and for gaining and getting, and for good success of his hands, asketh ability to do of him, that is most unable to do any thing.

14 Again, one preparing himself to sail, and about to pass through the raging waves, calleth upon a piece of wood more rotten than the vessel that carrieth him. ² For verily desire of gain devised that, and the workman built it by his skill. ³ But thy providence, O Father, governeth it: for thou hast made a way in the sea, and a safe path in the waves; ⁴ shewing that thou canst save from all danger: yea, though a man went to sea without art. ⁵ Nevertheless thou wouldest not that the works of thy wisdom should be idle, and therefore do men commit their lives to a small piece of wood, and passing the rough sea in a weak vessel are saved. ⁶ For in the old time also, when the proud giants perished, the hope of the world governed by thy hand escaped in a weak vessel, and left to all ages a seed of generation. ⁷ For blessed is the wood whereby righteousness cometh.

⁸ But that which is made with hands is cursed, as well it, as he that made it: he, because he made it; and it, because, being corruptible, it was called god. ⁹ For the ungodly and his ungodliness are both alike hateful unto God. ¹⁰ For that which is made shall be punished together with him that made it. ¹¹ Therefore even upon the idols of the Gentiles shall there be a visitation, because in the creature of God they are become an abomination, and stumbling-blocks to the souls of men, and a snare to the feet of the unwise.

¹² For the devising of idols was the beginning of spiritual fornication, and the invention of them the corruption of life. ¹³ For neither were they from the beginning, neither shall they be for ever. ¹⁴ For by the vain glory of men they entered

into the world, and therefore shall they come shortly to an end.

[15] For a father afflicted with untimely mourning, when he hath made an image of his child soon taken away, now honoured him as a god, which was then a dead man, and delivered to those that were under him ceremonies and sacrifices. [16] Thus in process of time an ungodly custom grown strong was kept as a law, and graven images were worshipped by the commandments of kings. [17] Whom men could not honour in presence, because they dwelt far off, they took the counterfeit of his visage from far, and made an express image of a king whom they honoured, to the end that by this their forwardness they might flatter him that was absent, as if he were present. [18] Also the singular diligence of the artificer did help to set forward the ignorant to more superstition. [19] For he, peradventure willing to please one in authority, forced all his skill to make the resemblance of the best fashion. [20] And so the multitude, allured by the grace of the work, took him now for a god, which a little before was but honoured as a man. [21] And this was an occasion to deceive the world; for men, serving either calamity or tyranny, did ascribe unto stones and stocks the incommunicable name.

[22] Moreover this was not enough for them, that they erred in the knowledge of God; but whereas they lived in the great war of ignorance, those so great plagues called they peace. [23] For whilst they slew their children in sacrifices, or used secret ceremonies, or made revellings of strange rites, [24] they

kept neither lives nor marriages any longer undefiled: but either one slew another traiterously, or grieved him by adultery. ²⁵ So that there reigned in all men without exception blood, manslaughter, theft, and dissimulation, corruption, unfaithfulness, tumults, perjury, ²⁶ disquieting of good men, forgetfulness of good turns, defiling of souls, changing of kind, disorder in marriages, adultery, and shameless uncleanness. ²⁷ For the worshipping of idols not to be named is the beginning, the cause, and the end, of all evil. ²⁸ For either they are mad when they be merry, or prophesy lies, or live unjustly, or else lightly forswear themselves. ²⁹ For insomuch as their trust is in idols, which have no life; though they swear falsely, yet they look not to be hurt. ³⁰ Howbeit for both causes shall they be justly punished: both because they thought not well of God, giving heed unto idols, and also unjustly swore in deceit, despising holiness. ³¹ For it is not the power of them by whom they swear: but it is the just vengeance of sinners, that punisheth always the offence of the ungodly.

15 But thou, O God, art gracious and true, longsuffering, and in mercy ordering all things. ²For if we sin, we are thine, knowing thy power; but we will not sin, knowing that we are counted thine. ³For to know thee is perfect righteousness: yea, to know thy power is the root of immortality. ⁴For neither did the mischievous invention of men deceive us, nor an image spotted with divers colours, the painter's fruitless labour; ⁵the sight whereof enticeth fools to lust after it, and so they desire the form of a dead image, that hath no breath. ⁶Both they that make them, they that desire them, and they that worship them, are lovers of evil things, and are worthy to have such things to trust upon.

⁷For the potter, tempering soft earth, fashioneth every vessel with much labour for our service: yea, of the same clay he maketh both the vessels that serve for clean uses, and likewise also all such as serve to the contrary; but what is the use of either sort, the potter himself is the judge. ⁸And employing his labours lewdly, he maketh a vain god of the same clay, even he which a little before was made of earth himself, and within a little while after returneth to the same, out of the which he was taken, when his life which was lent him shall be demanded. ⁹Notwithstanding his care is, not that he shall have much labour, nor that his life is short; but striveth to excel goldsmiths and silversmiths, and endeavoureth to do like the workers in brass, and counteth it his glory to make counterfeit things. ¹⁰His heart is ashes, his hope is more vile than earth, and his life of less value than clay: ¹¹forasmuch as he knew not his Maker, and him that

inspired into him an active soul, and breathed in a living spirit. ¹²But they counted our life a pastime, and our time here a market for gain; for, say they, we must be getting every way, though it be by evil means. ¹³For this man, that of earthly matter maketh brittle vessels and graven images, knoweth himself to offend above all others.

¹⁴And all the enemies of thy people, that hold them in subjection, are most foolish, and are more miserable than very babes. ¹⁵For they counted all the idols of the heathen to be gods, which neither have the use of eyes to see, nor noses to draw breath, nor ears to hear, nor fingers of hands to handle; and as for their feet, they are slow to go. ¹⁶For man made them, and he that borrowed his own spirit fashioned them; but no man can make a god like unto himself. ¹⁷For being mortal, he worketh a dead thing with wicked hands; for he himself is better than the things which he worshippeth: whereas he lived once, but they never.

¹⁸Yea, they worshipped those beasts also that are most hateful; for being compared together, some are worse than others. ¹⁹Neither are they beautiful, so much as to be desired in respect of beasts; but they went without the praise of God and his blessing.

16 Therefore by the like were they punished worthily, and by the multitude of beasts tormented. ²Instead of which punishment, dealing graciously with thine own people, thou preparedst for them meat of a strange taste, even quails to stir up their appetite; ³to the end that they, desiring food, might for the ugly sight of the beasts sent among them lothe even that, which they must needs desire; but these, suffering penury for a short space, might be made partakers of a strange taste. ⁴For it was requisite, that upon them exercising tyranny should come penury, which they could not avoid; but to these it should only be shewed how their enemies were tormented.

⁵For when the horrible fierceness of beasts came upon these, and they perished with the stings of crooked serpents, thy wrath endured not for ever; ⁶but they were troubled for a small season, that they might be admonished, having a sign of salvation, to put them in remembrance of the commandment of thy law.

⁷For he that turned himself toward it was not saved by the thing that he saw, but by thee, that art the Saviour of all. ⁸And in this thou madest thine enemies confess, that it is thou who deliverest from all evil. ⁹For them the bitings of grasshoppers and flies killed, neither was there found any remedy for their life; for they were worthy to be punished by such. ¹⁰But thy sons not the very teeth of venomous dragons overcame; for thy mercy was ever by them, and healed them. ¹¹For they were pricked, that they should remember thy words; and were quickly saved, that not falling into

deep forgetfulness, they might be continually mindful of thy goodness. ¹²For it was neither herb, nor mollifying plaister, that restored them to health, but thy word, O Lord, which healeth all things. ¹³For thou hast power of life and death: thou leadest to the gates of hell, and bringest up again. ¹⁴A man indeed killeth through his malice: and the spirit, when it is gone forth, returneth not; neither the soul received up cometh again.

¹⁵But it is not possible to escape thine hand. ¹⁶For the ungodly, that denied to know thee, were scourged by the strength of thine arm: with strange rains, hails, and showers, were they persecuted, that they could not avoid, and through fire were they consumed. ¹⁷For, which is most to be wondered at, the fire had more force in the water, that quencheth all things; for the world fighteth for the righteous. ¹⁸For sometime the flame was mitigated, that it might not burn up the beasts that were sent against the ungodly; but themselves might see and perceive that they were persecuted with the judgment of God. ¹⁹And at another time it burneth even in the midst of water above the power of fire, that it might destroy the fruits of an unjust land. ²⁰Instead whereof thou feddest thine own people with angels' food, and didst send them from heaven bread prepared without their labour, able to content every man's delight, and agreeing to every taste. ²¹For thy sustenance declared thy sweetness unto thy children, and serving to the appetite of the eater, tempered itself to every man's liking. ²²But snow and ice endured the fire, and melted not, that they might know that

fire burning in the hail, and sparkling in the rain, did destroy the fruits of the enemies. ²³ But this again did even forget his own strength, that the righteous might be nourished.

²⁴ For the creature that serveth thee, who art the Maker, increaseth his strength against the unrighteous for their punishment, and abateth his strength for the benefit of such as put their trust in thee. ²⁵ Therefore even then was it altered into all fashions, and was obedient to thy grace, that nourisheth all things, according to the desire of them that had need, ²⁶ that thy children, O Lord, whom thou lovest, might know, that it is not the growing of fruits that nourisheth man; but that it is thy word, which preserveth them that put their trust in thee. ²⁷ For that which was not destroyed of the fire, being warmed with a little sunbeam, soon melted away, ²⁸ that it might be known, that we must prevent the sun to give thee thanks, and at the dayspring pray unto thee. ²⁹ For the hope of the unthankful shall melt away as the winter's hoar frost, and shall run away as unprofitable water.

17 For great are thy judgments, and cannot be expressed: therefore unnurtured souls have erred. ²For when unrighteous men thought to oppress the holy nation; they being shut up in their houses, the prisoners of darkness, and fettered with the bonds of a long night, lay [there] exiled from the eternal providence. ³For while they supposed to lie hid in their secret sins, they were scattered under a dark veil of forgetfulness, being horribly astonished, and troubled with [strange] apparitions. ⁴For neither might the corner that held them keep them from fear; but noises [as of waters] falling down sounded about them, and sad visions appeared unto them with heavy countenances. ⁵No power of the fire might give them light: neither could the bright flames of the stars endure to lighten that horrible night. ⁶Only there appeared unto them a fire kindled of itself, very dreadful; for being much terrified, they thought the things which they saw to be worse than the sight they saw not. ⁷As for the illusions of art magick, they were put down, and their vaunting in wisdom was reproved with disgrace. ⁸For they, that promised to drive away terrors and troubles from a sick soul, were sick themselves of fear, worthy to be laughed at. ⁹For though no terrible thing did fear them; yet being scared with beasts that passed by, and hissing of serpents, ¹⁰they died for fear, denying that they saw the air, which could of no side be avoided. ¹¹For wickedness, condemned by her own witness, is very timorous, and being pressed with conscience, always forecasteth grievous things. ¹²For fear is nothing else but a betraying of the succours which reason

offereth. ¹³And the expectation from within, being less, counteth the ignorance more than the cause which bringeth the torment. ¹⁴But they sleeping the same sleep that night, which was indeed intolerable, and which came upon them out of the bottoms of inevitable hell, ¹⁵were partly vexed with monstrous apparitions, and partly fainted, their heart failing them; for a sudden fear, and not looked for, came upon them. ¹⁶So then whosoever there fell down was straitly kept, shut up in a prison without iron bars. ¹⁷For whether he were husbandman, or shepherd, or a labourer in the field, he was overtaken, and endured that necessity, which could not be avoided; for they were all bound with one chain of darkness. ¹⁸Whether it were a whistling wind, or a melodious noise of birds among the spreading branches, or a pleasing fall of water running violently, ¹⁹or a terrible sound of stones cast down, or a running that could not be seen of skipping beasts, or a roaring voice of most savage wild beasts, or a rebounding echo from the hollow mountains; these things made them to swoon for fear. ²⁰For the whole world shined with clear light, and none were hindered in their labour: ²¹over them only was spread an heavy night, an image of that darkness which should afterwards receive them; but yet were they unto themselves more grievous than the darkness.

18 Nevertheless thy saints had a very great light, whose voice they hearing, and not seeing their shape, because they also had not suffered the same things, they counted them happy. ²But for that they did not hurt them now, of whom they had been wronged before, they thanked them, and besought them pardon for that they had been enemies. ³Instead whereof thou gavest them a burning pillar of fire, both to be a guide of the unknown journey, and an harmless sun to entertain them honourably. ⁴For they were worthy to be deprived of light, and imprisoned in darkness, who had kept thy sons shut up, by whom the uncorrupt light of the law was to be given unto the world.

⁵And when they had determined to slay the babes of the saints, one child being cast forth, and saved, to reprove them, thou tookest away the multitude of their children, and destroyedst them altogether in a mighty water. ⁶Of that night were our fathers certified afore, that assuredly knowing unto what oaths they had given credence, they might afterwards be of good cheer. ⁷So of thy people was accepted both the salvation of the righteous, and destruction of the enemies. ⁸For wherewith thou didst punish our adversaries, by the same thou didst glorify us, whom thou hadst called. ⁹For the righteous children of good men did sacrifice secretly, and with one consent made a holy law, that the saints should be alike partakers of the same good and evil, the fathers now singing out the songs of praise. ¹⁰But on the other side there sounded an ill according cry of the enemies; and a lamentable noise was carried abroad for children that

were bewailed. "The master and the servant were punished after one manner; and like as the king, so suffered the common person. ¹²So they all together had innumerable dead with one kind of death; neither were the living sufficient to bury them; for in one moment the noblest offspring of them was destroyed. ¹³For whereas they would not believe any thing by reason of the enchantments; upon the destruction of the firstborn, they acknowledged this people to be the sons of God. ¹⁴For while all things were in quiet silence, and that night was in the midst of her swift course, ¹⁵thine Almighty word leaped down from heaven out of thy royal throne, as a fierce man of war into the midst of a land of destruction, ¹⁶and brought thine unfeigned commandment as a sharp sword, and standing up filled all things with death; and it touched the heaven, but it stood upon the earth. ¹⁷Then suddenly visions of horrible dreams troubled them sore, and terrors came upon them unlooked for. ¹⁸And one thrown here, and another there, half dead, shewed the cause of his death. ¹⁹For the dreams that troubled them did foreshew this, lest they should perish, and not know why they were afflicted.

²⁰Yea, the tasting of death touched the righteous also, and there was a destruction of the multitude in the wilderness; but the wrath endured not long. ²¹For then the blameless man made haste, and stood forth to defend them; and bringing the shield of his proper ministry, even prayer, and the propitiation of incense, set himself against the wrath, and so brought the calamity to an end, declaring that he was thy

servant. ²² So he overcame the destroyer, not with strength of body, nor force of arms, but with a word subdued he him that punished, alleging the oaths and covenants made with the fathers. ²³ For when the dead were now fallen down by heaps one upon another, standing between, he stayed the wrath, and parted the way to the living. ²⁴ For in the long garment was the whole world, and in the four rows of the stones was the glory of the fathers graven, and thy Majesty upon the diadem of his head. ²⁵ Unto these the destroyer gave place, and was afraid of them; for it was enough that they only tasted of the wrath.

19 As for the ungodly, wrath came upon them without mercy unto the end; for he knew before what they would do; ²how that having given them leave to depart, and sent them hastily away, they would repent and pursue them. ³For whilst they were yet mourning and making lamentation at the graves of the dead, they added another foolish device, and pursued them as fugitives, whom they had intreated to be gone. ⁴For the destiny, whereof they were worthy, drew them unto this end, and made them forget the things that had already happened, that they might fulfil the punishment which was wanting to their torments: ⁵and that thy people might pass a wonderful way; but they might find a strange death.

⁶For the whole creature in his proper kind was fashioned again anew, serving the peculiar commandments that were given unto them, that thy children might be kept without hurt, ⁷as namely, a cloud shadowing the camp; and where water stood before, dry land appeared; and out of the Red sea a way without impediment; and out of the violent stream a green field, ⁸wherethrough all the people went that were defended with thy hand, seeing thy marvellous strange wonders. ⁹For they went at large like horses, and leaped like lambs, praising thee, O Lord, who hadst delivered them. ¹⁰For they were yet mindful of the things that were done while they sojourned in the strange land, how the ground brought forth flies instead of cattle, and how the river cast up a multitude of frogs instead of fishes. ¹¹But afterwards they saw a new generation of fowls, when, being

led with their appetite, they asked delicate meats. ¹²For quails came up unto them from the sea for their contentment.

¹³And punishments came upon the sinners not without former signs by the force of thunders; for they suffered justly according to their own wickedness, insomuch as they used a more hard and hateful behaviour toward strangers. ¹⁴For the Sodomites did not receive those, whom they knew not when they came; but these brought friends into bondage, that had well deserved of them. ¹⁵And not only so, but peradventure some respect shall be had of those, because they used strangers not friendly; ¹⁶but these very grievously afflicted them, whom they had received with feastings, and were already made partakers of the same laws with them. ¹⁷Therefore even with blindness were these stricken, as those were at the doors of the righteous man, when, being compassed about with horrible great darkness, every one sought the passage of his own doors.

¹⁸For the elements were changed in themselves by a kind of harmony, like as in a psaltery notes change the name of the tune, and yet are always sounds; which may well be perceived by the sight of the things that have been done. ¹⁹For earthly things were turned into watery, and the things, that before swam in the water, now went upon the ground. ²⁰The fire had power in the water, forgetting his own virtue: and the water forgat his own quenching nature. ²¹On the other side, the flames wasted not the flesh of the corruptible living things, though they walked therein; neither melted they the

icy kind of heavenly meat, that was of nature apt to melt.

²² For in all things, O Lord, thou didst magnify thy people, and glorify them, neither didst thou lightly regard them, but didst assist them in every time and place.

the pocket canons

romans

the epistle of paul the apostle to the

romans

authorized king james version

grove press
new york

with an introduction by | ruth rendell

Introduction copyright © 1999 by Ruth Rendell
The Pocket Canon second series copyright © 2000 by Grove/Atlantic, Inc.

All rights reserved. No part of this book may be reproduced in any form
or by any electronic or mechanical means, including information storage
and retrieval systems, without permission in writing from the publisher,
except by a reviewer, who may quote brief passages in a review. Any
members of educational institutions wishing to photocopy part or all
of the work for classroom use, or publishers who would like to obtain
permission to include the work in an anthology, should send their
inquiries to Grove/Atlantic, Inc., 841 Broadway, New York, NY 10003.

Originally published in Great Britain in 1999 by Canongate Books,
Ltd., Edinburgh, Scotland.

Published simultaneously in Canada
Printed in the United States of America

FIRST AMERICAN EDITION

ISBN 0-8021-3759-8 (boxed set)

Design by Paddy Cramsie

Grove Press
841 Broadway
New York, NY 10003

00 01 02 03   10 9 8 7 6 5 4 3 2 1

a note about pocket canons

The Authorized King James Version of the Bible, translated between 1603 and 1611, coincided with an extraordinary flowering of English literature. This version, more than any other, and possibly more than any other work in history, has had an influence in shaping the language we speak and write today.

The books of the King James Bible encompass categories as diverse as history, philosophy, law, poetry and fiction. Each Pocket Canon volume has its own introduction, specially commissioned from an impressive range of writers, to provide a personal interpretation of the text and explore its contemporary relevance.

introduction by ruth rendell

Ruth Rendell is the author of more than forty novels, among them the Inspector Wexford series, and six volumes of short stories. She also writes under the pseudonym Barbara Vine. Many of her books have been adapted for television and feature films based on her work have been made by Claude Chabrol and Pedro Almodovar. She has received numerous fiction prizes, including the Arts Council's National Book Award for Genre Fiction, four Gold Daggers from the Crime Writers' Association, the Edgar Allan Poe Award and the Angel Award for Fiction. Ruth Rendell received a CBE *in 1996 and in the following year was made a Life Peer. Her latest novel is* A Sight for Sore Eyes.

The Road to Damascus is a phrase which has entered our language and our literature, becoming a metaphor for the sort of life-changing experience which strikes with suddenness and leaves its object transformed. It first happened to Paul the Apostle whose course of life, beliefs and objectives were all overturned by what happened to him on that actual road to that actual city.

He is believed to have been born in Tarsus, now part of Turkey, and was a Roman Citizen, a useful status which conferred certain judicial privileges, including that of *appellatio*, appeal to Caesar himself. He spoke Greek as his mother tongue, but in his letters he refers to his Jewishness – he had been a rabbinical student. Yet by profession he was a tentmaker, a trade somewhat frowned upon by strict Judaic orthodoxy. It will be seen that there were inconsistencies in his early life which modern scholars cannot account for and mysteries they cannot solve.

What is beyond doubt is that he was initially at the forefront of those who persecuted the Christians of Jerusalem. He might have been a temple guard and may possibly have been present at the arrest and crucifixion of Jesus. Certain it is that he played a significant part in the stoning of Stephen, a devout and active Christian. Stephen died and Paul 'made havoc of the [Christian] church, and entering every house and haling men and women, committed them to prison' (*Acts* 8:3). He asked the high priest for letters to the synagogues of Damascus, there to root out trouble-makers and bring them back as prisoners to Jerusalem. It was on this journey that the event took place which so immediately and entirely converted him.

Here, at one moment, we have a rabid oppressor and man of violence, 'breathing out threatenings and slaughter against the disciples of the Lord' (*Acts* 9:1), at the next the most obedient and devout of those disciples and an undoubted founder of the Christian religion. It is rather as if a camp guard suddenly became merciful to the inmates of Auschwitz and survived to become a great philosopher.

What happened to Paul on his Road to Damascus? Was he an epileptic, as some say, and this his first seizure? Had he been overworking and become, as we might put it today, 'stressed-out'? Or did he really hear the bidding of God? *Acts* says and he says himself that he saw a bright light and fell down, heard a voice call him by name and ask him, 'Why persecutest thou me?' (*Acts* 9:4) Paul inquired who this was and the voice replied he was Jesus and said, 'It is hard for thee to kick against the pricks.' The metaphor, of course, is that of the ass or ox kicking against the stings of the goad and the meaning that the speaker understood Saul's difficulties and the promptings of his conscience. From that moment, Saul now called Paul, saw himself as appointed to bear Christ's name 'before the Gentiles, and kings, and the children of Israel' (*Acts* 8:3).

He was somewhere between twenty and thirty years old, a small hook-nosed, bandy-legged man, humble and proud, brave and meek, the prisoner, as he joyfully (and sometimes with anguish) called himself, of Jesus Christ. Although he would have preferred everyone to be as he was, celibate and unencumbered by a family, he advocated marriage as 'honourable to all'. After his conversion he became a missionary and he wrote his epistles, thus becoming one of the greatest letter-writers the world has ever known and propounding principles and precepts of a startling originality. Of these the letter he wrote to the Romans, meaning to the Christians or 'church' of Rome, is generally thought the finest and perhaps the only one of whose sole and consistent authorship we can be certain.

Paul wrote this letter while staying in Corinth, capital of the Greek province of Achaia, during the cold months of the year, very probably a winter in the late fifties AD. When it was finished he appointed a woman called Phebe to carry it to Rome. In the final chapter, he asks its recipients to receive Phebe in a way becoming to them and to give her whatever assistance she may ask for, thus somewhat weakening the arguments of those critics who down the ages have called him a misogynist and despiser of women. Phebe must have travelled to Rome by sea, bringing to the beleaguered servants of the Roman church a foundation document of the faith.

Only by reading *Romans* in the knowledge of the kind of world Paul lived in can his letter be more fully understood. The Roman dominance of the known world was one of the most oppressive tyrannies nations have ever lived under. A huge proportion of the population was enslaved and few Romans, if any, thought of slavery as wrong. Punishment for any offences in the area of sedition was draconian. The Emperor Claudius had expelled the Jews from Rome and in a few years' time Titus was to sack Jerusalem, destroy the Temple and scatter the people of Israel. It was a superstitious world where sorcerers abounded, where signs and portents were part of everyday life, where cults of all kinds flourished, and where great religious ceremonies centred on blood sacrifice.

Today to believers, agnostics and atheists alike, crucifixion is a word both awesome and commonplace and one that brings to mind a single event: the execution of Jesus Christ. The sign of the cross is indicative of Christianity, and the idea of the cross is ineluctably bound up with Christ's death. But if we think about that death at all, even the most indifferent to the faith it gave rise to, think of it as honourable, a unique martyrdom. Anyone who travelled the Roman Empire at that time would have seen crosses on which the dead or dying hung, comparable perhaps to roadside gallows bearing their decaying corpses in mediaeval Britain. And to everyone, including Paul himself, crucifixion was a disgraceful manner of death, so that it is all the more extraordinary that he could write as he does in his letter to the Galatians, 'God forbid that I should glory save in the cross of our Lord Jesus Christ' (*Galatians* 6:14).

But perhaps the most important fact readers of this letter should know before they begin it, is how early it appears in the scheme of writings which form the New Testament. Most assume, and understandably, that the Gospels come first, then the *Acts of the Apostles* and after that the *Epistles of Paul*. Thus, Paul would have been writing with the Gospels as his source material. But none of those books existed when he set down his knowledge and beliefs. The earliest of the Gospels, that of *Mark*, cannot have been composed much before 70 AD, and by that time Paul's literary output was over and he was most probably dead. If readers today find a number of his precepts familiar, this is because they have come across them before, in church, in Sunday school, in literature and enshrined in Christian philosophy, as owing their provenance to the Gospels. But Paul came first.

Authorities have been commenting on *Romans* for nearly two thousand years. Every word Paul wrote in his letter has been minutely examined, both in translation and in the original, with commentators probing Greek prepositions and classical usage, in an effort to shed light on unfathomable obscurities. We shall approach it more humbly, remembering always that when Paul wrote it Jesus Christ had been crucified only about twenty-five years before.

He begins in the classical Greek fashion of starting a letter, with his name and his vocation: 'Paul, a servant of Jesus Christ, called to be an apostle,' then sets down the tenets of his faith. Kind and comforting messages for his letter's recipients follow; he mentions them always in his prayers and says how he longs to see them. Paul has never been to Rome but he intends to go, hoping for a safe journey in order to preach in person while there. He tells them he is not ashamed of the Gospel (in its sense of the good news). A tradition of shame prevails towards Christianity because Christ came not in majesty but in a way likely to be looked on as abjection and foolishness. Paul knows that this apparently weak message is in fact the supreme power of God himself directed towards man's salvation.

Faith can arise only through human beings' close contact with the Gospel. Paul explains the disastrous progress of evil in society as the natural process of cause and effect, not as the direct act of God. His first chapter ends with an exposure of certain kinds of 'unrighteousness' and here we come upon our first major difficulty in interpreting exactly what he meant. Through the ages men have taken six verses in particular to mean that all homosexuality was abhorrent to Christianity, 'men with men working that which is unseemly' being a phrase on which it is hard to put any other construction. Paul would have known of the importance of homosexuality in Greek thought where homosexual love was often glorified as superior to the heterosexual; he also knew that it was an abomination to the Jews which may be the reason for his harsh denunciations. Throughout his letters, though he comes to regard circumcision as unnecessary and certain dietary laws superfluous, and of course is confident that the Messiah has come, he otherwise holds fast to the Jewish Law. Certain authorities have sought to emphasise that his invective may be directed only against physical abuse in the kind of cult ceremonies Paul, coming as he did from Tarsus, would have been well acquainted with. Readers must draw their own conclusions.

The last four lines of the first chapter are interesting in a quite different way. They can be interpreted as meaning that those who watch, applaud and approve wrongdoing in others, though doing none themselves, are more guilty than those who commit it. An example would be that of the dictator who, rather than carry out torture himself, allow its use by his security forces and looks on with approbation.

He follows directly with a denunciation of hypocrisy. God will render to every man according to how he has behaved, for He cares nothing for rank, riches or status, and is no respector of persons. Perhaps it is at this point that we should remind ourselves that Paul was not writing for believers living centuries after Christ. He had no doubt that the end of the world was at hand, as had all Christians of his day, and to him the Second Coming was a reality to be expected at any moment. Therefore repentance, amendment of behaviour and a full knowledge of God and Jesus are matters of urgency. Circumcision, he tells us, is of no use in itself, the physical act that is, but 'circumcision is that of the heart'. In other words, to have faith is most important of all, but being a Jew (i.e. a circumcised person) matters too, the rite of circumcision affecting the spirit as well as the flesh, because it was to the Jews originally that the oracles of God were sent by Moses. All men, however, Jew and Gentile alike, are sinners and Jews need not think themselves better than the rest of the world.

Inheritance of the world was promised to Abraham and his descendants, and this gift was made not on condition that it was merited through fulfilment of the law, but simply on the basis of the rightness of the faith they upheld. The relevance to all Christians is in Abraham's faith as the paradigm of their own. It was quite a new thought that Abraham was the father of all who believe, not only of the Jews. But if those who have a claim to the inheritance do so on the basis of their obedience to the law alone, they will be disappointed, since no one is truly obedient but Christ Himself. Against all hope Abraham continued to believe in God's promise that he would be the ancestor of many nations, even though he and his wife were old and childless. By the conception and birth of his son Isaac his faith was proved. Just as he never doubted God's promise, so we must never doubt it.

Man's parent-and-child relationship with God is integral to forgiveness and absolution, and his purpose for humanity is altogether merciful. We were enemies of God, but by the death of his son became his friends, thus atonement through Christ should be a source of joy. (In the next chapter Paul points out that while it is rare for someone to give his life to save even a good man, and not much rarer to do so for someone who has been his benefactor, Christ died for the wicked.) But at the very place where sin most outrageously abounded, in Israel's rejection of Jesus, there grace abounded more and triumphed gloriously. Certain people would draw the inference that we must go on sinning that grace may be multiplied, but this Paul rejects utterly.

At the moment someone receives baptism, the dying and rising again of Christ takes place in him without any co-operation or exercise of will on his part. Baptism is a pledge of that death which, in God's sight, the person concerned has already succumbed to and of resurrection through union with Christ. Martin Luther, in his commentary, said that it was as if Paul 'wanted to give us impressive proof of the fact that ... every word in the Bible points to Christ.' Israel, says Paul, has misunderstood the law because it failed to comprehend that this was what it was all about.

Paul instructs the Romans on how to behave, and the Commandments not to kill, commit adultery, steal, bear false witness or covet are all summed up in the instruction to love one's neighbour as oneself. But one's enemy also must be loved. If an enemy is hungry, feed him, if thirsty, give him drink, for to do so is to heap 'coals of fire' on his head. The expression probably derives from the Egyptian ritual in which a man purged his offence by carrying on his head a dish containing burning charcoal on a bed of ashes. Paul goes on to speak of the imminence of the second coming, for the ministry of Jesus had ushered in the last days, the End-time. History's supreme events had taken place through Christ's life, death and resurrection.

Returning to one of his central themes, Paul has more to say about Judaism and Christianity. Dietary rules are no longer important. Now Christ's work on earth is done, the situation with regard to the ceremonial part of Old Testament eating and abstaining has been radically transformed. One obeys it by believing in him to whom it bears witness. Keep from hurting others with your dietary rules and remember that the Kingdom of God is not a matter of eating and drinking. But the strong Christian will not boast of his superior knowledge in this area. Paul explains that not everything which is delightful is to be avoided but one should not please oneself regardless of its effect on others.

He ends with greetings to a great many people and here women (Priscilla, Mary, Junia, Tryphena, Tryphosa, Julia, the sister of Nereus and the mother of Rufus) are accorded at least the same affection and admiration as men. Paul seems here to have tried to attach expressions of kindly commendation to all the individuals he mentions. At the end of this last chapter Tertius's declaration that he 'wrote this epistle' means not that he was its author but most probably that he wrote it from Paul's dictation.

What became of Paul? No one knows. The likelihood is that his fate was unknown even then, or Luke, who wrote the *Acts*, might have told us. What is known is that Paul came up for trial in Jerusalem and appealed, as he had the right to do, to Caesar. He was taken to the city to which he directed his letter and seems to have appeared twice before that Emperor whose very name causes a chill, Nero. In Rome he lived for two years under house arrest and the second of the letters to Timothy which bears his name sometimes includes the rather sinister note: '… written from Rome, when Paul was brought before Nero the second time.' Perhaps he died a martyr's death. No one can be sure. But if he did he would not have been thrown to wild beasts or made a human torch, but beheaded with a sword, as was prescribed for a Roman Citizen. He left behind him a book which is a blueprint for Christianity. Believers and non-believers alike cannot help but be stricken with awe by its temerity and Paul's genius.

the epistle of paul the apostle to the romans

Paul, a servant of Jesus Christ, called to be an apostle, separated unto the gospel of God ²(which he had promised afore by his prophets in the holy scriptures), ³concerning his Son Jesus Christ our Lord, which was made of the seed of David according to the flesh, ⁴and declared to be the Son of God with power, according to the spirit of holiness, by the resurrection from the dead, ⁵by whom we have received grace and apostleship, for obedience to the faith among all nations, for his name, ⁶among whom are ye also the called of Jesus Christ:

⁷To all that be in Rome, beloved of God, called to be saints: Grace to you and peace from God our Father, and the Lord Jesus Christ.

⁸First, I thank my God through Jesus Christ for you all, that your faith is spoken of throughout the whole world. ⁹For God is my witness, whom I serve with my spirit in the gospel of his Son, that without ceasing I make mention of you always in my prayers; ¹⁰making request, if by any means now at length I might have a prosperous journey by the will of God to come unto you. ¹¹For I long to see you, that I may impart unto you some spiritual gift, to the end ye may be established; ¹²That is, that I may be comforted together with you by the mutual faith both of you and me. ¹³Now I would not have you ignorant, brethren, that oftentimes I purposed to come unto you (but was let hitherto), that I might have some fruit among you also, even

1

as among other Gentiles. ¹⁴ I am debtor both to the Greeks, and to the Barbarians; both to the wise, and to the unwise. ¹⁵ So, as much as in me is, I am ready to preach the gospel to you that are at Rome also.

¹⁶ For I am not ashamed of the gospel of Christ, for it is the power of God unto salvation to every one that believeth; to the Jew first, and also to the Greek. ¹⁷ For therein is the righteousness of God revealed from faith to faith, as it is written, 'The just shall live by faith'.

¹⁸ For the wrath of God is revealed from heaven against all ungodliness and unrighteousness of men, who hold the truth in unrighteousness, ¹⁹ because that which may be known of God is manifest in them, for God hath shewed it unto them. ²⁰ For the invisible things of him from the creation of the world are clearly seen, being understood by the things that are made, even his eternal power and Godhead; so that they are without excuse, ²¹ because that, when they knew God, they glorified him not as God, neither were thankful; but became vain in their imaginations, and their foolish heart was darkened. ²² Professing themselves to be wise, they became fools, ²³ and changed the glory of the uncorruptible God into an image made like to corruptible man, and to birds, and four-footed beasts, and creeping things. ²⁴ Wherefore God also gave them up to uncleanness through the lusts of their own hearts, to dishonour their own bodies between themselves, ²⁵ who changed the truth of God into a lie, and worshipped and served the creature more than the Creator, who is blessed for ever. Amen.

²⁶ For this cause God gave them up unto vile affections, for even their women did change the natural use into that which is against nature: ²⁷ And likewise also the men, leaving the natural

use of the woman, burned in their lust one toward another; men with men working that which is unseemly, and receiving in themselves that recompence of their error which was meet. [28]And even as they did not like to retain God in their knowledge, God gave them over to a reprobate mind, to do those things which are not convenient; [29]being filled with all unrighteousness, fornication, wickedness, covetousness, maliciousness; full of envy, murder, debate, deceit, malignity; whisperers, [30]backbiters, haters of God, despiteful, proud, boasters, inventors of evil things, disobedient to parents, [31]without understanding, covenant-breakers, without natural affection, implacable, unmerciful, [32]who knowing the judgment of God, that they which commit such things are worthy of death, not only do the same, but have pleasure in them that do them.

2 Therefore thou art inexcusable, O man, whosoever thou art that judgest; for wherein thou judgest another, thou condemnest thyself; for thou that judgest doest the same things. [2]But we are sure that the judgment of God is according to truth against them which commit such things. [3]And thinkest thou this, O man, that judgest them which do such things, and does the same, that thou shalt escape the judgment of God? [4]Or despisest thou the riches of his goodness and forbearance and longsuffering; not knowing that the goodness of God leadeth thee to repentance? [5]But after thy hardness and impenitent heart treasurest up unto thyself wrath against the day of wrath and revelation of the righteous judgment of God; [6]who will render to every man according to his deeds: [7]to them who by patient continuance in well doing seek for glory and honour and immortality, eternal life: [8]but unto them that are con-

tentious, and do not obey the truth, but obey unrighteousness, indignation and wrath, [9] tribulation and anguish, upon every soul of man that doeth evil, of the Jew first, and also of the Gentile; [10] but glory, honour, and peace, to every man that worketh good, to the Jew first, and also to the Gentile, [11] for there is no respect of persons with God.

[12] For as many as have sinned without law shall also perish without law: and as many as have sinned in the law shall be judged by the law [13] (for not the hearers of the law are just before God, but the doers of the law shall be justified. [14] For when the Gentiles, which have not the law, do by nature the things contained in the law, these, having not the law, are a law unto themselves, [15] which shew the work of the law written in their hearts, their conscience also bearing witness, and their thoughts the mean while accusing or else excusing one another), [16] in the day when God shall judge the secrets of men by Jesus Christ according to my gospel.

[17] Behold, thou art called a Jew, and restest in the law, and makest thy boast of God, [18] and knowest his will, and approvest the things that are more excellent, being instructed out of the law; [19] and art confident that thou thyself art a guide of the blind, a light of them which are in darkness, [20] an instructor of the foolish, a teacher of babes, which hast the form of knowledge and of the truth in the law. [21] Thou therefore which teachest another, teachest thou not thyself? Thou that preachest a man should not steal, dost thou steal? [22] Thou that sayest a man should not commit adultery, dost thou commit adultery? Thou that abhorrest idols, dost thou commit sacrilege? [23] Thou that makest thy boast of the law, through breaking the law dishonourest thou God? [24] For the name of God is blasphemed among the Gentiles

through you, as it is written.

²⁵ For circumcision verily profiteth, if thou keep the law, but if thou be a breaker of the law, thy circumcision is made uncircumcision. ²⁶ Therefore if the uncircumcision keep the righteousness of the law, shall not his uncircumcision be counted for circumcision? ²⁷ And shall not uncircumcision which is by nature, if it fulfil the law, judge thee, who by the letter and circumcision dost transgress the law? ²⁸ For he is not a Jew, which is one outwardly; neither is that circumcision, which is outward in the flesh; ²⁹ but he is a Jew, which is one inwardly; and circumcision is that of the heart, in the spirit, and not in the letter; whose praise is not of men, but of God.

3 What advantage then hath the Jew? Or what profit is there of circumcision? ² Much every way: chiefly, because that unto them were committed the oracles of God. ³ For what if some did not believe? Shall their unbelief make the faith of God without effect? ⁴ God forbid: yea, let God be true, but every man a liar; as it is written, that thou mightest be justified in thy sayings, and mightest overcome when thou art judged. ⁵ But if our unrighteousness commend the righteousness of God, what shall we say? Is God unrighteous who taketh vengeance? (I speak as a man.) ⁶ God forbid, for then how shall God judge the world? ⁷ For if the truth of God hath more abounded through my lie unto his glory; why yet am I also judged as a sinner? ⁸ And not rather (as we be slanderously reported, and as some affirm that we say), 'Let us do evil, that good may come'? whose damnation is just.

⁹ What then? Are we better than they? No, in no wise, for we have before proved both Jews and Gentiles, that they are all

under sin, [10] as it is written, 'There is none righteous, no, not one; [11] there is none that understandeth, there is none that seeketh after God. [12] They are all gone out of the way, they are together become unprofitable; there is none that doeth good, no, not one.' [13] 'Their throat is an open sepulchre; with their tongues they have used deceit the poison of asps is under their lips.' [14] 'Whose mouth is full of cursing and bitterness.' [15] 'Their feet are swift to shed blood: [16] destruction and misery are in their ways: [17] and the way of peace have they not known.' [18] 'There is no fear of God before their eyes.'

[19] Now we know that what things soever the law saith, it saith to them who are under the law, that every mouth may be stopped, and all the world may become guilty before God. [20] Therefore by the deeds of the law there shall no flesh be justified in his sight, for by the law is the knowledge of sin.

[21] But now the righteousness of God without the law is manifested, being witnessed by the law and the prophets; [22] even the righteousness of God which is by faith of Jesus Christ unto all and upon all them that believe, for there is no difference, [23] for all have sinned, and come short of the glory of God; [24] being justified freely by his grace through the redemption that is in Christ Jesus, [25] whom God hath set forth to be a propitiation through faith in his blood, to declare his righteousness for the remission of sins that are past, through the forbearance of God; [26] to declare, I say, at this time his righteousness, that he might be just, and the justifier of him which believeth in Jesus.

[27] Where is boasting then? It is excluded. By what law? Of works? Nay, but by the law of faith. [28] Therefore we conclude that a man is justified by faith without the deeds of the law. [29] Is he the God of the Jews only? Is he not also of the Gentiles? Yes,

of the Gentiles also, ³⁰ seeing it is one God, which shall justify the circumcision by faith, and uncircumcision through faith. ³¹ Do we then make void the law through faith? God forbid: yea, we establish the law.

4 What shall we say then that Abraham our father, as pertaining to the flesh, hath found? ² For if Abraham were justified by works, he hath whereof to glory; but not before God. ³ For what saith the scripture? 'Abraham believed God, and it was counted unto him for righteousness.' ⁴ Now to him that worketh is the reward not reckoned of grace, but of debt. ⁵ But to him that worketh not, but believeth on him that justifieth the ungodly, his faith is counted for righteousness. ⁶ Even as David also describeth the blessedness of the man, unto whom God imputeth righteousness without works, ⁷ saying, 'Blessed are they whose iniquities are forgiven, and whose sins are covered. ⁸ Blessed is the man to whom the Lord will not impute sin.'

⁹ Cometh this blessedness then upon the circumcision only, or upon the uncircumcision also? For we say that faith was reckoned to Abraham for righteousness. ¹⁰ How was it then reckoned? When he was in circumcision, or in uncircumcision? Not in circumcision, but in uncircumcision. ¹¹ And he received the sign of circumcision, a seal of the righteousness of the faith which he had yet being uncircumcised, that he might be the father of all them that believe, though they be not circumcised, that righteousness might be imputed unto them also: ¹² and the father of circumcision to them who are not of the circumcision only, but who also walk in the steps of that faith of our father Abraham, which he had being yet uncircumcised.

¹³ For the promise, that he should be the heir of the world, was not to Abraham, or to his seed, through the law, but through the righteousness of faith. ¹⁴ For if they which are of the law be heirs, faith is made void, and the promise made of none effect, ¹⁵ because the law worketh wrath, for where no law is, there is no transgression.

¹⁶ Therefore it is of faith, that it might be by grace; to the end the promise might be sure to all the seed; not to that only which is of the law, but to that also which is of the faith of Abraham; who is the father of us all ¹⁷ (as it is written, I have made thee a father of many nations), before him whom he believed, even, God, who quickeneth the dead, and calleth those things which be not as though they were. ¹⁸ Who against hope believed in hope, that he might become the father of many nations, according to that which was spoken, 'So shall thy seed be.' ¹⁹ And being not weak in faith, he considered not his own body now dead, when he was about an hundred years old, neither yet the deadness of Sara's womb: ²⁰ he staggered not at the promise of God through unbelief; but was strong in faith, giving glory to God; ²¹ and being fully persuaded that, what he had promised, he was able also to perform. ²² And therefore it was imputed to him for righteousness. ²³ Now it was not written for his sake alone, that it was imputed to him; ²⁴ but for us also, to whom it shall be imputed, if we believe on him that raised up Jesus our Lord from the dead; ²⁵ who was delivered for our offences, and was raised again for our justification.

5 Therefore being justified by faith, we have peace with God through our Lord Jesus Christ, ² by whom also we have access by faith into this grace wherein we stand, and rejoice in

hope of the glory of God. ³And not only so, but we glory in tribulations also: knowing that tribulation worketh patience; ⁴and patience, experience; and experience, hope: ⁵and hope maketh not ashamed, because the love of God is shed abroad in our hearts by the Holy Ghost which is given unto us.

⁶For when we were yet without strength, in due time Christ died for the ungodly. ⁷For scarcely for a righteous man will one die: yet peradventure for a good man some would even dare to die. ⁸But God commendeth his love toward us, in that, while we were yet sinners, Christ died for us. ⁹Much more then, being now justified by his blood, we shall be saved from wrath through him. ¹⁰For if, when we were enemies, we were reconciled to God by the death of his Son, much more, being reconciled, we shall be saved by his life. ¹¹And not only so, but we also joy in God through our Lord Jesus Christ, by whom we have now received the atonement.

¹²Wherefore, as by one man sin entered into the world, and death by sin; and so death passed upon all men, for that all have sinned. ¹³For until the law sin was in the world, but sin is not imputed when there is no law. ¹⁴Nevertheless death reigned from Adam to Moses, even over them that had not sinned after the similitude of Adam's transgression, who is the figure of him that was to come.

¹⁵But not as the offence, so also is the free gift. For if through the offence of one many be dead, much more the grace of God, and the gift by grace, which is by one man, Jesus Christ, hath abounded unto many. ¹⁶And not as it was by one that sinned, so is the gift, for the judgment was by one to condemnation, but the free gift is of many offences unto justification. ¹⁷For if by one man's offence death reigned by one; much more they which

receive abundance of grace and of the gift of righteousness shall reign in life by one, Jesus Christ.)

[18] Therefore as by the offence of one judgment came upon all men to condemnation; even so by the righteousness of one the free gift came upon all men unto justification of life. [19] For as by one man's disobedience many were made sinners, so by the obedience of one shall many be made righteous. [20] Moreover the law entered, that the offence might abound. But where sin abounded, grace did much more abound, [21] that as sin hath reigned unto death, even so might grace reign through righteousness unto eternal life by Jesus Christ our Lord.

6 What shall we say then? Shall we continue in sin, that grace may abound? [2] God forbid. How shall we, that are dead to sin, live any longer therein? [3] Know ye not, that so many of us as were baptized into Jesus Christ were baptized into his death? [4] Therefore we are buried with him by baptism into death, that like as Christ was raised up from the dead by the glory of the Father, even so we also should walk in newness of life.

[5] For if we have been planted together in the likeness of his death, we shall be also in the likeness of his resurrection, [6] knowing this, that our old man is crucified with him, that the body of sin might be destroyed, that henceforth we should not serve sin. [7] For he that is dead is freed from sin. [8] Now if we be dead with Christ, we believe that we shall also live with him, [9] knowing that Christ being raised from the dead dieth no more; death hath no more dominion over him. [10] For in that he died, he died unto sin once; but in that he liveth, he liveth unto God. [11] Likewise reckon ye also yourselves to be dead indeed unto sin, but alive unto God through Jesus Christ our Lord.

¹²Let not sin therefore reign in your mortal body, that ye should obey it in the lusts thereof. ¹³Neither yield ye your members as instruments of unrighteousness unto sin; but yield yourselves unto God, as those that are alive from the dead, and your members as instruments of righteousness unto God. ¹⁴For sin shall not have dominion over you, for ye are not under the law, but under grace.

¹⁵What then? Shall we sin, because we are not under the law, but under grace? God forbid. ¹⁶Know ye not, that to whom ye yield yourselves servants to obey, his servants ye are to whom ye obey; whether of sin unto death, or of obedience unto righteousness? ¹⁷But God be thanked, that ye were the servants of sin, but ye have obeyed from the heart that form of doctrine which was delivered you. ¹⁸Being then made free from sin, ye became the servants of righteousness. ¹⁹I speak after the manner of men because of the infirmity of your flesh, for as ye have yielded your members servants to uncleanness and to iniquity unto iniquity; even so now yield your members servants to righteousness unto holiness.

²⁰For when ye were the servants of sin, ye were free from righteousness. ²¹What fruit had ye then in those things whereof ye are now ashamed? For the end of those things is death. ²²But now being made free from sin, and become servants to God, ye have your fruit unto holiness, and the end everlasting life. ²³For the wages of sin is death; but the gift of God is eternal life through Jesus Christ our Lord.

7 Know ye not, brethren (for I speak to them that know the law), how that the law hath dominion over a man as long as he liveth? ²For the woman which hath an husband is bound by

the law to her husband so long as he liveth; but if the husband be dead, she is loosed from the law of her husband. ³ So then if, while her husband liveth, she be married to another man, she shall be called an adulteress: but if her husband be dead, she is free from that law; so that she is no adulteress, though she be married to another man.

⁴ Wherefore, my brethren, ye also are become dead to the law by the body of Christ; that ye should be married to another, even to him who is raised from the dead, that we should bring forth fruit unto God. ⁵ For when we were in the flesh, the motions of sins, which were by the law, did work in our members to bring forth fruit unto death. ⁶ But now we are delivered from the law, that being dead wherein we were held; that we should serve in newness of spirit, and not in the oldness of the letter.

⁷ What shall we say then? Is the law sin? God forbid. Nay, I had not known sin, but by the law, for I had not known lust, except the law had said, 'Thou shalt not covet.' ⁸ But sin, taking occasion by the commandment, wrought in me all manner of concupiscence. For without the law sin was dead. ⁹ For I was alive without the law once: but when the commandment came, sin revived, and I died. ¹⁰ And the commandment, which was ordained to life, I found to be unto death. ¹¹ For sin, taking occasion by the commandment, deceived me, and by it slew me. ¹² Wherefore the law is holy, and the commandment holy, and just, and good.

¹³ Was then that which is good made death unto me? God forbid. But sin, that it might appear sin, working death in me by that which is good; that sin by the commandment might become exceeding sinful.

¹⁴ For we know that the law is spiritual: but I am carnal, sold under sin. ¹⁵ For that which I do I allow not; for what I would, that do I not; but what I hate, that do I. ¹⁶ If then I do that which I would not, I consent unto the law that it is good. ¹⁷ Now then it is no more I that do it, but sin that dwelleth in me. ¹⁸ For I know that in me (that is, in my flesh), dwelleth no good thing, for to will is present with me; but how to perform that which is good I find not. ¹⁹ For the good that I would I do not, but the evil which I would not, that I do. ²⁰ Now if I do that I would not, it is no more I that do it, but sin that dwelleth in me.

²¹ I find then a law, that, when I would do good, evil is present with me. ²² For I delight in the law of God after the inward man, ²³ but I see another law in my members, warring against the law of my mind, and bringing me into captivity to the law of sin which is in my members. ²⁴ O wretched man that I am! Who shall deliver me from the body of this death? ²⁵ I thank God through Jesus Christ our Lord. So then with the mind I myself serve the law of God; but with the flesh the law of sin.

8 There is therefore now no condemnation to them which are in Christ Jesus, who walk not after the flesh, but after the Spirit. ² For the law of the Spirit of life in Christ Jesus hath made me free from the law of sin and death. ³ For what the law could not do, in that it was weak through the flesh, God sending his own Son in the likeness of sinful flesh, and for sin, condemned sin in the flesh, ⁴ that the righteousness of the law might be fulfilled in us, who walk not after the flesh, but after the Spirit. ⁵ For they that are after the flesh do mind the things of the flesh; but they that are after the Spirit the things of the Spirit. ⁶ For to be carnally minded is death; but to be spiritually minded is life and

peace. [7] Because the carnal mind is enmity against God, for it is not subject to the law of God, neither indeed can be. [8] So then they that are in the flesh cannot please God.

[9] But ye are not in the flesh, but in the Spirit, if so be that the Spirit of God dwell in you. Now if any man have not the Spirit of Christ, he is none of his. [10] And if Christ be in you, the body is dead because of sin; but the Spirit is life because of righteousness. [11] But if the Spirit of him that raised up Jesus from the dead dwell in you, he that raised up Christ from the dead shall also quicken your mortal bodies by his Spirit that dwelleth in you.

[12] Therefore, brethren, we are debtors, not to the flesh, to live after the flesh. [13] For if ye live after the flesh, ye shall die, but if ye through the Spirit do mortify the deeds of the body, ye shall live. [14] For as many as are led by the Spirit of God, they are the sons of God. [15] For ye have not received the spirit of bondage again to fear; but ye have received the Spirit of adoption, whereby we cry, 'Abba, Father.' [16] The Spirit itself beareth witness with our spirit, that we are the children of God: [17] and if children, then heirs; heirs of God, and joint-heirs with Christ; if so be that we suffer with him, that we may be also glorified together.

[18] For I reckon that the sufferings of this present time are not worthy to be compared with the glory which shall be revealed in us. [19] For the earnest expectation of the creature waiteth for the manifestation of the sons of God. [20] For the creature was made subject to vanity, not willingly, but by reason of him who hath subjected the same in hope, [21] because the creature itself also shall be delivered from the bondage of corruption into the glorious liberty of the children of God. [22] For we know that the whole creation groaneth and travaileth in pain together until now. [23] And not only they, but ourselves also, which have the

firstfruits of the Spirit, even we ourselves groan within ourselves, waiting for the adoption, to wit, the redemption of our body. ²⁴ For we are saved by hope, but hope that is seen is not hope, for what a man seeth, why doth he yet hope for? ²⁵ But if we hope for that we see not, then do we with patience wait for it.

²⁶ Likewise the Spirit also helpeth our infirmities, for we know not what we should pray for as we ought, but the Spirit itself maketh intercession for us with groanings which cannot be uttered. ²⁷ And he that searcheth the hearts knoweth what is the mind of the Spirit, because he maketh intercession for the saints according to the will of God.

²⁸ And we know that all things work together for good to them that love God, to them who are the called according to his purpose. ²⁹ For whom he did foreknow, he also did predestinate to be conformed to the image of his Son, that he might be the firstborn among many brethren. ³⁰ Moreover whom he did predestinate, them he also called: and whom he called, them he also justified: and whom he justified, them he also glorified. ³¹ What shall we then say to these things? If God be for us, who can be against us? ³² He that spared not his own Son, but delivered him up for us all, how shall he not with him also freely give us all things? ³³ Who shall lay any thing to the charge of God's elect? It is God that justifieth. ³⁴ Who is he that condemneth? It is Christ that died, yea rather, that is risen again, who is even at the right hand of God, who also maketh intercession for us. ³⁵ Who shall separate us from the love of Christ? Shall tribulation, or distress, or persecution, or famine, or nakedness, or peril, or sword? ³⁶ As it is written, 'For thy sake we are killed all the day long; we are accounted as sheep for the slaughter.'

[37] Nay, in all these things we are more than conquerors through him that loved us. [38] For I am persuaded, that neither death, nor life, nor angels, nor principalities, nor powers, nor things present, nor things to come, [39] nor height, nor depth, nor any other creature, shall be able to separate us from the love of God, which is in Christ Jesus our Lord.

9 I say the truth in Christ, I lie not, my conscience also bearing me witness in the Holy Ghost, [2] that I have great heaviness and continual sorrow in my heart. [3] For I could wish that myself were accursed from Christ for my brethren, my kinsmen according to the flesh, [4] who are Israelites; to whom pertaineth the adoption, and the glory, and the covenants, and the giving of the law, and the service of God, and the promises; [5] whose are the fathers, and of whom as concerning the flesh Christ came, who is over all, God blessed for ever. Amen.

[6] Not as though the word of God hath taken none effect. For they are not all Israel, which are of Israel: [7] neither, because they are the seed of Abraham, are they all children, but, 'In Isaac shall thy seed be called.' [8] That is, 'They which are the children of the flesh, these are not the children of God, but the children of the promise are counted for the seed.' [9] For this is the word of promise, 'At this time will I come, and Sara shall have a son.' [10] And not only this; but when Rebecca also had conceived by one, even by our father Isaac. [11] (For the children being not yet born, neither having done any good or evil, that the purpose of God according to election might stand, not of works, but of him that calleth.) [12] It was said unto her, 'The elder shall serve the younger.' [13] As it is written, 'Jacob have I loved, but Esau have I hated.'

¹⁴ What shall we say then? Is there unrighteousness with God? God forbid. ¹⁵ For he saith to Moses, 'I will have mercy on whom I will have mercy, and I will have compassion on whom I will have compassion.' ¹⁶ So then it is not of him that willeth, nor of him that runneth, but of God that sheweth mercy. ¹⁷ For the scripture saith unto Pharaoh, 'Even for this same purpose have I raised thee up, that I might shew my power in thee, and that my name might be declared throughout all the earth.' ¹⁸ Therefore hath he mercy on whom he will have mercy, and whom he will he hardeneth.

¹⁹ Thou wilt say then unto me, 'Why doth he yet find fault? For who hath resisted his will?' ²⁰ Nay but, O man, who art thou that repliest against God? Shall the thing formed say to him that formed it, 'Why hast thou made me thus?' ²¹ Hath not the potter power over the clay, of the same lump to make one vessel unto honour, and another unto dishonour? ²² What if God, willing to shew his wrath, and to make his power known, endured with much longsuffering the vessels of wrath fitted to destruction; ²³ and that he might make known the riches of his glory on the vessels of mercy, which he had afore prepared unto glory, ²⁴ even us, whom he hath called, not of the Jews only, but also of the Gentiles? ²⁵ As he saith also in Osee, 'I will call them "my people", which were not my people; and her "beloved", which was not beloved.' ²⁶ And it shall come to pass, that in the place where it was said unto them, "Ye are not my people"; there shall they be called the children of the living God.'

²⁷ Esaias also crieth concerning Israel, 'Though the number of the children of Israel be as the sand of the sea, a remnant shall be saved, ²⁸ for he will finish the work, and cut it short in righteousness, because a short work will the Lord make upon the earth.'

[29] And as Esaias said before, 'Except the Lord of Sabaoth had left us a seed, we had been as Sodoma, and been made like unto Gomorrha.'

[30] What shall we say then? That the Gentiles, which followed not after righteousness, have attained to righteousness, even the righteousness which is of faith. [31] But Israel, which followed after the law of righteousness, hath not attained to the law of righteousness. [32] Wherefore? Because they sought it not by faith, but as it were by the works of the law. For they stumbled at that stumblingstone; [33] as it is written, 'Behold, I lay in Sion a stumblingstone and rock of offence: and whosoever believeth on him shall not be ashamed.'

10 Brethren, my heart's desire and prayer to God for Israel is, that they might be saved. [2] For I bear them record that they have a zeal of God, but not according to knowledge. [3] For they being ignorant of God's righteousness, and going about to establish their own righteousness, have not submitted themselves unto the righteousness of God. [4] For Christ is the end of the law for righteousness to every one that believeth.

[5] For Moses describeth the righteousness which is of the law, 'That the man which doeth those things shall live by them.' [6] But the righteousness which is of faith speaketh on this wise, 'Say not in thine heart, "Who shall ascend into heaven?" (that is, to bring Christ down from above) [7] Or, "Who shall descend into the deep?"' (That is, to bring up Christ again from the dead.) [8] But what saith it? The word is nigh thee, even in thy mouth, and in thy heart: that is, the word of faith, which we preach; [9] that if thou shalt confess with thy mouth the Lord Jesus, and shalt believe in thine heart that God hath raised him from the

dead, thou shalt be saved. [10] For with the heart man believeth unto righteousness; and with the mouth confession is made unto salvation. [11] For the scripture saith, 'Whosoever believeth on him shall not be ashamed.' [12] For there is no difference between the Jew and the Greek, for the same Lord over all is rich unto all that call upon him. [13] For whosoever shall call upon the name of the Lord shall be saved.

[14] How then shall they call on him in whom they have not believed? And how shall they believe in him of whom they have not heard? And how shall they hear without a preacher? [15] And how shall they preach, except they be sent? As it is written, 'How beautiful are the feet of them that preach the gospel of peace, and bring glad tidings of good things!' [16] But they have not all obeyed the gospel. For Esaias saith, 'Lord, who hath believed our report?' [17] So then faith cometh by hearing, and hearing by the word of God.

[18] But I say, 'Have they not heard? Yes verily, their sound went into all the earth, and their words unto the ends of the world.' [19] But I say, 'Did not Israel know?' First Moses saith, 'I will provoke you to jealousy by them that are no people, and by a foolish nation I will anger you.' [20] But Esaias is very bold, and saith, 'I was found of them that sought me not; I was made manifest unto them that asked not after me.' [21] But to Israel he saith, 'All day long I have stretched forth my hands unto a disobedient and gainsaying people.'

11 I say then, 'Hath God cast away his people?' God forbid. For I also am an Israelite, of the seed of Abraham, of the tribe of Benjamin. [2] God hath not cast away his people which he foreknew. Wot ye not what the scripture saith of Elias? How he

maketh intercession to God against Israel, saying, ³ 'Lord, they have killed thy prophets, and digged down thine altars; and I am left alone, and they seek my life.' ⁴ But what saith the answer of God unto him? 'I have reserved to myself seven thousand men, who have not bowed the knee to the image of Baal.' ⁵ Even so then at this present time also there is a remnant according to the election of grace. ⁶ And if by grace, then is it no more of works: otherwise grace is no more grace. But if it be of works, then is it no more grace: otherwise work is no more work.

⁷ What then? Israel hath not obtained that which he seeketh for; but the election hath obtained it, and the rest were blinded ⁸ according as it is written, 'God hath given them the spirit of slumber, eyes that they should not see, and ears that they should not hear unto this day. ⁹ And David saith, Let their table be made a snare, and a trap, and a stumbling-block, and a recompence unto them: ¹⁰ let their eyes be darkened, that they may not see, and bow down their back alway.'

¹¹ I say then, 'Have they stumbled that they should fall?' God forbid: but rather through their fall salvation is come unto the Gentiles, for to provoke them to jealousy. ¹² Now if the fall of them be the riches of the world, and the diminishing of them the riches of the Gentiles; how much more their fulness?

¹³ For I speak to you Gentiles, inas-much as I am the apostle of the Gentiles, I magnify mine office: ¹⁴ if by any means I may provoke to emulation them which are my flesh, and might save some of them. ¹⁵ For if the casting away of them be the reconciling of the world, what shall the receiving of them be, but life from the dead? ¹⁶ For if the firstfruit be holy, the lump is also holy: and if the root be holy, so are the branches.

¹⁷ And if some of the branches be broken off, and thou, being a wild olive tree, wert graffed in among them, and with them partakest of the root and fatness of the olive tree; ¹⁸ boast not against the branches. But if thou boast, thou bearest not the root, but the root thee. ¹⁹ Thou wilt say then, 'The branches were broken off, that I might be graffed in.' ²⁰ Well; because of unbelief they were broken off, and thou standest by faith. 'Be not highminded, but fear, ²¹ for if God spared not the natural branches, take heed lest he also spare not thee. ²² Behold therefore the goodness and severity of God: on them which fell, severity; but toward thee, goodness, if thou continue in his goodness: otherwise thou also shalt be cut off. ²³ And they also, if they abide not still in unbelief, shall be graffed in, for God is able to graff them in again. ²⁴ For if thou wert cut out of the olive tree which is wild by nature, and wert graffed contrary to nature into a good olive tree, how much more shall these, which be the natural branches, be graffed into their own olive tree?

²⁵ For I would not, brethren, that ye should be ignorant of this mystery, lest ye should be wise in your own conceits; that blindness in part is happened to Israel, until the fulness of the Gentiles be come in. ²⁶ And so all Israel shall be saved: as it is written, 'There shall come out of Sion the Deliverer, and shall turn away ungodliness from Jacob.' ²⁷ For this is my covenant unto them, when I shall take away their sins.' ²⁸ As concerning the gospel, they are enemies for your sakes; but as touching the election, they are beloved for the fathers' sakes. ²⁹ For the gifts and calling of God are without repentance. ³⁰ For as ye in times past have not believed God, yet have now obtained mercy through their unbelief, ³¹ even so have these also now not believed, that through your mercy they also may obtain mercy.

[32] For God hath concluded them all in unbelief, that he might have mercy upon all.

[33] O the depth of the riches both of the wisdom and knowledge of God! How unsearchable are his judgments, and his ways past finding out! [34] For who hath known the mind of the Lord? Or who hath been his counsellor? [35] Or who hath first given to him, and it shall be recompensed unto him again? [36] For of him, and through him, and to him, are all things: to whom be glory for ever. Amen.

12 I beseech you therefore, brethren, by the mercies of God, that ye present your bodies a living sacrifice, holy, acceptable unto God, which is your reasonable service. [2] And be not conformed to this world, but be ye transformed by the renewing of your mind, that ye may prove what is that good, and acceptable, and perfect, will of God.

[3] For I say, through the grace given unto me, to every man that is among you, not to think of himself more highly than he ought to think; but to think soberly, according as God hath dealt to every man the measure of faith. [4] For as we have many members in one body, and all members have not the same office: [5] so we, being many, are one body in Christ, and every one members one of another. [6] Having then gifts differing according to the grace that is given to us, whether prophecy, let us prophesy according to the proportion of faith; [7] or ministry, let us wait on our ministering: or he that teacheth, on teaching; [8] or he that exhorteth, on exhortation: he that giveth, let him do it with simplicity; he that ruleth, with diligence; he that sheweth mercy, with cheerfulness.

[9] Let love be without dissimulation. Abhor that which is evil;

cleave to that which is good. ¹⁰ Be kindly affectioned one to another with brotherly love; in honour preferring one another; ¹¹ not slothful in business; fervent in spirit; serving the Lord; ¹² rejoicing in hope; patient in tribulation; continuing instant in prayer; ¹³ Distributing to the necessity of saints; given to hospitality.

¹⁴ Bless them which persecute you: bless, and curse not. ¹⁵ Rejoice with them that do rejoice, and weep with them that weep. ¹⁶ Be of the same mind one toward another. Mind not high things, but condescend to men of low estate. Be not wise in your own conceits. ¹⁷ Recompense to no man evil for evil. Provide things honest in the sight of all men. ¹⁸ If it be possible, as much as lieth in you, live peaceably with all men. ¹⁹ Dearly beloved, avenge not yourselves, but rather give place unto wrath: for it is written, 'Vengeance is mine; I will repay,' saith the Lord. ²⁰ Therefore if thine enemy hunger, feed him; if he thirst, give him drink: for in so doing thou shalt heap coals of fire on his head. ²¹ Be not overcome of evil, but overcome evil with good.

13 Let every soul be subject unto the higher powers. For there is no power but of God: the powers that be are ordained of God. ² Whosoever therefore resisteth the power, resisteth the ordinance of God: and they that resist shall receive to themselves damnation. ³ For rulers are not a terror to good works, but to the evil. Wilt thou then not be afraid of the power? Do that which is good, and thou shalt have praise of the same, ⁴ for he is the minister of God to thee for good. But if thou do that which is evil, be afraid; for he beareth not the sword in vain; for he is the minister of God, a revenger to execute wrath upon him that doeth evil. ⁵ Wherefore ye must needs be subject, not only for wrath, but also for conscience sake. [6] For for this cause pay ye tribute also: for they are God's ministers, attending continually upon this very thing. [7] Render therefore to all their dues: tribute to whom tribute is due; custom to whom custom; fear to whom fear; honour to whom honour.

[8] Owe no man any thing, but to love one another, for he that loveth another hath fulfilled the law. [9] For this, 'Thou shalt not commit adultery, Thou shalt not kill, Thou shalt not steal, Thou shalt not bear false witness, Thou shalt not covet'; and if there be any other commandment, it is briefly comprehended in this saying, namely, 'Thou shalt love thy neighbour as thyself.' [10] Love worketh no ill to his neighbour: therefore love is the fulfilling of the law.

[11] And that, knowing the time, that now it is high time to awake out of sleep: for now is our salvation nearer than when we believed. [12] The night is far spent, the day is at hand: let us therefore cast off the works of darkness, and let us put on the armour of light. [13] Let us walk honestly, as in the day; not in rioting and drunkenness, not in chambering and wantonness, not in strife and envying. [14] But put ye on the Lord Jesus Christ, and make not provision for the flesh, to fulfil the lusts thereof.

14 Him that is weak in the faith receive ye, but not to doubtful disputations. [2] For one believeth that he may eat all things: another, who is weak, eateth herbs. [3] Let not him that eateth despise him that eateth not; and let not him which eateth not judge him that eateth, for God hath received him. [4] Who art thou that judgest another man's servant? To his own master he standeth or falleth. Yea, he shall be holden up, for God is able to make him stand.

⁵ One man esteemeth one day above another: another esteemeth every day alike. Let every man be fully persuaded in his own mind. ⁶ He that regardeth the day, regardeth it unto the Lord; and he that regardeth not the day, to the Lord he doth not regard it. He that eateth, eateth to the Lord, for he giveth God thanks; and he that eateth not, to the Lord he eateth not, and giveth God thanks.

⁷ For none of us liveth to himself, and no man dieth to himself. ⁸ For whether we live, we live unto the Lord; and whether we die, we die unto the Lord: whether we live therefore, or die, we are the Lord's. ⁹ For to this end Christ both died, and rose, and revived, that he might be Lord both of the dead and living.

¹⁰ But why dost thou judge thy brother? Or why dost thou set at nought thy brother? For we shall all stand before the judgment seat of Christ. ¹¹ For it is written, 'As I live,' saith the Lord, 'every knee shall bow to me, and every tongue shall confess to God.' ¹² So then every one of us shall give account of himself to God.

¹³ Let us not therefore judge one another any more, but judge this rather, that no man put a stumblingblock or an occasion to fall in his brother's way. ¹⁴ I know, and am persuaded by the Lord Jesus, that there is nothing unclean of itself, but to him that esteemeth any thing to be unclean, to him it is unclean. ¹⁵ But if thy brother be grieved with thy meat, now walkest thou not charitably. Destroy not him with thy meat, for whom Christ died. ¹⁶ Let not then your good be evil spoken of, ¹⁷ for the kingdom of God is not meat and drink; but righteousness, and peace, and joy in the Holy Ghost. ¹⁸ For he that in these things serveth Christ is acceptable to God, and approved of men. ¹⁹ Let us therefore follow after the things which make for peace, and

things wherewith one may edify another. ²⁰For meat destroy not the work of God. All things indeed are pure; but it is evil for that man who eateth with offence. ²¹It is good neither to eat flesh, nor to drink wine, nor any thing whereby thy brother stumbleth, or is offended, or is made weak. ²²Hast thou faith? Have it to thyself before God. Happy is he that condemneth not himself in that thing which he alloweth. ²³And he that doubteth is damned if he eat, because he eateth not of faith, for whatsoever is not of faith is sin.

15 We then that are strong ought to bear the infirmities of the weak, and not to please ourselves. ²Let every one of us please his neighbour for his good to edification. ³For even Christ pleased not himself; but, as it is written, 'The reproaches of them that reproached thee fell on me.' ⁴For whatsoever things were written aforetime were written for our learning, that we through patience and comfort of the scriptures might have hope. ⁵Now the God of patience and consolation grant you to be likeminded one toward another according to Christ Jesus, ⁶that ye may with one mind and one mouth glorify God, even the Father of our Lord Jesus Christ.

⁷Wherefore receive ye one another, as Christ also received us to the glory of God. ⁸Now I say that Jesus Christ was a minister of the circumcision for the truth of God, to confirm the promises made unto the fathers, ⁹and that the Gentiles might glorify God for his mercy; as it is written, 'For this cause I will confess to thee among the Gentiles, and sing unto thy name.' ¹⁰And again he saith, 'Rejoice, ye Gentiles, with his people.' ¹¹And again, 'Praise the Lord, all ye Gentiles; and laud him, all ye people.' ¹²And again, Esaias saith, 'There shall be a root of Jesse, and

he that shall rise to reign over the Gentiles; in him shall the Gentiles trust.' [13] Now the God of hope fill you with all joy and peace in believing, that ye may abound in hope, through the power of the Holy Ghost.

[14] And I myself also am persuaded of you, my brethren, that ye also are full of goodness, filled with all knowledge, able also to admonish one another. [15] Nevertheless, brethren, I have written the more boldly unto you in some sort, as putting you in mind, because of the grace that is given to me of God, [16] that I should be the minister of Jesus Christ to the Gentiles, ministering the gospel of God, that the offering up of the Gentiles might be acceptable, being sanctified by the Holy Ghost. [17] I have therefore whereof I may glory through Jesus Christ in those things which pertain to God. [18] For I will not dare to speak of any of those things which Christ hath not wrought by me, to make the Gentiles obedient, by word and deed, [19] through mighty signs and wonders, by the power of the Spirit of God; so that from Jerusalem, and round about unto Illyricum, I have fully preached the gospel of Christ. [20] Yea, so have I strived to preach the gospel, not where Christ was named, lest I should build upon another man's foundation, [21] but as it is written, 'To whom he was not spoken of, they shall see: and they that have not heard shall understand.'

[22] For which cause also I have been much hindered from coming to you. [23] But now having no more place in these parts, and having a great desire these many years to come unto you; [24] whensoever I take my journey into Spain, I will come to you, for I trust to see you in my journey, and to be brought on my way thitherward by you, if first I be somewhat filled with your company. [25] But now I go unto Jerusalem to minister unto the

saints. [26] For it hath pleased them of Macedonia and Achaia to make a certain contribution for the poor saints which are at Jerusalem. [27] It hath pleased them verily; and their debtors they are. For if the Gentiles have been made partakers of their spiritual things, their duty is also to minister unto them in carnal things. [28] When therefore I have performed this, and have sealed to them this fruit, I will come by you into Spain. [29]And I am sure that, when I come unto you, I shall come in the fulness of the blessing of the gospel of Christ.

[30] Now I beseech you, brethren, for the Lord Jesus Christ's sake, and for the love of the Spirit, that ye strive together with me in your prayers to God for me, [31] that I may be delivered from them that do not believe in Judæa; and that my service which I have for Jerusalem may be accepted of the saints; [32] that I may come unto you with joy by the will of God, and may with you be refreshed. [33] Now the God of peace be with you all. Amen.

16 I commend unto you Phebe our sister, which is a servant of the church which is at Cenchrea: [2] that ye receive her in the Lord, as becometh saints, and that ye assist her in whatsoever business she hath need of you, for she hath been a succourer of many, and of myself also.

[3] Greet Priscilla and Aquila my helpers in Christ Jesus, [4] who have for my life laid down their own necks, unto whom not only I give thanks, but also all the churches of the Gentiles. [5] Likewise greet the church that is in their house. Salute my well-beloved Epænetus, who is the firstfruits of Achaia unto Christ. [6] Greet Mary, who bestowed much labour on us. [7]Salute Andronicus and Junia, my kinsmen, and my fellowprisoners,

who are of note among the apostles, who also were in Christ before me. ⁸ Greet Amplias my beloved in the Lord. ⁹ Salute Urbane, our helper in Christ, and Stachys my beloved. ¹⁰ Salute Apelles approved in Christ. Salute them which are of Aristobulus' household. ¹¹ Salute Herodion my kinsman. Greet them that be of the household of Narcissus, which are in the Lord. ¹² Salute Tryphena and Tryphosa, who labour in the Lord. Salute the beloved Persis, which laboured much in the Lord. ¹³ Salute Rufus chosen in the Lord, and his mother and mine. ¹⁴ Salute Asyncritus, Phlegon, Hermas, Patrobas, Hermes, and the brethren which are with them. ¹⁵ Salute Philologus, and Julia, Nereus, and his sister, and Olympas, and all the saints which are with them. ¹⁶ Salute one another with an holy kiss. The churches of Christ salute you.

¹⁷ Now I beseech you, brethren, mark them which cause divisions and offences contrary to the doctrine which ye have learned; and avoid them. ¹⁸ For they that are such serve not our Lord Jesus Christ, but their own belly; and by good words and fair speeches deceive the hearts of the simple. ¹⁹ For your obedience is come abroad unto all men. I am glad therefore on your behalf, but yet I would have you wise unto that which is good, and simple concerning evil. ²⁰ And the God of peace shall bruise Satan under your feet shortly. The grace of our Lord Jesus Christ be with you. Amen.

²¹ Timotheus my workfellow, and Lucius, and Jason, and Sosipater, my kinsmen, salute you. ²² I Tertius, who wrote this epistle, salute you in the Lord. ²³ Gaius mine host, and of the whole church, saluteth you. Erastus the chamberlain of the city saluteth you, and Quartus a brother. ²⁴ The grace of our Lord Jesus Christ be with you all. Amen.

²⁵ Now to him that is of power to stablish you according to my gospel, and the preaching of Jesus Christ, according to the revelation of the mystery, which was kept secret since the world began, ²⁶ but now is made manifest, and by the scriptures of the prophets, according to the commandment of the everlasting God, made known to all nations for the obedience of faith: ²⁷ to God only wise, be glory through Jesus Christ for ever. Amen.

ruth and esther

the books of

ruth
and esther

authorized king james version

grove press
new york

with an introduction by | joanna trollope

Introduction copyright © 1999 by Joanna Trollope
The Pocket Canon second series copyright © 2000 by Grove/Atlantic, Inc.

All rights reserved. No part of this book may be reproduced in any form
or by any electronic or mechanical means, including information storage
and retrieval systems, without permission in writing from the publisher,
except by a reviewer, who may quote brief passages in a review. Any
members of educational institutions wishing to photocopy part or all
of the work for classroom use, or publishers who would like to obtain
permission to include the work in an anthology, should send their
inquiries to Grove/Atlantic, Inc., 841 Broadway, New York, NY 10003.

Originally published in Great Britain in 1999 by Canongate Books,
Ltd., Edinburgh, Scotland.

Published simultaneously in Canada
Printed in the United States of America

FIRST AMERICAN EDITION

ISBN 0-8021-3759-8 (boxed set)

Design by Paddy Cramsie

Grove Press
841 Broadway
New York, NY 10003

00 01 02 03   10 9 8 7 6 5 4 3 2 1

a note about pocket canons

The Authorized King James Version of the Bible, translated between 1603 and 1611, coincided with an extraordinary flowering of English literature. This version, more than any other, and possibly more than any other work in history, has had an influence in shaping the language we speak and write today.

The books of the King James Bible encompass categories as diverse as history, philosophy, law, poetry and fiction. Each Pocket Canon volume has its own introduction, specially commissioned from an impressive range of writers, to provide a personal interpretation of the text and explore its contemporary relevance.

introduction by joanna trollope

Author of eagerly awaited and bestselling novels often centred around the domestic nuances and dilemmas of life in contemporary England, Joanna Trollope is also the author of a number of historical novels and of Britannica's Daughters, *a study of women in the British Empire. In 1988 she wrote her first contemporary novel,* The Choir, *and this was followed by* A Village Affair, A Passionate Man, The Rector's Wife, The Men and the Girls, A Spanish Lover, The Best of Friends, Next of Kin *and most recently,* Other People's Children. *She lives in Gloucestershire.*

At first glance, it would seem natural, perhaps, to pair off the books of *Ruth* and *Esther* since they are the only two books in the Old Testament with women as their central characters, their heroines. At even a second glance, it might be tempting to see the two stories as applauding the courage and fortitude of women, a kind of remarkable early accolade to feminism. But a third glance reveals the reality. These two stories may *star* women, but only against the conventional biblical background of supreme male power; and if the women are celebrated, it is merely because of their ingenuity in exploiting that power. We are dealing it seems, with traditional, accepted romantic heroines – except that we are not.

Love may come into both stories, lust even, but the loyalties the women in these stories show is most fiercely directed in the one case to another, older woman, and in the second case, to a race, to a people. If these women had merely been feisty examples of romantic femininity, they would not have taken such a hold as they have, on Jewish and Christian minds and hearts down the ages. It is their breadth and their differences that have given them their enduring power.

There are thirty-nine books in the King James Old Testament, from the first book of Moses, called *Genesis*, to *Malachi*. In most bibles, this works out at about a thousand pages. And for the first five hundred pages, we know roughly where we are; not just following the revelation of God's will and purpose for mankind, but also pursuing the extraordinary story of the rise and fall of the nation of Israel, from the call of Abraham to the point in the fourth century BC when the Jews eventually emerged as a distinct religious community settled in a tiny corner of the Persian Empire.

So far, so reasonably manageable. But after the book of *Nehemiah*, the pattern disappears. The continuity of the story fragments and diffuses into something different and less accessible – into the (very broadly speaking) literature of the Hebrew people, into their prophecies and poetry, their wisdom and stories. Instead of reading the books of the Old Testament in sequence, we can read them individually. They aren't exactly random but they aren't, because of their separate natures, in narrative or development of thought order, either.

Some books, like those of the prophets, illuminate the

history that has gone before as well as foretell the future. Some, like *Psalms*, from which hymns were used in Temple services, describe the nature and mood of Jewish worship after the exile of its people. And some – *Ruth* and *Esther* among them – are stories that, for various reasons, plainly became interwoven into Jewish life and faith, into its attitudes as well as its rituals.

Like all stories – at least stories that endure – the stories of *Ruth* and *Esther* are metaphors. At one level they are simple narratives – one romantic, one dramatic – but at another they are illustrations, or images, of human behaviour, human attitudes, human arbitrariness, human trial and error, human failing, human (with divine assistance) triumph. We may not be able to identify with the time and place, but in some way, however small, we can identify with some aspect of the human condition.

They are also in violent contrast to one another. *Ruth* is a story of simplicity and gentleness; *Esther* one of hatred and savagery. Both books were of course written pre-Christ, but only the book of *Ruth*, with its quiet virtues, its extolling of compassion and tolerance and honourable conduct, found favour with later Christian thinking. The name of God is invoked, called upon and blessed. *Esther*, on the other hand, never even mentions the name of God. Yet both have their place, and particular point, in this rich and amazing history of a remarkable people and their remarkable faith.

The book of *Ruth*, in the authorised version, now sits between *Judges* and the first book of *Samuel*. The Greek translators put it there because there is reference, in the first chapter, to the story having taken place 'in the days when the judges ruled'. It could have been written before the Exile (598 BC), it could have been written some time after, but its exact date is nothing like as important as the question raised by the mere fact of its inclusion in the first place. It's a charming story, certainly, with an equally charming, peaceful, pastoral setting, among the Bethlehem barley fields at harvest time (a welcome relief after all the blood and thunder of *Judges*). But it's also something more significant and more muscular because it suggests that not all Jews of the period believed in the remorselessly tough racial laws that followed their return from exile – the ban on mixed marriage, the segregation of their people from any other, the open hostility to foreigners.

Ruth, you see, is not a Jew. She is a Moabitess. She marries a Jew who has come to live in Moabite country and, after his death, makes her immortal speech to her Jewish mother-in-law, Naomi: 'Whither thou goest, I will go; and where thou lodgest, I will lodge; thy people shall be my people and thy God my God; where thou diest will I die and there I will be buried: The Lord do so to me and more also, if aught but death part thee and me'(1:16-17).

Naomi takes Ruth home to Bethlehem. To sustain them both, Naomi sends Ruth out to glean barley after the reapers – a privilege accorded to widows and the poor – in a kinsman's field. 'Whose', demands the immediately interested kinsman, 'damsel is this?' Soon, after some delicate moonlight manoeuvrings, she is his, Moabite or not. And soon again, she, as his wife, bears him a son. The son is named

Obed. Obed was the father of Jesse who in turn was the father of the great king, David. And the great King David – honoured almost as much as Moses – was the grandson, not just of Obed, but naturally of his wife too, who was a Gentile. It is as if the storyteller of *Ruth* is saying, gently but firmly, either that even the blood of the great king was diluted or – more likely – that God's chosen people must make room for others who truly wish to join them, such as Moabites and other Gentiles.

This tiny hint of racial intolerance is the only link between the tender book of *Ruth* and the fierce book of *Esther*; both the Jewish canon and the Christian church have expressed huge reluctance in accepting *Esther*, and Martin Luther bluntly wished it had never been written.

Their repugnance isn't hard to understand. It's a horrible story, a tale of hatred and massacre and revenge, and at the heart of it stands the beautiful Jewish consort of the Persian king, Xerxes I, remorselessly defending her people. In fact – again unlike Ruth – it hardly seems a suitable Biblical story at all.

It is, instead, like something from the *Tales of the Arabian Nights*. Xerxes, ruling a seething court in an opulent palace – the architecture and furnishings are described in lavish detail – is displeased at some minor (and understandable) disobedience on his wife's part. So he commands the land to be scoured for beautiful virgins and, of all of them, Esther, the foster-child and cousin of a Jew named Mordecai, finds supreme favour and becomes queen, without disclosing her religion. But the king's vizier, Haman, is deeply offended that

Mordecai 'bowed not, nor did him reverence', and orders him to be hanged, as a punishment, and also that all Jews around shall be slaughtered as a warning against further contemptuous behaviour.

Only the queen, revealing her race to the besotted king, saves the day. And that should be the happy ending. But it isn't. Haman is hanged on his own gallows and the Jews rise up and massacre everyone who had intended to massacre them. Then they have a party in celebration, two days of 'feasting and gladness'. And, down the ages, that party has continued in these 'days of Purim', a festival when the Jewish people celebrate relief from their enemies '... the month which was turned unto them from sorrow to joy, and from mourning into a good day ... days of feasting and joy, and of sending portions one to another, and gifts to the poor'(9:22).

I have read both books over and over. I can see every reason – Jewish, Christian, humanitarian – for including the book of *Ruth*. But the book of *Esther* is another matter altogether. It incorporates everything that we all know fights strenuously against all the charities and harmonies we strive to achieve. But perhaps, on reflection, that is the point of it – it is a fascinating, glittering, gaudy, alarming reminder of how we can be, how we too often are. *Esther* is darkness in a beguiling mask of light.

the book of ruth

Now it came to pass in the days when the judges ruled, that there was a famine in the land. And a certain man of Bethlehem-judah went to sojourn in the country of Moab, he, and his wife, and his two sons. ²And the name of the man was Elimelech, and the name of his wife Naomi, and the name of his two sons Mahlon and Chilion, Ephrathites of Bethlehem-judah. And they came into the country of Moab, and continued there. ³And Elimelech Naomi's husband died; and she was left, and her two sons. ⁴And they took them wives of the women of Moab; the name of the one was Orpah, and the name of the other Ruth: and they dwelled there about ten years. ⁵And Mahlon and Chilion died also both of them; and the woman was left of her two sons and her husband.

⁶Then she arose with her daughters in law, that she might return from the country of Moab, for she had heard in the country of Moab how that the Lord had visited his people in giving them bread. ⁷Wherefore she went forth out of the place where she was, and her two daughters in law with her; and they went on the way to return unto the land of Judah. ⁸And Naomi said unto her two daughters in law, 'Go, return each to her mother's house: the Lord deal kindly with you, as ye have dealt with the dead, and with me. ⁹The Lord

grant you that ye may find rest, each of you in the house of her husband.' Then she kissed them; and they lifted up their voice, and wept. ¹⁰And they said unto her, 'Surely we will return with thee unto thy people.' ¹¹And Naomi said, 'Turn again, my daughters: why will ye go with me? Are there yet any more sons in my womb, that they may be your husbands? ¹²Turn again, my daughters, go your way; for I am too old to have an husband. If I should say, I have hope, if I should have an husband also to night, and should also bear sons, ¹³ would ye tarry for them till they were grown? Would ye stay for them from having husbands? Nay, my daughters; for it grieveth me much for your sakes that the hand of the Lord is gone out against me.' ¹⁴And they lifted up their voice, and wept again: and Orpah kissed her mother in law; but Ruth clave unto her. ¹⁵And she said, 'Behold, thy sister in law is gone back unto her people, and unto her gods: return thou after thy sister in law.' ¹⁶And Ruth said, 'Intreat me not to leave thee, or to return from following after thee: for whither thou goest, I will go; and where thou lodgest, I will lodge: thy people shall be my people, and thy God my God: ¹⁷where thou diest, will I die, and there will I be buried: the Lord do so to me, and more also, if ought but death part thee and me.' ¹⁸When she saw that she was stedfastly minded to go with her, then she left speaking unto her.

¹⁹So they two went until they came to Beth-lehem. And it came to pass, when they were come to Beth-lehem, that all the city was moved about them, and they said, 'Is this Naomi?' ²⁰And she said unto them, 'Call me not Naomi, call me Mara:

for the Almighty hath dealt very bitterly with me. ²¹I went out full, and the Lord hath brought me home again empty: why then call ye me Naomi, seeing the Lord hath testified against me, and the Almighty hath afflicted me?' ²²So Naomi returned, and Ruth the Moabitess, her daughter in law, with her, which returned out of the country of Moab: and they came to Beth-lehem in the beginning of barley harvest.

2 And Naomi had a kinsman of her husband's, a mighty man of wealth, of the family of Elimelech; and his name was Boaz. ²And Ruth the Moabitess said unto Naomi, 'Let me now go to the field, and glean ears of corn after him in whose sight I shall find grace.' And she said unto her, 'Go, my daughter.' ³And she went, and came, and gleaned in the field after the reapers: and her hap was to light on a part of the field belonging unto Boaz, who was of the kindred of Elimelech.

⁴And, behold, Boaz came from Beth-lehem, and said unto the reapers, 'The Lord be with you.' And they answered him, 'The Lord bless thee.' ⁵Then said Boaz unto his servant that was set over the reapers, 'Whose damsel is this?' ⁶And the servant that was set over the reapers answered and said, 'It is the Moabitish damsel that came back with Naomi out of the country of Moab. ⁷And she said, 'I pray you, let me glean and gather after the reapers among the sheaves': so she came, and hath continued even from the morning until now, that she tarried a little in the house.' ⁸Then said Boaz unto Ruth, 'Hearest thou not, my daughter? Go not to glean in another field, neither go from hence, but abide here fast by my maidens. ⁹Let thine eyes be on the field that they do reap, and go thou after them: have I not charged the young men that they shall not touch thee? And when thou art athirst, go unto the vessels, and drink of that which the young men have drawn.' ¹⁰Then she fell on her face, and bowed herself to the ground, and said unto him, 'Why have I found grace in thine eyes, that thou shouldest take knowledge of me, seeing I am a

stranger?' ¹¹And Boaz answered and said unto her, 'It hath fully been shewed me, all that thou hast done unto thy mother in law since the death of thine husband: and how thou hast left thy father and thy mother, and the land of thy nativity, and art come unto a people which thou knewest not heretofore.' ¹²The Lord recompense thy work, and a full reward be given thee of the Lord God of Israel, under whose wings thou art come to trust. ¹³Then she said, 'Let me find favour in thy sight, my lord; for that thou hast comforted me, and for that thou hast spoken friendly unto thine hand-maid, though I be not like unto one of thine handmaidens.' ¹⁴And Boaz said unto her, 'At mealtime come thou hither, and eat of the bread, and dip thy morsel in the vinegar.' And she sat beside the reapers: and he reached her parched corn, and she did eat, and was sufficed, and left. ¹⁵And when she was risen up to glean, Boaz commanded his young men, saying, 'Let her glean even among the sheaves, and reproach her not. ¹⁶And let fall also some of the handfuls of purpose for her, and leave them, that she may glean them, and rebuke her not.' ¹⁷So she gleaned in the field until even, and beat out that she had gleaned: and it was about an ephah of barley.

¹⁸And she took it up, and went into the city: and her mother in law saw what she had gleaned: and she brought forth, and gave to her that she had reserved after she was sufficed. ¹⁹And her mother in law said unto her, 'Where hast thou gleaned to day? And where wroughtest thou? Blessed be he that did take knowledge of thee.' And she shewed her mother in law with whom she had wrought, and said, 'The

man's name with whom I wrought to day is Boaz.' ²⁰And Naomi said unto her daughter in law, 'Blessed be he of the Lord, who hath not left off his kindness to the living and to the dead.' And Naomi said unto her, 'The man is near of kin unto us, one of our next kinsmen.' ²¹And Ruth the Moabitess said, 'He said unto me also, "Thou shalt keep fast by my young men, until they have ended all my harvest."' ²²And Naomi said unto Ruth her daughter in law, 'It is good, my daughter, that thou go out with his maidens, that they meet thee not in any other field.' ²³ So she kept fast by the maidens of Boaz to glean unto the end of barley harvest and of wheat harvest; and dwelt with her mother in law.

3 Then Naomi her mother in law said unto her, 'My daughter, shall I not seek rest for thee, that it may be well with thee? [2]And now is not Boaz of our kindred, with whose maidens thou wast? Behold, he winnoweth barley to night in the threshingfloor. [3]Wash thyself therefore, and anoint thee, and put thy raiment upon thee, and get thee down to the floor; but make not thyself known unto the man, until he shall have done eating and drinking. [4]And it shall be, when he lieth down, that thou shalt mark the place where he shall lie, and thou shalt go in, and uncover his feet, and lay thee down; and he will tell thee what thou shalt do.' [5]And she said unto her, 'All that thou sayest unto me I will do.'

[6]And she went down unto the floor, and did according to all that her mother in law bade her. [7]And when Boaz had eaten and drunk, and his heart was merry, he went to lie down at the end of the heap of corn: and she came softly, and uncovered his feet, and laid her down.

[8]And it came to pass at midnight, that the man was afraid, and turned himself: and, behold, a woman lay at his feet. [9]And he said, 'Who art thou?' And she answered, 'I am Ruth thine handmaid: spread therefore thy skirt over thine handmaid; for thou art a near kinsman.' [10]And he said, 'Blessed be thou of the Lord, my daughter, for thou hast shewed more kindness in the latter end than at the beginning, inasmuch as thou followedst not young men, whether poor or rich. [11]And now, my daughter, fear not; I will do to thee all that thou requirest; for all the city of my people doth

know that thou art a virtuous woman. ^{12}And now it is true that I am thy near kinsman: howbeit there is a kinsman nearer than I. ^{13}Tarry this night, and it shall be in the morning, that if he will perform unto thee the part of a kinsman, well; let him do the kinsman's part; but if he will not do the part of a kinsman to thee, then will I do the part of a kinsman to thee, as the Lord liveth: lie down until the morning.'

^{14}And she lay at his feet until the morning: and she rose up before one could know another. And he said, 'Let it not be known that a woman came into the floor.' ^{15}Also he said, 'Bring the vail that thou hast upon thee, and hold it.' And when she held it, he measured six measures of barley, and laid it on her: and she went into the city. ^{16}And when she came to her mother in law, she said, 'Who art thou, my daughter?' And she told her all that the man had done to her. ^{17}And she said, 'These six measures of barley gave he me; for he said to me, "Go not empty unto thy mother in law."' ^{18}Then said she, 'Sit still, my daughter, until thou know how the matter will fall, for the man will not be in rest, until he have finished the thing this day.'

4 Then went Boaz up to the gate, and sat him down there: and, behold, the kinsman of whom Boaz spake came by; unto whom he said, 'Ho, such a one! Turn aside, sit down here.' And he turned aside, and sat down. ²And he took ten men of the elders of the city, and said, 'Sit ye down here.' And they sat down. ³And he said unto the kinsman, 'Naomi, that is come again out of the country of Moab, selleth a parcel of land, which was our brother Elimelech's. ⁴And I thought to advertise thee, saying, "Buy it before the inhabitants, and before the elders of my people. If thou wilt redeem it, redeem it; but if thou wilt not redeem it, then tell me, that I may know; for there is none to redeem it beside thee; and I am after thee."' And he said, 'I will redeem it.' ⁵Then said Boaz, 'What day thou buyest the field of the hand of Naomi, thou must buy it also of Ruth the Moabitess, the wife of the dead, to raise up the name of the dead upon his inheritance.'

⁶And the kinsman said, 'I cannot redeem it for myself, lest I mar mine own inheritance: redeem thou my right to thyself; for I cannot redeem it.' ⁷Now this was the manner in former time in Israel concerning redeeming and concerning changing, for to confirm all things; a man plucked off his shoe, and gave it to his neighbour; and this was a testimony in Israel. ⁸Therefore the kinsman said unto Boaz, 'Buy it for thee.' So he drew off his shoe.

⁹And Boaz said unto the elders, and unto all the people, 'Ye are witnesses this day, that I have bought all that was Elimelech's, and all that was Chilion's and Mahlon's, of the hand of Naomi. ¹⁰Moreover Ruth the Moabitess, the wife of

Mahlon, have I purchased to be my wife, to raise up the name of the dead upon his inheritance, that the name of the dead be not cut off from among his brethren, and from the gate of his place: ye are witnesses this day.' ¹¹And all the people that were in the gate, and the elders, said, 'We are witnesses. The Lord make the woman that is come into thine house like Rachel and like Leah, which two did build the house of Israel; and do thou worthily in Ephratah, and be famous in Beth-lehem. ¹²And let thy house be like the house of Pharez, whom Tamar bare unto Judah, of the seed which the Lord shall give thee of this young woman.'

¹³ So Boaz took Ruth, and she was his wife: and when he went in unto her, the Lord gave her conception, and she bare a son. ¹⁴And the women said unto Naomi, 'Blessed be the Lord, which hath not left thee this day without a kinsman, that his name may be famous in Israel. ¹⁵And he shall be unto thee a restorer of thy life, and a nourisher of thine old age, for thy daughter in law, which loveth thee, which is better to thee than seven sons, hath born him.' ¹⁶And Naomi took the child, and laid it in her bosom, and became nurse unto it. ¹⁷And the women her neighbours gave it a name, saying, 'There is a son born to Naomi'; and they called his name Obed: he is the father of Jesse, the father of David.

¹⁸ Now these are the generations of Pharez: Pharez begat Hezron, ¹⁹and Hezron begat Ram, and Ram begat Amminadab, ²⁰and Amminadab begat Nahshon, and Nahshon begat Salmon, ²¹and Salmon begat Boaz, and Boaz begat Obed, ²²and Obed begat Jesse, and Jesse begat David.

the book of esther

Now it came to pass in the days of Ahasuerus (this is Ahasuerus which reigned, from India even unto Ethispia, over
an hundred and seven and twenty provinces) ²that in those
days, when the king Ahasuerus sat on the throne of his kingdom, which was in Shushan the palace, ³in the third year of
his reign, he made a feast unto all his princes and his servants; the power of Persia and Media, the nobles and princes
of the provinces, being before him, ⁴then he shewed the
riches of his glorious kingdom and the honour of his excellent majesty many days, even an hundred and fourscore
days. ⁵And when these days were expired, the king made a
feast unto all the people that were present in Shushan the
palace, both unto great and small, seven days, in the court of
the garden of the king's palace, ⁶where were white, green,
and blue, hangings, fastened with cords of fine linen and
purple to silver rings and pillars of marble: the beds were of
gold and silver, upon a pavement of red, and blue, and
white, and black, marble. ⁷And they gave them drink in vessels of gold (the vessels being diverse one from another), and
royal wine in abundance, according to the state of the king.
⁸And the drinking was according to the law; none did com-
pel: for so the king had appointed to all the officers of his

house, that they should do according to every man's pleasure. ⁹Also Vashti the queen made a feast for the women in the royal house which belonged to king Ahasuerus.

¹⁰On the seventh day, when the heart of the king was merry with wine, he commanded Mehuman, Biztha, Harbona, Bigtha, and Abagtha, Zethar, and Carcas, the seven chamberlains that served in the presence of Ahasuerus the king, ¹¹to bring Vashti the queen before the king with the crown royal, to shew the people and the princes her beauty, for she was fair to look on. ¹²But the queen Vashti refused to come at the king's commandment by his chamberlains: therefore was the king very wroth, and his anger burned in him.

¹³Then the king said to the wise men, which knew the times (for so was the king's manner toward all that knew law and judgment; ¹⁴and the next unto him was Carshena, Shethar, Admatha, Tarshish, Meres, Marsena, and Memucan, the seven princes of Persia and Media, which saw the king's face, and which sat the first in the kingdom), ¹⁵'What shall we do unto the queen Vashti according to law, because she hath not performed the commandment of the king Ahasuerus by the chamberlains?' ¹⁶And Memucan answered before the king and the princes, 'Vashti the queen hath not done wrong to the king only, but also to all the princes, and to all the people that are in all the provinces of the king Ahasuerus. ¹⁷For this deed of the queen shall come abroad unto all women, so that they shall despise their husbands in their eyes, when it shall be reported, "The king Ahasuerus commanded Vashti the queen to be brought in before him, but

she came not." ¹⁸ Likewise shall the ladies of Persia and Media say this day unto all the king's princes, which have heard of the deed of the queen. Thus shall there arise too much contempt and wrath. ¹⁹ If it please the king, let there go a royal commandment from him, and let it be written among the laws of the Persians and the Medes, that it be not altered, that Vashti come no more before king Ahasuerus; and let the king give her royal estate unto another that is better than she. ²⁰And when the king's decree which he shall make shall be published throughout all his empire (for it is great), all the wives shall give to their husbands honour, both to great and small.' ²¹And the saying pleased the king and the princes; and the king did according to the word of Memucan, ²² for he sent letters into all the king's provinces, into every province according to the writing thereof, and to every people after their language, that every man should bear rule in his own house, and that it should be published according to the language of every people.

2 After these things, when the wrath of king Ahasuerus was appeased, he remembered Vashti, and what she had done, and what was decreed against her. ²Then said the king's servants that ministered unto him, 'Let there be fair young virgins sought for the king: ³and let the king appoint officers in all the provinces of his kingdom, that they may gather together all the fair young virgins unto Shushan the palace, to the house of the women, unto the custody of Hege the king's chamberlain, keeper of the women; and let their things for purification be given them. ⁴And let the maiden which pleaseth the king be queen instead of Vashti.' And the thing pleased the king; and he did so.

⁵ Now in Shushan the palace there was a certain Jew, whose name was Mordecai, the son of Jair, the son of Shimei, the son of Kish, a Benjamite, ⁶ who had been carried away from Jerusalem with the captivity which had been carried away with Jeconiah king of Judah, whom Nebuchadnezzar the king of Babylon had carried away. ⁷And he brought up Hadassah, that is, Esther, his uncle's daughter, for she had neither father nor mother, and the maid was fair and beautiful, whom Mordecai, when her father and mother were dead, took for his own daughter.

⁸ So it came to pass, when the king's commandment and his decree was heard, and when many maidens were gathered together unto Shushan the palace, to the custody of Hegai, that Esther was brought also unto the king's house, to the custody of Hegai, keeper of the women. ⁹And the maiden pleased him, and she obtained kindness of him; and he

speedily gave her her things for purification, with such things as belonged to her, and seven maidens, which were meet to be given her, out of the king's house: and he preferred her and her maids unto the best place of the house of the women. ¹⁰ Esther had not shewed her people nor her kindred, for Mordecai had charged her that she should not shew it. ¹¹And Mordecai walked every day before the court of the women's house, to know how Esther did, and what should become of her.

¹² Now when every maid's turn was come to go in to king Ahasuerus, after that she had been twelve months, according to the manner of the women (for so were the days of their purifications accomplished, to wit, six months with oil of myrrh, and six months with sweet odours, and with other things for the purifying of the women); ¹³ then thus came every maiden unto the king; whatsoever she desired was given her to go with her out of the house of the women unto the king's house. ¹⁴ In the evening she went, and on the morrow she returned into the second house of the women, to the custody of Shaashgaz, the king's chamberlain, which kept the concubines: she came in unto the king no more, except the king delighted in her, and that she were called by name.

¹⁵ Now when the turn of Esther, the daughter of Abihail the uncle of Mordecai, who had taken her for his daughter, was come to go in unto the king, she required nothing but what Hegai the king's chamberlain, the keeper of the women, appointed. And Esther obtained favour in the sight of all them that looked upon her. ¹⁶ So Esther was taken unto

king Ahasuerus into his house royal in the tenth month, which is the month Tebeth, in the seventh year of his reign. [17]And the king loved Esther above all the women, and she obtained grace and favour in his sight more than all the virgins; so that he set the royal crown upon her head, and made her queen instead of Vashti. [18]Then the king made a great feast unto all his princes and his servants, even Esther's feast; and he made a release to the provinces, and gave gifts, according to the state of the king. [19]And when the virgins were gathered together the second time, then Mordecai sat in the king's gate. [20]Esther had not yet shewed her kindred nor her people, as Mordecai had charged her; for Esther did the commandment of Mordecai, like as when she was brought up with him.

[21]In those days, while Mordecai sat in the king's gate, two of the king's chamberlains, Bigthan and Teresh, of those which kept the door, were wroth, and sought to lay hand on the king Ahasuerus. [22]And the thing was known to Mordecai, who told it unto Esther the queen; and Esther certified the king thereof in Mordecai's name. [23]And when inquisition was made of the matter, it was found out; therefore they were both hanged on a tree; and it was written in the book of the chronicles before the king.

3 After these things did king Ahasuerus promote Haman the son of Hammedatha the Agagite, and advanced him, and set his seat above all the princes that were with him. ²And all the king's servants, that were in the king's gate, bowed, and reverenced Haman, for the king had so commanded concerning him. But Mordecai bowed not, nor did him reverence. ³Then the king's servants, which were in the king's gate, said unto Mordecai, 'Why transgressest thou the king's commandment?' ⁴Now it came to pass, when they spake daily unto him, and he hearkened not unto them, that they told Haman, to see whether Mordecai's matters would stand, for he had told them that he was a Jew.' ⁵And when Haman saw that Mordecai bowed not, nor did him reverence, then was Haman full of wrath. ⁶And he thought scorn to lay hands on Mordecai alone; for they had shewed him the people of Mordecai: wherefore Haman sought to destroy all the Jews that were throughout the whole kingdom of Ahasuerus, even the people of Mordecai.

⁷In the first month, that is, the month Nisan, in the twelfth year of king Ahasuerus, they cast Pur, that is, the lot, before Haman from day to day, and from month to month, to the twelfth month, that is, the month Adar.

⁸And Haman said unto king Ahasuerus, 'There is a certain people scattered abroad and dispersed among the people in all the provinces of thy kingdom; and their laws are diverse from all people; neither keep they the king's laws: therefore it is not for the king's profit to suffer them. ⁹If it please the king, let it be written that they may be destroyed: and I will

pay ten thousand talents of silver to the hands of those that have the charge of the business, to bring it into the king's treasuries.' ¹⁰And the king took his ring from his hand, and gave it unto Haman the son of Hammedatha the Agagite, the Jews' enemy. ¹¹And the king said unto Haman, 'The silver is given to thee, the people also, to do with them as it seemeth good to thee.' ¹²Then were the king's scribes called on the thirteenth day of the first month, and there was written according to all that Haman had commanded unto the king's lieutenants, and to the governors that were over every province, and to the rulers of every people of every province according to the writing thereof, and to every people after their language; in the name of king Ahasuerus was it written, and sealed with the king's ring. ¹³And the letters were sent by posts into all the king's provinces, to destroy, to kill, and to cause to perish, all Jews, both young and old, little children and women, in one day, even upon the thirteenth day of the twelfth month, which is the month Adar, and to take the spoil of them for a prey. ¹⁴The copy of the writing for a commandment to be given in every province was published unto all people, that they should be ready against that day. ¹⁵The posts went out, being hastened by the king's commandment, and the decree was given in Shushan the palace. And the king and Haman sat down to drink; but the city Shushan was perplexed.

4 When Mordecai perceived all that was done, Mordecai rent his clothes, and put on sackcloth with ashes, and went out into the midst of the city, and cried with a loud and a bitter cry; ²and came even before the king's gate, for none might enter into the king's gate clothed with sackcloth. ³And in every province, whithersoever the king's commandment and his decree came, there was great mourning among the Jews, and fasting, and weeping, and wailing; and many lay in sackcloth and ashes.

⁴So Esther's maids and her chamberlains came and told it her. Then was the queen exceedingly grieved; and she sent raiment to clothe Mordecai, and to take away his sackcloth from him: but he received it not. ⁵Then called Esther for Hatach, one of the king's chamberlains, whom he had appointed to attend upon her, and gave him a commandment to Mordecai, to know what it was, and why it was. ⁶So Hatach went forth to Mordecai unto the street of the city, which was before the king's gate. ⁷And Mordecai told him of all that had happened unto him, and of the sum of the money that Haman had promised to pay to the king's treasuries for the Jews, to destroy them. ⁸Also he gave him the copy of the writing of the decree that was given at Shushan to destroy them, to shew it unto Esther, and to declare it unto her, and to charge her that she should go in unto the king, to make supplication unto him, and to make request before him for her people. ⁹And Hatach came and told Esther the words of Mordecai.

¹⁰Again Esther spake unto Hatach, and gave him commandment unto Mordecai; ¹¹all the king's servants, and the

people of the king's provinces, do know, that whosoever, whether man or woman, shall come unto the king into the inner court, who is not called, there is one law of his to put him to death, except such to whom the king shall hold out the golden sceptre, that he may live; but I have not been called to come in unto the king these thirty days. ¹²And they told to Mordecai Esther's words. ¹³Then Mordecai commanded to answer Esther, 'Think not with thyself that thou shalt escape in the king's house, more than all the Jews. ¹⁴For if thou altogether holdest thy peace at this time, then shall there enlargement and deliverance arise to the Jews from another place; but thou and thy father's house shall be destroyed; and who knoweth whether thou art come to the kingdom for such a time as this?'

¹⁵Then Esther bade them return Mordecai this answer, ¹⁶'Go, gather together all the Jews that are present in Shushan, and fast ye for me, and neither eat nor drink three days, night or day: I also and my maidens will fast likewise; and so will I go in unto the king, which is not according to the law; and if I perish, I perish.' ¹⁷So Mordecai went his way, and did according to all that Esther had commanded him.

5 Now it came to pass on the third day, that Esther put on her royal apparel, and stood in the inner court of the king's house, over against the king's house; and the king sat upon his royal throne in the royal house, over against the gate of the house. ²And it was so, when the king saw Esther the queen standing in the court, that she obtained favour in his sight: and the king held out to Esther the golden sceptre that was in his hand. So Esther drew near, and touched the top of the sceptre. ³ Then said the king unto her, 'What wilt thou, queen Esther? And what is thy request? It shall be even given thee to the half of the kingdom.' ⁴And Esther answered, 'If it seem good unto the king, let the king and Haman come this day unto the banquet that I have prepared for him.' ⁵ Then the king said, 'Cause Haman to make haste, that he may do as Esther hath said.' So the king and Haman came to the banquet that Esther had prepared.

⁶And the king said unto Esther at the banquet of wine, 'What is thy petition? And it shall be granted thee: and what is thy request? Even to the half of the kingdom it shall be performed.' ⁷ Then answered Esther, and said, 'My petition and my request is: ⁸ if I have found favour in the sight of the king, and if it please the king to grant my petition, and to perform my request, let the king and Haman come to the banquet that I shall prepare for them, and I will do to morrow as the king hath said.'

⁹ Then went Haman forth that day joyful and with a glad heart; but when Haman saw Mordecai in the king's gate, that he stood not up, nor moved for him, he was full

of indignation against Mordecai. ¹⁰ Nevertheless Haman refrained himself: and when he came home, he sent and called for his friends, and Zeresh his wife. ¹¹And Haman told them of the glory of his riches, and the multitude of his children, and all the things wherein the king had promoted him, and how he had advanced him above the princes and servants of the king. ¹² Haman said moreover, 'Yea, Esther the queen did let no man come in with the king unto the banquet that she had prepared but myself; and to morrow am I invited unto her also with the king. ¹³ Yet all this availeth me nothing, so long as I see Mordecai the Jew sitting at the king's gate.'

¹⁴ Then said Zeresh his wife and all his friends unto him, 'Let a gallows be made of fifty cubits high, and to morrow speak thou unto the king that Mordecai may be hanged thereon: then go thou in merrily with the king unto the banquet.' And the thing pleased Haman; and he caused the gallows to be made.

6 On that night could not the king sleep, and he commanded to bring the book of records of the chronicles; and they were read before the king. ²And it was found written, that Mordecai had told of Bigthana and Teresh, two of the king's chamberlains, the keepers of the door, who sought to lay hand on the king Ahasuerus. ³And the king said, 'What honour and dignity hath been done to Mordecai for this?' Then said the king's servants that ministered unto him, 'There is nothing done for him.'

⁴And the king said, 'Who is in the court?' Now Haman was come into the outward court of the king's house, to speak unto the king to hang Mordecai on the gallows that he had prepared for him. ⁵And the king's servants said unto him, 'Behold, Haman standeth in the court.' And the king said, 'Let him come in.' ⁶So Haman came in. And the king said unto him, 'What shall be done unto the man whom the king delighteth to honour?' Now Haman thought in his heart, 'To whom would the king delight to do honour more than to myself?' ⁷And Haman answered the king, 'For the man whom the king delighteth to honour, ⁸let the royal apparel be brought which the king useth to wear, and the horse that the king rideth upon, and the crown royal which is set upon his head. ⁹And let this apparel and horse be delivered to the hand of one of the king's most noble princes, that they may array the man withal whom the king delighteth to honour, and bring him on horseback through the street of the city, and proclaim before him, "Thus shall it be done to the man whom the king delighteth to honour."'

[10] Then the king said to Haman, 'Make haste, and take the apparel and the horse, as thou hast said, and do even so to Mordecai the Jew, that sitteth at the king's gate: let nothing fail of all that thou hast spoken.' [11] Then took Haman the apparel and the horse, and arrayed Mordecai, and brought him on horseback through the street of the city, and proclaimed before him, 'Thus shall it be done unto the man whom the king delighteth to honour.'

[12] And Mordecai came again to the king's gate. But Haman hasted to his house mourning, and having his head covered. [13] And Haman told Zeresh his wife and all his friends every thing that had befallen him. Then said his wise men and Zeresh his wife unto him, 'If Mordecai be of the seed of the Jews, before whom thou hast begun to fall, thou shalt not prevail against him, but shalt surely fall before him.' [14] And while they were yet talking with him, came the king's chamberlains, and hasted to bring Haman unto the banquet that Esther had prepared.

7 So the king and Haman came to banquet with Esther the queen. ²And the king said again unto Esther on the second day at the banquet of wine, 'What is thy petition, queen Esther? And it shall be granted thee: and what is thy request? And it shall be performed, even to the half of the kingdom.' ³Then Esther the queen answered and said, 'If I have found favour in thy sight, O king, and if it please the king, let my life be given me at my petition, and my people at my request, ⁴for we are sold, I and my people, to be destroyed, to be slain, and to perish. But if we had been sold for bondmen and bondwomen, I had held my tongue, although the enemy could not countervail the king's damage.'

⁵Then the king Ahasuerus answered and said unto Esther the queen, 'Who is he, and where is he, that durst presume in his heart to do so?' ⁶And Esther said, 'The adversary and enemy is this wicked Haman.' Then Haman was afraid before the king and the queen.

⁷And the king arising from the banquet of wine in his wrath went into the palace garden: and Haman stood up to make request for his life to Esther the queen; for he saw that there was evil determined against him by the king. ⁸Then the king returned out of the palace garden into the place of the banquet of wine; and Haman was fallen upon the bed whereon Esther was. Then said the king, 'Will he force the queen also before me in the house?' As the word went out of the king's mouth, they covered Haman's face. ⁹And Harbonah, one of the chamberlains, said before the king, 'Behold also, the gallows fifty cubits high, which

Haman had made for Mordecai, who had spoken good for the king, standeth in the house of Haman.' Then the king said, 'Hang him thereon.' [10] So they hanged Haman on the gallows that he had prepared for Mordecai. Then was the king's wrath pacified.

8 On that day did the king Ahasuerus give the house of Haman the Jews' enemy unto Esther the queen. And Mordecai came before the king; for Esther had told what he was unto her. ²And the king took off his ring, which he had taken from Haman, and gave it unto Mordecai. And Esther set Mordecai over the house of Haman.

³And Esther spake yet again before the king, and fell down at his feet, and besought him with tears to put away the mischief of Haman the Agagite, and his device that he had devised against the Jews. ⁴Then the king held out the golden sceptre toward Esther. So Esther arose, and stood before the king. ⁵And said, 'If it please the king, and if I have found favour in his sight, and the thing seem right before the king, and I be pleasing in his eyes, let it be written to reverse the letters devised by Haman the son of Hammedatha the Agagite, which he wrote to destroy the Jews which are in all the king's provinces. ⁶For how can I endure to see the evil that shall come unto my people? or how can I endure to see the destruction of my kindred?'

⁷Then the king Ahasuerus said unto Esther the queen and to Mordecai the Jew, 'Behold, I have given Esther the house of Haman, and him they have hanged upon the gallows, because he laid his hand upon the Jews. ⁸Write ye also for the Jews, as it liketh you, in the king's name, and seal it with the king's ring, for the writing which is written in the king's name, and sealed with the king's ring, may no man reverse.' ⁹Then were the king's scribes called at that time in the third month, that is, the month Sivan, on the three and

twentieth day thereof; and it was written according to all that Mordecai commanded unto the Jews, and to the lieutenants, and the deputies and rulers of the provinces which are from India unto Ethiopia, an hundred twenty and seven provinces, unto every province according to the writing thereof, and unto every people after their language, and to the Jews according to their writing, and according to their language. ¹⁰And he wrote in the king Ahasuerus' name, and sealed it with the king's ring, and sent letters by posts on horseback, and riders on mules, camels, and young dromedaries: ¹¹wherein the king granted the Jews which were in every city to gather themselves together, and to stand for their life, to destroy, to slay, and to cause to perish, all the power of the people and province that would assault them, both little ones and women, and to take the spoil of them for a prey, ¹²upon one day in all the provinces of king Ahasuerus, namely, upon the thirteenth day of the twelfth month, which is the month Adar. ¹³The copy of the writing for a commandment to be given in every province was published unto all people, and that the Jews should be ready against that day to avenge themselves on their enemies. ¹⁴So the posts that rode upon mules and camels went out, being hastened and pressed on by the king's commandment. And the decree was given at Shushan the palace.

¹⁵And Mordecai went out from the presence of the king in royal apparel of blue and white, and with a great crown of gold, and with a garment of fine linen and purple: and the city of Shushan rejoiced and was glad. ¹⁶The Jews had light,

and gladness, and joy, and honour. [17]And in every province, and in every city, whithersoever the king's commandment and his decree came, the Jews had joy and gladness, a feast and a good day. And many of the people of the land became Jews; for the fear of the Jews fell upon them.

9 Now in the twelfth month, that is, the month Adar, on the thirteenth day of the same, when the king's commandment and his decree drew near to be put in execution, in the day that the enemies of the Jews hoped to have power over them (though it was turned to the contrary, that the Jews had rule over them that hated them), ²the Jews gathered themselves together in their cities throughout all the provinces of the king Ahasuerus, to lay hand on such as sought their hurt; and no man could withstand them, for the fear of them fell upon all people. ³And all the rulers of the provinces, and the lieutenants, and the deputies, and officers of the king, helped the Jews; because the fear of Mordecai fell upon them. ⁴For Mordecai was great in the king's house, and his fame went out throughout all the provinces; for this man Mordecai waxed greater and greater. ⁵Thus the Jews smote all their enemies with the stroke of the sword, and slaughter, and destruction, and did what they would unto those that hated them. ⁶And in Shushan the palace the Jews slew and destroyed five hundred men. ⁷And Parshandatha, and Dalphon, and Aspatha, ⁸and Poratha, and Adalia, and Aridatha, ⁹and Parmashta, and Arisai, and Aridai, and Vajezatha, ¹⁰the ten sons of Haman the son of Hammedatha, the enemy of the Jews, slew they; but on the spoil laid they not their hand. ¹¹On that day the number of those that were slain in Shushan the palace was brought before the king.

¹²And the king said unto Esther the queen, 'The Jews have slain and destroyed five hundred men in Shushan the

palace, and the ten sons of Haman; what have they done in the rest of the king's provinces? Now what is thy petition? And it shall be granted thee: or what is thy request further? And it shall be done. ¹³ Then said Esther, 'If it please the king, let it be granted to the Jews which are in Shushan to do to morrow also according unto this day's decree, and let Haman's ten sons be hanged upon the gallows.' ¹⁴And the king commanded it so to be done; and the decree was given at Shushan; and they hanged Haman's ten sons. ¹⁵ For the Jews that were in Shushan gathered themselves together on the fourteenth day also of the month Adar, and slew three hundred men at Shushan; but on the prey they laid not their hand. ¹⁶ But the other Jews that were in the king's provinces gathered themselves together, and stood for their lives, and had rest from their enemies, and slew of their foes seventy and five thousand, but they laid not their hands on the prey, ¹⁷on the thirteenth day of the month Adar; and on the fourteenth day of the same rested they, and made it a day of feasting and gladness. ¹⁸ But the Jews that were at Shushan assembled together on the thirteenth day thereof, and on the fourteenth thereof; and on the fifteenth day of the same they rested, and made it a day of feasting and gladness. ¹⁹ Therefore the Jews of the villages, that dwelt in the unwalled towns, made the fourteenth day of the month Adar a day of gladness and feasting, and a good day, and of sending portions one to another.

²⁰And Mordecai wrote these things, and sent letters unto all the Jews that were in all the provinces of the king

Ahasuerus, both nigh and far, ²¹to stablish this among them, that they should keep the fourteenth day of the month Adar, and the fifteenth day of the same, yearly, ²²as the days wherein the Jews rested from their enemies, and the month which was turned unto them from sorrow to joy, and from mourning into a good day, that they should make them days of feasting and joy, and of sending portions one to another, and gifts to the poor. ²³And the Jews undertook to do as they had begun, and as Mordecai had written unto them, ²⁴because Haman the son of Hammedatha, the Agagite, the enemy of all the Jews, had devised against the Jews to destroy them, and had cast Pur, that is, the lot, to consume them, and to destroy them; ²⁵but when Esther came before the king, he commanded by letters that his wicked device, which he devised against the Jews, should return upon his own head, and that he and his sons should be hanged on the gallows. ²⁶Wherefore they called these days Purim after the name of Pur. Therefore for all the words of this letter, and of that which they had seen concerning this matter, and which had come unto them, ²⁷the Jews ordained, and took upon them, and upon their seed, and upon all such as joined themselves unto them, so as it should not fail, that they would keep these two days according to their writing, and according to their appointed time every year; ²⁸and that these days should be remembered and kept throughout every generation, every family, every province, and every city; and that these days of Purim should not fail from among the Jews, nor the memorial of them perish from their seed. ²⁹ Then Esther the queen, the daughter of Abihail, and Mordecai the Jew, wrote with all authority, to confirm this second letter of Purim. ³⁰And he sent the letters unto all the Jews, to the hundred twenty and seven provinces of the kingdom of Ahasuerus, with words of peace and truth, ³¹ to confirm these days of Purim in their times appointed, according as Mordecai the Jew and Esther the queen had enjoined them, and as they had decreed for themselves and for their seed, the matters of the fastings and their cry. ³²And the decree of Esther confirmed these matters of Purim; and it was written in the book.

10 And the king Ahasuerus laid a tribute upon the land, and upon the isles of the sea. ²And all the acts of his power and of his might, and the declaration of the greatness of Mordecai, whereunto the king advanced him, are they not written in the book of the chronicles of the kings of Media and Persia? ³For Mordecai the Jew was next unto king Ahasuerus, and great among the Jews, and accepted of the multitude of his brethren, seeking the wealth of his people, and speaking peace to all his seed.

the pocket canons

song of solomon

the song of

solomon

authorized king james version

grove press
new york

with an introduction by | a. s. byatt

Introduction copyright © 1998 by A. S. Byatt
The Pocket Canon second series copyright © 2000 by Grove/Atlantic, Inc.

All rights reserved. No part of this book may be reproduced in any form
or by any electronic or mechanical means, including information storage
and retrieval systems, without permission in writing from the publisher,
except by a reviewer, who may quote brief passages in a review. Any
members of educational institutions wishing to photocopy part or all
of the work for classroom use, or publishers who would like to obtain
permission to include the work in an anthology, should send their
inquiries to Grove/Atlantic, Inc., 841 Broadway, New York, NY 10003.

Originally published in Great Britain in 1998 by Canongate Books,
Ltd., Edinburgh, Scotland.

Published simultaneously in Canada
Printed in the United States of America

FIRST AMERICAN EDITION

ISBN 0-8021-3759-8 (boxed set)

Design by Paddy Cramsie

Grove Press
841 Broadway
New York, NY 10003

00 01 02 03   10 9 8 7 6 5 4 3 2 1

a note about pocket canons

The Authorized King James Version of the Bible, translated between 1603 and 1611, coincided with an extraordinary flowering of English literature. This version, more than any other, and possibly more than any other work in history, has had an influence in shaping the language we speak and write today.

The books of the King James Bible encompass categories as diverse as history, philosophy, law, poetry and fiction. Each Pocket Canon volume has its own introduction, specially commissioned from an impressive range of writers, to provide a personal interpretation of the text and explore its contemporary relevance.

A S Byatt was born in Yorkshire. Her novels include Shadow of a Sun, The Game, The Virgin in the Garden *and* Still Life. *In 1990 her best-selling novel* Possession *won the Booker Prize and the Irish Times/Aer Lingus International Fiction Prize. Her other books include* Angels and Insects *and two short story collections,* The Matisse Stories *and* The Djinn in the Nightingale's Eye. *Her latest novel,* Babel Tower, *was published to great acclaim in 1996. As well as being a distinguished literary critic, she has served as a judge of various literary prizes, including the Booker. A S Byatt was appointed* CBE *in 1990 for her work as a writer. She lives in London.*

introduction by a s byatt

The Song of Songs is a cry of erotic longing and a description of erotic bliss. It is a lyrical drama whose speakers and episodes run into each other as in a dream or a vision. There is a female voice, which is both virginal and knowing, triumphant and lost. There is a male voice, impatient, exulting, wooing. There is a chorus of unseen commentators, and other groups, the women of Jerusalem, the watchmen, the threescore valiant men who stand around the bed of Solomon. The scene shifts from walled garden to walled city to green bedchamber to the mountains. The woman is black but comely; the man is white and ruddy, with a head like fine gold and with bushy locks, black as a raven. The ending is abrupt and the story is fragmentary. It is a canonical biblical text, and yet there is no mention of God or of religion. It haunts many cultures, eastern and western.

It was ascribed, along with *Ecclesiastes* and *Proverbs*, to King Solomon, son of David. Solomon, according to *The Book of Kings*, had 'seven hundred wives, princesses, and three hundred concubines'; he was famous both for his wisdom and his lechery. The *Song* was thought to refer to his marriage with the daughter of Pharoah, or to his fabled meeting with the Queen of Sheba, who tested him with riddles, the answers to which were to do with the bodies of women.* Jewish commentators saw the woman as Israel, black with her sins; the reading of the *Song* was prescribed during the festival of the Passover. The Fathers of the Christian church were perturbed by its erotic charge, its voluptuous incitation. They assumed that a sacred text must have a spiritual meaning. As Origen wrote in the third century, 'If these things are not to be understood spiritually, are they not simply fabulous tales? If they have no hidden mystery, are they not unworthy of God?' The *Song* became part of an intricate web of allegorical readings of Scripture. These readings constructed both the theology and the poetry of a religion centred on the historical incarnation of the eternal and spiritual. The *Song* became also an extraordinary paradox – a rich, fleshy metaphor for the divine longing that would cause the wise soul to reject the flesh and its desires. Origen's explication turned on the doubleness of the Latin word, *amor*, love, which was used to describe carnal desire and spiritual yearning. Origen himself went as far as self-castration in his search for pure spiritual love. He allegorised the Bride's withdrawal into the marriage chamber as the withdrawal of the pure soul from all extraneous earthly desires.

Origen identified the Bride with Ecclesia, the embattled,

---

* The queen said, 'Seven there are and nine that enter, two yield the draught and one drinks.' Said he to her: 'Seven are the days of a woman's defilement, and nine the months of pregnancy, two are the breasts that yield the draught and one the child that drinks it.' Whereupon she said to him, 'Thou art wise.' Louis Ginzberg, *Legends of the Bible*, pp. 560 ff.

sinful Christian church, who had to learn to respond to the loving care and demands of her Divine Spouse, Christ. The *Song*'s imagery of the bridegroom knocking at a locked door, the bride waking too late, became assimilated to Christ's own parable of the sleepy, unwatchful bridesmaidens. In the twelfth century commentators interpreted the *Song* in terms of the Virgin Mary, the Mother-Bride, the sister-spouse, the mediator. The allegory had for them a literal historical meaning, to be teased out. The Bride also became the Hetaira, romantic heroine and childlike maiden, wooed by Christ the very perfect knight. Poems about Mary Magdalene, repentant beauty, spiritual sinner, who broke an alabaster vase of precious ointment over her Lord's feet, used the imagery of the *Song*. The spiritual interpreters, most strikingly St Bernard of Clairvaux, in his sermons on *The Song of Songs*, saw the individual human soul itself as the Beloved, drawn towards Christ initially through love of the created world. The Latin word for the soul is *anima*, which is a feminine word, and it is striking that the allegorical commentaries and interpretations of the *Song* written by celibate monks, take the passive, open, receptive female consciousness as the central consciousness of the drama. The human soul, male or female, in this erotic mysticism, is a woman waiting for her master, her lord, her bridegroom. The saint's rhetoric, like his vision of the *Song*, includes the erotic, lingers over it, only to dismiss it.

> You must not give an earth-bound meaning to this colouring of corruptible flesh, to this red liquid suffused beneath her pearly skin, to enhance her bodily beauty

in the pink and white loveliness of her cheeks. For the substance of the soul is incorporeal and invisible ...

Or

Shall we imagine for ourselves a huge powerful man, gripped by love for an absent girl, rushing to her desired embraces, bounding over those mountains and hills which we see raised up so high over the plain that their summit seems to penetrate the clouds? It is certainly not proper to fabricate bodily fantasies in this way, and especially when treating of this spiritual Song ... *

And St Bernard, preaching to the abbots of his order, on 'remembering the breasts' makes them into imagined women and mothers: 'Be gentle, avoid harshness, give up blows, show your breasts: let your bosoms be fat with milk, not swollen with wrath.'

The fathers of the church were preaching an incarnate God to an incarnate congregation, creatures made up of flesh and spirit. They could rationalise their treatment of *The Song of Songs* – which is not a rational structure – by saying that its inspired author had used the language of the flesh to entice the incarnate souls to the love of the Incarnate Word, speaking through the flesh. Their ingenuity and resourceful reconstructions and deconstructions can seem both beautiful

---

* These passages are quoted, with some retranslation, from Anne W Astell, *The Song of Songs in the Middle Ages* (Cornell University Press, 1990). I am much indebted to this excellent book.

and absurd to an unbeliever seduced and baffled by the literal presence of the *Song* itself. Is it the nature of the text or the nature of the theology that brings about all the building of these airy places, such a reader may ask her or himself.

The Jungians, as we might expect, have an answer. They are drawn to the *Song* by the presence of the woman and the idea of a marriage. The female persona in the story, or stories, can be seen as the Jungian *anima*, the complementary female self who must be integrated into the psyche for wholeness. The four major feminine archetypes of Jungian psychoanalysis – Virgin, Mother, Medial Woman and Hetaira – can all be found easily in the *Song*. A Jungian reading of the *Song* includes the alchemical Coniunctio, the mystical marriage of opposites. In alchemical terms the Shulamite's blackness signifies the 'feminine personification of the prima materia in the *nigredo* stato'. Jung quotes alchemical texts in which the Shulamite attributes her blackness to the original sin of Eve: 'O that the serpent roused up Eve! To which I must testify with the black colour that clings to me.' * 'She is the *anima mundi* or Gnostic Sophia, caught in the dark embraces of *physis*.' Here is a psychoanalytical and alchemical version of the interpretative anxiety about incarnation, spirit and matter. It leads to a consideration of the extraordinary proliferation of quotations, objects, metaphors from the *Song* throughout many centuries and literatures.

Ann Astell gives some beautiful examples of love lyrics, sacred and profane, from the Middle Ages. I myself found

---

* Jung, *Mysterium Coniunctionis*, Collected Works 14, para 591.

The Song of Songs everywhere in the thesis I never finished, which was about sensuous metaphors for the spiritual in the seventeenth century, and turned out to be about narratives of fleshly temptations in gardens, from Spenser's 'Bower of Bliss' to *Paradise Lost* and the temptation of Christ in *Paradise Regained*. The words of the *Song* sing enchantingly in English, for instance in Henry Vaughan's 'The Night'.

> God's silent searching flight
> When my Lord's head is filled with dew and all
> His locks are wet with the clear drops of night
> His still, soft call;
> His knocking time; the soul's dumb watch,
> When spirits her fair kinred catch.

Marvell's delightful conceits in 'The Nymph Complaining for the Death of her Fawn' combine classical pastoral with the *Song*'s imagery of innocence in a closed garden, lilies and roses, the beloved as a hart or a roe deer on the mountains. And Milton compares his Paradise garden to

> Those gardens feigned
> Or of revived Adonis, or renowned
> Alcinous, host of old Laertes' son,
> Or that, not mystic, where the sapient king
> Held dalliance with his fair Egyptian spouse.
>
> (*Paradise Lost*, IX, ll. 439-43)

Alastair Fowler, a great editor, points out that Milton is here drawing an analogy between Solomon and Adam, both wise, both uxorious, both lovers in gardens. He points out

he ambiguity of the word 'sapient', meaning, in its Latin
oot, 'gaining knowledge by tasting'. This concept, like most
ommentary on the Song, finds the spirit in the flesh. Fowler
oes on to point out that Milton's references to 'sapience' in
he Song of Songs tend to associate Solomon with Satan, and
ith the latter's interest in Eve's beauty, and in the taste of
e apples of the Tree of the knowledge of Good and Evil. In
aradise Lost (Book v, ll. 40–8), Eve recounts to Adam a dream
n which Satan tempts her in a parody of the lover of the
ong. It is interesting in this context that Solomon turned to
e worship of Ashtaroth through the persuasion of his wives.

> For it came to pass, when Solomon was old, that his
> wives turned away his heart after other gods: and his
> heart was not perfect with the Lord his God, as was
> the heart of David his father.
> For Solomon went after Ashtoreth the goddess of
> the Zidonians, and after Milcom, the abomination of
> the Ammonites ... (1 *Kings* 11:4-5)

St Augustine, before Milton, compared the sins of Adam
nd Solomon, led into temptation by their love for their wives.
Modern scholars see *The Song of Songs* as an echo of some-
hing more ancient, the marriage songs of the sacred mar-
iages of the ancient Mesopotamian gods and goddesses,
nana and Dumuzi, Ishtar and Tammuz, gods whose wor-
hip entailed sacred prostitution, the making of gardens, the
nourning of the vanished young god and the celebration of
is return with the spring. These deities were, in some ver-
ions, brother and sister – 'my sister, my spouse'. The return

and the rebirth of Adonis (who was the same god as Tam
muz, since Adonis simply means 'Lord') coincided with the
Spring, and the return of vegetation.

> For, lo, the winter is past, the rain is over and gone;
> The flowers appear on the earth;
> the time of the singing of birds is come,
> and the voice of the turtle is heard in our land;
> The fig tree putteth forth her green figs,
> and the vines with the tender grape
> give a good smell. Arise, my love, my fair one,
> and come away.

Frazer, in *The Golden Bough*, compares the kings of the
Bible to the priest-kings of the Syrian Lord Adonis, and
quotes St Jerome, who 'tells us that Bethlehem, the tradi
tional birthplace of the Lord, was shaded by a grove of that
still older Syrian Lord Adonis, and that where the infant Jesu
had wept, the lover of Venus was bewailed.' Jerome, Frazer
says, appears to have believed that the grove was planted by
heathens to defile the sacred spot. Frazer himself believes
that the grove was older, and that in any case the Christian
god who was the bread of life, born in Bethlehem, 'the House
of Bread' was related to the older corn spirit.

Whatever the spiritual meanings and antecedents, the
immediate experience of reading the *Song* is both sensuously
exciting and baffling. As a narrative, it does not hold together
Moments of intense dramatic feeling – the Shulamite's
description of her rejected blackness, the knocking and
vanishing of the bridegroom, her wandering the streets of

Darwin celebrated also. Later English poets learned from it a kind of eastern poetry which was diffused and exceeding, rather than precise and contained. The mythical erotic English gardens of Tennyson's *Maud* owe much to the *Song*. Tennyson combines his Isle of Wight cedars with the cedars of Lebanon, as he combines the lilies and roses of the *Song* with an English garden. Browning complained that Tennyson had diffused the feeling that should have been applied to the woman into the landscape. But Tennyson knew what he was doing. He had been reading Persian poetry, and understanding the *Song* in his way.

The *Song* continues to haunt our imaginations, between the absurd and the sublime. Dorothy Sayers' *Busman's Honeymoon* quotes it absurdly. Harriet Vane, watching Lord Peter Wimsey in a blazer, reflects that she has 'married England'. But her lord, on waking after their wedding night, addresses her as 'my Shulamite'.

And in quite another world, the *Song* inhabits some of the greatest and most terrible poetry of our time, the poems in German of Paul Celan. The figure of Shulamith, whose name occurs only once in the Bible, appears in many forms in his work. His riddling poems about terror and loss, about the Holocaust and Israel, mourn both the Rose of Sharon, and, specifically, 'my sister, my spouse', the lost and destroyed. His biographer, John Felstiner, traces the tradition by which Shulamith, whose name is associated with *Shalom* * (peace),

---

* Edward F. Edinger, *The Bible and the Psyche* (Inner City Books, 1986) p. 137.

was seen by the mystical tradition as a figure both for the *Shechinah* (the divine light) and for the promised return to Zion. 'Return, return, O Shulamite; return, return, that we may look upon thee.' * She appears in *Todesfuge* (*Deathfugue*) in a repeated, chanted juxtaposition with the doomed Margaret of Goethe's *Faust*.

> Dein goldenes Haar Margarete
> Dein aschenes Haar Sulamith
>
> (your golden hair, Margareta,
> your ashen hair, Shulamith)

Here, Shulamith's burned blackness, her ashen hair, are irredeemable, made smoke, buried in the air. Her darkness cancels and darkens Margarete's innocent suffering. This new, dreadful figuration of Shulamith ends a poem as powerful and unforgettable as the *Song* itself. It adds a meaning and a figure that can never again be separated from the changing poetic world of the *Song*, whatever else may be added.

---

* John Felstiner, *Paul Celan, Poet, Survivor, Jew* (Yale, 1995).

the song of solomon

The song of songs, which is Solomon's.

> [2] Let him kiss me with the kisses of his mouth;
>> for thy love is better than wine.
> [3] Because of the savour of thy good ointments
>> thy name is as ointment poured forth,
>>> therefore do the virgins love thee.
> [4] Draw me, we will run after thee;
>> the king hath brought me into his chambers:
>>> we will be glad and rejoice in thee,
>> we will remember thy love more than wine:
>>> the upright love thee.
> [5] I am black, but comely,
>> O ye daughters of Jerusalem,
>>> as the tents of Kedar,
>> as the curtains of Solomon.
> [6] Look not upon me, because I am black,
>> because the sun hath looked upon me.
>>> My mother's children were angry with me;
>> they made me the keeper of the vineyards;
>>> but mine own vineyard have I not kept.
> [7] Tell me, O thou whom my soul loveth,
>> where thou feedest,

where thou makest thy flock to rest at noon;
for why should I be as one that turneth aside
by the flocks of thy companions?

8 If thou know not, O thou fairest among women,
go thy way forth by the footsteps of the flock,
and feed thy kids beside the shepherds' tents.

9 I have compared thee, O my love,
to a company of horses in Pharaoh's chariots.

10 Thy cheeks are comely with rows of jewels,
thy neck with chains of gold.

11 We will make thee borders of gold
with studs of silver.

12 While the king sitteth at his table,
my spikenard sendeth forth the smell thereof.

13 A bundle of myrrh is my wellbeloved unto me;
he shall lie all night betwixt my breasts.

14 My beloved is unto me as a cluster of camphire
in the vineyards of En-gedi.

15 Behold, thou art fair, my love;
behold, thou art fair; thou hast doves' eyes.

16 Behold, thou art fair, my beloved,
yea, pleasant:
also our bed is green.

17 The beams of our house are cedar,
and our rafters of fir.

2 I am the rose of Sharon,
and the lily of the valleys.

2 As the lily among thorns,

so is my love among the daughters.
³As the apple tree among the trees of the wood,
  so is my beloved among the sons.
      I sat down under his shadow with great delight,
  and his fruit was sweet to my taste.
⁴He brought me to the banqueting house,
  and his banner over me was love.
⁵Stay me with flagons, comfort me with apples;
  for I am sick of love.
⁶His left hand is under my head,
  and his right hand doth embrace me.
⁷I charge you, O ye daughters of Jerusalem,
  by the roes, and by the hinds of the field,
      that ye stir not up,
  nor awake my love, till he please.
⁸The voice of my beloved!
  Behold, he cometh leaping upon the mountains,
      skipping upon the hills.
⁹My beloved is like a roe or a young hart;
  behold, he standeth behind our wall,
      he looketh forth at the windows,
  shewing himself through the lattice.
¹⁰My beloved spake, and said unto me,
  'Rise up, my love, my fair one, and come away.
¹¹For, lo, the winter is past,
  the rain is over and gone;
¹²the flowers appear on the earth;
  the time of the singing of birds is come,
      and the voice of the turtle is heard in our land;

¹³ the fig tree putteth forth her green figs,
    and the vines with the tender grape
        give a good smell.
    Arise, my love, my fair one, and come away.
¹⁴ O my dove, that art in the clefts of the rock,
    in the secret places of the stairs,
        let me see thy countenance,
    let me hear thy voice;
        for sweet is thy voice,
    and thy countenance is comely.
¹⁵ Take us the foxes,
    the little foxes, that spoil the vines;
        for our vines have tender grapes.'
¹⁶ My beloved is mine, and I am his;
    he feedeth among the lilies.
¹⁷ Until the day break,
    and the shadows flee away,
        turn, my beloved, and be thou like a roe
    or a young hart upon the mountains of Bether.

3   By night on my bed I sought him
        whom my soul loveth;
            I sought him, but I found him not.
    ² I will rise now, and go about the city in the streets,
        and in the broad ways I will seek
            him whom my soul loveth:
        I sought him, but I found him not.
    ³ The watchmen that go about the city found me:
        to whom I said,

'Saw ye him whom my soul loveth?'
⁴ It was but a little that I passed from them,
  but I found him whom my soul loveth:
    I held him, and would not let him go,
    until I had brought him into my mother's house,
      and into the chamber of her that conceived me.
⁵ I charge you, O ye daughters of Jerusalem,
    by the roes, and by the hinds of the field,
      that ye stir not up,
    nor awake my love, till he please.
⁶ Who is this that cometh out of the wilderness
    like pillars of smoke,
      perfumed with myrrh and frankincense,
    with all powders of the merchant?
⁷ Behold his bed, which is Solomon's;
    threescore valiant men are about it,
      of the valiant of Israel.
⁸ They all hold swords, being expert in war;
    every man hath his sword upon his thigh
      because of fear in the night.
⁹ King Solomon made himself a chariot of
    the wood of Lebanon.
¹⁰ He made the pillars thereof of silver,
    the bottom thereof of gold,
      the covering of it of purple,
    the midst thereof being paved with love,
      for the daughters of Jerusalem.
¹¹ Go forth, O ye daughters of Zion,
    and behold king Solomon with the crown

wherewith his mother crowned him
in the day of his espousals,
and in the day of the gladness of his heart.

4 Behold, thou art fair, my love;
behold, thou art fair;
thou hast doves' eyes within thy locks;
thy hair is as a flock of goats,
that appear from mount Gilead.
² Thy teeth are like a flock of sheep that are even shorn,
which came up from the washing;
whereof every one bear twins,
and none is barren among them.
³ Thy lips are like a thread of scarlet,
and thy speech is comely:
thy temples are like a piece of
a pomegranate within thy locks.
⁴ Thy neck is like the tower of David
builded for an armoury,
whereon there hang a thousand bucklers,
all shields of mighty men.
⁵ Thy two breasts are like two young roes
that are twins, which feed among the lilies.
⁶ Until the day break, and the shadows flee away,
I will get me to the mountain of myrrh,
and to the hill of frankincense.
⁷ Thou art all fair, my love; there is no spot in thee.
⁸ Come with me from Lebanon, my spouse,
with me from Lebanon;

look from the top of Amana,
from the top of Shenir and Hermon,
from the lions' dens,
from the mountains of the leopards.

9 Thou hast ravished my heart, my sister, my spouse;
thou hast ravished my heart with
one of thine eyes, with one chain of thy neck.

10 How fair is thy love, my sister, my spouse!
How much better is thy love than wine!
And the smell of thine ointments than all spices!

11 Thy lips, O my spouse, drop as the honeycomb:
honey and milk are under thy tongue;
and the smell of thy garments
is like the smell of Lebanon.

12 A garden inclosed is my sister, my spouse;
a spring shut up, a fountain sealed.

13 Thy plants are an orchard of pomegranates,
with pleasant fruits;
camphire, with spikenard,

14 spikenard and saffron;
calamus and cinnamon,
with all trees of frankincense;
myrrh and aloes,
with all the chief spices:

15 a fountain of gardens,
a well of living waters,
and streams from Lebanon.

16 Awake, O north wind; and come, thou south;
blow upon my garden,

that the spices thereof may flow out.
Let my beloved come into his garden,
    and eat his pleasant fruits.

5 I am come into my garden, my sister, my spouse:
    I have gathered my myrrh with my spice;
        I have eaten my honeycomb with my honey;
    I have drunk my wine with my milk:
        eat, O friends; drink,
    yea, drink abundantly, O beloved.
²I sleep, but my heart waketh:
    it is the voice of my beloved that knocketh, saying,
        'Open to me, my sister, my love,
    my dove, my undefiled;
        for my head is filled with dew,
    and my locks with the drops of the night.'
³I have put off my coat; how shall I put it on?
    I have washed my feet; how shall I defile them?
⁴My beloved put in his hand by the hole of the door,
    and my bowels were moved for him.
⁵I rose up to open to my beloved;
    and my hands dropped with myrrh,
        and my fingers with sweet-smelling myrrh,
    upon the handles of the lock.
⁶I opened to my beloved;
    but my beloved had withdrawn himself,
        and was gone:
    my soul failed when he spake:
        I sought him, but I could not find him;

I called him, but he gave me no answer.
⁷ The watchmen that went about the city found me,
they smote me, they wounded me;
the keepers of the walls
took away my veil from me.
⁸ I charge you, O daughters of Jerusalem,
if ye find my beloved, that ye tell him,
that I am sick of love.
⁹ What is thy beloved more than another beloved,
O thou fairest among women?
What is thy beloved more than another beloved,
that thou dost so charge us?
¹⁰ My beloved is white and ruddy,
the chiefest among ten thousand.
¹¹ His head is as the most fine gold,
his locks are bushy, and black as a raven.
¹² His eyes are as the eyes of doves
by the rivers of waters,
washed with milk, and fitly set.
¹³ His cheeks are as a bed of spices,
as sweet flowers:
his lips like lilies,
dropping sweet smelling myrrh.
¹⁴ His hands are as gold rings set with the beryl:
his belly is as bright ivory
overlaid with sapphires.
¹⁵ His legs are as pillars of marble,
set upon sockets of fine gold;
his countenance is as Lebanon,

excellent as the cedars.
¹⁶ His mouth is most sweet;
    yea, he is altogether lovely.
        This is my beloved, and this is my friend,
        O daughters of Jerusalem.

6 Whither is thy beloved gone,
    O thou fairest among women?
        Whither is thy beloved turned aside?
    That we may seek him with thee.
² My beloved is gone down into his garden,
    to the beds of spices,
        to feed in the gardens, and to gather lilies.
³ I am my beloved's, and my beloved is mine;
    he feedeth among the lilies.
⁴ Thou art beautiful, O my love, as Tirzah,
    comely as Jerusalem,
        terrible as an army with banners.
⁵ Turn away thine eyes from me,
    for they have overcome me:
        thy hair is as a flock of goats
    that appear from Gilead.
⁶ Thy teeth are as a flock of sheep
    which go up from the washing,
        whereof every one beareth twins,
    and there is not one barren among them.
⁷ As a piece of a pomegranate
    are thy temples within thy locks.
⁸ There are threescore queens,

and fourscore concubines,
    and virgins without number.
⁹ My dove, my undefiled is but one;
    she is the only one of her mother,
        she is the choice one of her that bare her.
The daughters saw her, and blessed her;
    yea, the queens and the concubines,
    and they praised her.
¹⁰ Who is she that looketh forth as the morning,
    fair as the moon, clear as the sun,
        and terrible as an army with banners?
¹¹ I went down into the garden of nuts
    to see the fruits of the valley,
        and to see whether the vine flourished,
    and the pomegranates budded.
¹² Or ever I was aware,
    my soul made me like the chariots of Ammi-nadib.
¹³ Return, return, O Shulamite;
    return, return, that we may look upon thee.
        What will ye see in the Shulamite?
    As it were the company of two armies.

7   How beautiful are thy feet with shoes,
        O prince's daughter!
            The joints of thy thighs are like jewels,
        the work of the hands of a cunning workman.
² Thy navel is like a round goblet,
    which wanteth not liquor;
        thy belly is like an heap of wheat

set about with lilies.

³ Thy two breasts are like two young roes that are twins.

⁴ Thy neck is as a tower of ivory;

thine eyes like the fishpools in Heshbon,

by the gate of Bath-rabbim;

thy nose is as the tower of Lebanon

which looketh toward Damascus.

⁵ Thine head upon thee is like Carmel,

and the hair of thine head like purple;

the king is held in the galleries.

⁶ How fair and how pleasant art thou,

O love, for delights!

⁷ This thy stature is like to a palm tree,

and thy breasts to clusters of grapes.

⁸ I said, 'I will go up to the palm tree,

I will take hold of the boughs thereof:

now also thy breasts shall be

as clusters of the vine,

and the smell of thy nose like apples;

⁹ and the roof of thy mouth like the best wine

for my beloved, that goeth down sweetly,

causing the lips of those that are asleep

to speak.'

¹⁰ I am my beloved's, and his desire is toward me.

¹¹ Come, my beloved,

let us go forth into the field;

let us lodge in the villages.

¹² Let us get up early to the vineyards;

let us see if the vine flourish,

whether the tender grape appear,
and the pomegranates bud forth;
there will I give thee my loves.
¹³ The mandrakes give a smell,
and at our gates are all manner of pleasant fruits,
new and old, which I have laid up for thee,
O my beloved.

8

O that thou wert as my brother,
that sucked the breasts of my mother!
When I should find thee without,
I would kiss thee;
yea, I should not be despised.
² I would lead thee,
and bring thee into my mother's house,
who would instruct me;
I would cause thee to drink of spiced wine
of the juice of my pomegranate.
³ His left hand should be under my head,
and his right hand should embrace me.
⁴ I charge you, O daughters of Jerusalem,
that ye stir not up,
nor awake my love, until he please.
⁵ Who is this that cometh up from the wilderness,
leaning upon her beloved?
I raised thee up under the apple tree:
there thy mother brought thee forth;
there she brought thee forth that bare thee.
⁶ Set me as a seal upon thine heart,

as a seal upon thine arm;

 for love is strong as death;

jealousy is cruel as the grave;

 the coals thereof are coals of fire,

which hath a most vehement flame.

⁷ Many waters cannot quench love,

neither can the floods drown it;

 if a man would give

all the substance of his house for love,

 it would utterly be contemned.

⁸ We have a little sister, and she hath no breasts;

what shall we do for our sister

 in the day when she shall be spoken for?

⁹ If she be a wall,

we will build upon her a palace of silver;

 and if she be a door,

we will inclose her with boards of cedar.

¹⁰ I am a wall, and my breasts like towers;

then was I in his eyes as one that found favour.

¹¹ Solomon had a vineyard at Baalhamon;

he let out the vineyard unto keepers;

 every one for the fruit thereof

was to bring a thousand pieces of silver.

¹² My vineyard, which is mine, is before me;

thou, O Solomon, must have a thousand,

 and those that keep the fruit thereof

two hundred.

¹³ Thou that dwellest in the gardens,

the companions hearken to thy voice;

cause me to hear it.
14 Make haste, my beloved,
    and be thou like to a roe or to a young hart
        upon the mountains of spices.

the pocket canons

genesis – *introduced by e. l. doctorow*
exodus – *introduced by david grossman*
ruth – *introduced by joanna trollope*
samuel – *introduced by meir shalev*
job – *introduced by charles frazier*
selections from the book of psalms – *introduced by bono*
proverbs – *introduced by charles johnson*
ecclesiastes – *introduced by doris lessing*
song of solomon – *introduced by a. s. byatt*
isaiah – *introduced by peter ackroyd*
jonah – *introduced by alasdair gray*
wisdom – *introduced by peirs paul read*
matthew – *introduced by francisco goldman*
mark – *introduced by barry hannah*
luke – *introduced by thomas cahill*
john – *introduced by darcey steinke*
acts – *introduced by p. d. james*
romans – *introduced by ruth rendell*
corinthians – *introduced by fay weldon*
hebrews – *introduced by karen armstrong*
epistles – *introduced by his holiness the dalai lama
of tibet*
revelation – *introduced by kathleen norris*

jonah, micah and nahum

the books of

jonah

micah and nahum

authorized king james version

grove press
new york

with an introduction by | alasdair gray

Introduction copyright © 1999 by Alasdair Gray
Extract from *On the Mass Bombing of Iraq and Kuwait, Commonly Known as 'The Gulf War'* © 1991 by Tom Leonard
The Pocket Canon second series copyright © 2000 by Grove/Atlantic, Inc.

All rights reserved. No part of this book may be reproduced in any form or by any electronic or mechanical means, including information storage and retrieval systems, without permission in writing from the publisher, except by a reviewer, who may quote brief passages in a review. Any members of educational institutions wishing to photocopy part or all of the work for classroom use, or publishers who would like to obtain permission to include the work in an anthology, should send their inquiries to Grove/Atlantic, Inc., 841 Broadway, New York, NY 10003.

Originally published in Great Britain in 1999 by Canongate Books, Ltd., Edinburgh, Scotland.

Published simultaneously in Canada
Printed in the United States of America

FIRST AMERICAN EDITION

ISBN 0-8021-3759-8 (boxed set)

Design by Paddy Cramsie

Grove Press
841 Broadway
New York, NY 10003

00 01 02 03   10 9 8 7 6 5 4 3 2 1

a note about pocket canons

The Authorized King James Version of the Bible, translated between 1603 and 1611, coincided with an extraordinary flowering of English literature. This version, more than any other, and possibly more than any other work in history, has had an influence in shaping the language we speak and write today.

The books of the King James Bible encompass categories as diverse as history, philosophy, law, poetry and fiction. Each Pocket Canon volume has its own introduction, specially commissioned from an impressive range of writers, to provide a personal interpretation of the text and explore its contemporary relevance.

introduction by alasdair gray

Alasdair Gray is an old asthmatic Glaswegian who lives by paint-ing, writing and book design. His books are the novels Lanark, 1982 Janine, The Fall of Kelvin Walker, Something Leather, McGrotty and Ludmilla, Poor Things, A History Maker; *short story collections* Unlikely Stories Mostly, Lean Tales *(with Agnes Owens and James Kelman),* Ten Tales Tall & True, Mavis Belfrage; *poetry* Old Negatives; *polemic* Why Scots Should Rule Scotland 1992, Why Scots should Rule Scotland 1997; *play* Working Legs *(for people without them); autobiog-raphy* Saltire Self Portrait 4; *literary history* The Anthology of Prefaces. *His hobbies are socialism and liking the English.*

The thirty-nine books called *The Old Testament* in the King James Bible show the state of the Jews between 900 and 100 BC and preserve legends from more ancient times. They were edited into their present form by scholars defending their culture from an empire ruling the place where they lived: an empire of people equally clever and literate: Greeks whose books were as various as their gods. Jews were then unique in worshipping a single God: their folklore, laws, politics and poetry kept mentioning him. The editors arranged these books in the chronological order of the subject matter, producing a story of their people from prehistoric times and making their God the strongest character in world fiction. It began with a second-century BC poem telling how he made the universe and people like a poet, out of words, followed by a fifth-century BC tale of how he made man like a potter, out of clay. It then showed God adapting to his worshippers from prehistoric times to their own.

Adam, Cain and Noah find God punitive but soothed by the smell of burnt flesh, mostly animal. He connives with the tricks of Abraham and Isaac, polygamous nomads who get cattle or revenge by prostituting a wife or cheating foreigners and relatives. When Moses leads Jewish tribes out of Egypt God commands them like a Pharaoh, promising unlimited protection for unlimited obedience. He is a war god when they invade Palestine, smiting them with plague when they do not kill every man, woman, child and animal in a captured city. Their leaders (called prophets because God tells them the future) are fathers of tribal families and military commanders until they get land and cities of their own where (as in other lands) wealth is managed by official landlords and priests who exploit the poor. New kinds of prophet then arise: poets inspired by moral rage who speak for the exploited. They say that if Jewish rulers don't obey God by being just and merciful he will use the might of foreigners to smash their new-made kingdoms. That happens. From 680 BC to 1948 Jews are ruled by foreign empires, first Assyrian and at last British. They outlive so many empires that Norwegian Ibsen calls them the aristocrats of world history, for they can survive without a land and government.

That was not wholly true. They were governed by the words of their prophets, especially those in the last *Old Testament* books who said the Jewish God is also God of all people, even people who oppress them; that God has created Jews to keep his words alive until the whole world learns justice and mercy by obeying him; that before then Jews should welcome suffering as punishment for sin or tests of faith. After the first destruction of Jerusalem in 586 BC this must have sounded a new policy to those who wanted to repossess a national territory gained (as all nations have gained territory) by killing folk. No wonder many Jews assimilated with foreigners and the faithful sometimes sang psalms begging God to leave them alone.

The book of *Jonah* is a prose comedy about a Jew who wants God to leave him alone and cannot grasp that God's policy is now for those of every nation.

Jonah is an unwilling prophet. His Jewish conscience orders him to denounce the wicked Assyrian empire in its capital city so he at once sails towards a different city where he hopes foreign gods will prevail over his own. This breaks the first of the ten commandments: *You shall have no other God than me* (*Deuteronomy* 5): hence the tempest. The international crew see it is aimed at someone aboard. Many verses describe their reluctance to fling Jonah out, even when he tells them it is the one way to save themselves. The book is insisting that mercy is not just a Jewish virtue; but out Jonah goes and God saves him in the belly of a fish. Here the prophet chants a psalm saying God can save those who cry unto him from the belly of hell. This hell is not the eternal torture chamber later adopted by official Christianity. For Jews hell is the worst that living people can suffer and Jonah IS suffering it, unless the fish intestines are a cosy place. But now he knows that God is always with him and he need not fear death.

Then comes a parody of *Exodus*, Chapter 11, perhaps the cruellest book in the *Old Testament*. In it the God of Moses sends Pharaoh a message then hardens Pharaoh's heart to reject it, giving Moses an excuse to condemn all Egyptian first-born children and cattle to death by plague. But God uses Jonah to send the Assyrians a message that softens their king's heart. The king leads his people into abandoning their evil ways, so *God repented of the evil that he had said that he would do unto them; and he did it not* (Jonah 3:10). This contradicts the Mosaic code, which says evil MUST be rewarded with evil.

So Jonah learns he is not a scourge in the hand of God, like Moses, Joshua and Samson, but a reformer, and like many reformers he now looks stupid. It is obvious that the enemy king who thought his people might be persuaded to deserve mercy knew more about God than God's Hebrew prophet. Jonah's short but influential career ends not with a bang but with his dismal whimper: *I knew that thou art a gracious God, and merciful, ... Therefore now, O Lord, take, I beseech thee, my life from me, for it is better for me to die than to live* (Jonah 4:2–3). God cuts this self-pitying cackle with a short question: *Doest thou well to be angry?* (Jonah 4:4) Jonah is too cowardly or childish to admit anger and squats outside the city determined to die by sunstroke if the promise of destruction is not fulfilled. Not even the mercy of miraculous shade cast over him softens this determination. The shade is withdrawn. In a fever Jonah hears God repeat something like his last question. He now answers truthfully and is favoured by words framed like another question. They suggest reasons for both God's action and his inaction: most evil is caused by folly; widespread slaughter is not the best cure if a warning of disaster helps folk to change their ways. We are not told if Jonah learns these lessons because they are meant for *us*.

Believers and unbelievers have argued pointlessly about the truth of Jonah's book because they did not know great truths can be told in fantasies. It was known by editors who put *Jonah* before *Micah* and *Nahum*, realistic books about the destruction of Jerusalem and Nineveh.

Micah starts a prophetic sermon in verse by denouncing the Jews who live in Samaria: God has let Assyria enslave them for disobeying him; soon the princes and priests of Jerusalem will be conquered too, for they seek wealth and luxury instead of justice and mercy, oppressing the poor of their own nation while thinking God's forgiveness can be bought by animal sacrifices. Micah foretells a disastrous but not hopeless future: after much warfare the whole world will find peace by accepting the one true God, for a Jewish ruler from the little town of Bethlehem will become lord of every nation. This prophecy must have inspired hope and dread in every imaginative child born afterwards in Bethlehem.

Nahum came eighty years later. He was probably an

Assyrian slave when all Jewish territory had been conquered as Micah foretold. Nahum saw the destruction of Nineveh by the combined armies of Babylon and Persia: these killed and enslaved the people and washed the city away by channelling the River Tigris into it. The only grand truth in Nahum's triumphant song is that nations who keep living by armaments will perish by them. Most governments, including the British, think this only true of foreign nations. I quote from Tom Leonard's *On the Mass Bombing of Iraq and Kuwait, Commonly Known as 'The Gulf War' with Leonard's Shorter Catechism*. AK Press published it in 1991.

Q. What did Britain take part in on Tuesday, February 19, 1991?

A. It took part in what was at that point 'one of the most ferocious attacks on the centre of Baghdad', using bombers and Cruise missiles fired from ships.

Q. What did John Major say about the bombing the next day?

A. He said: 'One is bound to ask about attacks such as these: what sort of people is it that can carry them out? They certainly are consumed with hate. They are certainly sick of mind, and they can be certain of one thing – they will be hunted and hunted until they are found.'

(He was talking about 5 lb of explosive left in a litter basket at Victoria Station in London. This killed one person and critically injured three.)

Major's government contained people privately enriched by weapon sales to both Britain's army and the army of the dictator we fought. We fought him again before Christmas 1998 when our most highly respected newspapers said that, though wicked and undemocratic, this dictator had better stay in power to stop Iraq falling apart and increasing the cost of our petrol. Meanwhile, since our troops in 1991 fired bullets tipped with uranium, babies are now being born in Iraq with distorted bodies and heads, others without heads.

When a child, Ernest Levy lost faith in a purely national god by living through Auschwitz and Belsen. He became a cantor in a Glasgow synagogue and now believes God is the innocent, creative, spiritual part of everyone. This sounds like the merciful God of *Jonah* but can any God be merciful to a nation that does not repent of the evil it does? That makes, sells and uses what kills, cripples and warps even the unborn? Jesus learned from *Jonah*, *Micah* and *Nahum* what governments of Britain and the USA refuse to learn from Jesus. They act like Moses and Elijah, deliberately killing and diseasing thousands of civilians who cannot harm them. They do it without the old Hebrew excuse of being slaves wanting freedom or wanderers needing a homeland, without the Crusaders' excuse of defending a True Faith, without the Liberal excuse of spreading democracy. The one idea behind such war is that any number of foreigners can be killed to keep up global company profits, though politicians give nicer-sounding reasons. The inevitable victory of big arms-selling nations over small arms-buying ones has provoked counter-attacks. Just now these have killed very few, but enough to prove that this world ruled by greed is hatching one ruled by revenge. Old and New Testaments should teach us to reform our ways for our children's sake.

I belong to a small nation that for centuries has exported more soldiers and weapons than the defence of it ever needed. It now contains more destructive nuclear missiles and launching machines than any nation outside the USA. England has the good sense to contain hardly any. I hope the reform of Britain starts in Scotland.

jonah

Now the word of the Lord came unto Jonah the son of Amittai, saying, ²'Arise, go to Nineveh, that great city, and cry against it, for their wickedness is come up before me.' ³But Jonah rose up to flee unto Tarshish from the presence of the Lord, and went down to Joppa; and he found a ship going to Tarshish: so he paid the fare thereof, and went down into it, to go with them unto Tarshish from the presence of the Lord.

⁴But the Lord sent out a great wind into the sea, and there was a mighty tempest in the sea, so that the ship was like to be broken. ⁵Then the mariners were afraid, and cried every man unto his god, and cast forth the wares that were in the ship into the sea, to lighten it of them. But Jonah was gone down into the sides of the ship; and he lay, and was fast asleep. ⁶So the shipmaster came to him, and said unto him, 'What meanest thou, O sleeper? Arise, call upon thy God, if so be that God will think upon us, that we perish not.' ⁷And they said every one to his fellow, 'Come, and let us cast lots, that we may know for whose cause this evil is upon us.' So they cast lots, and the lot fell upon Jonah. ⁸Then said they unto him, 'Tell us, we pray thee, for whose cause this evil is upon us. What is thine occupation? And whence

comest thou? What is thy country? And of what people art thou?' ⁹And he said unto them, 'I am an Hebrew; and I fear the Lord, the God of heaven, which hath made the sea and the dry land.' ¹⁰Then were the men exceedingly afraid, and said unto him, 'Why hast thou done this?' For the men knew that he fled from the presence of the Lord, because he had told them.

¹¹Then said they unto him, 'What shall we do unto thee, that the sea may be calm unto us?' For the sea wrought, and was tempestuous. ¹²And he said unto them, 'Take me up, and cast me forth into the sea; so shall the sea be calm unto you: for I know that for my sake this great tempest is upon you.' ¹³Nevertheless the men rowed hard to bring it to the land; but they could not, for the sea wrought, and was tempestuous against them. ¹⁴Wherefore they cried unto the Lord, and said, 'We beseech thee, O Lord, we beseech thee, let us not perish for this man's life, and lay not upon us innocent blood: for thou, O Lord, hast done as it pleased thee.' ¹⁵So they took up Jonah, and cast him forth into the sea, and the sea ceased from her raging. ¹⁶Then the men feared the Lord exceedingly, and offered a sacrifice unto the Lord, and made vows.

¹⁷Now the Lord had prepared a great fish to swallow up Jonah. And Jonah was in the belly of the fish three days and three nights.

2 Then Jonah prayed unto the Lord his God out of the fish's belly, ²and said, 'I cried by reason of mine affliction

unto the Lord, and he heard me; out of the belly of hell cried I, and thou heardest my voice. ³For thou hadst cast me into the deep, in the midst of the seas; and the floods compassed me about: all thy billows and thy waves passed over me. ⁴Then I said, "I am cast out of thy sight; yet I will look again toward thy holy temple." ⁵The waters compassed me about, even to the soul: the depth closed me round about, the weeds were wrapped about my head. ⁶I went down to the bottoms of the mountains; the earth with her bars was about me for ever: yet hast thou brought up my life from corruption, O Lord my God. ⁷When my soul fainted within me I remembered the Lord: and my prayer came in unto thee, into thine holy temple. ⁸They that observe lying vanities forsake their own mercy. ⁹But I will sacrifice unto thee with the voice of thanksgiving; I will pay that that I have vowed. Salvation is of the Lord.'

¹⁰And the Lord spake unto the fish, and it vomited out Jonah upon the dry land.

3 And the word of the Lord came unto Jonah the second time, saying, ²'Arise, go unto Nineveh, that great city, and preach unto it the preaching that I bid thee.' ³So Jonah arose, and went unto Nineveh, according to the word of the Lord. Now Nineveh was an exceeding great city of three days' journey. ⁴And Jonah began to enter into the city a day's journey, and he cried, and said, 'Yet forty days, and Nineveh shall be overthrown.'

⁵So the people of Nineveh believed God, and proclaimed

a fast, and put on sackcloth, from the greatest of them even to the least of them. ⁶For word came unto the king of Nineveh, and he arose from his throne, and he laid his robe from him, and covered him with sackcloth, and sat in ashes. ⁷And he caused it to be proclaimed and published through Nineveh by the decree of the king and his nobles, saying, 'Let neither man nor beast, herd nor flock, taste any thing: let them not feed, nor drink water. ⁸But let man and beast be covered with sackcloth, and cry mightily unto God: yea, let them turn every one from his evil way, and from the violence that is in their hands. ⁹Who can tell if God will turn and repent, and turn away from his fierce anger, that we perish not?'

¹⁰And God saw their works, that they turned from their evil way; and God repented of the evil that he had said that he would do unto them; and he did it not.

4 But it displeased Jonah exceedingly, and he was very angry. ²And he prayed unto the Lord, and said, 'I pray thee, O Lord, was not this my saying, when I was yet in my country? Therefore I fled before unto Tarshish, for I knew that thou art a gracious God, and merciful, slow to anger, and of great kindness, and repentest thee of the evil. ³Therefore now, O Lord, take, I beseech thee, my life from me, for it is better for me to die than to live.'

⁴Then said the Lord, 'Doest thou well to be angry?' ⁵So Jonah went out of the city, and sat on the east side of the city, and there made him a booth, and sat under it in the shadow,

till he might see what would become of the city. ⁶And the Lord God prepared a gourd, and made it to come up over Jonah, that it might be a shadow over his head, to deliver him from his grief. So Jonah was exceeding glad of the gourd. ⁷But God prepared a worm when the morning rose the next day, and it smote the gourd that it withered. ⁸And it came to pass, when the sun did arise, that God prepared a vehement east wind; and the sun beat upon the head of Jonah, that he fainted, and wished in himself to die, and said, 'It is better for me to die than to live.' ⁹And God said to Jonah, 'Doest thou well to be angry for the gourd?' And he said, 'I do well to be angry, even unto death.' ¹⁰Then said the Lord, 'Thou hast had pity on the gourd, for the which thou hast not laboured, neither madest it grow; which came up in a night, and perished in a night. ¹¹And should not I spare Nineveh, that great city, wherein are more than sixscore thousand persons that cannot discern between their right hand and their left hand; and also much cattle?'

micah

The word of the Lord that came to Micah the Morasthite in the days of Jotham, Ahaz, and Hezekiah, kings of Judah, which he saw concerning Samaria and Jerusalem.

> [2] Hear, all ye people; hearken, O earth,
>> and all that therein is:
>>> and let the Lord God be witness against you,
>>> the Lord from his holy temple.
> [3] For, behold, the Lord cometh forth
>> out of his place,
>>> and will come down, and tread upon the high
>>> places of the earth.
> [4] And the mountains shall be molten under him,
>> and the valleys shall be cleft,
>>> as wax before the fire, and as the waters
>>> that are poured down a steep place.
> [5] For the transgression of Jacob is all this,
>> and for the sins of the house of Israel.
>>> What is the transgression of Jacob?
>> Is it not Samaria?
>>> And what are the high places of Judah?
>> Are they not Jerusalem?

⁶ Therefore I will make Samaria as an heap
of the field, and as plantings of a vineyard:
and I will pour down the stones thereof
into the valley,
and I will discover the foundations thereof.
⁷ And all the graven images thereof shall be
beaten to pieces,
and all the hires thereof shall be burned with
the fire,
and all the idols thereof will I lay desolate,
for she gathered it of the hire of an harlot,
and they shall return to the hire of an
harlot.
⁸ Therefore I will wail and howl,
I will go stripped and naked:
I will make a wailing like the dragons,
and mourning as the owls.
⁹ For her wound is incurable;
for it is come unto Judah;
he is come unto the gate of my people,
even to Jerusalem.
¹⁰ Declare ye it not at Gath, weep ye not at all:
in the house of Aphrah roll thyself in the dust.
¹¹ Pass ye away, thou inhabitant of Saphir,
having thy shame naked:
the inhabitant of Zaanan came not forth in the
mourning of Beth-ezel;
he shall receive of you his standing.

¹² For the inhabitant of Maroth waited carefully
    for good, but evil came down from the Lord
        unto the gate of Jerusalem.
¹³ O thou inhabitant of Lachish,
    bind the chariot to the swift beast:
        she is the beginning of the sin
    to the daughter of Zion,
        for the transgressions of Israel
    were found in thee.
¹⁴ Therefore shalt thou give presents
    to Moresheth-gath: the houses of Achzib
        shall be a lie to the kings of Israel.
¹⁵ Yet will I bring an heir unto thee,
    O inhabitant of Mareshah:
        he shall come unto Adullam
    the glory of Israel.
¹⁶ Make thee bald, and poll thee
    for thy delicate children;
        enlarge thy baldness as the eagle;
    for they are gone into captivity from
        thee.

2   Woe to them that devise iniquity,
        and work evil upon their beds!
            When the morning is light, they practise it,
        because it is in the power of their
            hand.

²And they covet fields, and take them by violence;
  and houses, and take them away,
    so they oppress a man and his house,
    even a man and his heritage.
³Therefore thus saith the Lord:
  Behold, against this family do I devise an evil,
    from which ye shall not remove your necks;
  neither shall ye go haughtily:
    for this time is evil.
⁴In that day shall one take up a parable against you,
  and lament with a doleful lamentation, and say,
    'We be utterly spoiled:
  he hath changed the portion of my people:
    how hath he removed it from me!
  Turning away he hath divided our fields.'
⁵Therefore thou shalt have none that shall cast
  a cord by lot in the congregation of the Lord.
⁶'Prophesy ye not,' say they to them that prophesy,
  they shall not prophesy to them,
    that they shall not take shame.'
⁷O thou that art named the house of Jacob,
  is the spirit of the Lord straitened?
    Are these his doings?
  Do not my words do good
    to him that walketh up-rightly?
⁸Even of late my people is risen up as an enemy:
  ye pull off the robe with the garment
    from them that pass by securely
  as men averse from war.

⁹ The women of my people have ye cast out
from their pleasant houses;
from their children have ye taken away
my glory for ever.
¹⁰ Arise ye, and depart; for this is not your rest:
because it is polluted, it shall destroy you,
even with a sore destruction.
¹¹ If a man walking in the spirit and falsehood do lie,
saying, 'I will prophesy unto thee of wine
and of strong drink,' he shall even be
the prophet of this people.
¹² I will surely assemble, O Jacob, all of thee;
I will surely gather the remnant of Israel;
I will put them together as the sheep of
Bozrah,
as the flock in the midst of their fold:
they shall make great noise by reason of
the multitude of men.
¹³ The breaker is come up before them:
they have broken up, and have passed
through the gate, and are gone out by it:
and their king shall pass before them,
and the Lord on the head
of them.

3   And I said: Hear, I pray you, O heads of Jacob,
and ye princes of the house of Israel,
is it not for you to know judgment?

² Who hate the good, and love the evil;
    who pluck off their skin from off them,
    and their flesh from off their bones;
³ who also eat the flesh of my people,
    and flay their skin from off them;
        and they break their bones and chop them
    in pieces, as for the pot, and as flesh
        within the caldron.
⁴ Then shall they cry unto the Lord,
    but he will not hear them: he will even
        hide his face from them at that time,
    as they have behaved themselves ill
        in their doings.
⁵ Thus saith the Lord concerning the prophets
    that make my people err,
        that bite with their teeth, and cry, 'Peace';
    and he that putteth not into their mouths,
        they even prepare war against him.
⁶ Therefore night shall be unto you,
    that ye shall not have a vision;
        and it shall be dark unto you,
    that ye shall not divine;
        and the sun shall go down over the prophets,
    and the day shall be dark over them.
⁷ Then shall the seers be ashamed,
    and the diviners confounded: yea,
        they shall all cover their lips,
    for there is no answer of God.

⁸ But truly I am full of power by the spirit
   of the Lord, and of judgment, and of might,
      to declare unto Jacob his transgression,
   and to Israel his sin.
⁹ Hear this, I pray you, ye heads of the house
   of Jacob, and princes of the house of Israel,
   that abhor judgment, and pervert all
      equity.
¹⁰ They build up Zion with blood,
   and Jerusalem with iniquity.
¹¹ The heads thereof judge for reward,
   and the priests thereof teach for hire,
      and the prophets thereof divine for money;
   yet will they lean upon the Lord, and say,
      'Is not the Lord among us?
   None evil can come upon us.'
¹² Therefore shall Zion for your sake be plowed
   as a field, and Jerusalem shall become heaps,
      and the mountain of the house
   as the high places of the
      forest.

4   But in the last days it shall come to pass,
         that the mountain of the house of the Lord
            shall be established
      in the top of the mountains,
         and it shall be exalted above the hills;
      and people shall flow unto it.

² And many nations shall come, and say, 'Come,
　　and let us go up to the mountain of the Lord,
　　　　and to the house of the God of Jacob;
　　and he will teach us of his ways,
　　　　and we will walk in his paths,'
　　for the law shall go forth of Zion,
　　　　and the word of the Lord from
　　Jerusalem.
³ And he shall judge among many people, and
　　rebuke strong nations afar off;
　　　　and they shall beat their swords into plow-
　　shares,
　　　　and their spears into pruninghooks:
　　nation shall not lift up a sword against
　　　　nation,
　　neither shall they learn war any more.
⁴ But they shall sit every man under his vine
　　and under his fig tree;
　　　　and none shall make them afraid;
　　for the mouth of the Lord of hosts hath
　　　　spoken it.
⁵ For all people will walk every one in the name
　　of his god, and we will walk in the name
　　　　of the Lord our God for ever and ever.
⁶ In that day, saith the Lord, will I assemble her
　　that halteth, and I will gather her
　　　　that is driven out, and her that I have
　　afflicted;

7and I will make her that halted a remnant,
and her that was cast far off a strong nation;
and the Lord shall reign over them
in mount Zion from henceforth, even for ever.
8And thou, O tower of the flock, the
strong hold of the daughter of Zion,
unto thee shall it come, even the first
dominion;
the kingdom shall come to the daughter of
Jerusalem.
9 Now why dost thou cry out aloud?
Is there no king in thee? Is thy counsellor
perished?
For pangs have taken thee as a woman in travail.
10 Be in pain, and labour to bring forth,
O daughter of Zion, like a woman in travail;
for now shalt thou go forth out of the city,
and thou shalt dwell in the field, and thou
shalt go even to Babylon; there shalt thou
be delivered; there the Lord shall redeem thee
from the hand of thine enemies.
11 Now also many nations are gathered against thee,
that say, 'Let her be defiled,
and let our eye look upon Zion.'
12 But they know not the thoughts of the Lord,
neither understand they his counsel:
for he shall gather them as the sheaves
into the floor.

¹³Arise and thresh, O daughter of Zion,
    for I will make thine horn iron,
        and I will make thy hoofs brass;
    and thou shalt beat in pieces many people,
        and I will consecrate their gain unto the Lord,
    and their substance unto the Lord
        of the whole earth.

5 Now gather thyself in troops, O daughter of troops:
    he hath laid siege against us: they shall smite
        the judge of Israel with a rod upon
    the cheek.
²But thou, Beth-lehem Ephratah, though thou be
    little among the thousands of Judah,
        yet out of thee shall he come forth unto me
    that is to be ruler in Israel; whose goings forth
        have been from of old, from
    everlasting.
³Therefore will he give them up, until the time
    that she which travaileth hath brought forth;
        then the remnant of his brethren shall return
    unto the children of Israel.
⁴And he shall stand and feed in the strength
    of the Lord, in the majesty of the name
        of the Lord his God; and they shall abide;
    for now shall he be great unto the ends of the
        earth.

⁵And this man shall be the peace,
    when the Assyrian shall come into our land:
        and when he shall tread in our palaces,
    then shall we raise against him seven shepherds,
        and eight principal men.
⁶And they shall waste the land of Assyria
    with the sword, and the land of Nimrod
        in the entrances thereof:
    thus shall he deliver us from the Assyrian,
        when he cometh into our land,
    and when he treadeth within our borders.
⁷And the remnant of Jacob shall be in the midst
    of many people as a dew from the Lord,
        as the showers upon the grass,
    that tarrieth not for man,
        nor waiteth for the sons of men.
⁸And the remnant of Jacob shall be
    among the Gentiles in the midst of many people
        as a lion among the beasts of the forest,
    as a young lion among the flocks of sheep,
        who, if he go through, both treadeth down,
    and teareth in pieces, and none can deliver.
⁹Thine hand shall be lifted up
    upon thine adversaries,
        and all thine enemies shall be cut off.
¹⁰And it shall come to pass in that day, saith the Lord,
    that I will cut off thy horses
        out of the midst of thee,
    and I will destroy thy chariots:

¹¹ and I will cut off the cities of thy land, and throw
 down all thy strong holds:
¹² and I will cut off witchcrafts out of thine hand;
 and thou shalt have no more soothsayers:
¹³ thy graven images also will I cut off,
 and thy standing images out of the midst of thee;
 and thou shalt no more worship the work
 of thine hands.
¹⁴ And I will pluck up thy groves
 out of the midst of thee:
 so will I destroy thy cities.
¹⁵ And I will execute vengeance in anger and fury
 upon the heathen, such as they have not heard.

6 Hear ye now what the Lord saith:
 Arise, contend thou before the mountains,
 and let the hills hear thy voice.
² Hear ye, O mountains, the Lord's controversy,
 and ye strong foundations of the earth;
 for the Lord hath a controversy with his
 people,
 and he will plead with Israel.
³ O my people, what have I done unto thee?
 And wherein have I wearied thee?
 Testify against me.
⁴ For I brought thee up out of the land of Egypt,
 and redeemed thee out of the house of servants;
 and I sent before thee Moses, Aaron,
 and Miriam.

⁵ O my people, remember now what Balak
    king of Moab consulted, and what Balaam
the son of Beor answered him
    from Shittim unto Gilgal;
        that ye may know the righteousness of the
    Lord.
⁶ Wherewith shall I come before the Lord,
    and bow myself before the high God?
        Shall I come before him with burnt offerings,
    with calves of a year old?
⁷ Will the Lord be pleased with thousands of rams,
    or with ten thousands of rivers of oil?
        Shall I give my firstborn for my transgression,
    the fruit of my body for the sin of my soul?
⁸ He hath shewed thee, O man, what is good;
    and what doth the Lord require of thee,
        but to do justly, and to love mercy,
    and to walk humbly with thy God?
⁹ The Lord's voice crieth unto the city,
    and the man of wisdom shall see thy name:
        hear ye the rod, and who hath
    appointed it.
¹⁰ Are there yet the treasures of wickedness
    in the house of the wicked,
        and the scant measure that is
    abominable?
¹¹ Shall I count them pure with the wicked balances,
    and with the bag of deceitful weights?

¹² For the rich men thereof are full of violence,
  and the inhabitants thereof have spoken lies
    and their tongue is deceitful in
    their mouth.
¹³ Therefore also will I make thee sick in smiting thee,
  in making thee desolate because of thy sins.
¹⁴ Thou shalt eat, but not be satisfied;
  and thy casting down
    shall be in the midst of thee;
  and thou shalt take hold, but shalt not deliver;
    and that which thou deliverest
  will I give up to the sword.
¹⁵ Thou shalt sow, but thou shalt not reap;
  thou shalt tread the olives,
    but thou shalt not anoint thee with oil;
  and sweet wine, but shalt not drink wine.
¹⁶ For the statutes of Omri are kept,
  and all the works of the house of Ahab,
    and ye walk in their counsels,
  that I should make thee a desolation,
    and the inhabitants thereof an hissing:
  therefore ye shall bear the reproach
    of my people.

7   Woe is me! For I am as when they have gathered
    the summer fruits, as the grapegleanings
      of the vintage: there is no cluster to eat:
    my soul desired the firstripe fruit.

² The good man is perished out of the earth,
 and there is none upright among men;
  they all lie in wait for blood;
 they hunt every man his brother with a net.
³ That they may do evil with both hands earnestly,
 the prince asketh, and the judge asketh
  for a reward; and the great man,
 he uttereth his mischievous desire:
  so they wrap it up.
⁴ The best of them is as a brier,
 the most upright is sharper than a thorn hedge:
  the day of thy watchmen
 and thy visitation cometh;
  now shall be their perplexity.
⁵ Trust ye not in a friend, put ye not confidence
 in a guide: keep the doors of thy mouth
  from her that lieth in thy bosom.
⁶ For the son dishonoureth the father,
 the daughter riseth up against her mother,
  the daughter in law against her
 mother in law;
  a man's enemies are the men
 of his own house.
⁷ Therefore I will look unto the Lord;
 I will wait for the God of my salvation:
  my God will hear me.
⁸ Rejoice not against me, O mine enemy:
 when I fall, I shall arise; when I sit in darkness,
  the Lord shall be a light unto me.

⁹ I will bear the indignation of the Lord,
   because I have sinned against him,
      until he plead my cause,
   and execute judgment for me:
      he will bring me forth to the light,
   and I shall behold his righteousness.
¹⁰ Then she that is mine enemy shall see it,
   and shame shall cover her which said unto me,
      'Where is the Lord thy God?'
   Mine eyes shall behold her:
      now shall she be trodden down
   as the mire of the streets.
¹¹ In the day that thy walls are to be built,
   in that day shall the decree be far
      removed.
¹² In that day also he shall come even to thee
   from Assyria, and from the fortified cities,
      and from the fortress even to the river,
   and from sea to sea,
      and from mountain to mountain.
¹³ Notwithstanding the land shall be desolate
   because of them that dwell therein,
      for the fruit of their doings.
¹⁴ Feed thy people with thy rod,
   the flock of thine heritage, which dwell solitarily
      in the wood, in the midst of Carmel:
   let them feed in Bashan and Gilead,
      as in the days of old.

¹⁵According to the days of thy coming out of the land
   of Egypt will I shew unto him marvellous things.
¹⁶ The nations shall see and be confounded
   at all their might:
      they shall lay their hand upon their mouth,
      their ears shall be deaf.
¹⁷ They shall lick the dust like a serpent,
   they shall move out of their holes
      like worms of the earth:
   they shall be afraid of the Lord our God,
      and shall fear because of thee.
¹⁸ Who is a God like unto thee,
   that pardoneth iniquity, and passeth by
      the transgression of the remnant of his
   heritage?
      He retaineth not his anger for ever,
      because he delighteth in mercy.
¹⁹ He will turn again, he will have compassion
   upon us; he will subdue our iniquities;
      and thou wilt cast all their sins
   into the depths of the sea.
²⁰ Thou wilt perform the truth to Jacob,
   and the mercy to Abraham,
      which thou hast sworn unto our fathers
   from the days of old.

nahum

The burden of Nineveh. The book of the vision of Nahum the Elkoshite.

> [2] God is jealous, and the Lord revengeth;
>> the Lord revengeth, and is furious;
>>> the Lord will take vengeance on his adversaries,
>>> and he reserveth wrath for his enemies.
> [3] The Lord is slow to anger, and great in power,
>> and will not at all acquit the wicked:
>>> the Lord hath his way in the whirlwind and in the storm,
>>> and the clouds are the dust of his feet.
> [4] He rebuketh the sea, and maketh it dry,
>> and drieth up all the rivers:
>>> Bashan languisheth, and Carmel,
>>> and the flower of Lebanon languisheth.
> [5] The mountains quake at him, and the hills melt,
>> and the earth is burned at his presence,
>>> yea, the world, and all that dwell therein.

⁶ Who can stand before his indignation?
And who can abide in the fierceness of his anger?
His fury is poured out like fire,
and the rocks are thrown down by him.
⁷ The Lord is good, a strong hold
in the day of trouble;
and he knoweth them that trust in him.
⁸ But with an overrunning flood he will make
an utter end of the place thereof,
and darkness shall pursue his enemies.
⁹ What do ye imagine against the Lord?
He will make an utter end:
affliction shall not rise up the second time.
¹⁰ For while they be folden together as thorns,
and while they are drunken as drunkards,
they shall be devoured as stubble
fully dry.
¹¹ There is one come out of thee,
that imagineth evil against the Lord,
a wicked counsellor.
¹² Thus saith the Lord, 'Though they be quiet,
and likewise many,
yet thus shall they be cut down,
when he shall pass through.
Though I have afflicted thee,
I will afflict thee no more.
¹³ For now will I break his yoke from off thee,
and will burst thy bonds in sunder.'

¹⁴And the Lord hath given a commandment
concerning thee,
that no more of thy name be sown;
out of the house of thy gods will I cut off
the graven image and the molten image:
I will make thy grave, for thou
art vile.
¹⁵Behold upon the mountains the feet of him
that bringeth good tidings, that publisheth peace!
O Judah, keep thy solemn feasts,
perform thy vows, for the wicked shall no more
pass through thee; he is utterly
cut off.

2 He that dasheth in pieces is come up before thy face:
keep the munition, watch the way,
make thy loins strong, fortify thy power
mightily.
²For the Lord hath turned away the excellency of Jacob,
as the excellency of Israel,
for the emptiers have emptied them out,
and marred their vine branches.
³The shield of his mighty men is made red,
the valiant men are in scarlet:
the chariots shall be with flaming torches
in the day of his preparation,
and the fir trees shall be terribly
shaken.

⁴ The chariots shall rage in the streets,
    they shall justle one against another
        in the broad ways: they shall seem like
    torches,
        they shall run like the lightnings.
⁵ He shall recount his worthies:
    they shall stumble in their walk;
        they shall make haste to the wall thereof,
    and the defence shall be prepared.
⁶ The gates of the rivers shall be opened,
    and the palace shall be dissolved.
⁷ And Huzzab shall be led away captive,
    she shall be brought up, and her maids
        shall lead her as with the voice of doves,
    tabering upon their breasts.
⁸ But Nineveh is of old like a pool of water,
    yet they shall flee away. 'Stand, stand,'
        shall they cry; but none shall
    look back.
⁹ 'Take ye the spoil of silver, take the spoil of gold:
    for there is none end of the store and glory
        out of all the pleasant furniture.'
¹⁰ She is empty, and void, and waste:
    and the heart melteth,
        and the knees smite together,
    and much pain is in all loins,
        and the faces of them all gather
    blackness.

¹¹ Where is the dwelling of the lions,
  and the feedingplace of the young lions,
    where the lion, even the old lion, walked,
  and the lion's whelp, and none made them
    afraid?
¹² The lion did tear in pieces enough for his whelps,
  and strangled for his lionesses,
    and filled his holes with prey,
  and his dens with ravin.
¹³ Behold, I am against thee, saith the Lord of hosts,
  and I will burn her chariots in the smoke,
    and the sword shall devour thy young lions:
  and I will cut off thy prey from the earth,
    and the voice of thy messengers
  shall no more be heard.

3 Woe to the bloody city!
  It is all full of lies and robbery;
    the prey departeth not.
² The noise of a whip, and the noise of the rattling of
  the wheels, and of the pransing horses,
    and of the jumping chariots.
³ The horseman lifteth up both the bright sword
  and the glittering spear:
    and there is a multitude of slain,
  and a great number of carcases;
    and there is none end of their corpses;
  they stumble upon their corpses:

⁴ because of the multitude of the whoredoms of
    the wellfavoured harlot, the mistress of
        witchcrafts,
    that selleth nations through her whoredoms,
        and families through her
    witchcrafts.
⁵ Behold, I am against thee, saith the Lord of hosts;
    and I will discover thy skirts upon thy face,
        and I will shew the nations thy nakedness,
    and the kingdoms thy shame.
⁶ And I will cast abominable filth upon thee,
    and make thee vile,
        and will set thee as a
    gazingstock.
⁷ And it shall come to pass, that all they that look
    upon thee shall flee from thee, and say,
        'Nineveh is laid waste: who will bemoan
    her?'
        Whence shall I seek comforters
    for thee?
⁸ Art thou better than populous No,
    that was situate among the rivers,
        that had the waters round about it,
    whose rampart was the sea,
        and her wall was from the sea?
⁹ Ethiopia and Egypt were her strength,
    and it was infinite;
        Put and Lubim were thy helpers.

¹⁰ Yet was she carried away, she went into captivity;
her young children also were dashed in pieces
at the top of all the streets;
and they cast lots for her honourable men,
and all her great men were bound in chains.
¹¹ Thou also shalt be drunken:
thou shalt be hid, thou also shalt seek strength
because of the enemy.
¹² All thy strong holds shall be like fig trees
with the firstripe figs: if they be shaken,
they shall even fall into the mouth of the
eater.
¹³ Behold, thy people in the midst of thee are women:
the gates of thy land shall be set wide open
unto thine enemies:
the fire shall devour thy bars.
¹⁴ Draw thee waters for the siege,
fortify thy strong holds:
go into clay, and tread the morter,
make strong the brickkiln.
¹⁵ There shall the fire devour thee;
the sword shall cut thee off, it shall eat thee up
like the canker-worm:
make thyself many as the canker-worm,
make thyself many as the locusts.
¹⁶ Thou hast multiplied thy merchants above
the stars of heaven: the canker-worm spoileth,
and flieth away.

¹⁷ Thy crowned are as the locusts, and thy captains
     as the great grasshoppers,
          which camp in the hedges in the cold day,
     but when the sun ariseth they flee away,
          and their place is not known where they are.
¹⁸ Thy shepherds slumber, O king of Assyria:
     thy nobles shall dwell in the dust:
          thy people is scattered upon the mountains,
     and no man gathereth them.
¹⁹ There is no healing of thy bruise;
     thy wound is grievous:
          all that hear the bruit of thee shall clap
     the hands over thee: for upon whom
          hath not thy wickedness passed continually?

the pocket canons

hebrews

the epistle of paul the apostle to the

hebrews

authorized king james version

grove press
new york

with an introduction by | karen armstrong

Introduction copyright © 1999 by Karen Armstrong
The Pocket Canon second series copyright © 2000 by Grove/Atlantic, Inc.

All rights reserved. No part of this book may be reproduced in any form
or by any electronic or mechanical means, including information storage
and retrieval systems, without permission in writing from the publisher,
except by a reviewer, who may quote brief passages in a review. Any
members of educational institutions wishing to photocopy part or all
of the work for classroom use, or publishers who would like to obtain
permission to include the work in an anthology, should send their
inquiries to Grove/Atlantic, Inc., 841 Broadway, New York, NY 10003.

Originally published in Great Britain in 1999 by Canongate Books,
Ltd., Edinburgh, Scotland.

Published simultaneously in Canada
Printed in the United States of America

FIRST AMERICAN EDITION

ISBN 0-8021-3759-8 (boxed set)

Design by Paddy Cramsie

Grove Press
841 Broadway
New York, NY 10003

00 01 02 03   10 9 8 7 6 5 4 3 2 1

a note about pocket canons

The Authorized King James Version of the Bible, translated between 1603 and 1611, coincided with an extraordinary flowering of English literature. This version, more than any other, and possibly more than any other work in history, has had an influence in shaping the language we speak and write today.

The books of the King James Bible encompass categories as diverse as history, philosophy, law, poetry and fiction. Each Pocket Canon volume has its own introduction, specially commissioned from an impressive range of writers, to provide a personal interpretation of the text and explore its contemporary relevance.

introduction by karen armstrong

Karen Armstrong's first book, the best-selling Through the Narrow Gate *(1981), described her seven years as a nun in a Roman Catholic order. She has published numerous books –* A History of God, *which has been translated into thirty languages,* A History of Jerusalem *and* In the Beginning: A New Reading of Genesis.

We are currently living in a time of religious transition. In many of the countries of Western Europe, atheism is on the increase, and the churches are emptying, being converted into art galleries, restaurants and warehouses. Even in the United States, where over ninety per cent of the population claim to believe in God, people are seeking new ways of thinking about religion and practising their faith. In our dramatically altered circumstances, the old symbols that once introduced people to a sacred dimension of existence no longer function so effectively. In the Christian world, some people are either abandoning the old forms, or trying to reinterpret such doctrines as the incarnation or the atonement in a way that makes sense to them at the beginning of the third Christian millennium.

The author of *The Epistle to the Hebrews* was writing at

another pivotal moment in religious history, when the traditional symbols of the divine in Judaism – the Law of Moses, the Jerusalem Temple, and the old covenant between God and the people of Israel – seemed increasingly unsatisfactory to a significant number of Jews who were also struggling to find new ways of being religious. During the first century CE, there were a number of different sects, which were attempting to reinterpret Judaism. The most popular of these sects was that of the Pharisees, who based their spirituality on the Law; they were the most progressive and innovative Jews of the period and wanted to bring the Law up to date, by amending the Law as found in scripture by developing an oral or customal law, based on the actual practice of Jews. They enjoyed the support of most of the ordinary people. The Saducees were mostly members of the aristocratic and priestly classes; they were traditionalists, who wanted to stick to the letter of the Law as found in the Bible; their piety centred on the ancient cult in the Temple. The Essenes were more radical; they believed that the End of Days was nigh and that the Judaism of their day was corrupt, and had withdrawn from mainstream society to await the final battle between the powers of good and evil; some had retreated to Qumran beside the Dead Sea, and lived in a quasi-monastic community.

Christianity began as yet another of these Jewish sects. Until St Paul took the new faith to the gentile world, the original disciples of Jesus had no intention of founding a new religion. They believed that Jesus had been the Messiah and that he would shortly return in glory to inaugurate

God's kingdom. They observed the Law and worshipped daily in the Temple, were regarded as devout and legitimate Jews, and were not eager to admit gentiles into their sect. The author of *Hebrews* was writing to a group of these Jewish Christians, but he was trying to persuade them to be more radical. He was almost certainly not St Paul, but was probably Paul's contemporary, writing during the 60s, some thirty years after Jesus's death. The Temple, whose rites he describes in such detail and which was destroyed by the Romans in 70 CE, was obviously still standing, but our author, like other Jews at this time, no longer felt that its rites and imagery yielded access to God. He and the Jewish Christians to whom he was writing were in a stage of transition; they were trying to decide what Jesus had meant to them and what his function was in their religious life. The recipients of his letter had various theories, but their roots were still in Judaism, whereas our author was beginning to break away from the traditional Jewish faith, and develop something new.

Our author is aware that he is being controversial, and that many of his readers still felt comfortable with the Temple liturgy. But he was not alone in discovering that these ancient rites, which had been profoundly satisfying to Jews for centuries and which had been crucial to their spiritual life, no longer spoke to him of God. The Qumran sect would have nothing whatever to do with the Temple; they believed that their community constituted a spiritual Temple and that when the Messiah returned at the End of Days, he would build a new Temple, not made by human hands but built miraculously by God himself. They denounced the Jerusalem priests as wicked and sinful, and looked forward to the arrival of a Messiah who would be a perfect priest of the House of Aaron. They clearly felt so uncomfortable with the Temple liturgy that they condemned it as perverse. The Pharisees were less extreme. They continued to worship in the Temple, but were also beginning to teach that charity and acts of loving kindness were just as effective a means of expiating sin as the old animal sacrifices. The loss of the Temple in 70 CE was a devastating blow, but Jews had already begun to retreat from it, and were thus able to make the transition to rabbinic Judaism with the minimum of fuss, encountering the divine presence in the sacred text of the Law rather than in a sacred building.

The author of *Hebrews*, like other Jewish Christians, shared many of the concerns of the Pharisees and the Essenes; like them, he was trying to find a new way to be Jewish, which put Jesus, the Messiah, at the centre of the picture instead of the Law and the Temple. The Temple liturgy seems to have died on him, and now left him cold. He was especially perturbed by the fact that the Jewish priests had to offer 'those sacrifices' 'continually', over and over again, 'year by year', and all to no avail, for these rituals 'can never take away sins' (10:1,11). He felt the same kind of frustration with the Temple as St Paul experienced about the Law, which, far from liberating Paul from his sins, had only made him more conscious of his sinfulness (*Romans* 7). Where the Pharisees and the Essenes found God in the Law and the sacred community, respectively, these Jewish Christians were making Jesus a symbol which brought them into the divine presence.

We should not underestimate the magnitude of this change. In almost every civilization in the ancient world, the Temple was one of the chief symbols of the divine. Indeed, religion was inconceivable without temple worship and animal sacrifice. When those Jews who had been deported to Babylon by Nebuchadnezzar in 586 BCE, when their Temple had been destroyed for the first time, asked how they could sing the Lord's song in an alien land (Psalm 137:4), they were not simply being maudlin or nostalgic about their ruined Temple on Mount Zion in Jerusalem. They were voicing a real theological difficulty. A deity was inaccessible to his worshippers if he did not have a shrine. Whereas today people feel they can encounter God and pray to him wherever they happen to be (in a field or a mountain-top, as well as a church), this was not so in the ancient world. A god could only meet his devotees in a place that he had chosen. The Temple was a replica of his home in the divine world, which mysteriously made him present here below. In premodern religion, the reproduction contained something of the original archetype and a symbol was inseparable from the spiritual entity to which it pointed. The effect of this was similar to the way the son of a dead friend brings the father into the room with him, because he reminds us physically of the deceased, and, at the same time, makes us feel his absence more acutely. The author of *Hebrews* takes this symbolic spirituality for granted; it is fundamental to his argument. The Jerusalem Temple, he explains, is a copy of God's spiritual Temple in the Heavenly Jerusalem; its rituals imitate the celestial liturgy in the Heavenly Sanctuary, and this process of *imitatio dei* (on which all premodern religion was based) brought something of that transcendent reality down to the world of men and women.

Our author understood the Temple symbolism, but, like other Jews, found that it no longer worked for him. The Temple and its cult seemed to him repetitious and pointless; these rites no longer yielded any sense of the divine. There are clear indications that Jews were not alone in this. In some parts of the Greek world, people were beginning to find Temple worship meaningless too, and had started to locate the divine in other symbols which did give them that sense of transcendance and ecstasy that human beings seem to need. Today those who do not find this enhanced life in religion, seek transcendence in art, music, literature, sport, or even in drugs. This shift from temple worship in late antiquity represented a major religious change. It would once have been considered the height of blasphemy to deny that the Temple gave men and women access to the divine, so essential had it been to the religious experience of humanity.

The Temple was an attempt to express an ineffable divine reality in human terms. Our doctrines (such as the Trinity, the Incarnation, the Atonement, or even the concept of a personal God) are also symbols, which attempt to give shape to our experience of the sacred. These doctrines cannot fully contain the reality of what we call 'God', any more than a building could. They can only point to a Reality which must surpass them, as it goes beyond all human categories and systems. Western Christians have tended to lose sight of the crucial fact that we can only speak of the divine in terms of signs and symbols. Since the scientific revolution of the sixteenth and seventeenth centuries, Western people have often assumed that 'God' was an objective but unseen reality (like the atom), and that our doctrines were accurate descriptions of this divine Fact. But theology should be regarded as poetry (Greek and Russian Orthodox Christians have always been aware of this). Theology is merely an attempt to express the inexpressible as felicitously as possible. But, as we all know, some of our poetic symbols lose their power and immediacy, as our circumstances change. Today many Christians feel that the ideas of a personal God or of the divinity of Jesus are absolutely essential to faith, but in the ancient world people felt just as strongly about the divine presence in the Temple. When a particular image of the sacred loses its valency, it does not mean that religion itself must die. The old symbol is often taken up and given fresh life in a new and different system.

That is what is happening in *The Epistle to the Hebrews*. Where once Temple worship gave all believers a direct experience of the numinous, our author clearly finds that the Temple is *only* a symbol. When the Prophet Isaiah had been able to see the divine presence and the heavenly sanctuary while he was worshipping in the Temple, seeing *through* the symbolism and the liturgy to the Reality behind it (*Isaiah* 6:1–4), our author can see no further than the physical rites. For him, they are simply rules about the outward life, and have no power to transform us interiorly; the Temple priests are obviously imperfect, since they are only human; the sacrifice of bulls and goats is messy and pointless; and the building itself clearly man-made. He can no longer see what Isaiah saw. In order to work effectively, a symbol has to be experienced as a direct link to the more elusive and transcendent reality to which it directs our attention, but our author can only see the Temple as a human artefact. Similarly, for many sceptics today, the conventional doctrines of Christianity, which for centuries gave people an immediate sense of God, seem nothing more than human constructs.

But instead of jettisoning the old symbol of the Temple, as the Qumran sect did, our author reinterprets it. He makes Christ the new High Priest. In the old cult, the High Priest entered the Holy of Holies (the innermost sanctum of the Temple, which re-presented [*sic*] the divine presence) once a year on the Day of Atonement. He alone could enter this most sacred place, and the people came into God's presence vicariously through this symbolic rite. The Holy of Holies was carefully designed to re-present God's Throne in the Heavenly Jerusalem. Now, by virtue of his sacrificial death, Christ had entered into the celestial sanctuary once and for all. He had bypassed the symbolism and introduced believers to the sacred Reality itself. For our author, the figure of Christ had become *the* new symbol that brought humanity to the divine; he was 'the express image of [God's] person' (1:3). (The Jerusalem Bible has been truer to the author's intention and to the old symbolic spirituality by rendering this 'a perfect copy of [God's] nature'). As a 'copy' of God in human form, Jesus gave our author a direct experience of the divine: when he contemplated the human figure of Jesus, he had a clear sense of what God was like. People had no further need of earthly symbols, therefore, since they had already gone directly into the divine presence with Christ; they had already passed over, in the person of their High Priest, into the next world:

> But ye are come unto mount Sion, and unto
> the city of the living God, the heavenly
> Jerusalem, and to an innumerable company
> of angels, to the general assembly and church
> of the firstborn, which are written in heaven,
> and to God, the Judge of all ... (12:22–3)

Again, the Jerusalem Bible has preserved the original more forcefully than the King James version, by translating this last sentence: 'You have come to God himself.' In the person of their new High Priest, Christians have already come directly into the divine presence. They may feel that they are living a mundane life here below, but they are really with God in the Heavenly Jerusalem.

But, as with any religious symbolism, there were difficulties. Our author is poignantly aware that it is hard to live a religious life without any tangible replicas of the divine here below. Jesus had gone away, into another dimension, and Christians had to have faith in what was unseen. Their lives, as the author makes clear, were hard and full of suffering; how could they believe that they were already in Heaven? The epistle also makes it clear that the figure of

karen armstrong   xv

Christ was by no means firmly established as the only symbol that gave Christians a sense of God. Some of the recipients of his letter thought that angels were more effective mediators than Jesus; others were still drawn to the figure of Moses and the Law. This reminds us that Christianity did not spring forth ready-made from the minds of the apostles after the Resurrection. Christians had to work hard to make Jesus a viable symbol of the divine, using all their creative expertise. They would continue to discuss who and what Jesus had been and what he had meant to them for centuries. Western Christians would finally accept the ruling of the Council of Chalcedon (451) that Jesus had both a divine and a human nature, something that neither Paul nor the author of *Hebrews* (who saw Jesus only as a human 'copy' of God) had claimed. The Greek Orthodox Christians were not satisfied with Chalcedon and went on discussing Christology for another two hundred years. They developed quite a different notion of Jesus. Maximus the Confessor (*c.* 580–662), the founder of Byzantine theology, believed that God would have become human even if Adam had not sinned; Jesus had not died to atone for our sins, but he was the first human being to be wholly deified; what he had been, all Christians could be.

The point is that people who call themselves Christians have had very different ideas about God and Jesus over the years. Our theology has changed dramatically in the past, and can do so again. Today the old conciliar definitions about God or Jesus do not always speak to Christians or would-be Christians. They seem to belong to another age, and can appear to be as fabricated and arbitrary to many people as the old Temple and its liturgy had become for our author. *The Epistle to the Hebrews* reminds us that there is no need to repine if a rite, an image, or a doctrine dies on us. We can, like our author, use our imaginations to build on the past and create a symbol that will speak to us more eloquently and directly of the sacred.

the epistle of paul the apostle to the hebrews

God, who at sundry times and in divers manners spake in time past unto the fathers by the prophets, ²hath in these last days spoken unto us by his Son, whom he hath appointed heir of all things, by whom also he made the worlds, ³who being the brightness of his glory, and the express image of his person, and upholding all things by the word of his power, when he had by himself purged our sins, sat down on the right hand of the Majesty on high, ⁴being made so much better than the angles, as he hath by inheritance obtained a more excellent name than they.

⁵For unto which of the angels said he at any time, 'Thou art my Son, this day have I begotten thee?' And again, 'I will be to him a Father, and he shall be to me a Son?' ⁶And again, when he bringeth in the firstbegotten into the world, he saith, 'And let all the angels of God worship him.' ⁷And of the angels he saith, 'Who maketh his angels spirits, and his ministers a flame of fire.' ⁸But unto the Son he saith, 'Thy throne, O God, is for ever and ever: a sceptre of righteousness is the sceptre of thy kingdom. ⁹Thou hast loved righteousness, and hated iniquity; therefore God, even thy God, hath anointed thee with the oil of gladness above thy fellows.' ¹⁰And, 'Thou, Lord, in the beginning hast laid the foundation of the earth;

and the heavens are the works of thine hands: ¹¹they shall perish, but thou remainest; and they all shall wax old as doth a garment; ¹²and as a vesture shalt thou fold them up, and they shall be changed; but thou art the same, and thy years shall not fail.' ¹³But to which of the angels said he at any time, 'Sit on my right hand, until I make thine enemies thy footstool?' ¹⁴Are they not all ministering spirits, sent forth to minister for them who shall be heirs of salvation?

2 Therefore we ought to give the more earnest heed to the things which we have heard, lest at any time we should let them slip. ² For if the word spoken by angels was stedfast, and every transgression and disobedience received a just recompence of reward, ³ how shall we escape, if we neglect so great salvation; which at the first began to be spoken by the Lord, and was confirmed unto us by them that heard him; ⁴ God also bearing them witness, both with signs and wonders, and with divers miracles, and gifts of the Holy Ghost, according to his own will?

⁵ For unto the angels hath he not put in subjection the world to come, whereof we speak. ⁶ But one in a certain place testified, saying, 'What is man, that thou art mindful of him? Or the son of man, that thou visitest him? ⁷ Thou madest him a little lower than the angels; thou crownedst him with glory and honour, and didst set him over the works of thy hands: ⁸ thou hast put all things in subjection under his feet.' For in that he put all in subjection under him, he left nothing that is not put under him. But now we see not yet all things put under him. ⁹ But we see Jesus, who was made a little lower than the angels for the suffering of death, crowned with glory and honour; that he by the grace of God should taste death for every man.

¹⁰ For it became him, for whom are all things, and by whom are all things, in bringing many sons unto glory, to make the captain of their salvation perfect through sufferings. ¹¹ For both he that sanctifieth and they who are sanctified are all of one, for which cause he is not ashamed to call

them brethren, [12] saying, 'I will declare thy name unto my brethren, in the midst of the church will I sing praise unto thee.' [13] And again, 'I will put my trust in him.' And again, 'Behold I and the children which God hath given me.'

[14] Forasmuch then as the children are partakers of flesh and blood, he also himself likewise took part of the same; that through death he might destroy him that had the power of death, that is, the devil; [15] and deliver them who through fear of death were all their lifetime subject to bondage. [16] For verily he took not on him the nature of angels; but he took on him the seed of Abraham. [17] Wherefore in all things it behoved him to be made like unto his brethren, that he might be a merciful and faithful high priest in things pertaining to God, to make reconciliation for the sins of the people. [18] For in that he himself hath suffered being tempted, he is able to succour them that are tempted.

3 Wherefore, holy brethren, partakers of the heavenly calling, consider the Apostle and High Priest of our profession, Christ Jesus, [2] who was faithful to him that appointed him, as also Moses was faithful in all his house. [3] For this man was counted worthy of more glory than Moses, inasmuch as he who hath builded the house hath more honour than the house. [4] For every house is builded by some man; but he that built all things is God. [5] And Moses verily was faithful in all his house, as a servant, for a testimony of those things which were to be spoken after; [6] but Christ as a son over his own house; whose house are we, if we hold fast the confidence and the rejoicing of the hope firm unto the end.

[7] Wherefore (as the Holy Ghost saith) 'To day if ye will hear his voice, [8] harden not your hearts, as in the provocation, in the day of temptation in the wilderness: [9] when your fathers tempted me, proved me, and saw my works forty years. [10] Wherefore I was grieved with that generation, and said, "They do alway err in their heart; and they have not known my ways." [11] So I sware in my wrath, "They shall not enter into my rest."' [12] Take heed, brethren, lest there be in any of you an evil heart of unbelief, in departing from the living God. [13] But exhort one another daily, while it is called 'To day'; lest any of you be hardened through the deceitfulness of sin. [14] For we are made partakers of Christ, if we hold the beginning of our confidence stedfast unto the end, [15] while it is said, 'To day if ye will hear his voice, harden not your hearts, as in the provocation.' [16] For some, when they

had heard, did provoke: howbeit not all that came out of Egypt by Moses. [17] But with whom was he grieved forty years? Was it not with them that had sinned, whose carcases fell in the wilderness? [18] And to whom sware he that they should not enter into his rest, but to them that believed not? [19] So we see that they could not enter in because of unbelief.

4 Let us therefore fear, lest, a promise being left us of entering into his rest, any of you should seem to come short of it. ²For unto us was the gospel preached, as well as unto them; but the word preached did not profit them, not being mixed with faith in them that heard it. ³For we which have believed to enter into rest, as he said, 'As I have sworn in my wrath, if they shall enter into my rest': although the works were finished from the foundation of the world. ⁴For he spake in a certain place of the seventh day on this wise, 'And God did rest the seventh day from all his works.' ⁵And in this place again, 'If they shall enter into my rest.' ⁶Seeing therefore it remaineth that some must enter therein, and they to whom it was first preached entered not in because of unbelief: ⁷again, he limiteth a certain day, saying in David, 'To day', after so long a time; as it is said, 'To day if ye will hear his voice, harden not your hearts.' ⁸For if Jesus had given them rest, then would he not afterward have spoken of another day. ⁹There remaineth therefore a rest to the people of God. ¹⁰For he that is entered into his rest, he also hath ceased from his own works, as God did from his. ¹¹Let us labour therefore to enter into that rest, lest any man fall after the same example of unbelief.

¹²For the word of God is quick, and powerful, and sharper than any two-edged sword, piercing even to the dividing asunder of soul and spirit, and of the joints and marrow, and is a discerner of the thoughts and intents of the heart. ¹³Neither is there any creature that is not manifest in his sight; but all things are naked and opened unto the eyes

of him with whom we have to do.

¹⁴ Seeing then that we have a great high priest, that is passed into the heavens, Jesus the Son of God, let us hold fast our profession. ¹⁵ For we have not an high priest which cannot be touched with the feeling of our infirmities; but was in all points tempted like as we are, yet without sin. ¹⁶ Let us therefore come boldly unto the throne of grace, that we may obtain mercy, and find grace to help in time of need.

5 For every high priest taken from among men is ordained for men in things pertaining to God, that he may offer both gifts and sacrifices for sins, ² who can have compassion on the ignorant, and on them that are out of the way; for that he himself also is compassed with infirmity. ³ And by reason hereof he ought, as for the people, so also for himself, to offer for sins. ⁴ And no man taketh this honour unto himself, but he that is called of God, as was Aaron.

⁵ So also Christ glorified not himself to be made an high priest; but he that said unto him, 'Thou art my Son, to day have I begotten thee.' ⁶ As he saith also in another place, 'Thou art a priest for ever after the order of Melchisedec.'

⁷ Who in the days of his flesh, when he had offered up prayers and supplications with strong crying and tears unto him that was able to save him from death, and was heard in that he feared; ⁸ though he were a Son, yet learned he obedience by the things which he suffered; ⁹ and being made perfect, he became the author of eternal salvation unto all them that obey him; ¹⁰ called of God an high priest after the order of Melchisedec.

¹¹ Of whom we have many things to say, and hard to be uttered, seeing ye are dull of hearing. ¹² For when for the time ye ought to be teachers, ye have need that one teach you again which be the first principles of the oracles of God; and are become such as have need of milk, and not of strong meat. ¹³ For every one that useth milk is unskilful in the word of righeousness: for he is a babe. ¹⁴ But strong meat belongeth to them that are of full age, even those who by reason of use have their senses exercised to discern both good and evil.

6 Therefore leaving the principles of the doctrine of Christ, let us go on unto perfection; not laying again the foundation of repentance from dead works, and of faith toward God, ²of the doctrine of baptisms, and of laying on of hands, and of resurrection of the dead, and of eternal judgment. ³And this will we do, if God permit. ⁴For it is impossible for those who were once enlightened, and have tasted of the heavenly gift, and were made partakers of the Holy Ghost, ⁵and have tasted the good word of God, and the powers of the world to come, ⁶if they shall fall away, to renew them again unto repentance; seeing they crucify to themselves the Son of God afresh, and put him to an open shame. ⁷For the earth which drinketh in the rain that cometh oft upon it, and bringeth forth herbs meet for them by whom it is dressed, receiveth blessing from God. ⁸But that which beareth thorns and briers is rejected, and is nigh unto cursing; whose end is to be burned.

⁹But, beloved, we are persuaded better things of you, and things that accompany salvation, though we thus speak. ¹⁰For God is not unrighteous to forget your work and labour of love, which ye have shewed toward his name, in that ye have ministered to the saints, and do minister. ¹¹And we desire that every one of you do shew the same diligence to the full assurance of hope unto the end, ¹²that ye be not slothful, but followers of them who through faith and patience inherit the promises.

¹³For when God made promise to Abraham, because he could swear by no greater, he sware by himself, ¹⁴saying,

'Surely blessing I will bless thee, and multiplying I will multiply thee.' ¹⁵And so, after he had patiently endured, he obtained the promise. ¹⁶For men verily swear by the greater, and an oath for confirmation is to them an end of all strife. ¹⁷Wherein God, willing more abundantly to shew unto the heirs of promise the immutability of his counsel, confirmed it by an oath: ¹⁸that by two immutable things, in which it was impossible for God to lie, we might have a strong consolation, who have fled for refuge to lay hold upon the hope set before us, ¹⁹which hope we have as an anchor of the soul, both sure and stedfast, and which entereth into that within the veil; ²⁰whither the forerunner is for us entered, even Jesus, made an high priest for ever after the order of Melchisedec.

7 For this Melchisedec, king of Salem, priest of the most high God, who met Abraham returning from the slaughter of the kings, and blessed him, ²to whom also Abraham gave a tenth part of all; first being by interpretation King of righteousness, and after that also King of Salem, which is, King of peace; ³without father, without mother, without descent, having neither beginning of days, nor end of life; but made like unto the Son of God; abideth a priest continually.

⁴Now consider how great this man was, unto whom even the patriarch Abraham gave the tenth of the spoils. ⁵And verily they that are of the sons of Levi, who receive the office of the priesthood, have a commandment to take tithes of the people according to the law, that is, of their brethren, though they come out of the loins of Abraham, ⁶but he whose descent is not counted from them received tithes of Abraham, and blessed him that had the promises. ⁷And without all contradiction the less is blessed of the better. ⁸And here men that die receive tithes; but there he receiveth them, of whom it is witnessed that he liveth. ⁹And as I may so say, Levi also, who receiveth tithes, payed tithes in Abraham. ¹⁰For he was yet in the loins of his father, when Melchisedec met him.

¹¹If therefore perfection were by the Levitical priesthood (for under it the people received the law), what further need was there that another priest should rise after the order of Melchisedec, and not be called after the order of Aaron? ¹²For the priesthood being changed, there is made of necessity a change also of the law. ¹³For he of whom these things are spoken pertaineth to another tribe, of which no man gave attendance at the altar. ¹⁴For it is evident that our Lord sprang out of Juda;

of which tribe Moses spake nothing concerning priesthood.

¹⁵And it is yet far more evident, for that after the similitude of Melchisedec there ariseth another priest, ¹⁶ who is made, not after the law of a carnal commandment, but after the power of an endless life. ¹⁷ For he testifieth, 'Thou art a priest for ever after the order of Melchisedec.' ¹⁸ For there is verily a disannulling of the commandment going before for the weakness and unprofitableness thereof. ¹⁹ For the law made nothing perfect, but the bringing in of a better hope did; by the which we draw nigh unto God. ²⁰And inasmuch as not without an oath he was made priest ²¹(for those priests were made without an oath; but this with an oath by him that said unto him, 'The Lord sware and will not repent, Thou art a priest for ever after the order of Melchisedec'). ²²By so much was Jesus made a surety of a better testament.

²³And they truly were many priests, because they were not suffered to continue by reason of death: ²⁴ But this man, because he continueth ever, hath an unchangeable priesthood. ²⁵ Wherefore he is able also to save them to the uttermost that come unto God by him, seeing he ever liveth to make intercession for them.

²⁶ For such an high priest became us, who is holy, harmless, undefiled, separate from sinners, and made higher than the heavens; ²⁷ who needeth not daily, as those high priests, to offer up sacrifice, first for his own sins, and then for the people's, for this he did once, when he offered up himself. ²⁸ For the law maketh men high priests which have infirmity; but the word of the oath, which was since the law, maketh the Son, who is consecrated for evermore.

8 Now of the things which we have spoken this is the sum: we have such an high priest, who is set on the right hand of the throne of the Majesty in the heavens; ²a minister of the sanctuary, and of the true tabernacle, which the Lord pitched, and not man. ³For every high priest is ordained to offer gifts and sacrifices: wherefore it is of necessity that this man have somewhat also to offer. ⁴For if he were on earth, he should not be a priest, seeing that there are priests that offer gifts according to the law, ⁵who serve unto the example and shadow of heavenly things, as Moses was admonished of God when he was about to make the tabernacle, for, 'See,' saith he, 'that thou make all things according to the pattern shewed to thee in the mount.' ⁶But now hath he obtained a more excellent ministry, by how much also he is the mediator of a better covenant, which was established upon better promises. ⁷For if that first convenant had been faultless, then should no place have been sought for the second.

⁸For finding fault with them, he saith, 'Behold, the days come,' saith the Lord, 'when I will make a new covenant with the house of Israel and with the house of Judah: ⁹not according to the covenant that I made with their fathers in the day when I took them by the hand to lead them out of the land of Egypt; because they continued not in my covenant, and I regarded them not,' saith the Lord. ¹⁰'For this is the covenant that I will make with the house of Israel after those days,' saith the Lord; 'I will put my laws into their mind, and write them in their hearts: and I will be to

them a God, and they shall be to me a people: "and they shall not teach every man his neighbour, and every man his brother, saying, "Know the Lord," for all shall know me, from the least to the greatest. [12] For I will be merciful to their unrighteousness, and their sins and their iniquities will I remember no more.' [13] In that he saith, 'A new covenant', he hath made the first old. Now that which decayeth and waxeth old is ready to vanish away.

9 Then verily the first covenant had also ordinances of divine service, and a worldly sanctuary. ² For there was a tabernacle made; the first, wherein was the candlestick, and the table, and the shewbread; which is called the sanctuary. ³And after the second veil, the tabernacle which is called the Holiest of all, ⁴ which had the golden censer, and the ark of the covenant overlaid round about with gold, wherein was the golden pot that had manna, and Aaron's rod that budded, and the tables of the covenant; ⁵and over it the cherubims of glory shadowing the mercyseat; of which we cannot now speak particularly.

⁶ Now when these things were thus ordained, the priests went always into the first tabernacle, accomplishing the service of God. ⁷ But into the second went the high priest alone once every year, not without blood, which he offered for himself, and for the errors of the people: ⁸ the Holy Ghost this signifying, that the way into the holiest of all was not yet made manifest, while as the first tabernacle was yet standing, ⁹ which was a figure for the time then present, in which were offered both gifts and sacrifices, that could not make him that did the service perfect, as pertaining to the conscience, ¹⁰ which stood only in meats and drinks, and divers washings, and carnal ordinances, imposed on them until the time of reformation.

¹¹But Christ being come an high priest of good things to come, by a greater and more perfect tabernacle, not made with hands, that is to say, not of this building; ¹² neither by the blood of goats and calves, but by his own blood he

entered in once into the holy place, having obtained eternal redemption for us. ¹³ For if the blood of bulls and of goats, and the ashes of an heifer sprinkling the unclean, sanctifieth to the purifying of the flesh: ¹⁴ how much more shall the blood of Christ, who through the eternal Spirit offered himself without spot to God, purge your conscience from dead works to serve the living God?

¹⁵ And for this cause he is the mediator of the new testament, that by means of death, for the redemption of the transgressions that were under the first testament, they which are called might receive the promise of eternal inheritance. ¹⁶ For where a testament is, there must also of necessity be the death of the testator. ¹⁷ For a testament is of force after men are dead: otherwise it is of no strength at all while the testator liveth. ¹⁸ Whereupon neither the first testament was dedicated without blood. ¹⁹ For when Moses had spoken every precept to all the people according to the law, he took the blood of calves and of goats, with water, and scarlet wool, and hyssop, and sprinkled both the book, and all the people, ²⁰ saying, 'This is the blood of the testament which God hath enjoined unto you.' ²¹ Moreover he sprinkled with blood both the tabernacle, and all the vessels of the ministry. ²² And almost all things are by the law purged with blood; and without shedding of blood is no remission.

²³ It was therefore necessary that the patterns of things in the heavens should be purified with these; but the heavenly things themselves with better sacrifices than these. ²⁴ For Christ is not entered into the holy places made with hands,

which are the figures of the true; but into heaven itself, now to appear in the presence of God for us, ²⁵ nor yet that he should offer himself often, as the high priest entereth into the holy place every year with blood of others, ²⁶ for then must he often have suffered since the foundation of the world; but now once in the end of the world hath he appeared to put away sin by the sacrifice of himself. ²⁷ And as it is appointed unto men once to die, but after this the judgment: ²⁸ so Christ was once offered to bear the sins of many; and unto them that look for him shall he appear the second time without sin unto salvation.

10 For the law having a shadow of good things to come, and not the very image of the things, can never with those sacrifices which they offered year by year continually make the comers thereunto perfect. ²For then would they not have ceased to be offered? Because that the worshippers once purged should have had no more conscience of sins. ³But in those sacrifices there is a remembrance again made of sins every year. ⁴For it is not possible that the blood of bulls and of goats should take away sins. ⁵Wherefore when he cometh into the world, he saith, 'Sacrifice and offering thou wouldest not, but a body hast thou prepared me: ⁶in burnt offerings and sacrifices for sin thou hast had no pleasure.' ⁷Then said I, 'Lo, I come (in the volume of the book it is written of me), to do thy will, O God.' ⁸Above when he said, 'Sacrifice and offering and burnt offerings and offering for sin thou wouldest not, neither hadst pleasure therein; which are offered by the law'; ⁹then said he, 'Lo, I come to do thy will, O God.' He taketh away the first, that he may establish the second. ¹⁰By the which will we are sanctified through the offering of the body of Jesus Christ once for all.

¹¹And every priest standeth daily ministering and offering oftentimes the same sacrifices, which can never take away sins; ¹²but this man, after he had offered one sacrifice for sins for ever, sat down on the right hand of God; ¹³from henceforth expecting till his enemies be made his footstool. ¹⁴For by one offering he hath perfected for ever them that are sanctified. ¹⁵Whereof the Holy Ghost also is a witness to us, for after that he had said before, ¹⁶'This is the covenant that I

will make with them after those days,' saith the Lord, 'I will put my laws into their hearts, and in their minds will I write them; ¹⁷and their sins and iniquities will I remember no more.' ¹⁸Now where remission of these is, there is no more offering for sin.

¹⁹Having therefore, brethren, boldness to enter into the holiest by the blood of Jesus, ²⁰by a new and living way, which he hath consecrated for us, through the veil, that is to say, his flesh; ²¹and having an high priest over the house of God; ²²let us draw near with a true heart in full assurance of faith, having our hearts sprinkled from an evil conscience, and our bodies washed with pure water ²³Let us hold fast the profession of our faith without wavering (for he is faithful that promised); ²⁴and let us consider one another to provoke unto love and to good works: ²⁵not forsaking the assembling of ourselves together, as the manner of some is; but exhorting one another; and so much the more, as ye see the day approaching.

²⁶For if we sin wilfully after that we have received the knowledge of the truth, there remaineth no more sacrifice for sins, ²⁷but a certain fearful looking for of judgment and fiery indignation, which shall devour the adversaries. ²⁸He that despised Moses' law died without mercy under two or three witnesses: ²⁹of how much sorer punishment, suppose ye, shall he be thought worthy, who hath trodden under foot the Son of God, and hath counted the blood of the covenant, wherewith he was sanctified, an unholy thing, and hath done despite unto the Spirit of grace? ³⁰For we know him

that hath said, 'Vengeance belongeth unto me, I will recompense,' saith the Lord. And again, 'The Lord shall judge his people.' [31] It is a fearful thing to fall into the hands of the living God.

[32] But call to remembrance the former days, in which, after ye were illuminated, ye endured a great fight of afflictions; [33] partly, whilst ye were made a gazing-stock both by reproaches and afflictions; and partly, whilst ye became companions of them that were so used. [34] For ye had compassion of me in my bonds, and took joyfully the spoiling of your goods, knowing in yourselves that ye have in heaven a better and an enduring substance. [35] Cast not away therefore your confidence, which hath great recompence of reward. [36] For ye have need of patience, that, after ye have done the will of God, ye might receive the promise. [37] For yet a little while, and he that shall come will come, and will not tarry. [38] Now the just shall live by faith; but if any man draw back, my soul shall have no pleasure in him. [39] But we are not of them who draw back unto perdition; but of them that believe to the saving of the soul.

11 Now faith is the substance of things hoped for, the evidence of things not seen. ²For by it the elders obtained a good report. ³Through faith we understand that the worlds were framed by the word of God, so that things which are seen were not made of things which do appear.

⁴By faith Abel offered unto God a more excellent sacrifice than Cain, by which he obtained witness that he was righteous, God testifying of his gifts: and by it he being dead yet speaketh. ⁵By faith Enoch was translated that he should not see death; and was not found, because God had translated him, for before his translation he had this testimony, that he pleased God. ⁶But without faith it is impossible to please him, for he that cometh to God must believe that he is, and that he is a rewarder of them that diligently seek him. ⁷By faith Noah, being warned of God of things not seen as yet, moved with fear, prepared an ark to the saving of his house; by the which he condemned the world, and became heir of the righteousness which is by faith.

⁸By faith Abraham, when he was called to go out into a place which he should after receive for an inheritance, obeyed; and he went out, not knowing whither he went. ⁹By faith he sojourned in the land of promise, as in a strange country, dwelling in tabernacles with Isaac and Jacob, the heirs with him of the same promise, ¹⁰for he looked for a city which hath foundations, whose builder and maker is God. ¹¹Through faith also Sara herself received strength to conceive seed, and was delivered of a child when she was past age, because she judged him faithful who had promised.

¹² Therefore sprang there even of one, and him as good as dead, so many as the stars of the sky in multitude, and as the sand which is by the sea shore innumerable.

¹³ These all died in faith, not having received the promises, but having seen them afar off, and were persuaded of them, and embraced them, and confessed that they were strangers and pilgrims on the earth. ¹⁴ For they that say such things declare plainly that they seek a country. ¹⁵ And truly, if they had been mindful of that country from whence they came out, they might have had opportunity to have returned. ¹⁶ But now they desire a better country, that is, an heavenly: wherefore God is not ashamed to be called their God, for he hath prepared for them a city.

¹⁷ By faith Abraham, when he was tried, offered up Isaac: and he that had received the promises offered up his only begotten son, ¹⁸ of whom it was said, 'That in Isaac shall thy seed be called,' ¹⁹ accounting that God was able to raise him up, even from the dead; from whence also he received him in a figure. ²⁰ By faith Isaac blessed Jacob and Esau concerning things to come. ²¹ By faith Jacob, when he was a dying, blessed both the sons of Joseph; and worshipped, leaning upon the top of his staff. ²² By faith Joseph, when he died, made mention of the departing of the children of Israel; and gave commandment concerning his bones.

²³ By faith Moses, when he was born, was hid three months of his parents, because they saw he was a proper child; and they were not afraid of the king's commandment. ²⁴ By faith Moses, when he was come to years, refused to be

called the son of Pharaoh's daughter; ²⁵ choosing rather to suffer affliction with the people of God, than to enjoy the pleasures of sin for a season; ²⁶ esteeming the reproach of Christ greater riches than the treasures in Egypt, for he had respect unto the recompence of the reward. ²⁷ By faith he forsook Egypt, not fearing the wrath of the king, for he endured, as seeing him who is invisible. ²⁸ Through faith he kept the passover, and the sprinkling of blood, lest he that destroyed the firstborn should touch them.

²⁹ By faith they passed through the Red sea as by dry land, which the Egyptians assaying to do were drowned. ³⁰ By faith the walls of Jericho fell down, after they were compassed about seven days. ³¹ By faith the harlot Rahab perished not with them that believed not, when she had received the spies with peace.

³² And what shall I more say? For the time would fail me to tell of Gedeon, and of Barak, and of Samson, and of Jephthae; of David also, and Samuel, and of the prophets; ³³ who through faith subdued kingdoms, wrought righteousness, obtained promises, stopped the mouths of lions, ³⁴ quenched the violence of fire, escaped the edge of the sword, out of weakness were made strong, waxed valiant in fight, turned to flight the armies of the aliens. ³⁵ Women received their dead raised to life again: and others were tortured, not accepting deliverance; that they might obtain a better resurrection: ³⁶ and others had trial of cruel mockings and scourgings, yea, moreover of bonds and imprisonment: ³⁷ they were stoned, they were sawn asunder, were tempted, were slain

with the sword: they wandered about in sheepskins and goatskins; being destitute, afflicted, tormented ³⁸(of whom the world was not worthy): they wandered in deserts, and in mountains, and in dens and caves of the earth.

³⁹And these all, having obtained a good report through faith, received not the promise, ⁴⁰God having provided some better thing for us, that they without us should not be made perfect.

12 Wherefore seeing we also are compassed about with so great a cloud of witnesses, let us lay aside every weight, and the sin which doth so easily beset us, and let us run with patience the race that is set before us, ² looking unto Jesus the author and finisher of our faith; who for the joy that was set before him endured the cross, despising the shame, and is set down at the right hand of the throne of God.

³ For consider him that endured such contradiction of sinners against himself, lest ye be wearied and faint in your minds. ⁴ Ye have not yet resisted unto blood, striving against sin. ⁵ And ye have forgotten the exhortation which speaketh unto you as unto children, 'My son, despise not thou the chastening of the Lord, nor faint when thou art rebuked of him, ⁶ for whom the Lord loveth he chasteneth, and scourgeth every son whom he receiveth.' ⁷ If ye endure chastening, God dealeth with you as with sons; for what son is he whom the father chasteneth not? ⁸ But if ye be without chastisement, whereof all are partakers, then are ye bastards, and not sons. ⁹ Furthermore we have had fathers of our flesh which corrected us, and we gave them reverence: shall we not much rather be in subjection unto the Father of spirits, and live? ¹⁰ For they verily for a few days chastened us after their own pleasure; but he for our profit, that we might be partakers of his holiness. ¹¹ Now no chastening for the present seemeth to be joyous, but grievous: nevertheless afterward it yieldeth the peaceable fruit of righteousness unto them which are exercised thereby.

¹² Wherefore lift up the hands which hang down, and the feeble knees; ¹³ and make straight paths for your feet, lest that which is lame be turned out of the way; but let it rather be healed.

¹⁴ Follow peace with all men, and holiness, without which no man shall see the Lord: ¹⁵ looking diligently lest any man fail of the grace of God; lest any root of bitterness springing up trouble you, and thereby many be defiled; ¹⁶ lest there be any fornicator, or profane person, as Esau, who for one morsel of meat sold his birthright. ¹⁷ For ye know how that afterward, when he would have inherited the blessing, he was rejected, for he found no place of repentance, though he sought it carefully with tears.

¹⁸ For ye are not come unto the mount that might be touched, and that burned with fire, nor unto blackness, and darkness, and tempest, ¹⁹ and the sound of a trumpet, and the voice of words; which voice they that heard intreated that the word should not be spoken to them any more ²⁰(for they could not endure that which was commanded, 'And if so much as a beast touch the mountain, it shall be stoned, or thrust through with a dart': ²¹ and so terrible was the sight, that Moses said, 'I exceedingly fear and quake'): ²² but ye are come unto mount Sion, and unto the city of the living God, the heavenly Jerusalem, and to an innumerable company of angels, ²³ to the general assembly and church of the firstborn, which are written in heaven, and to God the Judge of all, and to the spirits of just men made perfect, ²⁴ and to Jesus the mediator of the new covenant, and to the blood of sprink-

ling, that speaketh better things than that of Abel.

²⁵ See that ye refuse not him that speaketh. For if they escaped not who refused him that spake on earth, much more shall not we escape, if we turn away from him that speaketh from heaven, ²⁶ whose voice then shook the earth: but now he hath promised, saying, 'Yet once more I shake not the earth only, but also heaven.' ²⁷ And this word, 'Yet once more' signifieth the removing of those things that are shaken, as of things that are made, that those things which cannot be shaken may remain. ²⁸ Wherefore we receiving a kingdom which cannot be moved, let us have grace, whereby we may serve God acceptably with reverence and godly fear, ²⁹ for our God is a consuming fire.

13 Let brotherly love continue. [2] Be not forgetful to entertain strangers, for thereby some have entertained angels unawares. [3] Remember them that are in bonds, as bound with them; and them which suffer adversity, as being yourselves also in the body. [4] Marriage is honourable in all, and the bed undefiled, but whoremongers and adulterers God will judge. [5] Let your conversation be without covetousness; and be content with such things as ye have, for he hath said, 'I will never leave thee, nor forsake thee.' [6] So that we may boldly say, 'The Lord is my helper, and I will not fear what man shall do unto me.'

[7] Remember them which have the rule over you, who have spoken unto you the word of God, whose faith follow, considering the end of their conversation. [8] Jesus Christ the same yesterday, and to day, and for ever. [9] Be not carried about with divers and strange doctrines. For it is a good thing that the heart be established with grace; not with meats, which have not profited them that have been occupied therein. [10] We have an altar, whereof they have no right to eat which serve the tabernacle. [11] For the bodies of those beasts, whose blood is brought into the sanctuary by the high priest for sin, are burned without the camp. [12] Wherefore Jesus also, that he might sanctify the people with his own blood, suffered without the gate. [13] Let us go forth therefore unto him without the camp, bearing his reproach. [14] For here have we no continuing city, but we seek one to come. [15] By him therefore let us offer the sacrifice of praise to God continually, that is, the fruit of our lips giving thanks to his

name. ¹⁶But to do good and to communicate forget not, for with such sacrifices God is well pleased.

¹⁷Obey them that have the rule over you, and submit yourselves, for they watch for your souls, as they that must give account, that they may do it with joy, and not with grief, for that is unprofitable for you.

¹⁸Pray for us, for we trust we have a good conscience, in all things willing to live honestly. ¹⁹But I beseech you the rather to do this, that I may be restored to you the sooner.

²⁰Now the God of peace, that brought again from the dead our Lord Jesus, that great shepherd of the sheep, through the blood of the everlasting covenant, ²¹make you perfect in every good work to do his will, working in you that which is wellpleasing in his sight, through Jesus Christ; to whom be glory for ever and ever. Amen.

²²And I beseech you, brethren, suffer the word of exhortation, for I have written a letter unto you in few words. ²³Know ye that our brother Timothy is set at liberty; with whom, if he come shortly, I will see you. ²⁴Salute all them that have the rule over you, and all the saints. They of Italy salute you. ²⁵Grace be with you all. Amen.

samuel

the first and second books of

samuel

authorized king james version

grove press
new york

with an introduction by | meir shalev

Introduction copyright © 1999 by Meir Shalev
Translation of Introduction copyright © 1999 by Marsha Weinstein
The Pocket Canon second series copyright © 2000 by Grove/Atlantic, Inc.

All rights reserved. No part of this book may be reproduced in any form
or by any electronic or mechanical means, including information storage
and retrieval systems, without permission in writing from the publisher,
except by a reviewer, who may quote brief passages in a review. Any
members of educational institutions wishing to photocopy part or all
of the work for classroom use, or publishers who would like to obtain
permission to include the work in an anthology, should send their
inquiries to Grove/Atlantic, Inc., 841 Broadway, New York, NY 10003.

Originally published in Great Britain in 1999 by Canongate Books,
Ltd., Edinburgh, Scotland.

Published simultaneously in Canada
Printed in the United States of America

FIRST AMERICAN EDITION

ISBN 0-8021-3759-8 (boxed set)

Design by Paddy Cramsie

Grove Press
841 Broadway
New York, NY 10003

00 01 02 03   10 9 8 7 6 5 4 3 2 1

note about pocket canons

he Authorized King James Version of the Bible, translated
etween 1603 and 1611, coincided with an extraordinary
owering of English literature. This version, more than any
her, and possibly more than any other work in history, has
d an influence in shaping the language we speak and write
day.

The books of the King James Bible encompass categories
diverse as history, philosophy, law, poetry and fiction. Each
cket Canon volume has its own introduction, specially com-
issioned from an impressive range of writers, to provide a
rsonal interpretation of the text and explore its contempo-
ry relevance.

introduction by meir shalev

Meir Shalev, one of Israel's most celebrated young novelists, is the author of Four Meals, Esau *and* Roman Russi, *all of which have been literary and commercial successes. His latest novel,* Alone in the Desert, *has enjoyed best-seller status in Israel and in Holland. His books have been translated into thirteen languages. Shalev has also written a collection of biblical commentaries,* The Bible for Now, *and a book of literary criticism,* Mainly about Love. *He also writes children's books, and is a columnist with the Israeli daily newspaper,* Yediot Ahronot. *He lives in Jerusalem with his wife and children.*

'Ruddy, and Withal of a Beautiful Countenance'
Of the three main characters in the *Book of Samuel*, only two died. King Saul, a tragic, haunted figure, fell on his sword at Mount Gilboa. Samuel the prophet, a benighted religious zealot, is brought back from the dead once, then sinks into oblivion forever. Aside from the two books at hand, the books that bear his name, he left nothing worth pining for. But David, king of Israel – as we children of Israel are fond of singing – Lives and breathes.

Three thousand years after the death of David we still wait for him to reappear, we read the psalms attributed to him, we even let him participate in political discussions on the future of the Middle East. But like another ruddy, charming, shrewd war hero – Odysseus – David, too, has a deep, personal side, emotional and spiritual. Today, three thousand years later, it is far more interesting than his politics or liturgy.

Like many other Israelis, I met King David. I was nine at the time, and my father took me to the valley of Elah, between Shochoh and Azekah. Ceremoniously planting himself in the middle of the valley, he announced that here David had killed Goliath. He read me *I Samuel 17* and instructed me to pick up five pebbles; when I touched the smooth, rounded stones, I – a short, bespectacled boy – felt as though I were clasping Excalibur and fighting off all the evil Goliaths of the world.

The victory over Goliath is not David's first appearance on the Biblical stage. It was preceded by the prophet Samuel's visit to Bethlehem, where David was anointed king. In the finest tradition of fireside stories, Samuel saw before him a young man who 'was ruddy, and withal of a beautiful countenance, and goodly to look to' (1:16:12) and underestimated him. Samuel saw with his eyes, but the Lord, who saw into the heart, said: 'Arise, anoint him: for this is he' (1:16:12).

We next meet David when he comes to play for Saul. Here he is described with more impressive, magnanimous adjectives: '... [he] is cunning in playing, and a mighty valiant man, and a man of war, and prudent in matters, and a comely person, and the Lord is with him' (1:16:18). Without reservation, this is a description of the perfect man: he is wise, handsome, brave, an artist favoured by God. No wonder his star rises, no wonder he ascends higher and higher, and no one – friend or foe – can resist his charm, his might, or his wisdom.

All five of these characteristics – courage, wisdom, artistic ability, beauty, and good luck – will be manifested at one stage or another of David's life; this is obvious. But often the Bible requires a closer reading, even a creative understanding of the text.

Although not apparent on first reading, I am referring to one of David's most basic characteristics, which may result from the combination of the five traits listed above. That is, his ability to kindle love in the heart of another. On the wings of this love David ascended to lofty heights.

'And Jonathan Loved Him as His Own Soul'
The reader of the chronicle of David will discover that the word 'love' is used extensively in the *Book of Samuel*: 'And David came to Saul, and stood before him: and he loved him greatly'; '… the soul of Jonathan was knit with the soul of David, and Jonathan loved him as his own soul'; 'And Michal Saul's daughter loved David'; '… for Hiram was ever a lover of David'; 'But all Israel and Judah loved David …'

Not one Biblical figure was the object of as much love as David. But closer inspection reveals an additional phenomenon: every time the verb 'love' is connected to David's name, the love is directed at him, but does not emanate from him to another. Saul, Michal, Jonathan, Hiram king of Tyre, the people of Judah and Israel – all of them loved David, but who did David love? At the linguistic level, David did no love even one person – the verb 'love' is never used t describe *his* relation to anyone.

To return to the lovers of David, King Saul loved him and wanted his life at one and the same time. His children Jonathan and Michal, loved David fully and entirely, without reservation or score-keeping. In particular, this i ascribed to Jonathan. I do not see the relations between then as homosexual but they do seem to be 'soulmates'. One way or the other, Jonathan, like his sister Michal, loved Davic 'as his own soul' and, like her, betrayed the interests o both Saul's lineage and himself because of that love.

In his famous lamentation over the death of Saul and Jonathan, David says: 'I am distressed for thee, my brother Jonathan: very pleasant hast thou been unto me: thy love t me was wonderful, passing the love of women' (2:1:26). It i interesting that he says 'thy love to me' rather than 'my love to thee' or 'our love'.

David's lamentation over Saul and Jonathan is a politica and literary masterpiece. It expresses not only his grief, but also his perception of leadership. In effect, it is so polished and calculating that the reader is liable to think that David i either hiding his emotions or perhaps has none. But was David lacking in emotion? Absolutely not.

His terrible pain over the death of his son Absalom, with his horrifying, unpolished wail that rends the heart of the reader even today: '… would God I had died for thee, C Absalom, my son, my son!' (2:18:33) – these words testify t immense depths of soul and emotion. But strangely enough the word 'love' is absent even from David's relation to Absalom, and to his children in general. This is odd, because the text provides a picture of a devoted father, concerned and coddling, sometimes in excess, as with Amnon, Absalom and Adonijah, his unsavoury and debased sons, whom he refused to scold. The verb 'love' is absent from his relation to them, whereas it is prevalent in the descriptions of other Biblical fathers' relations with their children.

'Went … Along Weeping'

In the description of David's relationship to women, the writer refrains from using the specific word 'love', and here, too, this is in contrast to other relationships between men and women in the Bible: Isaac loved Rebekah, Jacob toiled for Rachel for seven years, 'and they seemed unto him but a few days, for the love he had to her' (*Gen.* 29:20). Of Samson it is said: 'he loved a woman in the valley of Sorek, and her name was Delilah' (*Jud.* 16:4). Amnon said of himself: 'I love Tamar, my brother Absalom's sister' (*Sam.* 2:13:4). Elkanah preferred Hannah to Peninnah, 'for he loved Hannah' (*Sam.* 1:1:5). Of Ahasuerus it is said: 'And the king loved Esther above all the women' (*Esther* 2:17), and King Solomon, emotional profligate that he was, 'loved many strange women' (*Kings* 1:11:1).

David, unlike all of them, did not love his women but rather made use of them: in Abigail he found an ally, and one who gave him a private lesson in eliminating opponents. Michal was his ticket into the royal family. And Abishag and Bath-sheba served to fulfil much more basic

meir shalev   xi needs. He, of all people, though famed in this regard, did not love a single woman.

This is never more noticeable than in regard to Michal, Saul's daughter. She is the first woman who loves him, and she is the tragic figure, the one who suffers most from lacking his love. David enters her father's palace as a victorious and handsome hero, he rises to greatness in his court and his army, he amazes Michal when he clasps a sword or plucks a harp, he brings her father two hundred Philistine foreskins to win her. Both Michal and Jonathan succumb to his charm. Both of them sacrifice their interests and those of their family for him. Both shield him, spy for him, save him from their father's hand – and neither wins reciprocal attention from him.

Like Jonathan, Michal, too, betrays her father for her beloved, and the climax is on the same night when she warns him: 'If thou save not thy life tonight, tomorrow thou shalt be slain' (*Sam*. 1:19:11). She lets David out through a window so that he can flee the palace. The next time the two meet, David will be married to other women, and a brief, lone, sad verse will tell what befell Michal after the escape of her husband: 'But Saul had given Michal his daughter, David's wife, to Phalti the son of Laish, which was of Gallim' (*Sam*. 1:25:49).

After the death of Saul, David reigned in Hebron and demanded his wife back. He said then to Abner, Saul's captain of the army: 'Thou shalt not see my face, except thou first bring Michal Saul's daughter, when thou comest to see my face' (*Sam*. 2:3:13). Thus Michal was taken from her second husband, who was devoted to her heart and soul. This is described in a heart-rending verse: 'And her husband went must not kill his opponents with his own hand. He must make sure that the eradication is accomplished by others.

'As the Lord liveth, and as thy soul liveth' she says to him, 'seeing the Lord hath withholden thee from coming to shed blood, and from avenging thyself with thine own hand' adding, 'now let thine enemies, and they that seek evil to my lord, be as Nabal' (*Sam.* 1:25:26). And indeed, within several days Nabal has died under mysterious circumstances, and David has hastily married the attractive widow.

Also from this tale, which contains elements of blood, sex, politics, and violence, the basis of love is lacking – and not by accident. From the beginning the relations between the two were based on a deal. Abigail, so it seems, did away with her husband – a coarse, violent, and stupid man – and won a husband many times more excellent. David has eliminated a very powerful enemy, and repaid her for her assistance. Abigail does not again appear on centre stage, but her spirit and ideas continue to hover over the chapters of the *Book of Samuel*. From that day forward, David never kills an opponent or foe with his own hand. This is especially notable when Joab son of Zeruiah kills Abner, a relative of Saul and captain of his army, who was the primary potential threat to David's early reign.

In a similar fashion David also rids himself of Saul's sons, whom he hands over to the Gibeonites who had a long association with Saul's tribe, the sons of Benjamin; and David, in his way, knew how to take advantage of this. David's permanent henchman was always Joab son of Zeruiah. It was he who killed Abner, he who killed the captain of the mutinous army of Absalom, as well as Absalom himself. It was he who arranged the elimination of the king's most famous victim – Uriah the Hittite, the unfortunate husband of Bath-sheba. But in this case three things indicate a change in fortune: the one – Joab acts on a written order of David, who for once is imprudent. The second – God responds severely. And the third – alongside the story of adultery and murder, the first cracks in David's apparent armour of perfection and good fortune become apparent.

'From the Roof He Saw a Woman Washing Herself'

The story of David, Uriah, and Bath-sheba takes place against the background of David's war against the Ammonites. This is thought-provoking because, in this war, as in the murder of Uriah, David acts for the first time with less logic and wisdom.

In contrast to his previous wars, which were primarily wars over existence and independence, here David goes to war for the dubious reason of honour. The king of Ammon has humiliated an Israeli diplomatic emissary, and David sees in this a just and worthwhile *causus belli*. Similarly, the murder of Uriah is the first time in which David eliminates a man who is not his political rival, but rather a good and loyal soldier whose only crime is being the husband of a woman the king desires. The same intoxicating and addictive charm with which he has been blessed, of arousing love in the heart of another, proves that such charm might pave the way for him who possesses it, but destroys his soul and morality over the years.

This is, then, the first time in which hasty rather than

rational elements are involved in David's actions. Until this incident, the king fully justified the description, 'prudent in matters'. Henceforth begins his great decline: from heights of glory and success to mistakes and failures whose culmination is an ignominious old age.

And so, Joab readies the army of Israel for a siege of Rabbah in Ammon, and David sits in Jerusalem. 'And it came to pass in an evening-tide, that David arose from off his bed, and walked upon the roof of the king's house; and from the roof he saw a woman washing herself; and the woman was very beautiful to look upon. And David sent and enquired after the woman ... And David sent messengers, and took her; and she came in unto him, and he lay with her; for she was purified from her uncleanness: and she returned unto her house. And the woman conceived, and sent and told David, and said, "I am with child." And David sent to Joab, saying, "Send me Uriah the Hittite"' (*Sam.* 2:11:2–6).

David's intention was that Uriah sleep with his wife, and the pregnancy be attributed to him. This incident, the most infamous and dramatic of all of the king's love affairs, again reveals his inability to love. After he has quenched his desire for Bath-sheba, he no longer has any interest in her. Now he plans to extricate himself from the situation in which he finds himself. But Uriah refuses to go up to his house. So David presents in his hand a signed letter. In the letter, which was intended for Joab, captain of the army, the order is given to place Uriah 'in the forefront of the hottest battle ... that he may be smitten, and die'(*Sam.* 2:11:15). The Bible, typically, does not say whether Uriah knew he was carrying

meir shalev   xvii his own death warrant, but it is very detailed in everything pertaining to David's punishment: the death of Bath-sheba's son, and the mutiny of Absalom. From here on, as I noted before, he declines ever further.

David suffers a miserable old age, of mental flaccidity and physical feebleness; there is no longer even a hint of the five good traits that were attributed to him in his youth. Not courage, not wisdom, not beauty, not musicianship, and not the supportive hand of God.

'But the King Knew Her Not'

Of what was David thinking during that chill Jerusalem winter, as he lay in the warm embrace of Abishag the Shunammite? The text, as usual, does not say. We get to read only the journalistic chronicle, which in this case is fairly sensationalist: 'King David was old … and they covered him with clothes, but he gat no heat. His servants said unto him, "Let there be sought for my lord the king a young virgin … and let her lie in thy bosom, that my lord the king may get heat." So they sought for a fair damsel … and found Abishag, a Shunammite, and brought her to the king. And the damsel was very fair, and cherished the king, and ministered to him: but the king knew her not' (*Kings* 1:1:1–5).

The familiar and always relevant question – to what extent can one delve into the private life of a leader – receives here a surprising answer: it is permissible to plumb depths that even modern newspapers agonize over descending to. But the motivation is different. The Biblical author is not reporting on the king's love life because of considerations of circulation and sales, but because this information concerns the functioning of David as a leader. King David is a man in whose life sex and politics have already mingled. He is a man whose ability to arouse love has already degraded his soul. He is a man who has already committed adultery and murdered because of his desire. If now he is in bed with the loveliest maiden in Israel, and does not sleep with her, it is a sign he is in very bad shape.

The Jewish joke tells that when Abishag returned to Shunam, the village from which she was taken to the palace, her friends asked her how it was. Abishag said: 'Now I understand the difference between, "it was an honour" and "it was a pleasure".' But our sages, in contrast, did not find anything humorous in the king's impotence, but adopted the purifying and apologetic approach that is characteristic of many of their other interpretations. It is said that David did not sleep with Abishag because she was forbidden to him, and when the young woman expressed her disappointment and puzzlement, the old king slept with Bath-sheba in front of her, until Bath-sheba 'wiped herself with thirteen cloths'. It is also said there that 'even in David's hour of infirmity, he observed the eighteen seasons' (that is, he was sure to perform his conjugal duties with all eighteen of his wives).

But the plain meaning, it seems, was different. Near the description of David's physical weakness are described the mental details and their political consequences: Adonijah son of Haggith and Solomon son of Bath-sheba, David's sons, are fighting over the inheritance. The court is divided and Adonijah crowns himself king while his father is yet alive. In other words, not only does David 'not know' Abishag, but he is also unaware of all that is happening around him.

In *I Kings*, we learn that Nathan the prophet and Bath-sheba take advantage of the king's weakness and bring about the coronation of Solomon, Bath-sheba's son. This is a most stunning matter, since Nathan the prophet is the man who told David the parable in which Bath-sheba was the poor man's ewe lamb, and it was he who shouted the harsh reprove of David: 'Thou art the man.' That is the power of corruption. It is no wonder that the *Book of Chronicles*, which was written many years after the events described in it transpired, invests great effort in eradicating David's love life from history.

The compiler of *Chronicles* wanted to clear David, to ignore his emotional world, to cleanse him of his own personality and to leave in our hands only his religious-political shell. But the guardian-angel of history and the editors of the Bible wanted otherwise. Despite the censorship of *Chronicles* and despite the generations of sanctimonious and apologetic religious commentary that followed in its footsteps, the *Book of Samuel* – informative, revelatory, and courageous – has not been erased from our chronicles or our consciousness.

And see what a wonder: in spite of everything written there, we still love David, we still contemplate him, we still long for him and wonder about the riddles and contradictions of his personality. Three thousand years after his death, David, king of Israel, lives and breathes. Three thousand years after his death, David still arouses love.

Translated from the Hebrew by Marsha Weinstein

the first book of samuel
otherwise called, the first book of the kings

Now there was a certain man of Ramathaim-zophim, of mount Ephraim, and his name was Elkanah, the son of Jeroham, the son of Elihu, the son of Tohu, the son of Zuph, an Ephrathite: ²and he had two wives; the name of the one was Hannah, and the name of the other Peninnah: and Peninnah had children, but Hannah had no children. ³And this man went up out of his city yearly to worship and to sacrifice unto the Lord of hosts in Shiloh. And the two sons of Eli, Hophni and Phinehas, the priests of the Lord, were there.

⁴And when the time was that Elkanah offered, he gave to Peninnah his wife, and to all her sons and her daughters, portions, ⁵but unto Hannah he gave a worthy portion; for he loved Hannah: but the Lord had shut up her womb. ⁶And her adversary also provoked her sore, for to make her fret, because the Lord had shut up her womb. ⁷And as he did so year by year, when she went up to the house of the Lord, so she provoked her; therefore she wept, and did not eat. ⁸Then said Elkanah her husband to her, 'Hannah, why weepest thou? And why eatest thou not? And why is thy heart grieved? Am not I better to thee than ten sons?'

⁹So Hannah rose up after they had eaten in Shiloh, and after they had drunk. Now Eli the priest sat upon a seat by a

post of the temple of the Lord. ¹⁰And she was in bitterness of soul, and prayed unto the Lord, and wept sore. ¹¹And she vowed a vow, and said, 'O Lord of hosts, if thou wilt indeed look on the affliction of thine handmaid, and remember me, and not forget thine handmaid, but wilt give unto thine handmaid a man child, then I will give him unto the Lord all the days of his life, and there shall no razor come upon his head.' ¹²And it came to pass, as she continued praying before the Lord, that Eli marked her mouth. ¹³ Now Hannah, she spake in her heart; only her lips moved, but her voice was not heard: therefore Eli thought she had been drunken. ¹⁴And Eli said unto her, 'How long wilt thou be drunken? Put away thy wine from thee.' ¹⁵And Hannah answered and said, 'No, my lord, I am a woman of a sorrowful spirit: I have drunk neither wine nor strong drink, but have poured out my soul before the Lord. ¹⁶ Count not thine handmaid for a daughter of Belial, for out of the abundance of my complaint and grief have I spoken hitherto.' ¹⁷ Then Eli answered and said, 'Go in peace, and the God of Israel grant thee thy petition that thou hast asked of him. ¹⁸And she said, 'Let thine handmaid find grace in thy sight.' So the woman went her way, and did eat, and her countenance was no more sad.

¹⁹And they rose up in the morning early, and worshipped before the Lord, and returned, and came to their house to Ramah, and Elkanah knew Hannah his wife; and the Lord remembered her. ²⁰ Wherefore it came to pass, when the time was come about after Hannah had conceived, that she bare a son, and called his name Samuel, saying, 'Because I have

asked him of the Lord.' [21]And the man Elkanah, and all his house, went up to offer unto the Lord the yearly sacrifice, and his vow. [22]But Hannah went not up; for she said unto her husband, 'I will not go up until the child be weaned, and then I will bring him, that he may appear before the Lord, and there abide for ever.' [23]And Elkanah her husband said unto her, 'Do what seemeth thee good; tarry until thou have weaned him; only the Lord establish his word.' So the woman abode, and gave her son suck until she weaned him.

[24]And when she had weaned him, she took him up with her, with three bullocks, and one ephah of flour, and a bottle of wine, and brought him unto the house of the Lord in Shiloh: and the child was young. [25]And they slew a bullock, and brought the child to Eli. [26]And she said, 'O my lord, as thy soul liveth, my lord, I am the woman that stood by thee here, praying unto the Lord. [27]For this child I prayed; and the Lord hath given me my petition which I asked of him: [28]therefore also I have lent him to the Lord; as long as he liveth he shall be lent to the Lord.' And he worshipped the Lord there.

2 And Hannah prayed, and said, 'My heart rejoiceth in the Lord, mine horn is exalted in the Lord; my mouth is enlarged over mine enemies, because I rejoice in thy salvation. [2]There is none holy as the Lord, for there is none beside thee: neither is there any rock like our God. [3]Talk no more so exceeding proudly; let not arrogancy come out of your mouth, for the Lord is a God of knowledge, and by him

actions are weighed. ⁴ The bows of the mighty men are broken, and they that stumbled are girded with strength. ⁵ They that were full have hired out themselves for bread; and they that were hungry ceased: so that the barren hath born seven; and she that hath many children is waxed feeble. ⁶ The Lord killeth, and maketh alive: he bringeth down to the grave, and bringeth up. ⁷ The Lord maketh poor, and maketh rich: he bringeth low, and lifteth up. ⁸ He raiseth up the poor out of the dust, and lifteth up the beggar from the dunghill, to set them among princes, and to make them inherit the throne of glory, for the pillars of the earth are the Lord's, and he hath set the world upon them. ⁹ He will keep the feet of his saints, and the wicked shall be silent in darkness; for by strength shall no man prevail. ¹⁰ The adversaries of the Lord shall be broken to pieces; out of heaven shall he thunder upon them: the Lord shall judge the ends of the earth; and he shall give strength unto his king, and exalt the horn of his anointed.' ¹¹ And Elkanah went to Ramah to his house. And the child did minister unto the Lord before Eli the priest.

¹² Now the sons of Eli were sons of Belial; they knew not the Lord. ¹³ And the priests' custom with the people was, that, when any man offered sacrifice, the priest's servant came, while the flesh was in seething, with a flesh-hook of three teeth in his hand; ¹⁴ and he struck it into the pan, or kettle, or caldron, or pot; all that the fleshhook brought up the priest took for himself. So they did in Shiloh unto all the Israelites that came thither. ¹⁵ Also before they burnt the fat, the priest's servant came, and said to the man that sacrificed, 'Give flesh

to roast for the priest; for he will not have sodden flesh of thee, but raw.' ¹⁶And if any man said unto him, 'Let them not fail to burn the fat presently, and then take as much as thy soul desireth', then he would answer him, 'Nay; but thou shalt give it me now: and if not, I will take it by force.' ¹⁷Wherefore the sin of the young men was very great before the Lord, for men abhorred the offering of the Lord.

¹⁸But Samuel ministered before the Lord, being a child, girded with a linen ephod. ¹⁹Moreover his mother made him a little coat, and brought it to him from year to year, when she came up with her husband to offer the yearly sacrifice.

²⁰And Eli blessed Elkanah and his wife, and said, 'The Lord give thee seed of this woman for the loan which is lent to the Lord.' And they went unto their own home. ²¹And the Lord visited Hannah, so that she conceived, and bare three sons and two daughters. And the child Samuel grew before the Lord.

²²Now Eli was very old, and heard all that his sons did unto all Israel; and how they lay with the women that assembled at the door of the tabernacle of the congregation. ²³And he said unto them, 'Why do ye such things? For I hear of your evil dealings by all this people. ²⁴Nay, my sons, for it is no good report that I hear: ye make the Lord's people to transgress. ²⁵If one man sin against another, the judge shall judge him, but if a man sin against the Lord, who shall intreat for him?' Notwithstanding they hearkened not unto the voice of their father, because the Lord would slay them.

²⁶And the child Samuel grew on, and was in favour both with the Lord, and also with men.

²⁷And there came a man of God unto Eli, and said unto him, 'Thus saith the Lord, "Did I plainly appear unto the house of thy father, when they were in Egypt in Pharaoh's house? ²⁸And did I choose him out of all the tribes of Israel to be my priest, to offer upon mine altar, to burn incense, to wear an ephod before me? And did I give unto the house of thy father all the offerings made by fire of the children of Israel? ²⁹Wherefore kick ye at my sacrifice and at mine offering, which I have commanded in my habitation; and honourest thy sons above me, to make yourselves fat with the chiefest of all the offerings of Israel my people?" ³⁰Wherefore the Lord God of Israel saith, "I said indeed that thy house, and the house of thy father, should walk before me for ever," but now the Lord saith, "Be it far from me; for them that honour me I will honour, and they that despise me shall be lightly esteemed. ³¹Behold, the days come, that I will cut off thine arm, and the arm of thy father's house, that there shall not be an old man in thine house. ³²And thou shalt see an enemy in my habitation, in all the wealth which God shall give Israel: and there shall not be an old man in thine house for ever. ³³And the man of thine, whom I shall not cut off from mine altar, shall be to consume thine eyes, and to grieve thine heart: and all the increase of thine house shall die in the flower of their age. ³⁴And this shall be a sign unto thee, that shall come upon thy two sons, on Hophni and Phinehas; in one day they shall die both of them. ³⁵And I

will raise me up a faithful priest, that shall do according to that which is in mine heart and in my mind; and I will build him a sure house; and he shall walk before mine anointed for ever. ³⁶And it shall come to pass, that every one that is left in thine house shall come and crouch to him for a piece of silver and a morsel of bread, and shall say, 'Put me, I pray thee, into one of the priests' offices, that I may eat a piece of bread.'"'

3 And the child Samuel ministered unto the Lord before Eli. And the word of the Lord was precious in those days; there was no open vision. ²And it came to pass at that time, when Eli was laid down in his place, and his eyes began to wax dim, that he could not see; ³and ere the lamp of God went out in the temple of the Lord, where the ark of God was, and Samuel was laid down to sleep; ⁴that the Lord called 'Samuel': and he answered, 'Here am I.' ⁵And he ran unto Eli, and said, 'Here am I; for thou calledst me.' And he said, 'I called not; lie down again.' And he went and lay down. ⁶And the Lord called yet again, 'Samuel.' And Samuel arose and went to Eli, and said, 'Here am I; for thou didst call me.' And he answered, 'I called not, my son; lie down again.' ⁷Now Samuel did not yet know the Lord, neither was the word of the Lord yet revealed unto him. ⁸And the Lord called Samuel again the third time. And he arose and went to Eli, and said, 'Here am I; for thou didst call me.' And Eli perceived that the Lord had called the child. ⁹Therefore Eli said unto Samuel, 'Go, lie down: and it shall be, if he call

thee, that thou shalt say, "Speak, Lord; for thy servant heareth."' So Samuel went and lay down in his place. ¹⁰And the Lord came, and stood, and called as at other times, 'Samuel, Samuel.' Then Samuel answered, 'Speak; for thy servant heareth.'

¹¹And the Lord said to Samuel, 'Behold, I will do a thing in Israel, at which both the ears of every one that heareth it shall tingle. ¹²In that day I will perform against Eli all things which I have spoken concerning his house: when I begin, I will also make an end. ¹³For I have told him that I will judge his house for ever for the iniquity which he knoweth; because his sons made themselves vile, and he restrained them not. ¹⁴And therefore I have sworn unto the house of Eli, that the iniquity of Eli's house shall not be purged with sacrifice nor offering for ever.'

¹⁵And Samuel lay until the morning, and opened the doors of the house of the Lord. And Samuel feared to shew Eli the vision. ¹⁶Then Eli called Samuel, and said, 'Samuel, my son.' And he answered, 'Here am I.' ¹⁷And he said, 'What is the thing that the Lord hath said unto thee? I pray thee hide it not from me: God do so to thee, and more also, if thou hide any thing from me of all the things that he said unto thee.' ¹⁸And Samuel told him every whit, and hid nothing from him. And he said, 'It is the Lord: let him do what seemeth him good.'

¹⁹And Samuel grew, and the Lord was with him, and did let none of his words fall to the ground. ²⁰And all Israel from Dan even to Beer-sheba knew that Samuel was established

to be a prophet of the Lord. ²¹And the Lord appeared again in Shiloh, for the Lord revealed himself to Samuel in Shiloh by the word of the Lord.

4 And the word of Samuel came to all Israel. Now Israel went out against the Philistines to battle, and pitched beside Eben-ezer: and the Philistines pitched in Aphek. ²And the Philistines put themselves in array against Israel; and when they joined battle, Israel was smitten before the Philistines; and they slew of the army in the field about four thousand men.

³And when the people were come into the camp, the elders of Israel said, 'Wherefore hath the Lord smitten us to day before the Philistines? Let us fetch the ark of the covenant of the Lord out of Shiloh unto us, that, when it cometh among us, it may save us out of the hand of our enemies.' ⁴So the people sent to Shiloh, that they might bring from thence the ark of the covenant of the Lord of hosts, which dwelleth between the cherubims: and the two sons of Eli, Hophni and Phinehas, were there with the ark of the covenant of God. ⁵And when the ark of the covenant of the Lord came into the camp, all Israel shouted with a great shout, so that the earth rang again. ⁶And when the Philistines heard the noise of the shout, they said, 'What meaneth the noise of this great shout in the camp of the Hebrews?' And they understood that the ark of the Lord was come into the camp. ⁷And the Philistines were afraid, for they said, 'God is come into the camp.' And they said, 'Woe unto us! For there hath

not been such a thing heretofore. ⁸ Woe unto us! Who shall deliver us out of the hand of these mighty Gods? These are the Gods that smote the Egyptians with all the plagues in the wilderness. ⁹ Be strong, and quit yourselves like men, O ye Philistines, that ye be not servants unto the Hebrews, as they have been to you: quit yourselves like men, and fight.'

¹⁰And the Philistines fought, and Israel was smitten, and they fled every man into his tent: and there was a very great slaughter; for there fell of Israel thirty thousand footmen. ¹¹And the ark of God was taken; and the two sons of Eli, Hophni and Phinehas, were slain.

¹²And there ran a man of Benjamin out of the army, and came to Shiloh the same day with his clothes rent, and with earth upon his head. ¹³And when he came, lo, Eli sat upon a seat by the wayside watching, for his heart trembled for the ark of God. And when the man came into the city, and told it, all the city cried out. ¹⁴And when Eli heard the noise of the crying, he said, 'What meaneth the noise of this tumult?' And the man came in hastily, and told Eli. ¹⁵ Now Eli was ninety and eight years old; and his eyes were dim, that he could not see. ¹⁶And the man said unto Eli, 'I am he that came out of the army, and I fled to day out of the army.' And he said, 'What is there done, my son?' ¹⁷And the messenger answered and said, 'Israel is fled before the Philistines, and there hath been also a great slaughter among the people, and thy two sons also, Hophni and Phinehas, are dead, and the ark of God is taken.' ¹⁸And it came to pass, when he made mention of the ark of God, that he fell from off the seat back-

ward by the side of the gate, and his neck brake, and he died, for he was an old man, and heavy. And he had judged Israel forty years.

¹⁹And his daughter in law, Phinehas' wife, was with child, near to be delivered: and when she heard the tidings that the ark of God was taken, and that her father in law and her husband were dead, she bowed herself and travailed; for her pains came upon her. ²⁰And about the time of her death the women that stood by her said unto her, 'Fear not; for thou hast born a son.' But she answered not, neither did she regard it. ²¹And she named the child I-chabod, saying, 'The glory is departed from Israel, because the ark of God was taken, and because of her father in law and her husband.' ²²And she said, 'The glory is departed from Israel, for the ark of God is taken.'

5 And the Philistines took the ark of God, and brought it from Ebenezer unto Ashdod. ²When the Philistines took the ark of God, they brought it into the house of Dagon, and set it by Dagon.

³And when they of Ashdod arose early on the morrow, behold, Dagon was fallen upon his face to the earth before the ark of the Lord. And they took Dagon, and set him in his place again. ⁴And when they arose early on the morrow morning, behold, Dagon was fallen upon his face to the ground before the ark of the Lord; and the head of Dagon and both the palms of his hands were cut off upon the threshold; only the stump of Dagon was left to him. ⁵Therefore

neither the priests of Dagon, nor any that come into Dagon's house, tread on the threshold of Dagon in Ashdod unto this day. ⁶But the hand of the Lord was heavy upon them of Ashdod, and he destroyed them, and smote them with emerods, even Ashdod and the coasts thereof. ⁷And when the men of Ashdod saw that it was so, they said, 'The ark of the God of Israel shall not abide with us, for his hand is sore upon us, and upon Dagon our god. ⁸They sent therefore and gathered all the lords of the Philistines unto them, and said, 'What shall we do with the ark of the God of Israel?' And they answered, 'Let the ark of the God of Israel be carried about unto Gath.' And they carried the ark of the God of Israel about thither. ⁹And it was so, that, after they had carried it about, the hand of the Lord was against the city with a very great destruction: and he smote the men of the city, both small and great, and they had emerods in their secret parts.

¹⁰Therefore they sent the ark of God to Ekron. And it came to pass, as the ark of God came to Ekron, that the Ekronites cried out, saying, 'They have brought about the ark of the God of Israel to us, to slay us and our people.' ¹¹So they sent and gathered together all the lords of the Philistines, and said, 'Send away the ark of the God of Israel, and let it go again to his own place, that it slay us not, and our people'; for there was a deadly destruction throughout all the city; the hand of God was very heavy there. ¹²And the men that died not were smitten with the emerods: and the cry of the city went up to heaven.

6 And the ark of the Lord was in the country of the Philistines seven months. ²And the Philistines called for the priests and the diviners, saying, 'What shall we do to the ark of the Lord? Tell us wherewith we shall send it to his place.' ³And they said, 'If ye send away the ark of the God of Israel, send it not empty; but in any wise return him a trespass offering: then ye shall be healed, and it shall be known to you why his hand is not removed from you.' ⁴Then said they, 'What shall be the trespass offering which we shall return to him?' They answered, 'Five golden emerods, and five golden mice, according to the number of the lords of the Philistines, for one plague was on you all, and on your lords. ⁵Wherefore ye shall make images of your emerods, and images of your mice that mar the land; and ye shall give glory unto the God of Israel: peradventure he will lighten his hand from off you, and from off your gods, and from off your land. ⁶Wherefore then do ye harden your hearts, as the Egyptians and Pharaoh hardened their hearts? When he had wrought wonderfully among them, did they not let the people go, and they departed? ⁷Now therefore make a new cart, and take two milch kine, on which there hath come no yoke, and tie the kine to the cart, and bring their calves home from them: ⁸and take the ark of the Lord, and lay it upon the cart; and put the jewels of gold, which ye return him for a trespass offering, in a coffer by the side thereof; and send it away, that it may go. ⁹And see, if it goeth up by the way of his own coast to Beth-shemesh, then he hath done us this great evil; but if not, then we shall know that it is not his

hand that smote us; it was a chance that happened to us.'

¹⁰And the men did so; and took two milch kine, and tied them to the cart, and shut up their calves at home: ¹¹and they laid the ark of the Lord upon the cart, and the coffer with the mice of gold and the images of their emerods. ¹²And the kine took the straight way to the way of Beth-shemesh, and went along the highway, lowing as they went, and turned not aside to the right hand or to the left; and the lords of the Philistines went after them unto the border of Beth-shemesh. ¹³And they of Beth-shemesh were reaping their wheat harvest in the valley: and they lifted up their eyes, and saw the ark, and rejoiced to see it. ¹⁴And the cart came into the field of Joshua, a Beth-shemite, and stood there, where there was a great stone: and they clave the wood of the cart, and offered the kine a burnt offering unto the Lord. ¹⁵And the Levites took down the ark of the Lord, and the coffer that was with it, wherein the jewels of gold were, and put them on the great stone: and the men of Beth-shemesh offered burnt offerings and sacrificed sacrifices the same day unto the Lord. ¹⁶And when the five lords of the Philistines had seen it, they returned to Ekron the same day. ¹⁷And these are the golden emerods which the Philistines returned for a trespass offering unto the Lord; for Ashdod one, for Gaza one, for Askelon one, for Gath one, for Ekron one; ¹⁸and the golden mice, according to the number of all the cities of the Philistines belonging to the five lords, both of fenced cities, and of country villages, even unto the great stone of Abel, whereon they set down the ark of the Lord, which stone remaineth

unto this day in the field of Joshua, the Beth-shemite.

¹⁹And he smote the men of Beth-shemesh, because they had looked into the ark of the Lord, even he smote of the people fifty thousand and threescore and ten men: and the people lamented, because the Lord had smitten many of the people with a great slaughter. ²⁰And the men of Beth-shemesh said, 'Who is able to stand before this holy Lord God? And to whom shall he go up from us?'

²¹And they sent messengers to the inhabitants of Kirjath-jearim, saying, 'The Philistines have brought again the ark of the Lord; come ye down, and fetch it up to you.'

7 And the men of Kirjath-jearim came, and fetched up the ark of the Lord, and brought it into the house of Abinadab in the hill, and sanctified Eleazar his son to keep the ark of the Lord. ²And it came to pass, while the ark abode in Kirjath-jearim, that the time was long; for it was twenty years: and all the house of Israel lamented after the Lord.

³And Samuel spake unto all the house of Israel, saying, 'If ye do return unto the Lord with all your hearts, then put away the strange gods and Ashtaroth from among you, and prepare your hearts unto the Lord, and serve him only: and he will deliver you out of the hand of the Philistines.' ⁴Then the children of Israel did put away Baalim and Ashtaroth, and served the Lord only. ⁵And Samuel said, 'Gather all Israel to Mizpeh, and I will pray for you unto the Lord.' ⁶And they gathered together to Mizpeh, and drew water, and poured it out before the Lord, and fasted on that day,

and said there, 'We have sinned against the Lord.' And Samuel judged the children of Israel in Mizpeh. ⁷And when the Philistines heard that the children of Israel were gathered together to Mizpeh, the lords of the Philistines went up against Israel. And when the children of Israel heard it, they were afraid of the Philistines. ⁸And the children of Israel said to Samuel, 'Cease not to cry unto the Lord our God for us, that he will save us out of the hand of the Philistines.'

⁹And Samuel took a sucking lamb, and offered it for a burnt offering wholly unto the Lord: and Samuel cried unto the Lord for Israel; and the Lord heard him. ¹⁰And as Samuel was offering up the burnt offering, the Philistines drew near to battle against Israel; but the Lord thundered with a great thunder on that day upon the Philistines, and discomfited them; and they were smitten before Israel. ¹¹And the men of Israel went out of Mizpeh, and pursued the Philistines, and smote them, until they came under Beth-car. ¹²Then Samuel took a stone, and set it between Mizpeh and Shen, and called the name of it Eben-ezer, saying, Hitherto hath the Lord helped us.

¹³So the Philistines were subdued, and they came no more into the coast of Israel: and the hand of the Lord was against the Philistines all the days of Samuel. ¹⁴And the cities which the Philistines had taken from Israel were restored to Israel, from Ekron even unto Gath; and the coasts thereof did Israel deliver out of the hands of the Philistines. And there was peace between Israel and the Amorites. ¹⁵And Samuel judged Israel all the days of his life. ¹⁶And he went from year

to year in circuit to Beth-el, and Gilgal, and Mizpeh, and judged Israel in all those places. ¹⁷And his return was to Ramah; for there was his house; and there he judged Israel; and there he built an altar unto the Lord.

8 And it came to pass, when Samuel was old, that he made his sons judges over Israel. ²Now the name of his firstborn was Joel; and the name of his second, Abiah: they were judges in Beer-sheba. ³And his sons walked not in his ways, but turned aside after lucre, and took bribes, and perverted judgment. ⁴Then all the elders of Israel gathered themselves together, and came to Samuel unto Ramah, ⁵and said unto him, 'Behold, thou art old, and thy sons walk not in thy ways: now make us a king to judge us like all the nations.'

⁶But the thing displeased Samuel, when they said, 'Give us a king to judge us.' And Samuel prayed unto the Lord. ⁷And the Lord said unto Samuel, 'Hearken unto the voice of the people in all that they say unto thee, for they have not rejected thee, but they have rejected me, that I should not reign over them. ⁸According to all the works which they have done since the day that I brought them up out of Egypt even unto this day, wherewith they have forsaken me, and served other gods, so do they also unto thee. ⁹Now therefore hearken unto their voice: howbeit yet protest solemnly unto them, and shew them the manner of the king that shall reign over them.'

¹⁰And Samuel told all the words of the Lord unto the

people that asked of him a king. ¹¹And he said, 'This will be the manner of the king that shall reign over you: he will take your sons, and appoint them for himself, for his chariots, and to be his horsemen; and some shall run before his chariots. ¹²And he will appoint him captains over thousands, and captains over fifties; and will set them to ear his ground, and to reap his harvest, and to make his instruments of war, and instruments of his chariots. ¹³And he will take your daughters to be confectionaries, and to be cooks, and to be bakers. ¹⁴And he will take your fields, and your vineyards, and your oliveyards, even the best of them, and give them to his servants. ¹⁵And he will take the tenth of your seed, and of your vineyards, and give to his officers, and to his servants. ¹⁶And he will take your menservants, and your maidservants, and your goodliest young men, and your asses, and put them to his work. ¹⁷He will take the tenth of your sheep: and ye shall be his servants. ¹⁸And ye shall cry out in that day because of your king which ye shall have chosen you; and the Lord will not hear you in that day.

¹⁹Nevertheless the people refused to obey the voice of Samuel; and they said, 'Nay; but we will have a king over us; ²⁰ that we also may be like all the nations; and that our king may judge us, and go out before us, and fight our battles.' ²¹And Samuel heard all the words of the people, and he rehearsed them in the ears of the Lord. ²²And the Lord said to Samuel, 'Hearken unto their voice, and make them a king.' And Samuel said unto the men of Israel, 'Go ye every man unto his city.'

9 Now there was a man of Benjamin, whose name was Kish, the son of Abiel, the son of Zeror, the son of Bechorath, the son of Aphiah, a Benjamite, a mighty man of power. ²And he had a son, whose name was Saul, a choice young man, and a goodly; and there was not among the children of Israel a goodlier person than he: from his shoulders and upward he was higher than any of the people. ³And the asses of Kish Saul's father were lost. And Kish said to Saul his son, 'Take now one of the servants with thee, and arise, go seek the asses.' ⁴And he passed through mount Ephraim, and passed through the land of Shalisha, but they found them not: then they passed through the land of Shalim, and there they were not: and he passed through the land of the Benjamites, but they found them not. ⁵And when they were come to the land of Zuph, Saul said to his servant that was with him, 'Come, and let us return; lest my father leave caring for the asses, and take thought for us.' ⁶And he said unto him, 'Behold now, there is in this city a man of God, and he is an honourable man; all that he saith cometh surely to pass: now let us go thither; peradventure he can shew us our way that we should go.' ⁷Then said Saul to his servant, 'But, behold, if we go, what shall we bring the man? For the bread is spent in our vessels, and there is not a present to bring to the man of God: what have we?' ⁸And the servant answered Saul again, and said, 'Behold, I have here at hand the fourth part of a shekel of silver: that will I give to the man of God, to tell us our way.' ⁹(Beforetime in Israel, when a man went to enquire of God, thus he spake, 'Come, and let us go to the

seer, for he that is now called a Prophet was beforetime called a Seer.) ¹⁰Then said Saul to his servant, 'Well said; come, let us go.' So they went unto the city where the man of God was.

¹¹And as they went up the hill to the city, they found young maidens going out to draw water, and said unto them, 'Is the seer here?' ¹²And they answered them, and said, 'He is; behold, he is before you: make haste now, for he came to day to the city; for there is a sacrifice of the people to day in the high place. ¹³As soon as ye be come into the city, ye shall straightway find him, before he go up to the high place to eat; for the people will not eat until he come, because he doth bless the sacrifice; and afterwards they eat that be bidden. Now therefore get you up; for about this time ye shall find him.' ¹⁴And they went up into the city: and when they were come into the city, behold, Samuel came out against them, for to go up to the high place.

¹⁵Now the Lord had told Samuel in his ear a day before Saul came, saying, ¹⁶'To morrow about this time I will send thee a man out of the land of Benjamin, and thou shalt anoint him to be captain over my people Israel, that he may save my people out of the hand of the Philistines; for I have looked upon my people, because their cry is come unto me.' ¹⁷And when Samuel saw Saul, the Lord said unto him, 'Behold the man whom I spake to thee of! This same shall reign over my people.' ¹⁸Then Saul drew near to Samuel in the gate, and said, 'Tell me, I pray thee, where the seer's house is.' ¹⁹And Samuel answered Saul, and said, 'I am the

seer: go up before me unto the high place; for ye shall eat with me to day, and to morrow I will let thee go, and will tell thee all that is in thine heart. ²⁰And as for thine asses that were lost three days ago, set not thy mind on them; for they are found. And on whom is all the desire of Israel? Is it not on thee, and on all thy father's house?' ²¹And Saul answered and said, 'Am not I a Benjamite, of the smallest of the tribes of Israel? And my family the least of all the families of the tribe of Benjamin? Wherefore then speakest thou so to me?' ²²And Samuel took Saul and his servant, and brought them into the parlour, and made them sit in the chiefest place among them that were bidden, which were about thirty persons. ²³And Samuel said unto the cook, 'Bring the portion which I gave thee, of which I said unto thee, "Set it by thee."' ²⁴And the cook took up the shoulder, and that which was upon it, and set it before Saul. And Samuel said, 'Behold that which is left! Set it before thee, and eat; for unto this time hath it been kept for thee since I said, I have invited the people.' So Saul did eat with Samuel that day.

²⁵And when they were come down from the high place into the city, Samuel communed with Saul upon the top of the house. ²⁶And they arose early: and it came to pass about the spring of the day, that Samuel called Saul to the top of the house, saying, 'Up, that I may send thee away.' And Saul arose, and they went out both of them, he and Samuel, abroad. ²⁷And as they were going down to the end of the city, Samuel said to Saul, 'Bid the servant pass on before us (and

he passed on), but stand thou still a while, that I may shew thee the word of God.'

10

Then Samuel took a vial of oil, and poured it upon his head, and kissed him, and said, 'Is it not because the Lord hath anointed thee to be captain over his inheritance? ²When thou art departed from me to day, then thou shalt find two men by Rachel's sepulchre in the border of Benjamin at Zelzah; and they will say unto thee, "The asses which thou wentest to seek are found: and, lo, thy father hath left the care of the asses, and sorroweth for you, saying, 'What shall I do for my son?'" ³Then shalt thou go on forward from thence, and thou shalt come to the plain of Tabor, and there shall meet thee three men going up to God to Beth-el, one carrying three kids, and another carrying three loaves of bread, and another carrying a bottle of wine: ⁴and they will salute thee, and give thee two loaves of bread; which thou shalt receive of their hands. ⁵After that thou shalt come to the hill of God, where is the garrison of the Philistines: and it shall come to pass, when thou art come thither to the city, that thou shalt meet a company of prophets coming down from the high place with a psaltery, and a tabret, and a pipe, and a harp, before them; and they shall prophesy: ⁶and the Spirit of the Lord will come upon thee, and thou shalt prophesy with them, and shalt be turned into another man. ⁷And let it be, when these signs are come unto thee, that thou do as occasion serve thee; for God is with thee. ⁸And thou shalt go down before me to Gilgal;

and, behold, I will come down unto thee, to offer burnt offerings, and to sacrifice sacrifices of peace offerings: seven days shalt thou tarry, till I come to thee, and shew thee what thou shalt do.'

⁹And it was so, that when he had turned his back to go from Samuel, God gave him another heart: and all those signs came to pass that day. ¹⁰And when they came thither to the hill, behold, a company of prophets met him; and the Spirit of God came upon him, and he prophesied among them. ¹¹And it came to pass, when all that knew him beforetime saw that, behold, he prophesied among the prophets, then the people said one to another, 'What is this that is come unto the son of Kish? Is Saul also among the prophets?' ¹²And one of the same place answered and said, 'But who is their father?' Therefore it became a proverb, 'Is Saul also among the prophets?' ¹³And when he had made an end of prophesying, he came to the high place.

¹⁴And Saul's uncle said unto him and to his servant, 'Whither went ye?' And he said, 'To seek the asses: and when we saw that they were no where, we came to Samuel.' ¹⁵And Saul's uncle said, 'Tell me, I pray thee, what Samuel said unto you.' ¹⁶And Saul said unto his uncle, 'He told us plainly that the asses were found.' But of the matter of the kingdom, whereof Samuel spake, he told him not.

¹⁷And Samuel called the people together unto the Lord to Mizpeh; ¹⁸and said unto the children of Israel, 'Thus saith the Lord God of Israel, "I brought up Israel out of Egypt, and delivered you out of the hand of the Egyptians, and out

of the hand of all kingdoms, and of them that oppressed you." ¹⁹And ye have this day rejected your God, who himself saved you out of all your adversities and your tribulations; and ye have said unto him, "Nay, but set a king over us." Now therefore present yourselves before the Lord by your tribes, and by your thousands.' ²⁰And when Samuel had caused all the tribes of Israel to come near, the tribe of Benjamin was taken. ²¹When he had caused the tribe of Benjamin to come near by their families, the family of Matri was taken, and Saul the son of Kish was taken: and when they sought him, he could not be found. ²²Therefore they enquired of the Lord further, if the man should yet come thither. And the Lord answered, 'Behold, he hath hid himself among the stuff.' ²³And they ran and fetched him thence: and when he stood among the people, he was higher than any of the people from his shoulders and upward. ²⁴And Samuel said to all the people, 'See ye him whom the Lord hath chosen, that there is none like him among all the people?' And all the people shouted, and said, 'God save the king.' ²⁵Then Samuel told the people the manner of the kingdom, and wrote it in a book, and laid it up before the Lord. And Samuel sent all the people away, every man to his house.

²⁶And Saul also went home to Gibeah; and there went with him a band of men, whose hearts God had touched. ²⁷But the children of Belial said, 'How shall this man save us?' And they despised him, and brought him no presents. But he held his peace.

11 Then Nahash the Ammonite came up, and encamped against Jabesh-gilead: and all the men of Jabesh said unto Nahash, 'Make a covenant with us, and we will serve thee.' ²And Nahash the Ammonite answered them, 'On this condition will I make a covenant with you, that I may thrust out all your right eyes, and lay it for a reproach upon all Israel.' ³And the elders of Jabesh said unto him, 'Give us seven days' respite, that we may send messengers unto all the coasts of Israel: and then, if there be no man to save us, we will come out to thee.'

⁴Then came the messengers to Gibeah of Saul, and told the tidings in the ears of the people: and all the people lifted up their voices, and wept. ⁵And, behold, Saul came after the herd out of the field; and Saul said, 'What aileth the people that they weep?' And they told him the tidings of the men of Jabesh. ⁶And the Spirit of God came upon Saul when he heard those tidings, and his anger was kindled greatly. ⁷And he took a yoke of oxen, and hewed them in pieces, and sent them throughout all the coasts of Israel by the hands of messengers, saying, 'Whosoever cometh not forth after Saul and after Samuel, so shall it be done unto his oxen.' And the fear of the Lord fell on the people, and they came out with one consent. ⁸And when he numbered them in Bezek, the children of Israel were three hundred thousand, and the men of Judah thirty thousand. ⁹And they said unto the messengers that came, 'Thus shall ye say unto the men of Jabesh-gilead, "To morrow, by that time the sun be hot, ye shall have help."' And the messengers came and shewed it to the men

of Jabesh; and they were glad. ¹⁰ Therefore the men of Jabesh said, 'To morrow we will come out unto you, and ye shall do with us all that seemeth good unto you.' ¹¹ And it was so on the morrow, that Saul put the people in three companies; and they came into the midst of the host in the morning watch, and slew the Ammonites until the heat of the day: and it came to pass, that they which remained were scattered, so that two of them were not left together.

¹² And the people said unto Samuel, 'Who is he that said, "Shall Saul reign over us?" Bring the men, that we may put them to death.' ¹³ And Saul said, 'There shall not a man be put to death this day, for to day the Lord hath wrought salvation in Israel.' ¹⁴ Then said Samuel to the people, 'Come, and let us go to Gilgal, and renew the kingdom there.' ¹⁵ And all the people went to Gilgal; and there they made Saul king before the Lord in Gilgal; and there they sacrificed sacrifices of peace offerings before the Lord; and there Saul and all the men of Israel rejoiced greatly.

12 And Samuel said unto all Israel, 'Behold, I have hearkened unto your voice in all that ye said unto me, and have made a king over you. ² And now, behold, the king walketh before you; and I am old and gray-headed; and, behold, my sons are with you; and I have walked before you from my childhood unto this day. ³ Behold, here I am: witness against me before the Lord, and before his anointed: whose ox have I taken? Or whose ass have I taken? Or whom have I defrauded? Whom have I oppressed? Or of

whose hand have I received any bribe to blind mine eyes therewith? And I will restore it you.' ⁴And they said, 'Thou hast not defrauded us, nor oppressed us, neither hast thou taken ought of any man's hand.' ⁵And he said unto them, 'The Lord is witness against you, and his anointed is witness this day, that ye have not found ought in my hand.' And they answered, 'He is witness.'

⁶And Samuel said unto the people, 'It is the Lord that advanced Moses and Aaron, and that brought your fathers up out of the land of Egypt. ⁷Now therefore stand still, that I may reason with you before the Lord of all the righteous acts of the Lord, which he did to you and to your fathers. ⁸When Jacob was come into Egypt, and your fathers cried unto the Lord, then the Lord sent Moses and Aaron, which brought forth your fathers out of Egypt, and made them dwell in this place. ⁹And when they forgat the Lord their God, he sold them into the hand of Sisera, captain of the host of Hazor, and into the hand of the Philistines, and into the hand of the king of Moab, and they fought against them. ¹⁰And they cried unto the Lord, and said, "We have sinned, because we have forsaken the Lord, and have served Baalim and Ashtaroth, but now deliver us out of the hand of our enemies, and we will serve thee." ¹¹And the Lord sent Jerubbaal, and Bedan, and Jephthah, and Samuel, and delivered you out of the hand of your enemies on every side, and ye dwelled safe. ¹²And when ye saw that Nahash the king of the children of Ammon came against you, ye said unto me, "Nay; but a king shall reign over us", when the Lord your

God was your king. [13] Now therefore behold the king whom ye have chosen, and whom ye have desired! And, behold, the Lord hath set a king over you. [14] If ye will fear the Lord, and serve him, and obey his voice, and not rebel against the commandment of the Lord, then shall both ye and also the king that reigneth over you continue following the Lord your God. [15] But if ye will not obey the voice of the Lord, but rebel against the commandment of the Lord, then shall the hand of the Lord be against you, as it was against your fathers.

[16] Now therefore stand and see this great thing, which the Lord will do before your eyes. [17] Is it not wheat harvest to day? I will call unto the Lord, and he shall send thunder and rain; that ye may perceive and see that your wickedness is great, which ye have done in the sight of the Lord, in asking you a king.' [18] So Samuel called unto the Lord; and the Lord sent thunder and rain that day: and all the people greatly feared the Lord and Samuel. [19] And all the people said unto Samuel, 'Pray for thy servants unto the Lord thy God, that we die not, for we have added unto all our sins this evil, to ask us a king.'

[20] And Samuel said unto the people, 'Fear not: ye have done all this wickedness; yet turn not aside from following the Lord, but serve the Lord with all your heart; [21] and turn ye not aside, for then should ye go after vain things, which cannot profit nor deliver; for they are vain. [22] For the Lord will not forsake his people for his great name's sake, because it hath pleased the Lord to make you his people. [23] Moreover

as for me, God forbid that I should sin against the Lord in ceasing to pray for you, but I will teach you the good and the right way. ²⁴ Only fear the Lord, and serve him in truth with all your heart, for consider how great things he hath done for you. ²⁵ But if ye shall still do wickedly, ye shall be consumed, both ye and your king.'

13 Saul reigned one year; and when he had reigned two years over Israel, ² Saul chose him three thousand men of Israel; whereof two thousand were with Saul in Michmash and in mount Bethel, and a thousand were with Jonathan in Gibeah of Benjamin: and the rest of the people he sent every man to his tent. ³ And Jonathan smote the garrison of the Philistines that was in Geba, and the Philistines heard of it. And Saul blew the trumpet throughout all the land, saying, 'Let the Hebrews hear.' ⁴ And all Israel heard say that Saul had smitten a garrison of the Philistines, and that Israel also was had in abomination with the Philistines. And the people were called together after Saul to Gilgal.

⁵ And the Philistines gathered themselves together to fight with Israel, thirty thousand chariots, and six thousand horsemen, and people as the sand which is on the sea shore in multitude: and they came up, and pitched in Michmash, eastward from Beth-aven. ⁶ When the men of Israel saw that they were in a strait (for the people were distressed), then the people did hide themselves in caves, and in thickets, and in rocks, and in high places, and in pits. ⁷ And some of the Hebrews went over Jordan to the land of Gad and Gilead.

As for Saul, he was yet in Gilgal, and all the people followed him trembling.

⁸And he tarried seven days, according to the set time that Samuel had appointed, but Samuel came not to Gilgal; and the people were scattered from him. ⁹And Saul said, 'Bring hither a burnt offering to me, and peace offerings.' And he offered the burnt offering. ¹⁰And it came to pass, that as soon as he had made an end of offering the burnt offering, behold, Samuel came; and Saul went out to meet him, that he might salute him.

¹¹And Samuel said, 'What hast thou done?' And Saul said, 'Because I saw that the people were scattered from me, and that thou camest not within the days appointed, and that the Philistines gathered themselves together at Michmash; ¹²therefore said I, "The Philistines will come down now upon me to Gilgal, and I have not made supplication unto the Lord": I forced myself therefore, and offered a burnt offering.' ¹³And Samuel said to Saul, 'Thou hast done foolishly: thou hast not kept the commandment of the Lord thy God, which he commanded thee; for now would the Lord have established thy kingdom upon Israel for ever. ¹⁴But now thy kingdom shall not continue: the Lord hath sought him a man after his own heart, and the Lord hath commanded him to be captain over his people, because thou hast not kept that which the Lord commanded thee.' ¹⁵And Samuel arose, and gat him up from Gilgal unto Gibeah of Benjamin. And Saul numbered the people that were present with him, about six hundred men. ¹⁶And Saul, and Jonathan

his son, and the people that were present with them, abode in Gibeah of Benjamin, but the Philistines encamped in Michmash.

¹⁷And the spoilers came out of the camp of the Philistines in three companies: one company turned unto the way that leadeth to Ophrah, unto the land of Shual: ¹⁸and another company turned the way to Beth-horon: and another company turned to the way of the border that looketh to the valley of Zeboim toward the wilderness.

¹⁹Now there was no smith found throughout all the land of Israel, for the Philistines said, 'Lest the Hebrews make them swords or spears.' ²⁰But all the Israelites went down to the Philistines, to sharpen every man his share, and his coulter, and his axe, and his mattock. ²¹Yet they had a file for the mattocks, and for the coulters, and for the forks, and for the axes, and to sharpen the goads. ²²So it came to pass in the day of battle, that there was neither sword nor spear found in the hand of any of the people that were with Saul and Jonathan, but with Saul and with Jonathan his son was there found. ²³And the garrison of the Philistines went out to the passage of Michmash.

14 Now it came to pass upon a day, that Jonathan the son of Saul said unto the young man that bare his armour, 'Come, and let us go over to the Philistines' garrison, that is on the other side.' But he told not his father. ²And Saul tarried in the uttermost part of Gibeah under a pomegranate tree which is in Migron: and the people that were with him

were about six hundred men; ³and Ahiah, the son of Ahitub, I-chabod's brother, the son of Phinehas, the son of Eli, the Lord's priest in Shiloh, wearing an ephod. And the people knew not that Jonathan was gone.

⁴And between the passages, by which Jonathan sought to go over unto the Philistines' garrison, there was a sharp rock on the one side, and a sharp rock on the other side: and the name of the one was Bozez, and the name of the other Seneh. ⁵The forefront of the one was situate northward over against Michmash, and the other southward over against Gibeah. ⁶And Jonathan said to the young man that bare his armour, 'Come, and let us go over unto the garrison of these uncircumcised: it may be that the Lord will work for us; for there is no restraint to the Lord to save by many or by few.' ⁷And his armourbearer said unto him, 'Do all that is in thine heart: turn thee; behold, I am with thee according to thy heart.' ⁸Then said Jonathan, 'Behold, we will pass over unto these men, and we will discover ourselves unto them. ⁹If they say thus unto us, "Tarry until we come to you," then we will stand still in our place, and will not go up unto them. ¹⁰But if they say thus, "Come up unto us"; then we will go up; for the Lord hath delivered them into our hand: and this shall be a sign unto us.' ¹¹And both of them discovered themselves unto the garrison of the Philistines: and the Philistines said, 'Behold, the Hebrews come forth out of the holes where they had hid themselves.' ¹²And the men of the garrison answered Jonathan and his armourbearer, and said, 'Come up to us, and we will shew you a thing.' And Jonathan said unto his

armourbearer, 'Come up after me, for the Lord hath delivered them into the hand of Israel.' ¹³And Jonathan climbed up upon his hands and upon his feet, and his armourbearer after him: and they fell before Jonathan; and his armourbearer slew after him. ¹⁴And that first slaughter, which Jonathan and his armourbearer made, was about twenty men, within as it were an half acre of land, which a yoke of oxen might plow. ¹⁵And there was trembling in the host, in the field, and among all the people: the garrison, and the spoilers, they also trembled, and the earth quaked; so it was a very great trembling. ¹⁶And the watchmen of Saul in Gibeah of Benjamin looked; and, behold, the multitude melted away, and they went on beating down one another. ¹⁷Then said Saul unto the people that were with him, 'Number now, and see who is gone from us.' And when they had numbered, behold, Jonathan and his armourbearer were not there. ¹⁸And Saul said unto Ahiah, 'Bring hither the ark of God.' For the ark of God was at that time with the children of Israel.

¹⁹And it came to pass, while Saul talked unto the priest, that the noise that was in the host of the Philistines went on and increased: and Saul said unto the priest, 'Withdraw thine hand.' ²⁰And Saul and all the people that were with him assembled themselves, and they came to the battle: and, behold, every man's sword was against his fellow, and there was a very great discomfiture. ²¹Moreover the Hebrews that were with the Philistines before that time, which went up with them into the camp from the country round about,

even they also turned to be with the Israelites that were with Saul and Jonathan. ²² Likewise all the men of Israel which had hid themselves in mount Ephraim, when they heard that the Philistines fled, even they also followed hard after them in the battle. ²³ So the Lord saved Israel that day: and the battle passed over unto Bethaven.

²⁴And the men of Israel were distressed that day, for Saul had adjured the people, saying, 'Cursed be the man that eateth any food until evening, that I may be avenged on mine enemies.' So none of the people tasted any food. ²⁵And all they of the land came to a wood; and there was honey upon the ground. ²⁶And when the people were come into the wood, behold, the honey dropped; but no man put his hand to his mouth: for the people feared the oath. ²⁷ But Jonathan heard not when his father charged the people with the oath: wherefore he put forth the end of the rod that was in his hand, and dipped it in an honeycomb, and put his hand to his mouth; and his eyes were enlightened. ²⁸ Then answered one of the people, and said, 'Thy father straitly charged the people with an oath, saying, "Cursed be the man that eateth any food this day." And the people were faint.' ²⁹ Then said Jonathan, 'My father hath troubled the land: see, I pray you, how mine eyes have been enlightened, because I tasted a little of this honey. ³⁰ How much more, if haply the people had eaten freely to day of the spoil of their enemies which they found? For had there not been now a much greater slaughter among the Philistines?' ³¹And they smote the Philistines that day from Michmash to Aijalon: and the people were very

faint. ³²And the people flew upon the spoil, and took sheep, and oxen, and calves, and slew them on the ground: and the people did eat them with the blood.

³³ Then they told Saul, saying, 'Behold, the people sin against the Lord, in that they eat with the blood.' And he said, 'Ye have transgressed: roll a great stone unto me this day.' ³⁴And Saul said, 'Disperse yourselves among the people, and say unto them, "Bring me hither every man his ox, and every man his sheep, and slay them here, and eat; and sin not against the Lord in eating with the blood."' And all the people brought every man his ox with him that night, and slew them there. ³⁵And Saul built an altar unto the Lord: the same was the first altar that he built unto the Lord.

³⁶And Saul said, 'Let us go down after the Philistines by night, and spoil them until the morning light, and let us not leave a man of them.' And they said, 'Do whatsoever seemeth good unto thee.' Then said the priest, 'Let us draw near hither unto God.' ³⁷And Saul asked counsel of God, 'Shall I go down after the Philistines? Wilt thou deliver them into the hand of Israel?' But he answered him not that day. ³⁸And Saul said, 'Draw ye near hither, all the chief of the people: and know and see wherein this sin hath been this day.' ³⁹ For, as the Lord liveth, which saveth Israel, though it be in Jonathan my son, he shall surely die. But there was not a man among all the people that answered him. ⁴⁰Then said he unto all Israel, 'Be ye on one side, and I and Jonathan my son will be on the other side.' And the people said unto Saul, 'Do what seemeth good unto thee.' ⁴¹Therefore Saul said unto the

Lord God of Israel, 'Give a perfect lot.' And Saul and Jonathan were taken: but the people escaped. ⁴²And Saul said, 'Cast lots between me and Jonathan my son.' And Jonathan was taken. ⁴³Then Saul said to Jonathan, 'Tell me what thou hast done.' And Jonathan told him, and said, 'I did but taste a little honey with the end of the rod that was in mine hand, and, lo, I must die.' ⁴⁴And Saul answered, 'God do so and more also, for thou shalt surely die, Jonathan.' ⁴⁵And the people said unto Saul, 'Shall Jonathan die, who hath wrought this great salvation in Israel? God forbid: as the Lord liveth, there shall not one hair of his head fall to the ground; for he hath wrought with God this day.' So the people rescued Jonathan, that he died not. ⁴⁶Then Saul went up from following the Philistines: and the Philistines went to their own place.

⁴⁷So Saul took the kingdom over Israel, and fought against all his enemies on every side, against Moab, and against the children of Ammon, and against Edom, and against the kings of Zobah, and against the Philistines: and whithersoever he turned himself, he vexed them. ⁴⁸And he gathered an host, and smote the Amalekites, and delivered Israel out of the hands of them that spoiled them. ⁴⁹Now the sons of Saul were Jonathan, and Ishui, and Melchi-shua: and the names of his two daughters were these; the name of the firstborn Merab, and the name of the younger Michal. ⁵⁰And the name of Saul's wife was Ahinoam, the daughter of Ahimaaz; and the name of the captain of his host was Abner, the son of Ner, Saul's uncle. ⁵¹And Kish was the father of Saul; and Ner

the father of Abner was the son of Abiel. ⁵²And there was sore war against the Philistines all the days of Saul; and when Saul saw any strong man, or any valiant man, he took him unto him.

15 Samuel also said unto Saul, 'The Lord sent me to anoint thee to be king over his people, over Israel: now therefore hearken thou unto the voice of the words of the Lord. ²Thus saith the Lord of hosts, "I remember that which Amalek did to Israel, how he laid wait for him in the way, when he came up from Egypt. ³Now go and smite Amalek, and utterly destroy all that they have, and spare them not; but slay both man and woman, infant and suckling, ox and sheep, camel and ass."' ⁴And Saul gathered the people together, and numbered them in Telaim, two hundred thousand footmen, and ten thousand men of Judah. ⁵And Saul came to a city of Amalek, and laid wait in the valley.

⁶And Saul said unto the Kenites, 'Go, depart, get you down from among the Amalekites, lest I destroy you with them, for ye shewed kindness to all the children of Israel, when they came up out of Egypt.' So the Kenites departed from among the Amalekites. ⁷And Saul smote the Amalekites from Havilah until thou comest to Shur, that is over against Egypt. ⁸And he took Agag the king of the Amalekites alive, and utterly destroyed all the people with the edge of the sword. ⁹But Saul and the people spared Agag, and the best of the sheep, and of the oxen, and of the fatlings, and the lambs, and all that was good, and would

not utterly destroy them; but every thing that was vile and refuse, that they destroyed utterly.

¹⁰ Then came the word of the Lord unto Samuel, saying, ¹¹ 'It repenteth me that I have set up Saul to be king, for he is turned back from following me, and hath not performed my commandments.' And it grieved Samuel; and he cried unto the Lord all night. ¹²And when Samuel rose early to meet Saul in the morning, it was told Samuel, saying, 'Saul came to Carmel, and, behold, he set him up a place, and is gone about, and passed on, and gone down to Gilgal.' ¹³And Samuel came to Saul; and Saul said unto him, 'Blessed be thou of the Lord: I have performed the commandment of the Lord.' ¹⁴And Samuel said, 'What meaneth then this bleating of the sheep in mine ears, and the lowing of the oxen which I hear?' ¹⁵And Saul said, 'They have brought them from the Amalekites, for the people spared the best of the sheep and of the oxen, to sacrifice unto the Lord thy God; and the rest we have utterly destroyed.' ¹⁶Then Samuel said unto Saul, 'Stay, and I will tell thee what the Lord hath said to me this night.' And he said unto him, 'Say on.' ¹⁷And Samuel said, 'When thou wast little in thine own sight, wast thou not made the head of the tribes of Israel, and the Lord anointed thee king over Israel? ¹⁸And the Lord sent thee on a journey, and said, "Go and utterly destroy the sinners the Amalekites, and fight against them until they be consumed." ¹⁹Wherefore then didst thou not obey the voice of the Lord, but didst fly upon the spoil, and didst evil in the sight of the Lord?' ²⁰And Saul said unto Samuel, 'Yea, I have obeyed

the voice of the Lord, and have gone the way which the Lord sent me, and have brought Agag the king of Amalek, and have utterly destroyed the Amalekites. ²¹ But the people took of the spoil, sheep and oxen, the chief of the things which should have been utterly destroyed, to sacrifice unto the Lord thy God in Gilgal.' ²²And Samuel said, 'Hath the Lord as great delight in burnt offerings and sacrifices, as in obeying the voice of the Lord? Behold, to obey is better than sacrifice, and to hearken than the fat of rams. ²³ For rebellion is as the sin of witchcraft, and stubbornness is as iniquity and idolatry. Because thou hast rejected the word of the Lord, he hath also rejected thee from being king.'

²⁴And Saul said unto Samuel, 'I have sinned, for I have transgressed the commandment of the Lord, and thy words, because I feared the people, and obeyed their voice. ²⁵ Now therefore, I pray thee, pardon my sin, and turn again with me, that I may worship the Lord.' ²⁶And Samuel said unto Saul, 'I will not return with thee, for thou hast rejected the word of the Lord, and the Lord hath rejected thee from being king over Israel.' ²⁷And as Samuel turned about to go away, he laid hold upon the skirt of his mantle, and it rent. ²⁸And Samuel said unto him, 'The Lord hath rent the kingdom of Israel from thee this day, and hath given it to a neighbour of thine, that is better than thou. ²⁹And also the Strength of Israel will not lie nor repent, for he is not a man, that he should repent.' ³⁰ Then he said, 'I have sinned: yet honour me now, I pray thee, before the elders of my people, and before Israel, and turn again with me, that I may worship the Lord

thy God.' ³¹ So Samuel turned again after Saul; and Saul worshipped the Lord.

³² Then said Samuel, 'Bring ye hither to me Agag the king of the Amalekites.' And Agag came unto him delicately. And Agag said, 'Surely the bitterness of death is past.' ³³ And Samuel said, 'As thy sword hath made women childless, so shall thy mother be childless among women.' And Samuel hewed Agag in pieces before the Lord in Gilgal.

³⁴ Then Samuel went to Ramah; and Saul went up to his house to Gibeah of Saul. ³⁵ And Samuel came no more to see Saul until the day of his death: nevertheless Samuel mourned for Saul; and the Lord repented that he had made Saul king over Israel.

16 And the Lord said unto Samuel, 'How long wilt thou mourn for Saul, seeing I have rejected him from reigning over Israel? Fill thine horn with oil, and go, I will send thee to Jesse the Beth-lehemite; for I have provided me a king among his sons.' ² And Samuel said, 'How can I go? If Saul hear it, he will kill me.' And the Lord said, 'Take an heifer with thee, and say, "I am come to sacrifice to the Lord." ³ And call Jesse to the sacrifice, and I will shew thee what thou shalt do: and thou shalt anoint unto me him whom I name unto thee.' ⁴ And Samuel did that which the Lord spake, and came to Beth-lehem. And the elders of the town trembled at his coming, and said, 'Comest thou peaceably?' ⁵ And he said, 'Peaceably: I am come to sacrifice unto the Lord: sanctify yourselves, and come with me to the sacri-

fice.' And he sanctified Jesse and his sons, and called them to the sacrifice.

⁶And it came to pass, when they were come, that he looked on Eliab, and said, 'Surely the Lord's anointed is before him.' ⁷But the Lord said unto Samuel, 'Look not on his countenance, or on the height of his stature; because I have refused him; for the Lord seeth not as man seeth; for man looketh on the outward appearance, but the Lord looketh on the heart. ⁸Then Jesse called Abinadab, and made him pass before Samuel. And he said, 'Neither hath the Lord chosen this.' ⁹Then Jesse made Shammah to pass by. And he said, 'Neither hath the Lord chosen this.' ¹⁰Again, Jesse made seven of his sons to pass before Samuel. And Samuel said unto Jesse, 'The Lord hath not chosen these.' ¹¹And Samuel said unto Jesse, 'Are here all thy children?' And he said, 'There remaineth yet the youngest, and, behold, he keepeth the sheep.' And Samuel said unto Jesse, 'Send and fetch him, for we will not sit down till he come hither.' ¹²And he sent, and brought him in. Now he was ruddy, and withal of a beautiful countenance, and goodly to look to. And the Lord said, 'Arise, anoint him, for this is he.' ¹³Then Samuel took the horn of oil, and anointed him in the midst of his brethren: and the Spirit of the Lord came upon David from that day forward. So Samuel rose up, and went to Ramah.

¹⁴But the Spirit of the Lord departed from Saul, and an evil spirit from the Lord troubled him. ¹⁵And Saul's servants said unto him, 'Behold now, an evil spirit from God

troubleth thee. ¹⁶ Let our lord now command thy servants, which are before thee, to seek out a man, who is a cunning player on an harp: and it shall come to pass, when the evil spirit from God is upon thee, that he shall play with his hand, and thou shalt be well.' ¹⁷And Saul said unto his servants, 'Provide me now a man that can play well, and bring him to me.' ¹⁸ Then answered one of the servants, and said, 'Behold, I have seen a son of Jesse the Beth-lehemite, that is cunning in playing, and a mighty valiant man, and a man of war, and prudent in matters, and a comely person, and the Lord is with him.'

¹⁹ Wherefore Saul sent messengers unto Jesse, and said, 'Send me David thy son, which is with the sheep.' ²⁰And Jesse took an ass laden with bread, and a bottle of wine, and a kid, and sent them by David his son unto Saul. ²¹And David came to Saul, and stood before him; and he loved him greatly; and he became his armourbearer. ²²And Saul sent to Jesse, saying, 'Let David, I pray thee, stand before me; for he hath found favour in my sight.' ²³And it came to pass, when the evil spirit from God was upon Saul, that David took an harp, and played with his hand: so Saul was refreshed, and was well, and the evil spirit departed from him.

17 Now the Philistines gathered together their armies to battle, and were gathered together at Shochoh, which belongeth to Judah, and pitched between Shochoh and Azekah, in Ephes-dammim. ²And Saul and the men of Israel were gathered together, and pitched by the valley of Elah,

and set the battle in array against the Philistines. ³And the Philistines stood on a mountain on the one side, and Israel stood on a mountain on the other side: and there was a valley between them.

⁴And there went out a champion out of the camp of the Philistines, named Goliath, of Gath, whose height was six cubits and a span. ⁵And he had an helmet of brass upon his head, and he was armed with a coat of mail; and the weight of the coat was five thousand shekels of brass. ⁶And he had greaves of brass upon his legs, and a target of brass between his shoulders. ⁷And the staff of his spear was like a weaver's beam; and his spear's head weighed six hundred shekels of iron; and one bearing a shield went before him. ⁸And he stood and cried unto the armies of Israel, and said unto them, 'Why are ye come out to set your battle in array? Am not I a Philistine, and ye servants to Saul? Choose you a man for you, and let him come down to me. ⁹If he be able to fight with me, and to kill me, then will we be your servants; but if I prevail against him, and kill him, then shall ye be our servants, and serve us.' ¹⁰And the Philistine said, 'I defy the armies of Israel this day; give me a man, that we may fight together.' ¹¹When Saul and all Israel heard those words of the Philistine, they were dismayed, and greatly afraid.

¹²Now David was the son of that Ephrathite of Beth-lehem-judah, whose name was Jesse; and he had eight sons; and the man went among men for an old man in the days of Saul. ¹³And the three eldest sons of Jesse went and followed Saul to the battle: and the names of his three sons that went

to the battle were Eliab the first-born, and next unto him Abinadab, and the third Shammah. ¹⁴And David was the youngest: and the three eldest followed Saul. ¹⁵But David went and returned from Saul to feed his father's sheep at Bethlehem. ¹⁶And the Philistine drew near morning and evening, and presented himself forty days. ¹⁷And Jesse said unto David his son, 'Take now for thy brethren an ephah of this parched corn, and these ten loaves, and run to the camp to thy brethren; ¹⁸and carry these ten cheeses unto the captain of their thousand, and look how thy brethren fare, and take their pledge.' ¹⁹Now Saul, and they, and all the men of Israel, were in the valley of Elah, fighting with the Philistines.

²⁰And David rose up early in the morning, and left the sheep with a keeper, and took, and went, as Jesse had commanded him; and he came to the trench, as the host was going forth to the fight, and shouted for the battle. ²¹For Israel and the Philistines had put the battle in array, army against army. ²²And David left his carriage in the hand of the keeper of the carriage, and ran into the army, and came and saluted his brethren. ²³And as he talked with them, behold, there came up the champion, the Philistine of Gath, Goliath by name, out of the armies of the Philistines, and spake according to the same words: and David heard them. ²⁴And all the men of Israel, when they saw the man, fled from him, and were sore afraid. ²⁵And the men of Israel said, 'Have ye seen this man that is come up? Surely to defy Israel is he come up: and it shall be, that the man who killeth him, the king will enrich him with great riches, and will give him his

daughter, and make his father's house free in Israel.' ²⁶And David spake to the men that stood by him, saying, 'What shall be done to the man that killeth this Philistine, and taketh away the reproach from Israel? For who is this uncircumcised Philistine, that he should defy the armies of the living God?' ²⁷And the people answered him after this manner, saying, 'So shall it be done to the man that killeth him.'

²⁸And Eliab his eldest brother heard when he spake unto the men; and Eliab's anger was kindled against David, and he said, 'Why camest thou down hither? And with whom hast thou left those few sheep in the wilderness? I know thy pride, and the naughtiness of thine heart; for thou art come down that thou mightest see the battle.' ²⁹And David said, 'What have I now done? Is there not a cause?'

³⁰And he turned from him toward another, and spake after the same manner; and the people answered him again after the former manner. ³¹And when the words were heard which David spake, they rehearsed them before Saul: and he sent for him.

³²And David said to Saul, 'Let no man's heart fail because of him; thy servant will go and fight with this Philistine.' ³³And Saul said to David, 'Thou art not able to go against this Philistine to fight with him, for thou art but a youth, and he a man of war from his youth.' ³⁴And David said unto Saul, 'Thy servant kept his father's sheep, and there came a lion, and a bear, and took a lamb out of the flock. ³⁵And I went out after him, and smote him, and delivered it out of his mouth: and when he arose against me, I caught him by

his beard, and smote him, and slew him. ³⁶ Thy servant slew both the lion and the bear: and this uncircumcised Philistine shall be as one of them, seeing he hath defied the armies of the living God.' ³⁷ David said moreover, 'The Lord that delivered me out of the paw of the lion, and out of the paw of the bear, he will deliver me out of the hand of this Philistine.' And Saul said unto David, 'Go, and the Lord be with thee.'

³⁸And Saul armed David with his armour, and he put an helmet of brass upon his head; also he armed him with a coat of mail. ³⁹And David girded his sword upon his armour, and he assayed to go; for he had not proved it. And David said unto Saul, 'I cannot go with these; for I have not proved them.' And David put them off him. ⁴⁰And he took his staff in his hand, and chose him five smooth stones out of the brook, and put them in a shepherd's bag which he had, even in a scrip; and his sling was in his hand; and he drew near to the Philistine. ⁴¹And the Philistine came on and drew near unto David; and the man that bare the shield went before him. ⁴²And when the Philistine looked about, and saw David, he disdained him; for he was but a youth, and ruddy, and of a fair countenance. ⁴³And the Philistine said unto David, 'Am I a dog, that thou comest to me with staves?' And the Philistine cursed David by his gods. ⁴⁴And the Philistine said to David, 'Come to me, and I will give thy flesh unto the fowls of the air, and to the beasts of the field.' ⁴⁵Then said David to the Philistine, 'Thou comest to me with a sword, and with a spear, and with a shield, but I come to thee in the name of the Lord of hosts, the God of the armies

of Israel, whom thou hast defied. ⁴⁶ This day will the Lord deliver thee into mine hand; and I will smite thee, and take thine head from thee; and I will give the carcases of the host of the Philistines this day unto the fowls of the air, and to the wild beasts of the earth; that all the earth may know that there is a God in Israel. ⁴⁷And all this assembly shall know that the Lord saveth not with sword and spear, for the battle is the Lord's, and he will give you into our hands.' ⁴⁸And it came to pass, when the Philistine arose, and came and drew nigh to meet David, that David hasted, and ran toward the army to meet the Philistine. ⁴⁹And David put his hand in his bag, and took thence a stone, and slang it, and smote the Philistine in his forehead, that the stone sunk into his forehead; and he fell upon his face to the earth. ⁵⁰ So David prevailed over the Philistine with a sling and with a stone, and smote the Philistine, and slew him; but there was no sword in the hand of David. ⁵¹Therefore David ran, and stood upon the Philistine, and took his sword, and drew it out of the sheath thereof, and slew him, and cut off his head therewith. And when the Philistines saw their champion was dead, they fled. ⁵²And the men of Israel and of Judah arose, and shouted, and pursued the Philistines, until thou come to the valley, and to the gates of Ekron. And the wounded of the Philistines fell down by the way to Shaaraim, even unto Gath, and unto Ekron. ⁵³And the children of Israel returned from chasing after the Philistines, and they spoiled their tents. ⁵⁴And David took the head of the Philistine, and brought it to Jerusalem; but he put his armour in his tent.

⁵⁵And when Saul saw David go forth against the Philistine, he said unto Abner, the captain of the host, 'Abner, whose son is this youth?' And Abner said, 'As thy soul liveth, O king, I cannot tell.' ⁵⁶And the king said, 'Enquire thou whose son the stripling is.' ⁵⁷And as David returned from the slaughter of the Philistine, Abner took him, and brought him before Saul with the head of the Philistine in his hand. ⁵⁸And Saul said to him, 'Whose son art thou, thou young man?' And David answered, 'I am the son of thy servant Jesse the Beth-lehemite.'

18 And it came to pass, when he had made an end of speaking unto Saul, that the soul of Jonathan was knit with the soul of David, and Jonathan loved him as his own soul. ²And Saul took him that day, and would let him go no more home to his father's house. ³Then Jonathan and David made a covenant, because he loved him as his own soul. ⁴And Jonathan stripped himself of the robe that was upon him, and gave it to David, and his garments, even to his sword, and to his bow, and to his girdle.

⁵And David went out whithersoever Saul sent him, and behaved himself wisely; and Saul set him over the men of war, and he was accepted in the sight of all the people, and also in the sight of Saul's servants. ⁶And it came to pass as they came, when David was returned from the slaughter of the Philistine, that the women came out of all cities of Israel, singing and dancing, to meet king Saul, with tabrets, with joy, and with instruments of musick. ⁷And the women

answered one another as they played, and said, 'Saul hath slain his thousands, and David his ten thousands.' ⁸And Saul was very wroth, and the saying displeased him; and he said, 'They have ascribed unto David ten thousands, and to me they have ascribed but thousands: and what can he have more but the kingdom?' ⁹And Saul eyed David from that day and forward.

¹⁰And it came to pass on the morrow, that the evil spirit from God came upon Saul, and he prophesied in the midst of the house: and David played with his hand, as at other times: and there was a javelin in Saul's hand. ¹¹And Saul cast the javelin; for he said, 'I will smite David even to the wall with it.' And David avoided out of his presence twice.

¹²And Saul was afraid of David, because the Lord was with him, and was departed from Saul. ¹³Therefore Saul removed him from him, and made him his captain over a thousand; and he went out and came in before the people. ¹⁴And David behaved himself wisely in all his ways; and the Lord was with him. ¹⁵Wherefore when Saul saw that he behaved himself very wisely, he was afraid of him. ¹⁶But all Israel and Judah loved David, because he went out and came in before them.

¹⁷And Saul said to David, 'Behold my elder daughter Merab, her will I give thee to wife: only be thou valiant for me, and fight the Lord's battles.' For Saul said, 'Let not mine hand be upon him, but let the hand of the Philistines be upon him.' ¹⁸And David said unto Saul, 'Who am I? And what is my life, or my father's family in Israel, that I should

be son in law to the king?' ¹⁹ But it came to pass at the time when Merab Saul's daughter should have been given to David, that she was given unto Adriel the Meholathite to wife. ²⁰And Michal Saul's daughter loved David: and they told Saul, and the thing pleased him. ²¹And Saul said, 'I will give him her, that she may be a snare to him, and that the hand of the Philistines may be against him.' Wherefore Saul said to David, 'Thou shalt this day be my son in law in the one of the twain.'

²²And Saul commanded his servants, saying, 'Commune with David secretly, and say, "Behold, the king hath delight in thee, and all his servants love thee: now therefore be the king's son in law."' ²³And Saul's servants spake those words in the ears of David. And David said, 'Seemeth it to you a light thing to be a king's son in law, seeing that I am a poor man, and lightly esteemed?' ²⁴And the servants of Saul told him, saying, 'On this manner spake David.' ²⁵And Saul said, 'Thus shall ye say to David, "The king desireth not any dowry, but an hundred foreskins of the Philistines, to be avenged of the king's enemies."' But Saul thought to make David fall by the hand of the Philistines. ²⁶And when his servants told David these words, it pleased David well to be the king's son in law: and the days were not expired. ²⁷ Wherefore David arose and went, he and his men, and slew of the Philistines two hundred men; and David brought their foreskins, and they gave them in full tale to the king, that he might be the king's son in law. And Saul gave him Michal his daughter to wife.

²⁸And Saul saw and knew that the Lord was with David, and that Michal Saul's daughter loved him. ²⁹And Saul was yet the more afraid of David; and Saul became David's enemy continually. ³⁰Then the princes of the Philistines went forth: and it came to pass, after they went forth, that David behaved himself more wisely than all the servants of Saul; so that his name was much set by.

19 And Saul spake to Jonathan his son, and to all his servants, that they should kill David. ²But Jonathan Saul's son delighted much in David: and Jonathan told David, saying, 'Saul my father seeketh to kill thee: now therefore, I pray thee, take heed to thyself until the morning, and abide in a secret place, and hide thyself. ³And I will go out and stand beside my father in the field where thou art, and I will commune with my father of thee; and what I see, that I will tell thee.'

⁴And Jonathan spake good of David unto Saul his father, and said unto him, 'Let not the king sin against his servant, against David; because he hath not sinned against thee, and because his works have been to thee-ward very good; ⁵for he did put his life in his hand, and slew the Philistine, and the Lord wrought a great salvation for all Israel. Thou sawest it, and didst rejoice: wherefore then wilt thou sin against innocent blood, to slay David without a cause?' ⁶And Saul hearkened unto the voice of Jonathan: and Saul sware, 'As the Lord liveth, he shall not be slain.' ⁷And Jonathan called David, and Jonathan shewed him all those things.

And Jonathan brought David to Saul, and he was in his presence, as in times past.

⁸And there was war again: and David went out, and fought with the Philistines, and slew them with a great slaughter; and they fled from him. ⁹And the evil spirit from the Lord was upon Saul, as he sat in his house with his javelin in his hand: and David played with his hand. ¹⁰And Saul sought to smite David even to the wall with the javelin; but he slipped away out of Saul's presence, and he smote the javelin into the wall: and David fled, and escaped that night. ¹¹Saul also sent messengers unto David's house, to watch him, and to slay him in the morning: and Michal David's wife told him, saying, 'If thou save not thy life to night, to morrow thou shalt be slain.'

¹²So Michal let David down through a window: and he went, and fled, and escaped. ¹³And Michal took an image, and laid it in the bed, and put a pillow of goats' hair for his bolster, and covered it with a cloth. ¹⁴And when Saul sent messengers to take David, she said, 'He is sick.' ¹⁵And Saul sent the messengers again to see David, saying, 'Bring him up to me in the bed, that I may slay him.' ¹⁶And when the messengers were come in, behold, there was an image in the bed, with a pillow of goats' hair for his bolster. ¹⁷And Saul said unto Michal, 'Why hast thou deceived me so, and sent away mine enemy, that he is escaped?' And Michal answered Saul, 'He said unto me, "Let me go; why should I kill thee?"'

¹⁸So David fled, and escaped, and came to Samuel to

Ramah, and told him all that Saul had done to him. And he and Samuel went and dwelt in Naioth. ¹⁹And it was told Saul, saying, 'Behold, David is at Naioth in Ramah.' ²⁰And Saul sent messengers to take David: and when they saw the company of the prophets prophesying, and Samuel standing as appointed over them, the Spirit of God was upon the messengers of Saul, and they also prophesied. ²¹And when it was told Saul, he sent other messengers, and they prophesied likewise. And Saul sent messengers again the third time, and they prophesied also. ²²Then went he also to Ramah, and came to a great well that is in Sechu: and he asked and said, 'Where are Samuel and David?' And one said, 'Behold, they be at Naioth in Ramah.' ²³And he went thither to Naioth in Ramah: and the Spirit of God was upon him also, and he went on, and prophesied, until he came to Naioth in Ramah. ²⁴And he stripped off his clothes also, and prophesied before Samuel in like manner, and lay down naked all that day and all that night. Wherefore they say, 'Is Saul also among the prophets?'

20 And David fled from Naioth in Ramah, and came and said before Jonathan, 'What have I done? What is mine iniquity? And what is my sin before thy father, that he seeketh my life?' ²And he said unto him, 'God forbid; thou shalt not die: behold, my father will do nothing either great or small, but that he will shew it me: and why should my father hide this thing from me? It is not so.' ³And David sware moreover, and said, 'Thy father certainly knoweth

that I have found grace in thine eyes; and he saith, "Let not Jonathan know this, lest he be grieved," but truly as the Lord liveth, and as thy soul liveth, there is but a step between me and death.' ⁴Then said Jonathan unto David, 'Whatsoever thy soul desireth, I will even do it for thee.' ⁵And David said unto Jonathan, 'Behold, to morrow is the new moon, and I should not fail to sit with the king at meat, but let me go, that I may hide myself in the field unto the third day at even. ⁶If thy father at all miss me, then say, "David earnestly asked leave of me that he might run to Beth-lehem his city, for there is a yearly sacrifice there for all the family." ⁷If he say thus, "It is well," thy servant shall have peace: but if he be very wroth, then be sure that evil is determined by him. ⁸Therefore thou shalt deal kindly with thy servant; for thou hast brought thy servant into a covenant of the Lord with thee: notwithstanding, if there be in me iniquity, slay me thyself; for why shouldest thou bring me to thy father?' ⁹And Jonathan said, 'Far be it from thee, for if I knew certainly that evil were determined by my father to come upon thee, then would not I tell it thee? ¹⁰Then said David to Jonathan, 'Who shall tell me? Or what if thy father answer thee roughly?'

¹¹And Jonathan said unto David, 'Come, and let us go out into the field.' And they went out both of them into the field. ¹²And Jonathan said unto David, 'O Lord God of Israel, when I have sounded my father about to morrow any time, or the third day, and, behold, if there be good toward David, and I then send not unto thee, and shew it thee: ¹³the Lord do so and much more to Jonathan: but if it please my father to do

thee evil, then I will shew it thee, and send thee away, that thou mayest go in peace: and the Lord be with thee, as he hath been with my father. ¹⁴And thou shalt not only while yet I live shew me the kindness of the Lord, that I die not: ¹⁵but also thou shalt not cut off thy kindness from my house for ever: no, not when the Lord hath cut off the enemies of David every one from the face of the earth.' ¹⁶So Jonathan made a covenant with the house of David, saying, 'Let the Lord even require it at the hand of David's enemies.' ¹⁷And Jonathan caused David to swear again, because he loved him; for he loved him as he loved his own soul. ¹⁸Then Jonathan said to David, 'To morrow is the new moon: and thou shalt be missed, because thy seat will be empty. ¹⁹And when thou hast stayed three days, then thou shalt go down quickly, and come to the place where thou didst hide thyself when the business was in hand, and shalt remain by the stone Ezel. ²⁰And I will shoot three arrows on the side thereof, as though I shot at a mark. ²¹And, behold, I will send a lad, saying, "Go, find out the arrows." If I expressly say unto the lad, "Behold, the arrows are on this side of thee, take them"; then come thou: for there is peace to thee, and no hurt; as the Lord liveth. ²²But if I say thus unto the young man, "Behold, the arrows are beyond thee", go thy way; for the Lord hath sent thee away. ²³And as touching the matter which thou and I have spoken of, behold, the Lord be between thee and me for ever.'

²⁴So David hid himself in the field: and when the new moon was come, the king sat him down to eat meat. ²⁵And

the king sat upon his seat, as at other times, even upon a seat by the wall: and Jonathan arose, and Abner sat by Saul's side, and David's place was empty. ²⁶ Nevertheless Saul spake not any thing that day; for he thought, 'Something hath befallen him, he is not clean; surely he is not clean.' ²⁷ And it came to pass on the morrow, which was the second day of the month, that David's place was empty: and Saul said unto Jonathan his son, 'Wherefore cometh not the son of Jesse to meat, neither yesterday, nor to day?' ²⁸ And Jonathan answered Saul, 'David earnestly asked leave of me to go to Beth-lehem, ²⁹ and he said, "Let me go, I pray thee; for our family hath a sacrifice in the city; and my brother, he hath commanded me to be there: and now, if I have found favour in thine eyes, let me get away, I pray thee, and see my brethren." Therefore he cometh not unto the king's table.' ³⁰ Then Saul's anger was kindled against Jonathan, and he said unto him, 'Thou son of the perverse rebellious woman, do not I know that thou hast chosen the son of Jesse to thine own confusion, and unto the confusion of thy mother's nakedness? ³¹ For as long as the son of Jesse liveth upon the ground, thou shalt not be established, nor thy kingdom. Wherefore now send and fetch him unto me, for he shall surely die.' ³² And Jonathan answered Saul his father, and said unto him, 'Wherefore shall he be slain? What hath he done?' ³³ And Saul cast a javelin at him to smite him, whereby Jonathan knew that it was determined of his father to slay David. ³⁴ So Jonathan arose from the table in fierce anger, and did eat no meat the second day of the month, for he was grieved for David, because his father had done him shame.

³⁵And it came to pass in the morning, that Jonathan went out into the field at the time appointed with David, and a little lad with him. ³⁶And he said unto his lad, 'Run, find out now the arrows which I shoot.' And as the lad ran, he shot an arrow beyond him. ³⁷And when the lad was come to the place of the arrow which Jonathan had shot, Jonathan cried after the lad, and said, 'Is not the arrow beyond thee?' ³⁸And Jonathan cried after the lad, 'Make speed, haste, stay not.' And Jonathan's lad gathered up the arrows, and came to his master. ³⁹But the lad knew not any thing: only Jonathan and David knew the matter. ⁴⁰And Jonathan gave his artillery unto his lad, and said unto him, 'Go, carry them to the city.'

⁴¹And as soon as the lad was gone, David arose out of a place toward the south, and fell on his face to the ground, and bowed himself three times: and they kissed one another, and wept one with another, until David exceeded. ⁴²And Jonathan said to David, 'Go in peace, forasmuch as we have sworn both of us in the name of the Lord, saying, "The Lord be between me and thee, and between my seed and thy seed for ever."' And he arose and departed: and Jonathan went into the city.

21 Then came David to Nob to Ahimelech the priest: and Ahimelech was afraid at the meeting of David, and said unto him, 'Why art thou alone, and no man with thee?' ²And David said unto Ahimelech the priest, 'The king

hath commanded me a business, and hath said unto me, "Let no man know any thing of the business whereabout I send thee, and what I have commanded thee": and I have appointed my servants to such and such a place. ³Now therefore what is under thine hand? Give me five loaves of bread in mine hand, or what there is present.' ⁴And the priest answered David, and said, 'There is no common bread under mine hand, but there is hallowed bread; if the young men have kept themselves at least from women.' ⁵And David answered the priest, and said unto him, 'Of a truth women have been kept from us about these three days, since I came out, and the vessels of the young men are holy, and the bread is in a manner common, yea, though it were sanctified this day in the vessel.' ⁶So the priest gave him hallowed bread, for there was no bread there but the shew-bread, that was taken from before the Lord, to put hot bread in the day when it was taken away. ⁷Now a certain man of the servants of Saul was there that day, detained before the Lord; and his name was Doeg, an Edomite, the chiefest of the herdmen that belonged to Saul.

⁸And David said unto Ahimelech, 'And is there not here under thine hand spear or sword? For I have neither brought my sword nor my weapons with me, because the king's business required haste.' ⁹And the priest said, 'The sword of Goliath the Philistine, whom thou slewest in the valley of Elah, behold, it is here wrapped in a cloth behind the ephod: if thou wilt take that, take it; for there is no other save that here.' And David said, 'There is none like that; give it me.'

¹⁰And David arose, and fled that day for fear of Saul, and went to Achish the king of Gath. ¹¹And the servants of Achish said unto him, 'Is not this David the king of the land? Did they not sing one to another of him in dances, saying, "Saul hath slain his thousands, and David his ten thousands"?' ¹²And David laid up these words in his heart, and was sore afraid of Achish the king of Gath. ¹³And he changed his behaviour before them, and feigned himself mad in their hands, and scrabbled on the doors of the gate, and let his spittle fall down upon his beard. ¹⁴Then said Achish unto his servants, 'Lo, ye see the man is mad: wherefore then have ye brought him to me? ¹⁵Have I need of mad men, that ye have brought this fellow to play the mad man in my presence? Shall this fellow come into my house?'

22 David therefore departed thence, and escaped to the cave Adullam: and when his brethren and all his father's house heard it, they went down thither to him. ²And every one that was in distress, and every one that was in debt, and every one that was discontented, gathered themselves unto him; and he became a captain over them; and there were with him about four hundred men.

³And David went thence to Mizpeh of Moab: and he said unto the king of Moab, 'Let my father and my mother, I pray thee, come forth, and be with you, till I know what God will do for me.' ⁴And he brought them before the king of Moab: and they dwelt with him all the while that David was in the hold.

⁵And the prophet Gad said unto David, 'Abide not in the hold; depart, and get thee into the land of Judah.' Then David departed, and came into the forest of Hareth.

⁶When Saul heard that David was discovered, and the men that were with him (now Saul abode in Gibeah under a tree in Ramah, having his spear in his hand, and all his servants were standing about him); ⁷then Saul said unto his servants that stood about him, 'Hear now, ye Benjamites; will the son of Jesse give every one of you fields and vineyards, and make you all captains of thousands, and captains of hundreds; ⁸that all of you have conspired against me, and there is none that sheweth me that my son hath made a league with the son of Jesse, and there is none of you that is sorry for me, or sheweth unto me that my son hath stirred up my servant against me, to lie in wait, as at this day?'

⁹Then answered Doeg the Edomite, which was set over the servants of Saul, and said, 'I saw the son of Jesse coming to Nob, to Ahimelech the son of Ahitub.' ¹⁰And he enquired of the Lord for him, and gave him victuals, and gave him the sword of Goliath the Philistine. ¹¹Then the king sent to call Ahimelech the priest, the son of Ahitub, and all his father's house, the priests that were in Nob: and they came all of them to the king. ¹²And Saul said, 'Hear now, thou son of Ahitub.' And he answered, 'Here I am, my lord.' ¹³And Saul said unto him, 'Why have ye conspired against me, thou and the son of Jesse, in that thou hast given him bread, and a sword, and hast enquired of God for him, that he should rise against me, to lie in wait, as at this day?' ¹⁴Then Ahimelech

answered the king, and said, 'And who is so faithful among all thy servants as David, which is the king's son in law, and goeth at thy bidding, and is honourable in thine house? ¹⁵ Did I then begin to enquire of God for him? Be it far from me: let not the king impute any thing unto his servant, nor to all the house of my father; for thy servant knew nothing of all this, less or more.' ¹⁶And the king said, 'Thou shalt surely die, Ahimelech, thou, and all thy father's house.'

¹⁷And the king said unto the footmen that stood about him, 'Turn, and slay the priests of the Lord; because their hand also is with David, and because they knew when he fled, and did not shew it to me.' But the servants of the king would not put forth their hand to fall upon the priests of the Lord. ¹⁸And the king said to Doeg, 'Turn thou, and fall upon the priests.' And Doeg the Edomite turned, and he fell upon the priests, and slew on that day fourscore and five persons that did wear a linen ephod. ¹⁹And Nob, the city of the priests, smote he with the edge of the sword, both men and women, children and sucklings, and oxen, and asses, and sheep, with the edge of the sword.

²⁰And one of the sons of Ahimelech the son of Ahitub, named Abiathar, escaped, and fled after David. ²¹And Abiathar shewed David that Saul had slain the Lord's priests. ²²And David said unto Abiathar, 'I knew it that day, when Doeg the Edomite was there, that he would surely tell Saul: I have occasioned the death of all the persons of thy father's house. ²³Abide thou with me, fear not; for he that seeketh my life seeketh thy life; but with me thou shalt be in safeguard.'

23 Then they told David, saying, 'Behold, the Philistines fight against Keilah, and they rob the threshing-floors.' ² Therefore David enquired of the Lord, saying, 'Shall I go and smite these Philistines?' And the Lord said unto David, 'Go, and smite the Philistines, and save Keilah.' ³And David's men said unto him, 'Behold, we be afraid here in Judah: how much more then if we come to Keilah against the armies of the Philistines?' ⁴Then David enquired of the Lord yet again. And the Lord answered him and said, 'Arise, go down to Keilah; for I will deliver the Philistines into thine hand.' ⁵So David and his men went to Keilah, and fought with the Philistines, and brought away their cattle, and smote them with a great slaughter. So David saved the inhabitants of Keilah. ⁶And it came to pass, when Abiathar the son of Ahimelech fled to David to Keilah, that he came down with an ephod in his hand.

⁷And it was told Saul that David was come to Keilah. And Saul said, 'God hath delivered him into mine hand; for he is shut in, by entering into a town that hath gates and bars.' ⁸And Saul called all the people together to war, to go down to Keilah, to besiege David and his men.

⁹And David knew that Saul secretly practised mischief against him; and he said to Abiathar the priest, 'Bring hither the ephod.' ¹⁰Then said David, 'O Lord God of Israel, thy servant hath certainly heard that Saul seeketh to come to Keilah, to destroy the city for my sake. ¹¹Will the men of Keilah deliver me up into his hand? Will Saul come down, as thy servant hath heard? O Lord God of Israel, I beseech

thee, tell thy servant.' And the Lord said, 'He will come down.' ¹²Then said David, 'Will the men of Keilah deliver me and my men into the hand of Saul?' And the Lord said, 'They will deliver thee up.'

¹³Then David and his men, which were about six hundred, arose and departed out of Keilah, and went whithersoever they could go. And it was told Saul that David was escaped from Keilah; and he forbare to go forth. ¹⁴And David abode in the wilderness in strong holds, and remained in a mountain in the wilderness of Ziph. And Saul sought him every day, but God delivered him not into his hand. ¹⁵And David saw that Saul was come out to seek his life: and David was in the wilderness of Ziph in a wood.

¹⁶And Jonathan Saul's son arose, and went to David into the wood, and strengthened his hand in God. ¹⁷And he said unto him, 'Fear not: for the hand of Saul my father shall not find thee; and thou shalt be king over Israel, and I shall be next unto thee; and that also Saul my father knoweth.' ¹⁸And they two made a covenant before the Lord: and David abode in the wood, and Jonathan went to his house.

¹⁹Then came up, the Ziphites to Saul to Gibeah, saying, 'Doth not David hide himself with us in strong holds in the wood, in the hill of Hachilah, which is on the south of Jeshimon? ²⁰Now therefore, O king, come down according to all the desire of thy soul to come down; and our part shall be to deliver him into the king's hand.' ²¹And Saul said, 'Blessed be ye of the Lord; for ye have compassion on me. ²²Go, I pray you, prepare yet, and know and see his place where his

haunt is, and who hath seen him there, for it is told me that he dealeth very subtilly. ²³ See therefore, and take knowledge of all the lurking places where he hideth himself, and come ye again to me with the certainty, and I will go with you: and it shall come to pass, if he be in the land, that I will search him out throughout all the thousands of Judah.' ²⁴And they arose, and went to Ziph before Saul, but David and his men were in the wilderness of Maon, in the plain on the south of Jeshimon. ²⁵ Saul also and his men went to seek him. And they told David: wherefore he came down into a rock, and abode in the wilderness of Maon. And when Saul heard that, he pursued after David in the wilderness of Maon. ²⁶And Saul went on this side of the mountain, and David and his men on that side of the mountain: and David made haste to get away for fear of Saul; for Saul and his men compassed David and his men round about to take them.

²⁷ But there came a messenger unto Saul, saying, 'Haste thee, and come; for the Philistines have invaded the land.' ²⁸ Wherefore Saul returned from pursuing after David, and went against the Philistines: therefore they called that place Sela-hammahlekoth.

²⁹And David went up from thence, and dwelt in strong holds at En-gedi.

24 And it came to pass, when Saul was returned from following the Philistines, that it was told him, saying, 'Behold, David is in the wilderness of En-gedi.' ² Then Saul took three thousand chosen men out of all Israel, and went

to seek David and his men upon the rocks of the wild goats. [3]And he came to the sheepcotes by the way, where was a cave; and Saul went in to cover his feet: and David and his men remained in the sides of the cave. [4]And the men of David said unto him, 'Behold the day of which the Lord said unto thee, "Behold, I will deliver thine enemy into thine hand, that thou mayest do to him as it shall seem good unto thee."' Then David arose, and cut off the skirt of Saul's robe privily. [5]And it came to pass afterward, that David's heart smote him, because he had cut off Saul's skirt. [6]And he said unto his men, 'The Lord forbid that I should do this thing unto my master, the Lord's anointed, to stretch forth mine hand against him, seeing he is the anointed of the Lord.' [7]So David stayed his servants with these words, and suffered them not to rise against Saul. But Saul rose up out of the cave, and went on his way. [8]David also arose afterward, and went out of the cave, and cried after Saul, saying, 'My lord the king.' And when Saul looked behind him, David stooped with his face to the earth, and bowed himself.

[9]And David said to Saul, 'Wherefore hearest thou men's words, saying, "Behold, David seeketh thy hurt"? [10]Behold, this day thine eyes have seen how that the Lord had delivered thee to day into mine hand in the cave; and some bade me kill thee; but mine eye spared thee; and I said, "I will not put forth mine hand against my lord; for he is the Lord's anointed." [11]Moreover, my father, see, yea, see the skirt of thy robe in my hand, for in that I cut off the skirt of thy robe, and killed thee not, know thou and see that there is neither

evil nor transgression in mine hand, and I have not sinned against thee; yet thou huntest my soul to take it. ¹²The Lord judge between me and thee, and the Lord avenge me of thee; but mine hand shall not be upon thee. ¹³As saith the proverb of the ancients, "Wickedness proceedeth from the wicked"; but mine hand shall not be upon thee. ¹⁴After whom is the king of Israel come out? After whom dost thou pursue? After a dead dog, after a flea. ¹⁵The Lord therefore be judge, and judge between me and thee, and see, and plead my cause, and deliver me out of thine hand.'

¹⁶And it came to pass, when David had made an end of speaking these words unto Saul, that Saul said, 'Is this thy voice, my son David?' And Saul lifted up his voice, and wept. ¹⁷And he said to David, 'Thou art more righteous than I, for thou hast rewarded me good, whereas I have rewarded thee evil. ¹⁸And thou hast shewed this day how that thou hast dealt well with me, forasmuch as when the Lord had delivered me into thine hand, thou killedst me not. ¹⁹For if a man find his enemy, will he let him go well away? Wherefore the Lord reward thee good for that thou hast done unto me this day. ²⁰And now, behold, I know well that thou shalt surely be king, and that the kingdom of Israel shall be established in thine hand. ²¹Swear now therefore unto me by the Lord, that thou wilt not cut off my seed after me, and that thou wilt not destroy my name out of my father's house.' ²²And David sware unto Saul. And Saul went home; but David and his men gat them up unto the hold.

25 And Samuel died; and all the Israelites were gathered together, and lamented him, and buried him in his house at Ramah. And David arose, and went down to the wilderness of Paran. ²And there was a man in Maon, whose possessions were in Carmel; and the man was very great, and he had three thousand sheep, and a thousand goats; and he was shearing his sheep in Carmel. ³Now the name of the man was Nabal; and the name of his wife Abigail; and she was a woman of good understanding, and of a beautiful countenance; but the man was churlish and evil in his doings; and he was of the house of Caleb.

⁴And David heard in the wilderness that Nabal did shear his sheep. ⁵And David sent out ten young men, and David said unto the young men, 'Get you up to Carmel, and go to Nabal, and greet him in my name. ⁶And thus shall ye say to him that liveth in prosperity, "Peace be both to thee, and peace be to thine house, and peace be unto all that thou hast. ⁷And now I have heard that thou hast shearers: now thy shepherds which were with us, we hurt them not, neither was there ought missing unto them, all the while they were in Carmel. ⁸Ask thy young men, and they will shew thee. Wherefore let the young men find favour in thine eyes, for we come in a good day: give, I pray thee, whatsoever cometh to thine hand unto thy servants, and to thy son David."' ⁹And when David's young men came, they spake to Nabal according to all those words in the name of David, and ceased.

¹⁰And Nabal answered David's servants, and said, 'Who

is David? And who is the son of Jesse? There be many servants now a days that break away every man from his master. ¹¹Shall I then take my bread, and my water, and my flesh that I have killed for my shearers, and give it unto men, whom I know not whence they be? ¹²So David's young men turned their way, and went again, and came and told him all those sayings. ¹³And David said unto his men, 'Gird ye on every man his sword.' And they girded on every man his sword; and David also girded on his sword; and there went up after David about four hundred men; and two hundred abode by the stuff.

¹⁴But one of the young men told Abigail, Nabal's wife, saying, 'Behold, David sent messengers out of the wilderness to salute our master; and he railed on them. ¹⁵But the men were very good unto us, and we were not hurt, neither missed we any thing, as long as we were conversant with them, when we were in the fields. ¹⁶They were a wall unto us both by night and day, all the while we were with them keeping the sheep. ¹⁷Now therefore know and consider what thou wilt do; for evil is determined against our master, and against all his household; for he is such a son of Belial, that a man cannot speak to him.'

¹⁸Then Abigail made haste, and took two hundred loaves, and two bottles of wine, and five sheep ready dressed, and five measures of parched corn, and an hundred clusters of raisins, and two hundred cakes of figs, and laid them on asses. ¹⁹And she said unto her servants, 'Go on before me; behold, I come after you.' But she told not her

husband Nabal. ²⁰And it was so, as she rode on the ass, that she came down by the covert of the hill, and, behold, David and his men came down against her; and she met them. ²¹Now David had said, 'Surely in vain have I kept all that this fellow hath in the wilderness, so that nothing was missed of all that pertained unto him: and he hath requited me evil for good. ²²So and more also do God unto the enemies of David, if I leave of all that pertain to him by the morning light any that pisseth against the wall.' ²³And when Abigail saw David, she hasted, and lighted off the ass, and fell before David on her face, and bowed herself to the ground, ²⁴and fell at his feet, and said, 'Upon me, my lord, upon me let this iniquity be: and let thine handmaid, I pray thee, speak in thine audience, and hear the words of thine handmaid. ²⁵Let not my lord, I pray thee, regard this man of Belial, even Nabal; for as his name is, so is he; Nabal is his name, and folly is with him; but I thine handmaid saw not the young men of my lord, whom thou didst send. ²⁶Now therefore, my lord, as the Lord liveth, and as thy soul liveth, seeing the Lord hath withholden thee from coming to shed blood, and from avenging thyself with thine own hand, now let thine enemies, and they that seek evil to my lord, be as Nabal. ²⁷And now this blessing which thine handmaid hath brought unto my lord, let it even be given unto the young men that follow my lord. ²⁸I pray thee, forgive the trespass of thine handmaid; for the Lord will certainly make my lord a sure house; because my lord fighteth the battles of the Lord, and evil hath not been found in thee all thy days. ²⁹Yet a man is risen to pursue thee, and to seek thy soul; but the soul of my lord shall be bound in the bundle of life with the Lord thy God; and the souls of thine enemies, them shall he sling out, as out of the middle of a sling. ³⁰And it shall come to pass, when the Lord shall have done to my lord according to all the good that he hath spoken concerning thee, and shall have appointed thee ruler over Israel; ³¹ that this shall be no grief unto thee, nor offence of heart unto my lord, either that thou hast shed blood causeless, or that my lord hath avenged himself; but when the Lord shall have dealt well with my lord, then remember thine handmaid.'

³²And David said to Abigail, 'Blessed be the Lord God of Israel, which sent thee this day to meet me. ³³And blessed be thy advice, and blessed be thou, which hast kept me this day from coming to shed blood, and from avenging myself with mine own hand. ³⁴ For in very deed, as the Lord God of Israel liveth, which hath kept me back from hurting thee, except thou hadst hasted and come to meet me, surely there had not been left unto Nabal by the morning light any that pisseth against the wall.' ³⁵ So David received of her hand that which she had brought him, and said unto her, 'Go up in peace to thine house; see, I have hearkened to thy voice, and have accepted thy person.'

³⁶And Abigail came to Nabal; and, behold, he held a feast in his house, like the feast of a king; and Nabal's heart was merry within him, for he was very drunken; wherefore she told him nothing, less or more, until the morning light. ³⁷ But it came to pass in the morning, when the wine was gone out

of Nabal, and his wife had told him these things, that his heart died within him, and he became as a stone. ³⁸And it came to pass about ten days after, that the Lord smote Nabal, that he died.

³⁹And when David heard that Nabal was dead, he said, 'Blessed be the Lord, that hath pleaded the cause of my reproach from the hand of Nabal, and hath kept his servant from evil; for the Lord hath returned the wickedness of Nabal upon his own head.' And David sent and communed with Abigail, to take her to him to wife. ⁴⁰And when the servants of David were come to Abigail to Carmel, they spake unto her, saying, 'David sent us unto thee, to take thee to him to wife.' ⁴¹And she arose, and bowed herself on her face to the earth, and said, 'Behold, let thine handmaid be a servant to wash the feet of the servants of my lord.' ⁴²And Abigail hasted, and arose, and rode upon an ass, with five damsels of hers that went after her; and she went after the messengers of David, and became his wife. ⁴³David also took Ahinoam of Jezreel; and they were also both of them his wives.

⁴⁴But Saul had given Michal his daughter, David's wife, to Phalti the son of Laish, which was of Gallim.

26 And the Ziphites came unto Saul to Gibeah, saying, 'Doth not David hide himself in the hill of Hachilah, which is before Jeshimon?' ²Then Saul arose, and went down to the wilderness of Ziph, having three thousand chosen men of Israel with him, to seek David in the wilderness

of Ziph. ³And Saul pitched in the hill of Hachilah, which is before Jeshimon, by the way. But David abode in the wilderness, and he saw that Saul came after him into the wilderness. ⁴David therefore sent out spies, and understood that Saul was come in very deed.

⁵And David arose, and came to the place where Saul had pitched; and David beheld the place where Saul lay, and Abner the son of Ner, the captain of his host; and Saul lay in the trench, and the people pitched round about him. ⁶Then answered David and said to Ahimelech the Hittite, and to Abishai the son of Zeruiah, brother to Joab, saying, 'Who will go down with me to Saul to the camp?' And Abishai said, 'I will go down with thee.' ⁷So David and Abishai came to the people by night; and, behold, Saul lay sleeping within the trench, and his spear stuck in the ground at his bolster; but Abner and the people lay round about him. ⁸Then said Abishai to David, 'God hath delivered thine enemy into thine hand this day: now therefore let me smite him, I pray thee, with the spear even to the earth at once, and I will not smite him the second time.' ⁹And David said to Abishai, 'Destroy him not, for who can stretch forth his hand against the Lord's anointed, and be guiltless?' ¹⁰David said furthermore, 'As the Lord liveth, the Lord shall smite him; or his day shall come to die; or he shall descend into battle, and perish. ¹¹The Lord forbid that I should stretch forth mine hand against the Lord's anointed; but, I pray thee, take thou now the spear that is at his bolster, and the cruse of water, and let us go.' ¹²So David took the spear and the cruse of

water from Saul's bolster; and they gat them away, and no man saw it, nor knew it, neither awaked; for they were all asleep; because a deep sleep from the Lord was fallen upon them.

¹³ Then David went over to the other side, and stood on the top of an hill afar off; a great space being between them. ¹⁴And David cried to the people, and to Abner the son of Ner, saying, 'Answerest thou not, Abner?' Then Abner answered and said, 'Who art thou that criest to the king?' ¹⁵And David said to Abner, 'Art not thou a valiant man? And who is like to thee in Israel? Wherefore then hast thou not kept thy lord the king? For there came one of the people in to destroy the king thy lord. ¹⁶ This thing is not good that thou hast done. As the Lord liveth, ye are worthy to die, because ye have not kept your master, the Lord's anointed. And now see where the king's spear is, and the cruse of water that was at his bolster.' ¹⁷And Saul knew David's voice, and said, 'Is this thy voice, my son David?' And David said, 'It is my voice, my lord, O king.' ¹⁸And he said, 'Wherefore doth my lord thus pursue after his servant? For what have I done? Or what evil is in mine hand? ¹⁹Now therefore, I pray thee, let my lord the king hear the words of his servant. If the Lord have stirred thee up against me, let him accept an offering; but if they be the children of men, cursed be they before the Lord; for they have driven me out this day from abiding in the inheritance of the Lord, saying, "Go, serve other gods." ²⁰Now therefore, let not my blood fall to the earth before the face of the Lord; for the king of Israel is come out

to seek a flea, as when one doth hunt a partridge in the mountains.'

²¹ Then said Saul, 'I have sinned: return, my son David; for I will no more do thee harm, because my soul was precious in thine eyes this day: behold, I have played the fool, and have erred exceedingly.' ²² And David answered and said, 'Behold the king's spear! And let one of the young men come over and fetch it. ²³ The Lord render to every man his righteousness and his faithfulness; for the Lord delivered thee into my hand to day, but I would not stretch forth mine hand against the Lord's anointed. ²⁴ And, behold, as thy life was much set by this day in mine eyes, so let my life be much set by in the eyes of the Lord, and let him deliver me out of all tribulation.' ²⁵ Then Saul said to David, 'Blessed be thou, my son David: thou shalt both do great things, and also shalt still prevail.' So David went on his way, and Saul returned to his place.

27 And David said in his heart, 'I shall now perish one day by the hand of Saul: there is nothing better for me than that I should speedily escape into the land of the Philistines; and Saul shall despair of me, to seek me any more in any coast of Israel: so shall I escape out of his hand.' ² And David arose, and he passed over with the six hundred men that were with him unto Achish, the son of Maoch, king of Gath. ³ And David dwelt with Achish at Gath, he and his men, every man with his household, even David with his two wives, Ahinoam the Jezreelitess, and Abigail the

Carmelitess, Nabal's wife. ⁴And it was told Saul that David was fled to Gath: and he sought no more again for him.

⁵And David said unto Achish, 'If I have now found grace in thine eyes, let them give me a place in some town in the country, that I may dwell there; for why should thy servant dwell in the royal city with thee?' ⁶Then Achish gave him Ziklag that day: wherefore Ziklag pertaineth unto the kings of Judah unto this day. ⁷And the time that David dwelt in the country of the Philistines was a full year and four months.

⁸And David and his men went up, and invaded the Geshurites, and the Gezrites, and the Amalekites; for those nations were of old the inhabitants of the land, as thou goest to Shur, even unto the land of Egypt. ⁹And David smote the land, and left neither man nor woman alive, and took away the sheep, and the oxen, and the asses, and the camels, and the apparel, and returned, and came to Achish. ¹⁰And Achish said, 'Whither have ye made a road to day?' And David said, 'Against the south of Judah, and against the south of the Jerahmeelites, and against the south of the Kenites.' ¹¹And David saved neither man nor woman alive, to bring tidings to Gath, saying, 'Lest they should tell on us, saying, "So did David",' and so will be his manner all the while he dwelleth in the country of the Philistines. ¹²And Achish believed David, saying, 'He hath made his people Israel utterly to abhor him; therefore he shall be my servant for ever.'

28 And it came to pass in those days, that the Philistines gathered their armies together for warfare, to fight with Israel. And Achish said unto David, Know thou assuredly, that thou shalt go out with me to battle, thou and thy men.' ²And David said to Achish, 'Surely thou shalt know what thy servant can do.' And Achish said to David, 'Therefore will I make thee keeper of mine head for ever.'

³Now Samuel was dead, and all Israel had lamented him, and buried him in Ramah, even in his own city. And Saul had put away those that had familiar spirits, and the wizards, out of the land. ⁴And the Philistines gathered themselves together, and came and pitched in Shunem: and Saul gathered all Israel together, and they pitched in Gilboa. ⁵And when Saul saw the host of the Philistines, he was afraid, and his heart greatly trembled. ⁶And when Saul enquired of the Lord, the Lord answered him not, neither by dreams, nor by Urim, nor by prophets.

⁷Then said Saul unto his servants, 'Seek me a woman that hath a familiar spirit, that I may go to her, and enquire of her.' And his servants said to him, 'Behold, there is a woman that hath a familiar spirit at En-dor.' ⁸And Saul disguised himself, and put on other raiment, and he went, and two men with him, and they came to the woman by night: and he said, 'I pray thee, divine unto me by the familiar spirit, and bring me him up, whom I shall name unto thee.' ⁹And the woman said unto him, 'Behold, thou knowest what Saul hath done, how he hath cut off those that have familiar spirits, and the wizards, out of the land: wherefore then layest thou a snare for my life, to cause me to die?' ¹⁰And Saul sware to her by the Lord, saying, 'As the

Lord liveth, there shall no punishment happen to thee for this thing.' ¹¹ Then said the woman, 'Whom shall I bring up unto thee?' And he said, 'Bring me up Samuel.' ¹² And when the woman saw Samuel, she cried with a loud voice: and the woman spake to Saul, saying, 'Why hast thou deceived me? For thou art Saul.' ¹³ And the king said unto her, 'Be not afraid: for what sawest thou?' And the woman said unto Saul, 'I saw gods ascending out of the earth.' ¹⁴ And he said unto her, 'What form is he of?' And she said, 'An old man cometh up; and he is covered with a mantle.' And Saul perceived that it was Samuel, and he stooped with his face to the ground, and bowed himself.

¹⁵ And Samuel said to Saul, 'Why hast thou disquieted me, to bring me up?' And Saul answered, 'I am sore distressed; for the Philistines make war against me, and God is departed from me, and answereth me no more, neither by prophets, nor by dreams: therefore I have called thee, that thou mayest make known unto me what I shall do.' ¹⁶ Then said Samuel, 'Wherefore then dost thou ask of me, seeing the Lord is departed from thee, and is become thine enemy?' ¹⁷ And the Lord hath done to him, as he spake by me; for the Lord hath rent the kingdom out of thine hand, and given it to thy neighbour, even to David, ¹⁸ because thou obeyedst not the voice of the Lord, nor executedst his fierce wrath upon Amalek, therefore hath the Lord done this thing unto thee this day. ¹⁹ Moreover the Lord will also deliver Israel with thee into the hand of the Philistines: and to morrow shalt thou and thy sons be with me: the Lord also shall

deliver the host of Israel into the hand of the Philistines. [20] Then Saul fell straightway all along on the earth, and was sore afraid, because of the words of Samuel: and there was no strength in him; for he had eaten no bread all the day, nor all the night.

[21] And the woman came unto Saul, and saw that he was sore troubled, and said unto him, 'Behold, thine handmaid hath obeyed thy voice, and I have put my life in my hand, and have hearkened unto thy words which thou spakest unto me.' [22] Now therefore, I pray thee, hearken thou also unto the voice of thine handmaid, and let me set a morsel of bread before thee; and eat, that thou mayest have strength, when thou goest on thy way. [23] But he refused, and said, 'I will not eat.' But his servants, together with the woman, compelled him; and he hearkened unto their voice. So he arose from the earth, and sat upon the bed. [24] And the woman had a fat calf in the house; and she hasted, and killed it, and took flour, and kneaded it, and did bake unleavened bread thereof: [25] and she brought it before Saul, and before his servants; and they did eat. Then they rose up, and went away that night.

29 Now the Philistines gathered together all their armies to Aphek: and the Israelites pitched by a fountain which is in Jezreel. [2] And the lords of the Philistines passed on by hundreds, and by thousands; but David and his men passed on in the rereward with Achish. [3] Then said the princes of the Philistines, 'What do these Hebrews here?'

And Achish said unto the princes of the Philistines, 'Is not this David, the servant of Saul the king of Israel, which hath been with me these days, or these years, and I have found no fault in him since he fell unto me unto this day?' ⁴And the princes of the Philistines were wroth with him; and the princes of the Philistines said unto him, 'Make this fellow return, that he may go again to his place which thou hast appointed him, and let him not go down with us to battle, lest in the battle he be an adversary to us, for wherewith should he reconcile himself unto his master? Should it not be with the heads of these men? ⁵Is not this David, of whom they sang one to another in dances, saying, "Saul slew his thousands, and David his ten thousands?"'

⁶Then Achish called David, and said unto him, 'Surely, as the Lord liveth, thou hast been upright, and thy going out and thy coming in with me in the host is good in my sight; for I have not found evil in thee since the day of thy coming unto me unto this day: nevertheless the lords favour thee not. ⁷Wherefore now return, and go in peace, that thou displease not the lords of the Philistines.

⁸And David said unto Achish, 'But what have I done? And what hast thou found in thy servant so long as I have been with thee unto this day, that I may not go fight against the enemies of my lord the king?' ⁹And Achish answered and said to David, 'I know that thou art good in my sight, as an angel of God: notwithstanding the princes of the Philistines have said, "He shall not go up with us to the battle." ¹⁰Wherefore now rise up early in the morning with thy

master's servants that are come with thee: and as soon as ye be up early in the morning, and have light, depart.' ¹¹So David and his men rose up early to depart in the morning, to return into the land of the Philistines. And the Philistines went up to Jezreel.

30 And it came to pass, when David and his men were come to Ziklag on the third day, that the Amalekites had invaded the south, and Ziklag, and smitten Ziklag, and burned it with fire; ²and had taken the women captives, that were therein: they slew not any, either great or small, but carried them away, and went on their way.

³So David and his men came to the city, and, behold, it was burned with fire; and their wives, and their sons, and their daughters, were taken captives. ⁴Then David and the people that were with him lifted up their voice and wept, until they had no more power to weep. ⁵And David's two wives were taken captives, Ahinoam the Jezreelitess, and Abigail the wife of Nabal the Carmelite. ⁶And David was greatly distressed; for the people spake of stoning him, because the soul of all the people was grieved, every man for his sons and for his daughters; but David encouraged himself in the Lord his God. ⁷And David said to Abiathar the priest, Ahimelech's son, 'I pray thee, bring me hither the ephod.' And Abiathar brought thither the ephod to David. ⁸And David enquired at the Lord, saying, 'Shall I pursue after this troop? Shall I overtake them?' And he answered him, 'Pursue; for thou shalt surely overtake them, and

without fail recover all.' ⁹ So David went, he and the six hundred men that were with him, and came to the brook Besor, where those that were left behind stayed. ¹⁰ But David pursued, he and four hundred men; for two hundred abode behind, which were so faint that they could not go over the brook Besor.

¹¹And they found an Egyptian in the field, and brought him to David, and gave him bread, and he did eat; and they made him drink water; ¹²and they gave him a piece of a cake of figs, and two clusters of raisins; and when he had eaten, his spirit came again to him; for he had eaten no bread, nor drunk any water, three days and three nights. ¹³And David said unto him, 'To whom belongest thou? And whence art thou?' And he said, 'I am a young man of Egypt, servant to an Amalekite; and my master left me, because three days agone I fell sick. ¹⁴We made an invasion upon the south of the Cherethites, and upon the coast which belongeth to Judah, and upon the south of Caleb; and we burned Ziklag with fire.' ¹⁵And David said to him, 'Canst thou bring me down to this company?' And he said, 'Swear unto me by God, that thou wilt neither kill me, nor deliver me into the hands of my master, and I will bring thee down to this company.'

¹⁶And when he had brought him down, behold, they were spread abroad upon all the earth, eating and drinking, and dancing, because of all the great spoil that they had taken out of the land of the Philistines, and out of the land of Judah. ¹⁷And David smote them from the twilight even unto the evening of the next day: and there escaped not a man of

them, save four hundred young men, which rode upon camels, and fled. ¹⁸And David recovered all that the Amalekites had carried away: and David rescued his two wives. ¹⁹And there was nothing lacking to them, neither small nor great, neither sons nor daughters, neither spoil, nor any thing that they had taken to them: David recovered all. ²⁰And David took all the flocks and the herds, which they drave before those other cattle, and said, 'This is David's spoil.'

²¹And David came to the two hundred men, which were so faint that they could not follow David, whom they had made also to abide at the brook Besor: and they went forth to meet David, and to meet the people that were with him: and when David came near to the people, he saluted them. ²²Then answered all the wicked men and men of Belial, of those that went with David, and said, 'Because they went not with us, we will not give them ought of the spoil that we have recovered, save to every man his wife and his children, that they may lead them away, and depart.' ²³Then said David, 'Ye shall not do so, my brethren, with that which the Lord hath given us, who hath preserved us, and delivered the company that came against us into our hand. ²⁴For who will hearken unto you in this matter? But as his part is that goeth down to the battle, so shall his part be that tarrieth by the stuff: they shall part alike. ²⁵And it was so from that day forward, that he made it a statute and an ordinance for Israel unto this day.

²⁶And when David came to Ziklag, he sent of the spoil

unto the elders of Judah, even to his friends, saying, 'Behold a present for you of the spoil of the enemies of the Lord'; [27] To them which were in Beth-el, and to them which were in south Ramoth, and to them which were in Jattir, [28] And to them which were in Aroer, and to them which were in Siphmoth, and to them which were in Eshtemoa, [29] And to them which were in Rachal, and to them which were in the cities of the Jerahmeelites, and to them which were in the cities of the Kenites, [30] And to them which were in Hormah, and to them which were in Chor-ashan, and to them which were in Athach, [31] And to them which were in Hebron, and to all the places where David himself and his men were wont to haunt.

31 Now the Philistines fought against Israel: and the men of Israel fled from before the Philistines, and fell down slain in mount Gilboa. [2] And the Philistines followed hard upon Saul and upon his sons; and the Philistines slew Jonathan, and Abinadab, and Malchi-shua, Saul's sons. [3] And the battle went sore against Saul, and the archers hit him; and he was sore wounded of the archers. [4] Then said Saul unto his armour-bearer, 'Draw thy sword, and thrust me through therewith; lest these uncircumcised come and thrust me through, and abuse me.' But his armourbearer would not; for he was sore afraid. Therefore Saul took a sword, and fell upon it. [5] And when his armourbearer saw that Saul was dead, he fell likewise upon his sword, and died with him. [6] So Saul died, and his three sons, and his armourbearer, and all his men, that same day together.

⁷And when the men of Israel that were on the other side of the valley, and they that were on the other side Jordan, saw that the men of Israel fled, and that Saul and his sons were dead, they forsook the cities, and fled; and the Philistines came and dwelt in them. ⁸And it came to pass on the morrow, when the Philistines came to strip the slain, that they found Saul and his three sons fallen in mount Gilboa. ⁹And they cut off his head, and stripped off his armour, and sent into the land of the Philistines round about, to publish it in the house of their idols, and among the people. ¹⁰And they put his armour in the house of Ashtaroth: and they fastened his body to the wall of Beth-shan.

¹¹And when the inhabitants of Jabesh-gilead heard of that which the Philistines had done to Saul, ¹²all the valiant men arose, and went all night, and took the body of Saul and the bodies of his sons from the wall of Beth-shan, and came to Jabesh, and burnt them there. ¹³And they took their bones, and buried them under a tree at Jabesh, and fasted seven days.

the second book of samuel
otherwise called, the second book of the kings

Now it came to pass after the death of Saul, when David was returned from the slaughter of the Amalekites, and David had abode two days in Ziklag. ²It came even to pass on the third day, that, behold, a man came out of the camp from Saul with his clothes rent, and earth upon his head: and so it was, when he came to David, that he fell to the earth, and did obeisance. ³And David said unto him, 'From whence comest thou?' And he said unto him, 'Out of the camp of Israel am I escaped.' ⁴And David said unto him, 'How went the matter? I pray thee, tell me.' And he answered, 'That the people are fled from the battle, and many of the people also are fallen and dead; and Saul and Jonathan his son are dead also.' ⁵And David said unto the young man that told him, 'How knowest thou that Saul and Jonathan his son be dead?' ⁶And the young man that told him said, 'As I happened by chance upon mount Gilboa, behold, Saul leaned upon his spear; and, lo, the chariots and horsemen followed hard after him. ⁷And when he looked behind him, he saw me and called unto me. And I answered, "Here am I." ⁸And he said unto me, "Who art thou?" And I answered him, "I am an Amalekite." ⁹He said unto me again, "Stand, I pray thee, upon me, and slay me, for anguish is come upon me, because my life is yet whole in me." ¹⁰ So I stood upon him, and slew him, because I was sure that he could not live after that he was fallen: and I took the crown that was upon his head, and the bracelet that was on his arm, and have brought them hither unto my lord.' ¹¹ Then David took hold on his clothes, and rent them; and likewise all the men that were with him: ¹² and they mourned, and wept, and fasted until even, for Saul, and for Jonathan his son, and for the people of the Lord, and for the house of Israel; because they were fallen by the sword.

¹³ And David said unto the young man that told him, 'Whence art thou?' And he answered, 'I am the son of a stranger, an Amalekite.' ¹⁴ And David said unto him, 'How wast thou not afraid to stretch forth thine hand to destroy the Lord's anointed?' ¹⁵ And David called one of the young men, and said, 'Go near, and fall upon him.' And he smote him that he died. ¹⁶ And David said unto him, 'Thy blood be upon thy head; for thy mouth hath testified against thee, saying, "I have slain the Lord's anointed."'

¹⁷ And David lamented with this lamentation over Saul and over Jonathan his son. ¹⁸ (Also he bade them teach the children of Judah the use of the bow: behold, it is written in the book of Jasher.)

¹⁹ The beauty of Israel is slain upon thy high places:
　　how are the mighty fallen!
²⁰ Tell it not in Gath, publish it not in the streets of Askelon;
　　lest the daughters of the Philistines rejoice,
　　　　lest the daughters of the uncircumcised triumph.

²¹ Ye mountains of Gilboa, let there be no dew,
 neither let there be rain, upon you,
  nor fields of offerings;
 for there the shield of the mighty
  is vilely cast away,
 the shield of Saul,
  as though he had not been anointed with oil.
²² From the blood of the slain, from the fat of the mighty,
 the bow of Jonathan turned not back,
  and the sword of Saul returned not empty.
²³ Saul and Jonathan were lovely and pleasant in their lives,
 and in their death they were not divided:
  they were swifter than eagles,
 they were stronger than lions.
²⁴ Ye daughters of Israel, weep over Saul,
 who clothed you in scarlet,
  with other delights, who put on ornaments of gold
 upon your apparel.
²⁵ How are the mighty fallen in the midst of the battle!
 O Jonathan, thou wast slain in thine high places.
²⁶ I am distressed for thee, my brother Jonathan:
 very pleasant hast thou been unto me:
  thy love to me was wonderful,
 passing the love of women.
²⁷ How are the mighty fallen,
 and the weapons of war perished!

2 And it came to pass after this, that David enquired of the Lord, saying, 'Shall I go up into any of the cities of

Judah?' And the Lord said unto him, 'Go up.' And David said, 'Whither shall I go up?' And he said, 'Unto Hebron.' ²So David went up thither, and his two wives also, Ahinoam the Jezreelitess, and Abigail Nabal's wife the Carmelite. ³And his men that were with him did David bring up, every man with his household: and they dwelt in the cities of Hebron. ⁴And the men of Judah came, and there they anointed David king over the house of Judah. And they told David, saying that the men of Jabesh-gilead were they that buried Saul.

⁵And David sent messengers unto the men of Jabesh-gilead, and said unto them, 'Blessed be ye of the Lord, that ye have shewed this kindness unto your lord, even unto Saul, and have buried him. ⁶And now the Lord shew kindness and truth unto you: and I also will requite you this kindness, because ye have done this thing. ⁷Therefore now let your hands be strengthened, and be ye valiant; for your master Saul is dead, and also the house of Judah have anointed me king over them.'

⁸But Abner the son of Ner, captain of Saul's host, took Ish-bosheth the son of Saul, and brought him over to Mahanaim; ⁹and made him king over Gilead, and over the Ashurites, and over Jezreel, and over Ephraim, and over Benjamin, and over all Israel. ¹⁰Ish-bosheth Saul's son was forty years old when he began to reign over Israel, and reigned two years. But the house of Judah followed David. ¹¹And the time that David was king in Hebron over the house of Judah was seven years and six months.

¹²And Abner the son of Ner, and the servants of Ish-bosheth the son of Saul, went out from Mahanaim to Gibeon. ¹³And Joab the son of Zeruiah, and the servants of David, went out, and met together by the pool of Gibeon; and they sat down, the one on the one side of the pool, and the other on the other side of the pool. ¹⁴And Abner said to Joab, 'Let the young men now arise, and play before us.' And Joab said, 'Let them arise.' ¹⁵Then there arose and went over by number twelve of Benjamin, which pertained to Ish-bosheth the son of Saul, and twelve of the servants of David. ¹⁶And they caught every one his fellow by the head, and thrust his sword in his fellow's side; so they fell down together: wherefore that place was called Helkath-hazzurim, which is in Gibeon. ¹⁷And there was a very sore battle that day; and Abner was beaten, and the men of Israel, before the servants of David.

¹⁸And there were three sons of Zeruiah there, Joab, and Abishai, and Asahel: and Asahel was as light of foot as a wild roe. ¹⁹And Asahel pursued after Abner; and in going he turned not to the right hand nor to the left from following Abner. ²⁰Then Abner looked behind him, and said, 'Art thou Asahel?' And he answered, 'I am.' ²¹And Abner said to him, 'Turn thee aside to thy right hand or to thy left, and lay thee hold on one of the young men, and take thee his armour.' But Asahel would not turn aside from following of him. ²²And Abner said again to Asahel, 'Turn thee aside from following me: wherefore should I smite thee to the ground? How then should I hold up my face to Joab thy brother?'

²³ Howbeit he refused to turn aside: wherefore Abner with the hinder end of the spear smote him under the fifth rib, that the spear came out behind him; and he fell down there, and died in the same place: and it came to pass, that as many as came to the place where Asahel fell down and died stood still. ²⁴ Joab also and Abishai pursued after Abner: and the sun went down when they were come to the hill of Ammah, that lieth before Giah by the way of the wilderness of Gibeon.

²⁵ And the children of Benjamin gathered themselves together after Abner, and became one troop, and stood on the top of an hill. ²⁶ Then Abner called to Joab, and said, 'Shall the sword devour for ever? Knowest thou not that it will be bitterness in the latter end? How long shall it be then, ere thou bid the people return from following their brethren?' ²⁷ And Joab said, 'As God liveth, unless thou hadst spoken, surely then in the morning the people had gone up every one from following his brother.' ²⁸ So Joab blew a trumpet, and all the people stood still, and pursued after Israel no more, neither fought they any more. ²⁹ And Abner and his men walked all that night through the plain, and passed over Jordan, and went through all Bithron, and they came to Mahanaim. ³⁰ And Joab returned from following Abner; and when he had gathered all the people together, there lacked of David's servants nineteen men and Asahel. ³¹ But the servants of David had smitten of Benjamin, and of Abner's men, so that three hundred and threescore men died.

³² And they took up Asahel, and buried him in the sepulchre of his father, which was in Beth-lehem. And Joab and

his men went all night, and they came to Hebron at break of day.

3 Now there was long war between the house of Saul and the house of David; but David waxed stronger and stronger, and the house of Saul waxed weaker and weaker.

²And unto David were sons born in Hebron: and his firstborn was Amnon, of Ahinoam the Jezreelitess; ³and his second, Chileab, of Abigail the wife of Nabal the Carmelite; and the third, Absalom the son of Maacah the daughter of Talmai king of Geshur; ⁴and the fourth, Adonijah the son of Haggith; and the fifth, Shephatiah the son of Abital; ⁵and the sixth, Ithream, by Eglah David's wife. These were born to David in Hebron.

⁶And it came to pass, while there was war between the house of Saul and the house of David, that Abner made himself strong for the house of Saul. ⁷And Saul had a concubine, whose name was Rizpah, the daughter of Aiah: and Ish-bosheth said to Abner, 'Wherefore hast thou gone in unto my father's concubine?' ⁸Then was Abner very wroth for the words of Ish-bosheth, and said, 'Am I a dog's head, which against Judah do shew kindness this day unto the house of Saul thy father, to his brethren, and to his friends, and have not delivered thee into the hand of David, that thou chargest me to day with a fault concerning this woman?' ⁹So do God to Abner, and more also, except, as the Lord hath sworn to David, even so I do to him; ¹⁰to translate the kingdom from the house of Saul, and to set up the throne of David over

Israel and over Judah, from Dan even to Beer-sheba. ¹¹And he could not answer Abner a word again, because he feared him.

¹²And Abner sent messengers to David on his behalf, saying, 'Whose is the land?' saying also, 'Make thy league with me, and, behold, my hand shall be with thee, to bring about all Israel unto thee.'

¹³And he said, 'Well; I will make a league with thee; but one thing I require of thee, that is, thou shalt not see my face, except thou first bring Michal Saul's daughter, when thou comest to see my face.' ¹⁴And David sent messengers to Ish-bosheth Saul's son, saying, 'Deliver me my wife Michal, which I espoused to me for an hundred foreskins of the Philistines.' ¹⁵And Ish-bosheth sent, and took her from her husband, even from Phaltiel the son of Laish. ¹⁶And her husband went with her along weeping behind her to Bahurim. Then said Abner unto him, 'Go, return.' And he returned.

¹⁷And Abner had communication with the elders of Israel, saying, 'Ye sought for David in times past to be king over you: ¹⁸ now then do it; for the Lord hath spoken of David, saying, 'By the hand of my servant David I will save my people Israel out of the hand of the Philistines, and out of the hand of all their enemies.' ¹⁹And Abner also spake in the ears of Benjamin; and Abner went also to speak in the ears of David in Hebron all that seemed good to Israel, and that seemed good to the whole house of Benjamin. ²⁰ So Abner came to David to Hebron, and twenty men with him. And David made Abner and the men that were with him a

feast. ²¹And Abner said unto David, 'I will arise and go, and will gather all Israel unto my lord the king, that they may make a league with thee, and that thou mayest reign over all that thine heart desireth.' And David sent Abner away; and he went in peace.

²²And, behold, the servants of David and Joab came from pursuing a troop, and brought in a great spoil with them; but Abner was not with David in Hebron; for he had sent him away, and he was gone in peace. ²³When Joab and all the host that was with him were come, they told Joab, saying, 'Abner the son of Ner came to the king, and he hath sent him away, and he is gone in peace.' ²⁴Then Joab came to the king, and said, 'What hast thou done? Behold, Abner came unto thee; why is it that thou hast sent him away, and he is quite gone? ²⁵Thou knowest Abner the son of Ner, that he came to deceive thee, and to know thy going out and thy coming in, and to know all that thou doest.' ²⁶And when Joab was come out from David, he sent messengers after Abner, which brought him again from the well of Sirah; but David knew it not. ²⁷And when Abner was returned to Hebron, Joab took him aside in the gate to speak with him quietly, and smote him there under the fifth rib, that he died, for the blood of Asahel his brother.

²⁸And afterward when David heard it, he said, 'I and my kingdom are guiltless before the Lord for ever from the blood of Abner the son of Ner: ²⁹let it rest on the head of Joab, and on all his father's house; and let there not fail from the house of Joab one that hath an issue, or that is a leper, or

that leaneth on a staff, or that falleth on the sword, or that lacketh bread.' ³⁰So Joab and Abishai his brother slew Abner, because he had slain their brother Asahel at Gibeon in the battle.

³¹And David said to Joab, and to all the people that were with him, 'Rend your clothes, and gird you with sack-cloth, and mourn before Abner.' And king David himself followed the bier. ³²And they buried Abner in Hebron; and the king lifted up his voice, and wept at the grave of Abner; and all the people wept. ³³And the king lamented over Abner, and said, 'Died Abner as a fool dieth?' ³⁴Thy hands were not bound, nor thy feet put into fetters: as a man falleth before wicked men, so fellest thou. And all the people wept again over him. ³⁵And when all the people came to cause David to eat meat while it was yet day, David sware, saying, 'So do God to me, and more also, if I taste bread, or ought else, till the sun be down.' ³⁶And all the people took notice of it, and it pleased them, as whatsoever the king did pleased all the people. ³⁷For all the people and all Israel understood that day that it was not of the king to slay Abner the son of Ner. ³⁸And the king said unto his servants, 'Know ye not that there is a prince and a great man fallen this day in Israel? ³⁹And I am this day weak, though anointed king; and these men the sons of Zeruiah be too hard for me: the Lord shall reward the doer of evil according to his wickedness.'

4 And when Saul's son heard that Abner was dead in Hebron, his hands were feeble, and all the Israelites

were troubled. ²And Saul's son had two men that were captains of bands: the name of the one was Baanah, and the name of the other Rechab, the sons of Rimmon a Beerothite, of the children of Benjamin (for Beeroth also was reckoned to Benjamin, ³and the Beerothites fled to Gittaim, and were sojourners there until this day). ⁴And Jonathan, Saul's son, had a son that was lame of his feet. He was five years old when the tidings came of Saul and Jonathan out of Jezreel, and his nurse took him up, and fled: and it came to pass, as she made haste to flee, that he fell, and became lame. And his name was Mephibosheth. ⁵And the sons of Rimmon the Beerothite, Rechab and Baanah, went, and came about the heat of the day to the house of Ish-bosheth, who lay on a bed at noon, ⁶and they came thither into the midst of the house, as though they would have fetched wheat; and they smote him under the fifth rib; and Rechab and Baanah his brother escaped. ⁷For when they came into the house, he lay on his bed in his bedchamber, and they smote him, and slew him, and beheaded him, and took his head, and gat them away through the plain all night. ⁸And they brought the head of Ish-bosheth unto David to Hebron, and said to the king, 'Behold the head of Ish-bosheth the son of Saul thine enemy, which sought thy life; and the Lord hath avenged my lord the king this day of Saul, and of his seed.'

⁹And David answered Rechab and Baanah his brother, the sons of Rimmon the Beerothite, and said unto them, 'As the Lord liveth, who hath redeemed my soul out of all adversity, ¹⁰when one told me, saying, "Behold, Saul is

dead", thinking to have brought good tidings, I took hold of him, and slew him in Ziklag, who thought that I would have given him a reward for his tidings. ¹¹How much more, when wicked men have slain a righteous person in his own house upon his bed? Shall I not therefore now require his blood of your hand, and take you away from the earth? ¹²And David commanded his young men, and they slew them, and cut off their hands and their feet, and hanged them up over the pool in Hebron. But they took the head of Ish-bosheth, and buried it in the sepulchre of Abner in Hebron.

5 Then came all the tribes of Israel to David unto Hebron, and spake, saying, 'Behold, we are thy bone and thy flesh. ²Also in time past, when Saul was king over us, thou wast he that leddest out and broughtest in Israel: and the Lord said to thee, "Thou shalt feed my people Israel, and thou shalt be a captain over Israel."' ³So all the elders of Israel came to the king to Hebron; and king David made a league with them in Hebron before the Lord: and they anointed David king over Israel.

⁴David was thirty years old when he began to reign, and he reigned forty years. ⁵In Hebron he reigned over Judah seven years and six months: and in Jerusalem he reigned thirty and three years over all Israel and Judah.

⁶And the king and his men went to Jerusalem unto the Jebusites, the inhabitants of the land, which spake unto David, saying, 'Except thou take away the blind and the lame, thou shalt not come in hither,' thinking, 'David cannot

come in hither.' ⁷ Nevertheless David took the strong hold of Zion: the same is the city of David. ⁸ And David said on that day, 'Whosoever getteth up to the gutter, and smiteth the Jebusites, and the lame and the blind, that are hated of David's soul, he shall be chief and captain.' Wherefore they said, 'The blind and the lame shall not come into the house.' ⁹ So David dwelt in the fort, and called it the city of David. And David built round about from Millo and inward. ¹⁰ And David went on, and grew great, and the Lord God of hosts was with him.

¹¹ And Hiram king of Tyre sent messengers to David, and cedar trees, and carpenters, and masons: and they built David an house. ¹² And David perceived that the Lord had established him king over Israel, and that he had exalted his kingdom for his people Israel's sake.

¹³ And David took him more concubines and wives out of Jerusalem, after he was come from Hebron: and there were yet sons and daughters born to David. ¹⁴ And these be the names of those that were born unto him in Jerusalem; Shammua, and Shobab, and Nathan, and Solomon, ¹⁵ Ibhar also, and Elishua, and Nepheg, and Japhia, ¹⁶ and Elishama, and Eliada, and Eliphalet.

¹⁷ But when the Philistines heard that they had anointed David king over Israel, all the Philistines came up to seek David; and David heard of it, and went down to the hold. ¹⁸ The Philistines also came and spread themselves in the valley of Rephaim. ¹⁹ And David enquired of the Lord, saying, 'Shall I go up to the Philistines? Wilt thou deliver them into

mine hand?' And the Lord said unto David, 'Go up, for I will doubtless deliver the Philistines into thine hand.' ²⁰And David came to Baal-perazim, and David smote them there, and said, 'The Lord hath broken forth upon mine enemies before me, as the breach of waters.' Therefore he called the name of that place Baal-perazim. ²¹And there they left their images, and David and his men burned them.

²²And the Philistines came up yet again, and spread themselves in the valley of Rephaim. ²³And when David enquired of the Lord, he said, 'Thou shalt not go up; but fetch a compass behind them, and come upon them over against the mulberry trees. ²⁴And let it be, when thou hearest the sound of a going in the tops of the mulberry trees, that then thou shalt bestir thyself, for then shall the Lord go out before thee, to smite the host of the Philistines.' ²⁵And David did so, as the Lord had commanded him; and smote the Philistines from Geba until thou come to Gazer.

6 Again, David gathered together all the chosen men of Israel, thirty thousand. ²And David arose, and went with all the people that were with him from Baale of Judah, to bring up from thence the ark of God, whose name is called by the name of the Lord of hosts that dwelleth between the cherubims. ³And they set the ark of God upon a new cart, and brought it out of the house of Abinadab that was in Gibeah: and Uzzah and Ahio, the sons of Abinadab, drave the new cart. ⁴And they brought it out of the house of Abinadab which was at Gibeah, accompanying the ark of

God: and Ahio went before the ark. ⁵And David and all the house of Israel played before the Lord on all manner of instruments made of fir wood, even on harps, and on psalteries, and on timbrels, and on cornets, and on cymbals.

⁶And when they came to Nachon's threshingfloor, Uzzah put forth his hand to the ark of God, and took hold of it; for the oxen shook it. ⁷And the anger of the Lord was kindled against Uzzah; and God smote him there for his error; and there he died by the ark of God. ⁸And David was displeased, because the Lord had made a breach upon Uzzah: and he called the name of the place Perez-uzzah to this day. ⁹And David was afraid of the Lord that day, and said, 'How shall the ark of the Lord come to me?' ¹⁰So David would not remove the ark of the Lord unto him into the city of David; but David carried it aside into the house of Obed-edom the Gittite. ¹¹And the ark of the Lord continued in the house of Obed-edom the Gittite three months: and the Lord blessed Obed-edom, and all his household.

¹²And it was told king David, saying, 'The Lord hath blessed the house of Obed-edom, and all that pertaineth unto him, because of the ark of God.' So David went and brought up the ark of God from the house of Obed-edom into the city of David with gladness. ¹³And it was so, that when they that bare the ark of the Lord had gone six paces, he sacrificed oxen and fatlings. ¹⁴And David danced before the Lord with all his might; and David was girded with a linen ephod. ¹⁵So David and all the house of Israel brought up the ark of the Lord with shouting, and with the sound of

the trumpet. ¹⁶And as the ark of the Lord came into the city of David, Michal Saul's daughter looked through a window, and saw king David leaping and dancing before the Lord; and she despised him in her heart.

¹⁷And they brought in the ark of the Lord, and set it in his place, in the midst of the tabernacle that David had pitched for it; and David offered burnt offerings and peace offerings before the Lord. ¹⁸And as soon as David had made an end of offering burnt offerings and peace offerings, he blessed the people in the name of the Lord of hosts. ¹⁹And he dealt among all the people, even among the whole multitude of Israel, as well to the women as men, to every one a cake of bread, and a good piece of flesh, and a flagon of wine. So all the people departed every one to his house.

²⁰ Then David returned to bless his household. And Michal the daughter of Saul came out to meet David, and said, 'How glorious was the king of Israel to day, who uncovered himself to day in the eyes of the handmaids of his servants, as one of the vain fellows shamelessly uncovereth himself!' ²¹And David said unto Michal, 'It was before the Lord, which chose me before thy father, and before all his house, to appoint me ruler over the people of the Lord, over Israel: therefore will I play before the Lord. ²²And I will yet be more vile than thus, and will be base in mine own sight: and of the maidservants which thou hast spoken of, of them shall I be had in honour.' ²³ Therefore Michal the daughter of Saul had no child unto the day of her death.

7 And it came to pass, when the king sat in his house, and the Lord had given him rest round about from all his enemies; [2] that the king said unto Nathan the prophet, 'See now, I dwell in an house of cedar, but the ark of God dwelleth within curtains.' [3] And Nathan said to the king, 'Go, do all that is in thine heart; for the Lord is with thee.'

[4] And it came to pass that night, that the word of the Lord came unto Nathan, saying: [5] Go and tell my servant David: Thus saith the Lord: Shalt thou build me an house for me to dwell in? [6] Whereas I have not dwelt in any house since the time that I brought up the children of Israel out of Egypt, even to this day, but have walked in a tent and in a tabernacle. [7] In all the places wherein I have walked with all the children of Israel spake I a word with any of the tribes of Israel, whom I commanded to feed my people Israel, saying, 'Why build ye not me an house of cedar?' [8] Now therefore so shalt thou say unto my servant David: Thus saith the Lord of hosts: I took thee from the sheepcote, from following the sheep, to be ruler over my people, over Israel; [9] and I was with thee whithersoever thou wentest, and have cut off all thine enemies out of thy sight, and have made thee a great name, like unto the name of the great men that are in the earth. [10] Moreover I will appoint a place for my people Israel, and will plant them, that they may dwell in a place of their own, and move no more; neither shall the children of wickedness afflict them any more, as beforetime, [11] and as since the time that I commanded judges to be over my people Israel, and have caused thee to rest from all thine enemies.

Also the Lord telleth thee that he will make thee an house.

¹²And when thy days be fulfilled, and thou shalt sleep with thy fathers, I will set up thy seed after thee, which shall proceed out of thy bowels, and I will establish his kingdom. ¹³He shall build an house for my name, and I will stablish the throne of his kingdom for ever. ¹⁴I will be his father, and he shall be my son. If he commit iniquity, I will chasten him with the rod of men, and with the stripes of the children of men. ¹⁵But my mercy shall not depart away from him, as I took it from Saul, whom I put away before thee. ¹⁶And thine house and thy kingdom shall be established for ever before thee: thy throne shall be established for ever. ¹⁷According to all these words, and according to all this vision, so did Nathan speak unto David.

¹⁸Then went king David in, and sat before the Lord, and he said, 'Who am I, O Lord God? And what is my house, that thou hast brought me hitherto? ¹⁹And this was yet a small thing in thy sight, O Lord God; but thou hast spoken also of thy servant's house for a great while to come. And is this the manner of man, O Lord God? ²⁰And what can David say more unto thee? For thou, Lord God, knowest thy servant. ²¹For thy word's sake, and according to thine own heart, hast thou done all these great things, to make thy servant know them. ²²Wherefore thou art great, O Lord God; for there is none like thee, neither is there any God beside thee, according to all that we have heard with our ears. ²³And what one nation in the earth is like thy people, even like Israel, whom God went to redeem for a people to himself, and to make

him a name, and to do for you great things and terrible, for thy land, before thy people, which thou redeemedst to thee from Egypt, from the nations and their gods? ²⁴For thou hast confirmed to thyself thy people Israel to be a people unto thee for ever: and thou, Lord, art become their God. ²⁵And now, O Lord God, the word that thou hast spoken concerning thy servant, and concerning his house, establish it for ever, and do as thou hast said. ²⁶And let thy name be magnified for ever, saying, "The Lord of hosts is the God over Israel": and let the house of thy servant David be established before thee. ²⁷For thou, O Lord of hosts, God of Israel, hast revealed to thy servant, saying, "I will build thee an house"; therefore hath thy servant found in his heart to pray this prayer unto thee. ²⁸And now, O Lord God, thou art that God, and thy words be true, and thou hast promised this goodness unto thy servant; ²⁹therefore now let it please thee to bless the house of thy servant, that it may continue for ever before thee; for thou, O Lord God, hast spoken it; and with thy blessing let the house of thy servant be blessed for ever.'

8 And after this it came to pass, that David smote the Philistines, and subdued them: and David took Methegammah out of the hand of the Philistines. ²And he smote Moab, and measured them with a line, casting them down to the ground; even with two lines measured he to put to death, and with one full line to keep alive. And so the Moabites became David's servants, and brought gifts.

³David smote also Hadadezer, the son of Rehob, king of

Zobah, as he went to recover his border at the river Euphrates. ⁴And David took from him a thousand chariots, and seven hundred horsemen, and twenty thousand footmen: and David houghed all the chariot horses, but reserved of them for an hundred chariots. ⁵And when the Syrians of Damascus came to succour Hadadezer king of Zobah, David slew of the Syrians two and twenty thousand men. ⁶Then David put garrisons in Syria of Damascus: and the Syrians became servants to David, and brought gifts. And the Lord preserved David whithersoever he went. ⁷And David took the shields of gold that were on the servants of Hadadezer, and brought them to Jerusalem. ⁸And from Betah, and from Berothai, cities of Hadadezer, king David took exceeding much brass.

⁹When Toi king of Hamath heard that David had smitten all the host of Hadadezer, ¹⁰then Toi sent Joram his son unto king David, to salute him, and to bless him, because he had fought against Hadadezer, and smitten him; for Hadadezer had wars with Toi. And Joram brought with him vessels of silver, and vessels of gold, and vessels of brass, ¹¹which also king David did dedicate unto the Lord, with the silver and gold that he had dedicated of all nations which he subdued; ¹²of Syria, and of Moab, and of the children of Ammon, and of the Philistines, and of Amalek, and of the spoil of Hadadezer, son of Rehob, king of Zobah. ¹³And David gat him a name when he returned from smiting of the Syrians in the valley of salt, being eighteen thousand men.

¹⁴And he put garrisons in Edom; throughout all Edom

put he garrisons, and all they of Edom became David's servants. And the Lord preserved David whithersoever he went. ¹⁵And David reigned over all Israel; and David executed judgment and justice unto all his people. ¹⁶And Joab the son of Zeruiah was over the host; and Jehoshaphat the son of Ahilud was recorder; ¹⁷and Zadok the son of Ahitub, and Ahimelech the son of Abiathar, were the priests; and Seraiah was the scribe; ¹⁸and Benaiah the son of Jehoiada was over both the Cherethites and the Pelethites; and David's sons were chief rulers.

9 And David said, 'Is there yet any that is left of the house of Saul, that I may shew him kindness for Jonathan's sake?' ²And there was of the house of Saul a servant whose name was Ziba. And when they had called him unto David, the king said unto him, 'Art thou Ziba?' And he said, 'Thy servant is he.' ³And the king said, 'Is there not yet any of the house of Saul, that I may shew the kindness of God unto him?' And Ziba said unto the king, 'Jonathan hath yet a son, which is lame on his feet.' ⁴And the king said unto him, 'Where is he?' And Ziba said unto the king, 'Behold, he is in the house of Machir, the son of Ammiel, in Lo-debar.'

⁵Then king David sent, and fetched him out of the house of Machir, the son of Ammiel, from Lo-debar. ⁶Now when Mephibosheth, the son of Jonathan, the son of Saul, was come unto David, he fell on his face, and did reverence. And David said, Mephibosheth. And he answered, 'Behold thy servant!'

⁷And David said unto him, 'Fear not, for I will surely shew thee kindness for Jonathan thy father's sake, and will restore thee all the land of Saul thy father; and thou shalt eat bread at my table continually. ⁸And he bowed himself, and said, 'What is thy servant, that thou shouldest look upon such a dead dog as I am?'

⁹Then the king called to Ziba, Saul's servant, and said unto him, 'I have given unto thy master's son all that pertained to Saul and to all his house. ¹⁰Thou therefore, and thy sons, and thy servants, shall till the land for him, and thou shalt bring in the fruits, that thy master's son may have food to eat; but Mephibosheth thy master's son shall eat bread alway at my table.' Now Ziba had fifteen sons and twenty servants. ¹¹Then said Ziba unto the king, 'According to all that my lord the king hath commanded his servant, so shall thy servant do.' 'As for Mephibosheth', said the king, 'he shall eat at my table, as one of the king's sons.' ¹²And Mephibosheth had a young son, whose name was Micha. And all that dwelt in the house of Ziba were servants unto Mephibosheth. ¹³So Mephibosheth dwelt in Jerusalem, for he did eat continually at the king's table, and was lame on both his feet.

10 And it came to pass after this, that the king of the children of Ammon died, and Hanun his son reigned in his stead. ²Then said David, 'I will shew kindness unto Hanun the son of Nahash, as his father shewed kindness unto me.' And David sent to comfort him by the hand of his

servants for his father. And David's servants came into the land of the children of Ammon. ³And the princes of the children of Ammon said unto Hanun their lord, 'Thinkest thou that David doth honour thy father, that he hath sent comforters unto thee? Hath not David rather sent his servants unto thee, to search the city, and to spy it out, and to overthrow it?' ⁴Wherefore Hanun took David's servants, and shaved off the one half of their beards, and cut off their garments in the middle, even to their buttocks, and sent them away. ⁵When they told it unto David, he sent to meet them, because the men were greatly ashamed: and the king said, Tarry at Jericho until your beards be grown, and then return.

⁶And when the children of Ammon saw that they stank before David, the children of Ammon sent and hired the Syrians of Beth-rehob, and the Syrians of Zoba, twenty thousand footmen, and of king Maacah a thousand men, and of Ish-tob twelve thousand men. ⁷And when David heard of it, he sent Joab, and all the host of the mighty men. ⁸And the children of Ammon came out, and put the battle in array at the entering in of the gate: and the Syrians of Zoba, and of Rehob, and Ish-tob, and Maacah, were by themselves in the field. ⁹When Joab saw that the front of the battle was against him before and behind, he chose of all the choice men of Israel, and put them in array against the Syrians. ¹⁰And the rest of the people he delivered into the hand of Abishai his brother, that he might put them in array against the children of Ammon. ¹¹And he said, 'If the Syrians be too strong for me, then thou shalt help me, but if the children of Ammon

be too strong for thee, then I will come and help thee. [12] Be of good courage, and let us play the men for our people, and for the cities of our God: and the Lord do that which seemeth him good.' [13] And Joab drew nigh, and the people that were with him, unto the battle against the Syrians: and they fled before him. [14] And when the children of Ammon saw that the Syrians were fled, then fled they also before Abishai, and entered into the city. So Joab returned from the children of Ammon, and came to Jerusalem.

[15] And when the Syrians saw that they were smitten before Israel, they gathered themselves together. [16] And Hadarezer sent, and brought out the Syrians that were beyond the river; and they came to Helam; and Shobach the captain of the host of Hadarezer went before them. [17] And when it was told David, he gathered all Israel together, and passed over Jordan, and came to Helam. And the Syrians set themselves in array against David, and fought with him. [18] And the Syrians fled before Israel; and David slew the men of seven hundred chariots of the Syrians, and forty thousand horsemen, and smote Shobach the captain of their host, who died there. [19] And when all the kings that were servants to Hadarezer saw that they were smitten before Israel, they made peace with Israel, and served them. So the Syrians feared to help the children of Ammon any more.

11 And it came to pass, after the year was expired, at the time when kings go forth to battle, that David sent Joab, and his servants with him, and all Israel; and they destroyed

the children of Ammon, and besieged Rabbah. But David tarried still at Jerusalem.

²And it came to pass in an eveningtide, that David arose from off his bed, and walked upon the roof of the king's house; and from the roof he saw a woman washing herself; and the woman was very beautiful to look upon. ³And David sent and enquired after the woman. And one said, 'Is not this Bath-sheba, the daughter of Eliam, the wife of Uriah the Hittite?' ⁴And David sent messengers, and took her; and she came in unto him, and he lay with her; for she was purified from her uncleanness: and she returned unto her house. ⁵And the woman conceived, and sent and told David, and said, 'I am with child.'

⁶And David sent to Joab, saying, 'Send me Uriah the Hittite.' And Joab sent Uriah to David. ⁷And when Uriah was come unto him, David demanded of him how Joab did, and how the people did, and how the war prospered. ⁸And David said to Uriah, 'Go down to thy house, and wash thy feet.' And Uriah departed out of the king's house, and there followed him a mess of meat from the king. ⁹But Uriah slept at the door of the king's house with all the servants of his lord, and went not down to his house. ¹⁰And when they had told David, saying, 'Uriah went not down unto his house,' David said unto Uriah, 'Camest thou not from thy journey? Why then didst thou not go down unto thine house?' ¹¹And Uriah said unto David, 'The ark, and Israel, and Judah, abide in tents; and my lord Joab, and the servants of my lord, are encamped in the open fields; shall I then go into mine house,

to eat and to drink, and to lie with my wife? As thou livest, and as thy soul liveth, I will not do this thing.' ¹²And David said to Uriah, 'Tarry here to day also, and to morrow I will let thee depart.' So Uriah abode in Jerusalem that day, and the morrow. ¹³And when David had called him, he did eat and drink before him; and he made him drunk; and at even he went out to lie on his bed with the servants of his lord, but went not down to his house.

¹⁴And it came to pass in the morning, that David wrote a letter to Joab, and sent it by the hand of Uriah. ¹⁵And he wrote in the letter, saying, 'Set ye Uriah in the forefront of the hottest battle, and retire ye from him, that he may be smitten, and die.' ¹⁶And it came to pass, when Joab observed the city, that he assigned Uriah unto a place where he knew that valiant men were. ¹⁷And the men of the city went out, and fought with Joab; and there fell some of the people of the servants of David; and Uriah the Hittite died also.

¹⁸Then Joab sent and told David all the things concerning the war, ¹⁹and charged the messenger, saying, 'When thou hast made an end of telling the matters of the war unto the king, ²⁰and if so be that the king's wrath arise, and he say unto thee, "Wherefore approached ye so nigh unto the city when ye did fight? Knew ye not that they would shoot from the wall? ²¹Who smote Abimelech the son of Jerubbesheth? Did not a woman cast a piece of a millstone upon him from the wall, that he died in Thebez? Why went ye nigh the wall?" Then say thou, "Thy servant Uriah the Hittite is dead also."'

²²So the messenger went, and came and shewed David all that Joab had sent him for. ²³And the messenger said unto David, 'Surely the men prevailed against us, and came out unto us into the field, and we were upon them even unto the entering of the gate. ²⁴And the shooters shot from off the wall upon thy servants; and some of the king's servants be dead, and thy servant Uriah the Hittite is dead also.' ²⁵Then David said unto the messenger, 'Thus shalt thou say unto Joab, "Let not this thing displease thee, for the sword devoureth one as well as another: make thy battle more strong against the city, and overthrow it," and encourage thou him.'

²⁶And when the wife of Uriah heard that Uriah her husband was dead, she mourned for her husband. ²⁷And when the mourning was past, David sent and fetched her to his house, and she became his wife, and bare him a son. But the thing that David had done displeased the Lord.

12 And the Lord sent Nathan unto David. And he came unto him, and said unto him, 'There were two men in one city; the one rich, and the other poor. ²The rich man had exceeding many flocks and herds: ³but the poor man had nothing, save one little ewe lamb, which he had bought and nourished up, and it grew up together with him, and with his children; it did eat of his own meat, and drank of his own cup, and lay in his bosom, and was unto him as a daughter. ⁴And there came a traveller unto the rich man, and he spared to take of his own flock and of his own herd, to

dress for the wayfaring man that was come unto him; but took the poor man's lamb, and dressed it for the man that was come to him.' ⁵And David's anger was greatly kindled against the man; and he said to Nathan, 'As the Lord liveth, the man that hath done this thing shall surely die; ⁶and he shall restore the lamb four-fold, because he did this thing, and because he had no pity.'

⁷And Nathan said to David, 'Thou art the man.' Thus saith the Lord God of Israel, 'I anointed thee king over Israel, and I delivered thee out of the hand of Saul; ⁸and I gave thee thy master's house, and thy master's wives into thy bosom, and gave thee the house of Israel and of Judah; and if that had been too little, I would moreover have given unto thee such and such things. ⁹Wherefore hast thou despised the commandment of the Lord, to do evil in his sight? Thou hast killed Uriah the Hittite with the sword, and hast taken his wife to be thy wife, and hast slain him with the sword of the children of Ammon. ¹⁰Now therefore the sword shall never depart from thine house; because thou hast despised me, and hast taken the wife of Uriah the Hittite to be thy wife. ¹¹Thus saith the Lord. Behold, I will raise up evil against thee out of thine own house, and I will take thy wives before thine eyes, and give them unto thy neighbour, and he shall lie with thy wives in the sight of this sun. ¹²For thou didst it secretly, but I will do this thing before all Israel, and before the sun.' ¹³And David said unto Nathan, 'I have sinned against the Lord.' And Nathan said unto David, 'The Lord also hath put away thy sin; thou shalt not die. ¹⁴Howbeit,

because by this deed thou hast given great occasion to the enemies of the Lord to blaspheme, the child also that is born unto thee shall surely die.'

¹⁵And Nathan departed unto his house. And the Lord struck the child that Uriah's wife bare unto David, and it was very sick. ¹⁶David therefore besought God for the child; and David fasted, and went in, and lay all night upon the earth. ¹⁷And the elders of his house arose, and went to him, to raise him up from the earth; but he would not, neither did he eat bread with them. ¹⁸And it came to pass on the seventh day, that the child died. And the servants of David feared to tell him that the child was dead, for they said, 'Behold, while the child was yet alive, we spake unto him, and he would not hearken unto our voice: how will he then vex himself, if we tell him that the child is dead?' ¹⁹But when David saw that his servants whispered, David perceived that the child was dead: therefore David said unto his servants, 'Is the child dead?' And they said, 'He is dead.' ²⁰Then David arose from the earth, and washed, and anointed himself, and changed his apparel, and came into the house of the Lord, and worshipped; then he came to his own house; and when he required, they set bread before him, and he did eat. ²¹Then said his servants unto him, 'What thing is this that thou hast done? Thou didst fast and weep for the child, while it was alive; but when the child was dead, thou didst rise and eat bread.' ²²And he said, 'While the child was yet alive, I fasted and wept, for I said, "Who can tell whether God will be gracious to me, that the child may live?" ²³But

now he is dead, wherefore should I fast? Can I bring him back again? I shall go to him, but he shall not return to me.'

²⁴And David comforted Bath-sheba his wife, and went in unto her, and lay with her; and she bare a son, and he called his name Solomon; and the Lord loved him. ²⁵And he sent by the hand of Nathan the prophet; and he called his name Jedidiah, because of the Lord.

²⁶And Joab fought against Rabbah of the children of Ammon, and took the royal city. ²⁷And Joab sent messengers to David, and said, 'I have fought against Rabbah, and have taken the city of waters. ²⁸ Now therefore gather the rest of the people together, and encamp against the city, and take it: lest I take the city, and it be called after my name.' ²⁹And David gathered all the people together, and went to Rabbah, and fought against it, and took it. ³⁰And he took their king's crown from off his head, the weight whereof was a talent of gold with the precious stones; and it was set on David's head. And he brought forth the spoil of the city in great abundance. ³¹And he brought forth the people that were therein, and put them under saws, and under harrows of iron, and under axes of iron, and made them pass through the brickkiln: and thus did he unto all the cities of the children of Ammon. So David and all the people returned unto Jerusalem.

13 And it came to pass after this, that Absalom the son of David had a fair sister, whose name was Tamar; and Amnon the son of David loved her. ²And Amnon was so

vexed, that he fell sick for his sister Tamar; for she was a virgin; and Amnon thought it hard for him to do any thing to her. ³But Amnon had a friend, whose name was Jonadab, the son of Shimeah David's brother: and Jonadab was a very subtil man. ⁴And he said unto him, 'Why art thou, being the king's son, lean from day to day? Wilt thou not tell me?' And Amnon said unto him, 'I love Tamar, my brother Absalom's sister.' ⁵And Jonadab said unto him, 'Lay thee down on thy bed, and make thyself sick: and when thy father cometh to see thee, say unto him, "I pray thee, let my sister Tamar come, and give me meat, and dress the meat in my sight, that I may see it, and eat it at her hand."'

⁶So Amnon lay down, and made himself sick: and when the king was come to see him, Amnon said unto the king, 'I pray thee, let Tamar my sister come, and make me a couple of cakes in my sight, that I may eat at her hand.' ⁷Then David sent home to Tamar, saying, 'Go now to thy brother Amnon's house, and dress him meat.' ⁸So Tamar went to her brother Amnon's house; and he was laid down. And she took flour, and kneaded it, and made cakes in his sight, and did bake the cakes. ⁹And she took a pan, and poured them out before him; but he refused to eat. And Amnon said, 'Have out all men from me.' And they went out every man from him. ¹⁰And Amnon said unto Tamar, 'Bring the meat into the chamber, that I may eat of thine hand.' And Tamar took the cakes which she had made, and brought them into the chamber to Amnon her brother. ¹¹And when she had brought them unto him to eat, he took hold of her, and said

unto her, 'Come lie with me, my sister.' ¹²And she answered him, 'Nay, my brother, do not force me; for no such thing ought to be done in Israel: do not thou this folly. ¹³And I, whither shall I cause my shame to go? And as for thee, thou shalt be as one of the fools in Israel. Now therefore, I pray thee, speak unto the king; for he will not withhold me from thee.' ¹⁴Howbeit he would not hearken unto her voice; but, being stronger than she, forced her, and lay with her.

¹⁵Then Amnon hated her exceedingly; so that the hatred wherewith he hated her was greater than the love wherewith he had loved her. And Amnon said unto her, 'Arise, be gone.' ¹⁶And she said unto him, 'There is no cause: this evil in sending me away is greater than the other that thou didst unto me.' But he would not hearken unto her. ¹⁷Then he called his servant that ministered unto him, and said, 'Put now this woman out from me, and bolt the door after her.' ¹⁸And she had a garment of divers colours upon her, for with such robes were the king's daughters that were virgins apparelled. Then his servant brought her out, and bolted the door after her.

¹⁹And Tamar put ashes on her head, and rent her garment of divers colours that was on her, and laid her hand on her head, and went on crying. ²⁰And Absalom her brother said unto her, 'Hath Amnon thy brother been with thee? But hold now thy peace, my sister: he is thy brother; regard not this thing.' So Tamar remained desolate in her brother Absalom's house.

²¹But when king David heard of all these things, he was

very wroth. ²²And Absalom spake unto his brother Amnon neither good nor bad, for Absalom hated Amnon, because he had forced his sister Tamar.

²³And it came to pass after two full years, that Absalom had sheepshearers in Baal-hazor, which is beside Ephraim, and Absalom invited all the king's sons. ²⁴And Absalom came to the king, and said, 'Behold now, thy servant hath sheepshearers; let the king, I beseech thee, and his servants go with thy servant.' ²⁵And the king said to Absalom, 'Nay, my son, let us not all now go, lest we be chargeable unto thee.' And he pressed him: howbeit he would not go, but blessed him. ²⁶Then said Absalom, 'If not, I pray thee, let my brother Amnon go with us.' And the king said unto him, 'Why should he go with thee?' ²⁷But Absalom pressed him, that he let Amnon and all the king's sons go with him.

²⁸Now Absalom had commanded his servants, saying, 'Mark ye now when Amnon's heart is merry with wine, and when I say unto you, "Smite Amnon", then kill him, fear not: have not I commanded you? Be courageous, and be valiant.' ²⁹And the servants of Absalom did unto Amnon as Absalom had commanded. Then all the king's sons arose, and every man gat him up upon his mule, and fled.

³⁰And it came to pass, while they were in the way, that tidings came to David, saying, 'Absalom hath slain all the king's sons, and there is not one of them left.' ³¹Then the king arose, and tare his garments, and lay on the earth; and all his servants stood by with their clothes rent. ³²And Jonadab, the son of Shimeah David's brother, answered and said, 'Let not

my lord suppose that they have slain all the young men the king's sons; for Amnon only is dead; for by the appointment of Absalom this hath been determined from the day that he forced his sister Tamar. ³³ Now therefore let not my lord the king take the thing to his heart, to think that all the king's sons are dead; for Amnon only is dead.' ³⁴ But Absalom fled. And the young man that kept the watch lifted up his eyes, and looked, and, behold, there came much people by the way of the hill side behind him. ³⁵ And Jonadab said unto the king, 'Behold, the king's sons come: as thy servant said, so it is.' ³⁶ And it came to pass, as soon as he had made an end of speaking, that, behold, the king's sons came, and lifted up their voice and wept: and the king also and all his servants wept very sore.

³⁷ But Absalom fled, and went to Talmai, the son of Ammihud, king of Geshur. And David mourned for his son every day. ³⁸ So Absalom fled, and went to Geshur, and was there three years. ³⁹ And the soul of king David longed to go forth unto Absalom; for he was comforted concerning Amnon, seeing he was dead.

14 Now Joab the son of Zeruiah perceived that the king's heart was toward Absalom. ² And Joab sent to Tekoah, and fetched thence a wise woman, and said unto her, 'I pray thee, feign thyself to be a mourner, and put on now mourning apparel, and anoint not thyself with oil, but be as a woman that had a long time mourned for the dead, ³ and come to the king, and speak on this manner unto

him.' So Joab put the words in her mouth.

⁴And when the woman of Tekoah spake to the king, she fell on her face to the ground, and did obeisance, and said, 'Help, O king.' ⁵And the king said unto her, 'What aileth thee?' And she answered, 'I am indeed a widow woman, and mine husband is dead. ⁶And thy handmaid had two sons, and they two strove together in the field, and there was none to part them, but the one smote the other, and slew him. ⁷And, behold, the whole family is risen against thine handmaid, and they said, "Deliver him that smote his brother, that we may kill him, for the life of his brother whom he slew; and we will destroy the heir also"; and so they shall quench my coal which is left, and shall not leave to my husband neither name nor remainder upon the earth.' ⁸And the king said unto the woman, 'Go to thine house, and I will give charge concerning thee.' ⁹And the woman of Tekoah said unto the king, 'My lord, O king, the iniquity be on me, and on my father's house: and the king and his throne be guiltless.' ¹⁰And the king said, 'Whosoever saith ought unto thee, bring him to me, and he shall not touch thee any more.' ¹¹Then said she, 'I pray thee, let the king remember the Lord thy God, that thou wouldest not suffer the revengers of blood to destroy any more, lest they destroy my son.' And he said, 'As the Lord liveth, there shall not one hair of thy son fall to the earth.' ¹²Then the woman said, 'Let thine handmaid, I pray thee, speak one word unto my lord the king.' And he said, 'Say on.' ¹³And the woman said, 'Wherefore then hast thou thought such a thing against the

people of God? For the king doth speak this thing as one which is faulty, in that the king doth not fetch home again his banished. ¹⁴ For we must needs die, and are as water spilt on the ground, which cannot be gathered up again; neither doth God respect any person: yet doth he devise means, that his banished be not expelled from him. ¹⁵ Now therefore that I am come to speak of this thing unto my lord the king, it is because the people have made me afraid: and thy handmaid said, "I will now speak unto the king; it may be that the king will perform the request of his handmaid. ¹⁶ For the king will hear, to deliver his handmaid out of the hand of the man that would destroy me and my son together out of the inheritance of God." ¹⁷ Then thine handmaid said, "The word of my lord the king shall now be comfortable," or as an angel of God, so is my lord the king to discern good and bad: therefore the Lord thy God will be with thee.' ¹⁸ Then the king answered and said unto the woman, 'Hide not from me, I pray thee, the thing that I shall ask thee.' And the woman said, 'Let my lord the king now speak.' ¹⁹ And the king said, 'Is not the hand of Joab with thee in all this?' And the woman answered and said, 'As thy soul liveth, my lord the king, none can turn to the right hand or to the left from ought that my lord the king hath spoken; for thy servant Joab, he bade me, and he put all these words in the mouth of thine handmaid. ²⁰ To fetch about this form of speech hath thy servant Joab done this thing: and my lord is wise, according to the wisdom of an angel of God, to know all things that are in the earth.'

²¹And the king said unto Joab, 'Behold now, I have done this thing: go therefore, bring the young man Absalom again.' ²²And Joab fell to the ground on his face, and bowed himself, and thanked the king; and Joab said, 'To day thy servant knoweth that I have found grace in thy sight, my lord, O king, in that the king hath fulfilled the request of his servant.' ²³So Joab arose and went to Geshur, and brought Absalom to Jerusalem. ²⁴And the king said, 'Let him turn to his own house, and let him not see my face.' So Absalom returned to his own house, and saw not the king's face.

²⁵But in all Israel there was none to be so much praised as Absalom for his beauty: from the sole of his foot even to the crown of his head there was no blemish in him. ²⁶And when he polled his head (for it was at every year's end that he polled it, because the hair was heavy on him, therefore he polled it); he weighed the hair of his head at two hundred shekels after the king's weight. ²⁷And unto Absalom there were born three sons, and one daughter, whose name was Tamar: she was a woman of a fair countenance.

²⁸So Absalom dwelt two full years in Jerusalem, and saw not the king's face. ²⁹Therefore Absalom sent for Joab, to have sent him to the king; but he would not come to him; and when he sent again the second time, he would not come. ³⁰Therefore he said unto his servants, 'See, Joab's field is near mine, and he hath barley there; go and set it on fire.' And Absalom's servants set the field on fire. ³¹Then Joab arose, and came to Absalom unto his house, and said unto him, 'Wherefore have thy servants set my field on fire?' ³²And

Absalom answered Joab, 'Behold, I sent unto thee, saying. Come hither, that I may send thee to the king, to say, "Wherefore am I come from Geshur? It had been good for me to have been there still": now therefore let me see the king's face; and if there be any iniquity in me, let him kill me.' ³³ So Joab came to the king, and told him; and when he had called for Absalom, he came to the king, and bowed himself on his face to the ground before the king; and the king kissed Absalom.

15 And it came to pass after this, that Absalom prepared him chariots and horses, and fifty men to run before him. ²And Absalom rose up early, and stood beside the way of the gate; and it was so, that when any man that had a controversy came to the king for judgment, then Absalom called unto him, and said, 'Of what city art thou?' And he said, 'Thy servant is of one of the tribes of Israel.' ³And Absalom said unto him, 'See, thy matters are good and right; but there is no man deputed of the king to hear thee.' ⁴Absalom said moreover, 'Oh that I were made judge in the land, that every man which hath any suit or cause might come unto me, and I would do him justice!' ⁵And it was so, that when any man came nigh to him to do him obeisance, he put forth his hand, and took him, and kissed him. ⁶And on this manner did Absalom to all Israel that came to the king for judgment; so Absalom stole the hearts of the men of Israel.

⁷And it came to pass after forty years, that Absalom said unto the king, 'I pray thee, let me go and pay my vow, which

I have vowed unto the Lord, in Hebron. ⁸ For thy servant vowed a vow while I abode at Geshur in Syria, saying: If the Lord shall bring me again indeed to Jerusalem, then I will serve the Lord.' ⁹ And the king said unto him, 'Go in peace.' So he arose, and went to Hebron.

¹⁰ But Absalom sent spies throughout all the tribes of Israel, saying, 'As soon as ye hear the sound of the trumpet, then ye shall say, "Absalom reigneth in Hebron."' ¹¹ And with Absalom went two hundred men out of Jerusalem, that were called; and they went in their simplicity, and they knew not any thing. ¹² And Absalom sent for Ahithophel the Gilonite, David's counsellor, from his city, even from Giloh, while he offered sacrifices. And the conspiracy was strong; for the people increased continually with Absalom.

¹³ And there came a messenger to David, saying, 'The hearts of the men of Israel are after Absalom.' ¹⁴ And David said unto all his servants that were with him at Jerusalem, 'Arise, and let us flee; for we shall not else escape from Absalom: make speed to depart, lest he overtake us suddenly, and bring evil upon us, and smite the city with the edge of the sword.' ¹⁵ And the king's servants said unto the king, 'Behold, thy servants are ready to do whatsoever my lord the king shall appoint.' ¹⁶ And the king went forth, and all his household after him. And the king left ten women, which were concubines, to keep the house. ¹⁷ And the king went forth, and all the people after him, and tarried in a place that was far off. ¹⁸ And all his servants passed on beside him; and all the Cherethites, and all the Pelethites, and all the Gittites,

six hundred men which came after him from Gath, passed on before the king.

¹⁹ Then said the king to Ittai the Gittite, 'Wherefore goest thou also with us? Return to thy place, and abide with the king, for thou art a stranger, and also an exile. ²⁰ Whereas thou camest but yesterday, should I this day make thee go up and down with us? Seeing I go whither I may, return thou, and take back thy brethren: mercy and truth be with thee.' ²¹ And Ittai answered the king, and said, 'As the Lord liveth, and as my lord the king liveth, surely in what place my lord the king shall be, whether in death or life, even there also will thy servant be.' ²² And David said to Ittai, 'Go and pass over.' And Ittai the Gittite passed over, and all his men, and all the little ones that were with him. ²³ And all the country wept with a loud voice, and all the people passed over: the king also himself passed over the brook Kidron, and all the people passed over, toward the way of the wilderness.

²⁴ And lo Zadok also, and all the Levites were with him, bearing the ark of the covenant of God; and they set down the ark of God; and Abiathar went up, until all the people had done passing out of the city. ²⁵ And the king said unto Zadok, 'Carry back the ark of God into the city: if I shall find favour in the eyes of the Lord, he will bring me again, and shew me both it, and his habitation. ²⁶ But if he thus say, "I have no delight in thee", behold, here am I, let him do to me as seemeth good unto him.' ²⁷ The king said also unto Zadok the priest, 'Art not thou a seer? Return into the city in peace, and your two sons with you, Ahimaaz thy son, and Jonathan

the son of Abiathar. ²⁸ See, I will tarry in the plain of the wilderness, until there come word from you to certify me.' ²⁹ Zadok therefore and Abiathar carried the ark of God again to Jerusalem; and they tarried there.

³⁰ And David went up by the ascent of mount Olivet, and wept as he went up, and had his head covered, and he went barefoot; and all the people that was with him covered every man his head, and they went up, weeping as they went up.

³¹ And one told David, saying, 'Ahithophel is among the conspirators with Absalom.' And David said, 'O Lord, I pray thee, turn the counsel of Ahithophel into foolishness.'

³² And it came to pass, that when David was come to the top of the mount, where he worshipped God, behold, Hushai the Archite came to meet him with his coat rent, and earth upon his head, ³³ unto whom David said, 'If thou passest on with me, then thou shalt be a burden unto me.' ³⁴ But if thou return to the city, and say unto Absalom, "I will be thy servant, O king; as I have been thy father's servant hitherto, so will I now also be thy servant". then mayest thou for me defeat the counsel of Ahithophel. ³⁵ And hast thou not there with thee Zadok and Abiathar the priests? Therefore it shall be, that what thing soever thou shalt hear out of the king's house, thou shalt tell it to Zadok and Abiathar the priests. ³⁶ Behold, they have there with them their two sons, Ahimaaz Zadok's son, and Jonathan Abiathar's son; and by them ye shall send unto me every thing that ye can hear.' ³⁷ So Hushai David's friend came into the city, and Absalom came into Jerusalem.

16 And when David was a little past the top of the hill, behold, Ziba the servant of Mephibosheth met him, with a couple of asses saddled, and upon them two hundred loaves of bread, and an hundred bunches of raisins, and an hundred of summer fruits, and a bottle of wine. ²And the king said unto Ziba, 'What meanest thou by these?' And Ziba said, 'The asses be for the king's household to ride on; and the bread and summer fruit for the young men to eat; and the wine, that such as be faint in the wilderness may drink.' ³And the king said, 'And where is thy master's son?' And Ziba said unto the king, 'Behold, he abideth at Jerusalem, for he said, "To day shall the house of Israel restore me the kingdom of my father."' ⁴Then said the king to Ziba, 'Behold, thine are all that pertained unto Mephibosheth.' And Ziba said, 'I humbly beseech thee that I may find grace in thy sight, my lord, O king.'

⁵And when king David came to Bahurim, behold, thence came out a man of the family of the house of Saul, whose name was Shimei, the son of Gera: he came forth, and cursed still as he came. ⁶And he cast stones at David, and at all the servants of king David; and all the people and all the mighty men were on his right hand and on his left. ⁷And thus said Shimei when he cursed, 'Come out, come out, thou bloody man, and thou man of Belial. ⁸The Lord hath returned upon thee all the blood of the house of Saul, in whose stead thou hast reigned; and the Lord hath delivered the kingdom into the hand of Absalom thy son; and, behold, thou art taken in thy mischief, because thou art a bloody man.'

⁹ Then said Abishai the son of Zeruiah unto the king, 'Why should this dead dog curse my lord the king? Let me go over, I pray thee, and take off his head.' ¹⁰ And the king said, 'What have I to do with you, ye sons of Zeruiah? So let him curse, because the Lord hath said unto him, "Curse David." Who shall then say, "Wherefore hast thou done so?"' ¹¹ And David said to Abishai, and to all his servants, 'Behold, my son, which came forth of my bowels, seeketh my life: how much more now may this Benjamite do it? Let him alone, and let him curse; for the Lord hath bidden him. ¹² It may be that the Lord will look on mine affliction, and that the Lord will requite me good for his cursing this day.' ¹³ And as David and his men went by the way, Shimei went along on the hill's side over against him, and cursed as he went, and threw stones at him, and cast dust. ¹⁴ And the king, and all the people that were with him, came weary, and refreshed themselves there.

¹⁵ And Absalom, and all the people the men of Israel, came to Jerusalem, and Ahithophel with him. ¹⁶ And it came to pass, when Hushai the Archite, David's friend, was come unto Absalom, that Hushai said unto Absalom, God save the king, God save the king. ¹⁷ And Absalom said to Hushai, 'Is this thy kindness to thy friend? Why wentest thou not with thy friend?' ¹⁸ And Hushai said unto Absalom, 'Nay; but whom the Lord, and this people, and all the men of Israel, choose, his will I be, and with him will I abide. ¹⁹ And again, whom should I serve? Should I not serve in the presence of his son? As I have served in thy father's presence, so will I be in thy presence.'

²⁰ Then said Absalom to Ahithophel, 'Give counsel among you what we shall do.' ²¹And Ahithophel said unto Absalom, 'Go in unto thy father's concubines, which he hath left to keep the house; and all Israel shall hear that thou art abhorred of thy father: then shall the hands of all that are with thee be strong.' ²²So they spread Absalom a tent upon the top of the house; and Absalom went in unto his father's concubines in the sight of all Israel. ²³And the counsel of Ahithophel, which he counselled in those days, was as if a man had enquired at the oracle of God: so was all the counsel of Ahithophel both with David and with Absalom.

17 Moreover Ahithophel said unto Absalom, 'Let me now choose out twelve thousand men, and I will arise and pursue after David this night. ²And I will come upon him while he is weary and weak handed, and will make him afraid; and all the people that are with him shall flee; and I will smite the king only. ³And I will bring back all the people unto thee: the man whom thou seekest is as if all returned; so all the people shall be in peace. ⁴And the saying pleased Absalom well, and all the elders of Israel. ⁵ Then said Absalom, 'Call now Hushai the Archite also, and let us hear likewise what he saith.' ⁶And when Hushai was come to Absalom, Absalom spake unto him, saying, 'Ahithophel hath spoken after this manner: shall we do after his saying? If not; speak thou.' ⁷And Hushai said unto Absalom, 'The counsel that Ahithophel hath given is not good at this time.' ⁸ 'For,' said Hushai, 'thou knowest thy father and his men,

that they be mighty men, and they be chafed in their minds, as a bear robbed of her whelps in the field: and thy father is a man of war, and will not lodge with the people. ⁹Behold, he is hid now in some pit, or in some other place: and it will come to pass, when some of them be overthrown at the first, that whosoever heareth it will say, "There is a slaughter among the people that follow Absalom." ¹⁰And he also that is valiant, whose heart is as the heart of a lion, shall utterly melt, for all Israel knoweth that thy father is a mighty man, and they which be with him are valiant men. ¹¹Therefore I counsel that all Israel be generally gathered unto thee, from Dan even to Beer-sheba, as the sand that is by the sea for multitude; and that thou go to battle in thine own person. ¹²So shall we come upon him in some place where he shall be found, and we will light upon him as the dew falleth on the ground: and of him and of all the men that are with him there shall not be left so much as one. ¹³Moreover, if he be gotten into a city, then shall all Israel bring ropes to that city, and we will draw it into the river, until there be not one small stone found there.' ¹⁴And Absalom and all the men of Israel said, 'The counsel of Hushai the Archite is better than the counsel of Ahithophel.' For the Lord had appointed to defeat the good counsel of Ahithophel, to the intent that the Lord might bring evil upon Absalom.

¹⁵Then said Hushai unto Zadok and to Abiathar the priests, 'Thus and thus did Ahithophel counsel Absalom and the elders of Israel; and thus and thus have I counselled. ¹⁶Now therefore send quickly, and tell David, saying,

"Lodge not this night in the plains of the wilderness, but speedily pass over; lest the king be swallowed up, and all the people that are with him."' ¹⁷ Now Jonathan and Ahimaaz stayed by En-rogel; for they might not be seen to come into the city; and a wench went and told them; and they went and told king David. ¹⁸ Nevertheless a lad saw them, and told Absalom; but they went both of them away quickly, and came to a man's house in Bahurim, which had a well in his court; whither they went down. ¹⁹ And the woman took and spread a covering over the well's mouth, and spread ground corn thereon; and the thing was not known. ²⁰ And when Absalom's servants came to the woman to the house, they said, 'Where is Ahimaaz and Jonathan?' And the woman said unto them, 'They be gone over the brook of water.' And when they had sought and could not find them, they returned to Jerusalem. ²¹ And it came to pass, after they were departed, that they came up out of the well, and went and told king David, and said unto David, 'Arise, and pass quickly over the water: for thus hath Ahithophel counselled against you.' ²² Then David arose, and all the people that were with him, and they passed over Jordan: by the morning light there lacked not one of them that was not gone over Jordan.

²³ And when Ahithophel saw that his counsel was not followed, he saddled his ass, and arose, and gat him home to his house, to his city, and put his household in order, and hanged himself, and died, and was buried in the sepulchre of his father. ²⁴ Then David came to Mahanaim. And Absalom

passed over Jordan, he and all the men of Israel with him.

²⁵And Absalom made Amasa captain of the host instead of Joab, which Amasa was a man's son, whose name was Ithra an Israelite, that went in to Abigail the daughter of Nahash, sister to Zeruiah Joab's mother. ²⁶So Israel and Absalom pitched in the land of Gilead.

²⁷And it came to pass, when David was come to Mahanaim, that Shobi the son of Nahash of Rabbah of the children of Ammon, and Machir the son of Ammiel of Lodebar, and Barzillai the Gileadite of Rogelim, ²⁸brought beds, and basons, and earthen vessels, and wheat, and barley, and flour, and parched corn, and beans, and lentiles, and parched pulse, ²⁹and honey, and butter, and sheep, and cheese of kine, for David, and for the people that were with him, to eat, for they said, 'The people is hungry, and weary, and thirsty, in the wilderness.'

18 And David numbered the people that were with him, and set captains of thousands and captains of hundreds over them. ²And David sent forth a third part of the people under the hand of Joab, and a third part under the hand of Abishai the son of Zeruiah, Joab's brother, and a third part under the hand of Ittai the Gittite. And the king said unto the people, 'I will surely go forth with you myself also.' ³But the people answered, 'Thou shalt not go forth, for if we flee away, they will not care for us; neither if half of us die, will they care for us; but now thou art worth ten

thousand of us: therefore now it is better that thou succour us out of the city. ⁴And the king said unto them, 'What seemeth you best I will do.' And the king stood by the gate side, and all the people came out by hundreds and by thousands. ⁵And the king commanded Joab and Abishai and Ittai, saying, 'Deal gently for my sake with the young man, even with Absalom.' And all the people heard when the king gave all the captains charge concerning Absalom.

⁶ So the people went out into the field against Israel: and the battle was in the wood of Ephraim, ⁷where the people of Israel were slain before the servants of David, and there was there a great slaughter that day of twenty thousand men. ⁸ For the battle was there scattered over the face of all the country: and the wood devoured more people that day than the sword devoured.

⁹And Absalom met the servants of David. And Absalom rode upon a mule, and the mule went under the thick boughs of a great oak, and his head caught hold of the oak, and he was taken up between the heaven and the earth; and the mule that was under him went away. ¹⁰And a certain man saw it, and told Joab, and said, 'Behold, I saw Absalom hanged in an oak.' ¹¹And Joab said unto the man that told him, 'And, behold, thou sawest him, and why didst thou not smite him there to the ground? And I would have given thee ten shekels of silver, and a girdle.' ¹²And the man said unto Joab, 'Though I should receive a thousand shekels of silver in mine hand, yet would I not put forth mine hand against the king's son; for in our hearing the king charged thee and

Abishai and Ittai, saying, "Beware that none touch the young man Absalom." [13] Otherwise I should have wrought falsehood against mine own life; for there is no matter hid from the king, and thou thyself wouldest have set thyself against me.' [14] Then said Joab, 'I may not tarry thus with thee.' And he took three darts in his hand, and thrust them through the heart of Absalom, while he was yet alive in the midst of the oak. [15] And ten young men that bare Joab's armour compassed about and smote Absalom, and slew him. [16] And Joab blew the trumpet, and the people returned from pursuing after Israel; for Joab held back the people. [17] And they took Absalom, and cast him into a great pit in the wood, and laid a very great heap of stones upon him: and all Israel fled every one to his tent.

[18] Now Absalom in his lifetime had taken and reared up for himself a pillar, which is in the king's dale; for he said, 'I have no son to keep my name in remembrance: and he called the pillar after his own name: and it is called unto this day, Absalom's place.'

[19] Then said Ahimaaz the son of Zadok, 'Let me now run, and bear the king tidings, how that the Lord hath avenged him of his enemies.' [20] And Joab said unto him, 'Thou shalt not bear tidings this day, but thou shalt bear tidings another day; but this day thou shalt bear no tidings, because the king's son is dead.' [21] Then said Joab to Cushi, 'Go tell the king what thou hast seen.' And Cushi bowed himself unto Joab, and ran. [22] Then said Ahimaaz the son of Zadok yet again to Joab, 'But howsoever, let me, I pray thee, also run after

Cushi.' And Joab said, 'Wherefore wilt thou run, my son, seeing that thou hast no tidings ready?' ²³ 'But howsoever,' said he, 'let me run.' And he said unto him, 'Run.' Then Ahimaaz ran by the way of the plain, and overran Cushi. ²⁴And David sat between the two gates: and the watchman went up to the roof over the gate unto the wall, and lifted up his eyes, and looked, and behold a man running alone. ²⁵And the watchman cried, and told the king. And the king said, 'If he be alone, there is tidings in his mouth.' And he came apace, and drew near. ²⁶And the watchman saw another man running: and the watchman called unto the porter, and said, 'Behold another man running alone.' And the king said, 'He also bringeth tidings.' ²⁷And the watchman said, 'Me thinketh the running of the foremost is like the running of Ahimaaz the son of Zadok.' And the king said, 'He is a good man, and cometh with good tidings.' ²⁸And Ahimaaz called, and said unto the king, 'All is well.' And he fell down to the earth upon his face before the king, and said, 'Blessed be the Lord thy God, which hath delivered up the men that lifted up their hand against my lord the king.' ²⁹And the king said, 'Is the young man Absalom safe?' And Ahimaaz answered, 'When Joab sent the king's servant, and me thy servant, I saw a great tumult, but I knew not what it was.' ³⁰And the king said unto him, 'Turn aside, and stand here.' And he turned aside, and stood still. ³¹And, behold, Cushi came; and Cushi said, 'Tidings, my lord the king; for the Lord hath avenged thee this day of all them that rose up against thee.' ³²And the king said unto Cushi, 'Is the young man Absalom safe?' And

Cushi answered, 'The enemies of my lord the king, and all that rise against thee to do thee hurt, be as that young man is.'

[33] And the king was much moved, and went up to the chamber over the gate, and wept: and as he went, thus he said, 'O my son Absalom, my son, my son Absalom! Would God I had died for thee, O Absalom, my son, my son!'

19 And it was told Joab, 'Behold, the king weepeth and mourneth for Absalom.' [2] And the victory that day was turned into mourning unto all the people; for the people heard say that day how the king was grieved for his son. [3] And the people gat them by stealth that day into the city, as people being ashamed steal away when they flee in battle. [4] But the king covered his face, and the king cried with a loud voice, 'O my son Absalom, O Absalom, my son, my son!' [5] And Joab came into the house to the king, and said, 'Thou hast shamed this day the faces of all thy servants, which this day have saved thy life, and the lives of thy sons and of thy daughters, and the lives of thy wives, and the lives of thy concubines; [6] in that thou lovest thine enemies, and hatest thy friends. For thou hast declared this day, that thou regardest neither princes nor servants; for this day I perceive, that if Absalom had lived, and all we had died this day, then it had pleased thee well. [7] Now therefore arise, go forth, and speak comfortably unto thy servants; for I swear by the Lord, if thou go not forth, there will not tarry one with thee this night: and that will be worse unto thee than all the evil that befell thee from thy youth until now.' [8] Then the

king arose, and sat in the gate. And they told unto all the people, saying, 'Behold, the king doth sit in the gate.' And all the people came before the king; for Israel had fled every man to his tent.

⁹And all the people were at strife throughout all the tribes of Israel, saying, 'The king saved us out of the hand of our enemies, and he delivered us out of the hand of the Philistines; and now he is fled out of the land for Absalom. ¹⁰And Absalom, whom we anointed over us, is dead in battle. Now therefore why speak ye not a word of bringing the king back?'

¹¹And king David sent to Zadok and to Abiathar the priests, saying, 'Speak unto the elders of Judah, saying, "Why are ye the last to bring the king back to his house? Seeing the speech of all Israel is come to the king, even to his house. ¹²Ye are my brethren, ye are my bones and my flesh: wherefore then are ye the last to bring back the king?" ¹³And say ye to Amasa, "Art thou not of my bone, and of my flesh? God do so to me, and more also, if thou be not captain of the host before me continually in the room of Joab."' ¹⁴And he bowed the heart of all the men of Judah, even as the heart of one man; so that they sent this word unto the king, 'Return thou, and all thy servants.' ¹⁵ So the king returned, and came to Jordan. And Judah came to Gilgal, to go to meet the king, to conduct the king over Jordan.

¹⁶And Shimei the son of Gera, a Benjamite, which was of Bahurim, hasted and came down with the men of Judah to meet king David. ¹⁷And there were a thousand men of

Benjamin with him, and Ziba the servant of the house of Saul, and his fifteen sons and his twenty servants with him; and they went over Jordan before the king. ¹⁸And there went over a ferry boat to carry over the king's household, and to do what he thought good. And Shimei the son of Gera fell down before the king, as he was come over Jordan; ¹⁹and said unto the king, 'Let not my lord impute iniquity unto me, neither do thou remember that which thy servant did perversely the day that my lord the king went out of Jerusalem, that the king should take it to his heart. ²⁰For thy servant doth know that I have sinned: therefore, behold, I am come the first this day of all the house of Joseph to go down to meet my lord the king.' ²¹But Abishai the son of Zeruiah answered and said, 'Shall not Shimei be put to death for this, because he cursed the Lord's anointed?' ²²And David said, 'What have I to do with you, ye sons of Zeruiah, that ye should this day be adversaries unto me? Shall there any man be put to death this day in Israel? For do not I know that I am this day king over Israel?' ²³Therefore the king said unto Shimei, 'Thou shalt not die.' And the king sware unto him.

²⁴And Mephibosheth the son of Saul came down to meet the king, and had neither dressed his feet, nor trimmed his beard, nor washed his clothes, from the day the king departed until the day he came again in peace. ²⁵And it came to pass, when he was come to Jerusalem to meet the king, that the king said unto him, 'Wherefore wentest not thou with me, Mephibosheth?' ²⁶And he answered, 'My lord, O

king, my servant deceived me; for thy servant said, "I will saddle me an ass, that I may ride thereon, and go to the king"; because thy servant is lame. ²⁷And he hath slandered thy servant unto my lord the king; but my lord the king is as an angel of God: do therefore what is good in thine eyes. ²⁸For all of my father's house were but dead men before my lord the king: yet didst thou set thy servant among them that did eat at thine own table. What right therefore have I yet to cry any more unto the king?' ²⁹And the king said unto him, 'Why speakest thou any more of thy matters? I have said, "Thou and Ziba divide the land."' ³⁰And Mephibosheth said unto the king, 'Yea, let him take all, forasmuch as my lord the king is come again in peace unto his own house.'

³¹And Barzillai the Gileadite came down from Rogelim, and went over Jordan with the king, to conduct him over Jordan. ³²Now Barzillai was a very aged man, even fourscore years old; and he had provided the king of sustenance while he lay at Mahanaim; for he was a very great man. ³³And the king said unto Barzillai, 'Come thou over with me, and I will feed thee with me in Jerusalem.' ³⁴And Barzillai said unto the king, 'How long have I to live, that I should go up with the king unto Jerusalem? ³⁵I am this day fourscore years old: and can I discern between good and evil? Can thy servant taste what I eat or what I drink? Can I hear any more the voice of singing men and singing women? Wherefore then should thy servant be yet a burden unto my lord the king? ³⁶Thy servant will go a little way over Jordan with the king:

and why should the king recompense it me with such a reward? [37] Let thy servant, I pray thee, turn back again, that I may die in mine own city, and be buried by the grave of my father and of my mother. But behold thy servant Chimham; let him go over with my lord the king; and do to him what shall seem good unto thee.' [38] And the king answered, 'Chimham shall go over with me, and I will do to him that which shall seem good unto thee: and whatsoever thou shalt require of me, that will I do for thee.' [39] And all the people went over Jordan. And when the king was come over, the king kissed Barzillai, and blessed him; and he returned unto his own place. [40] Then the king went on to Gilgal, and Chimham went on with him: and all the people of Judah conducted the king, and also half the people of Israel.

[41] And, behold, all the men of Israel came to the king, and said unto the king, 'Why have our brethren the men of Judah stolen thee away, and have brought the king, and his household, and all David's men with him, over Jordan?' [42] And all the men of Judah answered the men of Israel, 'Because the king is near of kin to us: wherefore then be ye angry for this matter? Have we eaten at all of the king's cost? Or hath he given us any gift?' [43] And the men of Israel answered the men of Judah, and said, 'We have ten parts in the king, and we have also more right in David than ye: why then did ye despise us, that our advice should not be first had in bringing back our king?' And the words of the men of Judah were fiercer than the words of the men of Israel.

20 And there happened to be there a man of Belial, whose name was Sheba, the son of Bichri, a Benjamite: and he blew a trumpet, and said, 'We have no part in David, neither have we inheritance in the son of Jesse: every man to his tents, O Israel.' ²So every man of Israel went up from after David, and followed Sheba the son of Bichri: but the men of Judah clave unto their king, from Jordan even to Jerusalem.

³And David came to his house at Jerusalem; and the king took the ten women his concubines, whom he had left to keep the house, and put them in ward, and fed them, but went not in unto them. So they were shut up unto the day of their death, living in widowhood.

⁴Then said the king to Amasa, 'Assemble me the men of Judah within three days, and be thou here present.' ⁵So Amasa went to assemble the men of Judah; but he tarried longer than the set time which he had appointed him. ⁶And David said to Abishai, 'Now shall Sheba the son of Bichri do us more harm than did Absalom: take thou thy lord's servants, and pursue after him, lest he get him fenced cities, and escape us.' ⁷And there went out after him Joab's men, and the Cherethites, and the Pelethites, and all the mighty men: and they went out of Jerusalem, to pursue after Sheba the son of Bichri. ⁸When they were at the great stone which is in Gibeon, Amasa went before them. And Joab's garment that he had put on was girded unto him, and upon it a girdle with a sword fastened upon his loins in the sheath thereof; and as he went forth it fell out. ⁹And Joab said to Amasa, 'Art

thou in health, my brother?' And Joab took Amasa by the beard with the right hand to kiss him. ¹⁰But Amasa took no heed to the sword that was in Joab's hand: so he smote him therewith in the fifth rib, and shed out his bowels to the ground, and struck him not again; and he died. So Joab and Abishai his brother pursued after Sheba the son of Bichri. ¹¹And one of Joab's men stood by him, and said, 'He that favoureth Joab, and he that is for David, let him go after Joab.' ¹²And Amasa wallowed in blood in the midst of the highway. And when the man saw that all the people stood still, he removed Amasa out of the highway into the field, and cast a cloth upon him, when he saw that every one that came by him stood still. ¹³When he was removed out of the highway, all the people went on after Joab, to pursue after Sheba the son of Bichri.

¹⁴And he went through all the tribes of Israel unto Abel, and to Beth-maachah, and all the Berites: and they were gathered together, and went also after him. ¹⁵And they came and besieged him in Abel of Beth-maachah, and they cast up a bank against the city, and it stood in the trench; and all the people that were with Joab battered the wall, to throw it down.

¹⁶Then cried a wise woman out of the city, 'Hear, hear; say, I pray you, unto Joab, "Come near hither, that I may speak with thee."' ¹⁷And when he was come near unto her, the woman said, 'Art thou Joab?' And he answered, 'I am he.' Then she said unto him, 'Hear the words of thine handmaid.' And he answered, 'I do hear.' ¹⁸Then she spake, saying,

'They were wont to speak in old time, saying, "They shall surely ask counsel at Abel"', and so they ended the matter. ¹⁹ I am one of them that are peaceable and faithful in Israel: thou seekest to destroy a city and a mother in Israel: why wilt thou swallow up the inheritance of the Lord?' ²⁰ And Joab answered and said, 'Far be it, far be it from me, that I should swallow up or destroy. ²¹ The matter is not so: but a man of mount Ephraim, Sheba the son of Bichri by name, hath lifted up his hand against the king, even against David: deliver him only, and I will depart from the city.' And the woman said unto Joab, 'Behold, his head shall be thrown to thee over the wall.' ²² Then the woman went unto all the people in her wisdom. And they cut off the head of Sheba the son of Bichri, and cast it out to Joab. And he blew a trumpet, and they retired from the city, every man to his tent. And Joab returned to Jerusalem unto the king.

²³ Now Joab was over all the host of Israel: and Benaiah the son of Jehoiada was over the Cherethites and over the Pelethites: ²⁴ and Adoram was over the tribute: and Jehoshaphat the son of Ahilud was recorder: ²⁵ and Sheva was scribe: and Zadok and Abiathar were the priests: ²⁶ and Ira also the Jairite was a chief ruler about David.

21 Then there was a famine in the days of David three years, year after year; and David enquired of the Lord. And the Lord answered, 'It is for Saul, and for his bloody house, because he slew the Gibeonites.' ² And the king called the Gibeonites, and said unto them (now the Gibeonites

were not of the children of Israel, but of the remnant of the Amorites; and the children of Israel had sworn unto them; and Saul sought to slay them in his zeal to the children of Israel and Judah). ³Wherefore David said unto the Gibeonites, 'What shall I do for you? And wherewith shall I make the atonement, that ye may bless the inheritance of the Lord?' ⁴And the Gibeonites said unto him, 'We will have no silver nor gold of Saul, nor of his house; neither for us shalt thou kill any man in Israel.' And he said, 'What ye shall say, that will I do for you.' ⁵And they answered the king, 'The man that consumed us, and that devised against us that we should be destroyed from remaining in any of the coasts of Israel, ⁶let seven men of his sons be delivered unto us, and we will hang them up unto the Lord in Gibeah of Saul, whom the Lord did choose.' And the king said, 'I will give them.' ⁷But the king spared Mephibosheth, the son of Jonathan the son of Saul, because of the Lord's oath that was between them, between David and Jonathan the son of Saul. ⁸But the king took the two sons of Rizpah the daughter of Aiah, whom she bare unto Saul, Armoni and Mephibosheth; and the five sons of Michal the daughter of Saul, whom she brought up for Adriel the son of Barzillai the Meholathite; ⁹and he delivered them into the hands of the Gibeonites, and they hanged them in the hill before the Lord; and they fell all seven together, and were put to death in the days of harvest, in the first days, in the beginning of barley harvest.

¹⁰And Rizpah the daughter of Aiah took sackcloth, and spread it for her upon the rock, from the beginning of harvest

until water dropped upon them out of heaven, and suffered neither the birds of the air to rest on them by day, nor the beasts of the field by night. ¹¹And it was told David what Rizpah the daughter of Aiah, the concubine of Saul, had done.

¹²And David went and took the bones of Saul and the bones of Jonathan his son from the men of Jabesh-gilead, which had stolen them from the street of Beth-shan, where the Philistines had hanged them, when the Philistines had slain Saul in Gilboa; ¹³and he brought up from thence the bones of Saul and the bones of Jonathan his son; and they gathered the bones of them that were hanged. ¹⁴And the bones of Saul and Jonathan his son buried they in the country of Benjamin in Zelah, in the sepulchre of Kish his father; and they performed all that the king commanded. And after that God was intreated for the land.

¹⁵Moreover the Philistines had yet war again with Israel; and David went down, and his servants with him, and fought against the Philistines; and David waxed faint. ¹⁶And Ishbi-benob, which was of the sons of the giant, the weight of whose spear weighed three hundred shekels of brass in weight, he being girded with a new sword, thought to have slain David. ¹⁷But Abishai the son of Zeruiah succoured him, and smote the Philistine, and killed him. Then the men of David sware unto him, saying, 'Thou shalt go no more out with us to battle, that thou quench not the light of Israel.' ¹⁸And it came to pass after this, that there was again a battle with the Philistines at Gob: then Sibbechai the Hushathite slew Saph, which was of the sons of the giant. ¹⁹And there

was again a battle in Gob with the Philistines, where Elhanan the son of Jaare-oregim, a Beth-lehemite, slew the brother of Goliath the Gittite, the staff of whose spear was like a weaver's beam. ²⁰And there was yet a battle in Gath, where was a man of great stature, that had on every hand six fingers, and on every foot six toes, four and twenty in number; and he also was born to the giant. ²¹And when he defied Israel, Jonathan the son of Shimea the brother of David slew him. ²²These four were born to the giant in Gath, and fell by the hand of David, and by the hand of his servants.

22 And David spake unto the Lord the words of this song in the day that the Lord had delivered him out of the hand of all his enemies, and out of the hand of Saul.

²And he said, 'The Lord is my rock,
　　and my fortress, and my deliverer;
³the God of my rock; in him will I trust:
　　he is my shield, and the horn of my salvation,
　　　　my high tower, and my refuge, my saviour;
　　thou savest me from violence.
⁴I will call on the Lord, who is worthy to be praised:
　　so shall I be saved from mine enemies.
⁵When the waves of death compassed me,
　　the floods of ungodly men made me afraid;
⁶the sorrows of hell compassed me about;
　　the snares of death prevented me;
⁷in my distress I called upon the Lord,
　　and cried to my God:

and he did hear my voice out of his temple,
and my cry did enter into his ears.

⁸ Then the earth shook and trembled;
the foundations of heaven moved and shook,
because he was wroth.

⁹ There went up a smoke out of his nostrils,
and fire out of his mouth devoured:
coals were kindled by it.

¹⁰ He bowed the heavens also, and came down;
and darkness was under his feet.

¹¹And he rode upon a cherub, and did fly:
and he was seen upon the wings of the wind.

¹²And he made darkness pavilions round about him,
dark waters, and thick clouds of the skies.

¹³ Through the brightness before him
were coals of fire kindled.

¹⁴ The Lord thundered from heaven,
and the most High uttered his voice.

¹⁵And he sent out arrows, and scattered them;
lightning, and discomfited them.

¹⁶And the channels of the sea appeared,
the foundations of the world were discovered,
at the rebuking of the Lord,
at the blast of the breath of his nostrils.

¹⁷ He sent from above, he took me;
he drew me out of many waters;

¹⁸ he delivered me from my strong enemy,
and from them that hated me;
for they were too strong for me.

¹⁹ They prevented me in the day of my calamity;
    but the Lord was my stay.
²⁰ He brought me forth also into a large place:
    he delivered me, because he delighted in me.
²¹ The Lord rewarded me
    according to my righteousness:
        according to the cleanness of my hands
    hath he recompensed me.
²² For I have kept the ways of the Lord,
    and have not wickedly departed from
        my God.
²³ For all his judgments were before me:
    and as for his statutes,
        I did not depart from them.
²⁴ I was also upright before him,
    and have kept myself from mine iniquity.
²⁵ Therefore the Lord hath recompensed me
    according to my righteousness;
        according to my cleanness in his eye sight.
²⁶ With the merciful thou wilt shew thyself merciful,
    and with the upright man
        thou wilt shew thyself upright.
²⁷ With the pure thou wilt shew thyself pure;
    and with the froward
        thou wilt shew thyself unsavoury.
²⁸ And the afflicted people thou wilt save;
    but thine eyes are upon the haughty,
        that thou mayest bring them down.

²⁹ For thou art my lamp, O Lord:
    and the Lord will lighten my darkness.
³⁰ For by thee I have run through a troop:
    by my God have I leaped over a wall.
³¹ As for God, his way is perfect;
    the word of the Lord is tried:
        he is a buckler to all them that trust in him.
³² For who is God, save the Lord?
    And who is a rock, save our God?
³³ God is my strength and power:
    and he maketh my way perfect.
³⁴ He maketh my feet like hinds' feet,
    and setteth me upon my high places.
³⁵ He teacheth my hands to war;
    so that a bow of steel is broken by mine arms.
³⁶ Thou hast also given me the shield of thy salvation,
    and thy gentleness hath made me great.
³⁷ Thou hast enlarged my steps under me;
    so that my feet did not slip.
³⁸ I have pursued mine enemies, and destroyed them;
    and turned not again until I had consumed them.
³⁹ And I have consumed them,
    and wounded them, that they could not arise:
        yea, they are fallen under my feet.
⁴⁰ For thou hast girded me with strength to battle:
    them that rose up against me
        hast thou subdued under me.
⁴¹ Thou hast also given me the necks of mine enemies,

that I might destroy them that hate me.
⁴² They looked, but there was none to save;
even unto the Lord, but he answered them not.
⁴³ Then did I beat them
as small as the dust of the earth,
I did stamp them as the mire of the street, and
did spread them abroad.
⁴⁴ Thou also hast delivered me
from the strivings of my people,
thou hast kept me to be head of the heathen:
a people which I knew not shall serve me.
⁴⁵ Strangers shall submit themselves unto me:
as soon as they hear,
they shall be obedient unto me.
⁴⁶ Strangers shall fade away,
and they shall be afraid out of their close places.
⁴⁷ The Lord liveth; and blessed be my rock;
and exalted be the God of the rock
of my salvation.
⁴⁸ It is God that avengeth me,
and that bringeth down the people under me,
⁴⁹ and that bringeth me forth from mine enemies:
thou also hast lifted me up on high
above them that rose up against me:
thou hast delivered me from the violent man.
⁵⁰ Therefore I will give thanks unto thee, O Lord,
among the heathen,
and I will sing praises unto thy name.

⁵¹ He is the tower of salvation for his king
    and sheweth mercy to his anointed, unto David,
    and to his seed for evermore.

23 Now these be the last words of David. David the son of Jesse said, and the man who was raised up on high, the anointed of the God of Jacob, and the sweet psalmist of Israel, said:

² The Spirit of the Lord spake by me,
    and his word was in my tongue.
³ The God of Israel said,
    the Rock of Israel spake to me:
        He that ruleth over men must be just,
    ruling in the fear of God.
⁴ And he shall be as the light of the morning,
    when the sun riseth,
        even a morning without clouds;
    as the tender grass springing out of the earth
    by clear shining after rain.
⁵ Although my house be not so with God;
    yet he hath made with me
        an everlasting covenant,
    ordered in all things, and sure:
        for this is all my salvation, and all my desire,
    although he make it not to grow.
⁶ But the sons of Belial shall be all of them
    as thorns thrust away,
        because they cannot be taken with hands;

⁷ but the man that shall touch them
　　must be fenced with iron and the staff of a spear;
　　and they shall be utterly burned with fire
　in the same place.

⁸ These be the names of the mighty men whom David had: the Tachmonite that sat in the seat, chief among the captains; the same was Adino the Eznite: he lift up his spear against eight hundred, whom he slew at one time. ⁹ And after him was Eleazar the son of Dodo the Ahohite, one of the three mighty men with David, when they defied the Philistines that were there gathered together to battle, and the men of Israel were gone away. ¹⁰ He arose, and smote the Philistines until his hand was weary, and his hand clave unto the sword; and the Lord wrought a great victory that day; and the people returned after him only to spoil. ¹¹ And after him was Shammah the son of Agee the Hararite. And the Philistines were gathered together into a troop, where was a piece of ground full of lentiles: and the people fled from the Philistines. ¹² But he stood in the midst of the ground, and defended it, and slew the Philistines; and the Lord wrought a great victory. ¹³ And three of the thirty chief went down, and came to David in the harvest time unto the cave of Adullam: and the troop of the Philistines pitched in the valley of Rephaim. ¹⁴ And David was then in an hold, and the garrison of the Philistines was then in Beth-lehem. ¹⁵ And David longed, and said, 'Oh that one would give me drink of the water of the well of Beth-lehem, which is by the gate!' ¹⁶ And the three mighty men brake through

the host of the Philistines, and drew water out of the well of Beth-lehem, that was by the gate, and took it, and brought it to David: nevertheless he would not drink thereof, but poured it out unto the Lord. ¹⁷And he said, 'Be it far from me, O Lord, that I should do this: is not this the blood of the men that went in jeopardy of their lives?' Therefore he would not drink it. These things did these three mighty men. ¹⁸And Abishai, the brother of Joab, the son of Zeruiah, was chief among three. And he lifted up his spear against three hundred, and slew them, and had the name among three. ¹⁹Was he not most honourable of three? Therefore he was their captain: howbeit he attained not unto the first three. ²⁰And Benaiah the son of Jehoiada, the son of a valiant man, of Kabzeel, who had done many acts, he slew two lionlike men of Moab: he went down also and slew a lion in the midst of a pit in time of snow. ²¹And he slew an Egyptian, a goodly man; and the Egyptian had a spear in his hand; but he went down to him with a staff, and plucked the spear out of the Egyptian's hand, and slew him with his own spear. ²²These things did Benaiah the son of Jehoiada, and had the name among three mighty men. ²³He was more honourable than the thirty, but he attained not to the first three. And David set him over his guard. ²⁴Asahel the brother of Joab was one of the thirty; Elhanan the son of Dodo of Beth-lehem, ²⁵Shammah the Harodite, Elika the Harodite, ²⁶Helez the Paltite, Ira the son of Ikkesh the Tekoite, ²⁷Abiezer the Anethothite, Mebunnai the Hushathite, ²⁸Zalmon the Ahohite, Maharai the Netophathite, ²⁹Heleb the son of Baanah, a

Netophathite, Ittai the son of Ribai out of Gibeah of the children of Benjamin, ³⁰Benaiah the Pirathonite, Hiddai of the brooks of Gaash, ³¹Abi-albon the Arbathite, Azmaveth the Barhumite, ³²Eliahba the Shaalbonite, of the sons of Jashen, Jonathan, ³³Shammah the Hararite, Ahiam the son of Sharar the Hararite, ³⁴Eliphelet the son of Ahasbai, the son of the Maachathite, Eliam the son of Ahithophel the Gilonite, ³⁵Hezrai the Carmelite, Paarai the Arbite, ³⁶Igal the son of Nathan of Zobah, Bani the Gadite, ³⁷Zelek the Ammonite, Naharai the Beerothite, armourbearer to Joab the son of Zeruiah, ³⁸Ira an Ithrite, Gareb an Ithrite, ³⁹Uriah the Hittite: thirty and seven in all.

24 And again the anger of the Lord was kindled against Israel, and he moved David against them to say, 'Go, number Israel and Judah.' ²For the king said to Joab the captain of the host, which was with him, 'Go now through all the tribes of Israel, from Dan even to Beer-sheba, and number ye the people, that I may know the number of the people.' ³And Joab said unto the king, 'Now the Lord thy God add unto the people, how many soever they be, an hundredfold, and that the eyes of my lord the king may see it; but why doth my lord the king delight in this thing?' ⁴Notwithstanding the king's word prevailed against Joab, and against the captains of the host. And Joab and the captains of the host went out from the presence of the king, to number the people of Israel.

⁵And they passed over Jordan, and pitched in Aroer, on

the right side of the city that lieth in the midst of the river of Gad, and toward Jazer. ⁶Then they came to Gilead, and to the land of Tahtim-hodshi; and they came to Dan-jaan, and about to Zidon, ⁷and came to the strong hold of Tyre, and to all the cities of the Hivites, and of the Canaanites: and they went out to the south of Judah, even to Beer-sheba. ⁸So when they had gone through all the land, they came to Jerusalem at the end of nine months and twenty days. ⁹And Joab gave up the sum of the number of the people unto the king; and there were in Israel eight hundred thousand valiant men that drew the sword; and the men of Judah were five hundred thousand men.

¹⁰And David's heart smote him after that he had numbered the people. And David said unto the Lord, 'I have sinned greatly in that I have done; and now, I beseech thee, O Lord, take away the iniquity of thy servant; for I have done very foolishly.' ¹¹For when David was up in the morning, the word of the Lord came unto the prophet Gad, David's seer, saying, ¹²'Go and say unto David: Thus saith the Lord, I offer thee three things; choose thee one of them, that I may do it unto thee.' ¹³So Gad came to David, and told him, and said unto him, 'Shall seven years of famine come unto thee in thy land? Or wilt thou flee three months before thine enemies, while they pursue thee? Or that there be three days' pestilence in thy land? Now advise, and see what answer I shall return to him that sent me.' ¹⁴And David said unto Gad, 'I am in a great strait: let us fall now into the hand of the Lord; for his mercies are great; and let me not

fall into the hand of man.'

¹⁵ So the Lord sent a pestilence upon Israel from the morning even to the time appointed: and there died of the people from Dan even to Beer-sheba seventy thousand men. ¹⁶And when the angel stretched out his hand upon Jerusalem to destroy it, the Lord repented him of the evil, and said to the angel that destroyed the people, 'It is enough: stay now thine hand.' And the angel of the Lord was by the threshingplace of Araunah the Jebusite. ¹⁷And David spake unto the Lord when he saw the angel that smote the people, and said, 'Lo, I have sinned, and I have done wickedly: but these sheep, what have they done? Let thine hand, I pray thee, be against me, and against my father's house.'

¹⁸And Gad came that day to David, and said unto him, 'Go up, rear an altar unto the Lord in the threshingfloor of Araunah the Jebusite.' ¹⁹And David, according to the saying of Gad, went up as the Lord commanded. ²⁰And Araunah looked, and saw the king and his servants coming on toward him: and Araunah went out, and bowed himself before the king on his face upon the ground. ²¹And Araunah said, 'Wherefore is my lord the king come to his servant?' And David said, 'To buy the threshingfloor of thee, to build an altar unto the Lord, that the plague may be stayed from the people.' ²²And Araunah said unto David, 'Let my lord the king take and offer up what seemeth good unto him: behold, here be oxen for burnt sacrifice, and threshing instruments and other instruments of the oxen for wood. ²³All these things did Araunah, as a king, give unto the king.' And Araunah

said unto the king, 'The Lord thy God accept thee.' ²⁴And the king said unto Araunah, 'Nay; but I will surely buy it of thee at a price: neither will I offer burnt offerings unto the Lord my God of that which doth cost me nothing.' So David bought the threshingfloor and the oxen for fifty shekels of silver. ²⁵And David built there an altar unto the Lord, and offered burnt offerings and peace offerings. So the Lord was intreated for the land, and the plague was stayed from Israel.

**the epistles of
james, peter, john, and jude**

he

epistles

f james, peter, john and jude

uthorized king james version

rove press
ew york

---

with an introduction by | his holiness the dalai lama

Introduction copyright © 2000 by His Holiness the Dalai Lama of Tibet
The Pocket Canon second series copyright © 2000 by Grove/Atlantic, Inc.

All rights reserved. No part of this book may be reproduced in any form
or by any electronic or mechanical means, including information storage
and retrieval systems, without permission in writing from the publisher,
except by a reviewer, who may quote brief passages in a review. Any
members of educational institutions wishing to photocopy part or all
of the work for classroom use, or publishers who would like to obtain
permission to include the work in an anthology, should send their
inquiries to Grove/Atlantic, Inc., 841 Broadway, New York, NY 10003.

Originally published in Great Britain in 2000 by Canongate Books,
Ltd., Edinburgh, Scotland.

Published simultaneously in Canada
Printed in the United States of America

FIRST AMERICAN EDITION

ISBN 0-8021-3759-8 (boxed set)

Design by Paddy Cramsie

Grove Press
841 Broadway
New York, NY 10003

00 01 02 03   10 9 8 7 6 5 4 3 2 1

a note about pocket canons

The Authorized King James Version of the Bible, translated
between 1603 and 1611, coincided with an extraordinary
flowering of English literature. This version, more than any
other, and possibly more than any other work in history, has
had an influence in shaping the language we speak and write
today.

The books of the King James Bible encompass categories
as diverse as history, philosophy, law, poetry and fiction. Each
Pocket Canon volume has its own introduction, specially commissioned from an impressive range of writers, to provide a
personal interpretation of the text and explore its contemporary relevance.

His Holiness the 14th Dalai Lama, Tenzin Gyatso, is the head of state and spiritual leader of the Tibetan people. He was born in 1935 to a peasant family and recognised as the reincarnation of the 13th Dalai Lama at the age of two. He began his monastic Buddhist education when he was six. 'Dalai Lama' is a Mongolian title meaning 'Ocean of Wisdom'. In 1959 he was forced into exile with the brutal suppression of the Tibetan National Uprising in Lhasa by Chinese troops. For the last 39 years he has been living in Dharamsala, India. As leader of the Tibetan Government-in-Exile he advocates democracy and autonomy for the Tibetan people from Chinese rule. In his lectures and tours around the world he emphasises the importance of love, compassion and forgiveness. His publications in English include Ancient Wisdom Modern World *and his autobiography* Freedom in Exile. *His Holiness was awarded the Noble Prize for Peace in 1989.*

introduction by his holiness the dalai lama

As I read the lines of this *Epistle of St James*, I am struck by the similarities between this beautiful letter in the Bible and some of the texts in my own Buddhist tradition, especially those that belong to a genre known as *lojong*, literally meaning 'training the mind'. As with *lojong* texts, I believe, this epistle can be read on different levels. On the practical level, however, it encapsulates many of the key principles that are crucial for learning how to be a better human being. More precisely, it teaches us how to bring our spiritual vision to life at the highest possible level.

I feel humbled to be invited to write an introduction to this important part of the Christian scriptures. As the world enters a new millennium and Christians all over the world celebrate two thousand years of their tradition, I am reminded that this holy scripture has been a powerful source of spiritual inspiration and solace to millions of fellow human beings world-wide. Needless to say, I am no expert on Christian scriptures. I have, however, accepted the invitation to comment personally on the epistle from the perspective of my own Buddhist tradition. I will particularly focus on passages that evoke values and principles also emphasised in the Buddhist scriptures.

The epistle begins by underlining the critical importance of developing a single-pointed commitment to our chosen spiritual path. It says, 'A double minded man is unstable in all his ways' (James 1:8), because lack of commitment and a wavering mind are among the greatest obstacles to a successful spiritual life. However, this need not be some kind of blind faith, but rather a commitment based on personal appreciation of the value and efficacy of the spiritual path. Such faith arises through a process of reflection and deep understanding. Buddhist texts describe three levels of faith, namely: faith as admiration, faith as reasoned conviction, and faith as emulation of high spiritual ideals. I believe that these three kinds of faith are applicable here as well.

The epistle reminds us of the power of the destructive tendencies that exist naturally in all of us. In what is, for me at least, the most poignant verse of the entire letter, we read, 'Wherefore, my beloved brethren, let every man be swift to hear, slow to speak, slow to wrath: for the wrath of man worketh not the righteousness of God.' (James 1:19-20.)

These two verses encapsulate principles that are of utmost importance to a spiritual practitioner, and for that matter, any individual who aspires to express his or her basic human goodness. This emphasis on hearing as opposed to speaking teaches us the need for open-heartedness. For without it we have no room to receive the blessings and positive transformation that we might otherwise experience in our interaction with our fellow human beings.

Open and receptive, swift to listen to others, we should be slow to speak, because speech is a powerful instrument that can be highly constructive or profoundly destructive. We are all aware how seemingly harmless speech can actually inflict deep hurt upon others. Therefore, the wise course is to follow the advice of one well-known Buddhist *lojong* text: 'When amongst many, guard your speech and alone, guard your thoughts.'

The instruction that we should be 'slow to wrath' reminds us that it is vital to ensure some degree of restraint over powerful negative emotions like anger, for actions motivated by such states of mind are almost invariably destructive. This is something we must both appreciate and strive to implement in our everyday lives. Only then can we hope to reap the fruit of living a spiritual life.

The real test of spiritual practice lies in the practitioner's behaviour. There is sometimes a tendency to think of the spiritual life as primarily introspective, divorced from the concerns of everyday life and society. This, I believe, is plainly wrong and is also rejected in this epistle. Faith that does not translate into actions is no faith at all, as the text says:

If a brother or sister be naked, and destitute of daily food, and any of you say unto them, 'Depart in peace, be ye warmed and filled'; notwithstanding ye give them not those things which are needful to the body; what doth it profit? Even so faith, if it hath not works, is dead, being alone. (James 2:16-17.)

We find a similar principle in Buddhist texts as well. They advise that when helping others, giving material aid comes first, speaking words of comfort comes second, giving spiritual counsel comes third, while fourth is demonstrating what you teach by your own personal example.

I have long been an admirer of the Christian tradition of charity and social work. The image of monks and nuns devoting their entire lives to the service of humanity in the fields of health, education and care of the poor is truly inspiring. To me, these are true followers of Christ, demonstrating their faith in compassionate action.

The epistle addresses what a Buddhist might call 'contemplation of the transient nature of life.' This is beautifully captured in the following verse: 'Whereas ye know not what shall be on the morrow. For what is your life? It is even a vapour, that appeareth for a little time, and then vanisheth away.' (James 4:24)

In the Buddhist context, contemplation of life's transient nature brings a sense of urgency to our spiritual life. We may be aware of the value of spiritual practice, but in our daily lives, we tend to behave as if we will live for a long time. We have a false sense of the permanence of our existence, which is one of the greatest obstacles to a dedicated spiritual life. More important, from an ethical point of view, it is the assumption of permanence that leads us to pursue what we see as the 'legitimate' desires and needs of our enduring 'self'. We ignore the impact of our behaviour on other people's lives. We might even be willing to exploit others for our own ends. So, profound contemplation of life's transient nature introduces a note of healthy realism into our life as it helps put things in proper perspective.

The epistle is passionate in its advocacy of respect for the poor. In fact, it presents a severe critique of the conceit and complacency of the rich and the powerful. Some of these criticisms may have a certain historical significance, but they underline an important spiritual principle, which is never to forget the fundamental equality of all human beings. A true spiritual practitioner appreciates what I often describe as our 'basic spirituality'. By this I am referring to the fundamental qualities of goodness, which exist naturally in all of us irrespective of our gender, race, social and religious backgrounds.

By criticising disdainful attitudes towards the poor, the epistle persuasively reminds us of the need to return to a deeper appreciation of our humanity. It reminds us to relate to fellow human beings at a level of basic humanity. I often tell people that when I meet someone for the first time, my primary feeling is that I am meeting a fellow human being. It does not matter to me, whether the person is considered 'important' or not. For me, what matters most is basic warm-heartedness.

Certainly, from the standpoint of mere humanity, there are no grounds for discrimination. In the language of the Bible, we are all equal in the face of creation. And in the language of Buddhism, we all equally aspire for happiness and shun suffering. Furthermore, we all have the right to fulfil this basic aspiration to be happy and overcome suffering. So if we truly relate to our fellow human beings with a recognition of our fundamental equality, considerations of whether someone is rich or poor, educated or uneducated, black or white, male or female, or whether he or she belongs to this or that religion naturally become secondary.

When we read this text from the Bible today, two thousand years after they were written, it reminds us that not only are many of our fundamental spiritual values universal, they are also perennial. So long as human beings' fundamental nature, aspiring for happiness and wishing to overcome suffering, remains unchanged, these basic values too will remain relevant to us both as individual human beings and as a society.

I would like to conclude by remembering my friend Thomas Merton, a Catholic monk of the Cistercian order, who opened my eyes to the richness of the Christian tradition. It is to him that I owe my first, real appreciation of the value of Christian teachings. Since we met in the early 1960s, I have dedicated a large part of my time and effort to promoting deeper understanding amongst the followers of the world's major religions. And it is to this noble objective that I dedicate the words I have written here.

the general epistle of james

James, a servant of God and of the Lord Jesus Christ, to the twelve tribes which are scattered abroad, greeting.

² My brethren, count it all joy when ye fall into divers temptations; ³ knowing this, that the trying of your faith worketh patience. ⁴ But let patience have her perfect work, that ye may be perfect and entire, wanting nothing.

⁵ If any of you lack wisdom, let him ask of God, that giveth to all men liberally, and upbraideth not; and it shall be given him. ⁶ But let him ask in faith, nothing wavering. For he that wavereth is like a wave of the sea driven with the wind and tossed. ⁷ For let not that man think that he shall receive any thing of the Lord. ⁸ A double minded man is unstable in all his ways.

⁹ Let the brother of low degree rejoice in that he is exalted: ¹⁰ but the rich, in that he is made low, because as the flower of the grass he shall pass away. ¹¹ For the sun is no sooner risen with a burning heat, but it withereth the grass, and the flower thereof falleth, and the grace of the fashion of it perisheth: so also shall the rich man fade away in his ways.

¹² Blessed is the man that endureth temptation, for when he is tried, he shall receive the crown of life, which the Lord hath promised to them that love him. ¹³ Let no man say when

he is tempted, I am tempted of God, for God cannot be tempted with evil, neither tempteth he any man. ¹⁴ But every man is tempted, when he is drawn away of his own lust, and enticed. ¹⁵ Then when lust hath conceived, it bringeth forth sin: and sin, when it is finished, bringeth forth death. ¹⁶ Do not err, my beloved brethren.

¹⁷ Every good gift and every perfect gift is from above, and cometh down from the Father of lights, with whom is no variableness, neither shadow of turning. ¹⁸ Of his own will begat he us with the word of truth, that we should be a kind of firstfruits of his creatures.

¹⁹ Wherefore, my beloved brethren, let every man be swift to hear, slow to speak, slow to wrath, ²⁰ for the wrath of man worketh not the righteousness of God. ²¹ Wherefore lay apart all filthiness and superfluity of naughtiness, and receive with meekness the engrafted word, which is able to save your souls.

²² But be ye doers of the word, and not hearers only, deceiving your own selves. ²³ For if any be a hearer of the word, and not a doer, he is like unto a man beholding his natural face in a glass, ²⁴ for he beholdeth himself, and goeth his way, and straightway forgetteth what manner of man he was. ²⁵ But whoso looketh into the perfect law of liberty, and continueth therein, he being not a forgetful hearer, but a doer of the work, this man shall be blessed in his deed.

²⁶ If any man among you seem to be religious, and bridleth not his tongue, but deceiveth his own heart, this man's religion is vain. ²⁷ Pure religion and undefiled before God and

the Father is this: to visit the fatherless and widows in their affliction, and to keep himself unspotted from the world.

2 My brethren, have not the faith of our Lord Jesus Christ, the Lord of glory, with respect of persons. ² For if there come unto your assembly a man with a gold ring, in goodly apparel, and there come in also a poor man in vile raiment; ³ and ye have respect to him that weareth the gay clothing, and say unto him, 'Sit thou here in a good place'; and say to the poor, 'Stand thou there', or 'sit here under my footstool', ⁴ are ye not then partial in yourselves, and are become judges of evil thoughts? ⁵ Hearken, my beloved brethren, hath not God chosen the poor of this world rich in faith, and heirs of the kingdom which he hath promised to them that love him? ⁶ But ye have despised the poor. Do not rich men oppress you, and draw you before the judgment seats? ⁷ Do not they blaspheme that worthy name by the which ye are called?

⁸ If ye fulfil the royal law according to the scripture, 'Thou shalt love thy neighbour as thyself', ye do well, ⁹ but if ye have respect to persons, ye commit sin, and are convinced of the law as transgressors. ¹⁰ For whosoever shall keep the whole law, and yet offend in one point, he is guilty of all. ¹¹ For he that said, 'Do not commit adultery', said also, 'Do not kill'. Now if thou commit no adultery, yet if thou kill, thou art become a transgressor of the law. ¹² So speak ye, and so do, as they that shall be judged by the law of liberty. ¹³ For he shall have judgment without mercy, that hath shewed no mercy; and mercy rejoiceth against judgment.

[14] What doth it profit, my brethren, though a man say he hath faith, and have not works? Can faith save him? [15] If a brother or sister be naked, and destitute of daily food, [16] and one of you say unto them, 'Depart in peace, be ye warmed and filled', notwithstanding ye give them not those things which are needful to the body; what doth it profit? [17] Even so faith, if it hath not works, is dead, being alone.

[18] Yea, a man may say, 'Thou hast faith, and I have works': shew me thy faith without thy works, and I will shew thee my faith by my works. [19] Thou believest that there is one God; thou doest well: the devils also believe, and tremble. [20] But wilt thou know, O vain man, that faith without works is dead? [21] Was not Abraham our father justified by works, when he had offered Isaac his son upon the altar? [22] Seest thou how faith wrought with his works, and by works was faith made perfect? [23] And the scripture was fulfilled which saith, 'Abraham believed God, and it was imputed unto him for righteousness': and he was called the Friend of God. [24] Ye see then how that by works a man is justified, and not by faith only. [25] Likewise also was not Rahab the harlot justified by works, when she had received the messengers, and had sent them out another way? [26] For as the body without the spirit is dead, so faith without works is dead also.

3 My brethren, be not many masters, knowing that we shall receive the greater condemnation. [2] For in many things we offend all. If any man offend not in word, the

same is a perfect man, and able also to bridle the whole body. ³Behold, we put bits in the horses' mouths, that they may obey us; and we turn about their whole body. ⁴Behold also the ships, which though they be so great, and are driven of fierce winds, yet are they turned about with a very small helm, whithersoever the governor listeth. ⁵Even so the tongue is a little member, and boasteth great things. Behold, how great a matter a little fire kindleth! ⁶And the tongue is a fire, a world of iniquity: so is the tongue among our members, that it defileth the whole body, and setteth on fire the course of nature; and it is set on fire of hell. ⁷For every kind of beasts, and of birds, and of serpents, and of things in the sea, is tamed, and hath been tamed of mankind, ⁸but the tongue can no man tame; it is an unruly evil, full of deadly poison. ⁹Therewith bless we God, even the Father; and therewith curse we men, which are made after the similitude of God. ¹⁰Out of the same mouth proceedeth blessing and cursing. My brethren, these things ought not so to be. ¹¹Doth a fountain send forth at the same place sweet water and bitter? ¹²Can the fig tree, my brethren, bear olive berries? Either a vine, figs? So can no fountain both yield salt water and fresh.

¹³Who is a wise man and endued with knowledge among you? Let him shew out of a good conversation his works with meekness of wisdom. ¹⁴But if ye have bitter envying and strife in your hearts, glory not, and lie not against the truth. ¹⁵This wisdom descendeth not from above, but is earthly, sensual, devilish. ¹⁶For where envying and strife

is, there is confusion and every evil work. [17] But the wisdom that is from above is first pure, then peaceable, gentle, and easy to be intreated, full of mercy and good fruits, without partiality, and without hypocrisy. [18]And the fruit of righteousness is sown in peace of them that make peace.

4 From whence come wars and fightings among you? Come they not hence, even of your lusts that war in your members? [2] Ye lust, and have not: ye kill, and desire to have, and cannot obtain: ye fight and war, yet ye have not, because ye ask not. [3] Ye ask, and receive not, because ye ask amiss, that ye may consume it upon your lusts. [4] Ye adulterers and adulteresses, know ye not that the friendship of the world is enmity with God? Whosoever therefore will be a friend of the world is the enemy of God. [5] Do ye think that the scripture saith in vain, 'The spirit that dwelleth in us lusteth to envy'? [6] But he giveth more grace. Wherefore he saith, 'God resisteth the proud, but giveth grace unto the humble.' [7]Submit yourselves therefore to God. Resist the devil, and he will flee from you. [8] Draw nigh to God, and he will draw nigh to you. Cleanse your hands, ye sinners; and purify your hearts, ye double minded. [9] Be afflicted, and mourn, and weep: let your laughter be turned to mourning, and your joy to heaviness. [10]Humble yourselves in the sight of the Lord, and he shall lift you up.

[11]Speak not evil one of another, brethren. He that speaketh evil of his brother, and judgeth his brother, speaketh evil of the law, and judgeth the law: but if thou judge the law,

thou art not a doer of the law, but a judge. ¹²There is one lawgiver, who is able to save and to destroy: who art thou that judgest another?

¹³Go to now, ye that say, 'To day or to morrow we will go into such a city, and continue there a year, and buy and sell, and get gain, ¹⁴whereas ye know not what shall be on the morrow. For what is your life? It is even a vapour, that appeareth for a little time, and then vanisheth away. ¹⁵For that ye ought to say, 'If the Lord will, we shall live, and do this, or that.' ¹⁶But now ye rejoice in your boastings: all such rejoicing is evil. ¹⁷Therefore to him that knoweth to do good, and doeth it not, to him it is sin.

5 Go to now, ye rich men, weep and howl for your miseries that shall come upon you. ²Your riches are corrupted, and your garments are motheaten. ³Your gold and silver is cankered; and the rust of them shall be a witness against you, and shall eat your flesh as it were fire. Ye have heaped treasure together for the last days. ⁴Behold, the hire of the labourers who have reaped down your fields, which is of you kept back by fraud, crieth: and the cries of them which have reaped are entered into the ears of the Lord of sabaoth. ⁵Ye have lived in pleasure on the earth, and been wanton; ye have nourished your hearts, as in a day of slaughter. ⁶Ye have condemned and killed the just; and he doth not resist you.

⁷Be patient therefore, brethren, unto the coming of the Lord. Behold, the husbandman waiteth for the precious fruit

of the earth, and hath long patience for it, until he receive the early and latter rain. ⁸ Be ye also patient; stablish your hearts, for the coming of the Lord draweth nigh. ⁹ Grudge not one against another, brethren, lest ye be condemned: behold, the judge standeth before the door. ¹⁰ Take, my brethren, the prophets, who have spoken in the name of the Lord, for an example of suffering affliction, and of patience. ¹¹ Behold, we count them happy which endure. Ye have heard of the patience of Job, and have seen the end of the Lord; that the Lord is very pitiful, and of tender mercy.

¹² But above all things, my brethren, swear not, neither by heaven, neither by the earth, neither by any other oath; but let your yea be yea; and your nay, nay; lest ye fall into condemnation.

¹³ Is any among you afflicted? Let him pray. Is any merry? Let him sing psalms. ¹⁴ Is any sick among you? Let him call for the elders of the church; and let them pray over him, anointing him with oil in the name of the Lord, ¹⁵ and the prayer of faith shall save the sick, and the Lord shall raise him up; and if he have committed sins, they shall be forgiven him. ¹⁶ Confess your faults one to another, and pray one for another, that ye may be healed. The effectual fervent prayer of a righteous man availeth much. ¹⁷ Elias was a man subject to like passions as we are, and he prayed earnestly that it might not rain: and it rained not on the earth by the space of three years and six months. ¹⁸ And he prayed again, and the heaven gave rain, and the earth brought forth her fruit.

¹⁹ Brethren, if any of you do err from the truth, and one

convert him; [20] let him know, that he which converteth the sinner from the error of his way shall save a soul from death, and shall hide a multitude of sins.

the first epistle general of peter

Peter, an apostle of Jesus Christ, to the strangers scattered throughout Pontus, Galatia, Cappadocia, Asia, and Bithynia, ² elect according to the foreknowledge of God the Father, through sanctification of the Spirit, unto obedience and sprinkling of the blood of Jesus Christ: Grace unto you, and peace, be multiplied.

³ Blessed be the God and Father of our Lord Jesus Christ, which according to his abundant mercy hath begotten us again unto a lively hope by the resurrection of Jesus Christ from the dead, ⁴ to an inheritance incorruptible, and undefiled, and that fadeth not away, reserved in heaven for you, ⁵ who are kept by the power of God through faith unto salvation ready to be revealed in the last time. ⁶ Wherein ye greatly rejoice, though now for a season, if need be, ye are in heaviness through manifold temptations, ⁷ that the trial of your faith, being much more precious than of gold that perisheth, though it be tried with fire, might be found unto praise and honour and glory at the appearing of Jesus Christ, ⁸ whom having not seen, ye love, in whom, though now ye see him not, yet believing, ye rejoice with joy unspeakable and full of glory, ⁹ receiving the end of your faith, even the salvation of your souls.

¹⁰ Of which salvation the prophets have enquired and searched diligently, who prophesied of the grace that should come unto you, ¹¹ searching what, or what manner of time the Spirit of Christ which was in them did signify, when it testified beforehand the sufferings of Christ, and the glory that should follow. ¹² Unto whom it was revealed, that not unto themselves, but unto us they did minister the things, which are now reported unto you by them that have preached the gospel unto you with the Holy Ghost sent down from heaven; which things the angels desire to look into.

¹³ Wherefore gird up the loins of your mind, be sober, and hope to the end for the grace that is to be brought unto you at the revelation of Jesus Christ; ¹⁴ as obedient children, not fashioning yourselves according to the former lusts in your ignorance, ¹⁵ but as he which hath called you is holy, so be ye holy in all manner of conversation, ¹⁶ because it is written, 'Be ye holy; for I am holy.'

¹⁷ And if ye call on the Father, who without respect of persons judgeth according to every man's work, pass the time of your sojourning here in fear, ¹⁸ forasmuch as ye know that ye were not redeemed with corruptible things, as silver and gold, from your vain conversation received by tradition from your fathers, ¹⁹ but with the precious blood of Christ, as of a lamb without blemish and without spot, ²⁰ who verily was foreordained before the foundation of the world, but was manifest in these last times for you, ²¹ who by him do believe in God, that raised him up from the dead, and gave him glory; that your faith and hope might be in God.

[22] Seeing ye have purified your souls in obeying the truth through the Spirit unto unfeigned love of the brethren, see that ye love one another with a pure heart fervently, [23] being born again, not of corruptible seed, but of incorruptible, by the word of God, which liveth and abideth for ever. [24] For all flesh is as grass, and all the glory of man as the flower of grass. The grass withereth, and the flower thereof falleth away, [25] but the word of the Lord endureth for ever. And this is the word which by the gospel is preached unto you.

2 Wherefore laying aside all malice, and all guile, and hypocrisies, and envies, and all evil speakings, [2] as new-born babes, desire the sincere milk of the word, that ye may grow thereby; [3] if so be ye have tasted that the Lord is gracious.

[4] To whom coming, as unto a living stone, disallowed indeed of men, but chosen of God, and precious, [5] ye also, as lively stones, are built up a spiritual house, an holy priest-hood, to offer up spiritual sacrifices, acceptable to God by Jesus Christ. [6] Wherefore also it is contained in the scripture, 'Behold, I lay in Sion a chief corner stone, elect, precious: and he that believeth on him shall not be confounded.' [7] Unto you therefore which believe he is precious: but unto them which be disobedient, the stone which the builders dis-allowed, the same is made the head of the corner, [8] and a stone of stumbling, and a rock of offence, even to them which stumble at the word, being disobedient: whereunto also they were appointed.

[9] But ye are a chosen generation, a royal priesthood, an

holy nation, a peculiar people; that ye should shew forth the praises of him who hath called you out of darkness into his marvellous light: ¹⁰ which in time past were not a people, but are now the people of God: which had not obtained mercy, but now have obtained mercy.

¹¹ Dearly beloved, I beseech you as strangers and pilgrims, abstain from fleshly lusts, which war against the soul; ¹² having your conversation honest among the Gentiles: that, whereas they speak against you as evildoers, they may by your good works, which they shall behold, glorify God in the day of visitation.

¹³ Submit yourselves to every ordinance of man for the Lord's sake, whether it be to the king, as supreme; ¹⁴ or unto governors, as unto them that are sent by him for the punishment of evildoers, and for the praise of them that do well. ¹⁵ For so is the will of God, that with well doing ye may put to silence the ignorance of foolish men, ¹⁶ as free, and not using your liberty for a cloke of maliciousness, but as the servants of God. ¹⁷ Honour all men. Love the brotherhood. Fear God. Honour the king.

¹⁸ Servants, be subject to your masters with all fear; not only to the good and gentle, but also to the froward. ¹⁹ For this is thankworthy, if a man for conscience toward God endure grief, suffering wrongfully. ²⁰ For what glory is it, if, when ye be buffeted for your faults, ye shall take it patiently? But if, when ye do well, and suffer for it, ye take it patiently, this is acceptable with God. ²¹ For even hereunto were ye called, because Christ also suffered for us, leaving

us an example, that ye should follow his steps; ²² who did no sin, neither was guile found in his mouth; ²³ who, when he was reviled, reviled not again; when he suffered, he threatened not; but committed himself to him that judgeth righteously; ²⁴ who his own self bare our sins in his own body on the tree, that we, being dead to sins, should live unto righteousness: by whose stripes ye were healed. ²⁵ For ye were as sheep going astray; but are now returned unto the Shepherd and Bishop of your souls.

3 Likewise, ye wives, be in subjection to your own husbands; that, if any obey not the word, they also may without the word be won by the conversation of the wives; ² while they behold your chaste conversation coupled with fear. ³ Whose adorning let it not be that outward adorning of plaiting the hair, and of wearing of gold, or of putting on of apparel; ⁴ but let it be the hidden man of the heart, in that which is not corruptible, even the ornament of a meek and quiet spirit, which is in the sight of God of great price. ⁵ For after this manner in the old time the holy women also, who trusted in God, adorned themselves, being in subjection unto their own husbands, ⁶ even as Sara obeyed Abraham, calling him lord, whose daughters ye are, as long as ye do well, and are not afraid with any amazement.

⁷ Likewise, ye husbands, dwell with them according to knowledge, giving honour unto the wife, as unto the weaker vessel, and as being heirs together of the grace of life; that your prayers be not hindered.

⁸ Finally, be ye all of one mind, having compassion one of another, love as brethren, be pitiful, be courteous: ⁹ not rendering evil for evil, or railing for railing: but contrariwise blessing; knowing that ye are thereunto called, that ye should inherit a blessing. ¹⁰ For he that will love life, and see good days, let him refrain his tongue from evil, and his lips that they speak no guile: ¹¹ let him eschew evil, and do good; let him seek peace, and ensue it. ¹² For the eyes of the Lord are over the righteous, and his ears are open unto their prayers, but the face of the Lord is against them that do evil.

¹³ And who is he that will harm you, if ye be followers of that which is good? ¹⁴ But and if ye suffer for righteousness' sake, happy are ye: and be not afraid of their terror, neither be troubled, ¹⁵ but sanctify the Lord God in your hearts: and be ready always to give an answer to every man that asketh you a reason of the hope that is in you with meekness and fear: ¹⁶ having a good conscience; that, whereas they speak evil of you, as of evildoers, they may be ashamed that falsely accuse your good conversation in Christ. ¹⁷ For it is better, if the will of God be so, that ye suffer for well doing, than for evil doing. ¹⁸ For Christ also hath once suffered for sins, the just for the unjust, that he might bring us to God, being put to death in the flesh, but quickened by the Spirit, ¹⁹ by which also he went and preached unto the spirits in prison, ²⁰ which sometime were disobedient, when once the longsuffering of God waited in the days of Noah, while the ark was a preparing, wherein few, that is, eight souls were saved by water. ²¹ The like figure whereunto even baptism doth also now

save us (not the putting away of the filth of the flesh, but the answer of a good conscience toward God) by the resurrection of Jesus Christ, ²²who is gone into heaven, and is on the right hand of God; angels and authorities and powers being made subject unto him.

4 Forasmuch then as Christ hath suffered for us in the flesh, arm yourselves likewise with the same mind, for he that hath suffered in the flesh hath ceased from sin; ²that he no longer should live the rest of his time in the flesh to the lusts of men, but to the will of God. ³For the time past of our life may suffice us to have wrought the will of the Gentiles, when we walked in lasciviousness, lusts, excess of wine, revellings, banquetings, and abominable idolatries: ⁴wherein they think it strange that ye run not with them to the same excess of riot, speaking evil of you, ⁵who shall give account to him that is ready to judge the quick and the dead. ⁶For for this cause was the gospel preached also to them that are dead, that they might be judged according to men in the flesh, but live according to God in the spirit.

⁷But the end of all things is at hand: be ye therefore sober, and watch unto prayer. ⁸And above all things have fervent charity among yourselves, for charity shall cover the multitude of sins. ⁹Use hospitality one to another without grudging. ¹⁰As every man hath received the gift, even so minister the same one to another, as good stewards of the manifold grace of God. ¹¹If any man speak, let him speak as the oracles of God; if any man minister, let him do it as of the

ability which God giveth: that God in all things may be glorified through Jesus Christ, to whom be praise and dominion for ever and ever. Amen.

¹²Beloved, think it not strange concerning the fiery trial which is to try you, as though some strange thing happened unto you, ¹³but rejoice, inasmuch as ye are partakers of Christ's sufferings; that, when his glory shall be revealed, ye may be glad also with exceeding joy. ¹⁴If ye be reproached for the name of Christ, happy are ye; for the spirit of glory and of God resteth upon you: on their part he is evil spoken of, but on your part he is glorified. ¹⁵But let none of you suffer as a murderer, or as a thief, or as an evildoer, or as a busybody in other men's matters. ¹⁶Yet if any man suffer as a Christian, let him not be ashamed; but let him glorify God on this behalf. ¹⁷For the time is come that judgment must begin at the house of God: and if it first begin at us, what shall the end be of them that obey not the gospel of God? ¹⁸And if the righteous scarcely be saved, where shall the ungodly and the sinner appear? ¹⁹Wherefore let them that suffer according to the will of God commit the keeping of their souls to him in well doing, as unto a faithful Creator.

5 The elders which are among you I exhort, who am also an elder, and a witness of the sufferings of Christ, and also a partaker of the glory that shall be revealed. ²Feed the flock of God which is among you, taking the oversight thereof, not by constraint, but willingly; not for filthy lucre, but of a ready mind; ³neither as being lords over God's

heritage, but being ensamples to the flock. ⁴And when the chief Shepherd shall appear, ye shall receive a crown of glory that fadeth not away. ⁵Likewise, ye younger, submit yourselves unto the elder. Yea, all of you be subject one to another, and be clothed with humility, for God resisteth the proud, and giveth grace to the humble.

⁶Humble yourselves therefore under the mighty hand of God, that he may exalt you in due time, ⁷casting all your care upon him; for he careth for you. ⁸Be sober, be vigilant; because your adversary the devil, as a roaring lion, walketh about, seeking whom he may devour, ⁹whom resist stedfast in the faith, knowing that the same afflictions are accomplished in your brethren that are in the world. ¹⁰But the God of all grace, who hath called us unto his eternal glory by Christ Jesus, after that ye have suffered a while, make you perfect, stablish, strengthen, settle you. ¹¹To him be glory and dominion for ever and ever. Amen.

¹²By Silvanus, a faithful brother unto you, as I suppose, I have written briefly, exhorting, and testifying that this is the true grace of God wherein ye stand. ¹³The church that is at Babylon, elected together with you, saluteth you; and so doth Marcus my son. ¹⁴Greet ye one another with a kiss of charity. Peace be with you all that are in Christ Jesus. Amen.

the second epistle general of peter

Simon Peter, a servant and an apostle of Jesus Christ, to them that have obtained like precious faith with us through the righteousness of God and our Saviour Jesus Christ:

²Grace and peace be multiplied unto you through the knowledge of God, and of Jesus our Lord.

³According as his divine power hath given unto us all things that pertain unto life and godliness, through the knowledge of him that hath called us to glory and virtue: ⁴whereby are given unto us exceeding great and precious promises: that by these ye might be partakers of the divine nature, having escaped the corruption that is in the world through lust. ⁵And beside this, giving all diligence, add to your faith virtue; and to virtue knowledge; ⁶and to knowledge temperance; and to temperance patience; and to patience godliness; ⁷and to godliness brotherly kindness; and to brotherly kindness charity. ⁸For if these things be in you, and abound, they make you that ye shall neither be barren nor unfruitful in the knowledge of our Lord Jesus Christ. ⁹But he that lacketh these things is blind, and cannot see afar off, and hath forgotten that he was purged from his old sins. ¹⁰Wherefore the rather, brethren, give diligence to make

your calling and election sure, for if ye do these things, ye shall never fall, ¹¹ for so an entrance shall be ministered unto you abundantly into the everlasting kingdom of our Lord and Saviour Jesus Christ.

¹² Wherefore I will not be negligent to put you always in remembrance of these things, though ye know them, and be established in the present truth. ¹³ Yea, I think it meet, as long as I am in this tabernacle, to stir you up by putting you in remembrance; ¹⁴ knowing that shortly I must put off this my tabernacle, even as our Lord Jesus Christ hath shewed me. ¹⁵ Moreover I will endeavour that ye may be able after my decease to have these things always in remembrance.

¹⁶ For we have not followed cunningly devised fables, when we made known unto you the power and coming of our Lord Jesus Christ, but were eyewitnesses of his majesty. ¹⁷ For he received from God the Father honour and glory, when there came such a voice to him from the excellent glory, 'This is my beloved Son, in whom I am well pleased.' ¹⁸ And this voice which came from heaven we heard, when we were with him in the holy mount.

¹⁹ We have also a more sure word of prophecy; whereunto ye do well that ye take heed, as unto a light that shineth in a dark place, until the day dawn, and the day star arise in your hearts: ²⁰ knowing this first, that no prophecy of the scripture is of any private interpretation. ²¹ For the prophecy came not in old time by the will of man, but holy men of God spake as they were moved by the Holy Ghost.

2 But there were false prophets also among the people, even as there shall be false teachers among you, who privily shall bring in damnable heresies, even denying the Lord that bought them, and bring upon themselves swift destruction. ²And many shall follow their pernicious ways; by reason of whom the way of truth shall be evil spoken of. ³And through covetousness shall they with feigned words make merchandise of you, whose judgment now of a long time lingereth not, and their damnation slumbereth not.

⁴For if God spared not the angels that sinned, but cast them down to hell, and delivered them into chains of darkness, to be reserved unto judgment; ⁵and spared not the old world, but saved Noah the eighth person, a preacher of righteousness, bringing in the flood upon the world of the ungodly; ⁶and turning the cities of Sodom and Gomorrha into ashes condemned them with an overthrow, making them an ensample unto those that after should live ungodly; ⁷and delivered just Lot, vexed with the filthy conversation of the wicked ⁸for that righteous man dwelling among them, in seeing and hearing, vexed his righteous soul from day to day with their unlawful deeds, ⁹the Lord knoweth how to deliver the godly out of temptations, and to reserve the unjust unto the day of judgment to be punished, ¹⁰but chiefly them that walk after the flesh in the lust of uncleanness, and despise government. Presumptuous are they, selfwilled, they are not afraid to speak evil of dignities. ¹¹Whereas angels, which are greater in power and might, bring not railing accusation against them before the Lord.

¹² But these, as natural brute beasts, made to be taken and destroyed, speak evil of the things that they understand not; and shall utterly perish in their own corruption; ¹³ and shall receive the reward of unrighteousness, as they that count it pleasure to riot in the day time. Spots they are and blemishes, sporting themselves with their own deceivings while they feast with you; ¹⁴ having eyes full of adultery, and that cannot cease from sin; beguiling unstable souls; an heart they have exercised with covetous practices; cursed children, ¹⁵ which have forsaken the right way, and are gone astray, following the way of Balaam the son of Bosor, who loved the wages of unrighteousness; ¹⁶ but was rebuked for his iniquity: the dumb ass speaking with man's voice forbad the madness of the prophet.

¹⁷ These are wells without water, clouds that are carried with a tempest, to whom the mist of darkness is reserved for ever. ¹⁸ For when they speak great swelling words of vanity, they allure through the lusts of the flesh, through much wantonness, those that were clean escaped from them who live in error. ¹⁹ While they promise them liberty, they themselves are the servants of corruption, for of whom a man is overcome, of the same is he brought in bondage. ²⁰ For if after they have escaped the pollutions of the world through the knowledge of the Lord and Saviour Jesus Christ, they are again entangled therein, and overcome, the latter end is worse with them than the beginning. ²¹ For it had been better for them not to have known the way of righteousness, than, after they have known it, to turn from the holy command-

ment delivered unto them. ²² But it is happened unto them according to the true proverb, 'The dog is turned to his own vomit again; and the sow that was washed to her wallowing in the mire.'

3 This second epistle, beloved, I now write unto you; in both which I stir up your pure minds by way of remembrance, ² that ye may be mindful of the words which were spoken before by the holy prophets, and of the commandment of us the apostles of the Lord and Saviour, ³ knowing this first, that there shall come in the last days scoffers, walking after their own lusts, ⁴ and saying, 'Where is the promise of his coming?' For since the fathers fell asleep, all things continue as they were from the beginning of the creation. ⁵ For this they willingly are ignorant of, that by the word of God the heavens were of old, and the earth standing out of the water and in the water, ⁶ whereby the world that then was, being overflowed with water, perished, ⁷ but the heavens and the earth, which are now, by the same word are kept in store, reserved unto fire against the day of judgment and perdition of ungodly men.

⁸ But, beloved, be not ignorant of this one thing, that one day is with the Lord as a thousand years, and a thousand years as one day. ⁹ The Lord is not slack concerning his promise, as some men count slackness; but is longsuffering to us-ward, not willing that any should perish, but that all should come to repentance. ¹⁰ But the day of the Lord will come as a thief in the night; in the which the heavens shall

pass away with a great noise, and the elements shall melt with fervent heat, the earth also and the works that are therein shall be burned up.

¹¹ Seeing then that all these things shall be dissolved, what manner of persons ought ye to be in all holy conversation and godliness, ¹² looking for and hasting unto the coming of the day of God, wherein the heavens being on fire shall be dissolved, and the elements shall melt with fervent heat? ¹³ Nevertheless we, according to his promise, look for new heavens and a new earth, wherein dwelleth righteousness.

¹⁴ Wherefore, beloved, seeing that ye look for such things, be diligent that ye may be found of him in peace, without spot, and blameless. ¹⁵ And account that the longsuffering of our Lord is salvation; even as our beloved brother Paul also according to the wisdom given unto him hath written unto you, ¹⁶ as also in all his epistles, speaking in them of these things; in which are some things hard to be understood, which they that are unlearned and unstable wrest, as they do also the other scriptures, unto their own destruction. ¹⁷ Ye therefore, beloved, seeing ye know these things before, beware lest ye also, being led away with the error of the wicked, fall from your own stedfastness. ¹⁸ But grow in grace, and in the knowledge of our Lord and Saviour Jesus Christ. To him be glory both now and for ever. Amen.

the first epistle general of john

That which was from the beginning, which we have heard, which we have seen with our eyes, which we have looked upon, and our hands have handled, of the Word of life, ² for the life was manifested, and we have seen it, and bear witness, and shew unto you that eternal life, which was with the Father, and was manifested unto us, ³ that which we have seen and heard declare we unto you, that ye also may have fellowship with us: and truly our fellowship is with the Father, and with his Son Jesus Christ. ⁴And these things write we unto you, that your joy may be full.

⁵This then is the message which we have heard of him, and declare unto you, that God is light, and in him is no darkness at all. ⁶If we say that we have fellowship with him, and walk in darkness, we lie, and do not the truth, ⁷ but if we walk in the light, as he is in the light, we have fellowship one with another, and the blood of Jesus Christ his Son cleanseth us from all sin. ⁸If we say that we have no sin, we deceive ourselves, and the truth is not in us. ⁹If we confess our sins, he is faithful and just to forgive us our sins, and to cleanse us from all unrighteousness. ¹⁰If we say that we have not sinned, we make him a liar, and his word is not in us.

2 My little children, these things write I unto you, that ye sin not. And if any man sin, we have an advocate with the Father, Jesus Christ the righteous, ²and he is the propitiation for our sins, and not for ours only, but also for the sins of the whole world. ³And hereby we do know that we know him, if we keep his commandments. ⁴He that saith, 'I know him', and keepeth not his commandments, is a liar, and the truth is not in him. ⁵But whoso keepeth his word, in him verily is the love of God perfected: hereby know we that we are in him. ⁶He that saith he abideth in him ought himself also so to walk, even as he walked.

⁷Brethren, I write no new commandment unto you, but an old commandment which ye had from the beginning. The old commandment is the word which ye have heard from the beginning. ⁸Again, a new commandment I write unto you, which thing is true in him and in you, because the darkness is past, and the true light now shineth. ⁹He that saith he is in the light, and hateth his brother, is in darkness even until now. ¹⁰He that loveth his brother abideth in the light, and there is none occasion of stumbling in him. ¹¹But he that hateth his brother is in darkness, and walketh in darkness, and knoweth not whither he goeth, because that darkness hath blinded his eyes. ¹²I write unto you, little children, because your sins are forgiven you for his name's sake. ¹³I write unto you, fathers, because ye have known him that is from the beginning. I write unto you, young men, because ye have overcome the wicked one. I write unto you, little children, because ye have known the Father. ¹⁴I have written

unto you, fathers, because ye have known him that is from the beginning. I have written unto you, young men, because ye are strong, and the word of God abideth in you, and ye have overcome the wicked one.

¹⁵ Love not the world, neither the things that are in the world. If any man love the world, the love of the Father is not in him. ¹⁶ For all that is in the world, the lust of the flesh, and the lust of the eyes, and the pride of life, is not of the Father, but is of the world. ¹⁷ And the world passeth away, and the lust thereof, but he that doeth the will of God abideth for ever.

¹⁸ Little children, it is the last time: and as ye have heard that antichrist shall come, even now are there many antichrists; whereby we know that it is the last time. ¹⁹ They went out from us, but they were not of us; for if they had been of us, they would no doubt have continued with us, but they went out, that they might be made manifest that they were not all of us. ²⁰ But ye have an unction from the Holy One, and ye know all things. ²¹ I have not written unto you because ye know not the truth, but because ye know it, and that no lie is of the truth. ²² Who is a liar but he that denieth that Jesus is the Christ? He is antichrist, that denieth the Father and the Son. ²³ Whosoever denieth the Son, the same hath not the Father, (but) he that acknowledgeth the Son hath the Father also. ²⁴ Let that therefore abide in you, which ye have heard from the beginning. If that which ye have heard from the beginning shall remain in you, ye also shall continue in the Son, and in the Father. ²⁵ And this is the

promise that he hath promised us, even eternal life.

²⁶ These things have I written unto you concerning them that seduce you. ²⁷ But the anointing which ye have received of him abideth in you, and ye need not that any man teach you, but as the same anointing teacheth you of all things, and is truth, and is no lie, and even as it hath taught you, ye shall abide in him.

²⁸ And now, little children, abide in him; that, when he shall appear, we may have confidence, and not be ashamed before him at his coming.

²⁹ If ye know that he is righteous, ye know that every one that doeth righteousness is born of him.

3 Behold, what manner of love the Father hath bestowed upon us, that we should be called the sons of God: therefore the world knoweth us not, because it knew him not. ² Beloved, now are we the sons of God, and it doth not yet appear what we shall be, but we know that, when he shall appear, we shall be like him, for we shall see him as he is. ³ And every man that hath this hope in him purifieth himself, even as he is pure.

⁴ Whosoever committeth sin transgresseth also the law, for sin is the transgression of the law. ⁵ And ye know that he was manifested to take away our sins; and in him is no sin. ⁶ Whosoever abideth in him sinneth not: whosoever sinneth hath not seen him, neither known him. ⁷ Little children, let no man deceive you: he that doeth righteousness is righteous, even as he is righteous. ⁸ He that committeth sin is of

the devil, for the devil sinneth from the beginning. For this purpose the Son of God was manifested, that he might destroy the works of the devil. ⁹Whosoever is born of God doth not commit sin, for his seed remaineth in him, and he cannot sin, because he is born of God. ¹⁰In this the children of God are manifest, and the children of the devil: whosoever doeth not righteousness is not of God, neither he that loveth not his brother.

¹¹For this is the message that ye heard from the beginning, that we should love one another. ¹²Not as Cain, who was of that wicked one, and slew his brother. And wherefore slew he him? Because his own works were evil, and his brother's righteous. ¹³Marvel not, my brethren, if the world hate you. ¹⁴We know that we have passed from death unto life, because we love the brethren. He that loveth not his brother abideth in death. ¹⁵Whosoever hateth his brother is a murderer: and ye know that no murderer hath eternal life abiding in him. ¹⁶Hereby perceive we the love of God, because he laid down his life for us: and we ought to lay down our lives for the brethren. ¹⁷But whoso hath this world's good, and seeth his brother have need, and shutteth up his bowels of compassion from him, how dwelleth the love of God in him?

¹⁸My little children, let us not love in word, neither in tongue; but in deed and in truth. ¹⁹And hereby we know that we are of the truth, and shall assure our hearts before him. ²⁰For if our heart condemn us, God is greater than our heart, and knoweth all things. ²¹Beloved, if our heart condemn us

not, then have we confidence toward God. ²²And whatsoever we ask, we receive of him, because we keep his commandments, and do those things that are pleasing in his sight.

²³And this is his commandment, 'That we should believe on the name of his Son Jesus Christ, and love one another', as he gave us commandment. ²⁴And he that keepeth his commandments dwelleth in him, and he in him. And hereby we know that he abideth in us, by the Spirit which he hath given us.

4 Beloved, believe not every spirit, but try the spirits whether they are of God, because many false prophets are gone out into the world. ²Hereby know ye the Spirit of God: every spirit that confesseth that Jesus Christ is come in the flesh is of God: ³and every spirit that confesseth not that Jesus Christ is come in the flesh is not of God: and this is that spirit of antichrist, whereof ye have heard that it should come; and even now already is it in the world. ⁴Ye are of God, little children, and have overcome them, because greater is he that is in you, than he that is in the world. ⁵They are of the world: therefore speak they of the world, and the world heareth them. ⁶We are of God: he that knoweth God heareth us; he that is not of God heareth not us. Hereby know we the spirit of truth, and the spirit of error.

⁷Beloved, let us love one another, for love is of God; and every one that loveth is born of God, and knoweth God. ⁸He that loveth not knoweth not God, for God is love. ⁹In this was

manifested the love of God toward us, because that God sent his only begotten Son into the world, that we might live through him. [10] Herein is love, not that we loved God, but that he loved us, and sent his Son to be the propitiation for our sins. [11] Beloved, if God so loved us, we ought also to love one another. [12] No man hath seen God at any time. If we love one another, God dwelleth in us, and his love is perfected in us.

[13] Hereby know we that we dwell in him, and he in us, because he hath given us of his Spirit. [14] And we have seen and do testify that the Father sent the Son to be the Saviour of the world. [15] Whosoever shall confess that Jesus is the Son of God, God dwelleth in him, and he in God. [16] And we have known and believed the love that God hath to us. God is love; and he that dwelleth in love dwelleth in God, and God in him. [17] Herein is our love made perfect, that we may have boldness in the day of judgment, because as he is, so are we in this world. [18] There is no fear in love, but perfect love casteth out fear, because fear hath torment. He that feareth is not made perfect in love. [19] We love him, because he first loved us. [20] If a man say, 'I love God', and hateth his brother, he is a liar, for he that loveth not his brother whom he hath seen, how can he love God whom he hath not seen? [21] And this commandment have we from him, 'That he who loveth God love his brother also.'

5 Whosoever believeth that Jesus is the Christ is born of God: and every one that loveth him that begat loveth him also that is begotten of him. [2] By this we know that we

love the children of God, when we love God, and keep his commandments. ³For this is the love of God, that we keep his commandments: and his commandments are not grievous. ⁴For whatsoever is born of God overcometh the world: and this is the victory that overcometh the world, even our faith. ⁵Who is he that overcometh the world, but he that believeth that Jesus is the Son of God?

⁶This is he that came by water and blood, even Jesus Christ; not by water only, but by water and blood. And it is the Spirit that beareth witness, because the Spirit is truth. ⁷For there are three that bear record in heaven, the Father, the Word, and the Holy Ghost: and these three are one. ⁸And there are three that bear witness in earth, the Spirit, and the water, and the blood: and these three agree in one. ⁹If we receive the witness of men, the witness of God is greater, for this is the witness of God which he hath testified of his Son. ¹⁰He that believeth on the Son of God hath the witness in himself: he that believeth not God hath made him a liar; because he believeth not the record that God gave of his Son. ¹¹And this is the record, that God hath given to us eternal life, and this life is in his Son. ¹²He that hath the Son hath life; and he that hath not the Son of God hath not life.

¹³These things have I written unto you that believe on the name of the Son of God; that ye may know that ye have eternal life, and that ye may believe on the name of the Son of God.

¹⁴And this is the confidence that we have in him, that, if we ask any thing according to his will, he heareth us, ¹⁵and

if we know that he hear us, whatsoever we ask, we know that we have the petitions that we desired of him. ¹⁶ If any man see his brother sin a sin which is not unto death, he shall ask, and he shall give him life for them that sin not unto death. There is a sin unto death: I do not say that he shall pray for it. ¹⁷ All unrighteousness is sin: and there is a sin not unto death.

¹⁸ We know that whosoever is born of God sinneth not; but he that is begotten of God keepeth himself, and that wicked one toucheth him not. ¹⁹ And we know that we are of God, and the whole world lieth in wickedness. ²⁰ And we know that the Son of God is come, and hath given us an understanding, that we may know him that is true, and we are in him that is true, even in his Son Jesus Christ. This is the true God, and eternal life.

²¹ Little children, keep yourselves from idols. Amen.

the second epistle of john

The elder unto the elect lady and her children, whom I love in the truth; and not I only, but also all they that have known the truth, [2] for the truth's sake, which dwelleth in us, and shall be with us for ever.

[3] Grace be with you, mercy, and peace, from God the Father, and from the Lord Jesus Christ, the Son of the Father, in truth and love.

[4] I rejoiced greatly that I found of thy children walking in truth, as we have received a commandment from the Father. [5] And now I beseech thee, lady, not as though I wrote a new commandment unto thee, but that which we had from the beginning, that we love one another. [6] And this is love, that we walk after his commandments. This is the commandment, 'That, as ye have heard from the beginning, ye should walk in it.'

[7] For many deceivers are entered into the world, who confess not that Jesus Christ is come in the flesh. This is a deceiver and an antichrist. [8] Look to yourselves, that we lose not those things which we have wrought, but that we receive a full reward. [9] Whosoever transgresseth, and abideth not in the doctrine of Christ, hath not God. He that abideth in the doctrine of Christ, he hath both the Father and

the Son. ¹⁰If there come any unto you, and bring not this doctrine, receive him not into your house, neither bid him God speed, ¹¹for he that biddeth him God speed is partaker of his evil deeds.

¹²Having many things to write unto you, I would not write with paper and ink; but I trust to come unto you, and speak face to face, that our joy may be full.

¹³The children of thy elect sister greet thee. Amen.

the third epistle of john

The elder unto the wellbeloved Gaius, whom I love in the truth.

² Beloved, I wish above all things that thou mayest prosper and be in health, even as thy soul prospereth. ³ For I rejoiced greatly, when the brethren came and testified of the truth that is in thee, even as thou walkest in the truth. ⁴ I have no greater joy than to hear that my children walk in truth.

⁵ Beloved, thou doest faithfully whatsoever thou doest to the brethren, and to strangers, ⁶ which have borne witness of thy charity before the church, whom if thou bring forward on their journey after a godly sort, thou shalt do well, ⁷ because that for his name's sake they went forth, taking nothing of the Gentiles. ⁸ We therefore ought to receive such, that we might be fellowhelpers to the truth.

⁹ I wrote unto the church, but Diotrephes, who loveth to have the pre-eminence among them, receiveth us not. ¹⁰ Wherefore, if I come, I will remember his deeds which he doeth, prating against us with malicious words: and not content therewith, neither doth he himself receive the brethren, and forbiddeth them that would, and casteth them out of the church.

¹¹ Beloved, follow not that which is evil, but that which is good. He that doeth good is of God, but he that doeth evil hath not seen God. ¹² Demetrius hath good report of all men, and of the truth itself; yea, and we also bear record; and ye know that our record is true.

¹³ I had many things to write, but I will not with ink and pen write unto thee, ¹⁴ but I trust I shall shortly see thee, and we shall speak face to face. Peace be to thee. Our friends salute thee. Greet the friends by name.

the general epistle of jude

Jude, the servant of Jesus Christ, and brother of James, to them that are sanctified by God the Father, and preserved in Jesus Christ, and called:

² Mercy unto you, and peace, and love, be multiplied.

³ Beloved, when I gave all diligence to write unto you of the common salvation, it was needful for me to write unto you, and exhort you that ye should earnestly contend for the faith which was once delivered unto the saints. ⁴ For there are certain men crept in unawares, who were before of old ordained to this condemnation, ungodly men, turning the grace of our God into lasciviousness, and denying the only Lord God, and our Lord Jesus Christ.

⁵ I will therefore put you in remembrance, though ye once knew this, how that the Lord, having saved the people out of the land of Egypt, afterward destroyed them that believed not. ⁶ And the angels which kept not their first estate, but left their own habitation, he hath reserved in everlasting chains under darkness unto the judgment of the great day. ⁷ Even as Sodom and Gomorrha, and the cities about them in like manner, giving themselves over to fornication, and going after strange flesh, are set forth for an example, suffering the vengeance of eternal fire.

⁸ Likewise also these filthy dreamers defile the flesh, despise dominion, and speak evil of dignities. ⁹ Yet Michael the archangel, when contending with the devil he disputed about the body of Moses, durst not bring against him a railing accusation, but said, 'The Lord rebuke thee.' ¹⁰ But these speak evil of those things which they know not, but what they know naturally, as brute beasts, in those things they corrupt themselves. ¹¹ Woe unto them! For they have gone in the way of Cain, and ran greedily after the error of Balaam for reward, and perished in the gainsaying of Core. ¹² These are spots in your feasts of charity, when they feast with you, feeding themselves without fear: clouds they are without water, carried about of winds; trees whose fruit withereth, without fruit, twice dead, plucked up by the roots; ¹³ raging waves of the sea, foaming out their own shame; wandering stars, to whom is reserved the blackness of darkness for ever.

¹⁴ And Enoch also, the seventh from Adam, prophesied of these, saying, 'Behold, the Lord cometh with ten thousands of his saints, ¹⁵ to execute judgment upon all, and to convince all that are ungodly among them of all their ungodly deeds which they have ungodly committed, and of all their hard speeches which ungodly sinners have spoken against him.' ¹⁶ These are murmurers, complainers, walking after their own lusts; and their mouth speaketh great swelling words, having men's persons in admiration because of advantage.

¹⁷ But, beloved, remember ye the words which were spoken before of the apostles of our Lord Jesus Christ; ¹⁸ how that they told you there should be mockers in the last time,

who should walk after their own ungodly lusts. ¹⁹ These be they who separate themselves, sensual, having not the Spirit. ²⁰ But ye, beloved, building up yourselves on your most holy faith, praying in the Holy Ghost, ²¹ keep yourselves in the love of God, looking for the mercy of our Lord Jesus Christ unto eternal life. ²² And of some have compassion, making a difference: ²³ and others save with fear, pulling them out of the fire, hating even the garment spotted by the flesh.

²⁴ Now unto him that is able to keep you from falling, and to present you faultless before the presence of his glory with exceeding joy, ²⁵ to the only wise God our Saviour, be glory and majesty, dominion and power, both now and ever. Amen.

the pocket canons

the

acts

of the apostles

authorized king james version

grove press
new york

with an introduction by | p. d. james

Introduction copyright © 1999 by P. D. James
The Pocket Canon second series copyright © 2000 by Grove/Atlantic, Inc.

All rights reserved. No part of this book may be reproduced in any form
or by any electronic or mechanical means, including information storage
and retrieval systems, without permission in writing from the publisher,
except by a reviewer, who may quote brief passages in a review. Any
members of educational institutions wishing to photocopy part or all
of the work for classroom use, or publishers who would like to obtain
permission to include the work in an anthology, should send their
inquiries to Grove/Atlantic, Inc., 841 Broadway, New York, NY 10003.

Originally published in Great Britain in 1999 by Canongate Books,
Ltd., Edinburgh, Scotland.

Published simultaneously in Canada
Printed in the United States of America

FIRST AMERICAN EDITION

ISBN 0-8021-3759-8 (boxed set)

Design by Paddy Cramsie

Grove Press
841 Broadway
New York, NY 10003

00 01 02 03   10 9 8 7 6 5 4 3 2 1

a note about pocket canons

The Authorized King James Version of the Bible, translated between 1603 and 1611, coincided with an extraordinary flowering of English literature. This version, more than any other, and possibly more than any other work in history, has had an influence in shaping the language we speak and write today.

The books of the King James Bible encompass categories as diverse as history, philosophy, law, poetry and fiction. Each Pocket Canon volume has its own introduction, specially commissioned from an impressive range of writers, to provide a personal interpretation of the text and explore its contemporary relevance.

introduction by p d james

P.D. James has won many awards for crime-writing from Britain, America, Italy and Scandinavia, and has received honorary degrees from six universities. In 1983 she received the OBE and in 1991 she was created a life peer. Her novels include An Unsuitable Job for a Woman, Innocent Blood, Shroud for a Nightingale, A Taste for Death, The Children of Men, Original Sin *and* A Certain Justice. *She lives in London.*

No book of the New Testament has a plainer and less ambiguous title than has the fifth, *The Acts of the Apostles*, but it is hardly an accurate description of this complex, fascinating and occasionally puzzling testimony in which the majority of the Apostles are only briefly named. To read *Acts* is to be drawn into a world of dramatic incident thronged with characters from all walks of life, a world of many nations and tongues; Parthians and Medes, Elamites, Cretes and Arabians, some of whom briefly appear and then as mysteriously disappear. This personal account of the formative years of the Christian Church is dominated by two very different characters, both of immense stature and importance: Peter, the rock on which Christ said He would build His Church, and Paul of Tarsus, the religious genius who, following his dramatic conversion, carried the new faith to the Gentile world and formulated its theology.

The story opens with the command of Jesus that His disciples should wait in Jerusalem for the promised baptism with the Holy Ghost, after which they would be empowered to be witnesses to Him, 'both in Jerusalem and in all Judaea, and in Samaria, and unto the uttermost part of the earth' (1:8). By the end of the book we have seen this promise fulfilled. By the power of the Holy Spirit the faith has spread like sparks from a fire, leaping from community to community through the Mediterranean world until it reaches the gates of Rome itself.

From the end of the second century the tradition of the Church has ascribed authorship of *Acts* to Luke, who wrote the first gospel. Both works are dedicated to Theophilus. The style and vocabulary of both are consistent with the same authorship and it would seem that the two books were intended to be read as one narrative. Luke is mentioned only three times in the New Testament, all in the letters of Paul. In *Colossians* 4:14 he writes: 'Luke, the beloved physician, and Demas, greet you'. When writing to Philemon he refers to Luke as one of his fellow workers, and in the fourth chapter of the second letter to Timothy, he writes: 'Only Luke is with me'(4:11). It does seem likely that Luke accompanied Paul on some of his journeys, particularly since sections in the second half of the book changed from the third-person to the first-person narrative, and are obviously a personal account. But it is extraordinary that we know so little of the man who, through his writing, was so influential in the life of the Church.

We know even less of the dedicatee Theophilus. Luke, in his gospel, gave him the title 'Excellency'. Was he a provincial governor or other powerful man drawn to the new religion but waiting to be convinced of its truth before accepting baptism? Was he even a real person? But he certainly stands for the very many people whom Luke was addressing and seeking to convince and convert by this extraordinary, richly-populated and complex mixture of religious apologia, adventure story and travelogue. *Acts* was probably written about 60 AD, although some authorities date it twenty years later. If 60 AD is roughly correct, then Luke may well have spoken to witnesses who actually met Jesus during His ministry.

The most dramatic and arguably the most important episode in *Acts*, apart from Christ's ascension and the coming of the Holy Spirit, is the conversion of Paul, then called Saul. He was an indefatigable persecutor of the Way and had been present at the stoning to death of Stephen, the first martyr. Now 'breathing out threatenings and slaughter against the disciples of the Lord'(9:1), he obtained from the high priest letters to the synagogue at Damascus authorising him to bring in men or women followers of the Way bound for Jerusalem.

While he was on the road and coming close to Damascus, there was a sudden light from Heaven shining around him. He fell to the ground and heard a voice saying: 'Saul, Saul, why persecutest thou me?' Trembling and astonished he asked, 'Lord, what wilt thou have me to do?(9:6)' He was

p d james

told to rise and go into the city and there wait to be told what would happen next. The men who were journeying with him stood speechless with amazement, hearing a voice but seeing no-one. When Saul got up from the earth he was blind and his companions had to lead him by the hand and take him into Damascus. There, after three days without sight and without food or drink, the disciple named Ananias came to him, restored his sight, confirmed to him that the Lord had indeed appeared to him on the way, and baptised him. In that extraordinary moment of revelation on the Damascus road Paul's life was irrevocably changed and the history of the Western world was set on a different course.

It would not, of course, be accurate to think of Paul's conversion in our present sense of the word; he did not abjure his old religion. He and the disciples remained Jews and, when they worshipped, did so in the synagogue. And when they preached the message of Christ crucified and risen, they could not possibly have envisioned that this new religion would spread to lands then undiscovered, or that Jesus of Nazareth would still be worshipped two thousand years after their deaths. They must, indeed, have been in expectation of Christ's early Second Coming.

No organisation with which human beings are concerned, even one divinely ordained or inspired, is ever free from controversy. The main problem facing the new Church was whether Christ's revelation was to the Jews alone or whether Gentiles could also receive the gift of the Spirit and be baptised. The decision, like many others, was preceded by a divine revelation following prayer. Peter, who was at

Joppa, went up on the roof to pray. He was hungry and, while food was being prepared, he fell into a trance. He saw Heaven opening and a great sheet, knotted by its four corners, descend and ascend three times, containing all manner of 'four-footed beasts of the earth, and wild beasts, and creeping things, and fowls of the air'(10:12). Peter heard a voice saying: 'Rise, Peter; kill and eat', but he replied, 'Not so, Lord, for I have never eaten any thing that is common or unclean.' Then the voice spoke to him again: 'What God has cleansed, that call not thou common'(10:13-15). Peter perceived that God is no respecter of persons; the new dispensation of love was to be taken to the whole world.

Inevitably this decision gave rise to further dissension; was it necessary for converts who were not Jews to be circumcised before they were received into the Church? It was decided that the Gentiles must be required to keep the Jewish dietary rules and abstain from fornication, but that they need not be circumcised. The decision was certainly not unanimous and was probably more controversial than Luke admits. It was, however, one more vital step on the journey of Christianity towards world acceptance.

Another decision which caused difficulty arose from the practice of the Church that possessions should be held in common and that distribution should be made according to need. A certain man named Ananias (the second of that name in *Acts*), with Sapphira his wife, sold their possessions, as they were required to do, but kept back part of the price. When Ananais laid the remainder at the apostles' feet, Peter asked Ananias: 'Why has Satan filled thine heart to lie to the

Holy Ghost and to keep back part of the price of the land?(5:3)' On hearing Peter's words, Ananias fell down dead. About three hours later, his wife, not knowing what had happened, came in and received the same question from Peter. She too fell down dead at his feet and was carried out. 'And great fear came upon all the church, and upon as many as heard these things'(5:11). I have always found this a disturbing story and can't help feeling some sympathy for Ananias and his wife. They probably felt it was prudent and not unreasonable, having sold all their possessions, to retain at least part of the proceeds; their punishment – since that is how it is presented in *Acts* – seems more typical of a vengeful Jehovah than of the God of love and forgiveness.

Acts is a restless book, full of comings and going, of dramatic incidents and violent events. We accompany Paul on his three great perilous journeys, but he is not the only traveller; almost all the characters are on the road, healing, raising the dead, preaching, defending themselves before the councils of the great, both in state and synagogue. Luke observes the dramatic events with the eye of a physician and describes them with the discriminating skill of a novelist, providing the human details which add verisimilitude and reinforce the story's humanity and universality.

An example is the release of Paul and Silas from prison in chapter 16, when a great earthquake at midnight shook the prison foundations and opened all the doors. The keeper of the prison, assuming that all his prisoners had fled, drew out his sword to commit suicide, but Paul cried with a loud voice, saying: 'Do thyself no harm for we are all here'(16:28).

Then the keeper called for a light and, falling down before Paul and Silas, asked what he must do to be saved. They said: 'Believe on the Lord Jesus Christ, and thou shalt be saved, and thy house'(16:31). That same night he took them home, washed their weals from the flogging and he and all his family were baptised. The next morning the magistrates sent the serjeants to free Paul and Silas. Paul, however, insisted that the magistrates come in person to do the job, saying that he and Silas had been beaten and imprisoned without having been condemned, despite the fact that they were Roman citizens. Small wonder that, hearing the prisoners were Romans, the magistrates came themselves and exhorted them to leave the city.

The final chapter of *Acts*, chapter 28, ends so suddenly that one wonders whether Luke intended to continue writing. We are left uncertain of Paul's future; the last two sentences merely say that he dwelt for two whole years at Rome in his hired house and received 'all that came in unto him. Preaching the kingdom of God, and teaching those things which concern the Lord Jesus Christ, with all confidence, no man forbidding him'(28:31). The Holy Spirit which had descended upon the disciples in Jerusalem had led the Church to the heart of the Roman Empire. Although Luke's account of Paul's life and ministry ends so abruptly, tradition has it that he was executed in Rome in AD 64–5, under Nero's persecution. The path on which he had set out after that dramatic encounter on the Damascus road, and which he had followed so faithfully, led him at last to a martyr's crown.

p d james

the acts of the apostles

The former treatise have I made, O Theophilus, of all that Jesus began both to do and teach, [2] until the day in which he was taken up, after that he through the Holy Ghost had given commandments unto the apostles whom he had chosen: [3] to whom also he shewed himself alive after his passion by many infallible proofs, being seen of them forty days, and speaking of the things pertaining to the kingdom of God; [4] and, being assembled together with them, commanded them that they should not depart from Jerusalem, but wait for the promise of the Father, which, saith he, ye have heard of me. [5] For John truly baptized with water; but ye shall be baptized with the Holy Ghost not many days hence. [6] When they therefore were come together, they asked of him, saying, 'Lord, wilt thou at this time restore again the kingdom to Israel?' [7] And he said unto them, 'It is not for you to know the times or the seasons, which the Father hath put in his own power. [8] But ye shall receive power, after that the Holy Ghost is come upon you; and ye shall be witnesses unto me both in Jerusalem, and in all Judaea, and in Samaria, and unto the uttermost part of the earth.' [9] And when he had spoken these things, while they beheld, he was taken up; and a cloud received him out of their sight. [10] And while they looked stedfastly toward heaven as he went up, behold, two men stood by them in white apparel, [11]which also said, 'Ye men of Galilee, why stand ye gazing up into heaven? This same Jesus, which is taken up from you into heaven, shall so come in like manner as ye have seen him go into heaven.' [12]Then returned they unto Jerusalem from the mount called Olivet, which is from Jerusalem a sabbath day's journey. [13]And when they were come in, they went up into an upper room, where abode both Peter, and James, and John, and Andrew, Philip, and Thomas, Bartholomew, and Matthew, James the son of Alphaeus, and Simon Zelotes, and Judas the brother of James. [14]These all continued with one accord in prayer and supplication, with the women, and Mary the mother of Jesus, and with his brethren.

[15]And in those days Peter stood up in the midst of the disciples, and said (the number of names together were about an hundred and twenty), [16]'Men and brethren, this scripture must needs have been fulfilled, which the Holy Ghost by the mouth of David spake before concerning Judas, which was guide to them that took Jesus. [17]For he was numbered with us, and had obtained part of this ministry.' [18]Now this man purchased a field with the reward of iniquity; and falling headlong, he burst asunder in the midst, and all his bowels gushed out. [19]And it was known unto all the dwellers at Jerusalem; insomuch as that field is called in their proper tongue, Aceldama, that is to say, 'The field of blood'. [20]'For it is written in the book of Psalms, "Let his habitation be desolate, and let no man dwell therein; and his bishoprick let another take." [21]Wherefore of these men which have companied with us all the time that the Lord

Jesus went in and out among us, ²² beginning from the baptism of John, unto that same day that he was taken up from us, must one be ordained to be a witness with us of his resurrection.' ²³And they appointed two, Joseph called Barsabas, who was surnamed Justus, and Matthias. ²⁴And they prayed, and said, 'Thou, Lord, which knowest the hearts of all men, shew whether of these two thou hast chosen, ²⁵ that he may take part of this ministry and apostleship, from which Judas by transgression fell, that he might go to his own place.' ²⁶And they gave forth their lots; and the lot fell upon Matthias; and he was numbered with the eleven apostles.

2 And when the day of Pentecost was fully come, they were all with one accord in one place. ²And suddenly there came a sound from heaven as of a rushing mighty wind, and it filled all the house where they were sitting. ³And there appeared unto them cloven tongues like as of fire, and it sat upon each of them. ⁴And they were all filled with the Holy Ghost, and began to speak with other tongues, as the Spirit gave them utterance. ⁵And there were dwelling at Jerusalem Jews, devout men, out of every nation under heaven. ⁶ Now when this was noised abroad, the multitude came together, and were confounded, because that every man heard them speak in his own language. ⁷And they were all amazed and marvelled, saying one to another, 'Behold, are not all these which speak Galilæans? ⁸And how hear we every man in our own tongue, wherein we were born? ⁹Parthians, and Medes, and Elamites, and the dwellers

in Mesopotamia, and in Judaea, and Cappadocia, in Pontus, and Asia, [10] Phrygia, and Pamphylia, in Egypt, and in the parts of Libya about Cyrene, and strangers of Rome, Jews and proselytes, [11] Cretes and Arabians, we do hear them speak in our tongues the wonderful works of God.' [12] And they were all amazed, and were in doubt, saying one to another, 'What meaneth this?' [13] Others mocking said, 'These men are full of new wine.'

[14] But Peter, standing up with the eleven, lifted up his voice, and said unto them, 'Ye men of Judaea, and all ye that dwell at Jerusalem, be this known unto you, and hearken to my words, [15] for these are not drunken, as ye suppose, seeing it is but the third hour of the day. [16] But this is that which was spoken by the prophet Joel: [17] "And it shall come to pass in the last days," saith God, "I will pour out of my Spirit upon all flesh: and your sons and your daughters shall prophesy, and your young men shall see visions, and your old men shall dream dreams. [18] And on my servants and on my hand-maidens I will pour out in those days of my Spirit; and they shall prophesy. [19] And I will shew wonders in heaven above, and signs in the earth beneath; blood, and fire, and vapour of smoke. [20] The sun shall be turned into darkness, and the moon into blood, before that great and notable day of the Lord come. [21] And it shall come to pass, that whosoever shall call on the name of the Lord shall be saved." [22] Ye men of Israel, hear these words; Jesus of Nazareth, a man approved of God among you by miracles and wonders and signs, which God did by him in the midst of you, as ye yourselves also know: [23] him, being delivered by the determinate counsel

and foreknowledge of God, ye have taken, and by wicked hands have crucified and slain, [24] whom God hath raised up, having loosed the pains of death, because it was not possible that he should be holden of it. [25] For David speaketh concerning him, "I foresaw the Lord always before my face, for he is on my right hand, that I should not be moved: [26] therefore did my heart rejoice, and my tongue was glad; moreover also my flesh shall rest in hope, [27] because thou wilt not leave my soul in hell, neither wilt thou suffer thine Holy One to see corruption. [28] Thou hast made known to me the ways of life; thou shalt make me full of joy with thy countenance." [29] Men and brethren, let me freely speak unto you of the patriarch David, that he is both dead and buried, and his sepulchre is with us unto this day. [30] Therefore being a prophet, and knowing that God had sworn with an oath to him, that of the fruit of his loins, according to the flesh, he would raise up Christ to sit on his throne; [31] he seeing this before spake of the resurrection of Christ, that his soul was not left in hell, neither his flesh did see corruption. [32] This Jesus hath God raised up, whereof we all are witnesses. [33] Therefore being by the right hand of God exalted, and having received of the Father the promise of the Holy Ghost, he hath shed forth this, which ye now see and hear. [34] For David is not ascended into the heavens; but he saith himself, "The Lord said unto my Lord, 'Sit thou on my right hand, [35] until I make thy foes thy footstool.'" [36] Therefore let all the house of Israel know assuredly, that God hath made that same Jesus, whom ye have crucified, both Lord and Christ.'

[37] Now when they heard this, they were pricked in their

heart, and said unto Peter and to the rest of the apostles, 'Men and brethren, what shall we do?' [38]Then Peter said unto them, 'Repent, and be baptized every one of you in the name of Jesus Christ for the remission of sins, and ye shall receive the gift of the Holy Ghost. [39]For the promise is unto you, and to your children, and to all that are afar off, even as many as the Lord our God shall call.' [40]And with many other words did he testify and exhort, saying, 'Save yourselves from this untoward generation.'

[41]Then they that gladly received his word were baptized: and the same day there were added unto them about three thousand souls. [42]And they continued stedfastly in the apostles' doctrine and fellowship, and in breaking of bread, and in prayers. [43]And fear came upon every soul: and many wonders and signs were done by the apostles. [44]And all that believed were together, and had all things common; [45]and sold their possessions and goods, and parted them to all men, as every man had need. [46]And they, continuing daily with one accord in the temple, and breaking bread from house to house, did eat their meat with gladness and singleness of heart, [47]praising God, and having favour with all the people. And the Lord added to the church daily such as should be saved.

3 Now Peter and John went up together into the temple at the hour of prayer, being the ninth hour. [2]And a certain man lame from his mother's womb was carried, whom they laid daily at the gate of the temple which is called Beautiful, to ask alms of them that entered into the temple, [3]who seeing

Peter and John about to go into the temple asked an alms. ⁴And Peter, fastening his eyes upon him with John, said, 'Look on us.' ⁵And he gave heed unto them, expecting to receive something of them. ⁶Then Peter said, 'Silver and gold have I none; but such as I have give I thee: in the name of Jesus Christ of Nazareth rise up and walk.' ⁷And he took him by the right hand, and lifted him up: and immediately his feet and ankle bones received strength. ⁸And he leaping up stood, and walked, and entered with them into the temple, walking, and leaping, and praising God. ⁹And all the people saw him walking and praising God; ¹⁰and they knew that it was he which sat for alms at the Beautiful gate of the temple; and they were filled with wonder and amazement at that which had happened unto him. ¹¹And as the lame man which was healed held Peter and John, all the people ran together unto them in the porch that is called Solomon's, greatly wondering.

¹²And when Peter saw it, he answered unto the people, 'Ye men of Israel, why marvel ye at this? Or why look ye so earnestly on us, as though by our own power or holiness we had made this man to walk? ¹³The God of Abraham, and of Isaac, and of Jacob, the God of our fathers, hath glorified his Son Jesus; whom ye delivered up, and denied him in the presence of Pilate, when he was determined to let him go. ¹⁴But ye denied the Holy One and the Just, and desired a murderer to be granted unto you; ¹⁵and killed the Prince of life, whom God hath raised from the dead; whereof we are witnesses. ¹⁶And his name through faith in his name hath made this man strong, whom ye see and know: yea, the faith

which is by him hath given him this perfect soundness in the presence of you all. ¹⁷And now, brethren, I wot that through ignorance ye did it, as did also your rulers. ¹⁸But those things, which God before had shewed by the mouth of all his prophets, that Christ should suffer, he hath so fulfilled.

¹⁹'Repent ye therefore, and be converted, that your sins may be blotted out, when the times of refreshing shall come from the presence of the Lord; ²⁰and he shall send Jesus Christ, which before was preached unto you, ²¹whom the heaven must receive until the times of restitution of all things, which God hath spoken by the mouth of all his holy prophets since the world began. ²²For Moses truly said unto the fathers, "A prophet shall the Lord your God raise up unto you of your brethren, like unto me; him shall ye hear in all things whatsoever he shall say unto you. ²³And it shall come to pass, that every soul, which will not hear that prophet, shall be destroyed from among the people." ²⁴Yea, and all the prophets from Samuel and those that follow after, as many as have spoken, have likewise foretold of these days. ²⁵Ye are the children of the prophets, and of the covenant which God made with our fathers, saying unto Abraham, "And in thy seed shall all the kindreds of the earth be blessed." ²⁶Unto you first God, having raised up his Son Jesus, sent him to bless you, in turning away every one of you from his iniquities.'

4 And as they spake unto the people, the priests, and the captain of the temple, and the Sadducees, came upon them, ²being grieved that they taught the people, and

preached through Jesus the resurrection from the dead.
³And they laid hands on them, and put them in hold unto
the next day, for it was now eventide. ⁴Howbeit many of
them which heard the word believed; and the number of the
men was about five thousand.

⁵And it came to pass on the morrow, that their rulers,
and elders, and scribes, ⁶and Annas the high priest, and
Caiaphas, and John, and Alexander, and as many as were of
the kindred of the high priest, were gathered together at
Jerusalem. ⁷And when they had set them in the midst, they
asked, 'By what power, or by what name, have ye done
this?' ⁸Then Peter, filled with the Holy Ghost, said unto
them, 'Ye rulers of the people, and elders of Israel, ⁹if we this
day be examined of the good deed done to the impotent
man, by what means he is made whole; ¹⁰be it known unto
you all, and to all the people of Israel, that by the name of
Jesus Christ of Nazareth, whom ye crucified, whom God
raised from the dead, even by him doth this man stand here
before you whole. ¹¹This is the stone which was set at nought
of you builders, which is become the head of the corner.
¹²Neither is there salvation in any other, for there is none
other name under heaven given among men, whereby we
must be saved.'

¹³Now when they saw the boldness of Peter and John,
and perceived that they were unlearned and ignorant men,
they marvelled; and they took knowledge of them, that they
had been with Jesus. ¹⁴And beholding the man which was
healed standing with them, they could say nothing against
it. ¹⁵But when they had commanded them to go aside out of

the council, they conferred among themselves, ¹⁶ saying, 'What shall we do to these men? For that indeed a notable miracle hath been done by them is manifest to all them that dwell in Jerusalem; and we cannot deny it. ¹⁷ But that it spread no further among the people, let us straitly threaten them, that they speak henceforth to no man in this name.' ¹⁸ And they called them, and commanded them not to speak at all nor teach in the name of Jesus. ¹⁹ But Peter and John answered and said unto them, 'Whether it be right in the sight of God to hearken unto you more than unto God, judge ye. ²⁰ For we cannot but speak the things which we have seen and heard.' ²¹ So when they had further threatened them, they let them go, finding nothing how they might punish them, because of the people, for all men glorified God for that which was done. ²² For the man was above forty years old, on whom this miracle of healing was shewed.

²³ And being let go, they went to their own company, and reported all that the chief priests and elders had said unto them. ²⁴ And when they heard that, they lifted up their voice to God with one accord, and said, 'Lord, thou art God, which hast made heaven, and earth, and the sea, and all that in them is, ²⁵ who by the mouth of thy servant David hast said, "Why did the heathen rage, and the people imagine vain things? ²⁶ The kings of the earth stood up, and the rulers were gathered together against the Lord, and against his Christ." ²⁷ For of a truth against thy holy child Jesus, whom thou hast anointed, both Herod, and Pontius Pilate, with the Gentiles, and the people of Israel, were gathered together, ²⁸ for to do whatsoever thy hand and thy counsel determined

before to be done. [29]And now, Lord, behold their threatenings; and grant unto thy servants, that with all boldness they may speak thy word, [30]by stretching forth thine hand to heal; and that signs and wonders may be done by the name of thy holy child Jesus.'

[31]And when they had prayed, the place was shaken where they were assembled together; and they were all filled with the Holy Ghost, and they spake the word of God with boldness. [32]And the multitude of them that believed were of one heart and of one soul: neither said any of them that ought of the things which he possessed was his own; but they had all things common. [33]And with great power gave the apostles witness of the resurrection of the Lord Jesus, and great grace was upon them all. [34]Neither was there any among them that lacked, for as many as were possessors of lands or houses sold them, and brought the prices of the things that were sold, [35]and laid them down at the apostles' feet, and distribution was made unto every man according as he had need. [36]And Joses, who by the apostles was surnamed Barnabas (which is, being interpreted, 'the son of consolation'), a Levite, and of the country of Cyprus, [37]having land, sold it, and brought the money, and laid it at the apostles' feet.

5 But a certain man named Ananias, with Sapphira his wife, sold a possession, [2]and kept back part of the price, his wife also being privy to it, and brought a certain part, and laid it at the apostles' feet. [3]But Peter said, 'Ananias, why hath Satan filled thine heart to lie to the Holy Ghost,

and to keep back part of the price of the land? ⁴Whiles it remained, was it not thine own? And after it was sold, was it not in thine own power? Why hast thou conceived this thing in thine heart? Thou hast not lied unto men, but unto God.' ⁵And Ananias hearing these words fell down, and gave up the ghost, and great fear came on all them that heard these things. ⁶And the young men arose, wound him up, and carried him out, and buried him. ⁷And it was about the space of three hours after, when his wife, not knowing what was done, came in. ⁸And Peter answered unto her, 'Tell me whether ye sold the land for so much?' And she said, 'Yea, for so much.' ⁹Then Peter said unto her, 'How is it that ye have agreed together to tempt the Spirit of the Lord? Behold, the feet of them which have buried thy husband are at the door, and shall carry thee out.' ¹⁰Then fell she down straightway at his feet, and yielded up the ghost; and the young men came in, and found her dead, and, carrying her forth, buried her by her husband. ¹¹And great fear came upon all the church, and upon as many as heard these things.

¹²And by the hands of the apostles were many signs and wonders wrought among the people (and they were all with one accord in Solomon's porch; ¹³and of the rest durst no man join himself to them; but the people magnified them; ¹⁴and believers were the more added to the Lord, multitudes both of men and women). ¹⁵Insomuch that they brought forth the sick into the streets, and laid them on beds and couches, that at the least the shadow of Peter passing by might overshadow some of them. ¹⁶There came also a multitude out of the cities round about unto Jerusalem, bringing

sick folks, and them which were vexed with unclean spirits; and they were healed every one.

¹⁷ Then the high priest rose up, and all they that were with him (which is the sect of the Sadducees), and were filled with indignation, ¹⁸ and laid their hands on the apostles, and put them in the common prison. ¹⁹ But the angel of the Lord by night opened the prison doors, and brought them forth, and said, ²⁰ 'Go, stand and speak in the temple to the people all the words of this life.' ²¹ And when they heard that, they entered into the temple early in the morning, and taught. But the high priest came, and they that were with him, and called the council together, and all the senate of the children of Israel, and sent to the prison to have them brought. ²² But when the officers came, and found them not in the prison, they returned, and told, ²³ saying, 'The prison truly found we shut with all safety, and the keepers standing without before the doors; but when we had opened, we found no man within.' ²⁴ Now when the high priest and the captain of the temple and the chief priests heard these things, they doubted of them whereunto this would grow. ²⁵ Then came one and told them, saying, 'Behold, the men whom ye put in prison are standing in the temple, and teaching the people.' ²⁶ Then went the captain with the officers, and brought them without violence, for they feared the people, lest they should have been stoned. ²⁷ And when they had brought them, they set them before the council; and the high priest asked them, ²⁸ saying, 'Did not we straitly command you that ye should not teach in this name? And, behold, ye have filled Jerusalem with your

doctrine, and intend to bring this man's blood upon us.'

²⁹ Then Peter and the other apostles answered and said, 'We ought to obey God rather than men. ³⁰ The God of our fathers raised up Jesus, whom ye slew and hanged on a tree. ³¹ Him hath God exalted with his right hand to be a Prince and a Saviour, for to give repentance to Israel, and forgiveness of sins. ³² And we are his witnesses of these things; and so is also the Holy Ghost, whom God hath given to them that obey him.'

³³ When they heard that, they were cut to the heart, and took counsel to slay them. ³⁴ Then stood there up one in the council, a Pharisee, named Gamaliel, a doctor of the law, had in reputation among all the people, and commanded to put the apostles forth a little space; ³⁵ and said unto them, 'Ye men of Israel, take heed to yourselves what ye intend to do as touching these men. ³⁶ For before these days rose up Theudas, boasting himself to be somebody, to whom a number of men, about four hundred, joined themselves; who was slain; and all, as many as obeyed him, were scattered, and brought to nought. ³⁷ After this man rose up Judas of Galilee in the days of the taxing, and drew away much people after him: he also perished; and all, even as many as obeyed him, were dispersed. ³⁸ And now I say unto you, "Refrain from these men, and let them alone, for if this counsel or this work be of men, it will come to nought; ³⁹ but if it be of God, ye cannot overthrow it; lest haply ye be found even to fight against God."' ⁴⁰ And to him they agreed; and when they had called the apostles, and beaten them, they commanded that they should not speak in the

name of Jesus, and let them go.

[41] And they departed from the presence of the council, rejoicing that they were counted worthy to suffer shame for his name. [42] And daily in the temple, and in every house, they ceased not to teach and preach Jesus Christ.

6 And in those days, when the number of the disciples was multiplied, there arose a murmuring of the Grecians against the Hebrews, because their widows were neglected in the daily ministration. [2] Then the twelve called the multitude of the disciples unto them, and said, 'It is not reason that we should leave the word of God, and serve tables. [3] Wherefore, brethren, look ye out among you seven men of honest report, full of the Holy Ghost and wisdom, whom we may appoint over this business. [4] But we will give ourselves continually to prayer, and to the ministry of the word.'

[5] And the saying pleased the whole multitude; and they chose Stephen, a man full of faith and of the Holy Ghost, and Philip, and Prochorus, and Nicanor, and Timon, and Parmenas, and Nicolas a proselyte of Antioch; [6] whom they set before the apostles; and when they had prayed, they laid their hands on them. [7] And the word of God increased; and the number of the disciples multiplied in Jerusalem greatly; and a great company of the priests were obedient to the faith. [8] And Stephen, full of faith and power, did great wonders and miracles among the people.

[9] Then there arose certain of the synagogue, which is called the synagogue of the Libertines, and Cyrenians, and Alexandrians, and of them of Cilicia and of Asia, disputing with

Stephen. ¹⁰And they were not able to resist the wisdom and the spirit by which he spake. ¹¹Then they suborned men, which said, 'We have heard him speak blasphemous words against Moses, and against God.' ¹²And they stirred up the people, and the elders, and the scribes, and came upon him, and caught him, and brought him to the council, ¹³and set up false witnesses, which said, 'This man ceaseth not to speak blasphemous words against this holy place, and the law, ¹⁴for we have heard him say that this Jesus of Nazareth shall destroy this place, and shall change the customs which Moses delivered us.' ¹⁵And all that sat in the council, looking stedfastly on him, saw his face as it had been the face of an angel.

7 Then said the high priest, 'Are these things so?' ²And he said, 'Men, brethren, and fathers, hearken: the God of glory appeared unto our father Abraham, when he was in Mesopotamia, before he dwelt in Charran, ³and said unto him, "Get thee out of thy country, and from thy kindred, and come into the land which I shall shew thee." ⁴Then came he out of the land of the Chaldaeans, and dwelt in Charran; and from thence, when his father was dead, he removed him into this land, wherein ye now dwell. ⁵And he gave him none inheritance in it, no, not so much as to set his foot on: yet he promised that he would give it to him for a possession, and to his seed after him, when as yet he had no child. ⁶And God spake on this wise, "That his seed should sojourn in a strange land; and that they should bring them into bondage, and entreat them evil four hundred years. ⁷And the nation to

whom they shall be in bondage will I judge," said God; "and after that shall they come forth, and serve me in this place." ⁸And he gave him the covenant of circumcision: and so Abraham begat Isaac, and circumcised him the eighth day; and Isaac begat Jacob; and Jacob begat the twelve patriarchs. ⁹And the patriarchs, moved with envy, sold Joseph into Egypt; but God was with him, ¹⁰and delivered him out of all his afflictions, and gave him favour and wisdom in the sight of Pharaoh king of Egypt; and he made him governor over Egypt and all his house. ¹¹Now there came a dearth over all the land of Egypt and Chanaan, and great affliction: and our fathers found no sustenance. ¹²But when Jacob heard that there was corn in Egypt, he sent out our fathers first. ¹³And at the second time Joseph was made known to his brethren; and Joseph's kindred was made known unto Pharaoh. ¹⁴Then sent Joseph, and called his father Jacob to him, and all his kindred, threescore and fifteen souls. ¹⁵So Jacob went down into Egypt, and died, he, and our fathers, ¹⁶and were carried over into Sychem, and laid in the sepulchre that Abraham bought for a sum of money of the sons of Emmor the father of Sychem. ¹⁷But when the time of the promise drew nigh, which God had sworn to Abraham, the people grew and multiplied in Egypt, ¹⁸till another king arose, which knew not Joseph. ¹⁹The same dealt subtilly with our kindred, and evil entreated our fathers, so that they cast out their young children, to the end they might not live. ²⁰In which time Moses was born, and was exceeding fair, and nourished up in his father's house three months; ²¹and when he was cast out, Pharaoh's daughter took him up, and nourished him for her own son. ²²And Moses was learned in all the wisdom of the Egyptians, and was mighty in words and in deeds. ²³And when he was full forty years old, it came into his heart to visit his brethren the children of Israel. ²⁴And seeing one of them suffer wrong, he defended him, and avenged him that was oppressed, and smote the Egyptian, ²⁵for he supposed his brethren would have understood how that God by his hand would deliver them: but they understood not. ²⁶And the next day he shewed himself unto them as they strove, and would have set them at one again, saying, "Sirs, ye are brethren; why do ye wrong one to another?" ²⁷But he that did his neighbour wrong thrust him away, saying, "Who made thee a ruler and a judge over us? ²⁸Wilt thou kill me, as thou diddest the Egyptian yesterday?" ²⁹Then fled Moses at this saying, and was a stranger in the land of Madian, where he begat two sons. ³⁰And when forty years were expired, there appeared to him in the wilderness of mount Sina an angel of the Lord in a flame of fire in a bush. ³¹When Moses saw it, he wondered at the sight; and as he drew near to behold it, the voice of the Lord came unto him, ³²saying, "I am the God of thy fathers, the God of Abraham, and the God of Isaac, and the God of Jacob." Then Moses trembled, and durst not behold. ³³Then said the Lord to him, "Put off thy shoes from thy feet, for the place where thou standest is holy ground. ³⁴I have seen, I have seen the affliction of my people which is in Egypt, and I have heard their groaning, and am come down to deliver them. And now come, I will send thee into Egypt." ³⁵This Moses whom they refused, saying, "Who made thee a ruler and a judge?", the same did God send to be a ruler and a deliverer by the hand of the angel which appeared to him in the bush. ³⁶ He brought them out, after that he had shewed wonders and signs in the land of Egypt, and in the Red Sea, and in the wilderness forty years.

³⁷ 'This is that Moses, which said unto the children of Israel, "A prophet shall the Lord your God raise up unto you of your brethren, like unto me; him shall ye hear." ³⁸ This is he, that was in the church in the wilderness with the angel which spake to him in the mount Sina, and with our fathers, who received the lively oracles to give unto us, ³⁹ to whom our fathers would not obey, but thrust him from them, and in their hearts turned back again into Egypt, ⁴⁰ saying unto Aaron, "Make us gods to go before us, for as for this Moses, which brought us out of the land of Egypt, we wot not what is become of him." ⁴¹ And they made a calf in those days, and offered sacrifice unto the idol, and rejoiced in the works of their own hands. ⁴² Then God turned, and gave them up to worship the host of heaven; as it is written in the book of the prophets, "O ye house of Israel, have ye offered to me slain beasts and sacrifices by the space of forty years in the wilderness? ⁴³ Yea, ye took up the tabernacle of Moloch, and the star of your god Remphan, figures which ye made to worship them, and I will carry you away beyond Babylon." ⁴⁴ Our fathers had the tabernacle of witness in the wilderness, as he had appointed, speaking unto Moses, that he should make it according to the fashion that he had seen. ⁴⁵ Which also our fathers that came after brought in with Jesus into the possession of the Gentiles, whom God drave

out before the face of our fathers, unto the days of David, ⁴⁶ who found favour before God, and desired to find a tabernacle for the God of Jacob. ⁴⁷ But Solomon built him an house. ⁴⁸ Howbeit the most High dwelleth not in temples made with hands; as saith the prophet, ⁴⁹"Heaven is my throne, and earth is my footstool: what house will ye build me? saith the Lord: or what is the place of my rest? ⁵⁰ Hath not my hand made all these things?"

⁵¹ 'Ye stiffnecked and uncircumcised in heart and ears, ye do always resist the Holy Ghost: as your fathers did, so do ye. ⁵² Which of the prophets have not your fathers persecuted? And they have slain them which shewed before of the coming of the Just One; of whom ye have been now the betrayers and murderers; ⁵³ who have received the law by the disposition of angels, and have not kept it.'

⁵⁴ When they heard these things, they were cut to the heart, and they gnashed on him with their teeth. ⁵⁵ But he, being full of the Holy Ghost, looked up stedfastly into heaven, and saw the glory of God, and Jesus standing on the right hand of God, ⁵⁶ and said, 'Behold, I see the heavens opened, and the Son of man standing on the right hand of God.' ⁵⁷ Then they cried out with a loud voice, and stopped their ears, and ran upon him with one accord, ⁵⁸ and cast him out of the city, and stoned him: and the witnesses laid down their clothes at a young man's feet, whose name was Saul. ⁵⁹ And they stoned Stephen, calling upon God, and saying, 'Lord Jesus, receive my spirit.' ⁶⁰ And he kneeled down, and cried with a loud voice, 'Lord, lay not this sin to their charge.' And when he had said this, he fell asleep.

8 And Saul was consenting unto his death. And at that time there was a great persecution against the church which was at Jerusalem; and they were all scattered abroad throughout the regions of Judaea and Samaria, except the apostles. ²And devout men carried Stephen to his burial, and made great lamentation over him. ³As for Saul, he made havock of the church, entering into every house, and haling men and women committed them to prison.

⁴Therefore they that were scattered abroad went every where preaching the word. ⁵Then Philip went down to the city of Samaria, and preached Christ unto them. ⁶And the people with one accord gave heed unto those things which Philip spake, hearing and seeing the miracles which he did. ⁷For unclean spirits, crying with loud voice, came out of many that were possessed with them: and many taken with palsies, and that were lame, were healed. ⁸And there was great joy in that city.

⁹But there was a certain man, called Simon, which before-time in the same city used sorcery, and bewitched the people of Samaria, giving out that himself was some great one, ¹⁰to whom they all gave heed, from the least to the greatest, saying, 'This man is the great power of God.' ¹¹And to him they had regard, because that of long time he had bewitched them with sorceries. ¹²But when they believed Philip preaching the things concerning the kingdom of God, and the name of Jesus Christ, they were baptized, both men and women. ¹³Then Simon himself believed also: and when he was baptized, he continued with Philip, and wondered, beholding the miracles and signs which were done.

¹⁴ Now when the apostles which were at Jerusalem heard that Samaria had received the word of God, they sent unto them Peter and John, ¹⁵ who, when they were come down, prayed for them, that they might receive the Holy Ghost ¹⁶(for as yet he was fallen upon none of them: only they were baptized in the name of the Lord Jesus). ¹⁷ Then laid they their hands on them, and they received the Holy Ghost. ¹⁸ And when Simon saw that through laying on of the apostles' hands the Holy Ghost was given, he offered them money, ¹⁹ saying, 'Give me also this power, that on whomsoever I lay hands, he may receive the Holy Ghost.' ²⁰ But Peter said unto him, 'Thy money perish with thee, because thou hast thought that the gift of God may be purchased with money. ²¹ Thou hast neither part nor lot in this matter, for thy heart is not right in the sight of God. ²² Repent therefore of this thy wickedness, and pray God, if perhaps the thought of thine heart may be forgiven thee. ²³ For I perceive that thou art in the gall of bitterness, and in the bond of iniquity.' ²⁴ Then answered Simon, and said, 'Pray ye to the Lord for me, that none of these things which ye have spoken come upon me.'

²⁵ And they, when they had testified and preached the word of the Lord, returned to Jerusalem, and preached the gospel in many villages of the Samaritans.

²⁶ And the angel of the Lord spake unto Philip, saying, 'Arise, and go toward the south unto the way that goeth down from Jerusalem unto Gaza, which is desert.' ²⁷ And he arose and went: and, behold, a man of Ethiopia, an eunuch of great authority under Candace queen of the Ethiopians,

who had the charge of all her treasure, and had come to Jerusalem for to worship, ²⁸ was returning, and sitting in his chariot read Esaias the prophet. ²⁹ Then the Spirit said unto Philip, 'Go near, and join thyself to this chariot.' ³⁰ And Philip ran thither to him, and heard him read the prophet Esaias, and said, 'Understandest thou what thou readest?' ³¹ And he said, 'How can I, except some man should guide me?' And he desired Philip that he would come up and sit with him. ³² The place of the scripture which he read was this, 'He was led as a sheep to the slaughter; and like a lamb dumb before his shearer, so opened he not his mouth. ³³ In his humiliation his judgment was taken away: and who shall declare his generation? For his life is taken from the earth.' ³⁴ And the eunuch answered Philip, and said, 'I pray thee, of whom speaketh the prophet this? Of himself, or of some other man?' ³⁵ Then Philip opened his mouth, and began at the same scripture, and preached unto him Jesus. ³⁶ And as they went on their way, they came unto a certain water: and the eunuch said, 'See, here is water; what doth hinder me to be baptized?' ³⁷ And Philip said, 'If thou believest with all thine heart, thou mayest.' And he answered and said, 'I believe that Jesus Christ is the Son of God.' ³⁸ And he commanded the chariot to stand still: and they went down both into the water, both Philip and the eunuch; and he baptized him. ³⁹ And when they were come up out of the water, the Spirit of the Lord caught away Philip, that the eunuch saw him no more: and he went on his way rejoicing. ⁴⁰ But Philip was found at Azotus: and passing through he preached in all the cities, till he came to Caesarea.

9 And Saul, yet breathing out threatenings and slaughter against the disciples of the Lord, went unto the high priest, ²and desired of him letters to Damascus to the synagogues, that if he found any of this way, whether they were men or women, he might bring them bound unto Jerusalem. ³And as he journeyed, he came near Damascus; and suddenly there shined round about him a light from heaven; ⁴and he fell to the earth, and heard a voice saying unto him, 'Saul, Saul, why persecutest thou me?' ⁵And he said, 'Who art thou, Lord?' And the Lord said, 'I am Jesus whom thou persecutest: it is hard for thee to kick against the pricks.' ⁶And he trembling and astonished said, 'Lord, what wilt thou have me to do?' And the Lord said unto him, 'Arise, and go into the city, and it shall be told thee what thou must do.' ⁷And the men which journeyed with him stood speechless, hearing a voice, but seeing no man. ⁸And Saul arose from the earth; and when his eyes were opened, he saw no man; but they led him by the hand, and brought him into Damascus. ⁹And he was three days without sight, and neither did eat nor drink.

¹⁰And there was a certain disciple at Damascus, named Ananias; and to him said the Lord in a vision, 'Ananias'. And he said, 'Behold, I am here, Lord.' ¹¹And the Lord said unto him, 'Arise, and go into the street which is called Straight, and enquire in the house of Judas for one called Saul, of Tarsus, for, behold, he prayeth, ¹²and hath seen in a vision a man named Ananias coming in, and putting his hand on him, that he might receive his sight.' ¹³Then Ananias answered, 'Lord, I have heard by many of this man, how

much evil he hath done to thy saints at Jerusalem, ¹⁴and here he hath authority from the chief priests to bind all that call on thy name.' ¹⁵But the Lord said unto him, 'Go thy way, for he is a chosen vessel unto me, to bear my name before the Gentiles, and kings, and the children of Israel, ¹⁶for I will shew him how great things he must suffer for my name's sake.' ¹⁷And Ananias went his way, and entered into the house; and putting his hands on him said, 'Brother Saul, the Lord, even Jesus, that appeared unto thee in the way as thou camest, hath sent me, that thou mightest receive thy sight, and be filled with the Holy Ghost.' ¹⁸And immediately there fell from his eyes as it had been scales; and he received sight forthwith, and arose, and was baptized. ¹⁹And when he had received meat, he was strengthened. Then was Saul certain days with the disciples which were at Damascus. ²⁰And straightway he preached Christ in the synagogues, that he is the Son of God. ²¹But all that heard him were amazed, and said, 'Is not this he that destroyed them which called on this name in Jerusalem, and came hither for that intent, that he might bring them bound unto the chief priests?' ²²But Saul increased the more in strength, and confounded the Jews which dwelt at Damascus, proving that this is very Christ.

²³And after that many days were fulfilled, the Jews took counsel to kill him, ²⁴but their laying await was known of Saul. And they watched the gates day and night to kill him. ²⁵Then the disciples took him by night, and let him down by the wall in a basket. ²⁶And when Saul was come to Jerusalem, he assayed to join himself to the disciples, but they were all afraid of him, and believed not that he was a

disciple. ²⁷ But Barnabas took him, and brought him to the apostles, and declared unto them how he had seen the Lord in the way, and that he had spoken to him, and how he had preached boldly at Damascus in the name of Jesus. ²⁸And he was with them coming in and going out at Jerusalem. ²⁹And he spake boldly in the name of the Lord Jesus, and disputed against the Grecians, but they went about to slay him, ³⁰ which when the brethren knew, they brought him down to Caesarea, and sent him forth to Tarsus. ³¹Then had the churches rest throughout all Judaea and Galilee and Samaria, and were edified; and walking in the fear of the Lord, and in the comfort of the Holy Ghost, were multiplied.

³²And it came to pass, as Peter passed throughout all quarters, he came down also to the saints which dwelt at Lydda. ³³And there he found a certain man named Aeneas, which had kept his bed eight years, and was sick of the palsy. ³⁴And Peter said unto him, 'Aeneas, Jesus Christ maketh thee whole: arise, and make thy bed.' And he arose immediately. ³⁵And all that dwelt at Lydda and Saron saw him, and turned to the Lord.

³⁶ Now there was at Joppa a certain disciple named Tabitha, which by interpretation is called Dorcas: this woman was full of good works and almsdeeds which she did. ³⁷And it came to pass in those days, that she was sick, and died, whom when they had washed, they laid her in an upper chamber. ³⁸And forasmuch as Lydda was nigh to Joppa, and the disciples had heard that Peter was there, they sent unto him two men, desiring him that he would not delay to come to them. ³⁹ Then Peter arose and went with

them. When he was come, they brought him into the upper chamber: and all the widows stood by him weeping, and shewing the coats and garments which Dorcas made, while she was with them. ⁴⁰ But Peter put them all forth, and kneeled down, and prayed; and turning him to the body said, 'Tabitha, arise.' And she opened her eyes, and when she saw Peter, she sat up. ⁴¹And he gave her his hand, and lifted her up, and when he had called the saints and widows, presented her alive. ⁴²And it was known throughout all Joppa; and many believed in the Lord. ⁴³And it came to pass, that he tarried many days in Joppa with one Simon a tanner.

10 There was a certain man in Caesarea called Cornelius, a centurion of the band called the Italian band, ²a devout man, and one that feared God with all his house, which gave much alms to the people, and prayed to God alway. ³He saw in a vision evidently about the ninth hour of the day an angel of God coming in to him, and saying unto him, 'Cornelius'. ⁴And when he looked on him, he was afraid, and said, 'What is it, Lord?' And he said unto him, 'Thy prayers and thine alms are come up for a memorial before God. ⁵And now send men to Joppa, and call for one Simon, whose surname is Peter: ⁶he lodgeth with one Simon a tanner, whose house is by the sea side: he shall tell thee what thou oughtest to do.' ⁷And when the angel which spake unto Cornelius was departed, he called two of his household servants, and a devout soldier of them that waited on him continually; ⁸and when he had declared all these things unto them, he sent them to Joppa.

⁹On the morrow, as they went on their journey, and drew nigh unto the city, Peter went up upon the housetop to pray about the sixth hour. ¹⁰And he became very hungry, and would have eaten, but while they made ready, he fell into a trance, ¹¹and saw heaven opened, and a certain vessel descending unto him, as it had been a great sheet knit at the four corners, and let down to the earth, ¹²wherein were all manner of four-footed beasts of the earth, and wild beasts, and creeping things, and fowls of the air. ¹³And there came a voice to him, 'Rise, Peter; kill, and eat.' ¹⁴But Peter said, 'Not so, Lord; for I have never eaten any thing that is common or unclean.' ¹⁵And the voice spake unto him again the second time, 'What God hath cleansed, that call not thou common.' ¹⁶This was done thrice, and the vessel was received up again into heaven. ¹⁷Now while Peter doubted in himself what this vision which he had seen should mean, behold, the men which were sent from Cornelius had made enquiry for Simon's house, and stood before the gate, ¹⁸and called, and asked whether Simon, which was surnamed Peter, were lodged there.

¹⁹While Peter thought on the vision, the Spirit said unto him, 'Behold, three men seek thee. ²⁰Arise therefore, and get thee down, and go with them, doubting nothing, for I have sent them.' ²¹Then Peter went down to the men which were sent unto him from Cornelius; and said, 'Behold, I am he whom ye seek: what is the cause wherefore ye are come?' ²²And they said, 'Cornelius the centurion, a just man, and one that feareth God, and of good report among all the nation of the Jews, was warned from God by an holy angel

to send for thee into his house, and to hear words of thee.' ²³ Then called he them in, and lodged them. And on the morrow Peter went away with them, and certain brethren from Joppa accompanied him. ²⁴And the morrow after they entered into Caesarea. And Cornelius waited for them, and had called together his kinsmen and near friends. ²⁵And as Peter was coming in, Cornelius met him, and fell down at his feet, and worshipped him. ²⁶ But Peter took him up, saying, 'Stand up; I myself also am a man.' ²⁷And as he talked with him, he went in, and found many that were come together. ²⁸And he said unto them, 'Ye know how that it is an unlawful thing for a man that is a Jew to keep company, or come unto one of another nation; but God hath shewed me that I should not call any man common or unclean. ²⁹ Therefore came I unto you without gainsaying, as soon as I was sent for: I ask therefore for what intent ye have sent for me?' ³⁰And Cornelius said, 'Four days ago I was fasting until this hour; and at the ninth hour I prayed in my house, and, behold, a man stood before me in bright clothing, ³¹and said, "Cornelius, thy prayer is heard, and thine alms are had in remembrance in the sight of God. ³² Send therefore to Joppa, and call hither Simon, whose surname is Peter; he is lodged in the house of one Simon a tanner by the sea side: who, when he cometh, shall speak unto thee." ³³ Immediately therefore I sent to thee; and thou hast well done that thou art come. Now therefore are we all here present before God, to hear all things that are commanded thee of God.'

³⁴ Then Peter opened his mouth, and said, 'Of a truth I perceive that God is no respecter of persons, ³⁵ but in every

nation he that feareth him, and worketh righteousness, is accepted with him. ³⁶ The word which God sent unto the children of Israel, preaching peace by Jesus Christ (he is Lord of all). ³⁷ That word, I say, ye know, which was published throughout all Judaea, and began from Galilee, after the baptism which John preached; ³⁸ how God anointed Jesus of Nazareth with the Holy Ghost and with power; who went about doing good, and healing all that were oppressed of the devil; for God was with him. ³⁹ And we are witnesses of all things which he did both in the land of the Jews, and in Jerusalem; whom they slew and hanged on a tree: ⁴⁰ Him God raised up the third day, and shewed him openly; ⁴¹ not to all the people, but unto witnesses chosen before of God, even to us, who did eat and drink with him after he rose from the dead. ⁴² And he commanded us to preach unto the people, and to testify that it is he which was ordained of God to be the Judge of quick and dead. ⁴³ To him give all the prophets witness, that through his name whosoever believeth in him shall receive remission of sins.'

⁴⁴ While Peter yet spake these words, the Holy Ghost fell on all them which heard the word. ⁴⁵ And they of the circumcision which believed were astonished, as many as came with Peter, because that on the Gentiles also was poured out the gift of the Holy Ghost. ⁴⁶ For they heard them speak with tongues, and magnify God. Then answered Peter, ⁴⁷ 'Can any man forbid water, that these should not be baptized, which have received the Holy Ghost as well as we?' ⁴⁸ And he commanded them to be baptized in the name of the Lord. Then prayed they him to tarry certain days.

11 And the apostles and brethren that were in Judaea heard that the Gentiles had also received the word of God. ²And when Peter was come up to Jerusalem, they that were of the circumcision contended with him, ³saying, 'Thou wentest in to men uncircumcised, and didst eat with them.' ⁴But Peter rehearsed the matter from the beginning, and expounded it by order unto them, saying, ⁵'I was in the city of Joppa praying: and in a trance I saw a vision, a certain vessel descend, as it had been a great sheet, let down from heaven by four corners; and it came even to me; ⁶upon the which when I had fastened mine eyes, I considered, and saw four-footed beasts of the earth, and wild beasts, and creeping things, and fowls of the air. ⁷And I heard a voice saying unto me, "Arise, Peter; slay and eat." ⁸But I said, "Not so, Lord: for nothing common or unclean hath at any time entered into my mouth." ⁹But the voice answered me again from heaven, "What God hath cleansed, that call not thou common." ¹⁰And this was done three times: and all were drawn up again into heaven. ¹¹And, behold, immediately there were three men already come unto the house where I was, sent from Caesarea unto me. ¹²And the Spirit bade me go with them, nothing doubting. Moreover these six brethren accompanied me, and we entered into the man's house: ¹³and he shewed us how he had seen an angel in his house, which stood and said unto him, "Send men to Joppa, and call for Simon, whose surname is Peter; ¹⁴who shall tell thee words, whereby thou and all thy house shall be saved." ¹⁵And as I began to speak, the Holy Ghost fell on them, as on us at the beginning. ¹⁶Then remembered I the word of the

Lord, how that he said, "John indeed baptized with water; but ye shall be baptized with the Holy Ghost." ¹⁷ Forasmuch then as God gave them the like gift as he did unto us, who believed on the Lord Jesus Christ; what was I, that I could withstand God?' ¹⁸ When they heard these things, they held their peace, and glorified God, saying, 'Then hath God also to the Gentiles granted repentance unto life.'

¹⁹ Now they which were scattered abroad upon the persecution that arose about Stephen travelled as far as Phenice, and Cyprus, and Antioch, preaching the word to none but unto the Jews only. ²⁰ And some of them were men of Cyprus and Cyrene, which, when they were come to Antioch, spake unto the Grecians, preaching the Lord Jesus. ²¹ And the hand of the Lord was with them: and a great number believed, and turned unto the Lord.

²² Then tidings of these things came unto the ears of the church which was in Jerusalem: and they sent forth Barnabas, that he should go as far as Antioch. ²³ Who, when he came, and had seen the grace of God, was glad, and exhorted them all, that with purpose of heart they would cleave unto the Lord. ²⁴ For he was a good man, and full of the Holy Ghost and of faith: and much people was added unto the Lord. ²⁵ Then departed Barnabas to Tarsus, for to seek Saul; ²⁶ and when he had found him, he brought him unto Antioch. And it came to pass, that a whole year they assembled themselves with the church, and taught much people. And the disciples were called Christians first in Antioch.

²⁷ And in these days came prophets from Jerusalem unto

Antioch. ²⁸And there stood up one of them named Agabus, and signified by the Spirit that there should be great dearth throughout all the world; which came to pass in the days of Claudius Caesar. ²⁹Then the disciples, every man according to his ability, determined to send relief unto the brethren which dwelt in Judaea; ³⁰which also they did, and sent it to the elders by the hands of Barnabas and Saul.

12 Now about that time Herod the king stretched forth his hands to vex certain of the church. ²And he killed James the brother of John with the sword. ³And because he saw it pleased the Jews, he proceeded further to take Peter also. (Then were the days of unleavened bread.) ⁴And when he had apprehended him, he put him in prison, and delivered him to four quaternions of soldiers to keep him; intending after Easter to bring him forth to the people. ⁵Peter therefore was kept in prison, but prayer was made without ceasing of the church unto God for him. ⁶And when Herod would have brought him forth, the same night Peter was sleeping between two soldiers, bound with two chains; and the keepers before the door kept the prison. ⁷And, behold, the angel of the Lord came upon him, and a light shined in the prison; and he smote Peter on the side, and raised him up, saying, 'Arise up quickly.' And his chains fell off from his hands. ⁸And the angel said unto him, 'Gird thyself, and bind on thy sandals.' And so he did. And he saith unto him, 'Cast thy garment about thee, and follow me.' ⁹And he went out, and followed him; and wist not that it was true which was done by the angel; but thought he saw a vision. ¹⁰When they

were past the first and the second ward, they came unto the iron gate that leadeth unto the city; which opened to them of his own accord: and they went out, and passed on through one street; and forthwith the angel departed from him. ¹¹And when Peter was come to himself, he said, 'Now I know of a surety, that the Lord hath sent his angel, and hath delivered me out of the hand of Herod, and from all the expectation of the people of the Jews.' ¹²And when he had considered the thing, he came to the house of Mary the mother of John, whose surname was Mark; where many were gathered together praying. ¹³And as Peter knocked at the door of the gate, a damsel came to hearken, named Rhoda. ¹⁴And when she knew Peter's voice, she opened not the gate for gladness, but ran in, and told how Peter stood before the gate. ¹⁵And they said unto her, 'Thou art mad.' But she constantly affirmed that it was even so. Then said they, 'It is his angel.' ¹⁶But Peter continued knocking: and when they had opened the door, and saw him, they were astonished. ¹⁷But he, beckoning unto them with the hand to hold their peace, declared unto them how the Lord had brought him out of the prison. And he said, 'Go shew these things unto James, and to the brethren.' And he departed, and went into another place. ¹⁸Now as soon as it was day, there was no small stir among the soldiers, what was become of Peter. ¹⁹And when Herod had sought for him, and found him not, he examined the keepers, and commanded that they should be put to death. And he went down from Judaea to Caesarea, and there abode.

²⁰And Herod was highly displeased with them of Tyre and Sidon; but they came with one accord to him, and, having

made Blastus the king's chamberlain their friend, desired peace; because their country was nourished by the king's country. ²¹And upon a set day Herod, arrayed in royal apparel, sat upon his throne, and made an oration unto them. ²²And the people gave a shout, saying, 'It is the voice of a god, and not of a man.' ²³And immediately the angel of the Lord smote him, because he gave not God the glory; and he was eaten of worms, and gave up the ghost.

²⁴ But the word of God grew and multiplied. ²⁵And Barnabas and Saul returned from Jerusalem, when they had fulfilled their ministry, and took with them John, whose surname was Mark.

13 Now there were in the church that was at Antioch certain prophets and teachers; as Barnabas, and Simeon that was called Niger, and Lucius of Cyrene, and Manaen, which had been brought up with Herod the tetrarch, and Saul. ²As they ministered to the Lord, and fasted, the Holy Ghost said, 'Separate me Barnabas and Saul for the work whereunto I have called them.' ³And when they had fasted and prayed, and laid their hands on them, they sent them away.

⁴So they, being sent forth by the Holy Ghost, departed unto Seleucia; and from thence they sailed to Cyprus. ⁵And when they were at Salamis, they preached the word of God in the synagogues of the Jews; and they had also John to their minister. ⁶And when they had gone through the isle unto Paphos, they found a certain sorcerer, a false prophet, a Jew, whose name was Bar-jesus; ⁷which was with the

deputy of the country, Sergius Paulus, a prudent man; who called for Barnabas and Saul, and desired to hear the word of God. ⁸ But Elymas the sorcerer (for so is his name by interpretation) withstood them, seeking to turn away the deputy from the faith. ⁹ Then Saul (who also is called Paul), filled with the Holy Ghost, set his eyes on him, ¹⁰ and said, 'O full of all subtilty and all mischief, thou child of the devil, thou enemy of all righteousness, wilt thou not cease to pervert the right ways of the Lord? ¹¹ And now, behold, the hand of the Lord is upon thee, and thou shalt be blind, not seeing the sun for a season.' And immediately there fell on him a mist and a darkness; and he went about seeking some to lead him by the hand. ¹² Then the deputy, when he saw what was done, believed, being astonished at the doctrine of the Lord. ¹³ Now when Paul and his company loosed from Paphos, they came to Perga in Pamphylia; and John departing from them returned to Jerusalem.

¹⁴ But when they departed from Perga, they came to Antioch in Pisidia, and went into the synagogue on the sabbath day, and sat down. ¹⁵ And after the reading of the law and the prophets the rulers of the synagogue sent unto them, saying, 'Ye men and brethren, if ye have any word of exhortation for the people, say on.' ¹⁶ Then Paul stood up, and beckoning with his hand said, 'Men of Israel, and ye that fear God, give audience. ¹⁷ The God of this people of Israel chose our fathers, and exalted the people when they dwelt as strangers in the land of Egypt, and with an high arm brought he them out of it. ¹⁸ And about the time of forty years suffered he their manners in the wilderness. ¹⁹ And when he had destroyed

seven nations in the land of Chanaan, he divided their land to them by lot. ²⁰And after that he gave unto them judges about the space of four hundred and fifty years, until Samuel the prophet. ²¹And afterward, they desired a king: and God gave unto them Saul the son of Cis, a man of the tribe of Benjamin, by the space of forty years. ²²And when he had removed him, he raised up unto them David to be their king; to whom also he gave testimony, and said, "I have found David the son of Jesse, a man after mine own heart, which shall fulfil all my will." ²³Of this man's seed hath God according to his promise raised unto Israel a Saviour, Jesus; ²⁴when John had first preached before his coming the baptism of repentance to all the people of Israel. ²⁵And as John fulfilled his course, he said, "Whom think ye that I am? I am not he. But, behold, there cometh one after me, whose shoes of his feet I am not worthy to loose." ²⁶Men and brethren, children of the stock of Abraham, and whosoever among you feareth God, to you is the word of this salvation sent. ²⁷For they that dwell at Jerusalem, and their rulers, because they knew him not, nor yet the voices of the prophets which are read every sabbath day, they have fulfilled them in condemning him. ²⁸And though they found no cause of death in him, yet desired they Pilate that he should be slain. ²⁹And when they had fulfilled all that was written of him, they took him down from the tree, and laid him in a sepulchre. ³⁰But God raised him from the dead; ³¹and he was seen many days of them which came up with him from Galilee to Jerusalem, who are his witnesses unto the people. ³²And we declare unto you glad tidings, how that the promise which was made unto the fathers, ³³ God hath fulfilled the same unto us their children, in that he hath raised up Jesus again; as it is also written in the second psalm, "Thou art my Son, this day have I begotten thee." ³⁴ And as concerning that he raised him up from the dead, now no more to return to corruption, he said on this wise, "I will give you the sure mercies of David." ³⁵ Wherefore he saith also in another psalm, "Thou shalt not suffer thine Holy One to see corruption." ³⁶ For David, after he had served his own generation by the will of God, fell on sleep, and was laid unto his fathers, and saw corruption, ³⁷ but he, whom God raised again, saw no corruption.

³⁸ 'Be it known unto you therefore, men and brethren, that through this man is preached unto you the forgiveness of sins; ³⁹ and by him all that believe are justified from all things, from which ye could not be justified by the law of Moses. ⁴⁰ Beware therefore, lest that come upon you, which is spoken of in the prophets: ⁴¹ "Behold, ye despisers, and wonder, and perish; for I work a work in your days, a work which ye shall in no wise believe, though a man declare it unto you."' ⁴² And when the Jews were gone out of the synagogue, the Gentiles besought that these words might be preached to them the next sabbath. ⁴³ Now when the congregation was broken up, many of the Jews and religious proselytes followed Paul and Barnabas; who, speaking to them, persuaded them to continue in the grace of God.

⁴⁴ And the next sabbath day came almost the whole city together to hear the word of God. ⁴⁵ But when the Jews saw the multitudes, they were filled with envy, and spake

against those things which were spoken by Paul, contradicting and blaspheming. ⁴⁶ Then Paul and Barnabas waxed bold, and said, 'It was necessary that the word of God should first have been spoken to you; but seeing ye put it from you, and judge yourselves unworthy of everlasting life, lo, we turn to the Gentiles.' ⁴⁷ For so hath the Lord commanded us, saying, 'I have set thee to be a light of the Gentiles, that thou shouldest be for salvation unto the ends of the earth.' ⁴⁸ And when the Gentiles heard this, they were glad, and glorified the word of the Lord: and as many as were ordained to eternal life believed. ⁴⁹ And the word of the Lord was published throughout all the region. ⁵⁰ But the Jews stirred up the devout and honourable women, and the chief men of the city, and raised persecution against Paul and Barnabas, and expelled them out of their coasts. ⁵¹ But they shook off the dust of their feet against them, and came unto Iconium. ⁵² And the disciples were filled with joy, and with the Holy Ghost.

14 And it came to pass in Iconium, that they went both together into the synagogue of the Jews, and so spake, that a great multitude both of the Jews and also of the Greeks believed. ² But the unbelieving Jews stirred up the Gentiles, and made their minds evil affected against the brethren. ³ Long time therefore abode they speaking boldly in the Lord, which gave testimony unto the word of his grace, and granted signs and wonders to be done by their hands. ⁴ But the multitude of the city was divided: and part held with the Jews, and part with the apostles. ⁵ And when

there was an assault made both of the Gentiles, and also of the Jews with their rulers, to use them despitefully, and to stone them, ⁶they were ware of it, and fled unto Lystra and Derbe, cities of Lycaonia, and unto the region that lieth round about; ⁷and there they preached the gospel.

⁸And there sat a certain man at Lystra, impotent in his feet, being a cripple from his mother's womb, who never had walked: ⁹the same heard Paul speak, who stedfastly beholding him, and perceiving that he had faith to be healed, ¹⁰said with a loud voice, 'Stand upright on thy feet.' And he leaped and walked. ¹¹And when the people saw what Paul had done, they lifted up their voices, saying in the speech of Lycaonia, 'The gods are come down to us in the likeness of men.' ¹²And they called Barnabas, Jupiter; and Paul, Mercurius, because he was the chief speaker. ¹³Then the priest of Jupiter, which was before their city, brought oxen and garlands unto the gates, and would have done sacrifice with the people. ¹⁴Which when the apostles, Barnabas and Paul, heard of, they rent their clothes, and ran in among the people, crying out, ¹⁵and saying, 'Sirs, why do ye these things? We also are men of like passions with you, and preach unto you that ye should turn from these vanities unto the living God, which made heaven, and earth, and the sea, and all things that are therein, ¹⁶who in times past suffered all nations to walk in their own ways. ¹⁷Nevertheless he left not himself without witness, in that he did good, and gave us rain from heaven, and fruitful seasons, filling our hearts with food and gladness.' ¹⁸And with these sayings scarce restrained they the people, that

they had not done sacrifice unto them.

¹⁹And there came thither certain Jews from Antioch and Iconium, who persuaded the people, and, having stoned Paul, drew him out of the city, supposing he had been dead. ²⁰Howbeit, as the disciples stood round about him, he rose up, and came into the city: and the next day he departed with Barnabas to Derbe. ²¹And when they had preached the gospel to that city, and had taught many, they returned again to Lystra, and to Iconium, and Antioch, ²²confirming the souls of the disciples, and exhorting them to continue in the faith, and that we must through much tribulation enter into the kingdom of God. ²³And when they had ordained them elders in every church, and had prayed with fasting, they commended them to the Lord, on whom they believed. ²⁴And after they had passed throughout Pisidia, they came to Pamphylia. ²⁵And when they had preached the word in Perga, they went down into Attalia, ²⁶and thence sailed to Antioch, from whence they had been recommended to the grace of God for the work which they fulfilled. ²⁷And when they were come, and had gathered the church together, they rehearsed all that God had done with them, and how he had opened the door of faith unto the Gentiles. ²⁸And there they abode long time with the disciples.

15 And certain men which came down from Judaea taught the brethren, and said, 'Except ye be circumcised after the manner of Moses, ye cannot be saved.' ²When therefore Paul and Barnabas had no small dissension and disputation with them, they determined that Paul and

Barnabas, and certain other of them, should go up to Jerusalem unto the apostles and elders about this question. ³And being brought on their way by the church, they passed through Phenice and Samaria, declaring the conversion of the Gentiles: and they caused great joy unto all the brethren. ⁴And when they were come to Jerusalem, they were received of the church, and of the apostles and elders, and they declared all things that God had done with them. ⁵But there rose up certain of the sect of the Pharisees which believed, saying, 'That it was needful to circumcise them, and to command them to keep the law of Moses.'

⁶And the apostles and elders came together for to consider of this matter. ⁷And when there had been much disputing, Peter rose up, and said unto them, 'Men and brethren, ye know how that a good while ago God made choice among us, that the Gentiles by my mouth should hear the word of the gospel, and believe. ⁸And God, which knoweth the hearts, bare them witness, giving them the Holy Ghost, even as he did unto us; ⁹and put no difference between us and them, purifying their hearts by faith. ¹⁰Now therefore why tempt ye God, to put a yoke upon the neck of the disciples, which neither our fathers nor we were able to bear? ¹¹But we believe that through the grace of the Lord Jesus Christ we shall be saved, even as they.'

¹²Then all the multitude kept silence, and gave audience to Barnabas and Paul, declaring what miracles and wonders God had wrought among the Gentiles by them.

¹³And after they had held their peace, James answered, saying, 'Men and brethren, hearken unto me: ¹⁴Simeon hath

declared how God at the first did visit the Gentiles, to take out of them a people for his name. ¹⁵And to this agree the words of the prophets; as it is written, ¹⁶"After this I will return, and will build again the tabernacle of David, which is fallen down; and I will build again the ruins thereof, and I will set it up, ¹⁷that the residue of men might seek after the Lord, and all the Gentiles, upon whom my name is called, saith the Lord, who doeth all these things. ¹⁸Known unto God are all his works from the beginning of the world." ¹⁹Wherefore my sentence is, that we trouble not them, which from among the Gentiles are turned to God, ²⁰but that we write unto them, that they abstain from pollutions of idols, and from fornication, and from things strangled, and from blood. ²¹For Moses of old time hath in every city them that preach him, being read in the synagogues every sabbath day.' ²²Then pleased it the apostles and elders, with the whole church, to send chosen men of their own company to Antioch with Paul and Barnabas; namely, Judas surnamed Barsabas, and Silas, chief men among the brethren; ²³and they wrote letters by them after this manner:

'The apostles and elders and brethren send greeting unto the brethren which are of the Gentiles in Antioch and Syria and Cilicia: ²⁴forasmuch as we have heard, that certain which went out from us have troubled you with words, subverting your souls, saying, "Ye must be circumcised, and keep the law"; to whom we gave no such commandment; ²⁵it seemed good unto us, being assembled with one accord, to send chosen men unto you with our beloved Barnabas and Paul, ²⁶ men that have hazarded their lives for the name of our Lord Jesus Christ. ²⁷ We have sent therefore Judas and Silas, who shall also tell you the same things by mouth. ²⁸ For it seemed good to the Holy Ghost, and to us, to lay upon you no greater burden than these necessary things, ²⁹ that ye abstain from meats offered to idols, and from blood, and from things strangled, and from fornication, from which if ye keep yourselves, ye shall do well. Fare ye well.'

³⁰ So when they were dismissed, they came to Antioch: and when they had gathered the multitude together, they delivered the epistle, ³¹ which when they had read, they rejoiced for the consolation. ³² And Judas and Silas, being prophets also themselves, exhorted the brethren with many words, and confirmed them. ³³ And after they had tarried there a space, they were let go in peace from the brethren unto the apostles. ³⁴ Notwithstanding it pleased Silas to abide there still. ³⁵ Paul also and Barnabas continued in Antioch, teaching and preaching the word of the Lord, with many others also.

³⁶ And some days after Paul said unto Barnabas, 'Let us go again and visit our brethren in every city where we have preached the word of the Lord, and see how they do.' ³⁷ And Barnabas determined to take with them John, whose surname was Mark. ³⁸ But Paul thought not good to take him with them, who departed from them from Pamphylia, and

went not with them to the work. [39]And the contention was so sharp between them, that they departed asunder one from the other: and so Barnabas took Mark, and sailed unto Cyprus; [40]and Paul chose Silas, and departed, being recommended by the brethren unto the grace of God. [41]And he went through Syria and Cilicia, confirming the churches.

16

Then came he to Derbe and Lystra: and, behold, a certain disciple was there, named Timotheus, the son of a certain woman, which was a Jewess, and believed; but his father was a Greek, [2]which was well reported of by the brethren that were at Lystra and Iconium. [3]Him would Paul have to go forth with him; and took and circumcised him because of the Jews which were in those quarters; for they knew all that his father was a Greek. [4]And as they went through the cities, they delivered them the decrees for to keep, that were ordained of the apostles and elders which were at Jerusalem. [5]And so were the churches established in the faith, and increased in number daily. [6]Now when they had gone throughout Phrygia and the region of Galatia, and were forbidden of the Holy Ghost to preach the word in Asia, [7]after they were come to Mysia, they assayed to go into Bithynia; but the Spirit suffered them not. [8]And they passing by Mysia came down to Troas. [9]And a vision appeared to Paul in the night: there stood a man of Macedonia, and prayed him, saying, 'Come over into Macedonia, and help us.' [10]And after he had seen the vision, immediately we endeavoured to go into Macedonia, assuredly gathering that the Lord had called us for to preach the gospel unto them. ¹¹Therefore loosing from Troas, we came with a straight course to Samothracia, and the next day to Neapolis; ¹²and from thence to Philippi, which is the chief city of that part of Macedonia, and a colony; and we were in that city abiding certain days. ¹³And on the sabbath we went out of the city by a river side, where prayer was wont to be made; and we sat down, and spake unto the women which resorted thither.

¹⁴And a certain woman named Lydia, a seller of purple, of the city of Thyatira, which worshipped God, heard us, whose heart the Lord opened, that she attended unto the things which were spoken of Paul. ¹⁵And when she was baptized, and her household, she besought us, saying, 'If ye have judged me to be faithful to the Lord, come into my house, and abide there.' And she constrained us.

¹⁶And it came to pass, as we went to prayer, a certain damsel possessed with a spirit of divination met us, which brought her masters much gain by soothsaying. ¹⁷The same followed Paul and us, and cried, saying, 'These men are the servants of the most high God, which shew unto us the way of salvation.' ¹⁸And this did she many days. But Paul, being grieved, turned and said to the spirit, 'I command thee in the name of Jesus Christ to come out of her.' And he came out the same hour.

¹⁹And when her masters saw that the hope of their gains was gone, they caught Paul and Silas, and drew them into the marketplace unto the rulers, ²⁰and brought them to the magistrates, saying, 'These men, being Jews, do exceedingly trouble our city, ²¹and teach customs, which are not lawful

for us to receive, neither to observe, being Romans.' [22]And the multitude rose up together against them: and the magistrates rent off their clothes, and commanded to beat them. [23]And when they had laid many stripes upon them, they cast them into prison, charging the jailor to keep them safely, [24] who, having received such a charge, thrust them into the inner prison, and made their feet fast in the stocks.

[25]And at midnight Paul and Silas prayed, and sang praises unto God: and the prisoners heard them. [26]And suddenly there was a great earthquake, so that the foundations of the prison were shaken: and immediately all the doors were opened, and every one's bands were loosed. [27]And the keeper of the prison awaking out of his sleep, and seeing the prison doors open, he drew out his sword, and would have killed himself, supposing that the prisoners had been fled. [28]But Paul cried with a loud voice, saying, 'Do thyself no harm: for we are all here.' [29]Then he called for a light, and sprang in, and came trembling, and fell down before Paul and Silas, [30]and brought them out, and said, 'Sirs, what must I do to be saved?' [31]And they said, 'Believe on the Lord Jesus Christ, and thou shalt be saved, and thy house.' [32]And they spake unto him the word of the Lord, and to all that were in his house. [33]And he took them the same hour of the night, and washed their stripes; and was baptized, he and all his, straightway. [34]And when he had brought them into his house, he set meat before them, and rejoiced, believing in God with all his house. [35]And when it was day, the magistrates sent the serjeants, saying, 'Let those men go.' [36]And the keeper of the prison told this saying to Paul, 'The magis-

trates have sent to let you go: now therefore depart, and go in peace.' ³⁷ But Paul said unto them, 'They have beaten us openly uncondemned, being Romans, and have cast us into prison; and now do they thrust us out privily? Nay verily; but let them come themselves and fetch us out.' ³⁸And the serjeants told these words unto the magistrates: and they feared, when they heard that they were Romans. ³⁹And they came and besought them, and brought them out, and desired them to depart out of the city. ⁴⁰And they went out of the prison, and entered into the house of Lydia: and when they had seen the brethren, they comforted them, and departed.

17 Now when they had passed through Amphipolis and Apollonia, they came to Thessalonica, where was a synagogue of the Jews. ²And Paul, as his manner was, went in unto them, and three sabbath days reasoned with them out of the scriptures, ³opening and alleging, that Christ must needs have suffered, and risen again from the dead; and that this Jesus, whom I preach unto you, is Christ. ⁴And some of them believed, and consorted with Paul and Silas; and of the devout Greeks a great multitude, and of the chief women not a few.

⁵ But the Jews which believed not, moved with envy, took unto them certain lewd fellows of the baser sort, and gathered a company, and set all the city on an uproar, and assaulted the house of Jason, and sought to bring them out to the people. ⁶And when they found them not, they drew Jason and certain brethren unto the rulers of the city, crying, 'These

that have turned the world upside down are come hither also, ⁷whom Jason hath received: and these all do contrary to the decrees of Caesar, saying that there is another king, one Jesus.' ⁸And they troubled the people and the rulers of the city, when they heard these things. ⁹And when they had taken security of Jason, and of the other, they let them go.

¹⁰And the brethren immediately sent away Paul and Silas by night unto Berea, who coming thither went into the synagogue of the Jews. ¹¹These were more noble than those in Thessalonica, in that they received the word with all readiness of mind, and searched the scriptures daily, whether those things were so. ¹²Therefore many of them believed; also of honourable women which were Greeks, and of men, not a few. ¹³But when the Jews of Thessalonica had knowledge that the word of God was preached of Paul at Berea, they came thither also, and stirred up the people. ¹⁴And then immediately the brethren sent away Paul to go as it were to the sea, but Silas and Timotheus abode there still. ¹⁵And they that conducted Paul brought him unto Athens; and receiving a commandment unto Silas and Timotheus for to come to him with all speed, they departed.

¹⁶Now while Paul waited for them at Athens, his spirit was stirred in him, when he saw the city wholly given to idolatry. ¹⁷Therefore disputed he in the synagogue with the Jews, and with the devout persons, and in the market daily with them that met with him. ¹⁸Then certain philosophers of the Epicureans, and of the Stoicks, encountered him. And some said, 'What will this babbler say?' Other some, 'He seemeth to be a setter forth of strange gods': because he

preached unto them Jesus, and the resurrection. ¹⁹And they took him, and brought him unto Areopagus, saying, 'May we know what this new doctrine, whereof thou speakest, is? ²⁰For thou bringest certain strange things to our ears: we would know therefore what these things mean.' ²¹(For all the Athenians and strangers which were there spent their time in nothing else, but either to tell, or to hear some new thing.)

²²Then Paul stood in the midst of Mars' hill, and said, 'Ye men of Athens, I perceive that in all things ye are too superstitious. ²³For as I passed by, and beheld your devotions, I found an altar with this inscription, "To the unknown god". Whom therefore ye ignorantly worship, him declare I unto you. ²⁴God that made the world and all things therein, seeing that he is Lord of heaven and earth, dwelleth not in temples made with hands; ²⁵neither is worshipped with men's hands, as though he needed any thing, seeing he giveth to all life, and breath, and all things; ²⁶and hath made of one blood all nations of men for to dwell on all the face of the earth, and hath determined the times before appointed, and the bounds of their habitation; ²⁷that they should seek the Lord, if haply they might feel after him, and find him, though he be not far from every one of us, ²⁸for in him we live, and move, and have our being; as certain also of your own poets have said, "For we are also his offspring." ²⁹Forasmuch then as we are the offspring of God, we ought not to think that the Godhead is like unto gold, or silver, or stone, graven by art and man's device. ³⁰And the times of this ignorance God winked at; but now commandeth all men every where to repent, ³¹because he hath appointed a day, in the which he

will judge the world in righteousness by that man whom he hath ordained; whereof he hath given assurance unto all men, in that he hath raised him from the dead.'

³²And when they heard of the resurrection of the dead, some mocked, and others said, 'We will hear thee again of this matter.' ³³So Paul departed from among them. ³⁴Howbeit certain men clave unto him, and believed: among the which was Dionysius the Areopagite, and a woman named Damaris, and others with them.

18 After these things Paul departed from Athens, and came to Corinth; ²and found a certain Jew named Aquila, born in Pontus, lately come from Italy, with his wife Priscilla (because that Claudius had commanded all Jews to depart from Rome), and came unto them. ³And because he was of the same craft, he abode with them, and wrought, for by their occupation they were tentmakers. ⁴And he reasoned in the synagogue every sabbath, and persuaded the Jews and the Greeks. ⁵And when Silas and Timotheus were come from Macedonia, Paul was pressed in the spirit, and testified to the Jews that Jesus was Christ. ⁶And when they opposed themselves, and blasphemed, he shook his raiment, and said unto them, 'Your blood be upon your own heads; I am clean: from henceforth I will go unto the Gentiles.'

⁷And he departed thence, and entered into a certain man's house, named Justus, one that worshipped God, whose house joined hard to the synagogue. ⁸And Crispus, the chief ruler of the synagogue, believed on the Lord with all his house; and many of the Corinthians hearing believed, and

were baptized. ⁹Then spake the Lord to Paul in the night by a vision, 'Be not afraid, but speak, and hold not thy peace, ¹⁰for I am with thee, and no man shall set on thee to hurt thee, for I have much people in this city.' ¹¹And he continued there a year and six months, teaching the word of God among them.

¹²And when Gallio was the deputy of Achaia, the Jews made insurrection with one accord against Paul, and brought him to the judgment seat, ¹³saying, 'This fellow persuadeth men to worship God contrary to the law.' ¹⁴And when Paul was now about to open his mouth, Gallio said unto the Jews, 'If it were a matter of wrong or wicked lewdness, O ye Jews, reason would that I should bear with you, ¹⁵but if it be a question of words and names, and of your law, look ye to it; for I will be no judge of such matters.' ¹⁶And he drave them from the judgment seat. ¹⁷Then all the Greeks took Sosthenes, the chief ruler of the synagogue, and beat him before the judgment seat. And Gallio cared for none of those things.

¹⁸And Paul after this tarried there yet a good while, and then took his leave of the brethren, and sailed thence into Syria, and with him Priscilla and Aquila; having shorn his head in Cenchrea; for he had a vow. ¹⁹And he came to Ephesus, and left them there, but he himself entered into the synagogue, and reasoned with the Jews. ²⁰When they desired him to tarry longer time with them, he consented not, ²¹but bade them farewell, saying, 'I must by all means keep this feast that cometh in Jerusalem, but I will return again unto you, if God will.' And he sailed from Ephesus.

²²And when he had landed at Caesarea, and gone up, and saluted the church, he went down to Antioch. ²³And after he had spent some time there, he departed, and went over all the country of Galatia and Phrygia in order, strengthening all the disciples.

²⁴And a certain Jew named Apollos, born at Alexandria, an eloquent man, and mighty in the scriptures, came to Ephesus. ²⁵This man was instructed in the way of the Lord; and being fervent in the spirit, he spake and taught diligently the things of the Lord, knowing only the baptism of John. ²⁶And he began to speak boldly in the synagogue, whom when Aquila and Priscilla had heard, they took him unto them, and expounded unto him the way of God more perfectly. ²⁷And when he was disposed to pass into Achaia, the brethren wrote, exhorting the disciples to receive him, who, when he was come, helped them much which had believed through grace; ²⁸for he mightily convinced the Jews, and that publickly, shewing by the scriptures that Jesus was Christ.

19 And it came to pass, that, while Apollos was at Corinth, Paul having passed through the upper coasts came to Ephesus: and finding certain disciples, ²he said unto them, 'Have ye received the Holy Ghost since ye believed?' And they said unto him, 'We have not so much as heard whether there be any Holy Ghost.' ³And he said unto them, 'Unto what then were ye baptized?' And they said, 'Unto John's baptism.' ⁴Then said Paul, John verily baptized with the baptism of repentance, saying unto the people, that they

should believe on him which should come after him, that is, on Christ Jesus. ⁵When they heard this, they were baptized in the name of the Lord Jesus. ⁶And when Paul had laid his hands upon them, the Holy Ghost came on them; and they spake with tongues, and prophesied. ⁷And all the men were about twelve. ⁸And he went into the synagogue, and spake boldly for the space of three months, disputing and persuading the things concerning the kingdom of God. ⁹But when divers were hardened, and believed not, but spake evil of that way before the multitude, he departed from them, and separated the disciples, disputing daily in the school of one Tyrannus. ¹⁰And this continued by the space of two years; so that all they which dwelt in Asia heard the word of the Lord Jesus, both Jews and Greeks. ¹¹And God wrought special miracles by the hands of Paul, ¹²so that from his body were brought unto the sick handkerchiefs or aprons, and the diseases departed from them, and the evil spirits went out of them.

¹³ Then certain of the vagabond Jews, exorcists, took upon them to call over them which had evil spirits the name of the Lord Jesus, saying, 'We adjure you by Jesus whom Paul preacheth.' ¹⁴And there were seven sons of one Sceva, a Jew, and chief of the priests, which did so. ¹⁵And the evil spirit answered and said, 'Jesus I know, and Paul I know; but who are ye?' ¹⁶And the man in whom the evil spirit was leaped on them, and overcame them, and prevailed against them, so that they fled out of that house naked and wounded. ¹⁷And this was known to all the Jews and Greeks also dwelling at Ephesus; and fear fell on them all, and the name of the Lord

Jesus was magnified. ¹⁸And many that believed came, and confessed, and shewed their deeds. ¹⁹Many of them also which used curious arts brought their books together, and burned them before all men; and they counted the price of them, and found it fifty thousand pieces of silver. ²⁰So mightily grew the word of God and prevailed.

²¹After these things were ended, Paul purposed in the spirit, when he had passed through Macedonia and Achaia, to go to Jerusalem, saying, 'After I have been there, I must also see Rome.' ²²So he sent into Macedonia two of them that ministered unto him, Timotheus and Erastus; but he himself stayed in Asia for a season. ²³And the same time there arose no small stir about that way. ²⁴For a certain man named Demetrius, a silversmith, which made silver shrines for Diana, brought no small gain unto the craftsmen, ²⁵whom he called together with the workmen of like occupation, and said, 'Sirs, ye know that by this craft we have our wealth. ²⁶Moreover ye see and hear, that not alone at Ephesus, but almost throughout all Asia, this Paul hath persuaded and turned away much people, saying that they be no gods, which are made with hands; ²⁷so that not only this our craft is in danger to be set at nought; but also that the temple of the great goddess Diana should be despised, and her magnificence should be destroyed, whom all Asia and the world worshippeth.' ²⁸And when they heard these sayings, they were full of wrath, and cried out, saying, 'Great is Diana of the Ephesians.' ²⁹And the whole city was filled with confusion: and having caught Gaius and Aristarchus, men of Macedonia, Paul's companions in travel, they rushed with

one accord into the theatre. ³⁰And when Paul would have entered in unto the people, the disciples suffered him not. ³¹And certain of the chief of Asia, which were his friends, sent unto him, desiring him that he would not adventure himself into the theatre. ³²Some therefore cried one thing, and some another, for the assembly was confused; and the more part knew not wherefore they were come together. ³³And they drew Alexander out of the multitude, the Jews putting him forward. And Alexander beckoned with the hand, and would have made his defence unto the people. ³⁴But when they knew that he was a Jew, all with one voice about the space of two hours cried out, 'Great is Diana of the Ephesians.' ³⁵And when the townclerk had appeased the people, he said, 'Ye men of Ephesus, what man is there that knoweth not how that the city of the Ephesians is a worshipper of the great goddess Diana, and of the image which fell down from Jupiter? ³⁶Seeing then that these things cannot be spoken against, ye ought to be quiet, and to do nothing rashly. ³⁷For ye have brought hither these men, which are neither robbers of churches, nor yet blasphemers of your goddess. ³⁸Wherefore if Demetrius, and the craftsmen which are with him, have a matter against any man, the law is open, and there are deputies: let them implead one another. ³⁹But if ye enquire any thing concerning other matters, it shall be determined in a lawful assembly. ⁴⁰For we are in danger to be called in question for this day's uproar, there being no cause whereby we may give an account of this concourse.' ⁴¹And when he had thus spoken, he dismissed the assembly.

20 And after the uproar was ceased, Paul called unto him the disciples, and embraced them, and departed for to go into Macedonia. ²And when he had gone over those parts, and had given them much exhortation, he came into Greece, ³and there abode three months. And when the Jews laid wait for him, as he was about to sail into Syria, he purposed to return through Macedonia. ⁴And there accompanied him into Asia Sopater of Berea; and of the Thessalonians, Aristarchus and Secundus; and Gaius of Derbe, and Timotheus; and of Asia, Tychicus and Trophimus. ⁵These going before tarried for us at Troas. ⁶And we sailed away from Philippi after the days of unleavened bread, and came unto them to Troas in five days; where we abode seven days. ⁷And upon the first day of the week, when the disciples came together to break bread, Paul preached unto them, ready to depart on the morrow; and continued his speech until midnight. ⁸And there were many lights in the upper chamber, where they were gathered together. ⁹And there sat in a window a certain young man named Eutychus, being fallen into a deep sleep: and as Paul was long preaching, he sunk down with sleep, and fell down from the third loft, and was taken up dead. ¹⁰And Paul went down, and fell on him, and embracing him said, 'Trouble not yourselves; for his life is in him.' ¹¹When he therefore was come up again, and had broken bread, and eaten, and talked a long while, even till break of day, so he departed. ¹²And they brought the young man alive, and were not a little comforted.

¹³And we went before to ship, and sailed unto Assos, there intending to take in Paul, for so had he appointed,

minding himself to go afoot. ¹⁴And when he met with us at Assos, we took him in, and came to Mitylene. ¹⁵And we sailed thence, and came the next day over against Chios; and the next day we arrived at Samos, and tarried at Trogyllium; and the next day we came to Miletus. ¹⁶For Paul had determined to sail by Ephesus, because he would not spend the time in Asia; for he hasted, if it were possible for him, to be at Jerusalem the day of Pentecost.

¹⁷And from Miletus he sent to Ephesus, and called the elders of the church. ¹⁸And when they were come to him, he said unto them, 'Ye know, from the first day that I came into Asia, after what manner I have been with you at all seasons, ¹⁹serving the Lord with all humility of mind, and with many tears, and temptations, which befell me by the lying in wait of the Jews; ²⁰and how I kept back nothing that was profitable unto you, but have shewed you, and have taught you publickly, and from house to house, ²¹testifying both to the Jews, and also to the Greeks, repentance toward God, and faith toward our Lord Jesus Christ. ²²And now, behold, I go bound in the spirit unto Jerusalem, not knowing the things that shall befall me there: ²³save that the Holy Ghost witnesseth in every city, saying that bonds and afflictions abide me. ²⁴But none of these things move me, neither count I my life dear unto myself, so that I might finish my course with joy, and the ministry, which I have received of the Lord Jesus, to testify the gospel of the grace of God. ²⁵And now, behold, I know that ye all, among whom I have gone preaching the kingdom of God, shall see my face no more. ²⁶Wherefore I take you to record this day, that I am pure from the blood of

all men. ²⁷ For I have not shunned to declare unto you all the counsel of God.

²⁸ 'Take heed therefore unto yourselves, and to all the flock, over the which the Holy Ghost hath made you overseers, to feed the church of God, which he hath purchased with his own blood. ²⁹ For I know this, that after my departing shall grievous wolves enter in among you, not sparing the flock. ³⁰ Also of your own selves shall men arise, speaking perverse things, to draw away disciples after them. ³¹ Therefore watch, and remember, that by the space of three years I ceased not to warn every one night and day with tears. ³² And now, brethren, I commend you to God, and to the word of his grace, which is able to build you up, and to give you an inheritance among all them which are sanctified. ³³ I have coveted no man's silver, or gold, or apparel. ³⁴ Yea, ye yourselves know, that these hands have ministered unto my necessities, and to them that were with me. ³⁵ I have shewed you all things, how that so labouring ye ought to support the weak, and to remember the words of the Lord Jesus, how he said, "It is more blessed to give than to receive."'

³⁶ And when he had thus spoken, he kneeled down, and prayed with them all. ³⁷ And they all wept sore, and fell on Paul's neck, and kissed him, ³⁸ sorrowing most of all for the words which he spake, that they should see his face no more. And they accompanied him unto the ship.

21 And it came to pass, that after we were gotten from them, and had launched, we came with a straight course unto Coos, and the day following unto Rhodes, and

from thence unto Patara. ²And finding a ship sailing over unto Phenicia, we went aboard, and set forth. ³Now when we had discovered Cyprus, we left it on the left hand, and sailed into Syria, and landed at Tyre, for there the ship was to unlade her burden. ⁴And finding disciples, we tarried there seven days, who said to Paul through the Spirit, that he should not go up to Jerusalem. ⁵And when we had accomplished those days, we departed and went our way; and they all brought us on our way, with wives and children, till we were out of the city; and we kneeled down on the shore, and prayed. ⁶And when we had taken our leave one of another, we took ship; and they returned home again.

⁷And when we had finished our course from Tyre, we came to Ptolemais, and saluted the brethren, and abode with them one day. ⁸And the next day we that were of Paul's company departed, and came unto Caesarea; and we entered into the house of Philip the evangelist, which was one of the seven; and abode with him. ⁹And the same man had four daughters, virgins, which did prophesy. ¹⁰And as we tarried there many days, there came down from Judaea a certain prophet, named Agabus. ¹¹And when he was come unto us, he took Paul's girdle, and bound his own hands and feet, and said, 'Thus saith the Holy Ghost, "So shall the Jews at Jerusalem bind the man that owneth this girdle, and shall deliver him into the hands of the Gentiles."' ¹²And when we heard these things, both we, and they of that place, besought him not to go up to Jerusalem. ¹³Then Paul answered, 'What mean ye to weep and to break mine heart? For I am ready not to be bound only, but also to die at Jerusalem for the

name of the Lord Jesus.' ¹⁴And when he would not be persuaded, we ceased, saying, 'The will of the Lord be done.'

¹⁵And after those days we took up our carriages, and went up to Jerusalem. ¹⁶There went with us also certain of the disciples of Caesarea, and brought with them one Mnason of Cyprus, an old disciple, with whom we should lodge.

¹⁷And when we were come to Jerusalem, the brethren received us gladly. ¹⁸And the day following Paul went in with us unto James; and all the elders were present. ¹⁹And when he had saluted them, he declared particularly what things God had wrought among the Gentiles by his ministry. ²⁰And when they heard it, they glorified the Lord, and said unto him, 'Thou seest, brother, how many thousands of Jews there are which believe; and they are all zealous of the law; ²¹and they are informed of thee, that thou teachest all the Jews which are among the Gentiles to forsake Moses, saying that they ought not to circumcise their children, neither to walk after the customs. ²²What is it therefore? The multitude must needs come together, for they will hear that thou art come. ²³Do therefore this that we say to thee: we have four men which have a vow on them; ²⁴them take, and purify thyself with them, and be at charges with them, that they may shave their heads; and all may know that those things, whereof they were informed concerning thee, are nothing; but that thou thyself also walkest orderly, and keepest the law. ²⁵As touching the Gentiles which believe, we have written and concluded that they observe no such thing, save only that they keep themselves from things offered to idols, and from blood, and from strangled, and

from fornication.' ²⁶ Then Paul took the men, and the next day purifying himself with them entered into the temple, to signify the accomplishment of the days of purification, until that an offering should be offered for every one of them.

²⁷And when the seven days were almost ended, the Jews which were of Asia, when they saw him in the temple, stirred up all the people, and laid hands on him, ²⁸ crying out, 'Men of Israel, help: this is the man, that teacheth all men every where against the people, and the law, and this place; and further brought Greeks also into the temple, and hath polluted this holy place.' ²⁹(For they had seen before with him in the city Trophimus an Ephesian, whom they supposed that Paul had brought into the temple.) ³⁰And all the city was moved, and the people ran together; and they took Paul, and drew him out of the temple; and forthwith the doors were shut. ³¹And as they went about to kill him, tidings came unto the chief captain of the band, that all Jerusalem was in an uproar. ³² Who immediately took soldiers and centurions, and ran down unto them: and when they saw the chief captain and the soldiers, they left beating of Paul. ³³ Then the chief captain came near, and took him, and commanded him to be bound with two chains; and demanded who he was, and what he had done. ³⁴And some cried one thing, some another, among the multitude: and when he could not know the certainty for the tumult, he commanded him to be carried into the castle. ³⁵And when he came upon the stairs, so it was, that he was borne of the soldiers for the violence of the people. ³⁶ For the multitude of the people followed after, crying, 'Away with him.'

[37]And as Paul was to be led into the castle, he said unto the chief captain, 'May I speak unto thee?' Who said, 'Canst thou speak Greek? [38]Art not thou that Egyptian, which before these days madest an uproar, and leddest out into the wilderness four thousand men that were murderers?' [39]But Paul said, 'I am a man which am a Jew of Tarsus, a city in Cilicia, a citizen of no mean city: and, I beseech thee, suffer me to speak unto the people.' [40]And when he had given him licence, Paul stood on the stairs, and beckoned with the hand unto the people. And when there was made a great silence, he spake unto them in the Hebrew tongue, saying,

22

'Men, brethren, and fathers, hear ye my defence which I make now unto you.' [2](And when they heard that he spake in the Hebrew tongue to them, they kept the more silence: and he saith,) [3]'I am verily a man which am a Jew, born in Tarsus, a city in Cilicia, yet brought up in this city at the feet of Gamaliel, and taught according to the perfect manner of the law of the fathers, and was zealous toward God, as ye all are this day. [4]And I persecuted this way unto the death, binding and delivering into prisons both men and women. [5]As also the high priest doth bear me witness, and all the estate of the elders, from whom also I received letters unto the brethren, and went to Damascus, to bring them which were there bound unto Jerusalem, for to be punished.

[6]'And it came to pass, that, as I made my journey, and was come nigh unto Damascus about noon, suddenly there shone from heaven a great light round about me. [7]And I fell

unto the ground, and heard a voice saying unto me, "Saul, Saul, why persecutest thou me?" [8]And I answered, "Who art thou, Lord?" And he said unto me, "I am Jesus of Nazareth, whom thou persecutest." [9]And they that were with me saw indeed the light, and were afraid; but they heard not the voice of him that spake to me. [10]And I said, "What shall I do, Lord?" And the Lord said unto me, "Arise, and go into Damascus; and there it shall be told thee of all things which are appointed for thee to do." [11]And when I could not see for the glory of that light, being led by the hand of them that were with me, I came into Damascus.

[12]'And one Ananias, a devout man according to the law, having a good report of all the Jews which dwelt there, [13]came unto me, and stood, and said unto me, "Brother Saul, receive thy sight." And the same hour I looked up upon him. [14]And he said, "The God of our fathers hath chosen thee, that thou shouldest know his will, and see that Just One, and shouldest hear the voice of his mouth. [15]For thou shalt be his witness unto all men of what thou hast seen and heard. [16]And now why tarriest thou? Arise, and be baptized, and wash away thy sins, calling on the name of the Lord."

[17]'And it came to pass, that, when I was come again to Jerusalem, even while I prayed in the temple, I was in a trance; [18]and saw him saying unto me, "Make haste, and get thee quickly out of Jerusalem, for they will not receive thy testimony concerning me." [19]And I said, "Lord, they know that I imprisoned and beat in every synagogue them that believed on thee: [20]and when the blood of thy martyr

Stephen was shed, I also was standing by, and consenting unto his death, and kept the raiment of them that slew him." ²¹And he said unto me, "Depart: for I will send thee far hence unto the Gentiles."'

²²And they gave him audience unto this word, and then lifted up their voices, and said, 'Away with such a fellow from the earth, for it is not fit that he should live.' ²³And as they cried out, and cast off their clothes, and threw dust into the air, ²⁴the chief captain commanded him to be brought into the castle, and bade that he should be examined by scourging; that he might know wherefore they cried so against him. ²⁵And as they bound him with thongs, Paul said unto the centurion that stood by, 'Is it lawful for you to scourge a man that is a Roman, and uncondemned?' ²⁶When the centurion heard that, he went and told the chief captain, saying, 'Take heed what thou doest, for this man is a Roman.' ²⁷Then the chief captain came, and said unto him, 'Tell me, art thou a Roman?' He said, 'Yea.' ²⁸And the chief captain answered, 'With a great sum obtained I this freedom.' And Paul said, 'But I was free born.' ²⁹Then straightway they departed from him which should have examined him: and the chief captain also was afraid, after he knew that he was a Roman, and because he had bound him.

³⁰On the morrow, because he would have known the certainty wherefore he was accused of the Jews, he loosed him from his bands, and commanded the chief priests and all their council to appear, and brought Paul down, and set him before them.

23 And Paul, earnestly beholding the council, said, 'Men and brethren, I have lived in all good conscience before God until this day.' ²And the high priest Ananias commanded them that stood by him to smite him on the mouth. ³Then said Paul unto him, 'God shall smite thee, thou whited wall, for sittest thou to judge me after the law, and commandest me to be smitten contrary to the law?' ⁴And they that stood by said, 'Revilest thou God's high priest?' ⁵Then said Paul, 'I wist not, brethren, that he was the high priest, for it is written, "Thou shalt not speak evil of the ruler of thy people."'

⁶But when Paul perceived that the one part were Sadducees, and the other Pharisees, he cried out in the council, 'Men and brethren, I am a Pharisee, the son of a Pharisee: of the hope and resurrection of the dead I am called in question.' ⁷And when he had so said, there arose a dissension between the Pharisees and the Sadducees: and the multitude was divided. ⁸For the Sadducees say that there is no resurrection, neither angel, nor spirit; but the Pharisees confess both. ⁹And there arose a great cry; and the scribes that were of the Pharisees' part arose, and strove, saying, 'We find no evil in this man; but if a spirit or an angel hath spoken to him, let us not fight against God.' ¹⁰And when there arose a great dissension, the chief captain, fearing lest Paul should have been pulled in pieces of them, commanded the soldiers to go down, and to take him by force from among them, and to bring him into the castle.

¹¹And the night following the Lord stood by him, and said, 'Be of good cheer, Paul, for as thou hast testified of me

in Jerusalem, so must thou bear witness also at Rome.'

¹²And when it was day, certain of the Jews banded together, and bound themselves under a curse, saying that they would neither eat nor drink till they had killed Paul. ¹³And they were more than forty which had made this conspiracy. ¹⁴And they came to the chief priests and elders, and said, 'We have bound ourselves under a great curse, that we will eat nothing until we have slain Paul. ¹⁵Now therefore ye with the council signify to the chief captain that he bring him down unto you to morrow, as though ye would enquire something more perfectly concerning him: and we, or ever he come near, are ready to kill him.'

¹⁶And when Paul's sister's son heard of their lying in wait, he went and entered into the castle, and told Paul. ¹⁷Then Paul called one of the centurions unto him, and said, 'Bring this young man unto the chief captain, for he hath a certain thing to tell him.' ¹⁸So he took him, and brought him to the chief captain, and said, 'Paul the prisoner called me unto him, and prayed me to bring this young man unto thee, who hath something to say unto thee.' ¹⁹Then the chief captain took him by the hand, and went with him aside privately, and asked him, 'What is that thou hast to tell me?' ²⁰And he said, 'The Jews have agreed to desire thee that thou wouldest bring down Paul to morrow into the council, as though they would enquire somewhat of him more perfectly. ²¹But do not thou yield unto them, for there lie in wait for him of them more than forty men, which have bound themselves with an oath, that they will neither eat nor drink till they have killed him: and now are they ready, looking for

a promise from thee.' ²²So the chief captain then let the young man depart, and charged him, 'See thou tell no man that thou hast shewed these things to me.'

²³And he called unto him two centurions, saying, 'Make ready two hundred soldiers to go to Caesarea, and horsemen threescore and ten, and spearmen two hundred, at the third hour of the night; ²⁴and provide them beasts, that they may set Paul on, and bring him safe unto Felix the governor.' ²⁵And he wrote a letter after this manner:

²⁶'Claudius Lysias unto the most excellent governor Felix sendeth greeting. ²⁷This man was taken of the Jews, and should have been killed of them: then came I with an army, and rescued him, having understood that he was a Roman. ²⁸And when I would have known the cause wherefore they accused him, I brought him forth into their council, ²⁹whom I perceived to be accused of questions of their law, but to have nothing laid to his charge worthy of death or of bonds. ³⁰And when it was told me how that the Jews laid wait for the man, I sent straightway to thee, and gave commandment to his accusers also to say before thee what they had against him. Farewell.'

³¹Then the soldiers, as it was commanded them, took Paul, and brought him by night to Antipatris. ³²On the morrow they left the horsemen to go with him, and returned to the castle, ³³who, when they came to Caesarea, and delivered the epistle to the governor, presented Paul also before

him. ³⁴And when the governor had read the letter, he asked of what province he was. And when he understood that he was of Cilicia, ³⁵'I will hear thee,' said he, 'when thine accusers are also come.' And he commanded him to be kept in Herod's judgment hall.

24 And after five days Ananias the high priest descended with the elders, and with a certain orator named Tertullus, who informed the governor against Paul. ²And when he was called forth, Tertullus began to accuse him, saying, 'Seeing that by thee we enjoy great quietness, and that very worthy deeds are done unto this nation by thy providence, ³we accept it always, and in all places, most noble Felix, with all thankfulness. ⁴Notwithstanding, that I be not further tedious unto thee, I pray thee that thou wouldest hear us of thy clemency a few words. ⁵For we have found this man a pestilent fellow, and a mover of sedition among all the Jews throughout the world, and a ringleader of the sect of the Nazarenes, ⁶who also hath gone about to profane the temple, whom we took, and would have judged according to our law. ⁷But the chief captain Lysias came upon us, and with great violence took him away out of our hands, ⁸commanding his accusers to come unto thee: by examining of whom thyself mayest take knowledge of all these things, whereof we accuse him.'

⁹And the Jews also assented, saying that these things were so.

¹⁰Then Paul, after that the governor had beckoned unto him to speak, answered, 'Forasmuch as I know that thou

hast been of many years a judge unto this nation, I do the more cheerfully answer for myself, ¹¹because that thou mayest understand, that there are yet but twelve days since I went up to Jerusalem for to worship. ¹²And they neither found me in the temple disputing with any man, neither raising up the people, neither in the synagogues, nor in the city: ¹³neither can they prove the things whereof they now accuse me. ¹⁴But this I confess unto thee, that after the way which they call heresy, so worship I the God of my fathers, believing all things which are written in the law and in the prophets, ¹⁵and have hope toward God, which they themselves also allow, that there shall be a resurrection of the dead, both of the just and unjust. ¹⁶And herein do I exercise myself, to have always a conscience void of offence toward God, and toward men. ¹⁷Now after many years I came to bring alms to my nation, and offerings. ¹⁸Whereupon certain Jews from Asia found me purified in the temple, neither with multitude, nor with tumult. ¹⁹Who ought to have been here before thee, and object, if they had ought against me. ²⁰Or else let these same here say, if they have found any evil doing in me, while I stood before the council, ²¹except it be for this one voice, that I cried standing among them, "Touching the resurrection of the dead I am called in question by you this day."'

²²And when Felix heard these things, having more perfect knowledge of that way, he deferred them, and said, 'When Lysias the chief captain shall come down, I will know the uttermost of your matter.' ²³And he commanded a centurion to keep Paul, and to let him have liberty, and that he

should forbid none of his acquaintance to minister or come unto him. ²⁴And after certain days, when Felix came with his wife Drusilla, which was a Jewess, he sent for Paul, and heard him concerning the faith in Christ. ²⁵And as he reasoned of righteousness, temperance, and judgment to come, Felix trembled, and answered, 'Go thy way for this time; when I have a convenient season, I will call for thee.' ²⁶He hoped also that money should have been given him of Paul, that he might loose him: wherefore he sent for him the oftener, and communed with him.

²⁷But after two years Porcius Festus came into Felix' room: and Felix, willing to shew the Jews a pleasure, left Paul bound.

25 Now when Festus was come into the province, after three days he ascended from Caesarea to Jerusalem. ²Then the high priest and the chief of the Jews informed him against Paul, and besought him, ³and desired favour against him, that he would send for him to Jerusalem, laying wait in the way to kill him. ⁴But Festus answered, that Paul should be kept at Caesarea, and that he himself would depart shortly thither. ⁵'Let them therefore,' said he, 'which among you are able, go down with me, and accuse this man, if there be any wickedness in him.'

⁶And when he had tarried among them more than ten days, he went down unto Caesarea; and the next day sitting on the judgment seat commanded Paul to be brought. ⁷And when he was come, the Jews which came down from Jerusalem stood round about, and laid many and grievous

complaints against Paul, which they could not prove. ⁸ While he answered for himself, 'Neither against the law of the Jews, neither against the temple, nor yet against Caesar, have I offended any thing at all.' ⁹ But Festus, willing to do the Jews a pleasure, answered Paul, and said, 'Wilt thou go up to Jerusalem, and there be judged of these things before me?' ¹⁰ Then said Paul, 'I stand at Caesar's judgment seat, where I ought to be judged: to the Jews have I done no wrong, as thou very well knowest. ¹¹ For if I be an offender, or have committed any thing worthy of death, I refuse not to die; but if there be none of these things whereof these accuse me, no man may deliver me unto them. I appeal unto Caesar.' ¹² Then Festus, when he had conferred with the council, answered, 'Hast thou appealed unto Caesar? Unto Caesar shalt thou go.'

¹³ And after certain days king Agrippa and Bernice came unto Caesarea to salute Festus. ¹⁴ And when they had been there many days, Festus declared Paul's cause unto the king, saying, 'There is a certain man left in bonds by Felix, ¹⁵ about whom, when I was at Jerusalem, the chief priests and the elders of the Jews informed me, desiring to have judgment against him, ¹⁶ to whom I answered, "It is not the manner of the Romans to deliver any man to die, before that he which is accused have the accusers face to face, and have licence to answer for himself concerning the crime laid against him." ¹⁷ Therefore, when they were come hither, without any delay on the morrow I sat on the judgment seat, and commanded the man to be brought forth, ¹⁸ against whom when the accusers stood up, they brought none accusation of such

things as I supposed, ¹⁹ but had certain questions against him of their own superstition, and of one Jesus, which was dead, whom Paul affirmed to be alive. ²⁰And because I doubted of such manner of questions, I asked him whether he would go to Jerusalem, and there be judged of these matters. ²¹But when Paul had appealed to be reserved unto the hearing of Augustus, I commanded him to be kept till I might send him to Caesar.' ²²Then Agrippa said unto Festus, 'I would also hear the man myself.' 'To morrow,' said he, 'thou shalt hear him.'

²³And on the morrow, when Agrippa was come, and Bernice, with great pomp, and was entered into the place of hearing, with the chief captains, and principal men of the city, at Festus' commandment Paul was brought forth. ²⁴And Festus said, 'King Agrippa, and all men which are here present with us, ye see this man, about whom all the multitude of the Jews have dealt with me, both at Jerusalem, and also here, crying that he ought not to live any longer. ²⁵But when I found that he had committed nothing worthy of death, and that he himself hath appealed to Augustus, I have determined to send him. ²⁶Of whom I have no certain thing to write unto my lord. Wherefore I have brought him forth before you, and specially before thee, O king Agrippa, that, after examination had, I might have somewhat to write. ²⁷For it seemeth to me unreasonable to send a prisoner, and not withal to signify the crimes laid against him.'

26 Then Agrippa said unto Paul, 'Thou art permitted to speak for thyself.' Then Paul stretched forth the

hand, and answered for himself:

² 'I think myself happy, king Agrippa, because I shall answer for myself this day before thee touching all the things whereof I am accused of the Jews, ³ especially because I know thee to be expert in all customs and questions which are among the Jews: wherefore I beseech thee to hear me patiently.

⁴ 'My manner of life from my youth, which was at the first among mine own nation at Jerusalem, know all the Jews, ⁵ which knew me from the beginning, if they would testify, that after the most straitest sect of our religion I lived a Pharisee. ⁶ And now I stand and am judged for the hope of the promise made of God unto our fathers, ⁷ unto which promise our twelve tribes, instantly serving God day and night, hope to come. For which hope's sake, king Agrippa, I am accused of the Jews. ⁸ Why should it be thought a thing incredible with you, that God should raise the dead?

⁹ 'I verily thought with myself, that I ought to do many things contrary to the name of Jesus of Nazareth, ¹⁰ which thing I also did in Jerusalem: and many of the saints did I shut up in prison, having received authority from the chief priests; and when they were put to death, I gave my voice against them. ¹¹ And I punished them oft in every synagogue, and compelled them to blaspheme; and being exceedingly mad against them, I persecuted them even unto strange cities.

¹² 'Whereupon as I went to Damascus with authority and commission from the chief priests, ¹³ at midday, O king, I saw in the way a light from heaven, above the brightness of the sun, shining round about me and them which journeyed

with me. ¹⁴And when we were all fallen to the earth, I heard a voice speaking unto me, and saying in the Hebrew tongue, "Saul, Saul, why persecutest thou me? It is hard for thee to kick against the pricks." ¹⁵And I said, "Who art thou, Lord?" And he said, "I am Jesus whom thou persecutest. ¹⁶But rise, and stand upon thy feet, for I have appeared unto thee for this purpose, to make thee a minister and a witness both of these things which thou hast seen, and of those things in the which I will appear unto thee; ¹⁷delivering thee from the people, and from the Gentiles, unto whom now I send thee, ¹⁸to open their eyes, and to turn them from darkness to light, and from the power of Satan unto God, that they may receive forgiveness of sins, and inheritance among them which are sanctified by faith that is in me."

¹⁹'Whereupon, O king Agrippa, I was not disobedient unto the heavenly vision, ²⁰but shewed first unto them of Damascus, and at Jerusalem, and throughout all the coasts of Judaea, and then to the Gentiles, that they should repent and turn to God, and do works meet for repentance. ²¹For these causes the Jews caught me in the temple, and went about to kill me. ²²Having therefore obtained help of God, I continue unto this day, witnessing both to small and great, saying none other things than those which the prophets and Moses did say should come, ²³that Christ should suffer, and that he should be the first that should rise from the dead, and should shew light unto the people, and to the Gentiles.'

²⁴And as he thus spake for himself, Festus said with a loud voice, 'Paul, thou art beside thyself; much learning doth make thee mad.' ²⁵But he said, 'I am not mad, most

noble Festus; but speak forth the words of truth and soberness. ²⁶ For the king knoweth of these things, before whom also I speak freely, for I am persuaded that none of these things are hidden from him, for this thing was not done in a corner. ²⁷ King Agrippa, believest thou the prophets? I know that thou believest.' ²⁸ Then Agrippa said unto Paul, 'Almost thou persuadest me to be a Christian.' ²⁹ And Paul said, 'I would to God, that not only thou, but also all that hear me this day, were both almost, and altogether such as I am, except these bonds.'

³⁰ And when he had thus spoken, the king rose up, and the governor, and Bernice, and they that sat with them: ³¹ and when they were gone aside, they talked between themselves, saying, 'This man doeth nothing worthy of death or of bonds.' ³² Then said Agrippa unto Festus, 'This man might have been set at liberty, if he had not appealed unto Caesar.'

27 And when it was determined that we should sail into Italy, they delivered Paul and certain other prisoners unto one named Julius, a centurion of Augustus' band. ² And entering into a ship of Adramyttium, we launched, meaning to sail by the coasts of Asia; one Aristarchus, a Macedonian of Thessalonica, being with us. ³ And the next day we touched at Sidon. And Julius courteously entreated Paul, and gave him liberty to go unto his friends to refresh himself. ⁴ And when we had launched from thence, we sailed under Cyprus, because the winds were contrary. ⁵ And when we had sailed over the sea of Cilicia and Pamphylia, we came to Myra, a city of Lycia. ⁶ And there the centurion

found a ship of Alexandria sailing into Italy; and he put us therein. ⁷And when we had sailed slowly many days, and scarce were come over against Cnidus, the wind not suffering us, we sailed under Crete, over against Salmone; ⁸and, hardly passing it, came unto a place which is called 'The fair havens'; nigh whereunto was the city of Lasea.

⁹Now when much time was spent, and when sailing was now dangerous, because the fast was now already past, Paul admonished them, ¹⁰and said unto them, 'Sirs, I perceive that this voyage will be with hurt and much damage, not only of the lading and ship, but also of our lives.' ¹¹Nevertheless the centurion believed the master and the owner of the ship, more than those things which were spoken by Paul. ¹²And because the haven was not commodious to winter in, the more part advised to depart thence also, if by any means they might attain to Phenice, and there to winter; which is an haven of Crete, and lieth toward the south west and north west.

¹³And when the south wind blew softly, supposing that they had obtained their purpose, loosing thence, they sailed close by Crete. ¹⁴But not long after there arose against it a tempestuous wind, called Euroclydon. ¹⁵And when the ship was caught, and could not bear up into the wind, we let her drive. ¹⁶And running under a certain island which is called Clauda, we had much work to come by the boat, ¹⁷which when they had taken up, they used helps, undergirding the ship; and, fearing lest they should fall into the quicksands, strake sail, and so were driven. ¹⁸And we being exceedingly tossed with a tempest, the next day they lightened the ship;

[19] and the third day we cast out with our own hands the tackling of the ship. [20] And when neither sun nor stars in many days appeared, and no small tempest lay on us, all hope that we should be saved was then taken away.

[21] But after long abstinence Paul stood forth in the midst of them, and said, 'Sirs, ye should have hearkened unto me, and not have loosed from Crete, and to have gained this harm and loss. [22] And now I exhort you to be of good cheer, for there shall be no loss of any man's life among you, but of the ship. [23] For there stood by me this night the angel of God, whose I am, and whom I serve, [24] saying, "Fear not, Paul; thou must be brought before Caesar; and, lo, God hath given thee all them that sail with thee." [25] Wherefore, sirs, be of good cheer: for I believe God, that it shall be even as it was told me. [26] Howbeit we must be cast upon a certain island.'

[27] But when the fourteenth night was come, as we were driven up and down in Adria, about midnight the shipmen deemed that they drew near to some country; [28] and sounded, and found it twenty fathoms; and when they had gone a little further, they sounded again, and found it fifteen fathoms. [29] Then fearing lest we should have fallen upon rocks, they cast four anchors out of the stern, and wished for the day. [30] And as the shipmen were about to flee out of the ship, when they had let down the boat into the sea, under colour as though they would have cast anchors out of the foreship, [31] Paul said to the centurion and to the soldiers, 'Except these abide in the ship, ye cannot be saved.' [32] Then the soldiers cut off the ropes of the boat, and let her fall off.

³³And while the day was coming on, Paul besought them all to take meat, saying, 'This day is the fourteenth day that ye have tarried and continued fasting, having taken nothing. ³⁴Wherefore I pray you to take some meat, for this is for your health, for there shall not an hair fall from the head of any of you.' ³⁵And when he had thus spoken, he took bread, and gave thanks to God in presence of them all: and when he had broken it, he began to eat. ³⁶Then were they all of good cheer, and they also took some meat. ³⁷And we were in all in the ship two hundred threescore and sixteen souls. ³⁸And when they had eaten enough, they lightened the ship, and cast out the wheat into the sea.

³⁹And when it was day, they knew not the land, but they discovered a certain creek with a shore, into the which they were minded, if it were possible, to thrust in the ship. ⁴⁰And when they had taken up the anchors, they committed themselves unto the sea, and loosed the rudder bands, and hoised up the mainsail to the wind, and made toward shore. ⁴¹And falling into a place where two seas met, they ran the ship aground; and the forepart stuck fast, and remained unmoveable, but the hinder part was broken with the violence of the waves. ⁴²And the soldiers' counsel was to kill the prisoners, lest any of them should swim out, and escape. ⁴³But the centurion, willing to save Paul, kept them from their purpose; and commanded that they which could swim should cast themselves first into the sea, and get to land, ⁴⁴and the rest, some on boards, and some on broken pieces of the ship. And so it came to pass, that they escaped all safe to land.

28 And when they were escaped, then they knew that the island was called Melita. ²And the barbarous people shewed us no little kindness, for they kindled a fire, and received us every one, because of the present rain, and because of the cold. ³And when Paul had gathered a bundle of sticks, and laid them on the fire, there came a viper out of the heat, and fastened on his hand. ⁴And when the barbarians saw the venomous beast hang on his hand, they said among themselves, 'No doubt this man is a murderer, whom, though he hath escaped the sea, yet vengeance suffereth not to live.' ⁵And he shook off the beast into the fire, and felt no harm. ⁶Howbeit they looked when he should have swollen, or fallen down dead suddenly, but after they had looked a great while, and saw no harm come to him, they changed their minds, and said that he was a god.

⁷ In the same quarters were possessions of the chief man of the island, whose name was Publius; who received us, and lodged us three days courteously. ⁸And it came to pass, that the father of Publius lay sick of a fever and of a bloody flux, to whom Paul entered in, and prayed, and laid his hands on him, and healed him. ⁹ So when this was done, others also, which had diseases in the island, came, and were healed, ¹⁰ who also honoured us with many honours; and when we departed, they laded us with such things as were necessary.

¹¹And after three months we departed in a ship of Alexandria, which had wintered in the isle, whose sign was Castor and Pollux. ¹²And landing at Syracuse, we tarried there three days. ¹³And from thence we fetched a compass,

and came to Rhegium: and after one day the south wind blew, and we came the next day to Puteoli, ¹⁴where we found brethren, and were desired to tarry with them seven days: and so we went toward Rome. ¹⁵And from thence, when the brethren heard of us, they came to meet us as far as Appii forum, and the three taverns, whom when Paul saw, he thanked God, and took courage.

¹⁶And when we came to Rome, the centurion delivered the prisoners to the captain of the guard, but Paul was suffered to dwell by himself with a soldier that kept him.

¹⁷And it came to pass that after three days Paul called the chief of the Jews together: and when they were come together, he said unto them, 'Men and brethren, though I have committed nothing against the people, or customs of our fathers, yet was I delivered prisoner from Jerusalem into the hands of the Romans, ¹⁸who, when they had examined me, would have let me go, because there was no cause of death in me. ¹⁹But when the Jews spake against it, I was constrained to appeal unto Caesar; not that I had ought to accuse my nation of. ²⁰For this cause therefore have I called for you, to see you, and to speak with you, because that for the hope of Israel I am bound with this chain.' ²¹And they said unto him, 'We neither received letters out of Judaea concerning thee, neither any of the brethren that came shewed or spake any harm of thee. ²²But we desire to hear of thee what thou thinkest, for as concerning this sect, we know that every where it is spoken against.'

²³And when they had appointed him a day, there came many to him into his lodging; to whom he expounded and

testified the kingdom of God, persuading them concerning Jesus, both out of the law of Moses, and out of the prophets, from morning till evening. ²⁴And some believed the things which were spoken, and some believed not. ²⁵And when they agreed not among themselves, they departed, after that Paul had spoken one word, 'Well spake the Holy Ghost by Esaias the prophet unto our fathers, ²⁶ saying, "Go unto this people, and say: Hearing ye shall hear, and shall not understand; and seeing ye shall see, and not perceive, ²⁷for the heart of this people is waxed gross, and their ears are dull of hearing, and their eyes have they closed, lest they should see with their eyes, and hear with their ears, and understand with their heart, and should be converted, and I should heal them." ²⁸ Be it known therefore unto you, that the salvation of God is sent unto the Gentiles, and that they will hear it.' ²⁹And when he had said these words, the Jews departed, and had great reasoning among themselves. ³⁰And Paul dwelt two whole years in his own hired house, and received all that came in unto him, ³¹ preaching the kingdom of God, and teaching those things which concern the Lord Jesus Christ, with all confidence, no man forbidding him.

isaiah

the book of

isaiah

authorized king james version

grove press
new york

with an introduction by | peter ackroyd

Introduction copyright © 1999 by Peter Ackroyd
The Pocket Canon second series copyright © 2000 by Grove/Atlantic, Inc.

All rights reserved. No part of this book may be reproduced in any form
or by any electronic or mechanical means, including information storage
and retrieval systems, without permission in writing from the publisher,
except by a reviewer, who may quote brief passages in a review. Any
members of educational institutions wishing to photocopy part or all
of the work for classroom use, or publishers who would like to obtain
permission to include the work in an anthology, should send their
inquiries to Grove/Atlantic, Inc., 841 Broadway, New York, NY 10003.

Originally published in Great Britain in 1999 by Canongate Books,
Ltd., Edinburgh, Scotland.

Published simultaneously in Canada
Printed in the United States of America

FIRST AMERICAN EDITION

ISBN 0-8021-3759-8 (boxed set)

Design by Paddy Cramsie

Grove Press
841 Broadway
New York, NY 10003

00 01 02 03   10 9 8 7 6 5 4 3 2 1

a note about pocket canons

The Authorized King James Version of the Bible, translated between 1603 and 1611, coincided with an extraordinary flowering of English literature. This version, more than any other, and possibly more than any other work in history, has had an influence in shaping the language we speak and write today.

The books of the King James Bible encompass categories as diverse as history, philosophy, law, poetry and fiction. Each Pocket Canon volume has its own introduction, specially commissioned from an impressive range of writers, to provide a personal interpretation of the text and explore its contemporary relevance.

introduction by peter ackroyd

Peter Ackroyd's most recent books include bestselling biographies of Dickens *(1990),* Blake *(1995) and* Thomas More *(1998), and the novels* Dan Leno and the Limehouse Golem *(1994) and* Milton in America *(1996). He is the winner of a Somerset Maugham Award, the Guardian Fiction Prize, the Whitbread Prize for Biography and the prestigious James Tait Black Memorial Prize. He lives in London.*

We must approach this sacred text with great respect, doubting the ability of our mind to comprehend it and of our tongue to describe it. The book of *Isaiah* is not the work of one writer or one prophet but, like the Homeric epics, incorporates the voices of many authors in a tradition of oral poetry. Yet even though it comprises various sources its shape, like a river made out of many streams, is fluent and harmonious. Within its 66 chapters passages of lyrical melody are pressed up against words of prophetic force, moments of vision vouchsafed beside occasions for denunciation; the narrative combines stories, poems, descriptions, revelations and lamentations. It is, in little, representative of the Bible itself.

The origins of the various texts, original or interpolated, date variously from the eighth to the sixth century BCE. Yet in a book where history and poetry mingle, for devotional or ritual purposes, there is no need to attempt to locate a substratum of real or observable fact; just as the original documents have long since crumbled to dust, so we cannot sift the episodes concerning forgotten battles and distant kings.

The composition of the book itself is more certain – chapters 1 to 39 are the work of several authors, but all moving within a realm concerning prophecies of redemption as well as fierce polemic against pagan idolaters and the profligate among the Lord's own people. The 40th chapter marks the beginning of the work of the 'Deutero-Isaiah', perhaps the single most eloquent and inspiring of all the biblical writers who within 15 verses offers a vision of hope and of redemption for the people of Israel at the same time as, in a magnificent panegyric, he launches an attack upon Babylon and all the powers of this world. The third part, verses 55 to 66, acts as a coda to the first two sections, where interpolated hands have provided passages of prophecy and eschatology.

Harmony itself is achieved through the introduction of very clear formal preoccupations, together with an abiding and overriding concern for rhetorical elaboration and amplitude. Scholars of the Hebrew text, for example, have enumerated instances of alliteration and onomatopoeia designed expressly to lift a cadence or emphasise a phrase. The construction of the phrase itself is of the utmost significance, where simplicity and force work together in unison. That is why some of the lines from *Isaiah* have entered folk memory beyond the tribes of Israel – 'and they shall beat their swords into plowshares (2:4) … For unto us a child is born, unto us a son is given (9:6) … The wolf also shall dwell with the lamb, and the leopard shall lie down with the kid (11:6) … How art thou fallen from heaven, O Lucifer, son of the morning! (14:12) … Let us eat and drink; for tomorrow we shall die (22:13) … All flesh is grass (40:6) … There is no peace, saith my God, to the wicked' (57:21) … No rest for the wicked. The provenance of some of these phrases is disputed as not springing from the lips of the 'historical' Isaiah, but their relevance and influence are not in dispute. These are words which have literally changed the consciousness of the world.

Yet they are important, too, in maintaining the urgency and relevance of a narrative which speaks to many nations concerning the central aspirations of humankind. That is also why the economy and brevity of *Isaiah* allow a single phrase to denote the passage of many years or the history of one city. The utter simplicity of the author's voice emerges in passages of perfect pitch and power – 'Then shalt thou call [upon the Lord] …, and he shall say, "Here I am." (58:9). Here I am. It is as if the whole world resounded with God's voice, and we may recall here William Blake's visionary conversation with Isaiah – 'I saw no God nor heard any,' the prophet informed the poet, 'in a finite organical perception; but my senses discover'd the infinite in everything.'

This in fact is one of the glories of *Isaiah*, where the grandeur or ineffability of the 'infinite' is expressed in terms of a local landscape or a specific activity, so that 'the burden of the valley of vision' (22:1) can be carried by details of weaving or of threshing. Here the aspiration towards the infinite and the illimitable is combined with a very clear and articulate presentation of contemporary realities. Israel is 'a lodge in a garden of cucumbers' (1:8), and the Lord tells Isaiah to walk towards 'the end of the conduit of the upper pool in the highway of the fuller's field' (7:3). The Lord shall tread down Moab 'even as straw is trodden down for the dunghill' (25:10) and will put forth his hands 'as he that swimmeth spreadeth forth his hands to swim' (25:11). *Isaiah* celebrates a universe in which the particulars of the social and natural world are revealed as tokens of spiritual activity, where world and spirit do indeed become one, like the swimmer, in a living pulse of energy – 'for the earth shall be full of the knowledge of the Lord, as the waters cover the sea' (11:9).

The economy of effect, together with the use of repetition, renders these sacred verses not unlike the texts of Anglo-Saxon poetry – or, indeed, the expression of any bardic people. The recitation may even have been accompanied by music, so that the whole narrative becomes a kind of performance in which the aspirations of both orator and audience alike are embodied. No one can ignore, either, the dramatic aspects of Isaiah where, for example, the anonymous author proclaims the fate of one unhappy man – 'He is despised and rejected of men; a man of sorrows, and acquainted with grief' (53:3). This has often been characterised as a prophecy of Christ's passion, yet it is more appropriately and less anachronistically seen as a most dramatic and human revelation of the outcast. In that sense, like the rest of *Isaiah*, it becomes a story of universal significance rather than a sample of pre-Christian revelation.

There has been much discussion, in recent years, of the

Bible as a literary rather than a sacred or historical text. Certainly the narrative devices are clear, with affiliations to western poetry and fiction. There is, for example, satire approaching an almost Swiftian vision of disgust at the flesh, in the description of the women of Zion 'with stretched forth necks and wanton eyes, walking and mincing as they go, and making a tinkling with their feet' (3:16), or in the depiction of the priests of Ephraim so drunk that 'all tables are full of vomit and filthiness' (28:8). But there are other forms of narrative in place here, as mysterious and as melodious as anything in epic poetry – 'And the posts of the door moved at the voice of him that cried, and the house was filled with smoke' (6:4). 'And his heart was moved, and the heart of his people, as the trees of the wood are moved with the wind' (7:2). 'For the heavens shall vanish away like smoke, and the earth shall wax old like a garment' (51:6).

Coleridge once remarked, of cadences like this, that the first chapter of *Isaiah* might be 'reduced to complete hexameters … so true is it that wherever passion was, the language became a sort of metre'. In truth the words of *Isaiah* are neither prose nor poetry but, rather, a series of incandescent utterances which effortlessly find their true form. That is why the question of whether this is a poetic rather than a sacred text is redundant – there is no necessary distinction between the two since the highest poetry is always a manifestation of the sacred, while the most sacred insights will necessarily take on the vesture of poetry.

As such the effect of *Isaiah* upon European literature has been extensive and profound; its plangent combination of prophetic passages, with visionary epiphanies and lyrical enchantments, have affected the understanding of epic and pastoral as well as the nature of poetry itself. It stands out like a great melody, informing the future and irradiating the past.

the book of the prophet isaiah

The vision of Isaiah the son of Amoz,
    which he saw concerning Judah and Jerusalem
        in the days of Uzziah, Jotham, Ahaz,
    and Hezekiah, kings of Judah.
² Hear, O heavens, and give ear, O earth;
    for the Lord hath spoken,
        I have nourished and brought up children,
    and they have rebelled against me.
³ The ox knoweth his owner,
    and the ass his master's crib,
        but Israel doth not know,
    my people doth not consider.
⁴ Ah sinful nation, a people laden with iniquity,
    a seed of evildoers,
        children that are corrupters:
    they have forsaken the Lord,
        they have provoked
    the Holy One of Israel unto anger,
        they are gone away backward.
⁵ Why should ye be stricken any more?
    Ye will revolt more and more:
        the whole head is sick,
    and the whole heart faint.

⁶ From the sole of the foot even unto the head
    there is no soundness in it;
        but wounds, and bruises,
    and putrifying sores:
        they have not been closed, neither bound up,
    neither mollified with ointment.
⁷ Your country is desolate,
    your cities are burned with fire;
        your land, strangers devour it
    in your presence,
        and it is desolate, as overthrown by strangers.
⁸ And the daughter of Zion is left
    as a cottage in a vineyard,
        as a lodge in a garden of cucumbers,
    as a besieged city.
⁹ Except the Lord of hosts had left unto us
    a very small remnant,
        we should have been as Sodom,
    and we should have been like unto Gomorrah.
¹⁰ Hear the word of the Lord, ye rulers of Sodom;
    give ear unto the law of our God,
        ye people of Gomorrah.
¹¹ To what purpose is the multitude of
    your sacrifices unto me? saith the Lord:
        I am full of the burnt offerings of rams,
    and the fat of fed beasts;
        and I delight not in the blood of bullocks,
    or of lambs, or of he goats.

¹² When ye come to appear before me,
    who hath required this at your hand,
        to tread my courts?
¹³ Bring no more vain oblations;
    incense is an abomination unto me;
        the new moons and sabbaths,
    the calling of assemblies, I cannot away with:
        it is iniquity, even the solemn meeting.
¹⁴ Your new moons and your appointed feasts
    my soul hateth;
        they are a trouble unto me;
    I am weary to bear them.
¹⁵ And when ye spread forth your hands,
    I will hide mine eyes from you;
        yea, when ye make many prayers,
    I will not hear;
        your hands are full of blood.
¹⁶ Wash you, make you clean;
    put away the evil of your doings
        from before mine eyes; cease to do evil;
¹⁷ learn to do well; seek judgment,
    relieve the oppressed, judge the fatherless,
        plead for the widow.
¹⁸ Come now, and let us reason together, saith the Lord:
    though your sins be as scarlet,
        they shall be as white as snow;
    though they be red like crimson,
        they shall be as wool.

¹⁹ If ye be willing and obedient,
ye shall eat the good of the land;
²⁰ but if ye refuse and rebel,
ye shall be devoured with the sword,
for the mouth of the Lord
hath spoken it.
²¹ How is the faithful city become an harlot!
It was full of judgment;
righteousness lodged in it;
but now murderers.
²² Thy silver is become dross,
thy wine mixed with water.
²³ Thy princes are rebellious,
and companions of thieves:
every one loveth gifts,
and followeth after rewards:
they judge not the fatherless,
neither doth the cause of the widow
come unto them.
²⁴ Therefore saith the Lord, the Lord of hosts,
the mighty One of Israel,
Ah, I will ease me of mine adversaries,
and avenge me of mine enemies.
²⁵ And I will turn my hand upon thee,
and purely purge away thy dross,
and take away all thy tin.
²⁶ And I will restore thy judges as at the first,
and thy counsellors as at the beginning:

  afterward thou shalt be called,
   'The city of righteousness, the faithful city.'
²⁷ Zion shall be redeemed with judgment,
  and her converts with righteousness.
²⁸ And the destruction of the transgressors
  and of the sinners shall be together,
   and they that forsake the Lord
  shall be consumed.
²⁹ For they shall be ashamed of the oaks
  which ye have desired,
   and ye shall be confounded for the gardens
  that ye have chosen.
³⁰ For ye shall be as an oak whose leaf fadeth,
  and as a garden that hath no water.
³¹ And the strong shall be as tow,
  and the maker of it as a spark,
   and they shall both burn together,
  and none shall quench them.

2 The word that Isaiah the son of Amoz saw
   concerning Judah and Jerusalem.
 ²And it shall come to pass in the last days,
  that the mountain of the Lord's house shall be
   established in the top of the mountains,
  and shall be exalted above the hills;
   and all nations shall flow unto it.

³And many people shall go and say,
   Come ye, and let us go up
      to the mountain of the Lord,
   to the house of the God of Jacob;
      and he will teach us of his ways,
      and we will walk in his paths:
         for out of Zion shall go forth the law,
      and the word of the Lord from Jerusalem.
⁴And he shall judge among the nations,
   and shall rebuke many people,
      and they shall beat their swords
   into plowshares,
      and their spears into pruninghooks:
   nation shall not lift up sword against nation,
      neither shall they learn war any more.
⁵O house of Jacob,
   come ye,
      and let us walk in the light of the Lord.
⁶Therefore thou hast forsaken thy people
   the house of Jacob,
      because they be replenished from the east,
   and are soothsayers like the Philistines,
      and they please themselves
   in the children of strangers.
⁷Their land also is full of silver and gold,
   neither is there any end of their treasures;
      their land is also full of horses,
   neither is there any end of their chariots.

[8] Their land also is full of idols;
     they worship the work of their own hands,
          that which their own fingers have made.
[9] And the mean man boweth down,
     and the great man humbleth himself:
          therefore forgive them not.
[10] Enter into the rock,
     and hide thee in the dust,
          for fear of the Lord
     and for the glory of his majesty.
[11] The lofty looks of man shall be humbled,
     and the haughtiness of men
          shall be bowed down,
     and the Lord alone shall be exalted
          in that day.
[12] For the day of the Lord of hosts shall be upon
     every one that is proud and lofty,
          and upon every one that is lifted up;
     and he shall be brought low:
[13] and upon all the cedars of Lebanon,
     that are high and lifted up,
          and upon all the oaks of Bashan,
[14] and upon all the high mountains,
     and upon all the hills that are lifted up,
[15] and upon every high tower,
     and upon every fenced wall,
[16] and upon all the ships of Tarshish,
     and upon all pleasant pictures.

¹⁷And the loftiness of man shall be bowed down,
and the haughtiness of men shall be made low:
and the Lord alone shall be exalted
in that day.
¹⁸And the idols he shall utterly abolish.
¹⁹And they shall go into the holes of the rocks,
and into the caves of the earth,
for fear of the Lord,
and for the glory of his majesty,
when he ariseth to shake terribly the earth.
²⁰In that day a man shall cast his idols of silver,
and his idols of gold,
which they made each one for himself
to worship,
to the moles and to the bats;
²¹to go into the clefts of the rocks,
and into the tops of the ragged rocks,
for fear of the Lord,
and for the glory of his majesty,
when he ariseth to shake terribly the earth.
²²Cease ye from man, whose breath is in his nostrils,
for wherein is he to be accounted of?

3   For, behold, the Lord, the Lord of hosts,
doth take away from Jerusalem and from Judah
the stay and the staff,

the whole stay of bread,
and the whole stay of water,
² the mighty man, and the man of war,
the judge, and the prophet,
and the prudent, and the ancient,
³ the captain of fifty, and the honourable man,
and the counsellor, and the cunning artificer,
and the eloquent orator.
⁴And I will give children to be their princes,
and babes shall rule over them.
⁵And the people shall be oppressed,
every one by another,
and every one by his neighbour:
the child shall behave himself
proudly against the ancient,
and the base against the honourable.
⁶ When a man shall take hold of his brother
of the house of his father, saying,
'Thou hast clothing, be thou our ruler,
and let this ruin be under thy hand.'
⁷ In that day shall he swear, saying,
'I will not be an healer;
for in my house is neither bread nor clothing:
make me not a ruler of the people.'
⁸ For Jerusalem is ruined, and Judah is fallen,
because their tongue and their doings
are against the Lord,
to provoke the eyes of his glory.

[9] The shew of their countenance
doth witness against them;
and they declare their sin as Sodom,
they hide it not. Woe unto their soul!
For they have rewarded evil unto themselves.
[10] Say ye to the righteous,
that it shall be well with him,
for they shall eat the fruit of their doings.
[11] Woe unto the wicked! It shall be ill with him,
for the reward of his hands shall be given him.
[12] As for my people,
children are their oppressors,
and women rule over them. O my people,
they which lead thee cause thee to err,
and destroy the way of thy paths.
[13] The Lord standeth up to plead,
and standeth to judge the people.
[14] The Lord will enter into judgment
with the ancients of his people,
and the princes thereof:
for ye have eaten up the vineyard;
the spoil of the poor is in your houses.
[15] 'What mean ye that ye beat my people to pieces,
and grind the faces of the poor?'
saith the Lord God of hosts.
[16] Moreover the Lord saith,
Because the daughters of Zion are haughty,
and walk with stretched forth necks

and wanton eyes,
   walking and mincing as they go,
   and making a tinkling with their feet,
¹⁷ therefore the Lord will smite with a scab the crown
   of the head of the daughters of Zion,
      and the Lord will discover their secret parts.
¹⁸ In that day the Lord will take away the bravery
   of their tinkling ornaments about their feet,
      and their cauls,
   and their round tires like the moon,
¹⁹ the chains, and the bracelets,
   and the mufflers,
²⁰ the bonnets, and the ornaments of the legs,
   and the headbands, and the tablets,
      and the earrings,
²¹ the rings, and nose jewels,
²² the changeable suits of apparel,
   and the mantles, and the wimples,
      and the crisping pins,
²³ the glasses, and the fine linen,
   and the hoods, and the vails.
²⁴ And it shall come to pass,
   that instead of sweet smell there shall be stink;
      and instead of a girdle a rent;
      and instead of well set hair baldness;
         and instead of a stomacher
      a girding of sackcloth;
         and burning instead of beauty.

[25] Thy men shall fall by the sword,
    and thy mighty in the war.
[26] And her gates shall lament and mourn;
    and she being desolate
        shall sit upon the ground.

4 And in that day seven women
    shall take hold of one man, saying,
        We will eat our own bread,
    and wear our own apparel:
        only let us be called by thy name,
    to take away our reproach?
[2] In that day shall the branch of the Lord
    be beautiful and glorious,
        and the fruit of the earth shall be excellent
    and comely for them that are escaped of Israel.
[3] And it shall come to pass,
    that he that is left in Zion,
        and he that remaineth in Jerusalem,
    shall be called holy,
        even every one that is written
    among the living in Jerusalem,
[4] when the Lord shall have washed away
    the filth of the daughters of Zion,
        and shall have purged the blood of Jerusalem

from the midst thereof by the spirit of judgment,
and by the spirit of burning.
⁵And the Lord will create upon every dwelling place
of mount Zion,
and upon her assemblies,
a cloud and smoke by day,
and the shining of a flaming fire by night:
for upon all the glory
shall be a defence.
⁶And there shall be a tabernacle for a shadow
in the daytime from the heat,
and for a place of refuge,
and for a covert from storm
and from rain.

5 Now will I sing to my wellbeloved
a song of my beloved touching his vineyard.
My wellbeloved hath a vineyard
in a very fruitful hill.
²And he fenced it, and gathered out the stones thereof,
and planted it with the choicest vine,
and built a tower in the midst of it,
and also made a winepress therein:
and he looked that it should bring forth grapes,
and it brought forth wild grapes.

³And now, O inhabitants of Jerusalem,
  and men of Judah,
      judge, I pray you, betwixt me and my vineyard.
⁴ What could have been done more to my vineyard,
  that I have not done in it?
      Wherefore, when I looked
  that it should bring forth grapes,
      brought it forth wild grapes?
⁵And now go to;
  I will tell you what I will do to my vineyard:
      I will take away the hedge thereof,
  and it shall be eaten up;
      and break down the wall thereof,
  and it shall be trodden down.
⁶And I will lay it waste:
  it shall not be pruned, nor digged;
      but there shall come up briers and thorns:
  I will also command the clouds
      that they rain no rain upon it.
⁷ For the vineyard of the Lord of hosts
  is the house of Israel,
      and the men of Judah his pleasant plant:
  and he looked for judgment,
      but behold oppression;
  for righteousness, but behold a cry.
⁸ Woe unto them that join house to house,
  that lay field to field, till there be no place,
      that they may be placed alone

in the midst of the earth!

⁹ In mine ears said the Lord of hosts,
    Of a truth many houses shall be desolate,
        even great and fair, without inhabitant.
¹⁰ Yea, ten acres of vineyard shall yield one bath,
    and the seed of an homer shall yield an ephah.
¹¹ Woe unto them that rise up early in the morning,
    that they may follow strong drink;
        that continue until night,
    till wine inflame them!
¹² And the harp, and the viol, the tabret,
    and pipe, and wine, are in their feasts but they
        regard not the work of the Lord,
    neither consider the operation of his hands.
¹³ Therefore my people are gone into captivity,
    because they have no knowledge:
        and their honourable men are famished,
    and their multitude dried up with thirst.
¹⁴ Therefore hell hath enlarged herself,
    and opened her mouth without measure:
        and their glory, and their multitude,
    and their pomp,
        and he that rejoiceth, shall descend into it.
¹⁵ And the mean man shall be brought down,
    and the mighty man shall be humbled,
        and the eyes of the lofty shall be humbled.
¹⁶ But the Lord of hosts shall be exalted in judgment,
    and God that is holy

shall be sanctified in righteousness.
¹⁷ Then shall the lambs feed after their manner,
and the waste places of the fat ones
shall strangers eat.
¹⁸ Woe unto them that draw iniquity with cords of vanity,
and sin as it were with a cart rope,
¹⁹ that say, 'Let him make speed, and hasten his work,
that we may see it,
and let the counsel of the Holy One of Israel
draw nigh and come,
that we may know it!'
²⁰ Woe unto them that call evil good, and good evil;
that put darkness for light,
and light for darkness;
that put bitter for sweet,
and sweet for bitter!
²¹ Woe unto them that are wise in their own eyes,
and prudent in their own sight!
²² Woe unto them that are mighty to drink wine,
and men of strength to mingle strong drink,
²³ which justify the wicked for reward,
and take away the righteousness
of the righteous from him!
²⁴ Therefore as the fire devoureth the stubble,
and the flame consumeth the chaff,
so their root shall be as rottenness,
and their blossom shall go up as dust,
because they have cast away

the law of the Lord of hosts,
> and despised the word of the Holy One of Israel.

²⁵ Therefore is the anger of the Lord
> kindled against his people,
>> and he hath stretched forth his hand
> against them,
>> and hath smitten them;
> and the hills did tremble, and their carcases
>> were torn in the midst of the streets.
> For all this his anger is not turned away,
>> but his hand is stretched out still.

²⁶ And he will lift up an ensign to the nations from far
> and will hiss unto them
>> from the end of the earth:
> and, behold, they shall come with speed swiftly.

²⁷ None shall be weary nor stumble among them;
> none shall slumber nor sleep;
>> neither shall the girdle of their loins
> be loosed,
>> nor the latchet of their shoes be broken:

²⁸ whose arrows are sharp, and all their bows bent,
> their horses' hoofs shall be counted like flint,
>> and their wheels like a whirlwind.

²⁹ Their roaring shall be like a lion,
> they shall roar like young lions: yea,
>> they shall roar, and lay hold of the prey,
> and shall carry it away safe,
>> and none shall deliver it.

³⁰And in that day they shall roar against them
　　like the roaring of the sea:
　　　　and if one look unto the land,
　　behold darkness and sorrow,
　　　　and the light is darkened
　　in the heavens thereof.

6 In the year that king Uzziah died I saw also
　　the Lord sitting upon a throne, high and lifted up,
　　　　and his train filled the temple.
²Above it stood the seraphims:
　　each one had six wings;
　　　　with twain he covered his face,
　　and with twain he covered his feet,
　　　　and with twain he did fly.
³And one cried unto another, and said,
　　'Holy, holy, holy, is the Lord of hosts:
　　　　the whole earth is full of his glory.'
⁴And the posts of the door moved
　　at the voice of him that cried,
　　　　and the house was filled with smoke.
⁵Then said I, 'Woe is me! for I am undone;
　　because I am a man of unclean lips,
　　　　and I dwell in the midst of a people
　　of unclean lips,
　　　　for mine eyes have seen the King,
　　the Lord of hosts.'

⁶ Then flew one of the seraphims unto me,
    having a live coal in his hand,
        which he had taken with the tongs
    from off the altar.
⁷ And he laid it upon my mouth, and said,
    'Lo, this hath touched thy lips;
        and thine iniquity is taken away,
    and thy sin purged.'
⁸ Also I heard the voice of the Lord, saying,
    'Whom shall I send, and who will go for us?'
        Then said I, 'Here am I; send me.'
⁹ And he said, 'Go, and tell this people;
    "Hear ye indeed, but understand not;
        and see ye indeed, but perceive not."
¹⁰ Make the heart of this people fat,
    and make their ears heavy, and shut their eyes;
        lest they see with their eyes,
    and hear with their ears,
        and understand with their heart,
    and convert, and be healed.'
¹¹ Then said I, 'Lord, how long?'
    And he answered, 'Until the cities be wasted
        without inhabitant,
    and the houses without man,
        and the land be utterly desolate,
¹² and the Lord have removed men far away,
    and there be a great forsaking
        in the midst of the land.

¹³ But yet in it shall be a tenth, and it shall return,
and shall be eaten, as a teil tree, and as an oak,
whose substance is in them,
when they cast their leaves.'
So the holy seed shall be
the substance thereof.

7   And it came to pass in the days of Ahaz the son
of Jotham, the son of Uzziah, king of Judah,
that Rezin the king of Syria,
and Pekah the son of Remaliah, king of Israel,
went up toward Jerusalem to war against it,
but could not prevail against it.
²And it was told the house of David, saying,
'Syria is confederate with Ephraim.'
And his heart was moved,
and the heart of his people,
as the trees of the wood are moved
with the wind.
³Then said the Lord unto Isaiah,
'Go forth now to meet Ahaz, thou,
and Shear-jashub thy son,
at the end of the conduit of the upper pool
in the highway of the fuller's field;
⁴and say unto him, "Take heed, and be quiet;
fear not, neither be fainthearted
for the two tails of these smoking firebrands,

for the fierce anger of Rezin with Syria,
and of the son of Remaliah."

5 Because Syria, Ephraim, and the son of Remaliah,
have taken evil counsel against thee, saying,

6 "Let us go up against Judah, and vex it,
and let us make a breach therein for us,
and set a king in the midst of it,
even the son of Tabeal".'

7 Thus saith the Lord God,
'It shall not stand, neither shall it come to pass.

8 For the head of Syria is Damascus,
and the head of Damascus is Rezin;
and within threescore and five years
shall Ephraim be broken,
that it be not a people.

9 And the head of Ephraim is Samaria,
and the head of Samaria is Remaliah's son.
If ye will not believe,
surely ye shall not be established.'

10 Moreover the Lord spake again unto Ahaz, saying,

11 'Ask thee a sign of the Lord thy God;
ask it either in the depth,
or in the height above.'

12 But Ahaz said,
'I will not ask, neither will I tempt the Lord.'

13 And he said, Hear ye now, O house of David;
is it a small thing for you to weary men,
but will ye weary my God also?

¹⁴ Therefore the Lord himself shall give you a sign.
　　Behold, a virgin shall conceive, and bear a son,
　　　　and shall call his name Immanuel.
¹⁵ Butter and honey shall he eat,
　　that he may know to refuse the evil,
　　　　and choose the good.
¹⁶ For before the child shall know to refuse the evil,
　　and choose the good,
　　　　the land that thou abhorrest shall be forsaken
　　of both her kings.
¹⁷ The Lord shall bring upon thee,
　　and upon thy people,
　　　　and upon thy father's house,
　　days that have not come,
　　　　from the day that Ephraim
　　departed from Judah;
　　　　even the king of Assyria.'
¹⁸ And it shall come to pass in that day,
　　that the Lord shall hiss for the fly that is in
　　　　the uttermost part of the rivers of Egypt,
　　and for the bee that is in the land
　　　　of Assyria.
¹⁹ And they shall come, and shall rest all of them
　　in the desolate valleys,
　　　　and in the holes of the rocks,
　　and upon all thorns,
　　　　and upon all bushes.
²⁰ In the same day shall the Lord shave

with a razor that is hired, namely,
  by them beyond the river,
by the king of Assyria,
  the head, and the hair of the feet;
and it shall also consume the beard.
²¹And it shall come to pass in that day,
  that a man shall nourish a young cow,
    and two sheep;
²²And it shall come to pass,
  for the abundance of milk
    that they shall give he shall eat butter,
  for butter and honey shall every one eat
    that is left in the land.
²³And it shall come to pass in that day,
  that every place shall be,
    where there were a thousand vines
  at a thousand silverlings,
    it shall even be for briers and thorns.
²⁴With arrows and with bows
  shall men come thither;
    because all the land shall become briers
  and thorns.
²⁵And on all hills that shall be digged
  with the mattock,
    there shall not come thither the fear of briers
  and thorns:
    but it shall be for the sending forth of oxen,
  and for the treading of lesser cattle.

8 Moreover the Lord said unto me,
'Take thee a great roll, and write in it
with a man's pen concerning
Maher-shalal-hash-baz.'
²And I took unto me faithful witnesses to record,
Uriah the priest, and Zechariah
the son of Jeberechiah.
³And I went unto the prophetess;
and she conceived, and bare a son.
Then said the Lord to me,
Call his name Maher-shalal-hash-baz.
⁴For before the child shall have knowledge to cry,
'My father', and 'My mother',
the riches of Damascus
and the spoil of Samaria
shall be taken away
before the king of Assyria.
⁵The Lord spake also unto me again, saying,
⁶Forasmuch as this people refuseth the waters
of Shiloah that go softly,
and rejoice in Rezin and Remaliah's son,
⁷now therefore, behold, the Lord bringeth up upon
them the waters of the river,
strong and many, even the king of Assyria,
and all his glory:
and he shall come up over all his channels,
and go over all his banks:
⁸and he shall pass through Judah;

he shall overflow and go over,
  he shall reach even to the neck;
and the stretching out of his wings
  shall fill the breadth of thy land,
O Immanuel.
⁹Associate yourselves, O ye people,
  and ye shall be broken in pieces;
    and give ear, all ye of far countries:
  gird yourselves, and ye shall be broken in pieces;
    gird yourselves,
  and ye shall be broken in pieces.
¹⁰Take counsel together, and it shall come to nought;
  speak the word, and it shall not stand,
    for God is with us.
¹¹For the Lord spake thus to me with a strong hand,
  and instructed me that I should not walk
    in the way of this people, saying,
¹²Say ye not, 'A confederacy',
  to all them to whom this people shall say
    'A confederacy';
  neither fear ye their fear, nor be afraid.
¹³Sanctify the Lord of hosts himself;
  and let him be your fear,
    and let him be your dread.
¹⁴And he shall be for a sanctuary;
  but for a stone of stumbling and for a rock
    of offence to both the houses of Israel,
  for a gin and for a snare
    to the inhabitants of Jerusalem.

¹⁵And many among them shall stumble, and fall,
    and be broken, and be snared,
        and be taken.
¹⁶Bind up the testimony,
    seal the law among my disciples.
¹⁷And I will wait upon the Lord,
    that hideth his face from the house of Jacob,
        and I will look for him.
¹⁸Behold, I and the children
    whom the Lord hath given me
        are for signs and for wonders in Israel
    from the Lord of hosts,
        which dwelleth in mount Zion.
¹⁹And when they shall say unto you,
    'Seek unto them that have familiar spirits,
        and unto wizards that peep, and that mutter:
    should not a people seek unto their God?
        For the living to the dead?
²⁰to the law and to the testimony':
    if they speak not according to this word,
        it is because there is no light in them.
²¹And they shall pass through it,
    hardly bestead and hungry:
        and it shall come to pass, that when
    they shall be hungry, they shall fret themselves,
        and curse their king and their God,
    and look upward.
²²And they shall look unto the earth;

and behold trouble and darkness,
      dimness of anguish;
and they shall be driven to darkness.

9 Nevertheless the dimness shall not be such
      as was in her vexation,
         when at the first he lightly afflicted
      the land of Zebulun and the land of Naphtali,
         and afterward did more grievously afflict her
      by the way of the sea,
         beyond Jordan, in Galilee of the nations.
² The people that walked in darkness
      have seen a great light:
         they that dwell in the land
      of the shadow of death,
         upon them hath the light shined.
³ Thou hast multiplied the nation,
      and not increased the joy:
         they joy before thee
      according to the joy in harvest,
         and as men rejoice when they divide the spoil.
⁴ For thou hast broken the yoke of his burden,
      and the staff of his shoulder,
         the rod of his oppressor,
      as in the day of Midian.

⁵For every battle of the warrior is with
  confused noise, and garments rolled in blood;
    but this shall be with burning
    and fuel of fire.
⁶For unto us a child is born, unto us a son is given;
  and the government shall be upon his shoulder;
    and his name shall be called
  Wonderful, Counsellor,
    The mighty God, The everlasting Father,
  The Prince of Peace.
⁷Of the increase of his government and peace
  there shall be no end,
    upon the throne of David,
  and upon his kingdom,
    to order it, and to establish it
  with judgment and with justice
    from henceforth even for ever.
  The zeal of the Lord of hosts will perform this.
⁸The Lord sent a word into Jacob,
  and it hath lighted upon Israel.
⁹And all the people shall know,
  even Ephraim and the inhabitant of Samaria,
    that say in the pride and stoutness of heart,
¹⁰'The bricks are fallen down,
  but we will build with hewn stones;
    the sycomores are cut down,
  but we will change them into cedars.'
¹¹Therefore the Lord shall set up

the adversaries of Rezin against him,
and join his enemies together;
¹² the Syrians before, and the Philistines behind;
and they shall devour Israel with open mouth.
For all this his anger is not turned away,
but his hand is stretched out still.
¹³ For the people turneth
not unto him that smiteth them,
neither do they seek the Lord of hosts.
¹⁴ Therefore the Lord will cut off from Israel
head and tail, branch and rush, in one day.
¹⁵ The ancient and honourable, he is the head;
and the prophet that teacheth lies, he is the tail.
¹⁶ For the leaders of this people cause them to err;
and they that are led of them are destroyed.
¹⁷ Therefore the Lord shall have no joy
in their young men,
neither shall have mercy
on their fatherless and widows,
for every one is an hypocrite and an evildoer,
and every mouth speaketh folly.
For all this his anger is not turned away,
but his hand is stretched out still.
¹⁸ For wickedness burneth as the fire:
it shall devour the briers and thorns,
and shall kindle in the thickets of the forest,
and they shall mount up
like the lifting up of smoke.

¹⁹ Through the wrath of the Lord of hosts
    is the land darkened,
        and the people shall be as the fuel of the fire:
    no man shall spare his brother.
²⁰ And he shall snatch on the right hand,
    and be hungry;
        and he shall eat on the left hand,
    and they shall not be satisfied;
        they shall eat every man
    the flesh of his own arm;
²¹ Manasseh, Ephraim; and Ephraim, Manasseh:
    and they together shall be against Judah.
        For all this his anger is not turned away,
    but his hand is stretched out still.

10   Woe unto them that decree unrighteous decrees,
    and that write grievousness
        which they have prescribed;
² to turn aside the needy from judgment,
    and to take away the right
    from the poor of my people,
        that widows may be their prey,
    and that they may rob the fatherless!
³ And what will ye do in the day of visitation,
    and in the desolation which shall come from far?

To whom will ye flee for help?
  And where will ye leave your glory?
⁴ Without me they shall bow down
    under the prisoners,
      and they shall fall under the slain.
  For all this his anger is not turned away,
    but his hand is stretched out still.
⁵ O Assyrian, the rod of mine anger,
  and the staff in their hand is mine indignation.
⁶ I will send him against an hypocritical nation,
  and against the people of my wrath
    will I give him a charge,
  to take the spoil, and to take the prey,
    and to tread them down
  like the mire of the streets.
⁷ Howbeit he meaneth not so,
  neither doth his heart think so;
    but it is in his heart to destroy
  and cut off nations not a few.
⁸ For he saith, 'Are not my princes altogether kings?
⁹ Is not Calno as Carchemish?
  Is not Hamath as Arpad?
    Is not Samaria as Damascus?
¹⁰ As my hand hath found the kingdoms of the idols,
  and whose graven images did excel them
    of Jerusalem and of Samaria,
¹¹ Shall I not, as I have done unto Samaria and her idols,
  so do to Jerusalem and her idols?'

¹² Wherefore it shall come to pass,
  that when the Lord hath performed
    his whole work upon mount Zion
  and on Jerusalem,
    I will punish the fruit of the stout heart
  of the king of Assyria,
    and the glory of his high looks.
¹³ For he saith,
  'By the strength of my hand I have done it,
    and by my wisdom,
  for I am prudent;
    and I have removed the bounds of the people,
  and have robbed their treasures,
    and I have put down the inhabitants
  like a valiant man.
¹⁴ And my hand hath found as a nest
  the riches of the people;
    and as one gathereth eggs that are left,
  have I gathered all the earth;
    and there was none that moved the wing,
  or opened the mouth, or peeped.'
¹⁵ Shall the axe boast itself against him
  that heweth therewith?
    Or shall the saw magnify itself
  against him that shaketh it?
    As if the rod should shake itself
  against them that lift it up,
    or as if the staff should lift up itself,
  as if it were no wood.

¹⁶ Therefore shall the Lord, the Lord of hosts,
  send among his fat ones leanness;
      and under his glory he shall kindle a burning
    like the burning of a fire.
¹⁷ And the light of Israel shall be for a fire,
    and his Holy One for a flame:
        and it shall burn and devour his thorns
      and his briers in one day.
¹⁸ and shall consume the glory of his forest,
    and of his fruitful field, both soul and body;
        and they shall be
      as when a standardbearer fainteth.
¹⁹ And the rest of the trees of his forest shall be few,
    that a child may write them.
²⁰ And it shall come to pass in that day,
    that the remnant of Israel,
        and such as are escaped of the house of Jacob,
      shall no more again stay upon
        him that smote them;
      but shall stay upon the Lord,
        the Holy One of Israel, in truth.
²¹ The remnant shall return, even the remnant of Jacob,
    unto the mighty God.
²² For though thy people Israel
    be as the sand of the sea,
        yet a remnant of them shall return:
      the consumption decreed shall overflow
        with righteousness.

²³ For the Lord God of hosts shall make a consumption,
   even determined, in the midst of all the land.
²⁴ Therefore thus saith the Lord God of hosts,
   O my people that dwellest in Zion,
      be not afraid of the Assyrian:
   he shall smite thee with a rod,
      and shall lift up his staff against thee
   after the manner of Egypt.
²⁵ For yet a very little while,
   and the indignation shall cease,
      and mine anger in their destruction.
²⁶ And the Lord of hosts shall stir up a scourge
   for him according to the slaughter of Midian
      at the rock of Oreb:
   and as his rod was upon the sea,
      so shall he lift it up after the manner of Egypt.
²⁷ And it shall come to pass in that day,
   that his burden shall be taken away
      from off thy shoulder,
   and his yoke from off thy neck,
      and the yoke shall be destroyed
   because of the anointing.
²⁸ He is come to Aiath, he is passed to Migron;
   at Michmash he hath laid up his carriages;
²⁹ they are gone over the passage;
   they have taken up their lodging at Geba;
      Ramah is afraid;
   Gibeah of Saul is fled.

³⁰ Lift up thy voice, O daughter of Gallim:
    cause it to be heard unto Laish,
        O poor Anathoth.
³¹ Madmenah is removed;
    the inhabitants of Gebim gather themselves to flee.
³² As yet shall he remain at Nob that day:
    he shall shake his hand
        against the mount of the daughter of Zion,
    the hill of Jerusalem.
³³ Behold, the Lord, the Lord of hosts,
    shall lop the bough with terror:
        and the high ones of stature
    shall be hewn down,
        and the haughty shall be humbled.
³⁴ And he shall cut down
    the thickets of the forest with iron,
        and Lebanon shall fall by a mighty one.

11 And there shall come forth a rod
        out of the stem of Jesse,
            and a Branch shall grow out of his roots.
    ² And the spirit of the Lord shall rest upon him,
        the spirit of wisdom and understanding,
            the spirit of counsel and might,
        the spirit of knowledge
            and of the fear of the Lord;

³ and shall make him of quick understanding
in the fear of the Lord;
and he shall not judge
after the sight of his eyes,
neither reprove after the hearing of his ears,
⁴ but with righteousness shall he judge the poor,
and reprove with equity
for the meek of the earth;
and he shall smite the earth
with the rod of his mouth,
and with the breath of his lips
shall he slay the wicked.
⁵ And righteousness shall be the girdle of his loins,
and faithfulness the girdle of his reins.
⁶ The wolf also shall dwell with the lamb,
and the leopard shall lie down with the kid;
and the calf and the young lion
and the fatling together;
and a little child shall lead them.
⁷ And the cow and the bear shall feed;
their young ones shall lie down together;
and the lion shall eat straw like the ox.
⁸ And the sucking child shall play
on the hole of the asp,
and the weaned child shall put his hand
on the cockatrice's den.
⁹ They shall not hurt nor destroy
in all my holy mountain;

for the earth shall be full
of the knowledge of the Lord,
as the waters cover the sea.
¹⁰And in that day there shall be a root of Jesse,
which shall stand for an ensign of the people;
to it shall the Gentiles seek:
and his rest shall be glorious.
¹¹And it shall come to pass in that day,
that the Lord shall set his hand again
the second time to recover
the remnant of his people, which shall be left,
from Assyria, and from Egypt,
and from Pathros, and from Cush, and from Elam,
and from Shinar, and from Hamath,
and from the islands of the sea.
¹²And he shall set up an ensign for the nations,
and shall assemble the outcasts of Israel,
and gather together the dispersed of Judah
from the four corners of the earth.
¹³The envy also of Ephraim shall depart,
and the adversaries of Judah shall be cut off:
Ephraim shall not envy Judah,
and Judah shall not vex Ephraim.
¹⁴But they shall fly upon the shoulders
of the Philistines toward the west;
they shall spoil them of the east together:
they shall lay their hand upon Edom and Moab;
and the children of Ammon shall obey them.

¹⁵And the Lord shall utterly destroy
the tongue of the Egyptian sea;
and with his mighty wind
shall he shake his hand over the river,
and shall smite it in the seven streams,
and make men go over dryshod.
¹⁶And there shall be an highway
for the remnant of his people,
which shall be left, from Assyria;
like as it was to Israel in the day
that he came up out of the land of Egypt.

12 And in that day thou shalt say,
O Lord, I will praise thee:
though thou wast angry with me,
thine anger is turned away,
and thou comfortedst me.
²Behold, God is my salvation;
I will trust, and not be afraid,
for the Lord Jehovah is my strength
and my song;
he also is become my salvation.
³Therefore with joy shall ye draw water
out of the wells of salvation.
⁴And in that day shall ye say,

Praise the Lord, call upon his name,
>> declare his doings among the people,
> make mention that his name is exalted.
⁵ Sing unto the Lord;
>> for he hath done excellent things:
>>> this is known in all the earth.
⁶ Cry out and shout, thou inhabitant of Zion,
>> for great is the Holy One of Israel
>>> in the midst of thee.

13 The burden of Babylon, which Isaiah
>> the son of Amoz did see.
² Lift ye up a banner upon the high mountain,
>> exalt the voice unto them, shake the hand,
>>> that they may go into the gates
> of the nobles.
³ I have commanded my sanctified ones,
>> I have also called my mighty ones for mine anger,
>>> even them that rejoice in my highness.
⁴ The noise of a multitude in the mountains,
>> like as of a great people;
>> a tumultuous noise
> of the kingdoms of nations gathered together:
>> the Lord of hosts mustereth
> the host of the battle.

⁵They come from a far country,
   from the end of heaven, even the Lord,
      and the weapons of his indignation,
   to destroy the whole land.
⁶Howl ye; for the day of the Lord is at hand;
   it shall come as a destruction from the Almighty.
⁷Therefore shall all hands be faint,
   and every man's heart shall melt,
⁸and they shall be afraid.
   Pangs and sorrows shall take hold of them;
      they shall be in pain
   as a woman that travaileth.
      They shall be amazed one at another;
   their faces shall be as flames.
⁹Behold, the day of the Lord cometh,
   cruel both with wrath and fierce anger,
      to lay the land desolate:
   and he shall destroy the sinners thereof
      out of it.
¹⁰For the stars of heaven and the constellations
   thereof shall not give their light:
      the sun shall be darkened in his going forth,
   and the moon shall not cause her light to shine.
¹¹And I will punish the world for their evil,
   and the wicked for their iniquity;
      and I will cause the arrogancy
   of the proud to cease,
      and will lay low the haughtiness
   of the terrible.

¹² I will make a man more precious than fine gold;
   even a man than the golden wedge of Ophir.
¹³ Therefore I will shake the heavens,
   and the earth shall remove out of her place,
      in the wrath of the Lord of hosts,
   and in the day of his fierce anger.
¹⁴And it shall be as the chased roe,
   and as a sheep that no man taketh up:
      they shall every man turn to his own people,
   and flee every one into his own land.
¹⁵ Every one that is found shall be thrust through;
   and every one that is joined unto them
      shall fall by the sword.
¹⁶ Their children also shall be dashed to pieces
   before their eyes;
      their houses shall be spoiled,
   and their wives ravished.
¹⁷ Behold, I will stir up the Medes against them,
   which shall not regard silver;
      and as for gold, they shall not delight in it.
¹⁸ Their bows also shall dash the young men to pieces;
      and they shall have no pity
   on the fruit of the womb;
      their eye shall not spare children.
¹⁹And Babylon, the glory of kingdoms,
   the beauty of the Chaldees' excellency,
      shall be as when God overthrew
   Sodom and Gomorrah.

²⁰ It shall never be inhabited,
   neither shall it be dwelt in
      from generation to generation:
   neither shall the Arabian pitch tent there;
      neither shall the shepherds make their fold there.
²¹ But wild beasts of the desert shall lie there;
   and their houses shall be full of doleful creatures;
      and owls shall dwell there,
      and satyrs shall dance there.
²² And the wild beasts of the islands shall cry
   in their desolate houses,
      and dragons in their pleasant palaces:
   and her time is near to come,
      and her days shall not be prolonged.

14 For the Lord will have mercy on Jacob,
   and will yet choose Israel,
      and set them in their own land;
   and the strangers shall be joined with them,
      and they shall cleave to the house of Jacob.
² And the people shall take them,
   and bring them to their place;
      and the house of Israel shall possess them in
   the land of the Lord for servants and handmaids;
      and they shall take them captives,
   whose captives they were;

and they shall rule over their oppressors.
³And it shall come to pass in the day that the Lord
shall give thee rest from thy sorrow,
and from thy fear,
and from the hard bondage
wherein thou wast made to serve,
⁴that thou shalt take up this proverb
against the king of Babylon,
and say, How hath the oppressor ceased!
The golden city ceased!
⁵The Lord hath broken the staff of the wicked,
and the sceptre of the rulers.
⁶He who smote the people in wrath
with a continual stroke,
he that ruled the nations in anger,
is persecuted, and none hindereth.
⁷The whole earth is at rest, and is quiet:
they break forth into singing.
⁸Yea, the fir trees rejoice at thee,
and the cedars of Lebanon,
saying, 'Since thou art laid down,
no feller is come up against us.'
⁹Hell from beneath is moved for thee
to meet thee at thy coming;
it stirreth up the dead for thee,
even all the chief ones of the earth;
it hath raised up from their thrones
all the kings of the nations.

¹⁰All they shall speak and say unto thee,
  'Art thou also become weak as we?
    Art thou become like unto us?'
¹¹Thy pomp is brought down to the grave,
  and the noise of thy viols:
    the worm is spread under thee,
  and the worms cover thee.
¹²How art thou fallen from heaven,
  O Lucifer, son of the morning!
    How art thou cut down to the ground,
  which didst weaken the nations!
¹³For thou hast said in thine heart,
  'I will ascend into heaven, I will exalt my throne
    above the stars of God;
  I will sit also upon the mount of the congregation,
    in the sides of the north;
¹⁴I will ascend above the heights of the clouds;
  I will be like the most High.'
¹⁵Yet thou shalt be brought down to hell,
  to the sides of the pit.
¹⁶They that see thee shall narrowly look upon thee,
  and consider thee, saying,
    'Is this the man
    that made the earth to tremble,
    that did shake kingdoms;
¹⁷That made the world as a wilderness,
  and destroyed the cities thereof;
    that opened not the house of his prisoners?'

¹⁸All the kings of the nations,
>even all of them, lie in glory,
>>every one in his own house.
¹⁹But thou art cast out of thy grave
>like an abominable branch,
>>and as the raiment of those that are slain,
>thrust through with a sword,
>>that go down to the stones of the pit;
>as a carcase trodden under feet.
²⁰Thou shalt not be joined with them in burial,
>because thou hast destroyed thy land,
>>and slain thy people:
>the seed of evildoers shall never
>be renowned.
²¹Prepare slaughter for his children
>for the iniquity of their fathers;
>>that they do not rise, nor possess the land,
>nor fill the face of the world with cities.
²²For I will rise up against them,
>saith the Lord of hosts,
>>and cut off from Babylon the name,
>and remnant, and son, and nephew,
>>saith the Lord.
²³I will also make it a possession for the bittern,
>and pools of water:
>>and I will sweep it with the besom
>of destruction,
>>saith the Lord of hosts.

[24] The Lord of hosts hath sworn, saying,
Surely as I have thought,
so shall it come to pass;
and as I have purposed, so shall it stand.
[25] that I will break the Assyrian in my land,
and upon my mountains tread him under foot;
then shall his yoke depart from off them,
and his burden depart from off their shoulders.
[26] This is the purpose that is purposed
upon the whole earth:
and this is the hand that is stretched out
upon all the nations.
[27] For the Lord of hosts hath purposed,
and who shall disannul it?
And his hand is stretched out,
and who shall turn it back?
[28] In the year that king Ahaz died was this burden.
[29] Rejoice not thou, whole Palestina,
because the rod of him that smote thee is broken,
for out of the serpent's root
shall come forth a cockatrice,
and his fruit shall be a fiery flying serpent.
[30] And the firstborn of the poor shall feed,
and the needy shall lie down in safety:
and I will kill thy root with famine,
and he shall slay thy remnant.
[31] Howl, O gate; cry, O city;
thou, whole Palestina, art dissolved,

for there shall come from the north a smoke,
and none shall be alone in his appointed times.
³² What shall one then answer
the messengers of the nation?
That the Lord hath founded Zion,
and the poor of his people shall trust in it.

15

The burden of Moab. Because in the night
Ar of Moab is laid waste, and brought to silence;
because in the night
Kir of Moab is laid waste, and brought to silence,
² he is gone up to Bajith, and to Dibon,
the high places, to weep:
Moab shall howl over Nebo,
and over Medeba:
on all their heads shall be baldness,
and every beard cut off.
³ In their streets they shall gird themselves
with sackcloth:
on the tops of their houses, and in their streets,
every one shall howl, weeping abundantly.
⁴ And Heshbon shall cry, and Elealeh:
their voice shall be heard even unto Jahaz:
therefore the armed soldiers of Moab
shall cry out; his life shall be grievous unto him.

⁵ My heart shall cry out for Moab;
　　his fugitives shall flee unto Zoar,
　　　　an heifer of three years old;
　　for by the mounting up of Luhith
　　　　with weeping shall they go it up;
　　for in the way of Horonaim they shall raise up
　　　　a cry of destruction.
⁶ For the waters of Nimrim shall be desolate;
　　for the hay is withered away, the grass faileth,
　　　　there is no green thing.
⁷ Therefore the abundance they have gotten,
　　and that which they have laid up,
　　　　shall they carry away to the brook
　　of the willows.
⁸ For the cry is gone round
　　about the borders of Moab;
　　　　the howling thereof unto Eglaim,
　　and the howling thereof unto Beer-elim.
⁹ For the waters of Dimon shall be full of blood;
　　for I will bring more upon Dimon,
　　　　lions upon him that escapeth of Moab,
　　and upon the remnant of the land.

16　Send ye the lamb to the ruler of the land
　　from Sela to the wilderness,
　　　　unto the mount of the daughter of Zion.
² For it shall be, that,

as a wandering bird
	cast out of the nest,
so the daughters of Moab
	shall be at the fords of Arnon.
³ Take counsel, execute judgment;
	make thy shadow as the night
		in the midst of the noonday; hide the outcasts;
	bewray not him that wandereth.
⁴ Let mine outcasts dwell with thee, Moab;
		be thou a covert to them
	from the face of the spoiler;
		for the extortioner is at an end,
	the spoiler ceaseth,
		the oppressors are consumed out of the land.
⁵ And in mercy shall the throne be established:
	and he shall sit upon it in truth
		in the tabernacle of David,
	judging, and seeking judgment,
		and hasting righteousness.
⁶ We have heard of the pride of Moab,
	(he is very proud),
		even of his haughtiness, and his pride,
	and his wrath;
		but his lies shall not be so.
⁷ Therefore shall Moab howl for Moab,
	every one shall howl;
		for the foundations of Kir-hareseth
	shall ye mourn;
		surely they are stricken.

⁸ For the fields of Heshbon languish,
   and the vine of Sibmah.
      The lords of the heathen have broken down
   the principal plants thereof,
      they are come even unto Jazer,
   they wandered through the wilderness:
      her branches are stretched out,
   they are gone over the sea.
⁹ Therefore I will bewail with the weeping of Jazer
   the vine of Sibmah.
      I will water thee with my tears,
   O Heshbon, and Elealeh;
      for the shouting for thy summer fruits
   and for thy harvest is fallen.
¹⁰ And gladness is taken away,
   and joy out of the plentiful field;
      and in the vineyards there shall be no singing,
   neither shall there be shouting;
      the treaders shall tread out no wine
   in their presses;
      I have made their vintage shouting to cease.
¹¹ Wherefore my bowels shall sound like
   an harp for Moab,
      and mine inward parts for Kir-haresh.
¹² And it shall come to pass, when it is seen that Moab
   is weary on the high place,
      that he shall come to his sanctuary to pray;
   but he shall not prevail.

¹³ This is the word that the Lord hath spoken
concerning Moab since that time.
¹⁴ But now the Lord hath spoken, saying,
Within three years, as the years of an hireling,
and the glory of Moab shall be contemned,
with all that great multitude;
and the remnant shall be very small and feeble.

17 The burden of Damascus. Behold,
Damascus is taken away from being a city,
and it shall be a ruinous heap.
² The cities of Aroer are forsaken:
they shall be for flocks, which shall lie down,
and none shall make them afraid.
³ The fortress also shall cease from Ephraim,
and the kingdom from Damascus,
and the remnant of Syria:
they shall be as the glory of the children of Israel,
saith the Lord of hosts.
⁴ And in that day it shall come to pass,
that the glory of Jacob shall be made thin,
and the fatness of his flesh shall wax lean.
⁵ And it shall be as when
the harvestman gathereth the corn,
and reapeth the ears with his arm;
and it shall be as he that gathereth ears
in the valley of Rephaim.

⁶ Yet gleaning grapes shall be left in it,
   as the shaking of an olive tree,
      two or three berries in the top of
   the uppermost bough,
      four or five in the outmost
   fruitful branches thereof,
      saith the Lord God of Israel.
⁷ At that day shall a man look to his Maker,
   and his eyes shall have respect
      to the Holy One of Israel.
⁸ And he shall not look to the altars,
   the work of his hands,
      neither shall respect that
   which his fingers have made,
      either the groves, or the images.
⁹ In that day shall his strong cities be
   as a forsaken bough,
      and an uppermost branch,
   which they left because of the children of Israel,
      and there shall be desolation.
¹⁰ Because thou hast forgotten
   the God of thy salvation,
      and hast not been mindful
   of the rock of thy strength,
      therefore shalt thou plant pleasant plants,
   and shalt set it with strange slips.
¹¹ In the day shalt thou make thy plant to grow,
   and in the morning
      shalt thou make thy seed to flourish,

but the harvest shall be a heap in the day
of grief and of desperate sorrow.
¹² Woe to the multitude of many people,
which make a noise like the noise of the seas;
and to the rushing of nations,
that make a rushing
like the rushing of mighty waters!
¹³ The nations shall rush
like the rushing of many waters,
but God shall rebuke them,
and they shall flee far off, and shall be chased
as the chaff of the mountains before the wind,
and like a rolling thing before the whirlwind.
¹⁴ And behold at eveningtide trouble;
and before the morning he is not.
This is the portion of them that spoil us,
and the lot of them that rob us.

18 Woe to the land shadowing with wings,
which is beyond the rivers of Ethiopia,
² that sendeth ambassadors by the sea,
even in vessels of bulrushes upon the waters,
saying, Go, ye swift messengers,
to a nation scattered and peeled, to a people
terrible from their beginning hitherto;
a nation meted out and trodden down,
whose land the rivers have spoiled!

³All ye inhabitants of the world,
    and dwellers on the earth,
        see ye, when he lifteth up an ensign
    on the mountains;
        and when he bloweth a trumpet, hear ye.
⁴For so the Lord said unto me,
    I will take my rest, and I will consider in my
        dwelling place
    like a clear heat upon herbs,
        and like a cloud of dew in the heat of harvest.
⁵For afore the harvest, when the bud is perfect,
    and the sour grape is ripening in the flower,
        he shall both cut off the sprigs
    with pruning hooks,
        and take away and cut down the branches.
⁶They shall be left together
    unto the fowls of the mountains,
        and to the beasts of the earth,
    and the fowls shall summer upon them,
        and all the beasts of the earth
    shall winter upon them.
⁷In that time shall the present
    be brought unto the Lord of hosts
        of a people scattered and peeled,
    and from a people terrible
        from their beginning hitherto;
    a nation meted out and trodden under foot,
        whose land the rivers have spoiled,

to the place of the name of the Lord of hosts,
the mount Zion.

19 The burden of Egypt. Behold, the Lord rideth
upon a swift cloud, and shall come into Egypt;
and the idols of Egypt shall be moved
at his presence,
and the heart of Egypt shall melt
in the midst of it.
²And I will set the Egyptians against the Egyptians,
and they shall fight every one against his brother,
and every one against his neighbour;
city against city, and kingdom against kingdom.
³And the spirit of Egypt shall fail
in the midst thereof;
and I will destroy the counsel thereof;
and they shall seek to the idols,
and to the charmers,
and to them that have familiar spirits,
and to the wizards.
⁴And the Egyptians will I give over
into the hand of a cruel lord;
and a fierce king shall rule over them,
saith the Lord, the Lord of hosts.
⁵And the waters shall fail from the sea,
and the river shall be wasted and dried up.

⁶And they shall turn the rivers far away;
 	and the brooks of defence shall be emptied
 		and dried up:
 	the reeds and flags shall wither.
⁷The paper reeds by the brooks,
 	by the mouth of the brooks,
 		and every thing sown by the brooks,
 	shall wither, be driven away, and be no more.
⁸The fishers also shall mourn,
 	and all they that cast angle into the brooks
 		shall lament,
 	and they that spread nets upon the waters
 		shall languish.
⁹Moreover they that work in fine flax,
 	and they that weave networks,
 		shall be confounded.
¹⁰And they shall be broken in the purposes thereof,
 	all that make sluices and ponds for fish.
¹¹Surely the princes of Zoan are fools,
 	the counsel of the wise counsellors of Pharaoh
 		is become brutish.
 	How say ye unto Pharaoh,
 		'I am the son of the wise,
 	the son of ancient kings'?
¹²Where are they? Where are thy wise men?
 	And let them tell thee now,
 		and let them know what the Lord of hosts
 	hath purposed upon Egypt.

¹³ The princes of Zoan are become fools,
   the princes of Noph are deceived;
         they have also seduced Egypt,
   even they that are the stay of the tribes thereof.
¹⁴ The Lord hath mingled a perverse spirit
   in the midst thereof;
         and they have caused Egypt to err in
   every work thereof,
         as a drunken man staggereth in his vomit.
¹⁵ Neither shall there be any work for Egypt,
   which the head or tail, branch or rush, may do.
¹⁶ In that day shall Egypt be like unto women;
   and it shall be afraid and fear because of
         the shaking of the hand of the Lord of hosts,
   which he shaketh over it.
¹⁷ And the land of Judah shall be a terror unto Egypt,
   every one that maketh mention thereof
         shall be afraid in himself,
   because of the counsel of the Lord of hosts,
         which he hath determined against it.
¹⁸ In that day shall five cities in the land of Egypt
   speak the language of Canaan,
         and swear to the Lord of hosts;
   one shall be called, 'The city of destruction'.
¹⁹ In that day shall there be an altar to the Lord
   in the midst of the land of Egypt,
         and a pillar at the border thereof to
   the Lord.

²⁰And it shall be for a sign and for a witness
    unto the Lord of hosts in the land of Egypt
        for they shall cry unto the Lord
    because of the oppressors,
        and he shall send them a saviour,
    and a great one, and he shall deliver them.
²¹And the Lord shall be known to Egypt,
    and the Egyptians shall know the Lord
        in that day,
    and shall do sacrifice and oblation;
        yea, they shall vow a vow unto the Lord,
    and perform it.
²²And the Lord shall smite Egypt;
    he shall smite and heal it;
        and they shall return even to the Lord,
    and he shall be intreated of them,
        and shall heal them.
²³In that day shall there be a highway
    out of Egypt to Assyria,
        and the Assyrian shall come into Egypt,
    and the Egyptian into Assyria,
        and the Egyptians shall serve
    with the Assyrians.
²⁴In that day shall Israel be the third
    with Egypt and with Assyria,
        even a blessing in the midst of the land,
²⁵whom the Lord of hosts shall bless, saying,
    'Blessed be Egypt my people,

and Assyria the work of my hands,
and Israel mine inheritance.'

20 In the year that Tartan came unto Ashdod
(when Sargon the king of Assyria sent him),
and fought against Ashdod,
and took it;
²at the same time spake the Lord by Isaiah
the son of Amoz, saying,
'Go and loose the sackcloth from off thy loins,
and put off thy shoe from thy foot.'
And he did so, walking naked and barefoot.
³And the Lord said, 'Like as my servant Isaiah
hath walked naked and barefoot three years
for a sign and wonder upon Egypt
and upon Ethiopia;
⁴so shall the king of Assyria lead away
the Egyptians prisoners,
and the Ethiopians captives, young and old,
naked and barefoot,
even with their buttocks uncovered,
to the shame of Egypt.
⁵And they shall be afraid and ashamed
of Ethiopia their expectation,
and of Egypt their glory.

⁶And the inhabitant of this isle shall say in that day,
"Behold, such is our expectation,
whither we flee for help to be delivered
from the king of Assyria:
and how shall we escape?"'

21

The burden of the desert of the sea.
As whirlwinds in the south pass through;
so it cometh from the desert,
from a terrible land.
²A grievous vision is declared unto me;
the treacherous dealer dealeth treacherously,
and the spoiler spoileth.
Go up, O Elam; besiege, O Media;
all the sighing thereof have I made to cease.
³Therefore are my loins filled with pain;
pangs have taken hold upon me,
as the pangs of a woman that travaileth;
I was bowed down at the hearing of it;
I was dismayed at the seeing of it.
⁴My heart panted, fearfulness affrighted me:
the night of my pleasure hath he turned
into fear unto me.
⁵Prepare the table, watch in the watch-tower,
eat, drink:
arise, ye princes, and anoint the shield.

⁶ For thus hath the Lord said unto me,
    'Go, set a watchman,
        let him declare what he seeth.'
⁷ And he saw a chariot with a couple of horsemen,
    a chariot of asses, and a chariot of camels;
        and he hearkened diligently with much heed.
⁸ And he cried, 'A lion; my lord,
    I stand continually upon the watchtower
        in the daytime,
    and I am set in my ward whole nights;
⁹ and, behold, here cometh a chariot of men,
    with a couple of horsemen.'
        And he answered and said,
    'Babylon is fallen, is fallen;
        and all the graven images of her gods
    he hath broken unto the ground.'
¹⁰ O my threshing, and the corn of my floor:
    that which I have heard of
        the Lord of hosts, the God of Israel,
    have I declared unto you.
¹¹ The burden of Dumah. He calleth to me out of Seir,
    'Watchman, what of the night?
        Watchman, what of the night?'
¹² The watchman said,
    'The morning cometh, and also the night:
        if ye will enquire, enquire ye; return, come.'
¹³ The burden upon Arabia.
    In the forest in Arabia shall ye lodge,
        O ye travelling companies of Dedanim.

¹⁴ The inhabitants of the land of Tema
    brought water to him that was thirsty,
        they prevented with their bread him that fled.
¹⁵ For they fled from the swords,
    from the drawn sword,
        and from the bent bow,
    and from the grievousness of war.
¹⁶ For thus hath the Lord said unto me,
    'Within a year, according to the years
        of an hireling,
    and all the glory of Kedar shall fail;
¹⁷and the residue of the number of archers,
    the mighty men of the children of Kedar,
        shall be diminished;
    for the Lord God of Israel hath spoken it.

22 The burden of the valley of vision.
    What aileth thee now,
        that thou art wholly gone up
    to the house-tops?
² Thou that art full of stirs, a tumultuous city,
    a joyous city:
        thy slain men are not slain with the sword,
    nor dead in battle.
³All thy rulers are fled together,
    they are bound by the archers:

all that are found in thee are bound together,
which have fled from far.

⁴Therefore said I, Look away from me;
I will weep bitterly, labour not to comfort me,
because of the spoiling of the daughter
of my people.

⁵For it is a day of trouble, and of treading down,
and of perplexity by the Lord God of hosts
in the valley of vision,
breaking down the walls,
and of crying to the mountains.

⁶And Elam bare the quiver with chariots
of men and horsemen,
and Kir uncovered the shield.

⁷And it shall come to pass,
that thy choicest valleys shall be full of chariots,
and the horsemen shall set themselves
in array at the gate.

⁸And he discovered the covering of Judah,
and thou didst look in that day to the armour
of the house of the forest.

⁹Ye have seen also the breaches of the city of David,
that they are many;
and ye gathered together the waters
of the lower pool.

¹⁰And ye have numbered the houses of Jerusalem,
and the houses have ye broken down
to fortify the wall.

¹¹ Ye made also a ditch between the two walls
for the water of the old pool,
but ye have not looked
unto the maker thereof,
neither had respect unto him
that fashioned it long ago.
¹²And in that day did the Lord God of hosts
call to weeping, and to mourning,
and to baldness,
and to girding with sack-cloth.
¹³And behold joy and gladness,
slaying oxen, and killing sheep,
eating flesh, and drinking wine:
let us eat and drink; for to morrow we shall die.
¹⁴And it was revealed in mine ears
by the Lord of hosts,
Surely this iniquity shall not be purged
from you till ye die, saith the Lord God of hosts.
¹⁵ Thus saith the Lord God of hosts,
Go, get thee unto this treasurer,
even unto Shebna,
which is over the house, and say,
¹⁶ What hast thou here?
And whom hast thou here,
that thou hast hewed thee
out a sepulchre here,
as he that heweth him out
a sepulchre on high,

and that graveth an habitation
for himself in a rock?
¹⁷ Behold, the Lord will carry thee away
with a mighty captivity,
and will surely cover thee.
¹⁸ He will surely violently turn and toss thee
like a ball into a large country:
there shalt thou die, and there the chariots of
thy glory shall be the shame of
thy lord's house.
¹⁹ And I will drive thee from thy station,
and from thy state shall he pull thee down.
²⁰ And it shall come to pass in that day,
that I will call my servant Eliakim
the son of Hilkiah,
²¹ and I will clothe him with thy robe,
and strengthen him with thy girdle,
and I will commit thy government
into his hand, and he shall be a father
to the inhabitants of Jerusalem,
and to the house of Judah.
²² And the key of the house of David
will I lay upon his shoulder;
so he shall open, and none shall shut;
and he shall shut, and none shall open.
²³ And I will fasten him as a nail in a sure place;
and he shall be for a glorious throne
to his father's house.

²⁴And they shall hang upon him
  all the glory of his father's house,
    the offspring and the issue,
  all vessels of small quantity,
    from the vessels of cups,
    even to all the vessels of flagons.
²⁵ In that day, saith the Lord of hosts,
  shall the nail that is fastened in the sure place
    be removed, and be cut down, and fall;
  and the burden that was upon it
    shall be cut off,
  for the Lord hath spoken it.

23 The burden of Tyre.
  Howl, ye ships of Tarshish; for it is laid waste,
    so that there is no house, no entering in:
  from the land of Chittim it is revealed to them.
² Be still, ye inhabitants of the isle;
  thou whom the merchants of Zidon,
    that pass over the sea, have replenished.
³ And by great waters the seed of Sihor,
  the harvest of the river, is her revenue;
    and she is a mart of nations.
⁴ Be thou ashamed, O Zidon; for the sea hath spoken,
  even the strength of the sea, saying,

'I travail not, nor bring forth children,
neither do I nourish up young men,
nor bring up virgins.'
⁵As at the report concerning Egypt,
so shall they be sorely pained
at the report of Tyre.
⁶Pass ye over to Tarshish;
howl, ye inhabitants of the isle.
⁷Is this your joyous city,
whose antiquity is of ancient days?
Her own feet shall carry her
afar off to sojourn.
⁸Who hath taken this counsel against Tyre,
the crowning city, whose merchants are princes,
whose traffickers are the honourable
of the earth?
⁹The Lord of hosts hath purposed it,
to stain the pride of all glory,
and to bring into contempt
all the honourable of the earth.
¹⁰Pass through thy land as a river,
O daughter of Tarshish:
there is no more strength.
¹¹He stretched out his hand over the sea,
he shook the kingdoms;
the Lord hath given a commandment
against the merchant city,
to destroy the strongholds thereof.

¹²And he said, 'Thou shalt no more rejoice,
　　O thou oppressed virgin, daughter of Zidon:
　　　　arise, pass over to Chittim;
　　there also shalt thou have no rest.'
¹³Behold the land of the Chaldeans;
　　this people was not, till the Assyrian founded it
　　　　for them that dwell in the wilderness:
　　they set up the towers thereof,
　　　　they raised up the palaces thereof;
　　and he brought it to ruin.
¹⁴Howl, ye ships of Tarshish,
　　for your strength is laid waste.
¹⁵And it shall come to pass in that day,
　　that Tyre shall be forgotten seventy years,
　　　　according to the days of one king:
　　after the end of seventy years shall Tyre sing
　　as an harlot.
¹⁶Take an harp, go about the city,
　　thou harlot that hast been forgotten;
　　　　make sweet melody, sing many songs,
　　that thou mayest be remembered.
¹⁷And it shall come to pass
　　after the end of seventy years,
　　　　that the Lord will visit Tyre,
　　and she shall turn to her hire,
　　　　and shall commit fornication
　　with all the kingdoms of the world
　　　　upon the face of the earth.

¹⁸And her merchandise and her hire
>   shall be holiness to the Lord.
>   It shall not be treasured nor laid up;
>   for her merchandise shall be for them that dwell
>   before the Lord,
>   to eat sufficiently, and for durable clothing.

24

Behold, the Lord maketh the earth empty,
>   and maketh it waste, and turneth it upside down,
>   and scattereth abroad
>   the inhabitants thereof.
²And it shall be, as with the people,
>   so with the priest;
>   as with the servant, so with his master;
>   as with the maid, so with her mistress;
>   as with the buyer, so with the seller;
>   as with the lender, so with the borrower;
>   as with the taker of usury,
>   so with the giver of usury to him.
³The land shall be utterly emptied,
>   and utterly spoiled,
>   for the Lord hath spoken this word.
⁴The earth mourneth and fadeth away,
>   the world languisheth and fadeth away,
>   the haughty people of the earth do languish.

⁵ The earth also is defiled
    under the inhabitants thereof;
        because they have transgressed the laws,
    changed the ordinance,
        broken the everlasting covenant.
⁶ Therefore hath the curse devoured the earth,
    and they that dwell therein are desolate;
        therefore the inhabitants
    of the earth are burned, and few men left.
⁷ The new wine mourneth, the vine languisheth,
    all the merryhearted do sigh.
⁸ The mirth of tabrets ceaseth,
    the noise of them that rejoice endeth,
        the joy of the harp ceaseth.
⁹ They shall not drink wine with a song;
    strong drink shall be bitter to them that drink it.
¹⁰ The city of confusion is broken down;
    every house is shut up,
        that no man may come in.
¹¹ There is a crying for wine in the streets;
    all joy is darkened,
        the mirth of the land is gone.
¹² In the city is left desolation,
    and the gate is smitten with destruction.
¹³ When thus it shall be in the midst of the land
    among the people,
        there shall be as the shaking of an olive tree,
    and as the gleaning grapes

when the vintage is done.
[14] They shall lift up their voice,
   they shall sing for the majesty of the Lord,
      they shall cry aloud from the sea.
[15] Wherefore glorify ye the Lord in the fires,
   even the name of the Lord God of Israel
      in the isles of the sea.
[16] From the uttermost part of the earth
   have we heard songs, even glory to the righteous.
      But I said,
   My leanness, my leanness, woe unto me!
      The treacherous dealers have dealt
   treacherously;
      yea, the treacherous dealers
   have dealt very treacherously.
[17] Fear, and the pit, and the snare,
   are upon thee, O inhabitant of the earth.
[18] And it shall come to pass,
   that he who fleeth from the noise of the fear
      shall fall into the pit;
   and he that cometh up out of the midst of the pit
      shall be taken in the snare;
   for the windows from on high are open,
      and the foundations of the earth
   do shake.
[19] The earth is utterly broken down,
   the earth is clean dissolved,
      the earth is moved exceedingly.

²⁰ The earth shall reel to and fro like a drunkard,
    and shall be removed like a cottage;
        and the transgression thereof
    shall be heavy upon it;
        and it shall fall, and not rise again.
²¹And it shall come to pass in that day,
    that the Lord shall punish the host
        of the high ones that are on high,
    and the kings of the earth upon the earth.
²²And they shall be gathered together,
    as prisoners are gathered in the pit,
        and shall be shut up in the prison,
    and after many days shall they be visited.
²³ Then the moon shall be confounded,
    and the sun ashamed,
        when the Lord of hosts shall reign
    in mount Zion, and in Jerusalem,
        and before his ancients gloriously.

25 Lord, thou art my God;
    I will exalt thee, I will praise thy name;
        for thou hast done wonderful things;
    thy counsels of old are faithfulness
        and truth.
² For thou hast made of a city an heap;
    of a defenced city a ruin:

a palace of strangers to be no city;
it shall never be built.
³ Therefore shall the strong people glorify thee,
the city of the terrible nations shall fear thee.
⁴ For thou hast been a strength to the poor,
a strength to the needy in his distress,
a refuge from the storm,
a shadow from the heat,
when the blast of the terrible ones
is as a storm against the wall.
⁵ Thou shalt bring down the noise of strangers,
as the heat in a dry place;
even the heat with the shadow of a cloud;
the branch of the terrible ones
shall be brought low.
⁶ And in this mountain shall the Lord of hosts
make unto all people a feast of fat things,
a feast of wines on the lees,
of fat things full of marrow,
of wines on the lees well refined.
⁷ And he will destroy in this mountain
the face of the covering cast over all people,
and the vail that is spread over all nations.
⁸ He will swallow up death in victory;
and the Lord God will wipe away tears
from off all faces;
and the rebuke of his people
shall he take away from off all the earth;
for the Lord hath spoken it.

⁹And it shall be said in that day, Lo, this is our God;
   we have waited for him, and he will save us:
      this is the Lord; we have waited for him,
   we will be glad and rejoice in his salvation.
¹⁰For in this mountain shall the hand of the Lord rest,
   and Moab shall be trodden down under him,
      even as straw is trodden down
   for the dunghill.
¹¹And he shall spread forth his hands
   in the midst of them,
      as he that swimmeth spreadeth forth
   his hands to swim;
      and he shall bring down their pride
   together with the spoils of their hands.
¹²And the fortress of the high fort of thy walls
   shall he bring down, lay low,
      and bring to the ground, even to the dust.

26 In that day shall this song be sung
   in the land of Judah:
      We have a strong city;
   salvation will God appoint
      for walls and bulwarks.
²Open ye the gates,
   that the righteous nation
      which keepeth the truth may enter in.
³Thou wilt keep him in perfect peace,

whose mind is stayed on thee,
　　because he trusteth in thee.
⁴ Trust ye in the Lord for ever,
　　for in the Lord Jehovah is everlasting strength.
⁵ For he bringeth down them that dwell on high;
　　the lofty city, he layeth it low;
　　　　he layeth it low, even to the ground;
　　he bringeth it even to the dust.
⁶ The foot shall tread it down,
　　even the feet of the poor,
　　　　and the steps of the needy.
⁷ The way of the just is uprightness:
　　thou, most upright,
　　　　dost weigh the path of the just.
⁸ Yea, in the way of thy judgments, O Lord,
　　have we waited for thee;
　　　　the desire of our soul is to thy name,
　　and to the remembrance of thee.
⁹ With my soul have I desired thee in the night;
　　yea, with my spirit within me
　　　　will I seek thee early;
　　for when thy judgments are in the earth,
　　　　the inhabitants of the world
　　will learn righteousness.
¹⁰ Let favour be shewed to the wicked,
　　yet will he not learn righteousness:
　　　　in the land of uprightness
　　will he deal unjustly,
　　　　and will not behold the majesty of the Lord.

¹¹ Lord, when thy hand is lifted up, they will not see:
    but they shall see, and be ashamed
        for their envy at the people;
    yea, the fire of thine enemies shall devour them.
¹² Lord, thou wilt ordain peace for us
    for thou also hast wrought all our works in us.
¹³ O Lord our God, other lords beside thee
    have had dominion over us,
        but by thee only will we make mention
    of thy name.
¹⁴ They are dead, they shall not live;
    they are deceased, they shall not rise;
        therefore hast thou visited
    and destroyed them,
        and made all their memory to perish.
¹⁵ Thou hast increased the nation, O Lord,
    thou hast increased the nation; thou art glorified;
        thou hadst removed it far unto
    all the ends of the earth.
¹⁶ Lord, in trouble have they visited thee,
    they poured out a prayer
        when thy chastening was upon them.
¹⁷ Like as a woman with child,
    that draweth near the time of her delivery,
        is in pain, and crieth out in her pangs;
    so have we been in thy sight, O Lord.
¹⁸ We have been with child, we have been in pain,
    we have as it were brought forth wind;

we have not wrought
any deliverance in the earth;
neither have the inhabitants
of the world fallen.
¹⁹ Thy dead men shall live,
together with my dead body shall they arise.
Awake and sing, ye that dwell in dust,
for thy dew is as the dew of herbs,
and the earth shall cast out the dead.
²⁰ Come, my people, enter thou into thy chambers,
and shut thy doors about thee:
hide thyself as it were for a little moment,
until the indignation be overpast.
²¹ For, behold, the Lord cometh out of his place
to punish the inhabitants of the earth
for their iniquity:
the earth also shall disclose her blood,
and shall no more cover her slain.

27 In that day the Lord with his sore
and great and strong sword
shall punish leviathan the piercing serpent,
even leviathan that crooked serpent;
and he shall slay the dragon that is in the sea.
² In that day sing ye unto her, a vineyard of red wine.
³ I the Lord do keep it; I will water it every moment:
lest any hurt it, I will keep it night and day.

⁴ Fury is not in me: who would set the briers
       and thorns against me in battle?
           I would go through them,
       I would burn them together.
⁵ Or let him take hold of my strength,
       that he may make peace with me;
           and he shall make peace with me.
⁶ He shall cause them that come of Jacob to take root:
       Israel shall blossom and bud,
           and fill the face of the world with fruit.
⁷ Hath he smitten him,
       as he smote those that smote him?
           Or is he slain according to the slaughter of
       them that are slain by him?
⁸ In measure, when it shooteth forth,
       thou wilt debate with it:
           he stayeth his rough wind in the day
       of the east wind.
⁹ By this therefore shall the iniquity
       of Jacob be purged;
           and this is all the fruit to take away his sin;
       when he maketh all the stones of the altar as
           chalkstones that are beaten in sunder,
       the groves and images shall not stand up.
¹⁰ Yet the defenced city shall be desolate,
       and the habitation forsaken,
           and left like a wilderness:
       there shall the calf feed,

and there shall he lie down,
and consume the branches thereof.
¹¹ When the boughs thereof are withered,
they shall be broken off;
the women come, and set them on fire,
for it is a people of no understanding;
therefore he that made them
will not have mercy on them,
and he that formed them
will shew them no favour.
¹² And it shall come to pass in that day,
that the Lord shall beat off from the channel
of the river unto the stream of Egypt,
and ye shall be gathered one by one,
O ye children of Israel.
¹³ And it shall come to pass in that day,
that the great trumpet shall be blown,
and they shall come which were ready
to perish in the land of Assyria,
and the outcasts in the land of Egypt,
and shall worship the Lord
in the holy mount at Jerusalem.

28

Woe to the crown of pride,
to the drunkards of Ephraim,
whose glorious beauty is a fading flower,
which are on the head of the fat valleys
of them that are overcome with wine!

² Behold, the Lord hath a mighty and strong one,
 which as a tempest of hail
  and a destroying storm,
 as a flood of mighty waters overflowing,
  shall cast down to the earth
 with the hand.
³ The crown of pride, the drunkards of Ephraim,
 shall be trodden under feet.
⁴ And the glorious beauty,
 which is on the head of the fat valley,
  shall be a fading flower,
 and as the hasty fruit before the summer;
  which when he that looketh upon it seeth,
 while it is yet in his hand he eateth it up.
⁵ In that day shall the Lord of hosts be
 for a crown of glory,
  and for a diadem of beauty,
 unto the residue of his people,
⁶ and for a spirit of judgment to him
 that sitteth in judgment,
  and for strength to them
 that turn the battle to the gate.
⁷ But they also have erred through wine,
 and through strong drink are out of the way;
  the priest and the prophet have erred
 through strong drink,
  they are swallowed up of wine,
 they are out of the way through strong drink;

they err in vision,
   they stumble in judgment.
⁸ For all tables are full of vomit and filthiness,
   so that there is no place clean.
⁹ Whom shall he teach knowledge?
   And whom shall he make
      to understand doctrine?
   Them that are weaned from the milk,
      and drawn from the breasts.
¹⁰ For precept must be upon precept,
   precept upon precept;
      line upon line, line upon line;
   here a little, and there a little.
¹¹ For with stammering lips and another tongue
   will he speak to this people.
¹² To whom he said,
   'This is the rest wherewith ye may cause
      the weary to rest; and this is the refreshing':
   yet they would not hear.
¹³ But the word of the Lord was unto them
   precept upon precept, precept upon precept;
      line upon line, line upon line;
   here a little, and there a little;
      that they might go, and fall backward,
   and be broken, and snared, and taken.
¹⁴ Wherefore hear the word of the Lord,
   ye scornful men, that rule this people
      which is in Jerusalem.

¹⁵ Because ye have said,
    'We have made a covenant with death,
    and with hell are we at agreement;
        when the overflowing scourge
    shall pass through,
        it shall not come unto us:
    for we have made lies our refuge,
        and under falsehood have we hid ourselves'.
¹⁶ Therefore thus saith the Lord God,
    Behold, I lay in Zion for a foundation a stone,
        a tried stone, a precious corner stone,
    a sure foundation:
        he that believeth shall not make haste.
¹⁷ Judgment also will I lay to the line,
    and righteousness to the plummet;
        and the hail shall sweep away
    the refuge of lies,
        and the waters shall overflow the hiding place.
¹⁸ And your covenant with death shall be disannulled,
    and your agreement with hell shall not stand;
        when the overflowing scourge
    shall pass through,
        then ye shall be trodden down by it.
¹⁹ From the time that it goeth forth it shall take you,
    for morning by morning shall it pass over,
        by day and by night;
    and it shall be a vexation

only to understand the report.

²⁰ For the bed is shorter than
that a man can stretch himself on it,
and the covering narrower than
that he can wrap himself in it.

²¹ For the Lord shall rise up as in mount Perazim,
he shall be wroth as in the valley of Gibeon,
that he may do his work, his strange work;
and bring to pass his act, his strange act.

²² Now therefore be ye not mockers,
lest your bands be made strong,
for I have heard from the Lord God of hosts
a consumption,
even determined upon the whole earth.

²³ Give ye ear, and hear my voice;
hearken, and hear my speech.

²⁴ Doth the plowman plow all day to sow?
Doth he open and break the clods
of his ground?

²⁵ When he hath made plain the face thereof,
doth he not cast abroad the fitches,
and scatter the cummin,
and cast in the principal wheat
and the appointed barley
and the rie in their place?

²⁶ For his God doth instruct him to discretion,
and doth teach him.

²⁷ For the fitches are not threshed
    with a threshing instrument,
        neither is a cart wheel turned about
    upon the cummin;
        but the fitches are beaten out with a staff,
    and the cummin with a rod.
²⁸ Bread corn is bruised;
    because he will not ever be threshing it,
        nor break it with the wheel of his cart,
    nor bruise it with his horsemen.
²⁹ This also cometh forth from the Lord of hosts,
    which is wonderful in counsel,
        and excellent in working.

29

Woe to Ariel, to Ariel, the city where David dwelt!
    Add ye year to year; let them kill sacrifices.
² Yet I will distress Ariel, and there shall be heaviness
    and sorrow,
        and it shall be unto me as Ariel.
³ And I will camp against thee round about,
    and will lay siege against thee with a mount,
        and I will raise forts against thee.
⁴ And thou shalt be brought down,
    and shalt speak out of the ground,
        and thy speech shall be low out of the dust,

and thy voice shall be,
  as of one that hath a familiar spirit,
out of the ground,
  and thy speech shall whisper
out of the dust.
⁵ Moreover the multitude of thy strangers
  shall be like small dust,
    and the multitude of the terrible ones
  shall be as chaff that passeth away:
    yea, it shall be at an instant suddenly.
⁶ Thou shalt be visited of the Lord of hosts
  with thunder, and with earthquake,
    and great noise, with storm and tempest,
  and the flame of devouring fire.
⁷ And the multitude of all the nations
  that fight against Ariel,
    even all that fight against her
  and her munition, and that distress her,
    shall be as a dream of a night vision.
⁸ It shall even be as when an hungry man dreameth,
  and, behold, he eateth;
    but he awaketh, and his soul is empty:
  or as when a thirsty man dreameth,
    and, behold, he drinketh;
  but he awaketh, and, behold, he is faint,
    and his soul hath appetite:
  so shall the multitude of all the nations be,
    that fight against mount Zion.

⁹ Stay yourselves, and wonder;
>   cry ye out, and cry: they are drunken,
>   but not with wine;
>   they stagger, but not with strong drink.
¹⁰ For the Lord hath poured out upon you the spirit of
>   deep sleep, and hath closed your eyes:
>   the prophets and your rulers,
>   the seers hath he covered.
¹¹ And the vision of all is become unto you
>   as the words of a book that is sealed,
>   which men deliver to one that is learned,
>   saying, 'Read this, I pray thee':
>   and he saith, 'I cannot; for it is sealed.'
¹² And the book is delivered to him that is not
>   learned, saying, 'Read this, I pray thee':
>   and he saith, 'I am not learned.'
¹³ Wherefore the Lord said,
>   Forasmuch as this people draw near me
>   with their mouth,
>   and with their lips do honour me,
>   but have removed their heart far from me,
>   and their fear toward me is taught
>   by the precept of men;
¹⁴ therefore, behold, I will proceed to do
>   a marvellous work among this people,
>   even a marvellous work and a wonder,
>   for the wisdom of their wise men shall perish,
>   and the understanding of their prudent men

shall be hid.

¹⁵ Woe unto them that seek deep to hide
  their counsel from the Lord,
    and their works are in the dark, and they say,
  'Who seeth us? And who knoweth us?'

¹⁶ Surely your turning of things upside down
  shall be esteemed as the potter's clay,
    for shall the work say of him that made it,
  'He made me not'?
    or shall the thing framed say of him that
  framed it, 'He had no understanding'?

¹⁷ Is it not yet a very little while,
  and Lebanon shall be turned into a fruitful field,
    and the fruitful field
  shall be esteemed as a forest?

¹⁸ And in that day shall the deaf hear
  the words of the book,
    and the eyes of the blind shall see
  out of obscurity, and out of darkness.

¹⁹ The meek also shall increase their joy in the Lord,
    and the poor among men shall rejoice
  in the Holy One of Israel.

²⁰ For the terrible one is brought to nought,
  and the scorner is consumed,
    and all that watch for iniquity are cut off:

²¹ that make a man an offender for a word,
  and lay a snare for him that reproveth in the gate,
    and turn aside the just for a thing of nought.

²² Therefore thus saith the Lord,
    who redeemed Abraham,
        concerning the house of Jacob,
    Jacob shall not now be ashamed,
        neither shall his face now wax pale.
²³ But when he seeth his children,
    the work of mine hands, in the midst of him,
        they shall sanctify my name,
    and sanctify the Holy One of Jacob,
        and shall fear the God of Israel.
²⁴ They also that erred in spirit
    shall come to understanding,
        and they that murmured
    shall learn doctrine.

30 Woe to the rebellious children, saith the Lord,
    that take counsel, but not of me;
        and that cover with a covering,
    but not of my spirit,
        that they may add sin to sin;
² that walk to go down into Egypt,
    and have not asked at my mouth;
        to strengthen themselves
    in the strength of Pharaoh,
        and to trust in the shadow of Egypt!

³ Therefore shall the strength of Pharaoh
   be your shame,
      and the trust in the shadow of Egypt
   your confusion.
⁴ For his princes were at Zoan,
   and his ambassadors came to Hanes.
⁵ They were all ashamed of a people
   that could not profit them,
      nor be an help nor profit,
   but a shame, and also a reproach.
⁶ The burden of the beasts of the south:
   into the land of trouble and anguish,
      from whence come the young and old lion,
   the viper and fiery flying serpent,
      they will carry their riches
   upon the shoulders of young asses,
      and their treasures upon the bunches of camels,
   to a people that shall not profit them.
⁷ For the Egyptians shall help in vain,
   and to no purpose;
      therefore have I cried concerning this,
   'Their strength is to sit still.'
⁸ Now go, write it before them in a table,
   and note it in a book,
      that it may be for the time to come
   for ever and ever:
⁹ that this is a rebellious people, lying children,
   children that will not hear the law of the Lord;

¹⁰ which say to the seers, 'See not', and to the prophets,
'Prophesy not unto us right things,
speak unto us smooth things, prophesy deceits.
¹¹ Get you out of the way, turn aside out of the path,
cause the Holy One of Israel
to cease from before us.'
¹² Wherefore thus saith the Holy One of Israel,
Because ye despise this word,
and trust in oppression and perverseness,
and stay thereon;
¹³ therefore this iniquity shall be to you
as a breach ready to fall, swelling out in a high wall,
whose breaking cometh
suddenly at an instant.
¹⁴ And he shall break it
as the breaking of the potters' vessel
that is broken in pieces; he shall not spare:
so that there shall not be found
in the bursting of it a sherd
to take fire from the hearth,
or to take water withal out of the pit.
¹⁵ For thus saith the Lord God,
the Holy One of Israel:
In returning and rest shall ye be saved;
in quietness and in confidence
shall be your strength; and ye would not.
¹⁶ But ye said, 'No; for we will flee upon horses';
therefore shall ye flee, and,

'We will ride upon the swift';
therefore shall they that pursue you
be swift.
¹⁷One thousand shall flee at the rebuke of one;
at the rebuke of five shall ye flee:
till ye be left as a beacon
upon the top of a mountain,
and as an ensign on an hill.
¹⁸And therefore will the Lord wait,
that he may be gracious unto you,
and therefore will he be exalted,
that he may have mercy upon you,
for the Lord is a God of judgment:
blessed are all they that wait for him.
¹⁹For the people shall dwell in Zion at Jerusalem:
thou shalt weep no more.
He will be very gracious unto thee
at the voice of thy cry;
when he shall hear it, he will answer thee.
²⁰And though the Lord give you
the bread of adversity, and the water of affliction,
yet shall not thy teachers be removed
into a corner any more,
but thine eyes shall see thy teachers:
²¹and thine ears shall hear a word behind thee,
saying, 'This is the way, walk ye in it',
when ye turn to the right hand,
and when ye turn to the left.

²² Ye shall defile also the covering of
    thy graven images of silver,
      and the ornament of
    thy molten images of gold:
      thou shalt cast them away
    as a menstruous cloth;
      thou shalt say unto it, 'Get thee hence.'
²³ Then shall he give the rain of thy seed,
    that thou shalt sow the ground withal;
      and bread of the increase of the earth,
    and it shall be fat and plenteous:
      in that day shall thy cattle feed in large pastures.
²⁴ The oxen likewise and the young asses
    that ear the ground shall eat clean provender,
      which hath been winnowed
    with the shovel and with the fan.
²⁵And there shall be upon every high mountain,
    and upon every high hill,
      rivers and streams of waters
    in the day of the great slaughter,
      when the towers fall.
²⁶ Moreover the light of the moon
    shall be as the light of the sun,
      and the light of the sun shall be sevenfold,
    as the light of seven days,
      in the day that the Lord bindeth up
    the breach of his people,
      and healeth the stroke of their wound.

²⁷ Behold, the name of the Lord cometh from far,
burning with his anger,
and the burden thereof is heavy:
his lips are full of indignation,
and his tongue as a devouring fire.
²⁸And his breath, as an overflowing stream,
shall reach to the midst of the neck,
to sift the nations with the sieve of vanity;
and there shall be a bridle
in the jaws of the people,
causing them to err.
²⁹ Ye shall have a song, as in the night
when a holy solemnity is kept;
and gladness of heart,
as when one goeth with a pipe to come into
the mountain of the Lord,
to the mighty One of Israel.
³⁰And the Lord shall cause his glorious voice
to be heard,
and shall shew the lighting down of his arm,
with the indignation of his anger,
and with the flame of a devouring fire,
with scattering, and tempest,
and hailstones.
³¹ For through the voice of the Lord
shall the Assyrian be beaten down,
which smote with a rod.

³²And in every place
 where the grounded staff shall pass,
   which the Lord shall lay upon him,
 it shall be with tabrets and harps;
   and in battles of shaking
 will he fight with it.
³³For Tophet is ordained of old;
 yea, for the king it is prepared;
   he hath made it deep and large:
 the pile thereof is fire and much wood;
   the breath of the Lord,
 like a stream of brimstone, doth kindle it.

31 Woe to them that go down to Egypt for help;
 and stay on horses, and trust in chariots,
   because they are many;
 and in horsemen, because they are very strong;
   but they look not unto the Holy One of Israel,
 neither seek the Lord!
²Yet he also is wise, and will bring evil,
 and will not call back his words,
   but will arise against the house
 of the evildoers,
   and against the help
 of them that work iniquity.
³Now the Egyptians are men, and not God;
 and their horses flesh, and not spirit.

When the Lord shall stretch out his hand,
both he that helpeth shall fall,
and he that is holpen shall fall down,
and they all shall fail together.
⁴ For thus hath the Lord spoken unto me,
Like as the lion and the young lion
roaring on his prey when a multitude
of shepherds is called forth against him,
he will not be afraid of their voice,
nor abase himself for the noise of them:
so shall the Lord of hosts come down to fight
for mount Zion, and for the hill thereof.
⁵ As birds flying, so will the Lord of hosts
defend Jerusalem;
defending also he will deliver it;
and passing over he will preserve it.
⁶ Turn ye unto him from whom
the children of Israel have deeply revolted.
⁷ For in that day every man shall cast away
his idols of silver, and his idols of gold,
which your own hands have made
unto you for a sin.
⁸ Then shall the Assyrian fall with the sword,
not of a mighty man;
and the sword, not of a mean man,
shall devour him;
but he shall flee from the sword,
and his young men shall be discomfited.

⁹And he shall pass over to his strong hold for fear,
    and his princes shall be afraid of the ensign,
        saith the Lord, whose fire is in Zion,
    and his furnace in Jerusalem.

32   Behold, a king shall reign in righteousness,
    and princes shall rule in judgment.
²And a man shall be
    as an hiding place from the wind,
        and a covert from the tempest;
    as rivers of water in a dry place,
        as the shadow of a great rock in a weary land.
³And the eyes of them that see shall not be dim,
    and the ears of them that hear shall hearken.
⁴The heart also of the rash
    shall understand knowledge,
        and the tongue of the stammerers
    shall be ready to speak plainly.
⁵The vile person shall be no more called liberal,
    nor the churl said to be bountiful.
⁶For the vile person will speak villany,
    and his heart will work iniquity,
        to practise hypocrisy,
    and to utter error against the Lord,
        to make empty the soul of the hungry,
    and he will cause
        the drink of the thirsty to fail.

[7] The instruments also of the churl are evil:
> he deviseth wicked devices
>> to destroy the poor with lying words,
> even when the needy speaketh right.
[8] But the liberal deviseth liberal things;
> and by liberal things shall he stand.
[9] Rise up, ye women that are at ease;
> hear my voice, ye careless daughters;
>> give ear unto my speech.
[10] Many days and years shall ye be troubled,
> ye careless women, for the vintage shall fail,
>> the gathering shall not come.
[11] Tremble, ye women that are at ease;
> be troubled, ye careless ones:
>> strip you, and make you bare,
> and gird sackcloth upon your loins.
[12] They shall lament for the teats,
> for the pleasant fields, for the fruitful vine.
[13] Upon the land of my people shall come up
> thorns and briers; yea,
>> upon all the houses of joy in the joyous city;
[14] because the palaces shall be forsaken;
> the multitude of the city shall be left;
>> the forts and towers shall be for dens for ever,
> a joy of wild asses, a pasture of flocks;
[15] until the spirit be poured upon us from on high,
> and the wilderness be a fruitful field,
>> and the fruitful field be counted for a forest.

¹⁶ Then judgment shall dwell in the wilderness,
and righteousness remain in the fruitful field.
¹⁷And the work of righteousness shall be peace;
and the effect of righteousness quietness
and assurance for ever.
¹⁸And my people shall dwell
in a peaceable habitation,
and in sure dwellings,
and in quiet resting places;
¹⁹ when it shall hail, coming down on the forest;
and the city shall be low in a low place.
²⁰ Blessed are ye that sow beside all waters,
that send forth thither
the feet of the ox and the ass.

33 Woe to thee that spoilest,
and thou wast not spoiled;
and dealest treacherously,
and they dealt not treacherously with thee!
When thou shalt cease to spoil,
thou shalt be spoiled;
and when thou shalt make an end
to deal treacherously,
they shall deal treacherously with thee.
² O Lord, be gracious unto us;
we have waited for thee:

be thou their arm every morning,
our salvation also in the time of trouble.
³At the noise of the tumult the people fled;
at the lifting up of thyself
the nations were scattered.
⁴And your spoil shall be gathered
like the gathering of the caterpiller:
as the running to and fro of locusts
shall he run upon them.
⁵The Lord is exalted; for he dwelleth on high:
he hath filled Zion with judgment
and righteousness.
⁶And wisdom and knowledge shall be the stability
of thy times, and strength of salvation:
the fear of the Lord is his treasure.
⁷Behold, their valiant ones shall cry without:
the ambassadors of peace shall weep bitterly.
⁸The highways lie waste,
the wayfaring man ceaseth:
he hath broken the covenant,
he hath despised the cities,
he regardeth no man.
⁹The earth mourneth and languisheth;
Lebanon is ashamed and hewn down;
Sharon is like a wilderness;
and Bashan and Carmel shake off their fruits.
¹⁰'Now will I rise,' saith the Lord;
'now will I be exalted; now will I lift up myself.

¹¹ Ye shall conceive chaff, ye shall bring forth stubble;
   your breath, as fire, shall devour you.
¹² And the people shall be as the burnings of lime:
   as thorns cut up shall they be burned in the fire.'
¹³ Hear, ye that are far off, what I have done;
   and, ye that are near, acknowledge my might.
¹⁴ The sinners in Zion are afraid;
   fearfulness hath surprised the hypocrites.
      Who among us shall dwell with
      the devouring fire?
      Who among us shall dwell with
      everlasting burnings?
¹⁵ He that walketh righteously,
   and speaketh uprightly;
      he that despiseth the gain of oppressions,
   that shaketh his hands from holding of bribes,
      that stoppeth his ears from hearing of blood,
   and shutteth his eyes from seeing evil;
¹⁶ he shall dwell on high:
   his place of defence
      shall be the munitions of rocks:
   bread shall be given him;
      his waters shall be sure.
¹⁷ Thine eyes shall see the king in his beauty:
   they shall behold the land that is very far off.
¹⁸ Thine heart shall meditate terror.
   Where is the scribe? Where is the receiver?

Where is he that counted the towers?
¹⁹ Thou shalt not see a fierce people,
    a people of a deeper speech
        than thou canst perceive;
    of a stammering tongue,
        that thou canst not understand.
²⁰ Look upon Zion, the city of our solemnities:
    thine eyes shall see Jerusalem a quiet habitation,
        a tabernacle that shall not be taken down;
    not one of the stakes thereof
        shall ever be removed,
    neither shall any of the cords thereof
        be broken.
²¹ But there the glorious Lord will be unto us
    a place of broad rivers and streams;
        wherein shall go no galley with oars,
    neither shall gallant ship pass thereby.
²² For the Lord is our judge, the Lord is our lawgiver,
    the Lord is our king; he will save us.
²³ Thy tacklings are loosed;
    they could not well strengthen their mast,
        they could not spread the sail:
    then is the prey of a great spoil divided;
        the lame take the prey.
²⁴ And the inhabitant shall not say, 'I am sick':
    the people that dwell therein
    shall be forgiven their iniquity.

34 Come near, ye nations, to hear;
and hearken, ye people: let the earth hear,
and all that is therein; the world,
and all things that come forth of it.
² For the indignation of the Lord is upon all nations,
and his fury upon all their armies:
he hath utterly destroyed them,
he hath delivered them to the slaughter.
³ Their slain also shall be cast out,
and their stink shall come up
out of their carcases,
and the mountains shall be melted
with their blood.
⁴ And all the host of heaven shall be dissolved,
and the heavens shall be rolled together
as a scroll;
and all their host shall fall down,
as the leaf falleth off from the vine,
and as a falling fig from the fig tree.
⁵ For my sword shall be bathed in heaven:
behold, it shall come down upon Idumea,
and upon the people of my curse,
to judgment.
⁶ The sword of the Lord is filled with blood,
it is made fat with fatness,
and with the blood of lambs and goats,
with the fat of the kidneys of rams,
for the Lord hath a sacrifice in Bozrah,
and a great slaughter in the land of Idumea.

⁷And the unicorns shall come down with them,
  and the bullocks with the bulls;
    and their land shall be soaked with blood,
    and their dust made fat with fatness.
⁸ For it is the day of the Lord's vengeance,
  and the year of recompences
    for the controversy of Zion.
⁹And the streams thereof shall be turned into pitch,
  and the dust thereof into brimstone,
    and the land thereof
    shall become burning pitch.
¹⁰ It shall not be quenched night nor day;
  the smoke thereof shall go up for ever:
    from generation to generation
    it shall lie waste;
      none shall pass through
      it for ever and ever.
¹¹ But the cormorant and the bittern shall possess it;
  the owl also and the raven shall dwell in it;
    and he shall stretch out upon it
    the line of confusion, and the stones
      of emptiness.
¹² They shall call the nobles thereof to the kingdom,
  but none shall be there,
    and all her princes shall be nothing.
¹³And thorns shall come up in her palaces,
  nettles and brambles in the fortresses thereof;
    and it shall be an habitation of dragons,
    and a court for owls.

¹⁴The wild beasts of the desert shall also meet
 with the wild beasts of the island,
  and the satyr shall cry to his fellow;
 the screech owl also shall rest there,
  and find for herself a place of rest.
¹⁵There shall the great owl make her nest,
 and lay, and hatch,
  and gather under her shadow;
 there shall the vultures also be gathered,
  every one with her mate.
¹⁶Seek ye out of the book of the Lord, and read:
 no one of these shall fail,
  none shall want her mate;
 for my mouth it hath commanded,
  and his spirit it hath gathered them.
¹⁷And he hath cast the lot for them,
 and his hand hath divided it unto them by line:
  they shall possess it for ever,
 from generation to generation
  shall they dwell therein.

35 The wilderness and the solitary place
  shall be glad for them;
   and the desert shall rejoice,
  and blossom as the rose.
²It shall blossom abundantly,
 and rejoice even with joy and singing:

the glory of Lebanon shall be given unto it,
the excellency of Carmel and Sharon,
they shall see the glory of the Lord,
and the excellency of our God.
³ Strengthen ye the weak hands,
and confirm the feeble knees.
⁴ Say to them that are of a fearful heart,
'Be strong, fear not:
behold, your God will come with vengeance,
even God with a recompence;
he will come and save you.'
⁵ Then the eyes of the blind shall be opened,
and the ears of the deaf shall be unstopped.
⁶ Then shall the lame man leap as an hart,
and the tongue of the dumb sing,
for in the wilderness shall waters break out,
and streams in the desert.
⁷ And the parched ground shall become a pool,
and the thirsty land springs of water:
in the habitation of dragons,
where each lay,
shall be grass with reeds and rushes.
⁸ And an highway shall be there, and a way,
and it shall be called 'The way of holiness';
the unclean shall not pass over it;
but it shall be for those:
the wayfaring men, though fools,
shall not err therein.

⁹No lion shall be there,
    nor any ravenous beast shall go up thereon,
      it shall not be found there;
    but the redeemed shall walk there.
¹⁰And the ransomed of the Lord shall return,
    and come to Zion with songs and
        everlasting joy upon their heads:
    they shall obtain joy and gladness,
        and sorrow and sighing shall flee away.

36 Now it came to pass in the fourteenth year
    of king Hezekiah,
        that Sennacherib king of Assyria
    came up against all the defenced cities of Judah,
        and took them.
²And the king of Assyria sent Rabshakeh
    from Lachish to Jerusalem
        unto king Hezekiah with a great army.
    And he stood by the conduit of the upper pool
        in the highway of the fuller's field.
³Then came forth unto him Eliakim, Hilkiah's son,
    which was over the house, and Shebna the scribe,
        and Joah, Asaph's son, the recorder.
⁴And Rabshakeh said unto them,
    'Say ye now to Hezekiah,
        Thus saith the great king,

the king of Assyria,
What confidence is this wherein thou trustest?
⁵ I say, sayest thou, (but they are but vain words)
I have counsel and strength for war:
now on whom dost thou trust,
that thou rebellest against me?
⁶ Lo, thou trustest in the staff of this broken reed,
on Egypt;
whereon if a man lean,
it will go into his hand, and pierce it:
so is Pharaoh king of Egypt
to all that trust in him.
⁷ But if thou say to me,
"We trust in the Lord our God"
is it not he, whose high places
and whose altars Hezekiah hath taken away,
and said to Judah and to Jerusalem,
"Ye shall worship before this altar"?
⁸ Now therefore give pledges, I pray thee,
to my master the king of Assyria,
and I will give thee two thousand horses,
if thou be able on thy part
to set riders
upon them.
⁹ How then wilt thou turn away the face of
one captain of the least of my master's servants,
and put thy trust on Egypt for chariots
and for horsemen?

¹⁰And am I now come up without the Lord
  against this land to destroy it?
    The Lord said unto me, 'Go up against this land,
    and destroy it.'
¹¹Then said Eliakim and Shebna and Joah
  unto Rabshakeh,
    'Speak, I pray thee, unto thy servants
    in the Syrian language, for we understand it;
      and speak not to us in the Jews' language,
      in the ears of the people that are on the wall.'
¹²But Rabshakeh said,
    'Hath my master sent me to thy master
      and to thee to speak these words?
    Hath he not sent me to the men
      that sit upon the wall,
    that they may eat their own dung,
      and drink their own piss with you?'
¹³Then Rabshakeh stood, and cried with a loud voice
  in the Jews' language, and said,
    'Hear ye the words of the great king,
    the king of Assyria.
¹⁴Thus saith the king, "Let not Hezekiah deceive you,
  for he shall not be able to deliver you.
¹⁵Neither let Hezekiah make you trust in the Lord,
  saying, 'The Lord will surely deliver us:
    this city shall not be delivered
    into the hand of the king of Assyria."
¹⁶Hearken not to Hezekiah,

for thus saith the king of Assyria,

"Make an agreement with me by a present,
and come out to me: and eat ye every one of his
vine,
and every one of his fig tree, and drink ye every
one
the waters of his own cistern,
¹⁷ until I come and take you away
to a land like your own land,
a land of corn and wine,
a land of bread and vineyards.
¹⁸ Beware lest Hezekiah persuade you, saying,
The Lord will deliver us.

Hath any of the gods of the nations
delivered his land out of the hand
of the king of Assyria?
¹⁹ Where are the gods of Hamath and Arphad?
Where are the gods of Sepharvaim?
And have they delivered Samaria
out of my hand?
²⁰ Who are they among all the gods of these lands,
that have delivered their land out of my hand,
that the Lord should deliver Jerusalem
out of my hand?"'
²¹ But they held their peace,
and answered him not a word;
for the king's commandment was, saying,
'Answer him not.'

²² Then came Eliakim, the son of Hilkiah,
   that was over the household,
      and Shebna the scribe,
   and Joah, the son of Asaph, the recorder,
      to Hezekiah with their clothes rent,
   and told him the words of Rabshakeh.

37 And it came to pass, when king Hezekiah heard it,
      that he rent his clothes,
         and covered himself with sackcloth,
      and went into the house of the Lord.
² And he sent Eliakim, who was over the household,
      and Shebna the scribe, and the elders
         of the priests covered with sackcloth,
      unto Isaiah the prophet
         the son of Amoz.
³ And they said unto him,
      'Thus saith Hezekiah,
         This day is a day of trouble,
      and of rebuke, and of blasphemy;
         for the children are come to the birth,
      and there is not strength to bring forth.
⁴ It may be the Lord thy God will hear the words
      of Rabshakeh,
         whom the king of Assyria his master

hath sent to reproach the living God,
   and will reprove the words
which the Lord thy God hath heard;
   wherefore lift up thy prayer
for the remnant that is left.'
⁵ So the servants of king Hezekiah came
   to Isaiah.
⁶ And Isaiah said unto them,
   'Thus shall ye say unto your master,
      "Thus saith the Lord,
Be not afraid
   of the words that thou hast heard,
wherewith the servants of the king of Assyria
   have blasphemed me.
⁷ Behold, I will send a blast upon him,
   and he shall hear a rumour,
      and return to his own land;
   and I will cause him to fall by the sword
      in his own land."'
⁸ So Rabshakeh returned, and found the king of
   Assyria warring against Libnah,
      for he had heard
   that he was departed from Lachish.
⁹ And he heard say concerning
   Tirhakah king of Ethiopia,
      'He is come forth to make war with thee.'
   And when he heard it,
      he sent messengers to Hezekiah, saying,

¹⁰ 'Thus shall ye speak to Hezekiah king of Judah,
saying, "Let not thy God,
in whom thou trustest, deceive thee, saying,
Jerusalem shall not be given
into the hand of the king of Assyria."
¹¹ Behold, thou hast heard
what the kings of Assyria have done
to all lands by destroying them utterly;
and shalt thou be delivered?
¹² Have the gods of the nations delivered them
which my fathers have destroyed,
as Gozan, and Haran, and Rezeph,
and the children of Eden which were in Telassar?
¹³ Where is the king of Hamath,
and the king of Arphad,
and the king of the city of Sepharvaim,
Hena, and Ivah?'
¹⁴ And Hezekiah received the letter
from the hand of the messengers, and read it;
and Hezekiah went up
unto the house of the Lord,
and spread it before the Lord.
¹⁵ And Hezekiah prayed unto the Lord, saying,
¹⁶ 'O Lord of hosts, God of Israel,
that dwellest between the cherubims,
thou art the God, even thou alone,
of all the kingdoms of the earth:
thou hast made heaven and earth.

¹⁷ Incline thine ear, O Lord, and hear;
open thine eyes, O Lord, and see:
and hear all the words of Sennacherib,
which hath sent to reproach the living God.
¹⁸ Of a truth, Lord, the kings of Assyria have laid waste
all the nations, and their countries,
¹⁹ and have cast their gods into the fire;
for they were no gods,
but the work of men's hands, wood and stone:
therefore they have destroyed them.
²⁰ Now therefore, O Lord our God,
save us from his hand,
that all the kingdoms of the earth
may know that thou art the Lord, even thou only.'
²¹ Then Isaiah the son of Amoz sent unto Hezekiah,
saying, 'Thus saith the Lord God of Israel,
Whereas thou hast prayed to me against
Senacherib king of Assyria:
²² this is the word which the Lord hath spoken concerning him.
The virgin, the daughter of Zion,
hath despised thee, and laughed thee to scorn;
the daughter of Jerusalem
hath shaken her head at thee.
²³ Whom hast thou reproached and blasphemed?
And against whom hast thou exalted thy voice,
and lifted up thine eyes on high?
Even against the Holy One of Israel.

²⁴ By thy servants hast thou reproached the Lord,
and hast said, "By the multitude of my chariots
am I come up to the height of the mountains,
to the sides of Lebanon;
and I will cut down the tall cedars thereof,
and the choice fir trees thereof;
and I will enter into the height of his border,
and the forest of his Carmel.
²⁵ I have digged, and drunk water;
and with the sole of my feet have I dried up
all the rivers of the besieged places."
²⁶ Hast thou not heard long ago, how I have done it;
and of ancient times, that I have formed it?
Now have I brought it to pass,
that thou shouldest be to lay waste
defenced cities into ruinous heaps.
²⁷ Therefore their inhabitants were of small power,
they were dismayed and confounded:
they were as the grass of the field,
and as the green herb,
as the grass on the housetops,
and as corn blasted before it be grown up.
²⁸ But I know thy abode, and thy going out,
and thy coming in, and thy rage against me.
²⁹ Because thy rage against me,
and thy tumult, is come up into mine ears,
therefore will I put my hook in thy nose,
and my bridle in thy lips,

and I will turn thee back
by the way by which thou camest.
³⁰And this shall be a sign unto thee.
Ye shall eat this year such as growth of itself;
and the second year
that which springeth of the same;
and in the third year sow ye, and reap,
and plant vineyards, and eat the fruit thereof.
³¹And the remnant that is escaped
of the house of Judah
shall again take root downward,
and bear fruit upward;
³²for out of Jerusalem shall go forth a remnant,
and they that escape out of mount Zion:
the zeal of the Lord of hosts shall do this.
³³Therefore thus saith the Lord
concerning the king of Assyria,
he shall not come into this city,
nor shoot an arrow there,
nor come before it with shields,
nor cast a bank against it.
³⁴By the way that he came,
by the same shall he return,
and shall not come into this city,
saith the Lord.
³⁵For I will defend this city
to save it for mine own sake,
and for my servant David's sake.'

³⁶ Then the angel of the Lord went forth,
    and smote in the camp of the Assyrians
        a hundred and fourscore and five thousand;
    and when they arose early in the morning,
        behold, they were all dead corpses.
³⁷ So Sennacherib king of Assyria departed,
    and went and returned,
        and dwelt at Nineveh.
³⁸ And it came to pass, as he was worshipping
    in the house of Nisroch his god,
        that Adrammelech and Sharezer his sons
    smote him with the sword;
        and they escaped into the land of Armenia;
    and Esar-haddon his son reigned in his stead.

38 In those days was Hezekiah sick unto death.
    And Isaiah the prophet the son of Amoz
        came unto him, and said unto him,
    'Thus saith the Lord, Set thine house in order:
        for thou shalt die, and not live.'
² Then Hezekiah turned his face toward the wall,
    and prayed unto the Lord,
³ and said, 'Remember now, O Lord,
    I beseech thee, how I have walked before thee
        in truth and with a perfect heart,
    and have done that which is good in thy sight.'

And Hezekiah wept sore.
⁴ Then came the word of the Lord to Isaiah, saying,
⁵ 'Go, and say to Hezekiah,
>Thus saith the Lord, the God of David thy father,
>>I have heard thy prayer, I have seen thy tears:
>behold, I will add unto thy days fifteen years.
⁶ And I will deliver thee and this city
>out of the hand of the king of Assyria;
>>and I will defend this city.
⁷ And this shall be a sign unto thee from the Lord,
>that the Lord will do this thing
>>that he hath spoken;
⁸ Behold, I will bring again
>the shadow of the degrees,
>>which is gone down in the sun dial of Ahaz,
>ten degrees backward.'
>>So the sun returned ten degrees,
>by which degrees it was gone down.
⁹ The writing of Hezekiah king of Judah,
>when he had been sick,
>>and was recovered of his sickness:
¹⁰ I said in the cutting off of my days,
>I shall go to the gates of the grave:
>>I am deprived of the residue of my years.
¹¹ I said, I shall not see the Lord,
>even the Lord, in the land of the living;
>>I shall behold man no more
>with the inhabitants of the world.

¹² Mine age is departed, and is removed from me
as a shepherd's tent;
I have cut off like a weaver my life;
he will cut me off with pining sickness;
from day even to night
wilt thou make an end of me.
¹³ I reckoned till morning, that,
as a lion, so will he break all my bones:
from day even to night
wilt thou make an end of me.
¹⁴ Like a crane or a swallow, so did I chatter;
I did mourn as a dove.
Mine eyes fail with looking upward:
O Lord, I am oppressed;
undertake for me.
¹⁵ What shall I say? He hath both spoken unto me,
and himself hath done it:
I shall go softly all my years in the
bitterness of my soul.
¹⁶ O Lord, by these things men live,
and in all these things is the life of my spirit:
so wilt thou recover me,
and make me to live.
¹⁷ Behold, for peace I had great bitterness;
but thou hast in love to my soul
delivered it from the pit of corruption;
for thou hast cast all my sins behind thy back.

¹⁸ For the grave cannot praise thee,
    death can not celebrate thee:
        they that go down into the pit
    cannot hope for thy truth.
¹⁹ The living, the living, he shall praise thee,
    as I do this day:
        the father to the children
    shall make known thy truth.
²⁰ The Lord was ready to save me;
    therefore we will sing my songs
        to the stringed instruments
    all the days of our life
        in the house of the Lord.
²¹ For Isaiah had said, 'Let them take a lump of figs,
    and lay it for a plaister
        upon the boil,
    and he shall recover.'
²² Hezekiah also had said,
    'What is the sign that I shall go up
        to the house of the Lord?'

39

At that time Merodach-baladan,
    the son of Baladan, king of Babylon,
        sent letters and a present to Hezekiah
    for he had heard that he had been sick,
        and was recovered.

²And Hezekiah was glad of them,
  and shewed them the house
    of his precious things,
  the silver, and the gold, and the spices,
    and the precious ointment,
  and all the house of his armour,
    and all that was found in his treasures:
  there was nothing in his house,
    nor in all his dominion,
  that Hezekiah shewed them not.
³ Then came Isaiah the prophet unto king Hezekiah,
  and said unto him, 'What said these men?
    and from whence came they unto thee?'
  And Hezekiah said,
    'They are come from a far country unto me,
  even from Babylon.'
⁴ Then said he, 'What have they seen in thine house?'
  And Hezekiah answered,
    'All that is in mine house have they seen:
  there is nothing among my treasures
    that I have not shewed them.'
⁵ Then said Isaiah to Hezekiah,
  Hear the word of the Lord of hosts:
⁶ Behold, the days come,
  that all that is in thine house,
    and that which thy fathers have laid up
  in store until this day,
    shall be carried to Babylon:

nothing shall be left, saith the Lord.
⁷And of thy sons that shall issue from thee,
    which thou shalt beget, shall they take away;
        and they shall be eunuchs
    in the palace of the king of Babylon.
⁸Then said Hezekiah to Isaiah,
    'Good is the word of the Lord
        which thou hast spoken.'
    He said moreover,
        'For there shall be peace and truth in my days.'

40   Comfort ye, comfort ye my people,
    saith your God.
²Speak ye comfortably to Jerusalem,
    and cry unto her,
        that her warfare is accomplished,
    that her iniquity is pardoned,
        for she hath received of the Lord's hand
    double for all her sins.
³The voice of him that crieth in the wilderness,
    'Prepare ye the way of the Lord,
        make straight in the desert a highway
    for our God.
⁴Every valley shall be exalted,
    and every mountain and hill shall be made low,
        and the crooked shall be made straight,
    and the rough places plain.

⁵And the glory of the Lord shall be revealed,
   and all flesh shall see it together,
      for the mouth of the Lord hath spoken it.'
⁶The voice said, 'Cry.'
   And he said, 'What shall I cry?'
      All flesh is grass, and all the goodliness
      thereof is as the flower of the field:
⁷The grass withereth, the flower fadeth,
   because the spirit of the Lord bloweth upon it:
      surely the people is grass.
⁸The grass withereth, the flower fadeth;
   but the word of our God
      shall stand for ever.
⁹O Zion, that bringest good tidings,
   get thee up into the high mountain;
      O Jerusalem, that bringest good tidings,
   lift up thy voice with strength;
      lift it up, be not afraid;
   say unto the cities of Judah,
      'Behold your God!'
¹⁰Behold, the Lord God will come with strong hand,
   and his arm shall rule for him:
      behold, his reward is with him,
   and his work before him.
¹¹He shall feed his flock like a shepherd:
   he shall gather the lambs with his arm,
      and carry them in his bosom,
   and shall gently lead those
      that are with young.

¹² Who hath measured the waters
  in the hollow of his hand,
    and meted out heaven with the span,
  and comprehended the dust of the earth
    in a measure,
  and weighed the mountains in scales,
    and the hills in a balance?
¹³ Who hath directed the Spirit of the Lord,
  or being his counsellor hath taught him?
¹⁴ With whom took he counsel,
  and who instructed him,
    and taught him in the path of judgment,
  and taught him knowledge,
    and shewed to him
  the way of understanding?
¹⁵ Behold, the nations are as a drop of a bucket,
  and are counted as the small dust of the balance:
    behold, he taketh up the isles
  as a very little thing.
¹⁶ And Lebanon is not sufficient to burn,
  nor the beasts thereof sufficient
    for a burnt offering.
¹⁷ All nations before him are as nothing;
  and they are counted to him less than nothing,
    and vanity.
¹⁸ To whom then will ye liken God?
  Or what likeness will ye compare
    unto him?

¹⁹ The workman melteth a graven image,
  and the goldsmith spreadeth it over with gold,
    and casteth silver chains.
²⁰ He that is so impoverished that he hath no oblation
  chooseth a tree that will not rot;
      he seeketh unto him a cunning workman
  to prepare a graven image,
    that shall not be moved.
²¹ Have ye not known? Have ye not heard?
  Hath it not been told you from the beginning?
    Have ye not understood
  from the foundations of the earth?
²² It is he that sitteth upon the circle of the earth,
  and the inhabitants thereof are as grasshoppers;
    that stretcheth out the heavens as a curtain,
  and spreadeth them out as a tent to dwell in;
²³ that bringeth the princes to nothing;
  he maketh the judges of the earth as vanity.
²⁴ Yea, they shall not be planted;
  yea, they shall not be sown;
    yea, their stock
  shall not take root in the earth;
    and he shall also blow upon them,
  and they shall wither,
    and the whirlwind
  shall take them away as stubble.
²⁵ To whom then will ye liken me, or shall I be equal?
  saith the Holy One.
²⁶ Lift up your eyes on high,

and behold who hath created these things,
>that bringeth out their host by number:
he calleth them all by names
>by the greatness of his might,
for that he is strong in power; not one faileth.

[27] Why sayest thou, O Jacob, and speakest, O Israel,
>'My way is hid from the Lord,
>>and my judgment is passed over from my God'?

[28] Hast thou not known? Hast thou not heard,
>that the everlasting God, the Lord,
>>the Creator of the ends of the earth,
>fainteth not, neither is weary?
>>There is no searching of his understanding.

[29] He giveth power to the faint;
>and to them that have no might
>>he increaseth strength.

[30] Even the youths shall faint and be weary,
>and the young men shall utterly fall:

[31] but they that wait upon the Lord
>shall renew their strength;
>>they shall mount up with wings as eagles;
>they shall run, and not be weary;
>>and they shall walk, and not faint.

41 Keep silence before me, O islands;
>and let the people renew their strength:
>>let them come near; then let them speak:
>let us come near together to judgment.

² Who raised up the righteous man from the east,
    called him to his foot,
        gave the nations before him,
    and made him rule over kings?
        He gave them as the dust to his sword,
    and as driven stubble to his bow.
³ He pursued them, and passed safely;
    even by the way that he had not gone
        with his feet.
⁴ Who hath wrought and done it,
    calling the generations from the beginning?
        I the Lord, the first, and with the last;
    I am he.
⁵ The isles saw it, and feared;
    the ends of the earth were afraid,
        drew near, and came.
⁶ They helped every one his neighbour;
    and every one said to his brother,
        'Be of good courage.'
⁷ So the carpenter encouraged the goldsmith,
    and he that smootheth with the hammer
        him that smote the anvil, saying,
    'It is ready for the sodering':
        and he fastened it with nails,
    that it should not be moved.
⁸ But thou, Israel, art my servant,
    Jacob whom I have chosen,
        the seed of Abraham my friend.

⁹ Thou whom I have taken from the ends of the earth,
    and called thee from the chief men thereof,
        and said unto thee, 'Thou art my servant;
    I have chosen thee, and not cast thee away.'
¹⁰ Fear thou not; for I am with thee:
    be not dismayed; for I am thy God:
        I will strengthen thee;
    yea, I will help thee; yea, I will uphold thee
        with the right hand of my righteousness.
¹¹ Behold, all they that were incensed against thee
    shall be ashamed and confounded;
        they shall be as nothing;
    and they that strive with thee shall perish.
¹² Thou shalt seek them, and shalt not find them,
    even them that contended with thee:
        they that war against thee shall be as nothing,
    and as a thing of nought.
¹³ For I the Lord thy God will hold thy right hand,
    saying unto thee, 'Fear not; I will help thee.'
¹⁴ Fear not, thou worm Jacob, and ye men of Israel;
    I will help thee, saith the Lord,
        and thy redeemer,
    the Holy One of Israel.
⁵ Behold, I will make thee a new sharp threshing
    instrument having teeth:
        thou shalt thresh the mountains,
    and beat them small,
        and shalt make the hills as chaff.

¹⁶ Thou shalt fan them,
>   and the wind shall carry them away,
>   and the whirlwind shall scatter them:
>   and thou shalt rejoice in the Lord,
>   and shalt glory in the Holy One of Israel.
¹⁷ When the poor and needy seek water,
>   and there is none,
>   and their tongue faileth for thirst,
>   I the Lord will hear them,
>   I the God of Israel will not forsake them.
¹⁸ I will open rivers in high places,
>   and fountains in the midst of the valleys:
>   I will make the wilderness a pool of water,
>   and the dry land springs of water.
¹⁹ I will plant in the wilderness the cedar,
>   the shittah tree, and the myrtle, and the oil tree;
>   I will set in the desert the fir tree,
>   and the pine, and the box tree together:
²⁰ that they may see, and know, and consider,
>   and understand together,
>   that the hand of the Lord hath done this,
>   and the Holy One of Israel hath created it.
²¹ Produce your cause, saith the Lord;
>   bring forth your strong reasons,
>   saith the King of Jacob.
²² Let them bring them forth,
>   and shew us what shall happen:
>   let them shew the former things, what they be,
>   that we may consider them,

and know the latter end of them;
or declare us things for to come.
²³ Shew the things that are to come hereafter,
that we may know that ye are gods:
yea, do good, or do evil,
that we may be dismayed, and behold it together.
²⁴ Behold, ye are of nothing,
and your work of nought:
an abomination is he that chooseth you.
²⁵ I have raised up one from the north,
and he shall come:
from the rising of the sun
shall he call upon my name:
and he shall come upon princes
as upon morter,
and as the potter treadeth clay.
²⁶ Who hath declared from the beginning,
that we may know?
And before-time, that we may say,
'He is righteous? Yea, there is none that sheweth,
yea, there is none that declareth,
yea, there is none that heareth your words.
²⁷ The first shall say to Zion, 'Behold, behold them:
and I will give to Jerusalem
one that bringeth good tidings.
²⁸ For I beheld, and there was no man;
even among them, and there was no counsellor,
that, when I asked of them,
could answer a word.

²⁹ Behold, they are all vanity;
　　their works are nothing:
　　　　their molten images are wind and confusion.

42 Behold my servant, whom I uphold;
　　mine elect, in whom my soul delighteth;
　　I have put my spirit upon him:
　　he shall bring forth judgment to the Gentiles.
² He shall not cry, nor lift up,
　　nor cause his voice to be heard in the street.
³ A bruised reed shall he not break,
　　and the smoking flax shall he not quench:
　　　　he shall bring forth judgment unto truth.
⁴ He shall not fail nor be discouraged,
　　till he have set judgment in the earth:
　　　　and the isles shall wait for his law.
⁵ Thus saith God the Lord, he that created
　　the heavens, and stretched them out;
　　　　he that spread forth the earth,
　　and that which cometh out of it;
　　　　he that giveth breath unto the people upon it,
　　and spirit to them that walk therein:
⁶ I the Lord have called thee in righteousness,
　　and will hold thine hand, and will keep thee,
　　　　and give thee for a covenant of the people,
　　for a light of the Gentiles,

⁷to open the blind eyes,
>to bring out the prisoners from the prison,
>>and them that sit in darkness
>out of the prison house.
⁸I am the Lord: that is my name:
>and my glory will I not give to another,
>>neither my praise to graven images.
⁹Behold, the former things are come to pass,
>and new things do I declare:
>>before they spring forth I tell you of them.
¹⁰Sing unto the Lord a new song,
>and his praise from the end of the earth,
>>ye that go down to the sea,
>and all that is therein;
>>the isles, and the inhabitants thereof.
¹¹Let the wilderness and the cities thereof
>lift up their voice,
>>the villages that Kedar doth inhabit:
>let the inhabitants of the rock sing,
>>let them shout from the top of the
mountains.
¹²Let them give glory unto the Lord,
>and declare his praise in the islands.
¹³The Lord shall go forth as a mighty man,
>he shall stir up jealousy like a man of war;
>>he shall cry, yea, roar;
>he shall prevail against his enemies.

¹⁴ I have long time holden my peace;
  I have been still, and refrained myself;
    now will I cry like a travailing woman;
  I will destroy and devour at once.
¹⁵ I will make waste mountains and hills,
  and dry up all their herbs;
    and I will make the rivers islands,
  and I will dry up the pools.
¹⁶ And I will bring the blind by a way
  that they knew not;
    I will lead them in paths
  that they have not known:
    I will make darkness light before them,
  and crooked things straight. These things will I
    do unto them, and not forsake them.
¹⁷ They shall be turned back,
  they shall be greatly ashamed,
    that trust in graven images,
  that say to the molten images, 'Ye are our gods.'
¹⁸ Hear, ye deaf; and look, ye blind, that ye may see.
¹⁹ Who is blind, but my servant?
  Or deaf, as my messenger that I sent?
    Who is blind as he that is perfect,
  and blind as the Lord's servant?
²⁰ Seeing many things, but thou observest not;
  opening the ears, but he heareth not.
²¹ The Lord is well pleased
  for his righteousness' sake;

he will magnify the law,
and make it honourable.

²² But this is a people robbed and spoiled;
they are all of them snared in holes,
and they are hid in prison houses:
they are for a prey, and none delivereth;
for a spoil, and none saith, 'Restore.'

²³ Who among you will give ear to this?
Who will hearken and hear for the time to come?

²⁴ Who gave Jacob for a spoil, and Israel to the robbers?
Did not the Lord,
he against whom we have sinned?
For they would not walk in his ways,
neither were they obedient unto his law.

²⁵ Therefore he hath poured upon him the fury
of his anger, and the strength of battle;
and it hath set him on fire round about,
yet he knew not; and it burned him,
yet he laid it not to heart.

43 But now thus saith the Lord that created thee,
O Jacob, and he that formed thee, O Israel,
Fear not, for I have redeemed thee,
I have called thee by thy name;
thou art mine.

² When thou passest through the waters,
  I will be with thee; and through the rivers,
    they shall not overflow thee:
  when thou walkest through the fire,
    thou shalt not be burned;
  neither shall the flame kindle upon thee.
³ For I am the Lord thy God, the Holy One of Israel,
  thy Saviour: I gave Egypt for thy ransom,
    Ethiopia and Seba for thee.
⁴ Since thou wast precious in my sight,
  thou hast been honourable,
    and I have loved thee:
  therefore will I give men for thee,
    and people for thy life.
⁵ Fear not, for I am with thee:
  I will bring thy seed from the east,
    and gather thee from the west;
⁶ I will say to the north, 'Give up';
  and to the south, 'Keep not back:
    bring my sons from far,
  and my daughters from the ends of the earth;
⁷ even every one that is called by my name,
  for I have created him for my glory,
    I have formed him;
  yea, I have made him.'
⁸ Bring forth the blind people that have eyes,
  and the deaf that have ears.
⁹ Let all the nations be gathered together,

and let the people be assembled:
>who among them can declare this,
and shew us former things?
>Let them bring forth their witnesses,
that they may be justified,
>or let them hear, and say, 'It is truth.'
¹⁰ Ye are my witnesses, saith the Lord,
and my servant whom I have chosen,
>that ye may know and believe me,
and understand that I am he:
>before me there was no God formed,
neither shall there be after me.
¹¹ I, even I, am the Lord;
and beside me there is no saviour.
¹² I have declared, and have saved,
and I have shewed,
>when there was no strange god among you:
therefore ye are my witnesses,
>saith the Lord, that I am God.
¹³ Yea, before the day was I am he;
and there is none that can deliver
>out of my hand;
I will work, and who shall let it?
¹⁴ Thus saith the Lord, your redeemer,
the Holy One of Israel;
>for your sake I have sent to Babylon,
and have brought down all their nobles,
>and the Chaldeans, whose cry is in the ships.

¹⁵ I am the Lord, your Holy One,
    the creator of Israel, your King.
¹⁶ Thus saith the Lord,
    which maketh a way in the sea,
        and a path in the mighty waters;
¹⁷ which bringeth forth the chariot and horse,
    the army and the power;
        they shall lie down together,
    they shall not rise;
        they are extinct, they are quenched as tow.
¹⁸ Remember ye not the former things,
    neither consider the things of old.
¹⁹ Behold, I will do a new thing;
    now it shall spring forth; shall ye not know it?
        I will even make a way in the wilderness,
    and rivers in the desert.
²⁰ The beast of the field shall honour me,
    the dragons and the owls,
        because I give waters in the wilderness,
    and rivers in the desert,
        to give drink to my people, my chosen.
²¹ This people have I formed for myself;
    they shall shew forth my praise.
²² But thou hast not called upon me, O Jacob;
    but thou hast been weary of me, O Israel.
²³ Thou hast not brought me the small cattle
    of thy burnt offerings;
        neither hast thou honoured me

with thy sacrifices.

I have not caused thee to serve with an offering,
nor wearied thee with incense.

²⁴ Thou hast bought me no sweet cane with money,
neither hast thou filled me
with the fat of thy sacrifices,
but thou hast made me to serve with thy sins,
thou hast wearied me with thine iniquities.

²⁵ I, even I, am he that blotteth out thy transgressions
for mine own sake,
and will not remember thy sins.

²⁶ Put me in remembrance: let us plead together:
declare thou, that thou mayest be justified.

²⁷ Thy first father hath sinned,
and thy teachers have transgressed against me.

²⁸ Therefore I have profaned
the princes of the sanctuary,
and have given Jacob to the curse,
and Israel to reproaches.

44 Yet now hear, O Jacob my servant;
and Israel, whom I have chosen:
² thus saith the Lord that made thee,
and formed thee from the womb,
which will help thee:
Fear not, O Jacob, my servant;
and thou, Jesurun, whom I have chosen.

³ For I will pour water upon him that is thirsty,
   and floods upon the dry ground:
      I will pour my spirit upon thy seed,
   and my blessing upon thine offspring.
⁴ And they shall spring up as among the grass,
   as willows by the water courses.
⁵ One shall say, I am the Lord's;
   and another shall call himself
      by the name of Jacob;
   and another shall subscribe
      with his hand unto the Lord,
   and surname himself by the name of Israel.
⁶ Thus saith the Lord the King of Israel,
   and his redeemer the Lord of hosts;
      I am the first, and I am the last;
   and beside me there is no God.
⁷ And who, as I, shall call, and shall declare it,
   and set it in order for me,
      since I appointed the ancient people?
   And the things that are coming,
      and shall come, let them shew unto them.
⁸ Fear ye not, neither be afraid:
   have not I told thee from that time,
      and have declared it?
   Ye are even my witnesses.
      Is there a God beside me?
   Yea, there is no God; I know not any.
⁹ They that make a graven image
   are all of them vanity;

and their delectable things shall not profit;
and they are their own witnesses;
they see not, nor know;
that they may be ashamed.

¹⁰ Who hath formed a god, or molten a graven image
that is profitable for nothing?

¹¹ Behold, all his fellows shall be ashamed,
and the workmen, they are of men:
let them all be gathered together,
let them stand up; yet they shall fear,
and they shall be ashamed together.

¹² The smith with the tongs both worketh in the coals,
and fashioneth it with hammers,
and worketh it with the strength of his arms:
yea, he is hungry, and his strength faileth:
he drinketh no water, and is faint.

¹³ The carpenter stretcheth out his rule;
he marketh it out with a line;
he fitteth it with planes,
and he marketh it out with the compass,
and maketh it after the figure of a man,
according to the beauty of a man;
that it may remain in the house.

¹⁴ He heweth him down cedars,
and taketh the cypress and the oak,
which he strengtheneth for himself
among the trees of the forest:
he planteth an ash,
and the rain doth nourish it.

¹⁵ Then shall it be for a man to burn;
   for he will take thereof, and warm himself;
      yea, he kindleth it, and baketh bread;
   yea, he maketh a god, and worshippeth it;
      he maketh it a graven image,
   and falleth down thereto.
¹⁶ He burneth part thereof in the fire;
   with part thereof he eateth flesh;
      he roasteth roast, and is satisfied:
   yea, he warmeth himself, and saith,
      'Aha, I am warm, I have seen the fire.'
¹⁷ And the residue thereof he maketh a god,
   even his graven image:
      he falleth down unto it, and worshippeth it,
   and prayeth unto it, and saith,
      'Deliver me; for thou art my god.'
¹⁸ They have not known nor understood;
   for he hath shut their eyes,
      that they cannot see;
   and their hearts,
      that they cannot understand.
¹⁹ And none considereth in his heart,
   neither is there knowledge nor understanding to say,
      'I have burned part of it in the fire;
   yea, also I have baked bread upon the coals thereof;
      I have roasted flesh, and eaten it:
   and shall I make the residue thereof
      an abomination?

Shall I fall down to the stock of a tree?'
²⁰ He feedeth on ashes:
    a deceived heart hath turned him aside,
        that he cannot deliver his soul, nor say,
    'Is there not a lie in my right hand?'
²¹ Remember these, O Jacob and Israel;
    for thou art my servant:
        I have formed thee; thou art my servant:
    O Israel; thou shalt not be forgotten of me.
²² I have blotted out, as a thick cloud,
    thy transgressions,
        and, as a cloud, thy sins:
    return unto me; for I have redeemed thee.
²³ Sing, O ye heavens; for the Lord hath done it:
    shout, ye lower parts of the earth:
        break forth into singing, ye mountains,
    O forest, and every tree therein;
        for the Lord hath redeemed Jacob,
    and glorified himself in Israel.
²⁴ Thus saith the Lord, thy redeemer,
    and he that formed thee from the womb,
        I am the Lord that maketh all things;
    that stretcheth forth the heavens alone;
        that spreadeth abroad the earth by myself;
²⁵ that frustrateth the tokens of the liars,
    and maketh diviners mad;
        that turneth wise men backward,
    and maketh their knowledge foolish;

²⁶ that confirmeth the word of his servant,
　　and performeth the counsel of his messengers;
　　　that saith to Jerusalem,
'Thou shalt be inhabited',
　　and to the cities of Judah, 'Ye shall be built,
　　and I will raise up the decayed places thereof;
²⁷ that saith to the deep,
　　'Be dry, and I will dry up thy rivers';
²⁸ that saith of Cyrus, 'He is my shepherd,
　　and shall perform all my pleasure';
　　　even saying to Jerusalem,
'Thou shalt be built'; and to the temple,
　　　'Thy foundation shall be laid.'

45 Thus saith the Lord to his anointed, to Cyrus,
　　whose right hand I have holden,
　　　to subdue nations before him;
　　and I will loose the loins of kings,
　　　to open before him the two leaved gates;
　　and the gates shall not be shut;
² I will go before thee,
　　and make the crooked places straight:
　　　I will break in pieces the gates of brass,
　　and cut in sunder the bars of iron;
³ and I will give thee the treasures of darkness,
　　and hidden riches of secret places,
　　　that thou mayest know that I, the Lord,

which call thee by thy name,
    am the God of Israel.
⁴ For Jacob my servant's sake, and Israel mine elect,
    I have even called thee by thy name:
        I have surnamed thee,
    though thou hast not known me.
⁵ I am the Lord, and there is none else,
    there is no God beside me: I girded thee,
        though thou hast not known me;
⁶ that they may know from the rising of the sun,
    and from the west,
        that there is none beside me.
    I am the Lord, and there is none else.
⁷ I form the light, and create darkness:
    I make peace, and create evil:
        I the Lord do all these things.
⁸ Drop down, ye heavens, from above,
    and let the skies pour down righteousness:
        let the earth open,
    and let them bring forth salvation,
        and let righteousness spring up together;
    I the Lord have created it.
⁹ Woe unto him that striveth with his Maker!
    Let the potsherd strive
        with the potsherds of the earth.
    Shall the clay say to him that fashioneth it,
        'What makest thou? 'or thy work,
    'He hath no hands'?

¹⁰ Woe unto him that saith unto his father,
'What begettest thou?'
or to the woman,
'What hast thou brought forth?'
¹¹ Thus saith the Lord, the Holy One of Israel,
and his Maker:
Ask me of things to come
concerning my sons,
and concerning the work of my hands
command ye me.
¹² I have made the earth, and created man upon it:
I, even my hands,
have stretched out the heavens,
and all their host have I commanded.
¹³ I have raised him up in righteousness,
and I will direct all his ways:
he shall build my city,
and he shall let go my captives,
not for price nor reward,
saith the Lord of hosts.
¹⁴ Thus saith the Lord: The labour of Egypt,
and merchandise of Ethiopia and of the Sabeans,
men of stature, shall come over unto thee,
and they shall be thine: they shall come after thee;
in chains they shall come over,
and they shall fall down unto thee,
they shall make supplication unto thee, saying,
'Surely God is in thee;
and there is none else, there is no God.'

¹⁵ Verily thou art a God that hidest thyself,
   O God of Israel, the Saviour.
¹⁶ They shall be ashamed,
      and also confounded, all of them:
         they shall go to confusion together
      that are makers of idols.
¹⁷ But Israel shall be saved in the Lord
      with an everlasting salvation:
         ye shall not be ashamed nor confounded
      world without end.
¹⁸ For thus saith the Lord that created the heavens;
      God himself that formed the earth and made it;
         he hath established it,
      he created it not in vain,
         he formed it to be inhabited:
      I am the Lord; and there is none else.
¹⁹ I have not spoken in secret,
      in a dark place of the earth:
         I said not unto the seed of Jacob,
      'Seek ye me in vain':
         I the Lord speak righteousness,
      I declare things that are right.
²⁰Assemble yourselves and come;
      draw near together,
         ye that are escaped of the nations:
      they have no knowledge
         that set up the wood of
      their graven image,
         and pray unto a god that cannot save.

²¹ Tell ye, and bring them near;
　　yea, let them take counsel together:
　　　　who hath declared this from ancient time?
　　Who hath told it from that time?
　　　　Have not I the Lord?
　　And there is no God else beside me;
　　　　a just God and a Saviour;
　　there is none beside me.
²² Look unto me, and be ye saved,
　　all the ends of the earth,
　　　　for I am God, and there is none else.
²³ I have sworn by myself, the word is gone out
　　of my mouth in righteousness,
　　　　and shall not return,
　　'That unto me every knee shall bow,
　　　　every tongue shall swear.'
²⁴ Surely, shall one say, in the Lord
　　have I righteousness and strength:
　　　　even to him shall men come;
　　and all that are incensed against him
　　　　shall be ashamed.
²⁵ In the Lord shall all the seed of Israel be justified,
　　and shall glory.

46　Bel boweth down, Nebo stoopeth,
　　　their idols were upon the beasts,
　　　　and upon the cattle:

your carriages were heavy loaden;
    they are a burden to the weary beast.
² They stoop, they bow down together,
    they could not deliver the burden,
        but themselves are gone into captivity.
³ Hearken unto me, O house of Jacob,
    and all the remnant of the house of Israel,
        which are borne by me from the belly,
    which are carried from the womb;
⁴ and even to your old age I am he;
    and even to hoar hairs will I carry you:
        I have made, and I will bear;
    even I will carry, and will deliver you.
⁵ To whom will ye liken me, and make me equal
    and compare me, that we may be like?
⁶ They lavish gold out of the bag,
    and weigh silver in the balance,
        and hire a goldsmith; and he maketh it a god:
    they fall down, yea, they worship.
⁷ They bear him upon the shoulder, they carry him,
    and set him in his place, and he standeth;
        from his place shall he not remove:
    yea, one shall cry unto him,
        yet can he not answer,
    nor save him out of his trouble.
⁸ Remember this, and shew yourselves men;
    bring it again to mind,
        O ye transgressors.

⁹Remember the former things of old, for I am God,
and there is none else;
I am God, and there is none like me,
¹⁰Declaring the end from the beginning,
and from ancient times
the things that are not yet done, saying,
'My counsel shall stand, and I will do
all my pleasure,'
¹¹calling a ravenous bird from the east,
the man that executeth my counsel
from a far country: yea, I have spoken it,
I will also bring it to pass;
I have purposed it, I will also do it.
¹²Hearken unto me, ye stouthearted,
that are far from righteousness;
¹³I bring near my righteousness;
it shall not be far off,
and my salvation shall not tarry;
and I will place salvation in Zion
for Israel my glory.

47 Come down, and sit in the dust,
O virgin daughter of Babylon, sit on the ground:
there is no throne,
O daughter of the Chaldeans;
for thou shalt no more be called
tender and delicate.
²Take the millstones, and grind meal;

uncover thy locks, make bare the leg,
uncover the thigh, pass over the rivers.
³ Thy nakedness shall be uncovered,
yea, thy shame shall be seen:
I will take vengeance,
and I will not meet thee as a man.
⁴ As for our redeemer, the Lord of hosts is his name,
the Holy One of Israel.
⁵ Sit thou silent, and get thee into darkness,
O daughter of the Chaldeans,
for thou shalt no more be called,
'The lady of kingdoms'.
⁶ I was wroth with my people,
I have polluted mine inheritance,
and given them into thine hand:
thou didst shew them no mercy;
upon the ancient hast thou
very heavily laid thy yoke.
⁷ And thou saidst, 'I shall be a lady for ever':
so that thou didst not
lay these things to thy heart,
neither didst remember the latter end of it.
⁸ Therefore hear now this,
thou that art given to pleasures,
that dwellest carelessly,
that sayest in thine heart,
'I am, and none else beside me;
I shall not sit as a widow,
neither shall I know the loss of children,'

⁹ but these two things shall come to thee
　　in a moment in one day,
　　　　the loss of children, and widowhood:
　　they shall come upon thee in their perfection
　　　　for the multitude of thy sorceries,
　　and for the great abundance
　　　　of thine enchantments.
¹⁰ For thou hast trusted in thy wickedness:
　　thou hast said, 'None seeth me.'
　　　　Thy wisdom and thy knowledge,
　　it hath perverted thee;
　　　　and thou hast said in thine heart,
　　'I am, and none else beside me.'
¹¹ Therefore shall evil come upon thee;
　　thou shalt not know from whence it riseth:
　　　　and mischief shall fall upon thee;
　　thou shalt not be able to put it off:
　　　　and desolation shall come upon thee
　　suddenly, which thou shalt not know.
¹² Stand now with thine enchantments,
　　and with the multitude of thy sorceries,
　　　　wherein thou hast laboured from thy youth;
　　if so be thou shalt be able to profit,
　　　　if so be thou mayest prevail.
¹³ Thou art wearied in the multitude of thy counsels.
　　Let now the astrologers, the stargazers,
　　　　the monthly prognosticators, stand up,

and save thee from these things
that shall come upon thee.
¹⁴ Behold, they shall be as stubble;
the fire shall burn them;
they shall not deliver themselves
from the power of the flame:
there shall not be a coal to warm at,
nor fire to sit before it.
¹⁵ Thus shall they be unto thee
with whom thou hast laboured,
even thy merchants, from thy youth:
they shall wander every one to his quarter;
none shall save thee.

48 Hear ye this, O house of Jacob,
which are called by the name of Israel,
and are come forth
out of the waters of Judah,
which swear by the name of the Lord,
and make mention of the God of Israel,
but not in truth, nor in righteousness.
² For they call themselves of the holy city,
and stay themselves upon the God of Israel;
the Lord of hosts is his name.

³I have declared the former things
   from the beginning;
      and they went forth out of my mouth,
   and I shewed them;
      I did them suddenly, and they came to pass.
⁴Because I knew that thou art obstinate,
   and thy neck is an iron sinew,
      and thy brow brass;
⁵I have even from the beginning declared it to thee;
   before it came to pass I shewed it thee:
      lest thou shouldest say,
   'Mine idol hath done them, and my graven
      image, and my molten image,
   hath commanded them.'
⁶Thou hast heard, see all this;
   and will not ye declare it?
      I have shewed thee new things
   from this time, even hidden things,
      and thou didst not know them.
⁷They are created now, and not from the beginning;
   even before the day when
      thou heardest them not;
      lest thou shouldest say, 'Behold, I knew them.'
⁸Yea, thou heardest not; yea, thou knewest not;
      yea, from that time that thine ear
   was not opened,
      for I knew that thou wouldest deal
   very treacherously,

and wast called a transgressor
from the womb.

⁹ For my name's sake will I defer mine anger,
and for my praise will I refrain for thee,
that I cut thee not off.

¹⁰ Behold, I have refined thee,
but not with silver;
I have chosen thee
in the furnace of affliction.

¹¹ For mine own sake,
even for mine own sake, will I do it;
for how should my name be polluted?
And I will not give my glory
unto another.

¹² Hearken unto me, O Jacob and Israel, my called;
I am he; I am the first,
I also am the last.

¹³ Mine hand also hath laid
the foundation of the earth,
and my right hand
hath spanned the heavens:
when I call unto them, they stand up
together.

¹⁴ All ye, assemble yourselves, and hear;
which among them hath declared these things?
The Lord hath loved him:
he will do his pleasure on Babylon,
and his arm shall be on the Chaldeans.

¹⁵ I, even I, have spoken; yea, I have called him:
    I have brought him,
    and he shall make his way prosperous.
¹⁶ Come ye near unto me, hear ye this;
    I have not spoken in secret from the beginning;
        from the time that it was, there am I:
    and now the Lord God, and his Spirit,
        hath sent me.
¹⁷ Thus saith the Lord, thy Redeemer,
    the Holy One of Israel;
        I am the Lord thy God
    which teacheth thee to profit,
        which leadeth thee by the way
    that thou shouldest go.
¹⁸ O that thou hadst hearkened
    to my commandments!
        Then had thy peace been as a river,
    and thy righteousness as the waves of the sea;
¹⁹ thy seed also had been as the sand,
    and the offspring of thy bowels
        like the gravel thereof;
    his name should not have been cut off
        nor destroyed from before me.
²⁰ Go ye forth of Babylon, flee ye from the Chaldeans,
    with a voice of singing declare ye,
        tell this, utter it even to the end of the earth;
    say ye, the Lord hath redeemed his servant Jacob.
²¹ And they thirsted not when he led them

through the deserts: he caused the waters to flow
out of the rock for them: he clave the rock also,
and the waters gushed out.
²² There is no peace, saith the Lord, unto the wicked.

49

Listen, O isles, unto me;
and hearken, ye people, from far;
the Lord hath called me from the womb;
from the bowels of my mother
hath he made mention of my name.

²And he hath made my mouth like a sharp sword;
in the shadow of his hand hath he hid me,
and made me a polished shaft;
in his quiver hath he hid me;

³and said unto me,
'Thou art my servant, O Israel,
in whom I will be glorified.'

⁴Then I said, 'I have laboured in vain,
I have spent my strength for nought, and in vain:
yet surely my judgment is with the Lord,
and my work with my God.'

⁵And now, saith the Lord that formed me
from the womb to be his servant,
to bring Jacob again to him.
'Though Israel be not gathered, yet
shall I be glorious in the eyes of the Lord,
and my God shall be my strength.'

⁶And he said, 'It is a light thing
   that thou shouldest be my servant
      to raise up the tribes of Jacob,
   and to restore the preserved of Israel:
      I will also give thee for a light to the Gentiles,
   that thou mayest be my salvation
      unto the end of the earth.'
⁷Thus saith the Lord, the Redeemer of Israel,
   and his Holy One, to him whom man despiseth,
      to him whom the nation abhorreth,
   to a servant of rulers, Kings shall see
      and arise, princes also shall worship,
   because of the Lord that is faithful,
      and the Holy One of Israel,
   and he shall choose thee.
⁸Thus saith the Lord,
   In an acceptable time have I heard thee,
      and in a day of salvation have I helped thee:
   and I will preserve thee,
      and give thee for a covenant of the people,
   to establish the earth,
      to cause to inherit the desolate heritages,
⁹that thou mayest say to the prisoners, 'Go forth';
   to them that are in darkness, 'Shew yourselves.'
      They shall feed in the ways,
   and their pastures shall be in all
      high places.

¹⁰ They shall not hunger nor thirst;
  neither shall the heat nor sun smite them;
    for he that hath mercy on them
  shall lead them, even by the springs of water
    shall he guide them.
¹¹ And I will make all my mountains a way,
  and my highways shall be exalted:
¹² Behold, these shall come from far;
  and, lo, these from the north and from the west;
    and these from the land of Sinim.
¹³ Sing, O heavens; and be joyful, O earth;
  and break forth into singing, O mountains;
    for the Lord hath comforted his people,
  and will have mercy upon his afflicted.
¹⁴ But Zion said, 'The Lord hath forsaken me,
  and my Lord hath forgotten me.'
¹⁵ Can a woman forget her sucking child,
  that she should not have compassion
    on the son of her womb?
  Yea, they may forget,
    yet will I not forget thee.
¹⁶ Behold, I have graven thee
  upon the palms of my hands;
    thy walls are continually before me.
¹⁷ Thy children shall make haste;
  thy destroyers and they that made thee waste
    shall go forth of thee.

¹⁸ Lift up thine eyes round about, and behold:
  all these gather themselves together,
    and come to thee.
  As I live, saith the Lord,
    thou shalt surely clothe thee with them all,
  as with an ornament,
    and bind them on thee, as a bride doeth.
¹⁹ For thy waste and thy desolate places,
  and the land of thy destruction,
    shall even now be too narrow
  by reason of the inhabitants,
    and they that swallowed thee up
  shall be far away.
²⁰ The children which thou shalt have,
  after thou hast lost the other,
    shall say again in thine ears,
  'The place is too strait for me:
    give place to me that I may dwell.'
²¹ Then shalt thou say in thine heart,
  'Who hath begotten me these,
    seeing I have lost my children,
  and am desolate, a captive,
    and removing to and fro?
  And who hath brought up these?
    Behold, I was left alone;
  these, where had they been?'
²² Thus saith the Lord God:
  Behold, I will lift up mine hand to the Gentiles,

and set up my standard to the people;
and they shall bring thy sons in their arms,
and thy daughters shall be carried
upon their shoulders.
²³And kings shall be thy nursing fathers,
and their queens thy nursing mothers:
they shall bow down to thee
with their face toward the earth,
and lick up the dust of thy feet;
and thou shalt know that I am the Lord;
for they shall not be ashamed
that wait for me.
²⁴ Shall the prey be taken from the mighty,
or the lawful captive delivered?
²⁵ But thus saith the Lord:
Even the captives of the mighty
shall be taken away,
and the prey of the terrible shall be delivered,
for I will contend with him
that contendeth with thee,
and I will save thy children.
²⁶And I will feed them
that oppress thee with their own flesh;
and they shall be drunken
with their own blood, as with sweet wine;
and all flesh shall know that I the Lord
am thy Saviour and thy Redeemer,
the mighty One of Jacob.

50 Thus saith the Lord.
Where is the bill of your mother's divorcement,
    whom I have put away?
Or which of my creditors is it
    to whom I have sold you?
Behold, for your iniquities
    have ye sold yourselves,
and for your transgressions
    is your mother put away.
² Wherefore, when I came, was there no man?
When I called, was there none to answer?
    Is my hand shortened at all,
that it cannot redeem?
    Or have I no power to deliver?
Behold, at my rebuke I dry up the sea,
    I make the rivers a wilderness:
their fish stinketh, because there is no water,
    and dieth for thirst.
³ I clothe the heavens with blackness,
    and I make sackcloth their covering.
⁴ The Lord God hath given me
    the tongue of the learned,
       that I should know how to speak a word
in season to him that is weary:
    he wakeneth morning by morning,
he wakeneth mine ear to hear as the learned.
⁵ The Lord God hath opened mine ear,
    and I was not rebellious,

neither turned away back.

⁶ I gave my back to the smiters, and my cheeks
    to them that plucked off the hair:
        I hid not my face from shame
    and spitting.

⁷ For the Lord God will help me;
    therefore shall I not be confounded;
        therefore have I set my face like a flint,
    and I know that I shall not be ashamed.

⁸ He is near that justifieth me;
    who will contend with me? Let us stand together:
        who is mine adversary?
    Let him come near to me.

⁹ Behold, the Lord God will help me;
    who is he that shall condemn me?
        Lo, they all shall wax old as a garment;
    the moth shall eat them up.

¹⁰ Who is among you that feareth the Lord,
    that obeyeth the voice of his servant,
        that walketh in darkness, and hath no light?
    Let him trust in the name of the Lord, and stay
        upon his God.

¹¹ Behold, all ye that kindle a fire, that compass your-
    selves about with sparks:
        walk in the light of your fire, and in the
    sparks that ye have kindled. This shall ye have of
        mine hand;
    ye shall lie down in sorrow.

51

Hearken to me, ye that follow after righteousness,
ye that seek the Lord:

look unto the rock whence ye are hewn,
and to the hole of the pit
whence ye are digged.

² Look unto Abraham your father,
and unto Sarah that bare you,

for I called him alone, and blessed him,
and increased him.

³ For the Lord shall comfort Zion;
he will comfort all her waste places;

and he will make her wilderness like Eden,
and her desert like the garden of the Lord;

joy and gladness shall be found therein,
thanksgiving, and the voice of melody.

⁴ Hearken unto me, my people;
and give ear unto me, O my nation;

for a law shall proceed from me,
and I will make my judgment to rest
for a light of the people.

⁵ My righteousness is near;
my salvation is gone forth,

and mine arms shall judge the people;
the isles shall wait upon me,
and on mine arm shall they trust.

⁶ Lift up your eyes to the heavens,
and look upon the earth beneath;

for the heavens shall vanish away like smoke,

and the earth shall wax old like a garment,
and they that dwell therein shall die
in like manner;
but my salvation shall be for ever,
and my righteousness shall not be abolished.
⁷ Hearken unto me, ye that know righteousness,
the people in whose heart is my law;
fear ye not the reproach of men,
neither be ye afraid of their revilings.
⁸ For the moth shall eat them up like a garment,
and the worm shall eat them like wool,
but my righteousness shall be for ever,
and my salvation from generation
to generation.
⁹ Awake, awake, put on strength, O arm of the Lord;
awake, as in the ancient days,
in the generations of old.
Art thou not it that hath cut Rahab,
and wounded the dragon?
¹⁰ Art thou not it which hath dried the sea,
the waters of the great deep;
that hath made the depths of the sea
a way for the ransomed to pass over?
¹¹ Therefore the redeemed of the Lord shall return,
and come with singing unto Zion;
and everlasting joy shall be upon their head:
they shall obtain gladness and joy;
and sorrow and mourning shall flee away.

¹² I, even I, am he that comforteth you;
   who art thou, that thou shouldest be afraid
      of a man that shall die,
   and of the son of man which shall be made
      as grass;
¹³ and forgettest the Lord thy maker,
   that hath stretched forth the heavens,
      and laid the foundations of the earth;
   and hast feared continually every day
      because of the fury of the oppressor,
   as if he were ready to destroy?
      And where is the fury of the oppressor?
¹⁴ The captive exile hasteneth that he may be loosed,
   and that he should not die in the pit,
      nor that his bread should fail.
¹⁵ But I am the Lord thy God, that divided the sea,
   whose waves roared:
      the Lord of hosts is his name.
¹⁶ And I have put my words in thy mouth,
   and I have covered thee
      in the shadow of mine hand,
   that I may plant the heavens,
      and lay the foundations of the earth,
   and say unto Zion,
      'Thou art my people.'
¹⁷ Awake, awake, stand up, O Jerusalem,
   which hast drunk at the hand of the Lord

the cup of his fury;
thou hast drunken the dregs of the cup
of trembling, and wrung them out.

 18 There is none to guide her among all the sons
whom she hath brought forth;
neither is there any that taketh her
by the hand of all the sons
that she hath brought up.

19 These two things are come unto thee;
who shall be sorry for thee?
Desolation, and destruction,
and the famine, and the sword:
by whom shall I comfort thee?

20 Thy sons have fainted,
they lie at the head of all the streets,
as a wild bull in a net:
they are full of the fury of the Lord,
the rebuke of thy God.

21 Therefore hear now this, thou afflicted,
and drunken, but not with wine:

22 thus saith thy Lord the Lord,
and thy God that pleadeth the cause
of his people.
Behold, I have taken out of thine hand
the cup of trembling,
even the dregs of the cup of my fury;
thou shalt no more drink it again.

²³ But I will put it into the hand of them
    that afflict thee; which have said to thy soul,
        'Bow down, that we may go over':
    and thou hast laid thy body as the ground,
        and as the street, to them that went over.

52 Awake, awake; put on thy strength, O Zion;
    put on thy beautiful garments, O Jerusalem,
        the holy city;
    for henceforth there shall no more come into thee
        the uncircumcised and the unclean.
² Shake thyself from the dust;
    arise, and sit down, O Jerusalem:
        loose thyself from the bands of thy neck,
    O captive daughter of Zion.
³ For thus saith the Lord:
    Ye have sold yourselves for nought;
        and ye shall be redeemed without money.
⁴ For thus saith the Lord God:
    My people went down aforetime into Egypt
        to sojourn there;
    and the Assyrian oppressed them
        without cause.
⁵ Now therefore, what have I here, saith the Lord,
    that my people is taken away for nought?
        They that rule over them make them to howl,

saith the Lord;

and my name continually every day
is blasphemed.
⁶ Therefore my people shall know my name;

therefore they shall know in that day that I am he
that doth speak: behold, it is I.
⁷ How beautiful upon the mountains
are the feet of him that bringeth good tidings,
that publisheth peace;
that bringeth good tidings of good,
that publisheth salvation;
that saith unto Zion, 'Thy God reigneth!'
⁸ Thy watchmen shall lift up the voice;
with the voice together shall they sing:
for they shall see eye to eye,
when the Lord shall bring again Zion.
⁹ Break forth into joy, sing together,
ye waste places of Jerusalem;
for the Lord hath comforted his people,
he hath redeemed Jerusalem.
¹⁰ The Lord hath made bare his holy arm
in the eyes of all the nations;
and all the ends of the earth
shall see the salvation of our God.
¹¹ Depart ye, depart ye, go ye out from thence,
touch no unclean thing;
go ye out of the midst of her;
be ye clean, that bear the vessels of the Lord.

¹²For ye shall not go out with haste, nor go by flight;
   for the Lord will go before you;
      and the God of Israel will be your reward.
¹³Behold, my servant shall deal prudently,
   he shall be exalted and extolled, and be very high.
¹⁴As many were astonied at thee;
      his visage was so marred more than any man,
         and his form more than the sons of men:
¹⁵so shall he sprinkle many nations;
      the kings shall shut their mouths at him;
         for that which had not been told them
      shall they see;
         and that which they had not heard
      shall they consider.

53 Who hath believed our report?
      And to whom is the arm of the Lord revealed?
²For he shall grow up before him as a tender plant,
      and as a root out of a dry ground:
         he hath no form nor comeliness;
      and when we shall see him,
         there is no beauty
      that we should desire him.
³He is despised and rejected of men;
      a man of sorrows, and acquainted with grief:

and we hid as it were our faces from him;
he was despised, and we esteemed him not.
⁴ Surely he hath borne our griefs,
and carried our sorrows;
yet we did esteem him stricken,
smitten of God, and afflicted.
⁵ But he was wounded for our transgressions,
he was bruised for our iniquities;
the chastisement of our peace was upon him;
and with his stripes we are healed.
⁶ All we like sheep have gone astray;
we have turned every one to his own way;
and the Lord hath laid on him
the iniquity of us all.
⁷ He was oppressed, and he was afflicted,
yet he opened not his mouth:
he is brought as a lamb to the slaughter,
and as a sheep before her shearers is dumb,
so he openeth not his mouth.
⁸ He was taken from prison and from judgment,
and who shall declare his generation?
For he was cut off out of the land of the living:
for the transgression of my people
was he stricken.
⁹ And he made his grave with the wicked,
and with the rich in his death;
because he had done no violence,
neither was any deceit in his mouth.

[10] Yet it pleased the Lord to bruise him;
　　he hath put him to grief: when thou shalt make
　　　his soul an offering for sin,
　　he shall see his seed, he shall prolong his days,
　　　and the pleasure of the Lord
　　shall prosper in his hand.
[11] He shall see of the travail of his soul,
　　and shall be satisfied:
　　　by his knowledge shall my righteous servant
　　justify many; for he shall bear their iniquities.
[12] Therefore will I divide him a portion with the great,
　　and he shall divide the spoil with the strong;
　　　because he hath poured out his soul unto death;
　　and he was numbered with the transgressors;
　　　and he bare the sin of many, and made
　　intercession for the transgressors.

54 Sing, O barren, thou that didst not bear;
　　break forth into singing, and cry aloud,
　　　thou that didst not travail with child;
　　for more are the children of the desolate
　　　than the children of the married wife,
　　saith the Lord.
[2] Enlarge the place of thy tent, and let them

stretch forth the curtains of thine habitations:
>> spare not, lengthen thy cords,
> and strengthen thy stakes;
3 for thou shalt break forth on the right hand
> and on the left;
>> and thy seed shall inherit the Gentiles,
> and make the desolate cities to be inhabited.
4 Fear not; for thou shalt not be ashamed:
> neither be thou confounded;
>> for thou shalt not be put to shame;
>> for thou shalt forget the shame of thy youth,
> and shalt not remember the reproach
> of thy widowhood any more.
5 For thy Maker is thine husband;
> the Lord of hosts is his name;
>> and thy Redeemer the Holy One of Israel;
> the God of the whole earth shall he be called.
6 For the Lord hath called thee as a woman forsaken
> and grieved in spirit, and a wife of youth,
>> when thou wast refused, saith thy God.
7 For a small moment have I forsaken thee;
> but with great mercies will I gather thee.
8 In a little wrath I hid my face from thee
> for a moment;
>> but with everlasting kindness
> will I have mercy on thee,
>> saith the Lord thy Redeemer.

⁹For this is as the waters of Noah unto me;
   for as I have sworn that the waters of Noah
      should no more go over the earth,
   so have I sworn that I would not be wroth
      with thee, nor rebuke thee.
¹⁰For the mountains shall depart,
   and the hills be removed;
      but my kindness shall not depart from thee,
   neither shall the covenant of my peace
      be removed,
   saith the Lord that hath mercy on thee.
¹¹O thou afflicted, tossed with tempest,
   and not comforted, behold,
      I will lay thy stones with fair colours,
   and lay thy foundations with sapphires.
¹²And I will make thy windows of agates,
   and thy gates of carbuncles,
      and all thy borders of pleasant stones.
¹³And all thy children shall be taught of the Lord;
   and great shall be the peace of thy children.
¹⁴In righteousness shalt thou be established:
   thou shalt be far from oppression;
      for thou shalt not fear:
   and from terror; for it shall not come near thee.
¹⁵Behold, they shall surely gather together,
   but not by me:
      whosoever shall gather together against thee
   shall fall for thy sake.

¹⁶ Behold, I have created the smith
    that bloweth the coals in the fire,
        and that bringeth forth an instrument
    for his work;
        and I have created the waster to destroy.
¹⁷ No weapon that is formed against thee
    shall prosper;
        and every tongue that shall rise against thee
    in judgment thou shalt condemn.
        This is the heritage of the servants
    of the Lord,
        and their righteousness is of me,
    saith the Lord.

55

Ho, every one that thirsteth, come ye to the waters,
    and he that hath no money;
        come ye, buy, and eat;
    yea, come, buy wine and milk without money
        and without price.
² Wherefore do ye spend money
    for that which is not bread?
        And your labour for that which satisfieth not?
    Hearken diligently unto me,
        and eat ye that which is good,
    and let your soul delight itself in fatness.

³ Incline your ear, and come unto me:
> hear, and your soul shall live;
>> and I will make an everlasting covenant
>> with you, even the sure mercies of David.
⁴ Behold, I have given him for a witness to the people,
> a leader and commander to the people.
⁵ Behold, thou shalt call a nation
> that thou knowest not,
>> and nations that knew not thee
>> shall run unto thee because of the Lord thy God,
>> and for the Holy One of Israel;
> for he hath glorified thee.
⁶ Seek ye the Lord while he may be found,
> call ye upon him while he is near;
⁷ let the wicked forsake his way,
> and the unrighteous man his thoughts;
>> and let him return unto the Lord,
>> and he will have mercy upon him; and to our God,
>> for he will abundantly pardon.
⁸ For my thoughts are not your thoughts,
> neither are your ways my ways,
>> saith the Lord.
⁹ For as the heavens are higher than the earth,
> so are my ways higher than your ways,
>> and my thoughts than your thoughts.
¹⁰ For as the rain cometh down,
> and the snow from heaven,
>> and returneth not thither,

but watereth the earth,
　　and maketh it bring forth and bud,
that it may give seed to the sower,
　　and bread to the eater;
[11] so shall my word be that goeth forth
　　out of my mouth;
　　　　it shall not return unto me void,
　　but it shall accomplish that which I please,
　　　　and it shall prosper in the thing
　　whereto I sent it.
[12] For ye shall go out with joy,
　　and be led forth with peace:
　　　　the mountains and the hills shall break forth
　　before you into singing,
　　　　and all the trees of the field
　　shall clap their hands.
[13] Instead of the thorn shall come up the fir tree,
　　and instead of the brier
　　　　shall come up the myrtle tree:
　　and it shall be to the Lord for a name,
　　　　for an everlasting sign that shall not be cut off.

56 Thus saith the Lord:
　　Keep ye judgment, and do justice;
　　　　for my salvation is near to come,
　　and my righteousness to be revealed.

² Blessed is the man that doeth this,
  and the son of man that layeth hold on it;
    that keepeth the sabbath from polluting it,
  and keepeth his hand from doing any evil.
³ Neither let the son of the stranger,
  that hath joined himself to the Lord, speak,
    saying, 'The Lord hath utterly separated me
  from his people';
    neither let the eunuch say,
  'Behold, I am a dry tree.'
⁴ For thus saith the Lord unto the eunuchs
  that keep my sabbaths,
    and choose the things that please me,
  and take hold of my covenant;
⁵ even unto them will I give in mine house
  and within my walls
    a place and a name better than of sons
  and of daughters:
    I will give them an everlasting name,
  that shall not be cut off.
⁶ Also the sons of the stranger, that join themselves
  to the Lord, to serve him,
    and to love the name of the Lord,
  to be his servants, every one
    that keepeth the sabbath
  from polluting it, and taketh hold of my covenant;
⁷ even them will I bring to my holy mountain,
  and make them joyful in my house of prayer:

their burnt offerings and their sacrifices
shall be accepted upon mine altar;
for mine house shall be called an house
of prayer for all people.
⁸ The Lord God which gathereth the outcasts of Israel
saith, Yet will I gather others to him,
beside those that are gathered unto him.
⁹ All ye beasts of the field, come to devour,
yea, all ye beasts in the forest.
¹⁰ His watchmen are blind: they are all ignorant,
they are all dumb dogs, they cannot bark;
sleeping, lying down, loving to slumber.
¹¹ Yea, they are greedy dogs
which can never have enough,
and they are shepherds
that cannot understand:
they all look to their own way,
every one for his gain, from his quarter.
¹² Come ye, say they, I will fetch wine,
and we will fill ourselves with strong drink;
and to morrow shall be as this day,
and much more abundant.

57 The righteous perisheth, and no man layeth it
to heart; and merciful men are taken away,
none considering that the righteous
is taken away from the evil to come.

²He shall enter into peace:
> they shall rest in their beds,
>> each one walking in his uprightness.
³But draw near hither, ye sons of the sorceress,
> the seed of the adulterer and the whore.
⁴Against whom do ye sport yourselves?
> Against whom make ye a wide mouth,
>> and draw out the tongue?
> Are ye not children of transgression,
>> a seed of falsehood,
⁵enflaming yourselves with idols
> under every green tree,
>> slaying the children in the valleys
> under the clifts of the rocks?
⁶Among the smooth stones of the stream
> is thy portion; they, they are thy lot:
>> even to them hast thou poured a drink offering,
> thou hast offered a meat offering.
>> Should I receive comfort in these?
⁷Upon a lofty and high mountain
> hast thou set thy bed:
>> even thither wentest thou up to offer sacrifice.
⁸Behind the doors also and the posts
> hast thou set up thy remembrance;
>> for thou hast discovered thyself
> to another than me, and art gone up;
>> thou hast enlarged thy bed,

and made thee a covenant with them;
  thou lovedst their bed where thou sawest it.
⁹And thou wentest to the king with ointment,
  and didst increase thy perfumes,
    and didst send thy messengers far off,
  and didst debase thyself even unto hell.
¹⁰Thou art wearied in the greatness of thy way;
  yet saidst thou not, 'There is no hope':
    thou hast found the life of thine hand;
  therefore thou wast not grieved.
¹¹And of whom hast thou been afraid or feared,
  that thou hast lied,
    and hast not remembered me,
  nor laid it to thy heart?
    Have not I held my peace even of old,
  and thou fearest me not?
¹²I will declare thy righteousness, and thy works;
  for they shall not profit thee.
¹³When thou criest, let thy companies deliver thee;
  but the wind shall carry them all away;
    vanity shall take them:
  but he that putteth his trust in me
    shall possess the land,
  and shall inherit my holy mountain;
¹⁴and shall say, 'Cast ye up, cast ye up,
  prepare the way, take up the stumbling-block
    out of the way of my people.'

¹⁵ For thus saith the high and lofty One
    that inhabiteth eternity, whose name is Holy;
        I dwell in the high and holy place,
    with him also that is of a contrite
        and humble spirit, to revive the spirit
of the humble,
        and to revive the heart of the contrite ones.
¹⁶ For I will not contend for ever,
    neither will I be always wroth
        for the spirit should fail before me,
    and the souls which I have made.
¹⁷ For the iniquity of his covetousness was I wroth,
    and smote him: I hid me, and was wroth,
        and he went on frowardly
    in the way of his heart.
¹⁸ I have seen his ways, and will heal him:
    I will lead him also, and restore comforts
        unto him and to his mourners.
¹⁹ I create the fruit of the lips.
    Peace, peace to him that is far off,
        and to him that is near, saith the Lord;
    and I will heal him.
²⁰ But the wicked are like the troubled sea,
    when it cannot rest,
        whose waters cast up mire and dirt.
²¹ There is no peace,
    saith my God, to the wicked.

58 Cry aloud, spare not, lift up thy voice
       like a trumpet,
               and shew my people their transgression,
       and the house of Jacob their sins.
2 Yet they seek me daily,
       and delight to know my ways,
               as a nation that did righteousness,
       and forsook not the ordinance of their God:
               they ask of me the ordinances of justice;
       they take delight in approaching to God.
3 Wherefore have we fasted, say they,
       and thou seest not?
               Wherefore have we afflicted our soul,
       and thou takest no knowledge?
               Behold, in the day of your fast
       ye find pleasure,
               and exact all your labours.
4 Behold, ye fast for strife and debate,
       and to smite with the fist of wickedness:
               ye shall not fast as ye do this day,
       to make your voice to be heard on high.
5 Is it such a fast that I have chosen?
       A day for a man to afflict his soul?
               Is it to bow down his head as a bulrush,
       and to spread sackcloth and ashes under him?
               Wilt thou call this a fast,
       and an acceptable day to the Lord?

⁶ Is not this the fast that I have chosen?
　　To loose the bands of wickedness,
　　　　to undo the heavy burdens,
　　and to let the oppressed go free,
　　　　and that ye break every yoke?
⁷ Is it not to deal thy bread to the hungry,
　　and that thou bring the poor
　　　　that are cast out to thy house?
　　When thou seest the naked,
　　　　that thou cover him;
　　and that thou hide not thyself
　　　　from thine own flesh?
⁸ Then shall thy light break forth as the morning,
　　and thine health shall spring forth speedily:
　　　　and thy righteousness shall go before thee;
　　the glory of the Lord shall be thy reward.
⁹ Then shalt thou call, and the Lord shall answer;
　　thou shalt cry, and he shall say, 'Here I am.'
　　　　If thou take away from the midst of thee
　　the yoke, the putting forth of the finger,
　　　　and speaking vanity;
¹⁰ and if thou draw out thy soul to the hungry,
　　and satisfy the afflicted soul;
　　　　then shall thy light rise in obscurity,
　　and thy darkness be as the noonday:
¹¹ and the Lord shall guide thee continually,
　　and satisfy thy soul in drought,
　　　　and make fat thy bones:

and thou shalt be like a watered garden,
and like a spring of water,
whose waters fail not.
¹²And they that shall be of thee
shall build the old waste places:
thou shalt raise up the foundations
of many generations; and thou shalt be called,
'The repairer of the breach',
'The restorer of paths to dwell in'.
¹³If thou turn away thy foot from the sabbath,
from doing thy pleasure on my holy day;
and call the sabbath a delight,
the holy of the Lord, honourable;
and shalt honour him,
not doing thine own ways,
nor finding thine own pleasure,
nor speaking thine own words:
¹⁴then shalt thou delight thyself in the Lord;
and I will cause thee to ride
upon the high places of the earth,
and feed thee with the heritage
of Jacob thy father;
for the mouth of the Lord hath spoken it.

59 Behold, the Lord's hand is not shortened,
that it cannot save; neither his ear heavy,
that it cannot hear.

² But your iniquities have separated between you
  and your God,
      and your sins have hid his face from you,
  that he will not hear.
³ For your hands are defiled with blood,
  and your fingers with iniquity;
      your lips have spoken lies,
  your tongue hath muttered perverseness.
⁴ None calleth for justice, nor any pleadeth for truth:
  they trust in vanity, and speak lies;
      they conceive mischief,
  and bring forth iniquity.
⁵ They hatch cockatrice' eggs,
  and weave the spider's web:
      he that eateth of their eggs dieth,
  and that which is crushed breaketh
      out into a viper.
⁶ Their webs shall not become garments,
  neither shall they cover themselves
      with their works:
  their works are works of iniquity,
      and the act of violence is in their hands.
⁷ Their feet run to evil,
  and they make haste to shed innocent blood:
      their thoughts are thoughts of iniquity;
  wasting and destruction are in their paths.
⁸ The way of peace they know not;

and there is no judgment in their goings:

    they have made them crooked paths:

    whosoever goeth therein shall not know peace.

9 Therefore is judgment far from us,

    neither doth justice overtake us:

      we wait for light, but behold obscurity;

    for brightness, but we walk in darkness.

10 We grope for the wall like the blind,

    and we grope as if we had no eyes;

      we stumble at noonday as in the night;

    we are in desolate places as dead men.

11 We roar all like bears, and mourn sore like doves:

    we look for judgment, but there is none;

      for salvation, but it is far off from us.

12 For our transgressions are multiplied before thee,

    and our sins testify against us;

      for our transgressions are with us;

    and as for our iniquities, we know them;

13 in transgressing and lying against the Lord,

    and departing away from our God,

      speaking oppression and revolt,

    conceiving and uttering from the heart

    words of falsehood.

14 And judgment is turned away backward,

    and justice standeth afar off;

      for truth is fallen in the street, and

    equity cannot enter.

¹⁵ Yea, truth faileth; and he that departeth from evil
    maketh himself a prey:

> and the Lord saw it, and it displeased him
> that there was no judgment.

¹⁶ And he saw that there was no man,
    and wondered that there was no intercessor:

> therefore his arm brought salvation unto him;
> and his righteousness, it sustained him.

¹⁷ For he put on righteousness as a breastplate,
    and an helmet of salvation upon his head;

> and he put on the garments of vengeance
> for clothing,
>   and was clad with zeal as a cloke.

¹⁸ According to their deeds, accordingly he will repay,
    fury to his adversaries,

> recompence to his enemies;
> to the islands he will repay recompence.

¹⁹ So shall they fear the name of the Lord
    from the west,

> and his glory from the rising of the sun.
> When the enemy shall come in like a flood,
>   the Spirit of the Lord shall lift up a standard
> against him.

²⁰ And the Redeemer shall come to Zion,
    and unto them that turn from transgression
        in Jacob, saith the Lord.

²¹ As for me, this is my covenant with them,

saith the Lord, my spirit that is upon thee,
> and my words which I have put in thy mouth,
shall not depart out of thy mouth,
> nor out of the mouth of thy seed,
nor out of the mouth of thy seed's seed,
> saith the Lord, from henceforth and for ever.

60

Arise, shine; for thy light is come,
> and the glory of the Lord is risen upon thee.
²For, behold, the darkness shall cover the earth,
> and gross darkness the people,
>> but the Lord shall arise upon thee,
> and his glory shall be seen upon thee.
³And the Gentiles shall come to thy light,
> and kings to the brightness of thy rising.
⁴Lift up thine eyes round about, and see:
> all they gather themselves together,
>> they come to thee: thy sons shall come from far,
> and thy daughters shall be nursed at thy side.
⁵Then thou shalt see, and flow together,
> and thine heart shall fear, and be enlarged;
>> because the abundance of the see
> shall be converted unto thee,
>> the forces of the Gentiles
> shall come unto thee.

⁶The multitude of camels shall cover thee,
   the dromedaries of Midian and Ephah;
      all they from Sheba shall come:
   they shall bring gold and incense;
      and they shall shew forth
   the praises of the Lord.
⁷All the flocks of Kedar
   shall be gathered together unto thee,
      the rams of Nebaioth
   shall minister unto thee:
      they shall come up with acceptance
   on mine altar,
      and I will glorify the house of my glory.
⁸Who are these that fly as a cloud,
   and as the doves to their windows?
⁹Surely the isles shall wait for me,
   and the ships of Tarshish first,
      to bring thy sons from far,
   their silver and their gold with them,
      unto the name of the Lord thy God,
   and to the Holy One of Israel,
      because he hath glorified thee.
¹⁰And the sons of strangers shall build up thy walls,
   and their kings shall minister unto thee,
      for in my wrath I smote thee,
   but in my favour have I had mercy
      on thee.

¹¹ Therefore thy gates shall be open continually;
they shall not be shut day nor night;
that men may bring unto thee
the forces of the Gentiles,
and that their kings may be brought.
¹² For the nation and kingdom that will not serve thee
shall perish;
yea, those nations shall be utterly wasted.
¹³ The glory of Lebanon shall come unto thee,
the fir tree, the pine tree, and the box together,
to beautify the place of my sanctuary;
and I will make the place of my feet glorious.
¹⁴ The sons also of them that afflicted thee shall come
bending unto thee;
and all they that despised thee shall bow
themselves down at the soles of thy feet;
and they shall call thee 'The city of the Lord',
'The Zion of the Holy One of Israel'.
¹⁵ Whereas thou hast been forsaken and hated,
so that no man went through thee,
I will make thee an eternal excellency,
a joy of many generations.
¹⁶ Thou shalt also suck the milk of the Gentiles,
and shalt suck the breast of kings;
and thou shalt know that I the Lord
am thy Saviour and thy Redeemer,
the mighty One of Jacob.

¹⁷ For brass I will bring gold,
   and for iron I will bring silver,
      and for wood brass, and for stones iron:
   I will also make thy officers peace,
      and thine exactors righteousness.
¹⁸ Violence shall no more be heard in thy land,
   wasting nor destruction within thy borders;
      but thou shalt call thy walls Salvation,
   and thy gates Praise.
¹⁹ The sun shall be no more thy light by day;
   neither for brightness
      shall the moon give light unto thee:
   but the Lord shall be
      unto thee an everlasting light,
   and thy God thy glory.
²⁰ Thy sun shall no more go down;
   neither shall thy moon withdraw itself,
      for the Lord shall be thine everlasting light,
   and the days of thy mourning shall be ended.
²¹ Thy people also shall be all righteous:
   they shall inherit the land for ever,
      the branch of my planting,
   the work of my hands,
      that I may be glorified.
²² A little one shall become a thousand, and a small
   one a strong nation:
      I the Lord will hasten it in his time.

61 The Spirit of the Lord God is upon me;
because the Lord hath anointed me to preach
good tidings unto the meek;
he hath sent me to bind up the brokenhearted,
to proclaim liberty to the captives,
and the opening of the prison to them
that are bound;
² to proclaim the acceptable year of the Lord,
and the day of vengeance of our God;
to comfort all that mourn;
³ to appoint unto them that mourn in Zion,
to give unto them beauty for ashes,
the oil of joy for mourning,
the garment of praise for the spirit of heaviness;
that they might be called
trees of righteousness, the planting of the Lord,
that he might be glorified.
⁴And they shall build the old wastes,
they shall raise up the former desolations,
and they shall repair the waste cities,
the desolations of many generations.
⁵And strangers shall stand and feed your flocks,
and the sons of the alien shall be your plowmen
and your vinedressers.
⁶ But ye shall be named the Priests of the Lord:
men shall call you the Ministers of our God:
ye shall eat the riches of the Gentiles,
and in their glory shall ye boast yourselves.

⁷ For your shame ye shall have double;
and for confusion they shall rejoice
in their portion: therefore in their land
they shall possess the double:
everlasting joy shall be unto them.
⁸ For I the Lord love judgment,
I hate robbery for burnt offering;
and I will direct their work in truth,
and I will make an everlasting covenant
with them.
⁹ And their seed shall be known among the Gentiles,
and their offspring among the people:
all that see them shall acknowledge them,
that they are the seed
which the Lord hath blessed.
¹⁰ I will greatly rejoice in the Lord,
my soul shall be joyful in my God;
for he hath clothed me
with the garments of salvation,
he hath covered me with the robe
of righteousness,
as a bridegroom decketh himself
with ornaments,
and as a bride adorneth herself with her jewels.
¹¹ For as the earth bringeth forth her bud,
and as the garden causeth the things
that are sown in it to spring forth;
so the Lord God will cause righteousness

and praise to spring forth before all
the nations.

62 For Zion's sake will I not hold my peace,
and for Jerusalem's sake I will not rest,
until the righteousness thereof
go forth as brightness, and the salvation thereof
as a lamp that burneth.
²And the Gentiles shall see thy righteousness,
and all kings thy glory;
and thou shalt be called by a new name,
which the mouth of the Lord shall name.
³Thou shalt also be a crown of glory
in the hand of the Lord,
and a royal diadem in the hand of thy God.
⁴Thou shalt no more be termed Forsaken;
neither shall thy land any more be termed
Desolate:
but thou shalt be called Hephzi-bah,
and thy land Beulah;
for the Lord delighteth in thee,
and thy land shall be married.
⁵For as a young man marrieth a virgin,
so shall thy sons marry thee: and as the bridegroom
rejoiceth over the bride,
so shall thy God rejoice over thee.

⁶ I have set watchmen upon thy walls, O Jerusalem,
  which shall never hold their peace day nor night:
    ye that make mention of the Lord,
    keep not silence,
⁷ and give him no rest, till he establish,
  and till he make Jerusalem a praise in the earth.
⁸ The Lord hath sworn by his right hand,
  and by the arm of his strength:
    Surely I will no more give thy corn
    to be meat for thine enemies;
      and the sons of the stranger
    shall not drink thy wine,
      for the which thou hast laboured;
⁹ But they that have gathered it shall eat it,
  and praise the Lord;
    and they that have brought it together
    shall drink it in the courts of my holiness.
¹⁰ Go through, go through the gates;
  prepare ye the way of the people;
    cast up, cast up the highway;
    gather out the stones;
      lift up a standard for the people.
¹¹ Behold, the Lord hath proclaimed
  unto the end of the world:
    Say ye to the daughter of Zion,
    'Behold, thy salvation cometh; behold, his
      reward is with him,
    and his work before him.'

¹²And they shall call them, 'The holy people,
the redeemed of the Lord':
and thou shalt be called,
'Sought out, A city not forsaken'.

63

Who is this that cometh from Edom,
with dyed garments from Bozrah?
This that is glorious in his apparel,
travelling in the greatness of his strength?
I that speak in righteousness,
mighty to save.
² Wherefore art thou red in thine apparel,
and thy garments like him
that treadeth in the winefat?
³ I have trodden the winepress alone;
and of the people there was none with me;
for I will tread them in mine anger,
and trample them in my fury;
and their blood shall be sprinkled
upon my garments, and I will stain all my raiment.
⁴ For the day of vengeance is in mine heart,
and the year of my redeemed is come.
⁵ And I looked, and there was none to help;
and I wondered that there was none to uphold:
therefore mine own arm brought salvation
unto me; and my fury, it upheld me.

⁶And I will tread down the people in mine anger,
  and make them drunk in my fury,
      and I will bring down their strength
  to the earth.
⁷I will mention the lovingkindnesses of the Lord,
  and the praises of the Lord,
      according to all that the Lord
  hath bestowed on us, and the great goodness
      toward the house of Israel,
  which he hath bestowed on them
      according to his mercies,
  and according to the multitude
      of his lovingkindnesses.
⁸For he said: Surely they are my people,
  children that will not lie,
      so he was their Saviour.
⁹In all their affliction he was afflicted,
  and the angel of his presence saved them;
      in his love and in his pity he redeemed them;
  and he bare them, and carried them
      all the days of old.
¹⁰But they rebelled, and vexed his holy Spirit:
  therefore he was turned to be their enemy,
      and he fought against them.
¹¹Then he remembered the days of old, Moses,
  and his people, saying,
      'Where is he that brought them up
  out of the sea with the shepherd of his flock?

Where is he that put his holy Spirit
within him?
¹²That led them by the right hand of Moses
with his glorious arm,
dividing the water before them,
to make himself an everlasting name?
¹³That led them through the deep,
as an horse in the wilderness,
that they should not stumble?'
¹⁴As a beast goeth down into the valley,
the Spirit of the Lord caused him to rest:
so didst thou lead thy people,
to make thyself a glorious name.
¹⁵Look down from heaven, and behold
from the habitation of thy holiness
and of thy glory:
where is thy zeal and thy strength,
the sounding of thy bowels and of thy mercies
toward me? Are they restrained?
¹⁶Doubtless thou art our father,
though Abraham be ignorant of us,
and Israel acknowledge us not:
thou, O Lord, art our father, our redeemer;
thy name is from everlasting.
¹⁷O Lord, why hast thou made us to err
from thy ways,
and hardened our heart from thy fear?
Return for thy servants' sake,
the tribes of thine inheritance.

¹⁸ The people of thy holiness have possessed it
    but a little while:
        our adversaries have trodden down
    thy sanctuary.
¹⁹ We are thine: thou never barest rule over them;
    they were not called by thy name.

64 Oh that thou wouldest rend the heavens,
    that thou wouldest come down,
        that the mountains might flow down
    at thy presence,
² as when the melting fire burneth,
    the fire causeth the waters to boil,
        to make thy name known to thine adversaries,
    that the nations may tremble at thy presence!
³ When thou didst terrible things
    which we looked not for, thou camest down,
        the mountains flowed down at thy presence.
⁴ For since the beginning of the world
    men have not heard, nor perceived by the ear,
        neither hath the eye seen, O God, beside thee,
    what he hath prepared for him
    that waiteth for him.
⁵ Thou meetest him that rejoiceth
    and worketh righteousness,

those that remember thee in thy ways:
    behold, thou art wroth; for we have sinned;
        in those is continuance,
    and we shall be saved.

⁶ But we are all as an unclean thing, and all our
    righteousnesses are as filthy rags;
        and we all do fade as a leaf;
    and our iniquities, like the wind,
        have taken us away.

⁷ And there is none that calleth upon thy name,
    that stirreth up himself to take hold of thee
        for thou hast hid thy face from us,
    and hast consumed us,
        because of our iniquities.

⁸ But now, O Lord, thou art our father;
    we are the clay, and thou our potter;
        and we all are the work of thy hand.

⁹ Be not wroth very sore, O Lord, neither remember
    iniquity for ever: behold, see, we beseech thee,
        we are all thy people.

¹⁰ Thy holy cities are a wilderness,
    Zion is a wilderness, Jerusalem a desolation.

¹¹ Our holy and our beautiful house, where our
    fathers praised thee, is burned up with fire:
        and all our pleasant things are laid waste.

¹² Wilt thou refrain thyself for these things, O Lord?
    Wilt thou hold thy peace,
        and afflict us very sore?

65 I am sought of them that asked not for me;
I am found of them that sought me not:
I said, 'Behold me, behold me,'
unto a nation that was not called by my name.
² I have spread out my hands all the day
unto a rebellious people,
which walketh in a way that was not good,
after their own thoughts;
³ a people that provoketh me to anger
continually to my face; that sacrificeth in gardens,
and burneth incense upon altars of brick;
⁴ which remain among the graves,
and lodge in the monuments,
which eat swine's flesh,
and broth of abominable things
is in their vessels;
⁵ which say, 'Stand by thyself, come not near to me;
for I am holier than thou.'
These are a smoke in my nose,
a fire that burneth all the day.
⁶ Behold, it is written before me:
I will not keep silence, but will recompense,
even recompense into their bosom,
⁷ your iniquities, and the iniquities of your fathers
together, saith the Lord,
which have burned incense upon the mountains,
and blasphemed me upon the hills:

therefore will I measure their former work
into their bosom.
⁸ Thus saith the Lord:
as the new wine is found in the cluster,
and one saith,
'Destroy it not; for a blessing is in it':
so will I do for my servants' sakes,
that I may not destroy them all.
⁹ And I will bring forth a seed out of Jacob,
and out of Judah an inheritor of my mountains:
and mine elect shall inherit it,
and my servants shall dwell there.
¹⁰ And Sharon shall be a fold of flocks,
and the valley of Achor a place for the herds
to lie down in,
for my people that have sought me.
¹¹ But ye are they that forsake the Lord,
that forget my holy mountain,
that prepare a table for that troop,
and that furnish the drink offering
unto that number.
¹² Therefore will I number you to the sword,
and ye shall all bow down to the slaughter:
because when I called, ye did not answer;
when I spake, ye did not hear;
but did evil before mine eyes,
and did choose that wherein I delighted not.

¹³ Therefore thus saith the Lord God:
Behold, my servants shall eat,
    but ye shall be hungry:
behold, my servants shall drink,
    but ye shall be thirsty:
behold, my servants shall rejoice,
    but ye shall be ashamed.
¹⁴ Behold, my servants shall sing for joy of heart,
    but ye shall cry for sorrow of heart
        and shall howl for vexation of spirit.
¹⁵ And ye shall leave your name for a curse
    unto my chosen,
        for the Lord God shall slay thee,
    and call his servants by another name:
¹⁶ that he who blesseth himself in the earth
    shall bless himself in the God of truth;
        and he that sweareth in the earth
    shall swear by the God of truth;
        because the former troubles are forgotten,
    and because they are hid from mine eyes.
¹⁷ For, behold, I create new heavens
    and a new earth:
        and the former shall not be remembered,
    nor come into mind.
¹⁸ But be ye glad and rejoice for ever
    in that which I create;
        for, behold, I create Jerusalem a rejoicing,
    and her people a joy.

¹⁹And I will rejoice in Jerusalem,
    and joy in my people:
        and the voice of weeping shall be no more
        heard in her, nor the voice of crying.
²⁰ There shall be no more thence an infant of days,
    nor an old man that hath not filled his days;
        for the child shall die an hundred years old;
        but the sinner being an hundred years old shall
        be accursed.
²¹And they shall build houses, and inhabit them;
    and they shall plant vineyards,
        and eat the fruit of them.
²² They shall not build, and another inhabit;
    they shall not plant, and another eat,
        for as the days of a tree
        are the days of my people, and mine elect
        shall long enjoy the work of their hands.
²³ They shall not labour in vain,
    nor bring forth for trouble;
        for they are the seed of the blessed of
        the Lord, and their offspring with them.
²⁴And it shall come to pass,
    that before they call, I will answer;
        and while they are yet speaking, I will hear.
²⁵ The wolf and the lamb shall feed together,
    and the lion shall eat straw like the bullock:
        and dust shall be the serpent's meat.
    They shall not hurt nor destroy in all
        my holy mountain, saith the Lord.

66 Thus saith the Lord: The heaven is my throne,
and the earth is my footstool:
where is the house that ye build unto me?
And where is the place of my rest?
² For all those things hath mine hand made,
and all those things have been, saith the Lord;
but to this man will I look,
even to him that is poor and of a contrite spirit,
and trembleth at my word.
³ He that killeth an ox is as if he slew a man;
he that sacrificeth a lamb,
as if he cut off a dog's neck;
he that offereth an oblation,
as if he offered swine's blood;
he that burneth incense, as if he blessed an idol.
Yea, they have chosen their own ways,
and their soul delighteth in their abominations.
⁴ I also will choose their delusions,
and will bring their fears upon them;
because when I called, none did answer;
when I spake, they did not hear;
but they did evil before mine eyes,
and chose that in which I delighted not.
⁵ Hear the word of the Lord,
ye that tremble at his word.
Your brethren that hated you,
that cast you out for my name's sake,
said, 'Let the Lord be glorified,

but he shall appear to your joy',
and they shall be ashamed.
⁶A voice of noise from the city,
a voice from the temple,
a voice of the Lord that rendereth
recompence to his enemies.
⁷Before she travailed, she brought forth;
before her pain came,
she was delivered of a man child.
⁸Who hath heard such a thing?
Who hath seen such things?
Shall the earth be made to bring forth
in one day?
Or shall a nation be born at once?
For as soon as Zion travailed,
she brought forth her children.
⁹Shall I bring to the birth,
and not cause to bring forth? saith the Lord.
Shall I cause to bring forth,
and shut the womb? saith thy God.
¹⁰Rejoice ye with Jerusalem,
and be glad with her, all ye that love her:
rejoice for joy with her,
all ye that mourn for her,
¹¹that ye may suck, and be satisfied
with the breasts of her consolations;
that ye may milk out, and be delighted
with the abundance of her glory.

¹² For thus saith the Lord.

>Behold, I will extend peace to her like a river,
>>and the glory of the Gentiles
>like a flowing stream: then shall ye suck,
>>ye shall be borne upon her sides,
>and be dandled upon her knees.

¹³As one whom his mother comforteth,
>so will I comfort you;
>>and ye shall be comforted in Jerusalem.

¹⁴And when ye see this, your heart shall rejoice,
>and your bones shall flourish like an herb:
>>and the hand of the Lord shall be known
>toward his servants,
>>and his indignation toward his enemies.

¹⁵ For, behold, the Lord will come with fire,
>and with his chariots like a whirlwind,
>>to render his anger with fury,
>and his rebuke with flames of fire.

¹⁶ For by fire and by his sword will the Lord
>plead with all flesh:
>>and the slain of the Lord shall be many.

¹⁷ They that sanctify themselves,
>and purify themselves in the gardens
>>behind one tree in the midst,
>eating swine's flesh, and the abomination,
>>and the mouse, shall be consumed together,
>saith the Lord.

¹⁸ For I know their works and their thoughts:
    it shall come, that I will gather all nations
        and tongues; and they shall come,
    and see my glory.
¹⁹ And I will set a sign among them,
    and I will send those that escape of them
        unto the nations, to Tarshish, Pul, and Lud,
    that draw the bow, to Tubal, and Javan,
        to the isles afar off,
    that have not heard my fame,
        neither have seen my glory;
    and they shall declare my glory
        among the Gentiles.
²⁰ And they shall bring all your brethren
    for an offering unto the Lord
        out of all nations upon horses,
    and in chariots, and in litters, and upon mules,
        and upon swift beasts,
    to my holy mountain Jerusalem,
        saith the Lord, as the children of Israel
    bring an offering in a clean vessel
        into the house of the Lord.
²¹ And I will also take of them for priests
    and for Levites, saith the Lord.
²² For as the new heavens and the new earth,
    which I will make, shall remain before me,
        saith the Lord,
    so shall your seed and your name remain.

²³And it shall come to pass,
 that from one new moon to another,
  and from one sabbath to another,
 shall all flesh come to worship before me,
  saith the Lord.
²⁴And they shall go forth, and look upon the carcases
 of the men that have transgressed against me;
  for their worm shall not die,
 neither shall their fire be quenched;
  and they shall be an abhorring unto all flesh.

the pocket canons

genesis – *introduced by e. l. doctorow*
exodus – *introduced by david grossman*
ruth – *introduced by joanna trollope*
samuel – *introduced by meir shalev*
job – *introduced by charles frazier*
selections from the book of psalms – *introduced by bono*
proverbs – *introduced by charles johnson*
ecclesiastes – *introduced by doris lessing*
song of solomon – *introduced by a. s. byatt*
isaiah – *introduced by peter ackroyd*
jonah – *introduced by alasdair gray*
wisdom – *introduced by peirs paul read*
matthew – *introduced by francisco goldman*
mark – *introduced by barry hannah*
luke – *introduced by thomas cahill*
john – *introduced by darcey steinke*
acts – *introduced by p. d. james*
romans – *introduced by ruth rendell*
corinthians – *introduced by fay weldon*
hebrews – *introduced by karen armstrong*
epistles – *introduced by his holiness the dalai lama
of tibet*
revelation – *introduced by kathleen norris*